INCOME TAX LAW

SECOND EDITION

INCOME TAX
LAW

SECOND EDITION

VERN KRISHNA

Professor of Common Law, University of Ottawa
Barrister at Law, Borden Ladner Gervais, LLP
CM, QC, FRSC, FCGA, MCIArb
B Comm (Manchester), MBA, LLB (Alberta),
DCL (Cambridge), LLM (Harvard)

IRWIN
LAW

Income Tax Law, second edition
© Irwin Law Inc., 2012

Published in 2012 by

Irwin Law Inc.
14 Duncan Street
Suite 206
Toronto, ON
M5H 3G8

www.irwinlaw.com

ISBN: 978-1-55221-235-6
e-book ISBN: 978-1-55221-236-3

Library and Archives Canada Cataloguing in Publication

Krishna, Vern
    Income tax law / Vern Krishna. -- 2nd ed.

(Essentials of Canadian law)
Includes bibliographical references and index.
Issued also in electronic format.
ISBN 978-1-55221-235-6

. 1. Income tax--Law and legislation--Canada. I. Title.
II. Series: Essentials of Canadian law

KE5759.K75 2011   343.7105'2   C2011-907274-2
KF6370.ZA2K75 2011

The publisher acknowledges the financial support of the Government of Canada through the Canada Book Fund for its publishing activities.

We acknowledge the assistance of the OMDC Book Fund, an initiative of Ontario Media Development Corporation.

Printed and bound in Canada.

1 2 3 4 5   16 15 14 13 12

To Savitri, Linda, Nicola, Sacha, Vivian & Biggie.

SUMMARY
TABLE OF CONTENTS

DETAILED
TABLE OF CONTENTS

CHAPTER 9:

CAPITAL GAINS AND LOSSES 257

CHAPTER 17:
CORPORATE BUSINESS INCOME 433

PART VIII: JUDICIAL PROCESS 581

CHAPTER 21:
OBJECTIONS AND APPEALS 583

PREFACE

The *Income Tax Act* is a public policy statute with broad socio-economic impact and is the most pervasive of all economic laws. It affects individuals and corporations in every aspect of their personal lives and business activities. It affects all transactions—domestic and international, legal or illegal—that involve an exchange of goods, services or intellectual property.

Notwithstanding its pervasive influence, tax law engenders paranoia and fear in students, who develop narcotaxis—a medical ailment that, within thirty seconds of hearing their professors begin to explain the law, causes glassy eyes, loss of bodily feeling and a shallow coma. The symptoms last for nearly ninety minutes. Fortunately, the condition is not enduring and most students recover completely by the end of their class.

This text introduces students and practitioners to income tax law in its broadest dimensions. It addresses the subject matter based on principles, policy and practice. The objective is to explain what the law is and, more importantly, why it is the way it is, and how it works (or does not work). The answers to these questions are not always obvious, but they are becoming increasingly important as we move, albeit slowly, toward purposive statutory interpretation, particularly in the venue of the general anti-avoidance rule.

The *Income Tax Act* is poorly drafted, uses obtuse language with circular definitions and contains sentences with minimal punctuation. For example, an "avoidance transaction" is one that confers a "tax benefit," which the Act defines, *inter alia*, as "avoidance" of tax. Thus, reading the statute, a must for students and tax lawyers alike, is a painful exercise. Politicians and bureaucrats should heed the observation of the Chinese philosopher Lao Tzu: "The more laws are enacted and taxes assessed, the greater the number of lawbreakers and tax evaders."[1]

However, we live with the statute as drafted—not with one we would wish for—and must stoically endure the pain. This text assumes no prior knowledge of the subject and will, I hope, make tax law less painful and more intellectually vibrant.

I am sensitive to the aversion to numbers of many law students, practising lawyers and judges. Hence, I have attempted to use numbers only to better explain the operation of complex and, often, dense statutory provisions. As with a picture, a numerical example can better explain a provision drafted in opaque language.

The text examines the policy, structural, constitutional and judicial framework of income tax law. Thus, we address five fundamental questions:

1) Who is taxable?
2) What is taxable?
3) How much tax is payable?
4) When is tax payable?
5) How do we administer the system and resolve disputes with the tax collector?

Tax law influences human behaviour and is the catalyst for the structure of most commercial transactions. An understanding of the principles, structure and methodology of the subject matter effectively facilitates policy making, business structuring, personal transactions and litigating. It also enlivens the subject and makes it fun to study. Yes, tax law can be the funniest subject in law school!

I am grateful to two people who made it easier for me to write the text and contributed towards its timely production. Ryma Nasrallah, an associate at Borden Ladner Gervais LLP (Ottawa), read through the entire manuscript diligently and improved it in a meaningful way. She was also fun to work with. Gabriella Bellina helped in producing the text in a timely manner. She did not have as much fun, but managed the multiple revisions with good grace and humour.

At the end of the day (and often late into the night), one asks: why am I writing this text? Dr. Samuel Johnson said that the only outcome of writing is to enable readers to enjoy life better or to better endure

---

1   Lao Tzu, Chinese philosopher, founder of Taoism, 600 BC–531 BC.

it. It is too much to hope for that a text on income tax law will enable readers to enjoy their life better. I am modestly hopeful, however, that it will allow students to better endure their narcotaxis attacks and reduce anxiety in their income tax courses. Indeed, I think they may even have some fun in the course if they read the materials before coming to class so that they can understand what their professor is talking about in the ninety minutes that they attend. I hope the text will inspire some to become tax lawyers.

Legal practitioners in business law and litigators may also find the text helpful in drafting pleadings and assessing damages when considering tax issues in civil litigation.

I would be pleased to receive constructive comments and suggestions. The law in this edition is current to 3 January 2012.

Vern Krishna, CM, QC
vkrishna@blg.com
vkrishna@uottawa.ca

ACKNOWLEDGMENT

I wish to acknowledge the generous assistance and support of the Fellows and Life Fellows of the Foundation of Legal Research in the preparation of this text.

"The art of taxation is so to pluck the goose that the maximum number of feathers is obtained with the minimum amount of hissing."

—Jean Colbert (1665)
Minister of Finance to Louis XIV of France

PART I

INTRODUCTION

CHAPTER 1

AN OVERVIEW OF TAX LAW AND CONCEPTS

"We are about to consider the unpleasant subject of taxes."[1]

"'Basic Tax,' as everyone knows, is the only genuinely funny subject in law school."

—attributed to Martin D. Ginsburg

A. THE NATURE OF TAX

This chapter provides a broad overview of the income tax system, policy objectives and constitutional limits on the power to tax. Tax law involves expropriating money from taxpayers for governmental purposes. Hence, there is a natural tension between the tax collector and the taxpayer. Governments legislate; taxpayers seek to legally minimize their tax bills.

Tax law has a reputation of being a difficult and dry subject. To be sure, it is difficult, but it is neither dry nor unpleasant. Yes, tax law is replete with obtuse language, has a great deal of technical detail and is often incomprehensible even to the brightest minds. Albert Einstein—an acknowledged genius—conceded: "The hardest thing in the world to understand is the Income Tax."

---

1   Louis Eisenstein, *The Ideologies of Taxation* (Cambridge: Harvard University Press, 2010) at 4.

Nevertheless, taxpayers must live with the statute as it is and not with the one that they wish they had written. We must comply with the law or face severe sanctions. Advisors must advise on uncertain, complex and poorly drafted provisions. Courts must interpret obscure legislation in lengthy court battles that can extend over a decade.

All laws are ultimately behavioural and nowhere more so than in money matters. When governments take approximately one-half of one's earned income as tax, it is understandable that taxpayers will expend considerable energy and resources devising creative ways to minimize the government's bite. Tax lawyers are always busy.

Revenue is an important, indeed imperative, justification of tax law. However, governments also use tax law to implement social and political policies. Thus, tax law balances different objectives: funding public expenditures, promoting economic policies, providing regional incentives, and redistributing income. A statute that serves so many diverse and, often, conflicting purposes is necessarily going to be more complex than a narrow single purpose statute.

As we work through this text, we should delve into the purpose of statutory provisions and ask

- Is the provision "normative" and necessary to accurately measure income?
- Is the provision intended to promote social, economic or cultural policy?
- How effectively does the provision achieve its objective?

The *Income Tax Act*[2] (the Act) is badly drafted and violates almost every principle of grammatical construction. The comments of a member of the British Parliament speaking about the Irish Home Rule bill in 1889 would equally describe the Canadian Act today:

> . . . it sweats difficulties at every paragraph; every provision breeds a dilemma; every clause ends in a cul-de-sac; dangers lurk in every line; mischiefs abound in every sentence and an air of evil hangs over it all.

Our high school English teachers would be horrified.

Shorn of its technical language, however, the Act is an instrument of policy that reflects the social, political, economic and moral values of society. Thus, the statute evolves as our values and policies change. There is a reason or purpose underlying every provision. The rationale is there for those who make an effort to search for it. As Frankfurter J said:

> Legislation has an aim: it seeks to obviate some mischief, to supply an inadequacy, to effect a change in policy, to formulate a plan of Govern-

---

2   RSC 1985, c 1 (5th Supp) [*ITA*].

ment. That aim, that policy is not drawn, like nitrogen, out of the air; it is evinced in the language of the statute as read in the light of other external manifestations of purpose.[3]

The study of income tax law involves five basic questions:

1) Who is taxable?
2) What is taxable?
3) When is income taxable?
4) How much tax is payable?
5) How do we enforce taxation and administer the system?

Each of these questions raises five more questions:

1) What is the law?
2) Why is the law?
3) How do the courts interpret it?
4) What are taxpayers' responses?
5) What are the government's responses?

The first step in answering these questions is to read the law carefully to determine its meaning. Thus, we start with the *Income Tax Act*, the principal source of tax law.

The next steps are closely related. We apply the plain meaning of words where the language is "clear and unambiguous." The meaning of words in tax statutes, however, is rarely as plain as its authors anticipate when they draft the legislation. Where the statutory language is not clear or unambiguous, we turn to the purpose of the provision and try to reconcile unclear statutory language with the underlying rationale of the provision.

1) Some Examples

In *Bailey v Canada*,[4] the taxpayer claimed private elementary school fees as "child care" expenses—which are deductible from income—and not as education expenses—which are not. The Tax Court (in an informal decision) looked at the "object and spirit" or purpose of the child care provisions and allowed the deduction. The court said that any education from the school was merely an *incidental* benefit.

In *Witthuhn v MNR*,[5] the taxpayer, an invalid, could claim a medical deduction for care if she was confined to a bed or wheelchair. She

---

3   Felix Frankfurter, "Some Reflections on the Reading of Statutes" (1947) 47 Colum L Rev 527 at 538–39.
4   2005 TCC 305 (Informal Procedure).
5   (1957), 57 DTC 174 (TAB).

could not afford a wheelchair and purchased a rocking chair instead. The Tax Review Board denied her deduction, saying a rocking chair is not a wheelchair.

Judges wrestle with unclear provisions to elicit their meaning and policy. They look at legislative history and engage in purposive analysis when the words of the statute are capable of different meanings. In *Hewlett-Packard (Canada) Co v Canada*,[6] for example, the Tax Court had to determine whether the word "lodge" included "luxury hotels." If it did, the taxpayer could not deduct expenses to entertain its employees in the particular hotels. The purpose of the rule prohibiting deduction of lodge expenses is to prevent expense-account living on the public purse. Although dictionaries sometimes use the word "hotel" to describe "lodge," the Tax Court did not think that most Canadians would describe large resort hotels with a range of modern amenities as "lodges." The court allowed the taxpayer to deduct its substantial expenses and sideswiped the underlying legislative policy against the deduction of such expenses.

Purposive analysis is not easy. It requires an understanding of the principles underlying tax law, which allows judges, consciously or unconsciously, to inject their perspective into statutory interpretation and apply their own normative beliefs of the appropriate policy. As Justice Benjamin N. Cardozo said in his classic 1949 work, *The Nature of the Judicial Process*:

> Deep below consciousness are other forces, the likes and the dislikes, the predilections and the prejudices, the complex of instincts and emotions and habits and convictions, which make the man, whether he be litigant or judge.

Hence, in litigation, it can be helpful if you "know" your judge.

B. BRIEF HISTORY

Income tax systems have their origins in the need to finance wars. Before World War I, the principal sources of revenue in Canada were customs duties and excise taxes. Sir Robert Borden, Prime Minister of Canada, introduced the federal income tax on business profits in 1916, and a tax on personal income in 1917. The taxes were temporary measures to finance World War I. As Sir Thomas White, Minister of Finance, said when he introduced the *Income War Tax Act*:

---

6   2005 TCC 398 (General Procedure).

I have placed no time limit upon this measure . . . a year or two after the war is over, the measure should be definitely reviewed.

It was thirty-two years later when Louis St Laurent formally made income taxes permanent on 1 January 1949.

The *Income War Tax Act* was all of ten pages in its first edition. Today, the Act is over 2,500 pages and growing annually.

The *Carter Commission* (1967) was the most comprehensive reform study of the tax system, culminating in the present version of the *Income Tax Act*, which came into effect on 1 January 1972. Since then, there have been various further attempts at reform and simplification of the statute, all with minimal success.

The Act grows and becomes increasingly complex each year. We hear the despair of the Joint Committee on Taxation of the Canadian Bar Association and the Canadian Institute of Chartered Accountants in its testimony before the House of Commons Committee on Finance and Economic Affairs in 1984:

> For any taxpayer to pick up some of this legislation we are looking at today and understand how these rules are going to impact on him when he sits down to fill out his tax return is almost impossible.
>
> There is no quick fix to the complexity issue. It is a very long-term problem, but I fear that the Government's priority for tax simplification has fallen down to the bottom of the various objectives set out for tax reform.

Tax simplification comes at a price because it involves giving up incentive and deterrent provisions that involve trade-offs.

C. THE POWER TO TAX

Democratic societies cherish the rule of law and accountability for the collection of taxes for public purposes. The Canadian Constitution gives the federal Parliament and provincial legislatures the power to impose taxes. The origin of this ancient power — no taxation without representation — goes as far back as *Magna Carta* (1215). Section 53 of the *Constitution Act, 1867* embodies these principles:[7]

> Bills for appropriating any Part of the Public Revenue, or for imposing any Tax or Impost, shall originate in the House of Commons.

---

7   See, for example, *SNEAA c Canada (PG)*, (*sub nom Confédération des syndicats nationaux v Canada (AG)*) 2008 SCC 68, for modern application of the principle.

The section enshrines the doctrine of control and accountability over taxation by elected representatives.

The Constitution[8] divides the authority to impose taxes between the federal and provincial governments. The federal Parliament has the power under subsection 91(3) to raise money by *any* mode or system of taxation. Subsection 92(2) allows the provinces to impose income taxes through direct taxation within the province and only for raising revenue for provincial purposes. This division of taxing power gives the federal government considerable leverage over the national economy and the distribution of wealth amongst the provinces.

A legislative body can delegate the details of taxation and its mechanism to another body, but it must do so in unambiguous language that clearly expresses its intention.[9] However, neither the Dominion nor a province may delegate to the other its power to legislate on taxation.[10]

The dual authority to levy income taxes results in differential income tax burdens in the country. The income tax burden for Nova Scotia residents, for example, is substantially higher (50 percent in 2010) than the equivalent tax in Alberta (39 percent) (see Appendix B: Tax Rates).

The *Income Tax Act* is the primary source of federal income tax law. However, the Act authorizes the enactment of *Income Tax Regulations* ("regulations"), under which the Executive Branch can make law. Parliament can amend the Act, but only through a bill introduced in the House of Commons. In contrast, an order in council is sufficient for the federal cabinet to enact a regulation.

The rationale for limiting provincial legislatures to direct taxation is to contain provincial powers within provincial boundaries. Thus, the provincial taxing power is limited to direct taxes, imposed within the province and for provincial purposes. These three requirements prevent provinces from using their taxing power for colourable purposes by concealing their real objectives. In economic terms, however, we cannot contain provincial taxes within provincial boundaries. Taxpayers can always pass on direct taxes through prices to others (for example, consumers) outside the province.

As a matter of law, however, there is an important distinction between direct and indirect taxation. In 1848, John Stuart Mill stated the distinction between the two forms of taxation as follows:

8   *Constitution Act, 1867* (UK), 30 & 31 Vict, c 3, reprinted in RSC 1985, App II, No 5.
9   *Ontario English Catholic Teachers' Assn v Ontario (AG)*, 2001 SCC 15 (provincial legislation authorizing the Minister of Finance to prescribe tax rates for school purposes was constitutional. The legislation set out the structure of the tax, the tax base, and the principles for imposing the tax).
10   *Re Constitutional Validity of Bill No 136 (Nova Scotia) (sub nom Nova Scotia (AG) v Canada (AG))* [1951] SCR 31.

A direct tax is one which is demanded from the very persons who it is intended or desired should pay it. Indirect taxes are those which are demanded from one person in the expectation and intention that he shall indemnify himself at the expense of another, such as the excise or customs.[11]

Ultimately, the constitutional validity of a tax depends upon its pith and substance.[12] Thus, the crucial inquiry is the object and primary purpose of the scheme to tax and not simply its formal or superficial characteristics.[13] The pith and substance approach contrasts with blanket categorizations whereby courts regard certain categories of taxes—such as property and income taxes—as direct taxes.[14] Lord Simonds explained the process in *Atlantic Smoke Shops Ltd v Conlon*:

> Their Lordships are of opinion that Lord Cave's reference in his judgment in the Fairbanks' case to "two separate and distinct categories" of taxes, "namely those that are direct and those which cannot be so described", should not be understood as relieving the courts from the obligation of examining the real nature and effect of the particular tax in the present instance, or as justifying the classification of the tax as indirect merely because it is in some sense associated with the purchase of an article.[15]

Hence, we look at the *legal* incidence of a tax, not its label, to determine its constitutional validity.[16]

---

11 See *Cotton v R*, [1914] AC 176 at 193 (JCPC from Quebec). See also *Atlantic Smoke Shops Ltd v Conlon*, [1943] CTC 294 (JCPC from New Brunswick). See, generally, GV La Forest, *The Allocation of Taxing Power under the Canadian Constitution*, Canadian Tax Paper No 45 (Toronto: Canadian Tax Foundation, 1967) at 81.

12 See, for example, the majority of the Supreme Court in *Reference re Questions set out in OC 1079/80, Concerning Tax Proposed by Parliament of Canada on Exported Natural Gas* (1982), 136 DLR (3d) 385 at 438 (SCC) [*Re Exported Natural Gas Tax*]: "The essential question here is no different than in any other constitutional case: what is the 'pith and substance' of the relevant legislation?"

13 *Ontario Home Builders' Assn v York (Region) Board of Education* (1996), 137 DLR (4th) 449 (SCC) [*Ontario Home Builders' Assn*].

14 See *Halifax (City) v Fairbanks Estate*, [1927] 4 DLR 945 (JCPC from Nova Scotia).

15 Above note 11 at 303, quoted with approval by Iacobucci J at para 34 of *Ontario Home Builders' Assn*, above note 13.

16 *Ibid* at para 41:

> Of course, it is the general tendency of the tax that is of concern, rather than the ultimate incidence of the tax in the circumstances of a particular case . . . the test of incidence is based on a legal, rather than an economic distinction . . . . When determining the incidence of a tax, it is important to bear in mind the context within which the tax operates as well as the purpose of the tax.

The categories approach is not always helpful because it does not provide an unequivocal answer to the nature of a tax. For example, a land tax would usually be a direct tax; it may, however, also be an indirect tax under the legal incidence test. As Iacobucci J said in *Ontario Home Builders' Association v York (Region) Board of Education*:

> The hallmarks of a land tax are that the tax is, of course, imposed on land against the owner of the land, and that the tax is assessed as a percentage of the value of the land, or a fixed charge per acre. The tax may be an annual, recurring assessment, or a one-time charge . . . . Although landowners, like everyone, may wish to pass on their tax burden to someone else or otherwise avoid taxation, this desire or ability does not transform the direct nature of the tax into an indirect one . . . the case law reveals that land taxes are generally direct taxes; but I do not believe the case law prevents a tax on land by itself from being treated as an indirect tax.[17]

Most economists consider Mill's definition of direct and indirect taxes to be narrow and rigid. Indeed, the question as to who actually bears the burden of a tax ("incidence of taxation") is an unsettled economic issue.

Nevertheless, in constitutional terms, Mill's distinction between the two forms of taxes is the legal yardstick[18] and the courts regularly use the test.[19] Given the uncertainty of the ultimate incidence of a tax, for the purposes of constitutional law, Mill's definition is a useful demarcation between direct and indirect taxes.[20]

See John Stuart Mill, *Principles of Political Economy* (London: Parker & Son, 1852) Book V.

17   *Ontario Home Builders' Assn*, above note 13 at para 46.

18   See *Lambe v North British & Mercantile Fire & Life Insurance Co (sub nom Bank of Toronto v Lambe)* (1887), LR 12 App Cas 575 (JCPC from Quebec) [*Lambe*].

19   *Re Eurig Estate*, [1998] 2 SCR 565 (taxpayer challenged Ontario's estate probate fees as being an indirect tax beyond the power of the provincial government. Applying Mill's definition, the tax would be indirect if the executor was personally liable for payment of probate fees, as the intention would clearly be that the executor would recover payment from the beneficiaries of the estate. However, the legislation did not make the executor personally liable for the fees. The executor would pay only in his or her representative capacity. The majority of the Supreme Court held that amounts collected in respect of grants of letters probate constituted a tax rather than a regulatory fee. The probate fee was a direct tax and, therefore, *intra vires* the Province of Ontario.)
See also *Hudson's Bay Co v Ontario (AG)* (2000), 49 OR (3d) 455 (SCJ), aff'd (2001), 52 OR (3d) 737 (CA).

20   *Lambe*, above note 18.

1) Restraint on Powers

Section 125 of the *Constitution Act, 1867* provides that no lands or property belonging to Canada or any province shall be liable to taxation. This provision provides inter-governmental immunity from taxation in respect of "lands or property" owned by the federal or provincial Crown. The restriction also extends to Crown agents such as Crown corporations.[21]

Section 125 applies not only to provincial lands or property but also to taxes levied on persons and transactions in respect of Crown property. Thus, the section overrides the express powers of taxation contained in subsections 91(3) (the federal power) and 92(2) (the provincial power) of the *Constitution Act, 1867* and provides constitutional immunity from federal taxation of provincial property.[22] The immunity is absolute and restrains the federal government from imposing tax on provincial lands, property, Crown agents and transactions directly involving provincial property, regardless of whether or not the province is involved in commercial activity.

2) *Charter of Rights and Freedoms*

The *Income Tax Act* is also subject to the *Canadian Charter of Rights and Freedoms*.[23] Two provisions of the *Charter* are particularly relevant in the context of income tax law: the provision of equal rights and the right to be secure against unreasonable search and seizure.

Section 15 of the *Charter* reads:

15. (1) Every individual is equal before and under the law and has the right to the equal protection and equal benefit of the law without discrimination and, in particular, without discrimination based on race, national or ethnic origin, colour, religion, sex, age or mental or physical disability.

(2) Subsection (1) does not preclude any law, program or activity that has as its object the amelioration of conditions of disadvantaged individuals or groups including those that are disadvantaged because of race, national or ethnic origin, colour, religion, sex, age or mental or physical disability.

---

21 See, for example, *Nova Scotia Power Inc v Canada*, 2004 SCC 51 (Nova Scotia Power Inc acting within its purposes as a Crown agent and thus entitled to immunity from legislation, including the *Income Tax Act* as provided by s 17 of the *Interpretation Act*, RSC 1985, c I-21).
22 *Re Exported Natural Gas Tax*, above note 12.
23 *Canadian Charter of Rights and Freedoms*, Part I of the *Constitution Act, 1982*, being Schedule B to the *Canada Act 1982* (UK), 1982, c 11.

Section 8 of the *Charter* reads:

Everyone has the right to be secure against unreasonable search or seizure.

Note the significant omission of "property rights" from Section 15(1) of the *Charter*, which significantly lowers the protection of taxpayer rights.

3) Territorial Limitations

The Act applies only to persons who have a physical or economic *nexus*, bond or link with Canada.[24] It is a well accepted principle in Anglo-Canadian law that fiscal statutes are not enforced outside the territorial scope of the country responsible for their legislation. Canada does not enforce foreign tax laws, and it will not, even indirectly, assist foreign countries in the enforcement of their tax laws in Canadian courts.[25]

4) Administration of Act

The Minister of Finance determines the policy of tax legislation that is within the authority of the federal power.[26] The Minister of National Revenue is responsible for administering the Act.[27] Thus, unlike most other countries, Canada divides the responsibility for enacting and administering fiscal legislation.

---

24   See, generally, *Allied Farm Equipment v MNR*, [1972] CTC 619 (FCA). See also *Lea-Don Canada Ltd v MNR*, [1969] CTC 85 (Ex Ct), aff'd [1970] CTC 346 (SCC) (CCA not claimable by non-residents unless carrying on business in Canada).

25   *Holman v Johnson* (1775), 98 ER 1120 (should individual with knowledge of smuggling scheme be permitted remedy for non-payment of price); *Queen of Holland v Drukker*, [1928] 1 Ch 877 (whether foreign national (Dutch sovereign) permitted to sue in English Courts for revenue claim against Dutch subject). See also, for example, *US v Harden*, [1963] CTC 450 (SCC), where the United States government sought to circumvent this rule, first by obtaining a judgment in the United States court and then by contending that it was seeking to apply, not the United States tax law, but merely the enforceability of a judgment of the United States courts. This was rejected by the Supreme Court of Canada as an indirect attempt to enforce foreign fiscal legislation. See also *AG of Canada v RJ Reynolds Tobacco Holdings* (30 June 2000), United States District Court (Northern District of New York) (United States courts will not normally enforce foreign tax judgments).

26   *Financial Administration Act*, RSC 1985, c F-11.

27   *Canada Customs and Revenue Agency Act*, SC 1999, c 17.

5) Federal-Provincial Agreements

Federal-provincial income tax arrangements are governed by the *Federal-Provincial Fiscal Arrangements Act*.[28] Under the arrangement with the provinces and territories, the federal Parliament unilaterally vacates a portion of the income tax field to the provinces. The withdrawal of the federal government allows the provinces to re-enter the income tax field and impose their own taxes.

The federal government has tax collection agreements (TCAs) with most of the provinces, under which the federal government collects the provincial income tax on behalf of the provinces. To facilitate tax collection and assessment, the agreements require the provinces to levy their tax by reference to a taxable base that is identical to that used for federal income tax purposes.

Participating provinces can use either of two methods: (1) "tax on tax" or (2) "tax on income." Under the "tax on tax" method, individuals pay provincial tax as a percentage of their federal tax. The "tax on income" method calculates provincial income tax as a percentage of the individual's *taxable income* rather than of their federal tax payable. Thus, the "tax on income" method allows the provinces to determine its own unique income tax brackets and rates and to create its own distinct block of non-refundable tax credits. This allows the provinces greater flexibility in setting their tax policy. However, the provinces must still use the federal definition of "taxable income" in order to ensure a common tax base.

Ensuring a common tax base not only facilitates tax collection and assessment, but also mitigates the problems that can arise where there are significant discrepancies in tax policy between provinces. For example, a province may wish to establish a very low tax rate on capital income, compared with other sources of income, in order to attract highly mobile capital from other provinces. If this was permitted, it could negatively impact the national economy.

The federal government has TCAs with all the provinces and territories (except Quebec) for the collection of personal income taxes. For corporate taxes, it has TCAs with all the provinces and territories except Quebec, Ontario and Alberta. Residents of Quebec receive an abatement of 16.5 percent from their basic federal tax, but must pay Quebec income tax according to a special scale of provincial rates.

---

28   *Federal-Provincial Fiscal Arrangements Act*, RSC 1985, c F-8.

6) The Executive Process

The responsibility for fiscal policy and legislation is with the Minister of Finance. The Department of Finance advises the Minister on changes to income tax legislation. The Department also prepares tax policy papers and most of the income tax legislation. The Tax Policy and Legislation Division of the Department reports through an Assistant Deputy Minister to the Deputy Minister of Finance.

The responsibility for administering the Act is with the Canada Revenue Agency (CRA), which also has a tax policy division. The Department of Finance and the CRA[29] liaise closely on income tax legislation.

7) The Legislative Process

Legislation in respect of income tax commences in the House of Commons on the recommendation of the Governor General.[30] Income tax legislation may not be introduced in the Senate. A private member cannot introduce tax legislation in the House of Commons.

8) The Budget

The Minister of Finance presents the government's budget[31] to the House of Commons, following which he tables a Notice of Ways and Means Motions to introduce amendments to the Act. The budget allows the government of the day an opportunity to review the state of the economy and to announce policies in respect of economic and fiscal programs. Following the budget, there is a debate in the House. The debate cannot exceed six sitting days of the House of Commons.

Some time after the budget debate, the Minister of Finance introduces amending legislation in the form of a bill to implement the proposals set out in the Notice of Ways and Means Motion. The bill is given a first reading in the House to make it a public document and is then debated in principle during second reading. Following second reading,

---

29 In December 2003, the Canada Customs and Revenue Agency became the Canada Revenue Agency. The Customs program is now part of the new Canada Border Services Agency.

30 *Constitution Act, 1867*, above note 8, ss 53 & 54.

31 "Budget" (contrary to the understanding of the term by accountants who view it as a financial statement) is a derivation from the old French *bougette*, meaning "a little bag." In British parliamentary tradition, the "little bag" was replaced by a "little box" (14½" by 10") made for Gladstone in about 1860. The box was replaced by a new one in 1996.

income tax bills are debated by the Committee of Ways and Means, which is a committee of the whole House.[32]

The bill may also be considered by specialized committees such as the Committee on Finance, Trade and Economic Affairs, where particular provisions of the bill may be amended. Following detailed examination of the bill by the Committee of the Whole House, it is given third reading and sent to the Senate.

The Senate does not have the power to initiate income tax legislation. It does, however, have the constitutional authority to debate tax bills that have been referred to it by the House of Commons. The Senate Committee on Banking, Trade and Commerce is an influential committee whose deliberations may have a substantial impact on such a bill. As a practical matter, with the exception of purely technical changes, the Senate does not amend income tax legislation without the approval of the Cabinet.

Finally, the bill is sent for Royal Assent and becomes law the day that it receives it and comes into force. Amendments enacted through a bill, however, are effective as of the date that the legislation stipulates. Thus, tax legislation has a retrospective aspect.

D. THE MEANING OF "TAX"

A "tax" is a compulsory contribution that governments levy on individuals, firms or property in order to fund government operations.[33] Thus, the primary purpose of any tax is to raise revenue. However, governments also use tax law for other purposes—for example, to implement socio-economic and political policies.

A levy may be a tax even if it is disguised by a more attractive name. For example, the Canada Pension Plan and Employment Insurance are compulsory transfer payments determined by reference to payroll income. Hence, they are payroll taxes on earned income. The benefits that individuals derive do not necessarily correspond to their contributions. Similarly, the airport and other security taxes[34] imposed after 11 September 2001 are, in fact, user taxes on air travel to finance security needs.

---

32   Unlike bills dealing with non-tax matters, it is the entire House that constitutes the Committee. The public may not make representations directly to the Committee of the Whole House.

33   *Re Eurig Estate*, above note 19.

34   Air Travellers Security Charge.

E. "TAXPAYERS"

An income tax system must identify the types of taxpayers that it shall tax. This seemingly obvious task causes a good deal of complexity in the tax system because most business is conducted through artificial entities, some with multiple dimensions. The Canadian income tax system applies to:

- Individuals;
- Corporations;
- Trusts; and
- Partnerships.

Each individual is a taxpayer in his own right and must file a tax return in respect of tax payable for the year. Corporations, trusts and estates are also taxpayers in their own right and file separate returns from their owners or beneficiaries.

A partnership is not a taxpayer, but we determine partnership income level *as if* it were an entity. The partners then declare their share of income in their individual tax returns.

F. TAX POLICY

A tax system should raise sufficient revenue to finance government operations. A good tax system, however, is about more than generating sufficient revenue. Tax policy concerns the manner in which we collect revenues and the effect that it has on the economy. A "good" tax system should be:

- Neutral;
- Efficient;
- Fair and equitable; and
- Administratively simple and certain.

Thus, tax law is necessarily a compromise of competing economic, social and political values. Tax policy analysis evaluates the efficiency and effectiveness of the compromises.

1) Revenue Generation

It is trite to say that we levy income taxes to generate sufficient revenues to finance government operations. The amount of revenue that a tax system raises is a simple mathematical function:

$$\text{Revenue} = \text{Tax Base} \times \text{Tax Rate}$$

Thus, there are only two variables that directly determine the amount of revenue that a tax system raises. The interplay between these two variables, however, influences the manner in which we achieve other non-revenue objectives of the system. The size and character of the tax base (what is taxed?) and tax rates (how much is taxed?) affect the fairness of the system, its economic efficiency and administrative simplicity.

We can increase or decrease revenue by enlarging or contracting the tax base, or by increasing or decreasing the tax rate. Governments use both variables to political advantage. The smaller the base, the higher the rate required to generate a given amount of revenue. Conversely, the larger the base, the lower the rate needed to generate a pre-determined amount of revenue. The formula, however, is not that simple. High rates can reduce the tax base through tax avoidance and flight of capital. We should be careful in international tax comparisons to consider both elements, tax base and tax rate, to get at the effective tax rate and the amount of tax actually paid.

The size of the tax base also has an effect on other aspects of the tax system. A system with a broad base is usually more certain and simpler than a system with a narrowly constrained base. This is because a broad-based system requires fewer lines of demarcation between classifications of income and expenditures than a narrowly based system.

A system that taxes gains (a comprehensive tax base), regardless of the types of transactions from which they derive, requires fewer rules to implement than a system that distinguishes between different types of economic gains. For example, a system that taxes income at full rates and capital gains at half-rates is necessarily more complex than one that does not.

We can generate the same amount of revenue from a broadly based concept of income as from a narrowly based system by adjusting tax rates. The trade-off between the two, however, effects the economic efficiency of the system and its complexity, which, in turn, affects the amount of avoidance, the cost of compliance and tax administration.

The timing of when tax is payable is also an important consideration in the collection of taxes. Given the time-value of money, the earlier that a government collects taxes, the greater the revenue. From the taxpayer's perspective, tax deferral is tax saving. In the chapters following, we will encounter numerous rules targeted at preventing tax deferral by taxpayers.

2) Neutrality

Neutrality means that a tax system should not draw artificial distinctions between identical transactions merely based on the legal form of transactions or their source. Thus, neutrality implies a level playing field that does not favour, or unfairly discriminate against, taxpayers based on their choice of entities or relationships to structure business and personal transactions. For example, in a perfectly neutral system, the tax consequences of a transaction that an individual, corporation, partnership or trust engages in would be the same.

As we will see, the Canadian tax system is far from neutral, and invites behavioural responses from taxpayers who are often motivated purely by tax considerations. This is inevitable. Taxpayers faced with choices respond to the system and attempt to minimize their tax burden. To do otherwise would be irrational.

For example, a Canadian-controlled private corporation pays federal tax at a rate of approximately 11 percent (2011) on the first $500,000 of active business income.[35] In contrast, an individual in the top bracket pays federal tax at approximately 29 percent on the same income. Since the low rate of tax is not available to foreign corporations or businesses conducted as proprietorships, partnerships or trusts, the system favours Canadian corporate business.[36] This systemic bias is an intrinsic part of the tax system to which taxpayers respond quite rationally. Hence, absent legal prohibition, an individual will almost invariably choose to conduct a profitable Canadian business through a corporation in order to save tax. To do otherwise would attract higher taxes.

3) Efficiency

Tax efficiency concerns the efficient allocation of economic resources to maximize production and economic growth. A tax policy is efficient if it promotes the optimal allocation of capital. A tax system can distort efficiency and capital flows by causing persons to make business decisions solely on tax considerations. This is true both in domestic and international markets. Thus, we should evaluate tax measures (for example, tax expenditures[37]) intended to stimulate or encourage economic activities based on their cost effectiveness in the light of the objectives. For example, we can evaluate an investment tax credit based

---

35 *ITA*, above note 2, subs 125(2).

36 See, generally, *ibid*, s 125(1).

37 Tax revenues foregone by the government. For example, the reduced rate of corporate tax for manufacturing and processing activities.

on the increased investment that it stimulates against its cost in lost revenues; an employment credit by its effect on employment rates.

Thus, we ask:

- Does the statutory provision deliver the objectives sought in a cost-efficient manner?
- Is the statutory provision target efficient so that only those persons it is intended to benefit take advantage of it?
- Can we achieve the same economic objectives more effectively or efficiently through an alternative non-tax mechanism?
- Does the statutory provision shift economic activity towards tax-saving projects that distort markets? and
- Does the statutory provision lead to a non-optimal allocation of resources?

Similarly in international tax, provisions can distort economic decisions and cause a non-optimal allocation of capital. The principle of capital export or international neutrality, for example, suggests that a taxpayer's choice between investing at home or abroad should not be affected by the pattern of taxation.[38] For example, a Canadian corporate tax rate that is significantly higher than international norms stimulates export of capital and jobs to countries with lower rates in order to enhance global after-tax return on equity. We have capital export neutrality if we tax a Multinational Enterprise's (MNE) foreign and domestic income at the same total rate. For example, if we tax the Royal Bank of Canada at 35 percent on its Canadian income and at 30 percent on its UK subsidiary's profits, the Canadian tax system is neutral only if it taxes RBC at a net rate (after foreign credits) of 5 percent on its foreign income. (This assumes that nominal and effective rates of tax are the same.)

4) Fairness

A tax system must be fair. Anything less than a fair system invites blatant tax avoidance and evasion. Tax equity is concerned with the optimality of distribution. An equitable tax policy is one that treats similarly situated taxpayers in a similar manner (horizontal equity) and promotes a fair distribution of income (vertical equity).

Despite the political rhetoric during elections, it is not easy to settle upon a common measure of fairness. Fairness incorporates social, pol-

---

38   See, for example, Peggy B Musgrave, *United States Taxation of Foreign Investment Income: Issues and Arguments* (Cambridge, MA: Harvard Law School, 1969) at 109; Lawrence B Krause & Kenneth W Dam, *Federal Tax Treatment of Foreign Income* (Washington: Brookings Institution, 1964) at 46–52.

itical and moral values. Hence, determining whether a tax system is fair (or in tax parlance, "equitable") is contentious.

There is, however, some consensus on the meaning of "fairness" in taxation. First, most people would agree that taxpayers in similar financial circumstances should pay similar amounts of tax. Thus, an individual who earns $100,000 from employment should be taxed at the same rate as another employee who earns $100,000. We refer to this aspect of fairness as horizontal equity: equal treatment of those with equal ability to pay.

Hence, the accurate measurement of "income" is integral to the fairness of a tax system. The measurement of non-cash benefits is particularly contentious. For example, consider two individuals, Jane and Harry, both of whom are in a 50 percent tax bracket. Jane earns $150,000 as a public servant in government; Harry is employed in the private sector, earns $100,000 in salary, but also gets free accommodation valued at $50,000. Applying the principle of horizontal equity, we should tax both Jane and Harry in a similar manner because they earn equal amounts of income, albeit in different forms. But what if Jane trades off $10,000 of her salary in exchange for her employer providing on-site child care services that previously cost her $20,000 (after-tax) a year? Should Jane be taxed on $140,000, $150,000, $160,000 or $180,000?

Equity also requires that we recognize a taxpayer's ability to pay, which may be quite different from the taxpayer's "income" in an accounting sense. Assume, for example, that Harry, a single father with four infant children, looks after his elderly mother who suffers from chronic dementia. Jane is single, in good health, and spends her money on sailing. We recognize all these personal elements in the measure of the taxpayer's "ability to pay." The debate is not about having a fair tax system, but about the scope and extent of "fairness."

Second, there is general agreement that individuals with higher incomes should pay "more tax" than individuals with lower incomes. Most people will agree that an individual who earns $100,000 in a year should pay more tax than an individual who earns $30,000. This is the principle of vertical equity. This principle, premised on the theory that a taxpayer should pay according to her ability to pay, does not, in itself, provide a ready answer to the more difficult question: How *much* more should the rich pay than the poor? In technical terms, what is the ideal slope of the tax rate curve?

a) Proportional Tax Rates
In a proportional rate system, an individual's entire taxable base is taxed at a flat rate. For example, if three taxpayers—A, B and C with

taxable incomes of $20,000, $40,000 and $60,000 respectively—are each taxed at a flat rate of 17 percent, they would pay taxes commensurately proportionate with their income as follows:

Taxpayer	Taxable Income	Tax	Average Rate
A	$20,000	$3,400	17%
B	$40,000	$6,800	17%
C	$60,000	$10,200	17%

Thus, in a proportional rate system, higher income levels bear a heavier tax burden. In the above example, C pays three times, and B pays twice, the total tax that A pays, each according to their income level. The description "flat tax" refers to the shape of the curve or line plotted on a graph that displays the tax rate on the vertical axis and income on the horizontal axis. It does not refer to the amount of tax paid. Thus, a true flat tax takes the same percentage of everyone's income; a family with twice the taxable income of another would pay twice the tax.

Sales and consumption taxes (such as the HST) are proportional taxes; that is, they apply at a flat rate to all sales, regardless of the amount expended. The shape of the tax rate curve should not be confused with the incidence of a tax. The HST, for example, is a flat tax on consumption, but is regressive when measured against income. It takes a higher percentage of income from lower income levels than it does from higher income levels. All flat taxes (gasoline, airline, alcohol, tobacco, entertainment, gaming and fishing, excise, environmental, energy, etc.) on use or consumption are regressive when measured against income. The policy issue is whether the incidence and degree of regressivity of a tax properly reflects the economic and social values of society. If it does not, we can rectify the situation's regressivity through tax rebates and credits.

b) Progressive Taxation

Most Canadians agree with the principle that individuals with higher incomes should pay more tax than individuals who earn less. The underlying premise is that higher income individuals have a greater ability to pay taxes and, therefore, it is fair that they pay more tax. But how much more is "fair"? The difficulty is that many believe that a tax system is fair if it taxes the other person.

No one seriously argues with the principle that an individual who earns $150,000 should pay more tax than an individual who earns $30,000. However, is it sufficient to pay proportionately more or does the principle compel us to inevitably conclude that higher income earners must also pay progressively more than lower income earners? If higher incomes should pay progressively more taxes, what is the appropriate rate of progression? There are no easy answers to these questions.

Canada taxes individuals on a progressive basis. The adjective "progressive" refers not to the quality of our Byzantine tax law, but to the aspect of our system by which the marginal rate of tax increases at various levels of taxable income. For example, in 2011, the four basic federal rates of tax for individuals were:

- 15 percent on the first $41,544 or less;
- 22 percent on the next $41,544;
- 26 percent on the next $45,712; and
- 29 percent on income over $128,800.[39]

Thus, a person who earns $150,000 pays not only more tax in absolute dollars than an individual who earns $30,000, but the rate of federal tax progresses from 15 percent to 29 percent as income rises.

We justify progressive taxation on the principle that an individual's ability (though not his enthusiasm) to pay tax increases as his income rises. This assumption, however, only starts the debate. One-third of Canadian taxpayers (of which there are approximately 22 million) do not pay any income tax at all. The non-payers file tax returns primarily to receive benefits paid out as income redistribution under the HST and child-tax benefits. That leaves the remaining two-thirds to make up the necessary revenues.

As we move up the income scale, the numbers of taxpayers drop off dramatically and the percentage of tax collected increases progressively. Contrary to popular myth, Canadian socio-economic demographics are not very egalitarian. In 2009, for example, only 1.6 percent of Canadians made more than $150,000. This group includes professionals such as lawyers, doctors, accountants, etc. Average income in 2009 was $37,300, while median income was $27,400, and 19.6 percent of the population made less than $10,000 per year. Another 19.2 percent made between $10,000 and $19,999 in 2009.

At the top of the heap (incomes above $250,000) society becomes even more elitist. Only 97,370 people in all of Canada, 0.4 percent of the taxable population, qualified for admission into this club. Nevertheless, this group paid $18 billion in taxes, 16 percent of the total taxes collected, or 40 times their proportional number.

Thus, contrary to popular opinion, the rich in Canada do actually pay substantial taxes. However, there is no consensus, and likely never will be, on the meaning of what is fair in taxation.

---

39   Online: www.cra-arc.gc.ca/tx/ndvdls/fq/txrts-eng.html.

c) Marginal Tax Rates

The basic federal tax rate for individuals starts out at 15 percent and rises to 29 percent. Coupled with provincial tax rates, combined federal-provincial rates start at approximately 22 percent and increase to nearly 50 percent as income increases. Since provincial rates vary between provinces, the ultimate tax burden is a function of where one resides. Are these rates high or low? Are they overly progressive or not progressive enough? The top Canadian marginal rate is about 48 percent.

The progressive tax rate structure for individuals (and to a lesser extent corporations) is an incentive for taxpayers to arrange their affairs to reduce their marginal rate. Since every dollar of tax saving is at the top marginal rate of tax, taxpayers have an incentive to siphon off income to family members with lower marginal tax rates. For example, anti-avoidance rules in section 74.1 prevent income shifting for the purposes of marginal tax rate minimization. Similarly, the low tax rate on corporate business income up to $500,000 is an incentive to create multiple corporations. Thus, anti-avoidance rules treat associated corporations as one entity for the purpose of the low rate of tax.[40]

The more comprehensive the taxable base, the lower the rate required to produce a given amount of revenue. Hence, exclusion of income from the taxable base invariably necessitates a higher tax rate to produce a given amount of revenue. Exclusions of income from the taxable base also distort horizontal equity. For example, the exclusion of gambling gains from taxable income has two separate effects. First, it is unfair because it creates a preference for a particular form of income. Why should a person who derives a million dollars from a lottery ticket be treated more generously than an individual who derives $60,000 from employment?

Second, the exclusion means that the tax rate on other forms of income must necessarily be higher to produce a given amount of revenue. Thus, it is important that policy-makers carefully consider exclusions from income and tax preferences (for example, non-taxation of gains on principal residences) both in the light of government revenue requirements and the principles of tax fairness.

5) Simplicity and Certainty

A good tax system is one that can be administered economically and should not impose unreasonable compliance costs on taxpayers. The more complex the system, the higher the compliance costs.

A tax system should also be simple. This is particularly important in the case of personal taxes—the majority of individuals should be

---

40   *ITA*, above note 2, subs 256(2.1).

able to comply with the law without being put to unnecessary professional fees for expert advice.

There is danger, however, in overstating these attributes. A tax system must be certain so that taxpayers can plan their affairs and business transactions secure in the knowledge that the consequences that attach to the transactions are as predicted. On the other hand, business transactions in a complex economy are inherently uncertain and some degree of complexity is inevitable.

6) Compromise of Values

Tax law is a compromise between competing values. Tax policy objectives of revenue generation, neutrality, efficiency, fairness and administrative feasibility pull in different directions.

At any given required level of revenue, a neutral tax system is less complex than one that has multiple distinctions between classes of taxpayers and types of income. A neutral system, however, may be less sensitive to the objective of fairness, which implies distinctions based on ability to pay. For example, income taxes are levied both on individuals and on corporations at different rates. This creates two tensions. First, there is an incentive to choose the form of organization that attracts the lowest rate of tax. There is a substantial difference between taxes imposed on Canadian small businesses and the top marginal rate of tax on individuals. This creates a bias in favour of the corporate form of organization and makes the tax system less neutral.

Second, the levy on corporations results in double taxation of income, once at the corporate level and then again at the personal shareholder level when profits, net of tax, are distributed. Double taxation is inefficient and unfair to taxpayers. The mechanism to minimize double taxation through shareholder credits for corporate taxes makes the system fairer, but also more complex.

The following grid sets out the variables that we should consider when we evaluate policy.

| | | Tax Policy Objectives | | | |
	Revenue	Fairness	Efficiency	Neutrality	Simplicity
Who is taxable?					
What is taxable?					
How much is taxed (rate)?					
When is income taxed?					
Administrative controls and compliance?					

Structure of Act

7) Tax Expenditures

A government can achieve its social and economic policies in several ways. It can spend directly on programs by providing grants and subsidies through its annual budget process. Such expenditures are generally referred to as "budgetary expenditures" because their estimates are tabled in Parliament as part of the annual budget process.

A government can also pursue its social and economic policies indirectly by using the tax system. It can provide incentives for particular initiatives or activities, and implement social policies by providing an exemption, deduction, credit or deferral through the tax system. We refer to such exemptions, deductions, credits and deferrals as "tax expenditures" because they entail costs by giving up revenues.

Thus, tax expenditures are an alternative form of government expenditures. They differ from budgetary expenditures because they are not tabled as direct outgoings and, therefore, do not require parliamentary spending approval. Instead, tax expenditures are approved indirectly through the legislative process that enacts income tax law.

The term "tax expenditure" is a neutral term. It simply refers to expenditures that deviate from a "benchmark" tax system. A benchmark tax system refers to a normative system that measures income without reference to special incentives to achieve social, economic and other policy objectives.

The definition of income is central to the determination of what is a tax expenditure. Tax provisions that provide for the deduction of normal current costs incurred to earn income are considered to be part of the benchmark system and, therefore, not tax expenditures. Tax provisions that fall outside of what are considered to be "normal" deductions are tax expenditures.

The measurement of income is crucial to the benchmark because any deviation from the benchmark is considered a tax expenditure. For example, the deduction of salaries and wages from income is considered a normal expenditure intrinsic to the measurement of net business income. Thus, the deduction of such expenditures in the measurement of business income are "normal."

In contrast, a tax credit for donations to political parties is not intrinsic to the measurement of net income. The purpose of the credit is to encourage support for a democratic system of government and to engage Canadians in the political process. Hence, the cost of the political contributions credit is a tax expenditure outside the benchmark tax system.

Identifying a proper benchmark tax structure is difficult and controversial. A benchmark necessarily implies value judgments. The debate is not on the usefulness of tax expenditure analysis, but upon what goes into the list of "tax expenditures" that require analysis. For example, if child-care expenses are viewed as personal and part of the living expenses of parents, the deduction for such expenses in computing income is a tax expenditure because they are not part of the normal benchmark for net income. On the other hand, if child-care expenses are seen as necessary expenditures incurred for the process of earning income, deductions for such expenses are not tax expenditures. In either case, the foregone revenue from the deduction for child-care expenses—whether as part of the benchmark determination of income or as a tax expenditure—represents a financial cost to the public treasury. The controversy is not so much about the fact that child-care expenses cost the federal treasury, but whether we should identify such expenses as "tax expenditures" for analytical purposes.

G. THE JUDICIAL PROCESS[41]

The responsibility for litigating income tax disputes rests primarily with the Department of Justice. A taxpayer who disagrees with the CRA's assessment of her income tax liability may appeal the assessment in the Tax Court of Canada. An appeal or review of a decision of the Tax Court lies with the Federal Court of Appeal and from there, with leave, to the Supreme Court of Canada.

1) The Tax Court

The Tax Court of Canada is the sole trier of facts in disputes under the *Income Tax Act*. Where the minister confirms the assessment, the taxpayer can appeal the assessment to the Tax Court.[42] The time limit for an appeal is generally ninety days from the date that the minister mails the Notice of Confirmation to the taxpayer. If the minister does not respond to the taxpayer's Notice of Objection within ninety days, the taxpayer can appeal at any time.

Appeals to the Tax Court follow one of two procedures: informal or general.

a) Informal Procedure
The Informal Procedure is the equivalent of a "small claims" process. It is available only if the aggregate of all tax amounts (other than interest

---

41   For a fuller discussion, see Chapter 21.
42   *ITA*, above note 2, s 169.

or provincial tax) in dispute does not exceed $12,000, the amount of the loss in issue does not exceed $24,000, or the only amount in dispute is the amount of interest assessed under the Act.[43]

b) General Procedure

The General Procedure is formal, full-blown civil litigation. It applies to disputes in which federal tax exceeds $12,000. A taxpayer can represent herself or be represented by a lawyer. Non-lawyer agents are not allowed to plead before the Tax Court in a General Procedure appeal. Formal rules of evidence govern the General Procedure and the decisions of the Tax Court following such an appeal are judicial precedents.

In contrast with the Informal Procedure, there is no pre-determined time frame for completion of an appeal in the General Procedure, and the process can take several years. The parties may appeal a decision of the Tax Court under the General Procedure to the Federal Court of Appeal, pursuant to the rules of the *Federal Court Act*.[44]

2) Federal Court of Appeal

A taxpayer must institute an appeal to the Federal Court within thirty days from the judgment of the Tax Court. The thirty-day limitation excludes the months of July and August.[45] An appeal commences by filing a Notice of Appeal with the Federal Court Registry and by serving all parties who are directly affected by the appeal with a true copy of the notice. The Federal Court of Appeal usually hears appeals with a panel of three judges.[46]

3) Supreme Court of Canada

The Supreme Court of Canada is the final arbiter of income tax matters. Recourse to the Supreme Court, however, is possible only with leave to appeal, which is difficult to obtain in tax cases. There is no automatic right of appeal to the Supreme Court. Hence, for all practical purposes, the Federal Court of Appeal is the final appellate tribunal in more than 95 percent of income tax cases.

A taxpayer must bring an appeal to the Supreme Court within sixty days from the date that the Court of Appeal hands down its decision. A copy of the Notice of Appeal must be filed with the Registrar of the

---

43   *Tax Court of Canada Act*, RSC 1985, T-2, subs 18(1).

44   RSC 1985, c F-7.

45   *Ibid*, subs 27(2).

46   *Ibid*, s 27, and *ITA*, above note 2, subs 180(1).

Supreme Court and all parties directly affected by the appeal must be served with a copy of the notice.

The technical requirements are that:

- The Federal Court of Appeal thinks that the question involved is one that ought to be decided by the Supreme Court; or
- The Supreme Court is of the view that the issue litigated is one of national importance. The dollar value of the dispute is irrelevant.[47]

As a practical matter, the Supreme Court rarely, if ever, grants leave in more than two tax cases in any year.

H. DECLARATION OF TAXPAYER RIGHTS

The role of taxation in history has been dramatic. King John's penchant for increasing feudal taxation in England without consultation with his lords precipitated the greatest constitutional document in the common law world, the *Magna Carta*.

Similarly, the underlying grievance of the Peasants' Revolt of 1381 was a poll tax on all males and females over the age of fifteen. The drama of the event is recorded in David Hume's *History of England:*

> The first disorder was raised by a blacksmith in a village of Essex. The tax-gatherers came to this man's shop while he was at work; and they demanded payment for his daughter, who he asserted to be below the age assigned by the statute. One of these fellows offered to produce a very indecent proof to the contrary, and at the same time laid hold of the maid: which the father resenting, immediately knocked out the ruffian's brains with his hammer.

The image of the modern tax collector has improved, but only slightly. *The Report of the Task Force on Revenue Canada,*[48] prepared by the Conservative Party in Opposition, commented on the tax collectors' proclivity towards oppressive conduct and insensitive behaviour. Concerning Revenue Canada's (now the Canada Revenue Agency's) tax collection methods, the Task Force stated:

---

47   See, for example, *Canada v Savage,* [1980] CTC 103 (FCTD), rev'd on other grounds [1981] CTC 332 (FCA), aff'd [1983] CTC 393 (SCC) (leave to appeal $300 assessment granted).

48   (Ottawa: Conservative Party of Canada, 1984).

What we heard disturbed us deeply. We were distressed by the fear with which ordinary Canadians greet a call from the tax department, a fear that is sometimes cultivated by Revenue Canada.

Another impression that was deeply instilled in us during our tour was that the tax burden is falling disproportionately on Canadians of modest means, as a result of Revenue Canada's actions.

The complexity of the many provisions affecting lower income Canadians often causes serious resentment. This is also the group that is most likely to be audited by less-experienced employees who may make serious errors. These taxpayers can least afford the costly professional assistance needed to defend their rights.

Another factor that undermines the rights of ordinary Canadians is the sweeping powers given to the Department. In some cases, they are even greater than the powers of the police.

Later that year, the Conservative Government, by then in power, issued a declaratory statement, impressively entitled the "Declaration of Taxpayer Rights" which addressed some of the Task Force's concerns. However, the government did not enact the Declaration into law.

The *Charter of Rights* does not protect property rights and taxpayers have few constitutional protections against the tax collector. A notable exception is in the area of search and seizures to prosecute tax evasion. Apart from this narrow exception, the courts view the *Income Tax Act* as a regulatory statute. Hence, for example, the courts uphold the reverse onus clause, which presumes the minister's assessment to be proper and correct unless the taxpayer proves it is not.

I. CONCLUSION

This chapter has highlighted the multi-faceted nature of the income tax system. Apart from raising revenues for government operations, income tax law also concerns various aspects of government economic and social policies. Since an income tax statute expropriates private property for public purposes, it is almost inevitable that taxpayers will attempt to resist, or at least minimize, the effect of expropriation. The tension between the taxpayer and the tax collector necessitates complex provisions to prevent undue leakage of tax revenues. The scope of coverage and the changing nature of domestic and international economies require frequent changes as taxpayers adapt and adopt new techniques of tax minimization.

FURTHER READINGS

History

BALE, GORDON. "The Individual and Tax Reform in Canada" (1971) 49 Can Bar Rev 24.

BITTKER, BORIS. "A Comprehensive Tax Base as a Goal of Income Tax Reform" (1967) 80 Harv L Rev 925.

BLUM, WALTER. "Federal Income Tax Reform: Twenty Questions" (November 1963) 41 Taxes 672.

BREAK, GEORGE, & JOSEPH PECHMAN. *Federal Tax Reform: The Impossible Dream* (Washington: Brookings Institution, 1975).

HEAD, JOHN. "The Carter Legacy: An International Perspective" (1987) 4:2 Australian Tax Forum 143.

KRISHNA, VERN. "A Law that Taxes our Understanding" (1986) 10:9 Can Law.

Constitutional Authority for Taxation

HOGG, PETER. *Constitutional Law of Canada*, loose-leaf (Scarborough: Carswell, 2007).

LA FOREST, GV. *The Allocation of Taxing Power under the Canadian Constitution*, Canadian Tax Paper No 45 (Toronto: Canadian Tax Foundation, 1967).

The Legislative Process

CANADIAN TAX FOUNDATION COMMITTEE ON THE BUDGET PROCESS. "The Canadian Budget Process" (1986) 34 Can Tax J 989.

The Executive Process

EDWARDS, STANLEY. "Drafting Fiscal Legislation" (1984) 32 Can Tax J 727.

The Income Tax Process

DAVIDSON, DLH. "The Reorganization of the Legislation Branch of Revenue Canada Taxation" (1978) 26 Can Tax J 429.

DRACHE, ARTHUR BC. "Income Tax Policy Formulation in Canada, 1972–76" (1978) 16 Osgoode Hall LJ 1.

Tax System Objectives

ANDREWS, WILLIAM. "A Consumption Type or Cash Flow Personal Income Tax" (April 1984) 87:6 Harv L Rev 1113.

System Characteristics

MCCAFFERY, EDWARD J. "The Holy Grail of Tax Simplification" [1990] Wis L Rev 1267.

PREBBLE, JOHN. "Why is Tax Law Incomprehensible?" (1994) Brit Tax Rev 380.

Other

ANDREWS, WILLIAM. "Personal Deductions in an Ideal Income Tax" (December 1972) 86:2 Harv L Rev 309.

EISENSTEIN, LOUIS. "Some Second Thoughts on Tax Ideologies" (1964–65) 20 Tax L Rev 453.

HAIG, ROBERT. "The Concept of Income: Economic and Legal Aspects" in *The Federal Income Tax* (New York: Columbia University Press, 1921) at 1–28.

KLEIN, WILLIAM. *Policy Analysis and the Federal Income Tax: Text and Readings* (Mineola, NY: Foundation Press, 1976).

SIMONS, HENRY. *Personal Income Taxation: The Definition of Income as a Problem of Fiscal Policy* (Chicago: University of Chicago Press, 1938).

CHAPTER 2

STATUTORY INTERPRETATION

"The difficulties of so-called interpretation arise when the Legislature has had no meaning at all; when the question which is raised on the statute never occurred to it; when what the judges have to do is, not to determine what the legislature did mean on a point which was present to its mind, but to guess what it would have intended on a point not present to its mind, if the point had been present."[1]

A. INTRODUCTION

In this chapter, we set out the rules of the road in interpreting tax law. Tax interpretation is not static; it evolves, particularly in the context of provisions designed to control tax avoidance, as we shift from literal to purposive construction.

The primary purpose of statutory interpretation is to unlock legislative intent. In addition to the ordinary rules, constitutional traditions also play an important role in the interpretation of tax law. Tax legislation is the product of elected legislatures. The language of the Act reflects the constitutional will of the people through its elected representatives. Thus, interpretation of tax law requires careful attention to

---

1   John Chipman Gray, *Nature and Sources of the Law: Statutes*, 2d ed (New York: Macmillan, 1921).

the words of the statute. There is a lesser role for judicial rulemaking in tax law, than there is, for example, in constitutional law.[2]

B. THE *INTERPRETATION ACT*

The construction of the Act is a question of law. Section 12 of the *Interpretation Act* states:[3]

> Every enactment is deemed remedial, and shall be given such fair, large and liberal construction and interpretation as best ensures the attainment of its objects.

Thus, we must interpret tax law in such a fair and liberal manner as best ensures the attainment of its purpose as articulated in the statute. The tension is in interpreting statutory language as expressed by Parliament according to the context and purpose (often unarticulated) of provisions.

C. GENERAL PRINCIPLES

The general principle of modern statutory construction is to interpret statutes in context, in harmony and within the scheme of the legislation. Dr Driedger, in the second edition of his work, *Construction of Statutes,* stated the principle as follows:[4]

> Today there is only one principle or approach, namely, the words of an Act are to be read in their entire context and in their grammatical and ordinary sense harmoniously with the scheme of the Act, the object of

---

2   See *Stewart v Canada*, 2002 SCC 46 [*Stewart*]; *Ludco Enterprises Ltd v Canada*, 2001 SCC 62 [*Ludco*].

3   *Interpretation Act*, RSC 1985, c. I-21, as amended. Section 3 reads:
      (1) Every provision of this Act applies, unless a contrary intention appears, to every enactment, whether enacted before or after the commencement of this Act.
      (2) The provisions of this Act apply to the interpretation of this Act.
      (3) Nothing in this Act excludes the application to an enactment of a rule of construction applicable to that enactment and not inconsistent with this Act.

4   Elmer A Driedger, *Construction of Statutes*, 2d ed (Toronto: Butterworths, 1983) at 87. See also *Canada v Antosko*, [1994] 2 SCR 312 at paras 24–25, 29 & 30 [*Antosko*].

the Act, and the intention of Parliament. . . . Earlier expressions, though in different form, are to the same effect; Lord Atkinson in *Victoria (City) v. Bishop of Vancouver Island*, ([1921] A.C. 384 at p. 387) put it this way:

> In the construction of statutes their words must be inter-preted in their ordinary grammatical sense, unless there be something in the context, or in the object of the statute in which they occur, or in the circumstances with reference to which they are used, to show that they were used in a special sense different from their ordinary grammatical sense.

The Supreme Court of Canada has endorsed this approach repeated-ly. See, for example, *Canada Trustco Mortgage Co v Canada (Canada Trustco)*:[5] "the words of an Act are to be read in their entire context and in their grammatical and ordinary sense harmoniously with the scheme of the Act, the object of the Act, and the intention of Parliament."[6]

Thus, we should read discrete sections of the Act in light of the other relevant provisions of the Act, the purpose of the legislation and in the context of economic and commercial reality. However, no approach can alter the result where the words of the statute are clear and plain and where the legal and practical effect of the transaction is undisputed.[7]

We interpret clear and unequivocal words in the statute according to their ordinary, everyday meaning (the plain meaning rule) *unless* the words are specifically assigned different definitions. This rule applies even if the interpretation produces an unfair result. It is for Parlia-ment to resolve the unfairness. For example, the requirement that a deduction for support payments be supported by a written agreement is strictly enforced even if it produces unforeseen hardship for those who do not reduce their agreement to writing.[8]

However, in interpreting what is a "written agreement," a court can look at context and purpose of the provision.

The meaning of a word or phrase that is capable of diverse interpret-ation depends upon the circumstances of its use. Language is not so pre-cise and certain as to always render one, and only one, possible meaning. It is in these circumstances that we encounter the greatest difficulties of statutory construction. As Lord Simon said in *Ransom v Higgs*:[9]

---

5   *Canada Trustco Mortgage Co v Canada*, 2005 SCC 54 [*Canada Trustco*]. See also *Lipson v Canada*, 2009 SCC 1 [*Lipson*].
6   See *65302 British Columbia Ltd v Canada*, [1999] 3 SCR 804 [*65302 BC Ltd*].
7   See *Mattabi Mines Ltd v Ontario (Minister of Revenue)*, [1988] 2 SCR 175 at 194; *Symes v Canada*, [1993] 4 SCR 695.
8   *Hodson v Canada*, [1988] 1 CTC 2 (FCA).
9   *Ransom v Higgs*, [1974] 1 WLR 1594 at 1618 (HL).

The meaning of a word or phrase in an Act of Parliament is a question of law not fact; even though the law may then declare that the word or phrase has no statutory meaning beyond its common acceptance and that is a question of fact whether the circumstances fall within such meaning (*Cozens v. Brutus*, [1973] A.C. 854). But many words and phrases in English have many shades of meaning and are capable of embracing a great diversity of circumstances. So the interpretation of the language of an Act of Parliament often involves declaring that certain conduct must as a matter of law fall within the statutory language (as was the actual decision in *Edwards v. Bairstow*, [1956] A.C. 14); that other conduct must as a matter of law fall outside the statutory language; but that whether yet a third category of conduct falls within the statutory language or outside it depends on the evaluation of such conduct by the tribunal of fact. This last question is often appropriately described as one of "fact and degree."

The principle that the Act should be interpreted textually, contextually and purposively to find a meaning that is harmonious with the Act as a whole is now well established.

D. AMBIGUITY

Where statutory language is clear and unambiguous, the plain meaning rule requires that we apply the language of the statute in its proper context. To do otherwise would have the judiciary usurp the function of the legislature. This is an easy rule to state, but difficult to apply.

Even the simplest words, however, are susceptible to misunderstanding and should be read in context.[10] Thus, when Holmes J was asked to determine whether an aircraft was a "motor vehicle" for the purposes of a motor vehicle theft statute, he disposed of the question as follows:

No doubt etymologically it is possible to use the word to signify a conveyance working on land, water or air, and sometimes legislation extends the use in that direction . . . . But in everyday speech "vehicle" calls up the picture of a thing moving on land.[11]

Harmonious interpretation requires that we interpret words and phrases in the context of the statutory provision in which they appear

---

10   As Cardozo J explained in *Panama Refining Co v Ryan*, 293 US 388 at 439 (1935): "The meaning of a statute is to be looked for, not in any single section, but in all the parts together and in their relation to the end in view."

11   *McBoyle v US*, 283 US 25 at 26 (1931).

and in the context of the *entire Act*. As Lord Herschell said in *Colquhoun v Brooks*:[12]

> It is beyond dispute, too, that we are entitled and indeed bound when construing the terms of any provision found in a statute to consider any other parts of the Act which throw light upon the intention of the legislature and which may serve to show that the particular provision ought not to be construed as it would be if considered alone and apart from the rest of the Act.

Where words are ambiguous and capable of various meanings, however, courts should select the interpretation that best promotes the smooth working of the system[13] and avoid interpretations that produce absurd, unjust, anomalous or inconvenient results.[14] In Lord Esher's words:

> If the words of an Act are clear, you must follow them, even though they lead to a manifest absurdity. The court has nothing to do with

---

12 *Colquhoun v Brooks* (1889), 14 App Cas 493 at 506 (HL); cited with approval by Pratte J in *Canada v Cie Immobilière BCN Ltée*, [1979] CTC 71 (SCC). See also *Highway Sawmills Ltd v MNR*, [1966] CTC 150 at 157–58 (SCC):

> The answer to the question what tax is payable in any given circumstances depends, of course, upon the words of the legislation imposing it. Where the meaning of those words is difficult to ascertain it may be of assistance to consider which of two constructions contended for brings about a result which conforms to the apparent scheme of the legislation.

See also *Canada Sugar Refining Co v Canada*, [1898] AC 735 at 741 (PC), Lord Davey: "Every clause of a statute should be construed with reference to the context and the other clauses of the Act, so as, so far as possible, to make a consistent enactment of the whole statute or series of statutes relating to the subject-matter"; *Canada v Cadboro Bay Holdings Ltd*, [1977] CTC 186 (FCTD) ("active business" defined as any quantum of activity giving rise to income); *Noranda Mines Ltd v Canada*, [1982] CTC 226 (FCTD) (words claimed to be ineffectual or surplusage).

13 *Shannon Realties Ltd v Ville de St Michel*, [1924] AC 185 (PC).

14 *R v Judge of City of London Court*, [1892] 1 QB 273 (CA) (whether amount received from employer for completing course constituted a "prize"). See also *Gill v Donald Humberstone & Co*, [1963] 1 WLR 929 (HL) (roofer not in "working place" when he fell off ladder); *Railton v Wood* (1890), 15 App Cas 363 (PC) ("distress for rent" includes holder of bill of sale taking back goods from bailiff); *Fry v IRC*, [1959] 1 Ch 86 (CA) (estate tax on reversionary interest in possession but not indefeasibly vested); *Arrow Shipping Co v Tyne Improvement Commissioners (The Crystal)*, [1894] AC 508 (HL) (interpretation of "possession" at time of salvage and destruction of vessel); *R v Overseers of Tonbridge* (1884), 13 QBD 339 (CA) (dispute over jurisdiction to levy rates by opposing burial boards; ordinary meaning conflicted with other Act).

the question whether the legislature has committed an absurdity. In my opinion, the rule has always been this—if the words of an Act admit of two interpretations, then they are not clear; and if one interpretation leads to an absurdity, and the other does not, the court will conclude that the legislature did not intend to lead to an absurdity, and will adopt the other interpretation.[15]

The case for avoiding absurd interpretation is easy to make. The more difficult case is resolving ambiguity to promote statutory purpose and harmony. As the Supreme Court said in *Canada Trustco*: "The relative effects of ordinary meaning, context and purpose on the interpretative process may vary, but in all cases the court must seek to read the provisions of an Act as a harmonious whole."[16] Faced with ambiguity, courts shift to purposive interpretation to avoid harsh results.[17]

E. STRICT INTERPRETATION

The doctrine of strict interpretation works well if legislative purpose is precisely captured in statutory language. In these circumstances, we implement the purpose simply by applying the words of the Act. Experience, however, has taught us that legislation is not susceptible to such precise drafting. As early as 1936, in an era of comparatively simple tax legislation, the Income Tax Codification Committee in England realized the futility of attempting to anticipate every situation with comprehensive legislative drafting:

---

15   R v *Judge of City of London Court*, ibid at 290; see also R v *Savage*, [1980] CTC 103 (FCTD), rev'd on other grounds [1981] CTC 332 (FCA), aff'd [1983] CTC 393 (SCC) (whether $500 exemption applicable to "prize" from employer); *Victoria City Corp v Bishop of Vancouver Island*, [1921] 2 AC 384 (PC) (should exemption for house of worship include land upon which building erected); *IRC v Hinchy*, [1960] AC 748 (HL) (whether fine of "treble the tax" owed should include surtax); *Cartledge v E Jopling & Sons Ltd*, [1963] AC 758 (HL) (statutory limitation period expired before workers aware noxious dust caused injury to lungs); *Mersey Docks & Harbour Bd v Henderson Bros* (1888), 13 App Cas 595 (HL) (dues in port payable when "trading inwards" or "trading outwards"; interpretation in respect of voyage with several ports); *Clerical, Medical & General Life Assurance Society v Carter* (1889), 22 QBD 444 (CA) (interpretation of "profits or gains" and "interest of money"); *Warburton v Loveland* (1832), 2 Dow & Cl 480 (HL); *Corp d'Administration et de Placements Ltée v Castonguay* (1970), 3 NBR (2d) 278 (Co Ct) (two interpretations of *Creditor's Relief Act*, one avoided injustice).

16   *Canada Trustco*, above note 5 at para 10.

17   See, for example, *Québec (Communauté urbaine) v Corporation Notre-Dame de Bon-Secours*, [1994] 3 SCR 3 [*Notre-Dame de Bon-Secours*].

The imagination which can draw an income tax statute to cover the myriad transactions of a society like ours, capable of producing the necessary revenue without producing a flood of litigation, has not yet revealed itself.

Literal interpretation does not work as well when we use tax law not only to raise revenue, but also promote socio-economic policies, which require purposive analysis to achieve their goals.

Literal interpretation has contributed substantially to the complexity of tax legislation. There is impressionistic evidence to suggest that as the courts interpreted the Act strictly, the legislative draftsman responded with ever more complex and comprehensive statutory language in an attempt to provide for, and anticipate, every conceivable factual nuance and circumstance.

Stubart Investments Ltd v Canada (*Stubart*)[18] was the first significant breach to the doctrine of strict construction. The Supreme Court of Canada shifted from six decades of literal interpretation towards purposive interpretation.[19] Following *Stubart*, the Supreme Court expanded on more specific aspects of interpretative methodology in *Golden*,[20] *Bronfman Trust*,[21] *Johns-Manville Canada*,[22] *Antosko*,[23] *Corporation Notre-Dame de Bon-Secours*,[24] *Friesen*,[25] *Shell Canada*,[26] *Ludco*,[27] and *Stewart*.[28]

The difficulty is in balancing the literal meaning of words with contextual and purposive analysis. However, we must be careful of purposive interpretation that puts a gloss on legislative language that was not contemplated by the legislator. If the words of the statute are clear

18   *Stubart Investments Ltd v Canada*, [1984] 1 SCR 536 [*Stubart*].
19   See also *Irving Oil Ltd v Canada*, [1988] 1 CTC 263 (FCTD), aff'd [1991] 1 CTC 350 (FCA); *Indalex Ltd v Canada*, [1986] 2 CTC 482 (FCA); *Consolidated Bathurst Ltd v Canada*, [1985] 1 CTC 142 (FCTD), aff'd in part [1987] 1 CTC 55 (FCA); *Orr v MNR*, [1989] 2 CTC 2348 (TCC); *Hickman Motors Ltd v Canada*, [1993] 1 CTC 36 (FCTD); *Earlscourt Sheet Metal Mechanical Ltd v MNR*, [1988] 1 CTC 2045 (TCC); *Montgomery v MNR*, [1987] 2 CTC 2023 (TCC); *Canada v Vivian*; *Canada v Parsons*, [1984] CTC 354 (FCA); *Bastion Management Ltd v MNR*, [1988] 1 CTC 2344 (TCC), aff'd [1994] 2 CTC 70 (FCTD); *Daggett v MNR*, [1992] 2 CTC 2764 (TCC); *454538 Ontario Ltd v MNR*, [1993] 1 CTC 2746 (TCC); *Goulard v MNR*, [1992] 1 CTC 2396 (TCC).
20   *Canada v Golden*, [1986] 1 SCR 209.
21   *Bronfman Trust v Canada*, [1987] 1 CTC 117 (SCC) [*Bronfman Trust*].
22   *Canada v Johns-Manville Corp*, [1985] 2 SCR 46.
23   *Antosko*, above note 4.
24   *Notre-Dame de Bon-Secours*, above note 17.
25   *Friesen v Canada*, [1995] 2 CTC 369 (SCC) [*Friesen*].
26   *Shell Canada Ltd v Canada* (1999), 99 DTC 5669 (SCC) [*Shell Canada*].
27   *Ludco*, above note 2.
28   *Stewart*, above note 2.

and plain, they should be given their effect and not altered by legislative purpose or object.[29] Purposive interpretation should not be used to alter the result of commercial transactions where the words of the Act are clear and plain and where the legal and practical effect of the transaction is undisputed. As the Supreme Court said in *Antosko*:

> In the absence of evidence that the transaction was a sham or an abuse of the provisions of the Act, it is not the role of the court to determine whether the transaction in question is one which renders the taxpayer deserving of a deduction. If the terms of the section are met, the taxpayer may rely on it, and it is the option of Parliament specifically to preclude further reliance in such situations.[30]

And:

> Where the words of the section are not ambiguous, it is not for this Court to find that the appellants should be disentitled to a deduction because they do not deserve a "windfall" . . . . In the absence of a situation of ambiguity, such that the Court must look to the result of a transaction to assist in ascertaining the intent of Parliament, a normative assessment of the consequences of the application of a given provision is within the ambit of the legislature, not the courts.[31]

And again in *Friesen*:

> [T]he clear language of the *Income Tax Act* takes precedence over a court's view of the object and purpose of a provision . . . . The object and purpose of a provision need only be resorted to when the statutory language admits of some doubt or ambiguity.[32]

We draw the line between strict and literal construction and pedantic application of the purposive approach in the face of clear and unambiguous legislative language. Courts should apply the teleological approach only when the words of the statute are not clear.[33]

As McLachlin J (as she then was) stated in *Shell Canada*:

> Finding unexpressed legislative intentions under the guise of purposive interpretation runs the risk of upsetting the balance Parliament has attempted to strike in the Act. . . . The courts' role is to interpret and apply the Act as it was adopted by Parliament. *Obiter* statements

---

29   *Antosko*, above note 4.
30   *Ibid* at para 29.
31   *Ibid* at para 34.
32   *Friesen*, above note 26 at paras 59–60.
33   See *Notre-Dame de Bon-Secours*, above note 17.

in earlier cases that might be said to support a broader and less certain interpretive principle have therefore been overtaken by our developing tax jurisprudence.[34]

The Act does not operate in a commercial vacuum, but draws upon the meaning of words in their broader commercial context. Thus, in applying the plain meaning rule, we should interpret words in the context of the general commercial law and settled legal definitions therein.[35]

Interpretation of tax treaties, however, is more expansive and courts consider the purpose of provisions even in the absence of ambiguity. The Supreme Court stated the rule as follows:

> In interpreting a treaty, the paramount goal is to find the meaning of the words in question. This process involves looking to the language used and the intentions of the parties.[36]

Purposive analysis must be temperate, rooted in the statutory text and must not circumvent the intention of the legislature.[37]

To summarize: purposive interpretation is not a substitute for the plain meaning rule. It is used where statutory language is obscure or ambiguous and a court needs help in determining legislative intention. Otherwise, unambiguous legislative language is interpreted according to its plain meaning, but not so literally as to produce absurd results. The plain meaning rule must be applied contextually.

The presumption in favour of the taxpayer is *residual* in nature and exceptional in the interpretation of tax legislation.[38] Thus, we should make every effort to determine the meaning of the Act. We apply the presumption only when it is impossible to determine unambiguous meaning. Of course, factual ambiguity in applying penalty provisions should always favour the taxpayer.

1) Summary of Rules

a) Contextual Interpretation

The fundamental rule of statutory construction is that a provision should be interpreted in a textual, contextual and purposive way giv-

---

34   *Shell Canada*, above note 27 at paras 43 and 45.

35   *Will-Kare Paving & Contracting Ltd v Canada*, 2000 SCC 36 (the word "sale" has an established meaning that the *Income Tax Act* should not broaden without clear parliamentary intention). See also *Re Rizzo & Rizzo Shoes Ltd*, [1998] 1 SCR 27 [*Rizzo*] and *65302 BC Ltd*, above note 6.

36   *Crown Forest Industries Ltd v Canada*, [1995] 2 SCR 802.

37   *Bastien Estate v Canada*, 2011 SCC 38 at para 25.

38   *Notre-Dame de Bon-Secours*, above note 17 at 16.

ing all sections of a related group of provisions a coherent meaning if at all possible.[39] The meaning of an ambiguous word or phrase should derive from its context in the document and other provisions or segments of the statute in which it appears. Thus, one should read the entire document and not just the particular provision that is at issue.

b) Ordinary Meaning of Words

Words are presumed to bear their ordinary meaning unless specifically defined. Commercial words or phrases are interpreted according to their usage in normal commercial practice.

c) Consistent Meaning

A word or phrase is presumed to have the same meaning throughout a document, provision or statute unless there is a clear contrary indication.

d) Harmonious Interpretation

A statutory provision should be interpreted to render it harmonious, and not contradictory with the other provisions of the enactment.

e) No Superfluous Provisions

If at all possible, a provision should not be interpreted so as to render it—or any other provision—superfluous, unlawful or invalid.

f) No Surplusage

Every word should, if possible, be given effect; no word should be read as surplusage.

g) Criminal Provisions

A legislative provision that defines a criminal offence or has a criminal sanction should, in cases of ambiguity, be interpreted to favour the person accused of the offence.

---

39   See, for example, *Redeemer Foundation v Canada (MNR)*, 2008 SCC 46; *Canada Trustco*, above note 5 at para 10, McLachlin CJ and Major J:

> The interpretation of a statutory provision must be made according to a textual, contextual and purposive analysis to find a meaning that is harmonious with the Act as a whole.

h) *Ut Magis Valeat Quam Pereat* ("So that It May Survive Rather than Perish")

An ambiguous provision should be interpreted in a way that makes it valid rather than invalid. Parliament does not intend to enact pointless legislation.[40]

i) *Inclusio Unius Est Exclusio Alterius* ("The Inclusion of One Implies the Exclusion of Others")

For example, a provision that provides benefits to a person up to the age of eighteen necessarily implies that the benefit is not available to any person over the age of eighteen.

j) *Ejusdem Generis* ("Of the Same Kind")

A general residual category following a list of other items refers to items of the same sort.

The following canons of statutory construction are not definitive. They can yield different conclusions and point in different directions, in which case one must choose from amongst the alternative interpretations bearing in mind the purpose of the provision and statute.

2) Form and Substance

It is trite to suggest that substance should take precedence over form to the extent that it is consistent with the wording and objective of the statute. This chestnut of interpretational technique is easier to state than it is to apply. We start with the following questions:

- What does the transaction or arrangement achieve?
- Does it fit within the plain meaning of the provision?
- Does the result fit within the purpose of the statutory provision(s)?
- If it does not fit within the purpose of the provision(s), should the taxpayer be allowed the benefit of the provision or be subject to the avoidance strictures of the Act?

The difficulty with the substance doctrine is that, despite its intuitive appeal, it does not offer any objective yardstick to measure against particular facts. If applied on an *ex-post* basis, the doctrine leaves commercial transactions in an uncertain state. It is an unpredictable doc-

---

40 See, for example, *Rizzo*, above note 36 at para 27: " . . . a label of absurdity can be attached to interpretations which defeat the purpose of a statute or render some aspect of it pointless or futile."

trine of varying reach. In 1936, Lord Tomlin referred to it disparagingly as the "so-called doctrine" in *CIR v The Duke of Westminster*:

> [I]t is said that in revenue cases there is a doctrine that the Court may ignore the legal position and regard what is called "the substance of the matter" . . . . [The] supposed doctrine . . . seems to rest for its support upon a misunderstanding of language used in some earlier cases. The sooner this misunderstanding is dispelled, and the supposed doctrine given its quietus, the better it will be for all concerned, for the doctrine seems to involve substituting "the incertain and crooked cord of discretion" for "the golden and streight metwand of the law." Every man is entitled if he can to order his affairs so as that the tax attaching under the appropriate Acts is less than it otherwise would be . . . . This so-called doctrine of "the substance" seems to me to be nothing more than an attempt to make a man pay and notwithstanding that he has so ordered his affairs that the amount of tax sought from him is not legally claimable.[41]

Notwithstanding these early reservations, the doctrine has had a pervasive, but uncertain, effect in tax law. In 1984, the Supreme Court knocked it down in *Stubart*,[42] but it rose three years later under the guise of the "commercial reality" test in *Bronfman Trust*,[43] where Dickson CJ stated:

> I acknowledge, however, that just as there has been a recent trend away from strict construction of taxation statutes . . . so too has the recent trend in tax cases been towards attempting to ascertain the *true commercial and practical nature of the taxpayer's transaction*. There has been, in this country and elsewhere, movement away from tests based on the form of transactions and towards tests based on what Lord Pearce has referred to as a "common sense appreciation of all the guiding features" of the events in question . . . . This is, I believe, a laudable trend *provided it is consistent* with the text and purposes of the taxation statute.[44]

Thus, for a limited period, we see the pendulum swinging from form towards a looser standard, a common sense appreciation of "commercial reality."

However, by 1999, the Supreme Court realigns the doctrine of statutory construction in tax law:

---

41   *CIR v The Duke of Westminster*, [1936] AC 1 at 19 (HL).
42   *Stubart*, above note 19.
43   *Bronfman Trust*, above note 22.
44   *Ibid* at paras 36–37 [emphasis added].

Unless the Act provides otherwise, a taxpayer is entitled to be taxed on what it actually did, not on what it could have done, and certainly not based on what a less sophisticated taxpayer may have done.[45]

And:

[I]n the absence of a specific statutory bar to the contrary, taxpayers are entitled to structure their affairs in a manner that reduces the tax payable . . . . An unrestricted application of an "economic effects" approach does indirectly what this Court has consistently held Parliament did not intend the Act to do directly.[46]

What do "substance," "commercial reality" and "common sense view" really mean? How do we accurately measure the substance of transactions in the context of a tax structure premised upon artificial distinctions of different sources of income? For example, a taxpayer who requires a capital asset for business use can acquire it in one of three ways. He can:

1) Purchase the asset outright and acquire title to it immediately, but pay for it over time;
2) Lease the asset and pay rent for its use, but without acquiring title in the property; or
3) Lease the asset with an option to purchase the property for a token amount of, say, $1 when the lease expires.

In the first case, the taxpayer clearly acquires title and ownership of the property. If the property is depreciable property, the taxpayer can write off the capital cost of the asset as capital cost allowance (tax depreciation).[47]

In the second case, the taxpayer does not acquire title to the property but has a user interest in exchange for rental payments, which may or may not coincide with the amount deductible as capital cost allowance or tax depreciation. The write-off would depend upon the term of the lease, the underlying cost of financing, etc. If the lease is for ninety-nine years, is it transformed into an outright purchase in fee simple? In legal terms, the lease remains a lease with no change in title. In economic terms the lease is the equivalent of an outright sale.

In the third case, the economic substance of the transaction is that the taxpayer purchases the property, but with delayed transmission of title. The economic effect or commercial reality of the transaction

---

45   *Shell Canada*, above note 27 at para 45.
46   *Ibid* at para 46.
47   See Chapter 8.

is identical to an outright purchase of the asset in the first case. As a matter of legal substance, however, the taxpayer is a lessee during the tenure of the lease and acquires legal title only when the lease expires and she pays the token sum of $1. Thus, the legal substance of the transaction is that it is a lease until the lessee acquires title to the property by exercising the option.

Although courts may be sensitive to the economic realities of a particular transaction, rather than being bound to what first appears to be its legal form,[48] the doctrine is subject to at least two important caveats. First, absent a specific provision of the Act to the contrary or a finding that they are a sham, the taxpayer's formal legal relationships should be respected in tax cases. Second, where the provision at issue is clear and unambiguous, its terms must simply be applied.[49]

F. BURDEN OF PROOF

The burden of proof in civil tax cases is on a balance of probabilities. In criminal tax cases of tax evasion, the burden is on the Crown to establish its case beyond a reasonable doubt.

1) Presumption of Validity

Subsection 152(8) of the Act sets out the onus in civil cases:

> An assessment shall . . . be *deemed* to be valid and binding notwithstanding any error, defect or omission in the assessment or in any proceeding under this Act relating thereto. [Emphasis added.]

The taxpayer carries the onus to establish on a balance of probabilities that the factual findings and the assumptions of fact upon which the minister based the assessment are wrong.[50] The minister must disclose the findings of fact upon which he bases an assessment. He does this in his Reply to the Notice of Appeal. The taxpayer's onus of proof lies in rebutting the facts disclosed by the minister in the assessment. This burden balances the scale in favour of the minister.

---

48 *Shell Canada*, above note 27.
49 *Ibid.*
50 *Johnston v MNR*, [1948] CTC 195 (SCC); *Anderson Logging Co v British Columbia* (1924), [1925] SCR 45. See, however, *Anchor Point Energy Ltd v Canada*, 2006 TCC 424 (General Procedure), rev'd 2007 FCA 188, leave to appeal to SCC refused, [2007] SCCA No 368.

2) Reversal of Onus

Subsection 163(2) of the Act authorizes the minister to impose a penalty on a person who has either "knowingly" or "under circumstances amounting to gross negligence" made a false statement or omission in an income tax return. In these circumstances, where the minister imposes a penalty on the basis of the taxpayer's gross negligence, the Act reverses the burden of proof and puts it on the minister to show the gross negligence on the basis of the particular facts.[51]

Subsection 163(2) requires that the minister show not only that there has been an act of omission or misstatement by the taxpayer (or his or her agent), but also that the taxpayer (or agent) had a state of mind that justifies a finding of gross negligence. In *Udell v MNR*,[52] for example, the court stated: "In my view the use of the verb 'made' in the context in which it is used also involves a deliberate and intentional consciousness on the part of the principal to the act done."

G. CONCLUSION

We see from the above that the rules of statutory construction of tax law are not as definitive as one might have anticipated. Unlocking legislative intention is an uncertain process. Taxpayers crave certainty and are entitled to know the legal consequences of their transactions and arrangements. However, we must also balance the needs of taxpayers for certainty with the role that Parliament has assigned the Act as a fiscal and socio-economic statute. The *Interpretation Act* contemplates remedial, fair and liberal interpretation for *every* enactment.

The line between legitimate and abusive tax avoidance also shifts as the courts develop new approaches to statutory construction of fiscal legislation. The courts have shifted away from interpreting the Act as a penal statute. Nevertheless, we continue with problems of statutory construction. Sometimes we lean towards the "plain meaning" rule and, at other times, in favour of "purposive" interpretation. As we will see in subsequent chapters, this tension in statutory construction leads to uncertainty and legislative complexity in tax law.

Finally, the introduction of the General Anti-Avoidance Rule[53] into our tax law raises additional interpretational uncertainty. The broad language of section 245 of the *Income Tax Act* stands in contrast to the

---

51 *Income Tax Act*, RSC 1985, c 1 (5th Supp), subs 163(3).
52 *Udell v MNR*, [1969] CTC 704 at 714 (Ex Ct), Cattanach J.
53 See Chapter 19.

other detailed provisions of the statute[54] and creates (or at least, adds to) uncertainty. To be sure, tax law is difficult, but it is not dry. On the contrary, its influence on human behaviour is probably greater than that of any other statute.

54   See, for example, *Lipson*, above note 5.

PART II

WHO IS TAXABLE?

CHAPTER 3

TAX NEXUS

A. INTRODUCTION

In this chapter we examine the first of the five basic tax questions: who is taxable? The answer to this question determines the substantive and administrative structure of the statute that one devises to raise revenue. Even the most rudimentary tax system based on head count (for example, a poll tax) raises the question: whose heads should we count for the purposes of tax collection? Thus, we start with the question: on what basis do we assert taxable nexus?

There are several options for taxing individuals. We can tax them based on citizenship or nationality on the theory that citizenship confers a legal status that is not constrained by geographical boundaries. One can argue that the citizens of a country should pay their taxes to it regardless of where they reside because they derive benefits from their citizenship. Even non-resident citizens of a state are entitled to its political protection and, therefore, should bear some of the costs to reflect the benefits of citizenship.

Citizenship implies duties and responsibilities that require a balancing of the costs and benefits of national belonging. During the Israeli incursion into Lebanon in 2006, for example, Canadian, American, British and Scandinavian governments evacuated their citizens from the war zone. Canada evacuated 15,000 of its citizens from Lebanon at a cost of $85 million. Approximately 7,000 of the evacuees then returned to Lebanon after hostilities ceased. Canadian taxpayers paid the bill.

However, using citizenship as the sole connecting factor has problems. Citizenship is the political connection between an individual and her country and has little bearing upon economic activities. There are also administrative difficulties in asserting claims against non-resident citizens and measuring the value of the benefits they derive during their absence from their country of citizenship. Thus, Canada decided early on that it would not use citizenship as a connecting factor for tax purposes.

Indeed, even those countries (and there are very few[1]) that use citizenship or nationality to establish taxable nexus usually couple it with other factors, such as taxpayer residence or source of income. The United States, for example, asserts full tax liability on the worldwide income of its citizens and aliens who reside in the country. Thus, Canadians with dual Canadian-US citizenship are required to annually file US tax returns even if they do not owe US taxes.

Domicile is another form of legal status. Unlike citizenship, however, domicile uses different criteria: physical presence and an intention to reside indefinitely in the country. We can justify taxation based upon domicile on the theory that an individual should pay tax commensurate with the individual's economic and social association with the country.

Domicile depends upon intention and free choice. Every person has a domicile of origin at birth, usually the father's domicile. An individual may also adopt a domicile of choice, which entails physical presence in a country coupled with an intention to reside there indefinitely. Depending as it does on physical presence and intention, domicile is never easy to administer for tax purposes. Unlike Britain, Canada does not use domicile for income tax purposes.

Residence is another option to connect legal status with a country. The theory underlying the use of residence as a connecting factor is that a person should pay taxes to the country with which she is currently most closely connected in economic and social terms. The obligation to pay tax based on residence derives from the principle that persons who benefit from their economic and social affiliation with a country should be obliged to contribute to its public finances. Residence as a connecting factor is also administratively practical and convenient. It is generally easy for a country to ensure compliance with its tax laws if the person over whom it asserts the law has close economic links with the country and has assets within its administrative reach.

Taxation based upon source of income is essentially a territorial form of jurisdiction. It is administratively practical and easily enforce-

---

1   Few countries (United States, Philippines, Korea, Vietnam and Eritrea, for example) use citizenship as a basis of personal taxation.

able if one can pinpoint the source of income. Using source of income as the primary connecting factor for taxation is, however, contrary to tax equity because it does not provide an accurate measure of a taxpayer's ability to pay. Corporate taxpayers in particular may derive all the economic, political and legal benefits of residence in a country and arrange their international transactions so as to source their income in low-tax countries or tax havens. The development of electronic commerce, which can assign the source of transactions to locations that have little bearing on the economic substance of transactions, are likely to increase the problems of source taxation. Hence, most developed economies use source taxation only as an adjunct to full tax liability based on some other connection: citizenship, domicile or residence.

Canada asserts income tax jurisdiction by reference to three factors: residence, territorial source of income and the place of management.

B. RESIDENCE

Canada uses residence as its primary connecting factor to assert domestic taxable jurisdiction. A Canadian resident is taxable on his worldwide income. The theory is that a person who enjoys the legal, political and economic benefits of associating with Canada should bear the appropriate share of the costs of association.

Subsection 2(1) of the Act is the charging provision:

An income tax shall be paid . . . on the taxable income for each taxation year of every person[2] resident in Canada at any time in the year.

The subsection is quite clear: a resident of Canada is taxable on his, her or its worldwide taxable income. In addition to residence, however, Canada also uses territorial nexus of source of income to tax non-resident persons. Thus, subject to tax treaty provisions,[3] Canada taxes non-residents on their Canadian-source income. Thus, our first task is to distinguish between residents and non-residents.

"Resident" includes a person who is "ordinarily resident" in Canada.[4] The rule ensures horizontal equity. For example, assume that A and B, both residents of Canada, each earn $100,000. A earns his income in

---

2   "Person" includes individuals and corporations.
3   See, for example, *OECD Model Tax Convention on Income and on Capital* [*OECD Model Convention*], Article 7.
4   See *Income Tax Act*, RSC 1985, c 1 (5th Supp) [*ITA*], subs 250(3); *Laurin v Canada*, 2006 TCC 634, aff'd 2008 FCA 58 (Air Canada pilot living in Turks and Caicos and flying out of Canada not ordinarily resident in Canada); *R v Reeder*, [1975]

Canada; B earns half of her income from foreign investments. The principle of horizontal equity requires that A and B should pay an equal amount of tax. Since they are Canadian residents, we can apply the principle only if both are fully liable to tax in Canada on their worldwide income. However, to prevent double taxation of B, who might also pay tax at source on her foreign investment income, Canada grants her a tax credit for her foreign taxes.

Source of income is a secondary connecting factor. Non-residents are taxable only on their Canadian-source income (the *situs* principle). Subsection 2(3) states that a non-resident is taxable in Canada if he or she is employed in Canada, carries on business in Canada or derives a capital gain from the disposition of taxable Canadian property. This rule is also subject to Canada's bilateral tax treaties, which can limit the right to tax a non-resident's income.

Residence for tax purposes refers to the legal and economic *nexus* that an individual has with Canada. Although physical presence is an important criterion for residence for tax purposes, it is not necessarily conclusive in establishing taxable nexus. Thus, the concept of residence for tax purposes is quite different from residence for immigration purposes. A Canadian resident for immigration purposes may be non-resident for tax purposes and vice versa.

Residence for tax purposes is not synonymous with physical presence in Canada. An individual who is physically present in Canada—for example, a transient visitor—is not necessarily a Canadian resident.[5] Conversely, an individual who is absent from Canada for a considerable period (for example, a Canadian diplomat) may be a Canadian resident for income tax purposes.

1) Individuals

An individual can be a resident, non-resident or part-time resident of Canada. Each of these categories marks a boundary of taxable nexus. A resident of Canada is taxable on her worldwide income, regardless of where she earns the income.[6] A non-resident is subject to Canadian income tax only if he is employed in Canada, carries on business in Canada, or disposes of taxable Canadian property.[7] A part-time resident of Can-

---

CTC 256 (FCTD) (employee can be ordinarily resident in Canada even if he is out of the country for extended period).

5   See, however, the 183-day rule in *ITA, ibid*, subs 250(1).

6   *Ibid*, subs 2(1). A resident taxpayer is, within limits, entitled to a credit for foreign taxes paid by her; see s 126.

7   *Ibid*, subs 2(3).

ada is subject to tax on his or her worldwide income, but only while he or she is resident in Canada.[8]

There are three rules to determine an individual's residence: statutory, common law and (if applicable) international tax treaty rules.

a) Statutory Rules

The statutory rules deem individuals with substantial economic connections with Canada to reside in Canada, regardless of their physical presence in the country. The Act deems an individual to be a resident of Canada if he or she:[9]

- Sojourns in Canada for 183 days or more in a year;
- Is a member of the Canadian Forces;
- Is a member of the Canadian diplomatic or quasi-diplomatic service;
- Performs services in a foreign country under a prescribed international development assistance program of the Canadian government;
- Is a member of the Canadian Forces school staff; or
- Is a child of a person holding a position referred to in the above categories (other than a sojourner), if he or she is wholly dependent upon that person for support.

Since a statutory deeming provision is a conclusive presumption of law, the rules ensure that individuals who have substantial economic connections with Canada are subject to Canadian tax even if they are absent from the country for extended periods of time. The rationale is that all of the above taxpayers either have substantial Canadian connections or receive Canadian taxpayer support.

i) Sojourners

The Act deems an individual who sojourns in Canada for more than 182 days in a year to reside in Canada throughout the taxation year.[10] A presence of more than half a year in the country as a "sojourner" is sufficient economic and social connection with Canada to create a taxable nexus. The term "day" means a twenty-four-hour period or part thereof.[11] The days need not be consecutive.

---

8   *Ibid*, s 114.
9   *Ibid*, subs 250(1). An individual cannot, however, be deemed to be resident in Canada by virtue of subs 250(1) if he or she is considered resident in Canada on the basis of the case law rules. In certain circumstances, subs 250(1)(g) may deem spouses of Canadian diplomats to be resident in Canada if the diplomat marries a non-resident.
10 *Ibid*.
11 See Interpretation Bulletin IT-221R3, "Determination of an Individual's Residence Status" (4 October 2002) for similar reference under the *Canada-United*

The concept of sojourning is not easy to grasp and the Act does not define the term. Sojourning implies a temporary stay in a place, as opposed to ordinary residence. As Estey J said, "One sojourns at a place where he unusually, casually or intermittently visits or stays."[12] Thus, we must determine whether the individual's stay is usual, casual or intermittent. "Sojourning" is something less than establishing a permanent abode in Canada. Its effect, however, is to deem the individual to be resident in Canada *throughout* the particular taxation year.

We must distinguish between Canadian tax residents who acquire their status by virtue of the sojourning rule and those who acquire status under the common law "facts and circumstances" tests. The Act deems an individual who sojourns in Canada for more than 182 days to be a resident of Canada. However, the fact that an individual is present in Canada for fewer than 183 days does not, *by itself*, mean that he or she is not a Canadian resident. An individual who is in Canada for fewer than 183 days may be a resident under the "facts and circumstances" common law test.[13] Thus, an individual may be considered a Canadian resident for tax purposes even though he or she has only "visitor status" under the immigration rules.[14]

"Sojourning" is also different from permanent residence. For example, an individual who ceases to be a Canadian resident after 183 days in the year cannot be deemed to reside in Canada throughout the year by virtue of the sojourning rule. Rather, the individual is considered a part-time permanent resident for the particular year and a non-resident thereafter.[15]

ii) Government Personnel

Subsection 250(1) deems members of the Canadian Forces, certain development workers, Canadian Forces school staff, and officers and employees of the Government of Canada or a province to be Canadian residents, regardless of where they are posted and the length of time they are out of the country. A person who ceases to hold a position

---

States Income Tax Convention, 1980, Can TS 1984/15 [*Canada-US Tax Treaty*].

12 *Thomson v MNR*, [1946] SCR 209 at 231–32.

13 This rule is subject to treaty provisions to the contrary. See, for example, Article XV of the *Canada-US Tax Treaty*, above note 11, re exemption of employment income where an individual spends fewer than 183 days in Canada.

14 *Lee v MNR*, [1990] 1 CTC 2082 (TCC) (individual considered resident prior to obtaining landed immigrant status on basis of marriage to Canadian resident and purchase of matrimonial residence).

15 The Agency accepts this position in IT-221R3, above note 11; but see *Truchon v MNR* (1970), 70 DTC 1277 (TAB) (incorrectly decided and rule not followed).

described above is considered to have been resident in Canada for the part of the year during which he or she held that position.[16]

iii) Prescribed Agencies

Individuals who perform services at any time in the year in a foreign country under a "prescribed international development assistance program of the Government of Canada" are also deemed to be resident in Canada during the period of their absence from Canada if they were resident in Canada at any time in the three-month period immediately prior to commencing their service.[17]

b) Common Law Rules

The case law rules are essentially "facts and circumstances" tests that apply in the absence of statutory provisions to determine whether an individual has a taxable nexus with Canada. The common law rules determine an individual's residence by her links with Canada. Where the links are sufficiently strong, we consider the individual to have a nexus with Canada and she is a resident for tax purposes.[18] The sufficiency of connecting factors is a question that depends upon particular circumstances, including:

- Nationality and background;
- Physical presence;
- Ownership of dwelling in Canada;
- Location of family home;
- Presence of business interests;
- Presence of social interests;
- Mode of life and family ties; and
- Social connections by reason of birth or marriage.

The relative weight that one attaches to these factors is a question of fact in each case.[19] There are, however, certain generally accepted legal propositions:

- A taxpayer must reside somewhere;[20]

---

16   *ITA*, above note 4, subs 250(2).
17   *Ibid*, para 250(1)(d); *Income Tax Regulations*, CRC, c 945, s 3400. See *Petersen v MNR*, [1969] Tax ABC 682; *Bell v Canada*, [1996] 2 CTC 2191 (TCC) (shifting of onus to minister to prove that program qualifies).
18   *Weymyss v Weymyss's Trustees*, [1921] Sess Cas 30.
19   See, for example, *MacLean v MNR*, [1985] CTC 2207 (TCC) (taxpayer resident on the basis of continued connections with Canada despite the CRA's waiver of source deductions).
20   *Rogers v IRC* (1897), 1 Tax Cas 225 (Scot Ct of Ex).

- A taxpayer need not have a fixed place of abode to be resident in the jurisdiction;[21]
- Residence requires more than mere physical presence within the jurisdiction;[22]
- Residence does not require constant personal presence;[23]
- A taxpayer may have more than one residence;[24]
- The number of days[25] that a taxpayer spends within Canada is not determinative;
- Residence may be established by presence within Canada even though the presence is compelled by the authorities, business necessity or otherwise;[26]
- "Residing" and "ordinarily resident" do not have special or technical meanings. Whether a person is "residing or ordinarily resident in Canada" is a question of fact;[27] and
- Intention and free choice, which are essential elements in domicile, are not necessary to establish residence. Residence is quite different from domicile of choice.[28]

"Residing" is not a term of invariable elements. As Rand J said in *Thomson v MNR*:

> [It] is quite impossible to give it a precise and inclusive definition. It is highly flexible, and its many shades of meaning vary not only in the contexts of different matters, but also in different aspects of the same matter. In one case it is satisfied by certain elements, in another by others, some common, some new.[29]

---

21 *Reid v IRC* (1926), 10 Tax Cas 673 (Scot Ct of Sess).
22 *Levene v IRC* (1928), 13 Tax Cas 486 (HL).
23 *Re Young* (1875), 1 Tax Cas 57 (Scot Ct of Ex).
24 *Lloyd v Sulley* (1884), 2 Tax Cas 37 (Scot Ct of Ex).
25 *Reid v IRC*, above note 21.
26 *IRC v Lysaght*, [1928] AC 234 (HL).
27 *Ibid.*
28 *Schujahn v MNR*, [1962] CTC 364 (Ex Ct) (change of domicile depends on will of individual).
29 *Thomson v MNR*, above note 12 at 224, aff'g (1945), [1946] CTC 51 (Ex Ct). See also *Beament v MNR*, [1952] 2 SCR 486 (taxpayer not resident where he was physically absent from Canada, did not maintain any dwelling place in Canada, and maintained matrimonial home in UK); *Russell v MNR*, [1949] CTC 13 (Ex Ct) (examination of indicia of residence during active service overseas); *Schujahn v MNR*, *ibid* (taxpayer not resident though family remained in Canada for purpose of selling home); *Griffiths v Canada*, [1978] CTC 372 (FCTD) (established residence was yacht in Caribbean despite spouse, assets and income in Canada).

The following are relevant indicia in determining Canadian residence:

- Past and present habits of life;
- Regularity and length of visits to Canada;
- Ties within Canada;
- Ties elsewhere;
- Purpose of stay;
- Ownership of a home in Canada or rental of a dwelling on a long-term basis (for example, a lease for one or more years);
- Residence of spouse, children and other dependent family members in a dwelling that the individual maintains in Canada;
- Memberships with Canadian churches or synagogues, recreational and social clubs, unions and professional organizations;
- Registration and maintenance of automobiles, boats and airplanes in Canada;
- Credit cards issued by Canadian financial institutions and commercial entities, including stores, car rental agencies, etc.;
- Local newspaper subscriptions sent to a Canadian address;
- Rental of a Canadian safety deposit box or post office box;
- Subscriptions for life or general insurance, including health insurance, through a Canadian insurance company;
- Mailing address in Canada;
- Telephone listing in Canada;
- Business cards showing a Canadian address;
- Magazine and other periodical subscriptions sent to a Canadian address;
- Canadian bank accounts other than a non-resident bank account;
- Active securities accounts with Canadian brokers;
- Canadian driver's licence;
- Membership in a Canadian pension plan;
- Frequent visits to Canada for social or business purposes;
- Burial plot in Canada;
- Will prepared in Canada;
- Legal documentation indicating Canadian residence;
- Filing a Canadian income tax return as a Canadian resident;
- Ownership of a Canadian vacation property;
- Active involvement in business activities in Canada;
- Employment in Canada;
- Maintenance or storage in Canada of personal belongings, including clothing, furniture, family pets, etc.;
- Landed immigrant status in Canada; and
- Severing substantially all ties with former country of residence.

c) International Tax Treaties

Tax treaty rules usually apply to prevent double taxation of individuals when two countries both claim taxable jurisdiction over the taxpayer. An individual may be a resident of more than one country in the same year. For example, a Canadian resident who is a US citizen is potentially liable to taxation by both Canada (based on his residence) and the United States (based on his citizenship).

Similarly, an individual with international investments may be liable to tax in multiple jurisdictions. For example, a US resident who sojourns for 200 days in the year in Canada and receives dividends from a UK corporation might be liable for tax on his dividend income both in Canada and the United States under the domestic rules of the two countries. In addition, the individual would also be liable for any taxes the UK government withholds at source on the dividends. Thus, without specific relief, the individual would be potentially liable for tax on the same income in three countries.

Multiple taxation of income is unfair and inefficient in economic terms. Thus, countries negotiate bilateral tax treaties to prevent (or minimize) double taxation of income and capital.

Treaties resolve dual residency claims by allocating each country's jurisdiction to tax to either one or other of the countries, generally the country with the closer taxable nexus. The process involves applying a series of tiebreaker rules so that only one of the two countries will have the primary right to tax the individual as its resident. The tiebreakers determine the degree of attachment that an individual has with a country, and are ranked in descending order of significance.

Article 4(2) of the *OECD Model Double Taxation Convention on Income and on Capital,* which Canada uses as the model for most of its treaties, specifies the hierarchy of tiebreakers as follows:

> Where . . . an individual is a resident of both Contracting States, then his status shall be determined as follows:
>
> (a) he shall be deemed to be a resident of the State in which he has a permanent home available to him; if he has a permanent home available to him in both States, he shall be deemed to be a resident of the State with which his personal and economic relations are closer (centre of vital interests);
>
> (b) if the State in which he has his centre of vital interests cannot be determined, or if he has not a permanent home available to him in either State, he shall be deemed to be a resident of the State in which he has an habitual abode;

(c) if he has an habitual abode in both States or in neither of them, he shall be deemed to be a resident of the State of which he is a national;

(d) if he is a national of both States or of neither of them, the competent authorities of the Contracting States shall settle the question by mutual agreement.

If one cannot resolve the issue of dual residency by applying the above criteria, the revenue agencies (competent authorities) of the two countries shall settle the question by mutual agreement. The Model Treaty, however, does not provide a solution if the two countries cannot, or will not, settle the question.

i) Permanent Home

Treaties typically deem a dual resident individual to reside in the country in which he has a permanent home. Permanence implies that the individual must have arranged and retained the home for his permanent use.

A "home" includes any form of residential establishment, for example, a house, apartment, or even rented furnished rooms. It is the permanence of the home, rather than its size or nature of ownership or tenancy, that determines attachment to the country.

ii) Centre of Vital Interests

Where an individual has a permanent home in both of the countries that consider the individual a resident under their domestic laws, the treaty deems the individual to reside in the country with which he has closer personal and economic relations ("centre of vital interests").[30] Personal and economic relations mean family and social relations, occupation, political and cultural activities, place of business, and the place of administration of property. The OECD Commentary describes the centre of vital interests as follows:

> The circumstances must be examined as a whole, but it is nevertheless obvious that considerations based on the personal acts of the individual must receive special attention. If a person who has a home in one State sets up a second in the other State while retaining the first, the fact that he retains the first in the environment where he has always lived, where he has worked, and where he has his family and possessions, can, together with other elements, go to demonstrate that he has retained his centre of vital interests in the first State.[31]

---

30   OECD Model Convention, above note 3, Article 4(2).
31   Commentary on Article 4(2), para 15.

iii) Habitual Abode

If one cannot determine an individual's centre of vital interests or if the individual does not have a permanent home in either country, the OECD Model deems the individual to reside in the country in which he maintains a habitual abode. Alternatively, where an individual has a permanent home available to him in both countries, a habitual abode in one, rather than in the other, will tip the balance towards the country where he stays more frequently.[32]

Where, however, an individual does not have a permanent home in either country, one must consider all of his stays in the country without reference to the reason for the stay. The essential issue is whether the individual's residence in each of the two countries is sufficiently "habitual."

iv) Nationality

We saw earlier that very few countries use nationality to establish tax nexus. Nationality is important, however, if none of the above criteria are sufficient to break the deadlock. Then, treaties typically deem the individual to reside in the country of which he or she is a national.[33]

v) Competent Authorities

Finally, if one cannot resolve dual residency through the application of any of the specific attachment criteria, we refer the matter to the "competent authorities." The CRA is the designated competent authority under Canada's bilateral treaties.

d) Part-Year Residents

An individual is a part-year resident if he gives, or takes, up Canadian residence part way through the year. For example, a resident may emigrate on 30 May in a year and take up residence elsewhere. In these circumstances, the individual would be a resident of Canada until his departure on 30 May and a non-resident for the remainder of the year. As a resident, the individual would be taxable on his global income. As a non-resident, he would be taxable in Canada only if he was employed, or carrying on a business, in Canada or if he realized a capital gain from taxable Canadian property.[34]

---

32   *Allchin v Canada*, 2004 FCA 206 (resident of both Canada and the United States had her "habitual abode" in the US under Article IV(2)(b) of the *Canada-US Tax Treaty*, above note 11. Hence, not subject to tax under subs 2(1) of the *ITA*).

33   See, for example, Article IV of the *Canada-US Tax Treaty*, *ibid*.

34   *ITA*, above note 4, subs 2(3) and subject to any treaty provisions.

A resident who gives up residence during a taxation year may claim her tax deductions for that year, but only on a proportional basis.[35] We determine an individual's non-refundable tax credits for the period of residency based on reasonableness, such as the number of days of residency. For example, an individual who becomes a Canadian resident on 1 September of a year is liable for Canadian tax on his global income between 1 September and 31 December of the year. The individual's personal exemptions would be 122/365 (122 being the number of days of the year spent in Canada) of the annual deductions otherwise available. An individual may also claim—subject to annual maximums—additional tax credits for the period of non-residency if he earns at least 90 percent of his income for the period of non-residency in Canada.[36]

i)   Giving Up Residence
It is not easy to relinquish Canadian residence. Canada likes its taxpayers. An individual must produce convincing evidence that he has severed ties with Canada on a fairly permanent basis in order to cease residence. To give up Canadian residence, the taxpayer should minimize (preferably eliminate) his or her ties with Canada.[37]

The CRA looks at four principal factors to determine whether an individual has given up Canadian residence:

1)   Permanence and purpose of stay abroad;
2)   Residential ties within Canada;
3)   Residential ties elsewhere; and
4)   Regularity and length of visits to Canada.

Thus, at the very least, an individual giving up residence should:

- Sell or long-term lease his dwelling in Canada;
- Sell his motor vehicle;
- Cancel any lease in respect of a dwelling in Canada that he occupies, or sublease the dwelling for the period of his absence;
- Cancel bank accounts, club memberships and similar social and business connections within Canada; and
- Stay out of Canada.

---

35   *Ibid*, ss 114 and 118.91.
36   *Ibid*, s 118.94.
37   See, for example, *Ferguson v MNR*, [1989] 2 CTC 2387 (TCC) (Canadian in Saudi Arabia for five years considered Canadian resident because he retained Ontario driver's licence and union membership, and his spouse remained in Canada).

However, there is no bright-line factual test for the minimum length of time that an individual should be out of Canada to claim non-resident status.

ii) Becoming a Resident
It is much easier for an individual to become a Canadian resident than to relinquish residence. An individual who takes up residence in Canada is taxed as a part-year resident for the portion of the year after her arrival and as a non-resident prior to her arrival.

Residence for immigration purposes is different from residence for tax purposes. An individual can establish permanent residence status for immigration purposes without becoming a resident for tax purposes. "Landed immigrant" status is determined on the basis of selection standards that are quite different from those used to determine residence for tax purposes. For immigration purposes, a landed immigrant must spend 183 days in Canada in a *12-month period*. For tax purposes, the Act deems an individual to be a resident of Canada if he spends more than 182 days in Canada in a *calendar year*. Thus, an individual can arrange to take up landed immigrant status in Canada in a particular year and maintain non-resident status for income tax purposes.

It is generally advantageous for an individual to deliberately establish residence in Canada rather than be deemed a "sojourner" in Canada in the year of arrival. The Act deems a sojourner to be a Canadian resident for the *entire year* and taxable on his worldwide income.[38] In contrast, an incoming resident is taxable on his or her worldwide income only after arrival in Canada. Thus, timing immigration is important. An immigrant can minimize tax by splitting income between Canada and the country of departure.

2) Corporations

The residence of a corporation is a little more difficult because a corporation is an artificial legal entity, a person and a taxpayer in its own right. A corporation resident in Canada is taxable on its worldwide income. Non-resident corporations are taxable in Canada only on their Canadian-source income.

As with individuals, we determine the residence of a corporation in one of three ways: under statutory rules, at "common law," or by virtue of international tax treaty provisions. Canada, like many countries—for example, Australia, Germany, the Netherlands and the United

---

38   *ITA*, above note 4, para 250(1)(a), subs 2(1).

States—uses two tests of corporate residence: the place of incorporation (the statutory rule) and the place of management.

a) Statutory Rules

The statutory rule is simple. The Act deems a corporation incorporated in Canada to be resident in Canada for tax purposes.[39] This rule applies to corporations incorporated in Canada, regardless of where they are managed or controlled.[40]

The Act also deems a corporation incorporated in Canada prior to 26 April 1965 to be resident in Canada in a taxation year but only if after that date it:[41]

- Becomes resident in Canada at any time under the "common law" rules; or
- Carries on business in Canada.[42]

A corporation incorporated in Canada is a "Canadian corporation."[43] This concept is important because of special incentive provisions that apply only to Canadian corporations.[44]

Finally, the Act deems a corporation that is continued into or outside Canada to have been incorporated in its new jurisdiction.[45] Thus, a corporation that is incorporated in Canada and continued outside Canada escapes the deemed residence rules,[46] which are based on the jurisdiction of incorporation. For example, a corporation that is initially incorporated in the United States and then continued under federal or provincial corporate law in Canada, but which remains resident in both countries because of the "central management and control" test, is deemed a resident of Canada. Thus, US corporations continued into Canada can acquire "Canadian corporation" status, even if they are effectively managed from the United States. Such US corporations are eligible for favourable treatment under the Act.[47]

---

39 *Ibid*, para 250(4)(a). This deeming provision only applies to corporations incorporated in Canada after 26 April 1965.
40 *Ibid*, para 250(4)(a).
41 *Ibid*, para 250(4)(c).
42 See meaning of "carrying on business in Canada" in s 253, *ibid*.
43 *Ibid*, subs 89(1) "Canadian corporation."
44 See Chapter 17.
45 *ITA*, above note 4, subs 250(5.1).
46 *Ibid*, subs 250(4).
47 For example, for tax-deferred rollovers on transfers of property to the corporation on a merger with another taxable Canadian corporation.

b) Common Law Rules

The statutory incorporation test would, by itself, be an open gate to avoid Canadian tax by incorporating in a foreign jurisdiction. Thus, there is a supplementary common law test, which acts as an anti-avoidance rule.

The determination of corporate residence at "common law" is essentially a question of fact and circumstances. The classic rule, which originated in the Court of Exchequer in 1876 in *Calcutta Jute Mills v Nicholson*[48] and *Cesena Sulphur Co Ltd v Nicholson*,[49] is that a corporation is resident where its "central management and control" resides. Thirty years later, the House of Lords adopted the test in *De Beers Consolidated Mines Ltd v Howe* (*De Beers*), now considered the seminal authority on corporate residence. As Lord Loreburn said:

> In applying the conception of residence to a company, we ought, I think, to proceed as nearly as we can upon the analogy of an individual. A company cannot eat or sleep, but it can keep house and do business. We ought, therefore, to see where it really keeps house and does business . . . . [A] company resides for purposes of income tax where its real business is carried on . . . . I regard that as the true rule, and the real business is carried on where the central management and control actually abides.[50]

Corporate residence is different from corporate capacity. Corporate capacity is a legal test determined under the law of the jurisdiction of incorporation. Central management and control is where a company's board of directors actually controls its business and affairs—generally in the jurisdiction where the board meets. We use *de facto* "central management and control" to determine corporate residence.

i) *General Propositions*

The following propositions apply to corporate residence:

- A corporation can have more than one residence if its central management and control is located in more than one jurisdiction.[51]
- Central management and control refers to the exercise of power and control by the corporation's board of directors and not to the power

---

48   (1876), 1 TC 83 (Eng Ex Div).

49   (1876), 1 TC 88 (Eng Ex Div).

50   *De Beers Consolidated Mines Ltd v Howe*, [1906] AC 455 at 458.

51   *Swedish Central Ry Co v Thompson*, [1925] AC 495 (HL) (company resident in location of registered office and where controlled and managed); *MNR v Crossley Carpets (Canada) Ltd*, [1969] 1 Ex CR 405 (paramount authority for businesses divided between two countries).

of the corporation's shareholders. Thus, the residence of shareholders is irrelevant for the purposes of determining corporate residence.[52]

- Determine the residence of a subsidiary corporation, even a wholly owned subsidiary, independently of its parent corporation.
- A subsidiary corporation's residence may coincide with its parent corporation if the parent exercises effective control over the subsidiary's activities and management.[53]

There is no bright-line test that determines corporate residence in every case. To determine the central management and control of a corporation one must carefully evaluate all the surrounding factors, including:

- The location of meetings of its directors;
- The degree of independent control exercised by its directors; and
- The relative influence and power that domestic directors exercise, as compared with foreign directors (the "rubber stamp" test).

Ultimately, each case depends upon an evaluation of where the corporation is actually managed and controlled.

ii) Dual Residence

Since different countries use different connecting factors to assert taxable jurisdiction over corporations, a corporation may be resident in more than one country. For example, a corporation that is incorporated in the United States and managed and controlled in Canada would be resident in both countries.

The *OECD Model Convention* uses the "place of effective management" as a tiebreaker to determine the residence of persons other than individuals. Article 4(3) of the Model Convention states:

> Where . . . a person other than an individual is a resident of both Contracting States, then it shall be deemed to be a resident of the State in which its place of effective management is situated.

Both Canada and the United States, however, reserve the right to use place of incorporation as the determinative test for corporate residence. Article IV(3) of the *Canada-US Treaty*, for example, provides that:

> Where . . . a company is a resident of both Contracting States, then if it was created under the laws in force in a Contracting State, it shall be deemed to be a resident of that State.

---

52 *Gramophone & Typewriter Co v Stanley*, [1908] 2 KB 89 (CA).
53 *Unit Construction Co Ltd v Bullock*, [1960] AC 351 (HL).

Some jurisdictions allow local incorporation of an entity that is already organized and incorporated under the laws of another country. Under the *Canada-US Treaty*, however, the determinative factor is the location of the corporation's original creation.[54]

c) International Tax Treaties

A Canadian resident corporation is taxable in Canada on its worldwide income. A non-resident corporation is taxable in Canada only if it carries on business in Canada or disposes taxable Canadian property.[55]

However, a non-resident enterprise of a country with which Canada has a bilateral tax treaty is taxable only if it carries on business in Canada through a "permanent establishment." The permanent establishment test for determining source liability for Canadian tax of a non-resident from a treaty country raises the threshold from the simple test of carrying on business in Canada. "Permanent establishment" is the taxable nexus for source taxation of non-resident corporations.

i) Permanent Establishment

The term "permanent establishment" is essentially a tax treaty concept. Tax treaties typically provide that a "permanent establishment" means a *"fixed* place of business in which an enterprise wholly or partly carries on its business."[56] In *Re Consolidated Premium Iron Ores*, the United States Tax Court explained the concept:[57]

> The term "permanent establishment," normally interpreted, suggests something more substantial than a license, a letterhead and isolated activities. It implies the existence of an office, staffed and capable of carrying on the day-to-day business of the corporation and its use for such purpose, or it suggests the existence of a plant or facilities equipped to carry on the ordinary routine of such business activity. The descriptive word "permanent" in the characterization "permanent establishment" is vital in analysing the treaty provisions . . . . It indicates permanence and stability.

In determining whether a corporation has "an office" in a particular place, one looks to:

---

54 See *Revised Technical Explanation: Canada-U.S. Income Tax Convention 1980* (US Treasury Department), online: www.treasury.gov/resource-center/tax-policy/treaties/Documents/tecanada.pdf.

55 *ITA*, above note 4, subs 2(3) and s 253.

56 *OECD Model Convention*, above note 3, Article 5.

57 *Re Consolidated Premium Iron Ores*, 28 TC 127 at 152 (1957), aff'd 265 F 2d 320 (6th Circuit 1959).

- Presence of permanent physical premises;
- Presence of directors or employees;
- Bank accounts and books of account;
- Telephone listings; and
- Employees or agents established with the general authority to contract for the taxpayer in that jurisdiction.

Consolidated Premium Iron Ores was decided in 1957. It is questionable how valid the "bricks and mortar" test is in the context of electronic commerce.

ii) Treaty Shopping

There is increasing concern in the international community that treaties should limit, or at least restrain, tax planning motivated solely by tax avoidance. Corporate taxpayers, in particular, can quite easily arrange their affairs to take advantage of the rules that determine residence by virtue of specific statutory and treaty provisions.[58] For example, a corporation can be incorporated in the United States so that it is a resident there. This would allow the corporation to take advantage of US bilateral tax treaties that it might not otherwise be able to invoke.

There is little doubt that the trend in international communities is towards placing greater restrictions on the "improper" use of tax treaties. Thus, just as domestic statutory provisions (for example, the General Anti-Avoidance Rule[59]) restrict the application of the *Westminster*[60] principle, so also we are seeing increasing restrictions intended to curtail tax avoidance appearing in bilateral tax treaties. Article XXIX(A) of the *Canada-US Treaty*, for example, limits the benefits of the treaty to "qualifying persons." The Article also allows the authorities to deny taxpayers the benefits of the Treaty where they use it in an abusive manner.

The Commentary on Article 1 of the *OECD Model Convention* discusses the improper use of bilateral tax conventions:

> True, taxpayers have the possibility, double tax conventions being left aside, to exploit the differences in tax levels as between States and the tax advantages provided by various country's taxation laws, but it is for the States concerned to adopt provisions in their domestic laws to counter possible manoeuvres. Such States will then wish, in their bilateral double taxation conventions, to preserve the application of provisions of this kind contained in their domestic laws

---

58   *MIL (Investments) SA v Canada*, 2006 TCC 460, aff'd 2007 FCA 236.
59   *ITA*, above note 4, s 245 (discussed in Chapter 19).
60   *CIR v The Duke of Westminster*, [1936] AC 1 (HL) (taxpayer entitled to order affairs so as to minimize tax payable).

. . . . For example, if a person . . . acted through a legal entity created in a State essentially to obtain treaty benefits which would not be available directly to such person. Another case would be one of an individual having in a Contracting State both his permanent home and all his economic interests, including a substantial participation in a company of that State, and who, essentially in order to sell the participation and escape taxation in that State on the capital gains from the alienation . . . transferred his permanent home to the other Contracting State, where such gains were subject to little or no tax . . . . It may be appropriate for Contracting States to agree in bilateral negotiations that any relief from tax should not apply in certain cases, or to agree that the application of the provisions of domestic laws against tax avoidance should not be affected by the Convention.

The Commentary goes on to discuss various approaches that member countries may consider in combating the problem of tax avoidance through conduit companies. One approach is "look-through" provisions to disallow treaty benefits to corporations that are not owned, directly or indirectly, by residents of the country in which the corporation is a resident. The Commentary suggests the following wording for such a provision:

A company which is a resident of a Contracting State shall not be entitled to relief from taxation under this Convention with respect to any item of income, gains or profits unless it is neither owned nor controlled directly or through one or more companies, wherever resident, by persons who are not residents of the first-mentioned State.

Such provisions in Canadian bilateral tax treaties would prevent residents of third party countries from incorporating in Canada in order to take advantage of Canada's treaty network with other countries. The United States has negotiated similar anti-treaty shopping provisions in all (but one) of its treaties.[61]

Canada's anti-treaty-shopping rules vary in scope. Article 27(3) of the *Canada-Mexico Income Tax Convention*, for example, states:

The Convention shall not apply to any company, trust or partnership that is a resident of a Contracting State and is beneficially owned or controlled directly or indirectly by one or more persons who are not residents of that State, if the amount of the tax imposed on the income or capital of the company, trust or partnership by that State

---

61   See, for example, Article 28 of the *US-Germany Treaty* and Article 17 of the *US-Mexico Treaty*.

is substantially lower than the amount that would be imposed by the State if all of the shares of the capital stock of the company or all of the interests in the trust or partnership, as the case may be, were beneficially owned by one or more individuals who were residents of that State.[62]

In other cases, Canada's treaties state that treaty benefits may not apply to certain corporations established in particular jurisdictions. Article XXX(3) of the *Canada-Barbados Income Tax Agreement*,[63] for example, states that it

> shall not apply to companies entitled to any special tax benefit under the Barbados *International Business Companies (Exemption from Income Tax) Act* . . . or to companies entitled to any special tax benefits under any similar law enacted by Barbados in addition to or in place of that law.

3) Trusts

A trust is a legal relationship that arises when a person (the trustee) is compelled by law to hold property for the benefit of some other person (the beneficiary). The property is to be held in such a manner that the real benefit of the property accrues to the beneficiary and not to the trustee.

A trust is *not* a separate legal entity. For tax purposes, however, a trust is taxable as a separate person.[64] The residence of a trust for tax purposes is a question of fact determined according to the common law rules applicable to individuals.

A trust with a single trustee is resident where its trustee resides.[65] Where a trust has more than one trustee, it is resident where a majority of its trustees reside if the trust instrument permits majority decisions

---

62   *Canada-Mexico Income Tax Convention*, 8 April 1991, Can TS 1992 No 15, Article 27(3).

63   *Canada-Barbados Income Tax Agreement*, 22 January 1980, Can TS 1980 No 29.

64   *ITA*, above note 4, subs 104(2).

65   *McLeod v Canada (Minister of Customs and Excise)* (*sub nom Curry Estate v Canada (Minister of Customs and Excise)*), [1926] SCR 457 (taxation of accumulated income in hands of trustee); *MNR v Royal Trust Co* (1931), 1 DTC 217 (SCC) (trust with non-resident beneficiaries but resident trustee taxable); *MNR v McMartin Estate*, [1932] SCR 655, var'd on other grounds (*sub nom Holden v MNR*), [1933] AC 526 (trust taxed on undistributed income whether beneficiaries resident or not); *Williams v Singer*, [1921] 1 AC 65 (HL) (trust not taxed on foreign dividends received for non-resident beneficiary); *IRC v Gull*, [1937] 4 All ER 290 (KB) (English charitable trust exempt where one trustee non-resident).

on all matters within the discretion of the trustees *and* the trustees actually discharge their fiduciary duties.[66] A trust cannot have dual residence. In this respect, trusts are quite unlike individuals and corporations, which can have dual residences.[67]

In the event that a trust has multiple trustees, some of whom are individuals and others corporations, one must determine the residence of each of the trustees according to the common law and statutory rules. For example, we might determine the individual trustee's residence according to the common law tests and the residence of a corporate trustee by reference to its place of incorporation. The determination of a trust's residence is much more complicated if its trustees reside in different jurisdictions, each with bilateral tax treaties with Canada.

4) Partnerships

A partnership is the relationship that subsists between persons carrying on business in common with a view to profit.[68] A partnership is *not* a separate legal entity. The liability of partners for partnerships may be unlimited (general partnerships) or limited (limited liability partnerships). A "Canadian partnership" is a partnership in which all the members are resident in Canada.[69]

For tax purposes, partnership income is calculated *as if* the partnership were a separate person.[70] Thus, we calculate a partnership's income as if the partnership were an entity, and then allocate the income to the partners according to the terms of the partnership agreement. Hence, a partnership is a conduit, and its income flows through to the partners. Individual partners are taxed as individuals; corporate partners are taxed as corporations.

5) Provincial Residence

A Canadian resident is liable for federal income tax on his worldwide income. In addition to federal tax, however, a Canadian resident may

---

66   See *Garron (Trustee of)* v *Canada*, 2009 TCC 450 (court looked at actual management and control of Barbados trust); *Thibodeau Estate (Trustees of)* v *Canada*, [1978] CTC 539 (FCTD); see also Interpretation Bulletin IT-447, "Residence of a Trust or Estate" (30 May 1980).

67   IT-447, *ibid.*

68   *Partnerships Act*, RSO 1990, c P.5, s 2.

69   *ITA*, above note 4, subs 102(1).

70   *Ibid*, para 96(1)(a).

also be liable for provincial tax. Provincial income tax liability is generally calculated in a way similar to that of federal income tax liability.

We determine an individual's provincial income tax liability (except for Quebec) by applying the provincial income tax rates to the individual's "taxable income." "Taxable income" is defined by the federal government and is the tax base used by both levels of government for the calculation of income taxes.

For the purpose of provincial income tax liability, an individual resides in a province throughout the taxation year if she resides in the province on 31 December of the year. For example, an individual who moves from Ontario to Alberta on 30 December of a year is taxable on her income for the entire year in Alberta. This rule, although somewhat imperfect in its technical accuracy, is easy and convenient for individuals to apply and for the provinces to administer. Thus, we trade-off some loss of revenue for the province from which the individual moves in exchange for administrative simplicity and certainty for the individual.

The calculation of corporate provincial tax is more complex. A corporation must allocate its Canadian source income to each of the provinces in which it maintains a permanent establishment.[71] A formula based on the proportion of revenue and payroll attributable to a province determines the allocation.

C. NON-RESIDENTS

Non-residents are taxable in Canada, but only on their Canadian-source income. Thus, Canada exercises source or territorial jurisdiction over non-residents who earn income in Canada.

There are two broad categories of Canadian-source income — active and passive. Active income is taxable under Part I of the Act; passive income is subject to withholding tax under Part XIII.

A non-resident person has active Canadian source income if he or she:

- was employed in Canada;
- carried on business in Canada; or
- disposed of taxable Canadian property

at any time either in the current year or in a previous year.

---

71   *Ibid*, s 124; *Income Tax Regulations*, above note 17, s 400.

An individual is employed in Canada if she performs the duties of an office or employment in Canada. This rule applies whether or not the individual's employer resides in Canada.

A non-resident person carries on business in Canada if she engages in any business activity, solicits orders or offers anything for sale in Canada.[72] Subsection 248(1) defines a "business" to include a profession, calling, trade, manufacture or undertaking of any kind whatever, and an adventure or concern in the nature of trade. This is a broad definition that casts a wide net to catch non-resident businesses.

However, the liability of a non-resident person for Canadian income tax is curtailed if the person resides in a country with which Canada has a tax treaty. The general treaty rule is that business profits earned by a non-resident in Canada are taxable only if the non-resident has a "permanent establishment" in Canada and the profits are attributable to the establishment.

Taxable Canadian property includes real property in Canada, shares of resident Canadian corporations (other than most public corporations), and capital property used in carrying on a business in Canada.[73]

A non-resident who earns passive Canadian-source income (for example, dividends, interest or royalties) is liable for Canadian withholding tax of 25 percent under Part XIII of the Act. Canada reduces the withholding rate, however, in its tax treaties and has eliminated withholding on interest income under the *Canada-US Treaty*.

D. EXEMPT PERSONS

Regardless of their statutory or common law affiliations with Canada, the Act exempts from tax the following persons who might otherwise be taxable under Part I of the Act:[74]

- Persons holding diplomatic and quasi-diplomatic positions in Canada, members of their families and their servants;
- Municipal authorities;
- Corporations owned by the Crown;
- Registered charities;
- Labour organizations;

---

72   *ITA, ibid*, s 253.
73   *Ibid*, subs 248(1) "taxable Canadian property."
74   *Ibid*, s 149. The persons listed in this section are exempt from Part I tax. Subsection 227(14) extends the exemption for taxes under other parts to corporations exempt under s 149.

- Non-profit clubs, societies or associations (NPOs);[75]
- Prescribed small business investment corporations;[76]
- Registered pension funds and trusts;
- Trusts created for:
  - » Employee profit-sharing plans;
  - » Registered supplementary unemployment benefit plans;
  - » Registered retirement savings and income plans;
  - » Deferred profit-sharing plans;
  - » Registered education savings plans; and
  - » Retirement compensation arrangements.

These persons are exempt from tax only if they satisfy all of the conditions necessary for attaining exempt status.

E. INDIANS

Indians enjoy special tax status. Indian reserves are "tax havens" for Indians who derive income from property (real or personal) situated on a reserve in Canada.[77] The *Indian Act*[78] also provides immunity from seizure of property. Thus, an Indian can earn income off-reserve, import his capital onto a reserve and invest it on a tax-free basis if there are sufficient connecting factors between his income and the reserve.

Section 87 of the *Indian Act* provides:

Notwithstanding any other Act of the Parliament of Canada or any Act of the legislature of a province . . . the following property is exempt from taxation, namely:

(a) the interest of an Indian or a band in reserve or surrendered lands; and

(b) the personal property of an Indian or band situated on a reserve; and no Indian or band is subject to taxation in respect of the ownership, occupation, possession, or use of any property mentioned in paragraph (a) or (b) or is otherwise subject to taxation in respect of any such property . . . .

---

75   An election by an NPO for the purposes of GST legislation does not, in and of itself, adversely affect its tax-exempt status for income tax purposes: Technical Interpretation (27 August 1990), CRA.

76   *ITA*, above note 4, para 149(1)(o.3); *Income Tax Regulations*, above note 17, s 5101(1).

77   Section 87 of the *Indian Act* of 1876, SC 1876, c 18.

78   RSC 1985, c I-5.

The tax exemption derives from the *Royal Proclamation* of 1763[79] in which the Crown acknowledged that it is honour-bound to shield Indians from any efforts by non-natives to dispossess Indians of their property that they hold *qua* Indians. The rationale is to protect reserve Indians from government, which might otherwise use its taxing power to erode the benefits that Indians derive from the government. In effect, the exemption prevents one branch of government from emasculating the very benefits that another branch of the government gives Indians.[80]

The exemption applies only to property situated within the boundaries of a reserve.[81] The phrase "on a reserve" has its plain and ordinary meaning.[82] The taxpayer claiming the exemption does not have to reside on the same reserve as the property.[83]

The availability of the exemption does not depend on whether the property is integral to the life of the reserve or to the preservation of the traditional Indian way of life.

It is a relatively simple matter to determine the location of real property. The location of personal property, however, is more complex and uncertain. There are various factors that can connect personal property to income. For example, there is no simple or bright-line test to determine the location of investment income, unemployment insurance benefits or pension benefits. In each case, one must determine the *situs* of the particular property and its connection to the income. The connecting factors may depend upon the residence of the payor and the payee, the place of payment, the place of employment, and the place of the contract or the location of the investment activity.[84]

We evaluate each case on its particular merits. The connecting factors do not all have the same weight in each case. One connecting factor may have more weight than another in determining the sufficiency of connections to locate the particular property, which makes the entire process somewhat uncertain.

---

79   RSC 1985, App II, No 1.
80   See, for example, *Mitchell v Peguis Indian Band*, [1990] 2 SCR 85 at 133, La Forest J: "purpose [of the exemptions] is simply to insulate the property interests of Indians in their reserve lands from the intrusions and the interference of the larger society so as to ensure than Indians are not dispossessed of their entitlements."
81   *Bastien Estate v Canada*, 2011 SCC 38.
82   *R v Nowegijick*, [1983] SCR 29 at 41.
83   *Dubé v Canada*, 2011 SCC 39.
84   See, for example, *Williams v Canada*, [1992] 1 SCR 877 and *Bastien Estate v. Canada*, above note 81.

What is certain, however, is that if there is sufficient nexus between the income and the reserve, the reserve is a tax haven.

F. CONCLUSION

The answer to the question "Who is Taxable" depends upon economic, political and legal considerations. While countries want taxable bases that are revenue-secure and fair, the system must also be capable of efficient administration at a reasonable cost.

The concept of residence creates taxable nexus through economic, political and social links. Taxation of residents on their worldwide income is fair, equitable and tax neutral. However, taxing a resident's worldwide income creates problems of double taxation where the same income is also taxed at source in another country. This is why we address double taxation through domestic credits for foreign taxes and in negotiated bilateral tax treaties.[85]

FURTHER READINGS

General

BALE, GORDON. "The Basis of Taxation" in Brian Hansen, Vern Krishna, & James Rendall, eds, *Canadian Taxation* (Toronto: Richard De Boo, 1981).

Residence: Individuals

HANSEN, BRIAN. "Individual Residence" (1977) 29 Can Tax Found 682.

Residence: Corporations

FARNSWORTH, ALBERT. *The Residence and Domicile of Corporations* (London: Butterworth & Co, 1939).

---

85   See Chapter 15.

CHAPTER 4

THE MEANING
OF INCOME

"A word is not a crystal; transparent and unchanged, it is the skin of a living thought and may vary in colour and content according to the circumstances and the time in which it is used."[1]

A. INTRODUCTION

We turn now to the second of our five questions: what is taxable? The answer to this question is the *sine qua non* of every taxing statute. In the *Income Tax Act*, however, the answer is both obvious and obscure.

The income tax is a tax on income. Thus, the concept of income determines the size of the tax base and, implicitly, the structure of the system. We must answer two fundamental questions:

1) What is income for tax purposes? and
2) What is the source of the income?

In answering these questions, we start with the general concept of economic income and then see how our jurisprudence has modified the concept for pragmatic considerations.

It may be surprising, but the Act does not define the term "income" for tax purposes. Although the Act sometimes speaks of what we must

---

1   Justice Holmes in *Towne v Eisner*, 245 US 418 at 425.

include in, or can exclude from, income, it neither identifies nor describes the legal characteristics of income.[2]

We include a receipt in the taxable base if it is income unless, even though of an income nature, the Act specifically excludes it. The statute may exempt income because of the status of the recipient (for example, the Governor General's salary and allowances are exempt from income)[3] or the location where the taxpayer earns it (for example, income of an Indian on a reserve.)

The following figure is a bird's eye view of the Act's characterization of receipts into taxable and non-taxable components:

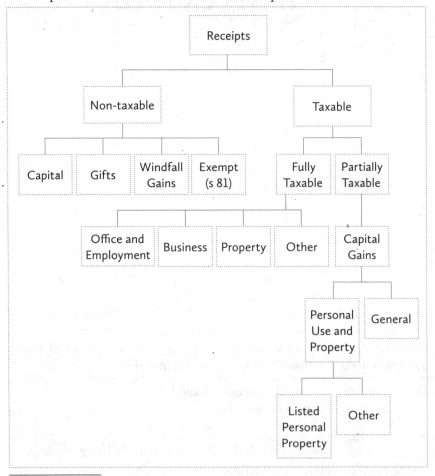

2   For example, in the *Income Tax Act*, RSC 1985, c 1 (5th Supp) [*ITA*], para 6(1)(a) specifies that the value of board and lodging is included in employment income; s 7 deems certain stock option benefits to be employment income; subs 6(9) deems imputed interest from an interest-free loan to be income, etc. See, for example, paras 12(1)(c) (interest), 12(1)(j) (dividends) and 12(1)(m) (benefits from trusts).
3   *Ibid*, para 81(1)(n).

The seemingly simple tasks of identifying and characterizing receipts creates considerable difficulty. For example, suppose an employer gives his employee $1,000 at Christmas. Is the $1,000 income or a gift to the employee? The distinction is crucial to the employee who will be taxed if the $1,000 is remuneration, but will not be taxable if it is a gift. We can determine taxability quite easily after we draw the line between remuneration and gifts. The difficulty is in determining where to draw the line.

B. THE MEANING OF INCOME

The term "income" means, literally, "incoming" or "what comes in" to a person. The literal meaning is not very helpful, because we must identify the character of the incoming.

Webster's Dictionary defines "income" as "a gain which proceeds from labour, business, property, or capital of any kind, as the produce of a farm, rent of houses, proceeds of professional business, the profits of commerce, or of occupation, or the interest of money or stock in funds."

The *Oxford Dictionary* describes income as "periodical (usually annual) receipts from one's business, lands, work, investments, etc."

These definitions, which are useful starting points, provide an intuitive response that income represents an increment ("incoming") to wealth over a period of time. This intuitive view was an important influence on the early thinking on the nature of income. In *Eisner v Macomber*,[4] for example, the US Supreme Court said that "income may be defined as the gain derived from labour, from capital, or from both combined." But what of incomings in the absence of labour or capital (for example, prizes, scholarships, damages, found property, etc.)?

Economists use the term "income" to mean net accretion of wealth. Two tax theorists formulated the most famous definition of economic income: Robert M Haig, a professor of Columbia University; and HC Simons, a professor of economics at the University of Chicago. Working independently in the 1920s and the 1930s, they developed what has become the standard economic definition of income: "the algebraic sum of (1) the market value of rights exercised in consumption and (2) the change in the value of the store of property rights between the beginning and end of the period in question."[5]

---

4   *Eisner v Macomber*, 252 US 189 (1920).

5   In Haig's language, income is "the increase or accretion in one's power to satisfy his wants in a given period in so far as that power consists of (a) money itself or, (b) anything susceptible of valuation in terms of money." Simons equates per-

Haig-Simons saw income as the accretion in the *value* of assets on hand at the end of the period over the *value* of assets on hand at the beginning of the period after adjustments for the value of goods consumed. Using this approach, a taxpayer who begins a year with $1,000, consumes $20,000 during the year and has $5,000 in assets at the end of the year, has $24,000 income for the year.

Two aspects of the above formulation of income warrant emphasis: (1) the formula does not distinguish between sources of income; and (2) net *accretion* of wealth includes all unrealized gains, imputed income[6] (for example, from owner-occupied housing), and increases in human capital resulting from education or acquired skills. Thus, the Haig-Simons concept of income is broad, all-inclusive, and without preferences.

The Haig-Simons formulation of income may appear bizarre to the average person. The definition has politically explosive elements and few politicians would rise to the level of theory that one should tax imputed income from owner-occupied housing or housework. Similarly, the debate on the capital gains preferential rate is intense and is long in the tooth. Nevertheless, tax policy-makers view the Haig-Simons formula as the ideal to which we should aspire. Hence, they see any deviation from the definition as inherently unjustifiable.

There are also other definitions of "income." For example:

- According to Richard Posner, income can be defined as "The broadest definition of income would be all pecuniary and non-pecuniary receipts, including leisure and gifts."[7]
- Professor Irving Fisher, of Yale, considered income to be "a flow of benefits during a period of time."[8]

The common feature of these definitions of income is that they are comprehensive and inclusive. The Carter Commission in its report on the Canadian tax system endorsed this approach:[9]

---

sonal income with the algebraic sum of consumption and change in net worth. See "The Concept of Income: Economic and Legal Aspects" in RM Haig, ed, *The Federal Income Tax* (New York: Columbia University Press, 1921).

6   We speak of imputed income as the benefit that we derive from consumption or use of our own assets.

7   Richard Posner, *Economic Analysis of Law* (Boston: Little Brown, 1973) at 231–32.

8   Irving Fisher, *Elementary Principles of Economics* (New York: MacMillan, 1911) at 34.

9   *Report of the Royal Commission on Taxation*, vol 1 (Ottawa: R Duhamel, Queen's Printer, 1966) at 9 (Chair: KM Carter); see also Henry Simons, *Personal Income Taxation: The Definition of Income as a Problem of Fiscal Policy* (Chicago: University of Chicago Press, 1938).

We are completely persuaded that taxes should be allocated according to the changes in the economic power of individuals and families. If a man obtains increased command over goods and services for his personal satisfaction, we do not believe it matters, from the point of view of taxation, whether he earned it through working, made it through operating a business, received it because he held property, made it by selling property, or was given it by a relative. Nor do we believe it matters whether the increased command over goods and services was in cash or in kind. Nor do we believe it matters whether the increase in economic power was expected or unexpected, whether it was a unique or recurrent event, whether the man suffered to get the increase in economic power, or it fell in his lap without effort.

To paraphrase Carter: a buck at a buck.

The implementation of abstract concepts (such as benefits, utilities and satisfactions) into a working formula that provides a simple and accurate measure of income is difficult. The concept of income for tax purposes must be one that we can administer at a reasonable cost. As Professor Taussig of Harvard said:[10]

> [F]or almost all purposes of economic study, it is best to content ourselves with a statement, and an attempt at measurement, in terms not of utility but of money income . . . . The reason for this rejection of a principle which is in itself sound lies in the conclusion . . . regarding total utility and consumer's surplus: they cannot be measured.

The Haig-Simons formulation of income would be difficult and expensive to administer. The cost, for example, of measuring the "value" of assets at the end of every fiscal year would be prohibitive. How do we measure whether a taxpayer is "as well off" at the end of a year? Would one measure income in terms of "real" or nominal dollars? Even assuming that it is possible to track one's expenditures accurately for a given period, the periodic valuation of assets would present great difficulties and create considerable uncertainty leading to disputes and litigation.

---

10   Frank Taussig, *Principles of Economics*, 2d ed, rev (New York: MacMillan, 1916) vol 10 at 134.

C. THE LEGAL CONCEPT OF INCOME

"Income" in tax law is a measure of *gain*. This means that income does not include the realized value of the capital component of the gain.[11] For example, where a taxpayer buys goods at a cost of $10 per unit and sells the goods for $30 per unit, income is $20 per unit. The first $10 from the sale merely recovers the capital investment in the goods. The income tax is a tax on income and not on capital or wealth. Thus, in the absence of specific statutory rules, "income" means *net* income determined in accordance with ordinary commercial principles.[12]

Again, assume that an individual buys merchandise for $10 per unit and pays $1 per unit on account of freight to have the goods delivered to her business premises. The taxpayer then sells the goods for $30 per unit and pays shipping costs of $2 per unit. The taxpayer's gross revenue is $30 per unit, but her "income" for tax purposes is only $17 per unit, the net realized *accretion* to her wealth. The taxpayer recovers her capital investment of $10 and expenses of $3 in calculating her gain.

The legal concept of income has evolved, more so in some countries than others. In the US, for example, the concept of income evolved from the narrow focus in *Eisner v Macomber* (gains derived from labour or capital) to a more comprehensive and inclusive meaning in *Glenshaw Glass Co*[13] (the entire treble damage award under anti-trust laws was income even though two-thirds of the award was for punitive damages)[14].

. The legal concept of income for Canadian tax purposes is less comprehensive than in economic theory in two important ways: (1) the exclusion of unrealized gains; and (2) the classification of income by source.

---

11   This principle underlies the oft-quoted statement that income is the fruit only and never the tree; see, for example, *Stratton's Independence Ltd v Howbert*, 231 US 399 (1913); *Ryall v Hoare* (1923), 8 Tax Cas 521. This principle is modified by statutory provisions in certain circumstances; for example, para 12(1)(g) taxes as income any amounts paid that are calculated by reference to production, regardless of whether or not the payment actually represents an instalment of the sale price of the property.

12   *Dominion Natural Gas Co v MNR*, [1940-41] CTC 144 at 147–48 (Ex Ct), rev'd on facts [1940-41] CTC 155 (SCC).

13   *Commissioner v Glenshaw Glass Co*, 348 US 426 (1955).

14   The US Supreme Court stated, *ibid* at 431: "Here, we have instances of undeniable accessions to wealth, clearly realized, and over which the taxpayers have complete dominion. The mere fact that the payments were extracted from the wrongdoers as punishment for unlawful conduct cannot detract from their character as taxable income to the recipients."

1) Realized Gains

We recognize income only when we realize it in a market transaction such as a sale, exchange or disposition. In contrast, economists refer to income as an "accretion" to wealth, whether or not the taxpayer has realized the increased value in a market transaction. For example, assume that an individual purchases shares at a price of $10 per share and the shares increase in value to $25 per share by the end of the year. Under the Haig-Simons concept of income, the individual's income for the year is $15 per share. This amount represents the net accretion in the value of the shares and, therefore, measures the increase in wealth. For most tax purposes, however, the taxpayer need not report any income until he actually sells the shares and realizes the gain.[15]

There are some special rules that deviate from the realization principle. For example, financial institutions must use unrealized changes—"mark-to-market"—from certain shares and debt to measure income.[16] These are, however, exceptions from the general requirement of realization.

The realization requirement is a compromise between the theoretical purity of the economic concept of income and the administrative feasibility of applying the theory in practice. Taxation based on annual valuations to determine the net accretion of one's wealth would be financially inconvenient, create uncertainty and result in disputes over valuations. For most purposes, we are content to tax only actual realized gains. Thus, the realization requirement makes the income tax a tax on transactions rather than a tax on economic income.

As well, the realization principle creates other problems, such as the bunching of income in the year of sale. A taxpayer who receives "bunched income" can be bumped up into a higher marginal tax bracket in the year that she realizes the investment. In other circumstances (for example, death), the Act deems the realization of assets in order to trigger gains and prevent prolonged tax deferral.

The realization requirement raises two issues: (1) when do we realize income? and (2) what are the consequences of not taxing income until we realize it?

Generally, we realize income when we complete a transaction—when we sell or dispose of an asset or complete a service. For example, if A buys shares at a cost of $1,000 and the shares appreciate in value to

---

15   In certain circumstances, the Act deems a disposition even where there has been none. For example, a deceased is *deemed* to have disposed of all her property immediately before death: *ITA*, above note 2, subs 70(5). The provision creates a deemed realization.

16   *Ibid*, ss 142.2 to 142.6.

$3,000, A generates economic income of $2,000, the amount of the appreciation. On paper, A is $2,000 wealthier. For tax purposes, however, the gain is not taxable because A has not realized it. In contrast, if B purchases shares at a cost of $10,000 and the shares pay a dividend of $2,000, the dividend is taxable because B realizes it in cash. Thus, although both A and B are both wealthier by $2,000, only B is taxable on her gain. A defers his tax until he disposes of the appreciated shares.

The realization rule trades off equity against administrative convenience. Although both A and B are equally able to pay, taxing A on his unrealized appreciation would cause a cash flow problem. Of course, A could sell a portion of his shares to meet the tax obligations. This would work well with publicly traded shares. It might not be as easy, however, to realize their value in the absence of a public market. Liquidity is an even greater problem if the asset involved is land.

What are the consequences of the realization requirement in tax law? First, we see that the principle of realization converts the tax system from a tax on income to a tax on transactions. This affects the timing of the tax payable on a transaction. The requirement allows us to defer our tax liabilities and, apart from certain events such as death, control when we will recognize income from appreciated property. The value of the tax deferral depends upon the prevailing interest rate and the length of time that we delay realization.

The realization requirement is an opportunity for tax planning and a clear incentive for taxpayers to invest in shares (which have a greater likelihood of capital gains that we can defer) rather than bonds that pay interest on a current and, therefore, taxable basis. Thus, the tax system is not neutral. From the treasury's perspective, tax deferral is a revenue loss. As between taxpayers who are similarly well off, the requirement allows some to delay paying taxes. These trade-offs are a compromise between administrative convenience and equity.

2) Income by Source

Economic theory is not concerned with the source of income: all net accretions of wealth are income, regardless of their source. Source is irrelevant as a measure of economic well-being. After all, a taxpayer's ability to pay depends not upon her source of income, but on her enrichment. Equity requires that we tax all gains equally, regardless of their source.

The Canadian income tax system, however, is solidly based on the source concept. To be taxable, income must have a source. We calculate income from each source separately and aggregate income according to strict rules applicable to each particular source.

The segregation of income by source was first conceived in the United Kingdom in *Addington's Act*[17] in 1803: taxpayers filed separate tax returns for each source of income so that no single government official would know the total of each person's income. Thus, the source doctrine (known as the schedule system in the UK) was originally intended to protect the privacy of taxpayers.

There is an important difference between the English schedular system and the Canadian source doctrine. Under the English tax system,[18] a receipt is not taxable as income unless it comes within one of the named schedules, which are mutually exclusive.[19] Thus, the schedules mark the outside boundaries of the tax net.[20]

Under the Canadian Act, the named sources of income (office, employment, business, property and capital gains) in section 3 are not exhaustive and income can arise from *any* other unnamed source. Income from *any* source inside or outside Canada is taxable.[21] This is justifiable both on the basis of the statutory language and on principle. Horizontal equity measured by the ability to pay is an important objective of the tax system. Thus, all income should be taxable, regardless of its particular source. The touchstone of income in law is realized enrichment, regardless of source.

The scope of the source doctrine, however, is not settled. Canadian courts have excluded many payments as not constituting income from a source even though the payment enhances the taxpayer's wealth. Understandably, taxpayers make every effort to have their receipts classified as something other than income from a source.

---

17   1803 (43 Geo III), c 122.

18   *Income and Corporation Taxes Act,* 1970 (UK), c 10, repealed 1992.

19   *Ibid,* s 1. As Lord Radcliffe said in *Mitchell v Ross,* [1961] 3 All ER 49 at 55, 40 Tax Cas 11:

> Before you can assess a profit to tax you must be sure that you have properly identified its source or other description according to the correct Schedule; but once you have done that, it is obligatory that it should be charged, if at all, under that Schedule and strictly in accordance with the Rules that are there laid down for assessments under it. It is a necessary consequence of this conception that the sources of profit in the different Schedules are mutually exclusive.

20   There are six schedules, some of which are subdivided into cases. Each schedule deals with a particular type of income.

21   *ITA,* above note 2, para 3(a) requires income "from a source inside or outside Canada" to be included in income.

In *Fries v MNR* (*Fries*),[22] for example, the Supreme Court held that strike pay paid to union members is not income because the Act does not *specifically* provide for its inclusion in the taxable base:

> The board need express no opinion on the principle involved — whether "strike pay" should or should not be taxable even though that principle was vigorously contested by the parties. It is only required that the Board express an opinion on whether the Act as it now stands provides for the taxation of the amount in question as well as it can be identified and described. The Act *does not provide for such taxation.*[23]

Thus, the Tax Review Board and the Supreme Court bypassed the critical issue whether income from "any source" is taxable under paragraph 3(a). Thus, the Supreme Court bypassed the fundamental issue: should section 3 be read expansively or narrowly?

In *Schwartz v Canada* (*Schwartz*),[24] the Supreme Court once again had the opportunity to fully explore the scope of paragraph 3(a). The taxpayer, a lawyer, received damages as compensation for the cancellation of his employment contract. The taxpayer had accepted an offer of employment from a company and, as a consequence thereof, resigned his partnership in a law firm. The parties agreed that the taxpayer would start working only on completion of an interim assignment he had undertaken to perform for the government of Ontario. Before he could complete his assignment, however, the company advised the taxpayer that it would not require his services. The parties reached a settlement under which the company agreed to pay the taxpayer $360,000 as damages plus $40,000 on account of costs.

The Supreme Court held that the damages in respect of the intended employment were not taxable as a "retiring allowance" and disposed of the case on that basis. Four of the seven judges maintained in *obiter*, however, that paragraph 3(a) should be read expansively:

> [W]hen Parliament used the words "without restricting the generality of the foregoing," great care was taken to emphasize that the first step in calculating a taxpayer's "income for the year" was to determine the total of all amounts constituting income inside or outside Canada and that the enumeration that followed merely identified examples of such sources. The phrasing adopted by Parliament, in paragraph

22 *Fries v MNR*, [1990] 2 SCR 1322, [1990] 2 CTC 439.
23 Adopting the decision of the Tax Review Board, *Fries v MNR*, [1983] CTC 2124 at 2128 (TRB) [emphasis added].
24 *Schwartz v Canada*, [1996] 1 SCR 254. See, generally, Interpretation Bulletin IT-426R, "Shares Sold Subject to an Earnout Agreement" (26 October 2004).

3(a) and in the introductory part of subsection 56(1) is probably the strongest that could have been used to express the idea that income from *all* sources, enumerated or not, expressly provided for in subdivision d or not was taxable under the Act.[25]

The *obiter* reflects the underlying policy of paragraph 3(a) and the principle of equity that equates the burden of tax with the ability to pay. However, the Court would not overturn the jurisprudence. As Major J noted: "If paragraph 3(a) were applied literally to provide for taxation of income from any source, then again it is arguable the existing jurisprudence would be placed in jeopardy."[26]

Following *Fries* and *Schwartz*, Canadian courts have (as they must) applied paragraph 3(a) restrictively. Income from other than the named sources is generally non taxable.

D. RECOVERY OF CAPITAL

Income tax is a tax on net realized gains. The accurate measurement of gains is essential to a fair and efficient tax system. There are two aspects to accurate measurement: (1) the recovery of basis (costs), and (2) the matching of income flows against capital.

The net gain from the sale of an asset can be straightforward or complicated, depending upon the number of assets that one holds and the time period over which one acquires the assets. In the simplest case, a gain or loss from the sale of an asset is the difference between its selling price and its cost or "basis." For example, where an individual buys 100 shares for $10,000 and later sells the shares for $15,000, the gain on the sale is $5,000. If the individual also incurs $300 in selling costs, the *net* gain is $4,700. The first $10,000, that is, the cost basis of the shares, is not taxable because it represents recovery of the investor's capital.

Measurement is more complicated, however, where an individual acquires several batches of shares over a period of years and then disposes of only a part of his shareholding. In these circumstances, we need a method for determining the cost basis of the shares sold so as to obtain an accurate measure of the taxpayer's net gain. We need rules for scheduling the recovery of the capital in the shares. The rules determine whether the taxpayer pays tax on the full amount of his economic net gain or on some lesser portion.

---

25 *Schwartz v Canada*, ibid at para 50.
26 *Ibid* at para 69.

Assume in the above example that the individual purchases an additional 200 shares at a cost of $30,000 before he sells any shares. If the taxpayer then sells 100 shares for $15,000, we must determine the cost basis of his shares in order to calculate the gain. There are at least four possibilities. We can assume that the taxpayer sells:

1) The first batch of 100 shares;
2) Half of the second batch of 200 shares;
3) Half from the first batch (50) and half from the second batch (50); or
4) One-third from the first batch (33) and two-thirds from the second batch (67).

Each of these assumptions produces a different amount of cost recovery to be deducted from the amount realized and, hence, a different net income.

Option	Cost Basis	Sales	Net Gain
1	$10,000	$15,000	$5,000
2	$15,000	$15,000	NIL
3	$12,500	$15,000	$2,500
4	$13,350	$15,000	$1,650

There is no absolute logic for selecting one basis over the other for tax purposes. The important point is that each method of cost recovery produces a different result. Each method produces a different allocation between the amount of tax currently payable and the tax deferred. Any definitive accounting must wait until a final disposition (for example, on death) of the remaining 200 shares.

There is a second, and more subtle, aspect of cost recovery if we attempt to match income flows against the recovery of capital. Assume that in the above example the shares yield an annual dividend of 5 percent, or $500 on the first batch of 100 shares. Should the shareholder be taxed on the $500 on a current basis or should she be taxable only after she recovers the entire capital cost of her investment (say in 20 years if the dividend rate remains unchanged)? If the current annual dividend is taxable on a current basis, the full recovery of capital is delayed until the shareholder sells her shares in 20 years.

Under the latter option, the annual dividend would reduce the basis of the capital invested in the shares until such time as it was zero. Of course, when the shares are ultimately disposed of, the net gain would be that much higher because the cost base of the shares would have been reduced to zero. If the shareholder sold her shares in 20 years for $40,000, the entire $40,000 would be the realized net gain because the full cost would have been previously recovered.

Although the ultimate nominal result under both options is the same, the timing of the net gain is significantly different. The net present value of the tax payable under the second option is considerably less than the amount payable under the first. As we will see in subsequent chapters, the Act generally prefers current basis taxation of annual income flows.

E. IMPUTED INCOME

"Imputed income" refers to income that is derived from the personal use and consumption of one's own assets and from the performance of services for one's own benefit. For example, assume that Harry, a lawyer, earns $80,000 a year from his law practice. Joseph, a farmer, earns $70,000 from his farming operations and consumes $10,000 of the meat and produce that he farms. It is clear that both individuals have the same financial ability to pay taxes. Each earns the same amount of income, albeit in different forms. Harry earns all his income in the marketplace and must buy his meat and produce in the market. Joseph earns less cash income, but has the advantage that he consumes what he grows or cultivates. Thus, Joseph enhances his economic well-being and his ability to pay by consuming his own produce. The principle of fairness suggests that, other things being equal, the two taxpayers should each pay the same amount of tax.

However, other things are rarely equal. The Canadian income tax system does not generally impute income — home repairs, homegrown food, owner-occupied home occupancy, etc. — in measuring income for tax purposes.

There are several reasons for excluding imputed income from the taxable base. First, it is clear that the valuation of goods and services to be imputed would present a substantial problem for taxpayers. One would need to obtain the value of "equivalent market" transactions under comparable circumstances. It would be a nightmare for taxpayers.

Second, the nightmare for taxpayers would soon translate into an administrative nightmare for the CRA, which would be faced with innumerable and prolonged debates with taxpayers on the appropriate value of the imputed value of goods and services. It is also more than likely that there would be substantial non-declaration of imputed goods and services. This would ultimately undermine the integrity and credibility of the tax system.

Third, there is political peril in taxing, as Britain once did, imputed income from owner-occupied housing. The mere suggestion of such a tax would be career-limiting.

To be sure, excluding imputed income from the taxable base offends the principle of tax neutrality and equity. The exclusion encourages taxpayers to engage in non-market transactions, such as home improvements. For example, assume that Jennifer and Lorrie each own homes. Jennifer, an accountant and an accomplished carpenter, regularly does her own home repairs, thereby saving herself $6,000 each year that she would otherwise pay to a professional. In contrast, Lorrie, a hairdresser, is completely incompetent when it comes to home repairs and must pay $6,000 annually to have someone come in and do her home repairs. If both Jennifer and Lorrie earn $50,000 cash income per year, it is clear that Jennifer has the greater ability to pay taxes. She will also be more inclined toward performing her own home repairs than working longer to earn more income in the marketplace. Lorrie, must first earn her marketplace income, pay tax on that income, and use her after-tax dollars to pay for her home repairs. If Lorrie has a tax rate of 40 percent, she must earn an additional $10,000 (in order to have an after-tax amount of $6,000) with which to pay for her home repairs and have the same ability to pay as Jennifer.

We see the tax advantages inherent in the exclusion of imputed income from the taxable base when we look at home ownership. Assume that two individuals, Martha and Larry, each inherit $200,000 from their parents. Martha invests her $200,000 in a home in which she lives. Larry takes his $200,000 and purchases bonds that yield 8 percent. Assume further that both individuals have a marginal tax rate of 50 percent. In these circumstances, Larry earns $16,000 interest income, on which he pays tax of $8,000. He can use his after-tax income of $8,000 to rent a home or an apartment. In contrast, Martha derives the economic benefit of owner-occupancy and uses her $200,000 without any intervention from the tax system. In other words, Martha derives the benefit of pre-tax investment in her home occupancy, while Larry must pay for equivalent accommodation with after-tax dollars.

Thus, the tax system clearly makes it advantageous (even ignoring considerations of potential appreciation in property values) for taxpayers to own and occupy their own homes. This bias affects decisions concerning the allocation of resources between rental housing and owner-occupied homes.

F. THE STATUTORY STRUCTURE

Section 3 is the anchor of the *Income Tax Act*. It contains the basic rules for determining income for a taxation year. Unavoidably, the definition of income in the section is tautological: "The income of a taxpayer for a taxation year . . . is the taxpayer's income for the year." The section then sets out a sequence for the aggregation of the different sources of income and losses. The sequence is rigid and adds to complexity of the tax system. The inflexibility of section 3 is also the impetus for tax planning by taxpayers who seek to shepherd their transactions from higher taxed sources of income into lower taxed sources — for example, from business income to capital gains.

Section 3 identifies at least five major categories for the classification of income and losses. Some of the categories (such as capital gains) are further divided into subcategories. The rules in respect of the computation of income and losses from each source are then set out neatly, but not simply, in separate subdivisions of the Act.

One of the basic objectives of tax planning is to convert income that is taxable at a high marginal rate into income that is either tax-exempt or taxable on a deferred basis. Thus, income conversion and tax deferral are two of the cornerstones of tax planning. The distinction between business income and capital gains, for example, has been the subject of hundreds of litigated cases because of the lower effective rate of tax on capital gains. Equally difficult, and sometimes even more subtle, is the distinction between business and investment income, which are also taxed at different rates.

Each class of income in section 3 is referred to as "income from a source" and we must calculate the income from each source separately.[27] For example, employment income is a category of income separate and apart from income from business or investments, which, in turn, are different from capital gains. Different rules apply to the computation of income from each source.

The process of determining income is as follows:

1) Characterize receipts as being on account of income or capital;
2) If the receipt is income, classify it by its source;
3) Deduct expenses applicable to the particular source to determine net income; and
4) Aggregate net income from the various sources in the sequence set out in section 3.

---

27 *ITA*, above note 2, subs 4(1). The source concept derives from the United Kingdom's tax system under which income is taxable if it falls into one of the schedules of the *Income and Corporation Taxes Act*, 1970, above note 18.

1) The Named Sources

There are five named sources of income:

- Office;
- Employment;
- Business;
- Property; and
- Capital gains.

This is not an exhaustive list. Apart from the named sources, section 3 states that income from *any* other source is also taxable. Thus, the section should bring into income all income (whether or not specifically named) that has a source. As we saw earlier, however, the *Fries* and *Schwartz* decisions constrain the meaning of "income" for tax purposes. Thus, there is a long list of judicial precedents for exclusions from income.[28]

---

28   The following have been held non-taxable: amateur hockey team's allowance and stipend paid to player: *Grenier v Canada*, 2007 TCC 93; amount received following expropriation: *Bellingham v Canada*, [1996] 1 CTC 187 (FCA); amounts paid for injurious affection to lands when expropriating other lands: *Hurley v Canada*, 2003 TCC 22; assistance (one-time) to hurricane and typhoon victims who are family members of employees: CRA doc 2009-0349581E5; British Columbia tax refunds under the BC *International Financial Activity Act*: CRA doc 2004-0086581E5; bus passes given by a church to street people who volunteer at a soup kitchen and shelter: CRA doc 2004-0056061I7; Chinese head tax immigration compensation $20,000 payments (Revenu Québec interpretation letter 06-010463 (14 September 2006); CRA would likely apply the same interpretation); compensation for entering into non-competition agreement: *Fortino v Canada*, [2000] 1 CTC 349 (FCA); *Manrell v Canada*, 2003 FCA 128 (giving up a right to do business, shared with everyone, is not giving up "property") (but see now *ITA, ibid*, s 56.4); damages due to company's inability to relocate its business, paid by city for civic purpose not business purpose: *Toronto Refiners & Smelters Ltd v Canada*, 2002 FCA 476; damages for human rights violations: Interpretation Bulletin IT-337R4, "Retiring Allowances" (1 February 2006) at para 12; CRA docs 2002-0172217, 2003-0014105, 2004-00167118117, 2004-0079731E5, 2005-0126912E5, 2008-0292081R3 (but see also notes to *ITA, ibid*, subs 248(1) "retiring allowance"); damages to an employee for mental distress, harassment or to reimburse for losses: *Bédard v MNR*, [1991] 1 CTC 2323 (TCC); *Mendes-Roux v Canada*, [1998] 2 CTC 2274 (TCC); *Fournier v Canada*, [1999] 4 CTC 2247 (TCC); *Saardi v Canada*, [1999] 4 CTC 2488 (TCC); deceased person's retroactive pay increase: CRA doc 2003-0018835; Duplessis Orphans national reconciliation program payments: CRA doc 2007-0226801E5; fishing licence surrender in exchange for voluntary payment by government: *Canada v Haché*, 2011 FCA 104; foreign government one-time payment to all its residents to share gains from buoyant economy: CRA doc 2008-0293241E5; gambling extensively on sports lotteries: *Leblanc v Canada*, 2006 TCC 680; Can-

Some of the named sources of income are subdivided. For example, capital gains are divided into personal use property gains, which are further subdivided into listed personal property (LPP) gains; business investment losses are a subsource of capital losses,[29] etc. Special rules apply to each of these subsources of income. For example, LPP losses may be offset only against LPP gains and not against any other capital gains. The compartmentalization of income into a myriad of segregated sources requires special rules to prevent the leakage of income between sources.

Example

The following data applies to an individual. All amounts shown are net of deductions in each category.

Employment income	$30,000
Business (No 1) income	12,000
Business (No 2) loss	(6,000)
Property income	6,000
Taxable capital gains (shares)	1,500
Taxable listed personal property (LLP) *net* gain	1,500
Allowable capital losses (*including* allowable business investment losses)	(4,900)
Moving expenses	(800)
Allowable business investment losses	(4,000)

The individual's income for the year is as follows:

Paragraph 3(a)

Employment income		$30,000
Business income		12,000
Property income		6,000
		48,000

ADD Paragraph 3(b)

Taxable capital gains	$1,500	
Taxable *net* LPP gain	1,500	
	3,000	

Exceeds:

Allowable capital losses in excess of allowable business investment losses ($4,900−4,000)	(900)	
		2,100
		50,100

---

adian Tax Foundation, *2008 Conference Report*, CRA Roundtable, q.7 at 3:6-7; golf marshal's free rounds of golf: CRA doc 2009-0323331E5.

29 *ITA*, above note 2, ss 54 "listed personal property" and 41, paras 39(1)(b) & (c); see Chapters 13 & 14 on computation of tax.

EXCEEDS Paragraph 3(c)		
Moving expenses		(800)
		49,300
EXCEEDS Paragraph 3(d)		
Business loss	$(6,000)	
Allowable business investment losses	(4,000)	(10,000)
Income for the year		$39,300

2) Losses by Source

The characterization of losses by source is also important. Business losses, for example, are fully deductible against any source of income; capital losses are only partially deductible from income and then only against net taxable capital gains. Unused business losses may be carried forward for 20 years; unused capital losses may be carried forward indefinitely. Similarly, listed personal property losses are deductible only against net gains from listed personal property and not from other types of capital gains, etc.

A taxpayer must compute income as though *each* source of income was his *only* source of income. Deductions from income are similarly limited: a deduction may be taken against a source of income only if it may be regarded as applicable to that source.[30]

Note, however, that certain amounts—for example, moving and child care expenses—do not derive from any specific source and, therefore, we account for them separately.[31] The following example illustrates the operation of the source doctrine and its impact on the concept of net income.

> **Example**
> Assume that the following data applies to three corporations:
>
> | | Corporation | | |
> |---|---|---|---|
> | | A | B | C |
> | Business income | $1,000 | $2,000 | $6,000 |
> | Property income | (1,000) | $2,000 | – |
> | Taxable capital gains (losses) | 2,000 | (2,000) | (4,000) |
> | Aggregate income | $2,000 | $2,000 | $2,000 |
> | Income for tax purposes is: | | | |
> | Business income | $1,000 | $2,000 | $6,000 |

---

30   *Ibid*, subs 4(1).
31   *Ibid*, subs 4(2).

Property income	–	2,000	–
Taxable capital gains	2,000	–	–
	3,000	4,000	6,000
Exceeds:			
Property or business losses	(1,000)	–	–
Income for the year	$2,000	$4,000	$6,000

* Capital losses may only be offset against capital gains.

G. DEDUCTIONS VS. CREDITS

The difference between a deduction from income and a tax credit is that a deduction has the effect of reducing income, which indirectly reduces the amount of tax payable, whereas a tax credit directly reduces the amount of tax payable without reducing income.

Example

Assume that an individual with a marginal tax rate of 50 percent earns $100,000. The following example illustrates the effect of a $20,000 deduction from income compared to a credit of $20,000 against tax.

	Deduction from income	Tax credit
Income	$100,000	$100,000
Less: deduction	($20,000)	–
Taxable income	$80,000	$100,000
Tax at 50%	$40,000	$50,000
Tax credit	–	($20,000)
Net payable	$40,000	$30,000

The above example illustrates that a dollar of tax credit is worth more to a taxpayer than a dollar deduction from income. The reason for this is that a deduction is only worth its face value multiplied by the taxpayer's marginal rate of tax. For instance, a $100 deduction to an individual with a marginal rate of 50 percent is worth $50 tax savings; at a marginal rate of 25 percent, the saving is only $25. Thus, the value of a deduction increases as the marginal rate rises. In contrast, the value of a tax credit remains constant through all marginal tax rates. This distinction is important in determining the distributional effect of taxes, exemptions and credits.

H. EXCLUSIONS FROM INCOME

As we have seen, economists measure income by reference to the net accretion of wealth between two points in time. On the other hand, the tax measure of income is based on realized gains from sources and a judicial understanding of what constitutes "income," supplemented by numerous *ad hoc* statutory inclusions[32] and exclusions based upon various policy considerations.[33] As Professor Rendall said:

> [T]he fact is that our notions of income have been intuitive rather than logical and that our jurisprudence has developed on a case-by-case basis and has often reflected primarily a gut feeling about the characterization of a particular amount. What this means is that "income," for tax purposes, is not at all a single, consistent, concept.[34]

Similarly, income for tax purposes is quite different from income for the purposes of accounting and financial statements.

There are three prominent exclusions from income for tax purposes:

- Gambling gains;
- Gifts and inheritances; and
- Windfall gains.

1) Gambling Gains

There are three broad categories of gambling gains: (1) casual or pleasurable; (2) as an adjunct to a business; and (3) professional.

Winnings from casual betting and incidental gambling are not income, even if the individual is a compulsive gambler.[35] Some judges have explained this exclusion on the theory that gambling is an irrational activity:

> What is a bet? A bet is merely an irrational agreement that one person should pay another person something on the happening of an event. A agrees to pay B something if C's horse runs quicker than D's or if a coin comes down one side up rather than the other side up. There is no relevance at all between the event and the acquisition of property.

---

32   See, for example, s 12, *ibid*.
33   See, for example, s 81, *ibid*.
34   James Rendall, "Defining the Tax Base" in Brian Hansen, Vern Krishna, & James Rendall, eds, *Canadian Taxation* (Toronto: Richard De Boo, 1981).
35   *Leblanc v Canada*, above note 28.

The event does not really produce it at all. It rests, as I say, on a mere irrational agreement.[36]

The essential issue in determining income is net accretion to realized wealth, not the rationality of the bet. All games of chance are nothing more or less than payouts based on probability distributions. A horse race is no more irrational than the trading on commodities futures on a stock exchange. The English courts said that such gains do not flow from a source and, hence, are not included under any of the UK schedules of income. This interpretation, however, is not helpful in the Canadian context. It ignores the statutory language of section 3, which includes income from *any* source inside or outside Canada.[37]

A better reason for excluding gambling gains from income is administrative and revenue considerations. Accounting for casual betting for pleasure would impose an unreasonable burden on individuals. One can only speculate how many would voluntarily comply. Any attempt to tax such gains would result in flagrant disregard of the rule and bring the administration of tax into disrepute.

Further, if losses were deductible, the net revenue gains would be minimal. Thus, we exclude gambling gains from income where the taxpayer realizes the gain in pursuit of a hobby and is not engaged in the business of gambling.[38] Similarly, losses from gambling are not deductible unless they are incurred in the conduct of a gambling business.

The exclusion from income, however, applies only to the capital sum of the gambling gain and not to any income earned from its investment. For example, the exclusion does not extend to "cash for life" lotteries.[39]

A gambling gain is taxable if the individual gambles as an adjunct to her business—for example, a race horse owner who bets on the races.

Similarly, a professional gambler's gains are taxable. A professional is a person who uses his expertise and skill to earn a livelihood from gambling—for example, a pool shark or river boat gambler.

---

36 Justice Rowlatt in *Graham v Green (Inspector of Taxes)*, [1925] 2 KB 37 at 39–40; *MNR v Morden*, [1961] CTC 484 (Ex Ct).

37 See, for example, *Rumack v MNR*, [1992] 1 CTC 57 at 59 (FCA).

38 See, for example, *MNR v Walker*, [1951] CTC 334 (Ex Ct) (gambling winnings taxable when achieved by taxpayer who himself owned and raced horses, had inside information, and could not afford to lose).

39 *Rumack v MNR*, above note 37.

2) Gifts and Inheritances

Gifts and inheritances are not income for tax purposes. "Gift" is defined in *Halsbury's Laws of England* (3d Edition, Volume 18):

> A gift *inter vivos* may be defined shortly as the transfer of any property from one person to another gratuitously while the donor is alive and not in expectation of death.

A "gift" is a voluntary and gratuitous transfer of property from one person to another.[40] It may be subject to a pre-condition, but, this apart, it is not revocable or terminable. Thus, a transfer of property qualifies as a gift only if the transfer is both voluntary and made without any expectation of reward or return. A payment that requires a *quid pro quo* is not a gift.

A gift represents an accretion to the recipient's wealth and, as such, would be considered income in economic theory. For tax purposes, however, gifts and inheritances are not taxable and are considered capital transfers.[41]

3) Windfall Gains

The exclusion of "windfall gains" from income is problematic. Windfall gains are clearly accretions to wealth and enhance the taxpayer's ability to pay. Windfalls are not usually capital transfers. The only unusual feature of a windfall is that it is unexpected. If the policy of the income tax is to impose similar taxes on those in similar financial circumstances, there is little merit in distinguishing between increments to wealth based on their source or expectations of return.

It is difficult to identify a "windfall." The phrase generally implies a gain that is unexpected or unplanned and one that we cannot link to one of the named sources of income (office, employment, business, property, and capital gains). In fact, "windfall gains" represent nothing more than an unarticulated, and irrational, bias against taxing certain types of gains. Income can arise only from *expected* returns. "Un-

---

40   *Black's Law Dictionary* defines a "gift" as: "A voluntary transfer of personal property without consideration . . . . A parting by owner with property without pecuniary consideration"; the *Shorter Oxford English Dictionary* defines "giving" as: "A transfer of property in a thing, voluntarily and without any valuable consideration."

41   The Carter Commission proposed that, subject to a minimum exemption, gifts and inheritances should be included in the income of the recipient; see *Report of the Royal Commission on Taxation*, above note 9, vol 3, ch 17.

expected" gains are windfalls and are not taxable as income. In *Canada v Cranswick*, for example:

> In the absence of a special statutory definition . . . income from a source will be that which is typically earned by it or which typically flows from it as the expected return.[42]

This approach harks back to the old *Eisner v Macomber* concept that income is the expected return from labour or capital.

To summarize: a windfall gain is a gain that is unexpected, unplanned and unrelated to any of the named sources of income.[43] More precisely, a windfall is defined as a gain that:

- Does not result from a legally enforceable claim;
- Is not expected, either specifically or customarily;
- Is not likely to recur;
- Is not customarily a source of income for the recipient of the gain;
- Is not given as consideration for services rendered, to garner favour, or anything else provided; and
- Is not earned as a result of an activity or pursuit of gain.

The general scheme for determining tax payable under Part I is as follows:

---

42   *Canada v Cranswick* (1982), 82 DTC 6073 at 6076 (FCA), leave to appeal to SCC refused (1982), 42 NR 35; *Frank Beban Logging Ltd v Canada*, [1998] 2 CTC 2493 (TCC) (*Ex gratia* payment of $800,000 by government to logging company was windfall as taxpayer did not expect the payment.) See Interpretation Bulletin IT-334R2, "Miscellaneous Receipts" (21 February 1992) at para 3.

43   *MacEachern v MNR*, [1977] CTC 2139 (TRB) (proceeds from sale of gold and silver coins found by three deep-sea divers was income from organized activity that was more than a hobby); *Charles R Bell Ltd v Canada*, [1992] 2 CTC 260 (FCA) (lump sum payment to corporate taxpayer upon termination of exclusive distributorship agreement was income); *Johnson & Johnson Inc v Canada*, [1994] 1 CTC 244 (FCA) (unexpected refund was business income and not windfall when looked at in context); *Federal Farms Ltd v MNR*, [1959] CTC 98 (Ex Ct) (voluntary payments to help taxpayer whose farm was flooded during hurricane was gift, not income); *Canada v Cranswick*, *ibid* (majority shareholder paid minority shareholder sum to avoid controversy over reorganization; unexpected and unusual payment was windfall).

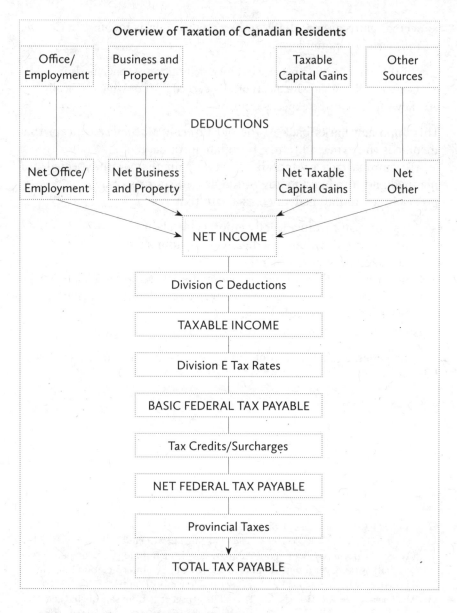

Overview of Taxation of Canadian Residents

| Office/Employment | Business and Property | | Taxable Capital Gains | Other Sources |

DEDUCTIONS

| Net Office/Employment | Net Business and Property | | Net Taxable Capital Gains | Net Other |

NET INCOME

Division C Deductions

TAXABLE INCOME

Division E Tax Rates

BASIC FEDERAL TAX PAYABLE

Tax Credits/Surcharges

NET FEDERAL TAX PAYABLE

Provincial Taxes

TOTAL TAX PAYABLE

I. BARTER TRANSACTIONS

A barter transaction occurs where two or more persons agree to a re-ciprocal exchange of goods or services without the use of money. In its simplest form, barter is a market transaction where the medium of exchange is goods or services instead of legal tender.[44]

---

44   Interpretation Bulletin IT-490, "Barter Transactions" (5 July 1982).

Payments in kind are governed by the same principles applicable to payments in cash. A payment or benefit in kind is an accretion to wealth and enhances the taxpayer's ability to pay. Payments in kind may involve bilateral or multilateral exchanges of property. For example, a lawyer who renders legal services to a farmer may accept a cow in settlement of his account. Alternatively, the lawyer may accept a non-cash credit which can be exchanged in a barter "pool" for other goods and services; for example, he may exchange the cow credit for plumbing services.

Barter transactions create valuation problems. Should the payment in kind be valued based on its *value in use* to the recipient or its *value in exchange* for the goods or services sold or rendered? For example, suppose a lawyer renders legal services for which she would usually charge $2,000 in exchange for a cow that has a market value of $1,600. How much should the lawyer include in her income, $2,000 (value of the services) or $1,600 (value of the exchange)? The CRA says that the recipient's income is increased by the price that she would "normally have charged" for the goods or services provided;[45] in this example, $2,000. That ignores the discount of $400 in the lawyer's fee, which she might also have given in a cash transaction.

In multilateral barter schemes with restrictions on exchange of barter credits, the value of consideration received may be considerably less than the "theoretical" value of goods and services sold or rendered. Since barter credits are a substitute medium of exchange, it is the value of the medium that should determine the price. In effect, a taxpayer who renders services for credits that have a restricted exchange value discounts the price normally charged for such services.[46]

J. EXEMPT INCOME

The Act also specifically exempts certain forms of income from tax. It is important to note the distinction between a taxpayer who is exempt from tax[47] and income that is tax-exempt.[48] In the former case, the recipient is exempt from tax, regardless of the nature of the income that he earns. In the latter case, only specific types of income are exempt from tax, regardless of who receives it.

---

45   *Ibid.*
46   *Linett v MNR*, [1985] 2 CTC 2037 (TCC).
47   *ITA*, above note 2, s 149.
48   *Ibid*, s 81.

Section 81 contains a long list of exemptions, each of which has its own theory, policy or political history. There is no coherent theory that connects the exemptions.

K. CONCLUSION

There is no categorical and definitive definition of income. The legal measure of income—which is central to the determination of the taxable base—is an amalgam of economic theory tempered with pragmatism, refined by jurisprudence and burdened by historical accident. Starting with the "pure" economist's concept of income, as represented by the Haig-Simons formulation, we have adapted it to accommodate the needs of taxpayers in daily life and commerce, and political considerations. Thus, we modify the economic concept of income to include only realized gains, exclude most imputed income and enumerate a long list of statutory exclusions. Finally, we top off the legal concept of income with the source doctrine.

FURTHER READINGS

General

RENDALL, JAMES. "Defining the Tax Base" in Brian Hansen, Vern Krishna, & James Rendall, eds, *Canadian Taxation* (Toronto: Richard De Boo, 1981).

SIMONS, HENRY C. *Personal Income Taxation* (Chicago: University of Chicago Press, 1938).

LABRIE, FRANCIS. *The Meaning of Income in the Law of Income Tax* (Toronto: University of Toronto Press, 1953).

THURONYI, VICTOR. "The Concept of Income" (1990) 46 Tax L Rev 45.

PART III

WHAT IS TAXABLE?

CHAPTER 5

WHOSE INCOME IS IT?

A. GENERAL COMMENT

Thus far, we have looked at who is taxable and, in a preliminary way, at what is the nature of income. However, the individual in receipt of income is not always the person taxable on it. In some cases, income may be attributed to an individual who becomes taxable on it even though she does not legally own the income.

Canada taxes each individual as a separate taxpayer. Unlike the United States, Canada does not recognize joint tax returns. To prevent income splitting between family members, the *Income Tax Act* has strict attribution and assignment rules for intra-family property transfers between spouses. The concept of spouse for tax purposes is broad and includes common-law partners and same-sex married relationships.[1]

The attribution rules are essentially anti-avoidance rules, but with numerous exceptions and carve-outs. Since the individual income tax structure is progressive,[2] income increments are taxable at higher marginal rates. This means that a single income family will pay higher taxes than a two-income family with identical income. Thus, high-income taxpayers have an incentive to reduce their taxes by shifting income to members of their family in lower tax brackets and splitting

---

1   See *Income Tax Act*, RSC 1985, c 1 (5th Supp) [*ITA*], subs 248(1) "common-law partner."
2   See *ibid*, s 117.

the tax payable. The more that one can sprinkle income amongst family members, the lower the overall family taxes. For example, two gross incomes of $100,000 each are much more valuable in after-tax terms than one gross income of $200,000.

Tax savings induce high marginal rate individuals to shift income to lower marginal rates. For example, a father with income of $200,000 and a marginal tax rate of 45 percent might transfer part of his port- folio of securities to his minor daughter to reduce his investment in- come and potential future capital gains. If his daughter's tax rate is only 15 percent, he saves 30 percentage points of tax. The problem is exacerbated if the father can retrieve the securities at any time from his daughter and have the title revert to him.

Professionals and entrepreneurs can also split business income. For example, an individual can incorporate a company and have it issue dif- ferent classes of shares to each member of his family. The corporation can then sprinkle dividends amongst the family members according to their financial circumstances. Dividend-sprinkling would reduce each family member's marginal rate of tax and the overall family tax burden.

There are attribution rules that prevent certain blatant forms of in- come-splitting amongst the immediate family and in certain non-arm's length relationships. The rules protect the integrity of the progressive tax rate structure by preventing downward rate-shifting from high-rate taxpayers to their children.

The rules do not affect the underlying commercial rights of the parties in the property transfer. In the above example, the transfer of securities by the father to his daughter is valid for purposes of commer- cial law. The attribution rules apply only for tax purposes.

Apart from the specific attribution rules, however, there is no gen- eral scheme in tax law to prevent income-splitting.[3] Indeed, the Act even promotes income-splitting in certain cases;[4] for example, Canada Pension Plan splitting and spousal Registered Retirement Savings Plans. The opportunities for income splitting and shifting also depend upon tax planning. Some are for sophisticated individuals with good profes- sional advisors. For example, the simplest method involves the high-rate taxpayer loaning (with appropriate documents) to his spouse at the pre- vailing prescribed rate (1 percent as of June 2011). The plan works and saves net tax dollars if the spouse can use the loan to earn investment income at more than the prescribed rate. For example, if the spouse can

---

3   *Neuman v Canada (MNR)*, [1998] 1 SCR 770 [*Neuman*].
4   See, for example, the rules permitting deductions to spousal RRSPs (*ITA*, above note 1, para 74.5(12)(a) and subs 146(5.1)).

invest the money at 6 percent and pay 1 percent to the transferor, there is an approximate benefit of 5 percent minus the tax payable.

The attribution rules are deeming provisions and apply regardless of taxpayer intent. They are, in effect, specific anti-avoidance rules (SAARs) to prevent income splitting in the specified circumstances. Nevertheless, the courts can override their deeming effect if the underlying transactions are "abusive." In *Lipson v Canada*,[5] for example, the Supreme Court applied GAAR to negate the deeming specific effect of three attribution rules.

B. INDIRECT PAYMENTS

Individuals can also reduce their taxes by shifting income to others—generally family members and related corporations.

A taxpayer who transfers income or property to another taxpayer may be deemed to have constructively received the diverted income or property.[6] For example, an individual who directs his employer to deposit his paycheque directly into his spouse's savings account is liable for tax on the salary, even though he relinquishes actual ownership and control over the property. For tax purposes, the taxpayer retains constructive ownership of the property. This rule prevents taxpayers from artificially reducing their taxable income by diverting funds to family members with lower marginal tax rates.

The doctrine of constructive receipt of income applies where a taxpayer transfers property:[7]

- To a person;
- At the taxpayer's direction or with the taxpayer's concurrence;
- For the benefit of the taxpayer or a person whom she wishes to benefit; *and*
- The payment or transfer is of a type that would ordinarily have been included in the taxpayer's income if she received it directly.

In these circumstances, the Act deems the transferor to receive the payment or transfer directly.[8]

---

5   2009 SCC 1.
6   *ITA*, above note 1, subs 56(2); see also Interpretation Bulletin IT-335R2, "Indirect Payments" (14 July 2004).
7   *Ibid*.
8   *Neuman*, above note 3; *McClurg v Canada*, [1990] 3 SCR 1020 (income not attributed to director of corporation for participating in declaration of corporate dividend); *Boardman v Canada*, [1986] 1 CTC 103 (FCTD) (shareholder taxable

The doctrine does not normally apply to corporate dividends. Directors of a corporation who declare a dividend do so in their capacity as directors and fiduciaries. The fourth condition requires that the taxpayer would have received the dividend if it had not been paid to the shareholder of record. An unpaid dividend remains in the corporation's retained earnings. Subsection 56(2) cannot apply to dividends if the fourth test is not satisfied.[9]

In a closely held family corporation, for example, dividends to the taxpayer's spouse do not come within the doctrine of constructive receipt. This is so even if the taxpayer waives his right to receive a dividend because the waived dividend merely remains in the corporation's retained earnings. The situation is different, however, if the shareholder of record directs the corporation to pay his share of the dividend to his spouse.

Subsections 56(2), (4) and (4.1) do not apply in respect of amounts included in a minor's split income. Thus, amounts taxed as split income in the hands of a minor child are not also attributable to another person.[10]

The constructive ownership doctrine does not apply where a taxpayer directs that a portion of his Canada Pension Plan be paid to his spouse.[11]

1) Transfers of Rights to Income

The doctrine of constructive receipt also applies where a taxpayer transfers rights to receive income (as opposed to the income itself) to another individual.[12] The essence of this type of transfer is that the individual transfers the right to all future income, but not the ownership

---

on diversion of corporate assets to settle financial obligations on divorce); *MNR v Bronfman*, [1965] CTC 378 (Ex Ct) (directors of corporation liable for taxes on account of gifts to relatives in need of financial assistance; combining subss 15(1) and 56(2)); *Reininger v MNR* (1958), 58 DTC 608 (TAB) (corporate loan to wife of principal shareholder taxable to him under subss 15(2) and 56(2)); *Perrault v Canada*, [1978] CTC 395 (FCA) (waiver of dividend by majority shareholder in favour of minority shareholder was dividend income); *New v MNR*, 70 DTC 1415 (TAB) (controlling shareholder in receipt of income for benefit conferred on son through rental of corporate property to son at less than fair market value).

9   *Neuman, ibid* (dividends paid to controlling shareholder's spouse not taxable in his hands despite absence of any "contribution" by spouse). *McClurg v Canada, ibid*, aff'g [1988] 1 CTC 75 (FCA). See Vern Krishna & J. Anthony VanDuzer, "Corporate Share Capital Structures and Income Splitting: *McClurg v Canada*" (1992–93) 21 Can Bus LJ 335 at 367.

10   *ITA*, above note 1, subs 56(5).

11   Including a prescribed provincial pension plan (see *Income Tax Regulations*, CRC, c 945, s 7800).

12   *ITA*, above note 1, subs 56(4).

of the underlying income-generating property. Thus, the transferee then owns the right to all future income or revenues that the property may yield, but does not own the property itself.

2) Interest-Free or Low-Interest Loan

A taxpayer can shift her tax burden by loaning money to another person at a rate lower than the market rate of interest. For example, in the simplest case, an individual can make an interest-free loan. Where the purpose of the loan is to reduce or avoid tax in a non-arm's length transaction, the Act deems the borrower's income from the loan to be the income of the lender.[13] The lender is taxable on any income from property substituted for the loan and from property purchased with the loan.

> Examples
> Jane loans $50,000 to her spouse who earns 10 percent by depositing the money in a GIC. Jane is taxable on the $5,000 interest income for the year.
>
> Mark loans $100,000 to his niece at 5 percent interest per year. The niece purchases an investment certificate yielding 8 percent per year. Mark is taxable on the net income of $3,000 from the investment certificate.

3) Transfers/Loans to Spouse

An individual who transfers or loans property, directly or indirectly, to her spouse — or to a person who becomes her spouse after the transfer or loan of property — is taxable on any income from the property or from any property that he substitutes for the transferred property. The Act attributes any income or loss from the property to the transferor during her lifetime as long as she resides in Canada and lives with her spouse.[14] The transferor is also taxable on any taxable capital gains or allowable capital losses from dispositions of the transferred or loaned property.[15] In both cases, the Act deems the transferor to have constructively received the transferred income (loss) or taxable gain (loss). These rules apply only to income and losses from *property*, not to income and losses from a business.[16]

---

13   *Ibid*, subs 56(4.1).
14   *Ibid*, subs 74.1(1). *MNR v Kieboom*, [1992] 2 CTC 59 (FCA) (income from taxpayer's gift of non-voting shares to wife and children subject to attribution).
15   *ITA, ibid*, subs 74.2(1).
16   See *Robins v MNR*, [1963] CTC 27 (Ex Ct). See also *Wertman v MNR*, [1964] CTC 252 (Ex Ct) (spouses' joint investment in building with funds from community property); *MNR v Minden*, [1963] CTC 364 (Ex Ct) (lawyer advanced money to spouse for investments without documentation, interest or security).

The attribution rules do not apply if the transferor and transferee spouses are living separate and apart by reason of a breakdown of their marriage.[17] In the case of capital gains, however, the parties must file a joint election not to have the rules apply.

Similarly, the attribution rules in respect of transfers to corporations (other than small business corporations)[18] in which a spouse has a direct or indirect interest generally do not apply to the period during which the spouses are living separate and apart by reason of a breakdown of their marriage.[19]

4) Transfers/Loans to Persons under Eighteen Years of Age

An individual who transfers or loans property to a person under eighteen years of age who is the transferor's niece or nephew—or does not deal at arm's length with the transferor—is taxable on any income earned on the property.[20] Thus, income and losses realized by the recipient of the transferred property are attributed to the person who transferred or loaned the property.

C. NON-ARM'S LENGTH LOANS

The rules discussed above (loans and transfers to spouses and to individuals under eighteen years of age) prevent taxpayers from engaging in blatant income-splitting. There is, however, an additional rule that is even broader: Income from any property (for example, money) loaned to a non-arm's length borrower may be attributed and taxed to the lender if one of the main purposes of the loan is to reduce or avoid tax, for example, by income-splitting.[21] This rule is considerably broader in scope than the more specific attribution rules in that it applies to low-cost or interest-free loans to any individual with whom the lender does not deal at arm's length. This rule does not apply to transfers of property; it only applies to loaned property.

Unlike the more specific attribution rules, the non-arm's length rule requires motive: the lender must loan the property for the purpos-

---

17   *ITA*, above note 1, para 74.5(3)(a).
18   *Ibid*, para 74.4(2)(c).
19   *Ibid*, subs 74.5(4).
20   *Ibid*, subs 74.1(2).
21   *Ibid*, subs 56(4.1).

es of reducing or avoiding tax on income that he would otherwise earn on the property. There is no attribution of income if the lender does not lend the money for the purposes of tax reduction or avoidance (for example, a loan to a relative or friend for altruistic reasons). Further, the attribution rules do not apply to loans at "commercial" rates of interest if the borrower pays the interest no later than thirty days after the end of the taxation year in which the interest is due.[22]

D. INTERPRETATION AND APPLICATION

The following aspects of the attribution rules warrant particular attention:

* The term "transfer" includes any divestiture of property from one person to another and includes gifts.[23]
* The attribution applies to income and losses from *property*, and not to income and losses from a business.[24]
* The attribution rules do not generally apply to sales at fair market value if the purchaser pays the vendor for the property.[25]
* The attribution rules do not apply to loans that bear a commercial rate of interest. A loan is considered to bear a commercial rate of interest if the rate charged is at least equal to the prescribed rate or the arm's length market rate.[26]
* A transfer or loan to an individual under the age of eighteen, income attribution continues until she reaches eighteen years of age.

---

22 *Ibid*, subs 56(4.2). The Act prescribes the appropriate rate of interest each quarter according to commercial market rates (*Income Tax Regulations*, above note 11, s 4301).

23 *Fasken Estate v MNR*, [1948] CTC 265 at 279 (Ex Ct); see also *St Aubyn v AG*, [1952] AC 15 at 53 (HL), Lord Radcliffe:

> If the word "transfer" is taken in its primary sense, a person makes a transfer of property to another person if he does the act or executes the instrument which divests him of the property and at the same time vests it in that other person.

24 See *Robins v MNR*, above note 16. See also *Wertman v MNR*, above note 16 (spouses' joint investment in building with funds from community property); *MNR v Minden*, above note 16 (lawyer advanced money to spouse for investments without documentation, interest or security).

25 *ITA*, above note 1, subs 74.5(1).

26 *Ibid*, subs 74.5(2).

- The attribution rules do not apply to a parent (or other transferor) on amounts that the Act taxes as split income[27] in the hands of a minor child.[28]
- The liability for tax from the application of the attribution rules is joint and several.[29]
- The income attribution rules apply to spouses only during the period that they are married *and* living together. The rules do not apply upon divorce or separation by reason of matrimonial breakdown.[30]
- There is no attribution of capital gains and losses following divorce or separation pursuant to matrimonial breakdown[31] if the parties file a joint election precluding attribution. The parties may file the election in the year after they begin to live separate and apart.

E. THE "KIDDIE TAX"

Although the attribution rules apply to transfers of property to minor children, they do not prevent all forms of income-splitting between family members. Since dividends are eligible for the dividend tax credit, minor children could receive substantial dividends without tax — the dividend tax credit would wipe out any tax payable on the income.

The "kiddie tax" prevents income-splitting with children under eighteen years of age. The "kiddie tax" is a special flat tax that applies at the highest rate to certain forms of passive income of individuals under the age of eighteen years. The tax applies to:[32]

- Taxable dividends and other shareholder benefits[33] on unlisted shares of Canadian and foreign companies; and
- Income from a partnership or trust where the partnership or trust derives the income from the business of providing property or services to a business that a relative of the child carries on or in which the relative participates.

This tax prevents some of the more blatant forms of income-splitting.[34] Any income that is taxable as "split income" is deductible from

---

27   *Ibid*, s 120.4.
28   *Ibid*, subs 74.5(13).
29   *Ibid*, para 160(1)(d).
30   *Ibid*, para 74.5(3)(a).
31   *Ibid*, para 74.5(3)(b).
32   *Ibid*, s 120.4.
33   See s 15, *ibid*.
34   See, for example, *Ferrel v Canada*, [1999] 2 CTC 101 (FCA).

the individual's income from business or property for the year. Hence, the regular income tax does not apply to any portion of the split income. Liability for the kiddie tax is joint and several.[35]

The only amounts deductible from the tax are the dividend tax credit and the foreign tax credit in respect of amounts that the minor includes in her split income. Thus, the tax has a substantial bite in that it effectively applies to gross income at the highest marginal tax rate.

The "kiddie tax" does not apply to:

- Income paid to individuals over eighteen years of age,
- Reasonable remuneration to minors,
- Capital gains, or
- Interest income.

Hence, it is still possible to split income unless the Act specifically prohibits it in particular circumstances.

F. TRANSFERS AND LOANS TO CORPORATIONS

An individual who transfers or loans property to a corporation may be taxable on investment income attributable to him on account of the transfer or loan.

In the case of equity investments, the Act attributes to the transferor the grossed-up amount of taxable dividends that she receives on shares that the corporation issues for the transfer. The gross-up will be either 25 or 45 percent. Where the transfer involves a loan, the amount attributed is the amount by which interest at the prescribed rate on the loan exceeds the total of any interest that she actually receives on the loan.

In both cases, the attribution rules apply only if one of the main purposes of the transfer is to reduce the transferor's income and benefit a person who is her spouse, common-law partner, a related person under eighteen years of age, or niece or nephew.[36]

These rules do not apply if the transferee corporation is a small business corporation. This is an important exclusion that allows individuals to split income.

A small business corporation[37] is a Canadian-controlled private corporation that uses all or substantially all of its assets in an "active

---

35   *ITA*, above note 1, subs 160(1.2).
36   *Ibid*, subs 74.5(5).
37   *Ibid*, subs 248(1) "small business corporation."

business"[38] that it carries on primarily in Canada. A corporation also qualifies as a small business corporation if a related corporation uses the assets in an active business in Canada.

CRA interprets the phrase "all or substantially all" as 90 percent of the corporation's assets. Hence, if a corporation permanently uses more than 10 percent of its total assets for investment purposes, it may not qualify as a small business corporation. The CRA interprets "primarily" as being more than 50 percent in respect of the business.

G. ARTIFICIAL TRANSACTIONS

Taxpayers sometimes structure transactions to take advantage of the attribution rules and generate "reverse attribution." For example, Harry might guarantee his high-income spouse's borrowing from a bank and assert that the income from the borrowed funds is attributable to him.[39] Subsection 74.5(11) is an anti-avoidance provision that prevents the attribution rules from applying if "one of the main reasons" for the transfer or loan is to reduce the tax payable on income or gains from loaned or transferred property.

FURTHER READINGS

Indirect Payments

INNES, WILLIAM I. "The Taxation of Indirect Benefits: An Examination of Subsections 56(2), 56(3), 56(4), 245(2) and 245(3) of the *Income Tax Act*" (1986) 38 Can Tax Found 42:1.

KRISHNA, VERN. "Corporate Share Capital Structures and Income Splitting" (1991) 3 Can Curr. Tax C-71.

———. "Indirect Payments and Transfer of Income" (1986) 1 Can Curr Tax J-137.

———. "Designing Share Capital Structures for Income Splitting" (1984) 1 Can Curr Tax C-51.

———. "Corporate Share Structures and Estate Planning" (1983) 6 E & TQ 168.

---

38 *Ibid*, subs 125(7) "active business carried on by a corporation."
39 See subs 74.5(7), *ibid*.

Non-Arm's Length Loans

DRACHE, ARTHUR BC, ED. "Income Splitting Needs Advance Planning" (1991) 13 Can Taxpayer 181.

———. "Income Splitting through Lending" (1991) 13 Can Taxpayer 174.

CHAPTER 6

OFFICE AND EMPLOYMENT INCOME

"Classification is the beginning of wisdom."[1]

A. GENERAL COMMENT

In this and the chapters immediately following, we begin to parse income according to its source. Section 3 specifies the manner and sequence in which income from each source flows into the computation of net income.

Section 3 identifies the following sources:

- Office;
- Employment;
- Business;
- Property;
- Capital gains; and
- Other income.

The section is mandatory and rigid, and neatly, but not easily, compartmentalizes the sources into segregated pigeonholes. Segregation by source adds a considerable amount of complexity in the statute.

Employment income is the single largest source of government revenues. Hence, tax revenues from this source play a critical role in

---

1   Edwin Robert Anderson Seligman, *Double Taxation and International Fiscal Cooperation* (New York: The Macmillan Company, 1928) at 58.

government financing. Even a small leak in the taxation of employment income can have substantial revenue consequences to federal and provincial treasuries. Thus, we see the CRA fighting cases involving as little as $300 all the way up to the Supreme Court of Canada.

The employment income rules affect individuals, each of whom is a potential voter. Thus, although the law is sensitive to the need for government revenues, it must also be seen as fair.

There are three basic issues in the taxation of employment income:

1) *Characterization*: What is the nature of the relationship that gives rise to income?
2) *Timing*: When do we tax it?
3) *Scope*: What is taxable?

There are four distinguishing features of employment-source income. First, deductions from employment income are strictly controlled: subsection 8(2) prohibits the deduction of any employment-related expense unless the Act specifically authorizes it. This rule keeps a tight rein on employment deductions. In contrast, we presume that deductions from business or investment income are acceptable if they comply with commercial and accounting principles. The presumption is that business expenses are deductible unless the statute specifically prohibits them.[2] Thus, deducting expenses against business income is much easier than against employment income. This difference between business and employment income is a powerful incentive for taxpayers to characterize their income as business income.

We withhold tax on employment income at source,[3] and hold the tax in trust for the Crown.[4] In contrast, there is no systematic withholding at source on business income. Taxpayers who earn business

---

2   *Income Tax Act*, RSC 1985, c 1 (5th Supp) [*ITA*], subs 9(1); *Royal Trust Co v MNR*, [1957] CTC 32 (Ex Ct) (payment of dues and memberships in community and social clubs on behalf of employees deductible where employees expected to make contacts and generate business); *Dominion Taxicab Assn v MNR*, [1954] SCR 82 (fees to company contracting with taxicab owners not deductible; funds contingently received not income); *Bank of Nova Scotia v Canada*, [1980] CTC 57 (FCTD), aff'd [1981] CTC 162 (FCA) (value of foreign tax credit determined in accordance with ordinary commercial principles, taking weighted rate of exchange at time tax payable).

3   *ITA*, *ibid*, para 153(1)(a).

4   *Ibid*, subs 227(4). Failure to withhold tax on employment income renders the employer liable to a civil penalty of 10 percent plus interest at a prescribed rate (subs 227(8)) and to criminal penalties (subs 238(1)). Directors of a corporation who fail to withhold and remit taxes may be personally liable (subs 227.1(1)).

income must make instalment payments on account of their estimated tax payable.[5]

Employment income is generally taxable on a cash basis.[6] Business and investment income are taxable on an accrual or as-earned basis, no matter when the taxpayer receives the income.[7]

Because of these restrictions on the computation of employment income, individuals generally prefer independent contractor status for tax purposes. This distinction causes some tension in the characterization of employment relationships.

Hence, we must address six issues:

- Is the taxpayer an employee?
- Does the taxpayer hold an office?
- Has the taxpayer received remuneration or taxable benefits?
- What is the value of the remuneration or benefit?
- When did the taxpayer receive the remuneration or benefit?
- Is the taxpayer entitled to any statutory deductions from employment income?

B. CHARACTERIZATION OF EMPLOYMENT RELATIONSHIP

There is a fair volume of litigation concerning the nature of working relationships. The issue occurs in different contexts — tax law, Canada Pension Plan claims, Employment Insurance, and labour law. The doctrine of employee relationships has evolved, and continues to do so, as working conditions and workplace relationships change.

"Employment" is the position of an individual in the service of some other person.[8] Thus, the first step in the characterization of employment income is to determine whether a contract of service relationship exists between the taxpayer and the source of his or her income.

In traditional relationships, characterization depends on the degree of control and supervision that a person exercises over another in the provision of services. In an employment relationship, the employee is under the direct control and supervision of the employer and is obliged

---

5   *Ibid*, subs 156(1).
6   *Ibid*, subs 5(1). There is an important exception for "salary deferral arrangements"; see para 6(1)(i), subs 248(1)"salary deferral arrangement" and subs 6(11).
7   *Ibid*, s 9.
8   *Ibid*, subs 248(1).

to obey that person's lawful orders. The employer controls not only what the employee does but also how she does it. Hence, older cases refer to a contract of employment as a master-servant relationship.

In an independent contract for services, a person engages another to perform services in order to achieve a prescribed objective, but does not prescribe the manner of achieving it. An independent contractor offers his services for a fee. Baron Bramwell described the distinction between the two types of relationships as follows: "the difference between the relations of master and servant and of principal and his agent is this: a principal has the right to direct what the agent has to do; but a master has not only that right, but also the right to say how it is to be done."[9]

Thus, we must evaluate a relationship to distinguish a contract of employment from a contract for service. The traditional essential elements are:

- The degree of supervision and control between the parties;
- The method of remuneration for services;
- Arrangements for holidays;
- Provisions for sick leave;
- Opportunities for outside employment;
- Provision of medical coverage;
- Compensation for work-related travel; and
- The nature of termination clauses.

Determining an employment relationship is essentially a question of fact. There is no absolute formula or bright-line test by which one conclusively determines whether a person is an employee or an independent contractor. No single test invariably yields a clear answer.[10] Indeed, in some situations, an employee may also provide independent contractor services to his employer outside the scope of his regular employment relationship.[11]

There are several legal tests for determining employment status in different situations. None of the tests, however, is definitive in every circumstance. The law continues to evolve as our economy shifts from conventional "bricks and mortar" commerce to electronic global networks. Thus, the law is uncertain, which leads to increasing disputes and litigation.

---

9   Baron Bramwell in *R v Walker* (1858), 27 LJMC 207 at 208 (CCR).
10   *671122 Ontario Ltd v Sagaz Industries Canada Inc*, 2001 SCC 59 [*Sagaz*].
11   See, for example, *Criterion Capital Corp v Canada*, [2001] 4 CTC 2844 (TCC [General Procedure]). See also *Wolf v Canada*, 2002 FCA 96.

1) Supervision and Control

The traditional test to determine whether a person retains another as an employee or as an independent contractor was to look almost exclusively at the degree of control over the service provider, the test Baron Bramwell used in 1858,[12] and which the Supreme Court of Canada adopted in 1978 in *Hôpital Notre-Dame de l'Espérance v Laurent*.[13] Since then, however, we have moved to a more flexible approach that looks at the total relationship (including control) of the parties.[14]

We evaluate control by four principal criteria:[15]

1) Power to select the person who renders the service;
2) Mode and time of payment;
3) Evaluation of the method and performance of work; and
4) Right to suspend or dismiss the person engaged to perform the work.

In a conventional employment relationship, the employer selects her employee, sets the amount of wages, benefits, and time of payment, and evaluates the employee's performance. The employer can terminate the relationship with appropriate notice. Further, depending on the employer's policies, it may provide supplementary medical coverage and set out policies in respect of travel, sick leave, disability, outside employment and vacations.

To be sure, each of these facets of the "control test" is useful in characterizing conventional employment relationships. As professionals have become increasingly qualified and technical in new technologies, the control test is of limited value in characterizing newer working relationships. As MacGuigan J said in *Wiebe Door Services Ltd v MNR*:

---

12   *Sagaz*, above note 10 at para 37.

13   *Hôpital Notre-Dame de l'Espérance v Laurent*, [1978] 1 SCR 605 [*Hôpital Notre-Dame*].

14   See, for example, *Sagaz*, above note 10; *Royal Winnipeg Ballet v MNR*, 2006 FCA 87 (expressed intention of parties in contractual arrangement given weight).

15   See *Gould v Minister of National Insurance*, [1951] All ER 368 (KB) (contract for services of a music hall artist contained restrictions and elements of control but only those necessary for proper working of the theatre); *Bell v MNR* (1951), 52 DTC 8 (TAB) (physician to rural villages contracted to provide services; still maintained private practice); *Fainstein v MNR* (1952), 52 DTC 102 (TAB) (physician and others setting up health departments). See also *Hôpital Notre-Dame*, above note 13 at 613 where Pigeon J quoted with approval the following passage from *Traité pratique de la responsabilité civile délictuelle* by André Nadeau (translation):

> The essential criterion of employer-employee relations is the right to give orders and instructions to the employee regarding the manner in which to carry out his work.

"the test has broken down completely in relation to highly skilled and professional workers, who possess skills far beyond the ability of their employers to direct."[16] Thus, the "organization and integration" test is a useful supplement in the case of professionals.

2) Organization and Integration

Characterizing the working relationships of skilled professionals involves more than merely identifying who has the power to dictate how one is to work. In relationships involving skilled persons, the user of services may not have the technical expertise or "know-how" to dictate how the service provider is to work. Any power or control in these circumstances is more illusory than real. After all, the very reason for hiring a skilled professional person is so he can instruct management in the performance of complex and technical tasks that are beyond the competence of the user of the service. We hire professionals to provide expertise, not to tell him how to do the job.

Thus, the question becomes: is the person an intrinsic part of the organization or merely an adjunct to it? There is no simple formula or single test that supplies the answer. One looks to the whole scheme of operations to elicit the nature of the relationship between the parties. Here, too, the mode and manner of compensation (vacations, sick leave, disability policies, medical coverage, etc.) provide an indication of the nature of a relationship. The greater the number and value of ancillary benefits that are attached to the service provider, the greater the likelihood of an employment relationship.

3) Total Relationship Test

Although the control and the organization/integration tests are useful in appropriate situations, they are not always determinative. Both tests have an overly narrow focus. The better approach is a more broadly based examination of the "total relationship" between the parties,[17] including:

- Supervision and control;
- Ownership of assets;
- Chance of profit; and
- Risk of loss.

---

16   *Wiebe Door Services Ltd v MNR*, [1986] 2 CTC 200 at 203 (FCA); *Sagaz*, above note 10 at para. 33.

17   See *Montreal (City) v Montreal Locomotive Works Ltd* (1946), [1947] 1 DLR 161 at 169–70 (PC), Lord Wright.

These are not four separate and independent tests. They are different aspects of the same test. We determine the nature of the relationship of persons on an analysis of the whole scheme of operations. However, no single test is conclusive.[18]

Although the degree of control will vary from case to case, an employment relationship implies at least some supervision and control over the employee. Further, in such relationships the employer usually owns the assets, carries the risk of the enterprise or working relationship, and derives the benefits of profit. The shared intention of the parties to the contract is also important if the evidence supports their view of the relationship.

As with most cases requiring characterization, the extremes of the spectrum are easy to identify. The bank teller is an employee of the bank and under its stringent supervision and control. A partner in a law firm serves clients, but is not an employee of any client. What of the lawyer with only one large client, who provides all the lawyer's revenue, reimburses all her expenses, and permits the lawyer to participate in a bonus arrangement that depends on profits?

In the final analysis, the determination of a relationship depends upon the nature of the evidence before the court. There may be clear evidence of shared intention between the parties or other contractual and control indicia that prevail. The onus is on the individual to establish the nature of her particular relationship.[19]

4) Office

Section 5 brings into income a taxpayer's income from an office. The Act defines the term "office" as a position that entitles an individual to a fixed or ascertainable stipend or remuneration.[20] If the stipend is pre-determined in amount, it is fixed. If it is not pre-determined in amount, but may be determined by reference to some formula, it is ascertainable.

The distinction between an "office" and "employment" is that the former does not require the individual to be in the service of some other person, which would imply an employment relationship. For example, judges, ministers of the Crown, and members of a legislative

---

18 For a good synthesis, see *Market Investigations Ltd v Minister of Social Security*, [1968] 3 All ER 732 (QB); *Lee Ting Sang v Chung Chi-Keung*, [1990] 2 AC 374 (PC from Hong Kong).
19 *Lang v MNR*, 2007 TCC 547 (Employment Insurance) (shared intention of parties determined they were independent contractors).
20 *ITA*, above note 2, subs 248(1) "office."

assembly or parliament are "officers" and are not employees for tax purposes. The distinction between an "officer" and an "employee" is not particularly significant for most tax purposes because both categories are taxable on their remuneration and benefits.

5) Administrative View

The CRA does not have a general administrative position on employment contracts,[21] but in practice is reasonably dogmatic in applying the supervision and control test. Interpretation Bulletin IT-525R, "Performing Artists," considers limited aspects of relationships involving musicians and other performing artists. The bulletin does, however, address the particular problems of persons who have special skills and expertise.[22] For example, it considers an artist is self-employed if she:[23]

- Has a chance of profit or risk of loss;
- Provides instruments and other equipment;
- Has a number of engagements with different persons during the course of a year;
- Regularly auditions or makes applications for engagements;
- Retains the services of an agent regularly;
- Selects or hires employees or helpers, fixes their salary, directs them, etc.;
- Arranges the time, place and nature of performances; or
- Earns remuneration that is directly related to particular rehearsals and performances.

6) International Dimensions

Employment status is also an important issue in international tax treaties. For example, under Article XIV of the *Canada-US Tax Treaty*, Canada has the primary right to tax an independent contractor's income that he earns in the United States. The US, however, can also tax the income if the individual has a fixed base or permanent establishment in that country. This may result in double taxation, for which we provide relief under other provisions.

---

21   The CRA published guidelines on the employed or self-employed issue in RC4110, online: www.cra-arc.gc.ca/E/pub/tg/rc4110/.

22   Interpretation Bulletin IT-525 R, "Performing Artists" (17 August 1995) at para 4.

23   *Ibid* at para 7.

C. TIMING

We tax employment income on a calendar-year basis.[24] Thus, an employee cannot choose any other fiscal year in respect of employment-source income. In contrast, we determine business income based on a fiscal period. This distinction allows individuals some flexibility in tax planning with business income. These are rules of administrative convenience that allow employees to comply with the tax system with minimum accounting records.

To be sure, cash-basis accounting allows employees some flexibility in tax planning. For example, an owner-manager of a corporation is taxable on his salary in the year that he receives payment, whereas the corporation may deduct the salary payable on an accrual basis.[25] This imbalance between deduction and inclusion permits modest tax deferral. If the corporation accrues the deduction on 31 December of a year and it pays the employee on 1 January of the year following, the employee can defer her tax on the income for an entire year. The Act tolerates this minor mismatch of deductions and inclusions in the interests of administrative convenience. It does, however, limit the deferral advantage from mismatching income and expenses to a maximum of 180 days after the end of the employer's fiscal period.[26]

D. SCOPE OF EMPLOYMENT INCOME

An employee (or a person who holds an office) is taxable on her salary, wages, and any other remuneration (including gratuities) that she receives in the year.[27] Of course, what constitutes "salary or wages" depends on whether there is an employment relationship between the parties. "Remuneration" is compensation for services from an employment relationship, whether past, present or future.[28]

---

24   *ITA*, above note 2; subs 5(1) and para 249(1)(b).
25   *Earlscourt Sheet Metal Mechanical Ltd v MNR*, [1988] 1 CTC 2045 (TCC).
26   *ITA*, above note 2, subs 78(4).
27   *Ibid*, s 5.
28   Note that the definition of "salary or wages" in *ibid*, subs 248(1) does not apply for the purposes of calculating employment income under s 5. See *Adam v MNR*, [1985] 2 CTC 2383 (TCC) (mere bookkeeping entries not capable of converting salary into something else, for example, dividends); *Hochstrasser v Mayes*, [1959] Ch 22 at 33 (CA); *Brumby v Milner*, [1976] 3 All ER 636 (HL); *Tyrer v Smart (Inspector of Taxes)*, [1979] 1 All ER 321 (HL); *Nicoll v Austin* (1935), 19 Tax Cas 531 (employer requested continued residence of director in costly

1) Benefits

Employment income must also include non-cash benefits in income if the tax system is to be equitable among taxpayers. Thus, section 6 reinforces the equitable principle in section 5 and taxes the value of any benefits that the taxpayer receives or enjoys in the year.

A benefit is an economic advantage, measurable in monetary terms, that an employer (or related person) confers on an employee in his capacity as an employee. It is not always easy, however, to draw the line between taxable and non-taxable benefits and timing issues. For example:

- Should "bargain purchases" and employee discounts be taxable?
- Should a promise to pay in the future be taken into income when the employer makes the promise or when he makes the payment?
- When is an employer-provided benefit (for example, child care services) merely a cost to the employer, and when does it become income to the employee?

Benefits constitute compensation and are taxable because their inclusion in income reflects the taxpayer's ability to pay. We saw in Chapter 1 that the principle of horizontal equity requires taxpayers in comparable financial and personal circumstances to bear comparable burdens of tax. The tax treatment of benefits is important to the principle of fairness in taxation. Exclusion of benefits from income would distort the tax system, undermine its integrity, and erode taxpayer confidence in the self-assessment and voluntary compliance system. Thus, we need to be particularly careful in considering the effect on the tax system of excluding benefits from income.

It is not always easy, however, to determine what is a taxable benefit and how much of it we should tax. Consider, for example, the tax status of three individuals: A works for X company, which pays him $4,000 per month and provides him with low-cost meals in its cafeteria, dental coverage for his entire family, access to a club that provides social and recreational facilities, and discount purchases on its goods. The fringe benefits cost the company $400 per month per employee. B is employed by Y Company, a competitor, and receives $4,400 per month in salary. Y company does not give its employees any fringe benefits. C is paid $4,200 per month to work at Z Company, which also does not pay any fringe benefits, but has a better and a more comfortable working

---

manor, but paid stipend to compensate for expenses); *Jaworski v Institution of Polish Engineers in Great Britain Ltd*, [1951] 1 KB 768 (CA) (oral contract for foreign national stipulated deductions and taxes borne by "employer"; held to be contract for services).

environment than either X Company or Y Company. Z Company's premises have better lighting, air conditioning, and are surrounded by attractive parks and gardens. These environmental facilities cost Z Company an average of $200 per month per employee. Should A, B and C pay tax only on their cash income or on their cash income and work environment benefits? If they should pay tax on benefits, which of the benefits should we consider "taxable" and which, if any, should we exclude from income? If we consider all the benefits to be "taxable," what value should we attach to the benefits—market value, cost to the employer or value to the employee? What if C suffers from allergies that are aggravated by Z Company's gardens: should C be taxable at all on any portion of her environmental "benefits"?

a)   Meaning of Benefits

Subsection 6(1) states that a taxpayer must include in his income "the value of board, lodging and other benefits of any kind whatever received or enjoyed" by the taxpayer in the year in respect of, in the course of, or by virtue of his office or employment. A benefit is an economic advantage or material acquisition, measurable in monetary terms, conferred on an employee in his capacity as an employee. Thus, there are several elements requiring analysis:

- Did the employee receive or enjoy an economic advantage?
- Is the economic advantage measurable in monetary terms?
- Was the economic advantage for the benefit of the employee or for the benefit of his employer? and
- Did the employer confer the economic advantage on the employee in respect of, in the course of, or by virtue of the employment relationship with the employee?

If we answer all these questions in the affirmative, the economic advantage or material acquisition is a taxable benefit from employment *unless* the statute specifically exempts it from tax.[29]

---

29   See *Canada v Savage*, [1983] CTC 393 at 399 (SCC) approving the judgment of Evans JA in *R v Poynton* (1972), 72 DTC 6329 at 6335–36 (Ont CA):

> I do not believe the language to be restricted to benefits that are related to the office or employment in the sense that they represent a form of remuneration for services rendered. If it is a material acquisition which confers an economic benefit on the taxpayer and does not constitute an exemption, e.g., loan or gift, then it is within the all-embracing definition of s. 3. A gift is a gesture of goodwill and is made without regard to services rendered by the recipient of the gift. For example, if an employer distributes turkeys to all employees at Christmas, the value of the turkey is not considered to be a benefit which must be included in an employee's income.

"Benefit" has a broader meaning under the Canadian statute than under its counterpart in the United Kingdom. In the UK, a benefit in kind was considered income only if it was readily convertible into cash.[30] For example, rent-free accommodation was considered to be a non-taxable benefit because the employee could not readily convert the accommodation into cash. As the House of Lords said in *Tennant v Smith*: "A person is chargeable for income tax . . . not on what saves his pocket but what goes into his pocket."[31] Paragraph 6(1)(a) clearly displaces the principle (sometimes described as the "money's worth" principle) in *Tennant v Smith*.

The first step in the analysis is whether the taxpayer derives an economic advantage. Benefits come in all sorts of varieties and guises. Some, such as payment of an individual's personal vacation and living expenses by an employer, are obvious benefits. Others are more subtle: for example, the payment of a grievance settlement to a unionized employee,[32] the discharge of a mortgage upon dismissal from employment,[33] or the issuance of stock options by a person other than the employer.[34]

Canadian tax law has wrestled with the concept of economic advantage for several decades. *Ransom v MNR* (*Ransom*)[35] was the first of many such decisions. The taxpayer sold his residence at a loss of approximately $4,000 when his employer relocated him from Sarnia to Montreal. The employer compensated the taxpayer for his loss. The Exchequer Court held that the reimbursement for the loss was not taxable because the taxpayer did not benefit from the payment — it did not put any money in his pocket, but merely saved his pocket. The court applied the "money's worth" principle.

Ransom clearly offends the principle of horizontal equity. A taxpayer who receives compensation for his capital loss on the sale of a home is clearly better off than an individual who is not so compensated. Nevertheless, many courts applied *Ransom* in relocation cases. In *Canada (AG) v Hoefele* (*Hoefele*),[36] for example, the taxpayer moved from Calgary to Toronto and purchased a house in Toronto that was more

---

30 *Tennant v Smith*, [1892] AC 150 (HL).
31 *Ibid* at 164. The law in the UK has been changed by statute, which now requires all payment of expenses, including reimbursements, to be included in income.
32 *Norman v MNR*, [1987] 2 CTC 2261 (TCC).
33 *Galanov v MNR*, [1987] 2 CTC 2353 (TCC).
34 *Robertson v Canada*, [1988] 1 CTC 111 (FCTD), aff'd [1990] 1 CTC 114 (FCA), leave to appeal to SCC refused (1990), 113 NR 319n (SCC).
35 *Ransom v MNR*, [1967] CTC 346 (Ex Ct).
36 [1996] 1 CTC 131 (FCA) [*Hoefele*].

expensive than the one he had left in Calgary. His employer picked up the increased mortgage interest on the differential between the two houses, thereby reducing his personal living expenses. The Federal Court of Appeal held that the mortgage interest subsidy was not taxable because the taxpayer was not enriched, but merely restored to his original position. The court said:[37]

> If, on the whole of a transaction, an employee's economic position is not improved, that is, if the transaction is a zero-sum situation when viewed in its entirety, a receipt is not a benefit and, therefore, is not taxable under paragraph 6(1)(a).

In contrast, compensation for the higher cost of a new home in a new location was a taxable benefit because it increases the taxpayer's net worth. In *Phillips v MNR*,[38] for example, the taxpayer moved from Moncton to Winnipeg. His employer paid him $10,000 to compensate for his increased housing costs in Winnipeg. The $10,000 subsidy was a taxable benefit because it "did more than save his pocket—it put money into it." Here, the court applied the money's worth principle to arrive at the right decision for the wrong reasons.

It is difficult to rationalize the difference between enhancing one's wealth through employer-subsidized financing[39] and subsidized capital costs.[40] Thus, subsection 6(20) provides special tax treatment for eligible housing losses. Generally, one-half of employer reimbursements in excess of $15,000 in respect of eligible housing losses are taxable as an employment benefit to the taxpayer.[41] The one-half exclusion is a compromise for those who move from one city to another and incur a loss as a consequence of their move.

The law on the taxation of reimbursements on relocation is neither clear, nor consistent, nor rational. In *Gernhart v MNR (Gernhart)*,[42] for example, the Tax Court of Canada refused to extend the reasoning of *Ransom* to reimbursements of income tax to accommodate a differential tax burden between Canada and the United States. The taxpayer, an employee of General Motors, moved from Ohio to Windsor. Her employer compensated her for Canada's higher income tax rates by paying her the tax differential between Canadian and US rates in

37   *Ibid* at 137. See also *Splane v MNR*, [1992] 2 CTC 224 (FCA).
38   (1994), 94 DTC 6177 (FCA) [*Phillips*].
39   *Hoefele*, above note 36.
40   *Phillips*, above note 38.
41   ITA, above note 2, subs 6(20).
42   *Gernhart v Canada*, [1996] 3 CTC 2369 (TCC), aff'd (1997), [1998] 2 CTC 102 (FCA), leave to appeal to SCC refused, [1998] SCCA No 46.

order to equalize her net after-tax income. The court characterized the reimbursement as a form of salary compensation. It is difficult in principle to distinguish *Gernhart* from *Hoefele*. In both cases, the taxpayer was not enriched, but merely restored to his or her original position. Nevertheless, *Gernhart* is preferable, in that the taxpayer was taxed on her benefit based on her enhanced ability to pay.[43]

Thus, the taxability of a benefit depends on the answers to several questions. First, has the taxpayer received or enjoyed an economic advantage? If so, was the economic advantage measurable in monetary terms? We tax an employee on benefits that he derives from his office but not on the pleasure of pleasant working conditions. Pleasure or psychic income is not a taxable perk of employment.

Although somewhat dated, "Kleinwachter's conundrum" illustrates the difficulty with taxing working conditions as income to the employee:

> We are asked to measure the relative incomes of the ordinary officer serving with his troops and a *Flugeladjutant* to the sovereign. Both receive the same nominal pay; but the latter receives quarters in the palace, food at the royal table, servants, and horses for sport. He accompanies the prince to the theatre and opera, and, in general, lives royally at no expense to himself and is able to save generously from his salary. But suppose, as one possible complication, that the *Flugeladjutant* detests opera and hunting.
>
> The problem is clearly hopeless. To neglect all compensation in kind is obviously inappropriate. On the other hand, to include the perquisites as a major addition to the salary implies that all income should be measured with regard to the relative pleasurableness of different activities—which would be the negation of measurement. There is hardly more reason for imputing additional income to the *Flugeladjutant* on account of his luxurious wardrobe than for bringing into account the prestige and social distinction of a (German) university professor. Fortunately, however, such difficulties in satisfactory measurement of relative incomes do not bulk large in modern times; and, again, these elements of unmeasurable psychic income may be presumed to vary in a somewhat continuous manner along the income scale.[44]

The third question to consider is whether the economic advantage was for the benefit of the taxpayer or for the benefit of the employer who conferred it. A payment that is primarily for the convenience of

---

43   Amount treated as income under *ITA*, above note 2, subs 5(1). See also subs 6(20) for eligible housing losses.

44   Henry Simons, *Personal Income Taxation* (Chicago: The University of Chicago Press, 1938) at 53,

the employer is not taxable to the employee. Thus, the key is: who is the *primary* beneficiary of the payment? For example, where an employer requires an employee to take computer courses so that she is better trained for her job, the cost of the job training is not a taxable benefit to the employee, even though she becomes a better qualified and more valuable person in the labour market. The benefit to the employee is ancillary to the benefits that the employer derives.

Similarly, where an employer sends her employee for second language training, the expenses are primarily for the benefit of the employer, even though the employee is better trained and marketable. What if the employer sends one of its senior executives on a fully reimbursed basis to Paris for three years? Would it make a difference if the executive was forty-five years of age or seventy years?

There is no bright-line test to determine what constitutes a benefit to the employee and convenience to the employer, particularly where there are mutual benefits.[45] The convenience-to-the-employer test does not imply that the employee cannot derive pleasure from the task entrusted to her. For example, a hotel manager who is "compelled" to live in a luxury suite in a resort hotel is not taxable on the value of the suite if the manager's job requires her to be on the premises.[46]

The final question to consider is: did the employee derive the economic advantage in respect of, in the course of or by virtue of the employment relationship between the taxpayer and her employer? Did the employer confer the economic advantage on his employee *qua* employee or in his personal capacity? The former may be taxable; the latter are not taxable as employment income. A gift to an employee in her personal capacity, for example, is not a benefit for tax purposes.[47]

The fourth question, characterization of capacity, can be difficult.[48] *Canada v Savage*[49] is the classic case. The taxpayer, a junior employee of a life insurance company, took three courses offered by the Life Office

---

45   See, for example, *Cutmore v MNR*, [1986] 1 CTC 2230 (TCC) (employees taxed on fees paid for preparation of personal tax returns despite employer's policy requiring such preparation).

46   *Benaglia v Comm'r*, 36 BTA 838 (1937).

47   See, for example, *Busby v Canada*, [1986] 1 CTC 147 (FCTD) [*Busby*]; *Phaneuf Estate v Canada*, [1978] CTC 21 at 27 (FCTD). See also *Seymour v Reed*, [1927] AC 554 at 559 (HL).

48   *Ball v Johnson* (1971), 47 Tax Cas 155; *Hochstrasser v Mayes*, [1960] AC 376 (HL) (court must be satisfied that the service agreement was *causa causans* and not merely *causa sine qua non* of receipt of benefit); *Bridges v Hewitt*, [1957] 2 All ER 281 (CA).

49   *Canada v Savage*, [1980] CTC 103 (FCTD), rev'd on other grounds [1981] CTC 332 (FCA), aff'd [1983] CTC 393 (SCC).

Management Association that were designed to provide a broad under-standing of insurance company operations. She undertook the courses of her own volition and without pressure from her employer. Never-theless, pursuant to its enlightened corporate policy, which was well known to employees, the employer reimbursed the taxpayer $100 for each course that she successfully completed. The reimbursements were taxable benefits. The phrase "in respect of an office or employment" in paragraph 6(1)(a) has wide scope.[50] Thus, the payments were taxable as benefits from employment because they were paid to the taxpayer in her capacity as an employee and primarily for her advantage.[51] The case involved only $300 of taxable benefits. The issue, however, was one of national importance to the public treasury.

b) Timing of Benefits

Timing and valuations of benefits are inextricably linked to each other. An employee is taxable on benefits that he *receives or enjoys* in the year. The word "enjoys" enlarges the benefit rule beyond actual receipt of the benefit.

---

50   *Canada v Savage, ibid* at 399 (SCC). The Court endorses its earlier decision in
      R v Nowegijick (1983), 83 DTC 5041 at 5045 (SCC):

> [T]he words "in respect of" are, in my opinion, words of the widest possible
> scope. They import such meanings as "in relation to," "with reference to" or
> "in connection with." The phrase "in respect of" is probably the widest of any
> expression intended to convey some connection between two related subject
> matters.

The Court in *Canada v Savage, ibid* at 399, also distinguishes earlier English
jurisprudence on benefits:

> Our Act contains the stipulation not found in the English statutes referred to,
> "benefits of any kind whatever . . . in respect of, in the course of, or by virtue
> of an office or employment." The meaning of "benefit of whatever kind" is
> clearly quite broad.

See also *Jex v Canada*, [1998] 2 CTC 2688 (TCC) (CRA employee taxed on
reimbursement of professional course fees in the absence of any requirement by
employer to take courses); *Faubert v Canada*, 98 DTC 1380 (TCC).

51   Dickson, Ritchie, Lamer and Wilson JJ specifically addressed the question with
      reference to para 6(1)(a)); McIntyre J left the issue open by excluding payment
      from income under para 56(1)(n) and not addressing para 6(1)(a). According to
      their Lordships (*Canada v Savage, ibid* at 398):

> . . . the *Hochstrasser* case and *Ball v Johnson* are of little assistance. The provi-
> sions of s. 156 of the *Income Tax Act, 1952* of England are not unlike s. 5(1) of the
> Canadian *Income Tax Act* but our Act goes further in s. 6(1)(a). In addition to the
> salary, wages and other remuneration referred to in s. 5(1), s. 6(1)(a) includes in
> income the value of benefits "of any kind whatever . . . received or enjoyed . . . in
> respect of, in the course of, or by virtue of an office or employment."

Section 6 does not distinguish between cash and "in kind" benefits. To illustrate: assume that on 1 September of Year 1 a corporation gives its employee 100 shares of its capital stock, which are trading at $100 per share. On 31 December (Year 1) the shares trade at $125. The employee sells the shares on 1 March (Year 2) for $160 per share. The total gain is $16,000. There are two issues: (1) how much should we include in the employee's income in the first year when he receives the stock? and (2) what should be the employee's gain when he sells the stock?

Paragraph 6(1)(a) taxes "in kind" and cash benefits equally in the year of receipt. The employee is taxable on $10,000, the market value of the shares, when he gets the stock. In effect, the shares are the equivalent of a cash bonus. If the taxpayer's marginal tax rate is 50 percent, he must pay tax of $5,000 even though he did not receive cash. Thus, the taxpayer must either come up with the $5,000 or sell sufficient shares to raise the cash.

· The answer to the second question depends upon the answer to the first. If we tax the employee on the value of the $10,000 benefit in Year 1 when he receives the shares, we must allow the employee to bump up his cost basis in the shares from zero to $10,000. Otherwise we would tax him twice on the same amount when he sells the shares in Year 2. The gain when the employee sells the shares is only $6,000, even though he did not pay anything for the shares. Thus, the employee must recognize $10,000 of his total economic gain in the first year and can defer recognizing $6,000 until he sells the shares.

The difference in timing is important. The present value of the $5,000 tax liability in the first year is $5,000. Assuming an interest rate of 8 percent, the present value of the $3,000 tax liability in Year 2 is only $2,778. Thus, the employee's decision to delay selling the shares affects not only the timing of his liability but also its net present value.

If we assume that the employee is not taxable in the year that he receives the shares but only when he sells them, the results are quite different. The employee's income inclusion in Year 1 is nil and does not trigger any tax. In the subsequent year, however, his gain on sale is $16,000. At a tax rate of 50 percent, he is liable to pay $8,000. The present value of the tax at an interest rate of 8 percent is now only $7,407. Thus, the delay of only one year results in a tax saving of $371. Deferring taxes means saving taxes.

A benefit is taxable only when it vests in the employee.[52] There are considerable difficulties in determining when rights vest in an employee and, if they have vested, the present value of benefits that are payable in the future. For example, how do we determine when an employee "re-

---

52   *Hogg v Canada*, [1987] 2 CTC 257 (FCTD).

ceives or enjoys" a benefit from her employer's contribution to her pension plan? Should the employee be taxable on the present value of her employer's contribution in the year that the employer contributes it or when it vests in the employee? To circumvent these difficulties of timing and value, the Act specifies a detailed scheme for the taxation of deferred income plans.[53] For example, employer contributions to an employee's registered pension plan are not taxable upon payment into the plan, but are taxable when the plan pays out the pension to the employee.[54]

c) Valuation

What is the taxable amount of an "in kind" benefit or "perk" from employment? Should the employee pay tax on the fair market value of the benefit, the cost of the benefit to the employer or on its exchange value? For example, suppose an airline allows its employees to travel free of charge on its planes on a space-available basis. Should an employee who takes advantage of the facility be taxable on the equivalent of full-fare, advanced booking fare or standby fare? What is the value of the trip if the employee is "bumped up" into business class because that is the only available space on the flight?

There is no single formula for the valuation of benefits. We value some benefits at their cost to the employer,[55] others according to market prices for similar products[56] and others by their opportunity cost.[57]

---

53   See Chapter 10.

54   *ITA*, above note 2, subpara 6(1)(a)(i) and para 56(1)(a).

55   See, for example, *Rendell v Went* (1964), 41 Tax Cas 654 (HL) (assumption by employer of costs of employee's criminal defence taxable benefit equal in value to amount of cost assumed); see also Interpretation Bulletin IT-470R, "Employees' Fringe Benefits" (8 April 1988) (cost of subsidized meals).

56   See, for example, *Wilkins v Rogerson* (1961), 39 Tax Cas 344 (CA) (second-hand value, rather than cost, of suits supplied by employer to employees was amount of taxable benefit); Harman LJ at 353:

> [T]he only controversy was whether he was to pay tax on the cost of the prerequisite to his employer, or on the value of it to him. It appears to me that this prerequisite is a taxable subject-matter because it is money's worth. It is money's worth because it can be turned into money, and when turned into money the taxable subject-matter is the value received. I cannot myself see how it is connected directly with the cost to the employer . . . . The taxpayer has to pay on what he gets. Here he has got a suit. He can realize it only for £5. The advantage to him is therefore, £5. The detriment to his employer has been considerably more, but that seems to me to be irrelevant. The validity of the Court's reasoning is dubious. Had His Lordship asked the question "what is the value in use?" instead of "what is the value in exchange?", he may have arrived at a different conclusion.

57   *Youngman v Canada*, [1986] 2 CTC 475 (FCTD), rev'd [1990] 2 CTC 10 (FCA)

The valuation of benefits is a contentious issue between taxpayers and the CRA. Thus, in the interests of administration and certainty, the Act prescribes valuation formulas for some of the more contentious benefits, such as those from automobiles, stock options and low-cost loans.[58] In other cases, the CRA simply ignores the value of certain perks. The result is that the tax system is riddled with benefits rules and exceptions that distort comparative tax burdens between similarly situated taxpayers.

The CRA does not tax a benefit unless it can measure the value of the benefit in monetary terms. For example, it does not attribute an amount to an employee who is given free parking on his employer's premises if such facilities are available to all employees *and* it is not possible to appraise the value of the benefit. It will, however, attribute tax benefits if the perk is given selectively and it can be valued by commercial standards. Similar considerations apply to employer-provided child care facilities. These exclusions are premised more on administrative convenience than on principles of tax equity. Why, for example, should we exclude a benefit from income merely because similar benefits are extended to all employees? Why not tax all the employees on the value of the benefit?

d) Taxable Benefits

Benefits come in various forms and guises. For example, travel rewards are taxable as benefits, but only if the reward mileage was accumulated by virtue of the frequent flyer's employment relationship and the employer paid the travel. Reward miles are taxable in the year in which the individual uses the miles for airline travel or other personal expenditures. The taxable amount is the fair market value of the benefit.

The following are some common forms of taxable benefits:

- Board and lodging furnished at an unreasonably low rate (except for the value of board and lodging at special work sites);
- Rent-free or low-rent housing provided by the employer;
- Personal use of employer's automobile;
- Gifts in cash or in kind, including Christmas gifts (with minor exceptions), if the gift is disguised as remuneration;
- Holiday trips, prizes and incentive awards in recognition of job performance;

(shareholder benefit measured by reference to capital cost of house supplied by corporation rather than by reference to its rental value).

58   See, for example, *ITA*, above note 2, subs 6(2) (formula for automobile benefits), s 7 (formula for stock option benefits), s 804 (formula for benefit of low-cost loans).

- Premiums paid by an employer under provincial hospitalization and medical care insurance plans, and certain Government of Canada plans;
- Tuition fees paid for, or reimbursed to, employees in respect of their private education;
- Travelling expenses of employee's spouse; and
- Interest-free or low-interest loans.

e) Excluded Benefits
Paragraph 6(1)(a) excludes the following from taxable benefits:

- Employer contributions to a registered pension plan, group sickness or accident insurance plan, private health services plan, supplementary unemployment benefit plan, deferred profit-sharing plan or group term life insurance policy;
- A retirement compensation arrangement, an employee benefit plan or an employee trust;
- A benefit in respect of the use of an automobile (taxed under other provisions);
- Benefits derived from counselling services; and
- Benefits under a salary deferral arrangement (taxed under other provisions).

f) Administrative Exclusions
As a matter of administrative policy, the CRA does not generally consider the following as taxable benefits:[59]

- Discounts on merchandise for employees of merchandising businesses;
- Subsidized meals to employees, staff lunchrooms and canteens;
- Uniforms and special protective clothing supplied by employers, including cost of laundry and dry-cleaning;
- Subsidized school services for families of employees in remote areas;
- Transportation to the job in a vehicle supplied by the employer free or for a nominal charge;
- Social or athletic club fees where it is to the employer's advantage for the employee to be a member;
- Moving expenses of an employee paid or reimbursed by the employer;
- Premiums under private health services plans paid on the employee's behalf by the employer; and
- Contributions by employers to provincial hospitalization and medical care insurance plans to the extent that the employer is required to pay amounts to the plan.

---

59   See Interpretation Bulletin IT-470R, above note 55, consolidated 11 August 1999.

2) Allowances

A taxpayer must include in his income all amounts that he receives in the year "as an allowance for personal or living expenses or as an allowance for any other purpose."[60] An "allowance" is a limited and pre-determined sum of money paid to an individual, who is not required to account for it. In contrast, a "reimbursement" is a payment to indemnify an individual against actual expenses. The individual must account for it by providing receipts to substantiate the expenditure.[61]

There is no consistent rationale for the taxation of allowances. Most allowances are taxable as income.[62] There are some, however, that the Act specifically excludes. For example, salespeople who are employed for the purpose of selling property or negotiating contracts may exclude a reasonable allowance paid for travelling expenses. Employees (other than salespeople) may exclude a reasonable allowance paid to them to cover travelling expenses if the allowance is calculated by reference to time spent by the employee travelling away from the municipality where he or she ordinarily works. Hence, employees in receipt of a *per diem* travelling allowance are not taxable on the allowance if the amount of the allowance is reasonable.

3) Personal and Living Expenses

Allowances and reimbursements for personal or living expenses are generally taxable as income. For example, if an employer reimburses her employee's credit card bills for personal travel and entertainment, the amount reimbursed is a taxable benefit under paragraph 6(1)(a). If, instead, the employer provides her employee with an allowance of $5,000 per month for personal and living expenses, the allowance is taxable under paragraph 6(1)(b).

The Act excludes the following allowances from income:

- Allowances fixed by an Act of Parliament or by the Treasury Board;
- Travel and separation allowances paid to members of the Canadian Forces;
- Representation or other special allowances paid to diplomats and Canadian officials posted abroad;

---

60   *ITA*, above note 2, para 6(1)(b).
61   *Gagnon v Canada*, [1986] 1 SCR 264 ("allowance" linked to spouse's ability to dispose of it for own benefit regardless of restriction that it be applied to particular purpose); *Canada v Pascoe*, [1975] CTC 656 (FCA) (court defines "allowance" and "payable on periodic basis"; note CTC editorial note at 656).
62   *ITA*, above note 2, para 6(1)(b).

- Reasonable allowances for travel expenses paid to an employee who is employed to sell property or negotiate contracts for his or her employer;
- Reasonable allowances for travel expenses paid to an employee where the employee is required to travel away from the municipality where his or her employer's establishment is located; and
- Reasonable allowances for the use of motor vehicles received by an employee from the employer for travelling in the performance of the duties of an office or employment.

4) Advances and Loans

Employees are taxable on a cash basis on their employment income. Thus, advances against salary are taxable in the year in which the employee receives the advance.[63] An "advance" is a payment on account of future salary or wages. Typically, the employee is not expected to repay the advance, but to work off his financial obligation by rendering service to the employer.[64]

In contrast, a loan is a capital transfer and, therefore, is not income. A loan is a debt with provision for repayment within some reasonable time. Thus, the distinction between an advance and a loan lies not in the fact of repayment but in the mode in which the employee will discharge the obligation.

5) Automobiles

Employees are generally taxable on the benefit that they derive from employer-supplied automobiles. Taxable benefits from employer-supplied automobiles come in two forms: (1) operating expenses, and (2) standby charges. The Act defines an automobile as a motor vehicle that is designed primarily to carry individuals on highways and that has a maximum seating capacity, including the driver, of nine persons.[65]

a) Operating Costs
An employee is taxable on the value of any personal net operating costs that her employer pays on her behalf. Thus, employees must allocate gas, oil, maintenance and insurance costs to determine their personal component.[66]

---

63   *Randall v MNR*, [1987] 2 CTC 2265 (TCC).
64   Interpretation Bulletin IT-421R2, "Benefits to Individuals, Corporations and Shareholders from Loans or Debt" (9 September 1992).
65   *ITA*, above note 2, subs 248(1).
66   *Ibid*, para 6(1)(l).

b) Standby Charge

The purpose of the standby charge is to tax employees on the benefit that they derive from the availability of their employer's car for personal use. The employee must pay the charge if he has access to the car for personal use, regardless whether he actually uses it. The benefit derives from availability, not from use.[67]

The amount of the standby charge is set by formula. The essence of the formula is that the benefit is equal to 2 percent of the original cost (including taxes) of the automobile for every month that it is available to the employee. The word "reasonable" in the phrase "reasonable standby charge" is misleading. The formula is a deeming provision that dictates the *exact* amount to be included in the employee's income. The calculation, which has little to do with the value of the benefit, is precise. Thus, it is administratively convenient.

Example

Assume that an employer pays $3,600 toward his employee's personal-use operating expenses, for which the employee reimburses the employer $1,600.

Then:

(1) Benefit under para. 6(1)(l)—	$3,600
Amount reimbursed	(1,600)
Inclusion in income	$2,000
(2) Standby charge (see next example)	
2% × $23,000 × 12	5,520
Taxable benefits	$7,520

To simplify record keeping, however, an employee who uses his employer's automobile primarily (that is, more than 50 percent) for employment purposes can opt to include an additional one-half of the automobile standby charge in income in lieu of his share of operating costs.[68] Hence, the employee could include 3, instead of 2, percent per month of the cost of the automobile as a taxable benefit.

The basic standby charge in respect of an employer-owned automobile is equal to:

$$\frac{(\text{cost} \times 2\% \times (\text{no of days available}))}{30}$$

The number of days divided by 30 is rounded to the next whole number.

---

67 *Adams v Canada*, [1998] 2 CTC 353 (FCA) (mere right of usage is sufficient to trigger standby charge).

68 *ITA*, above note 2, subpara 6(1)(k)(iv).

Example

Assume:

Personal use	24,000 kms
Basic cost of automobile	$20,354
Taxes	2,646
Total cost of automobile	$23,000
Number of days available	365 days
Expenses reimbursed by employee	NIL

Then, a reasonable standby charge is:

2% x $23,000 x 12*	$5,520

Note: 365 ÷ 30 is rounded to 12

The standby charge for automobile salespeople is calculated somewhat differently. The rate applicable is 75 percent of the rate applicable to all other employees.[69] Also, the charge is calculated by reference to the average cost of all automobiles purchased by the employer in the year.

The benefit from leased automobiles is calculated as two-thirds of the cost of leasing the automobile (excepting any portion related to insurance) for the period that the automobile is made available to the employee. The cost of the automobile, in the formula, is its actual cost and not the cost that the employer is entitled to depreciate for tax purposes.[70]

6) Imputed Interest

Employees are taxable on the imputed benefit that they derive from low cost loans by virtue of their employment.[71] The Act deems a benefit to the employee where it is reasonable to conclude that but for the employment, the loan would not have been made to the employee.[72] For example, a loan to the employee's spouse is taxable to the employee if she obtains it by virtue of his employment.

The taxable benefit is equal to the interest imputed on the loan[73] at a rate that is determined quarterly. The rate is based on the average treasury bill rate of the first month during the preceding quarter.[74]

---

69   *Ibid*, subs 6(2.1).
70   See *Income Tax Regulations*, CRC, c 945, Schedule II, Class 10.1. The maximum is updated from time to time per s 7307(1)(b).
71   *ITA*, above note 2, subs 6(9).
72   *Ibid*, s 80.4(1.1).
73   *Ibid*, s 80.4(1).
74   *Income Tax Regulations*, above note 70, s 4301.

The *effective* after-tax cost of a low-cost loan is considerably lower than the cost of commercial loans.

Example

Assume that a taxpayer with a marginal tax rate of 50 percent receives an interest-free loan of $100,000 from her employer when the prescribed rate is 8 percent. The imputed interest is calculated as follows:

Taxable benefit (8% × $100,000)	$8,000
Tax thereon (50% × $8,000)	$4,000
Effective after-tax cost of loan	
($4,000 ÷ $100,000)	4%

Example

Assume that an individual receives a loan of $150,000 by virtue of her employment. She pays $8,000 interest on the loan and a corporation related to the employer pays $3,000 interest on her behalf. The prescribed rate of interest is 12 percent and the loan is outstanding throughout the year.

Then:

Prescribed rate × loan amount	
(12% × $150,000)	$18,000
Add amounts paid by third party	3,000
	21,000
Less amounts paid on loan	
($8,000 + $3,000)	(11,000)
Taxable benefit	$10,000

---

a) Exclusions

The imputed interest rules do not apply if the rate at which an employee borrows from his or her employer is equal to, or greater than, the prevailing commercial rate for parties dealing with each other at arm's length.[75] In these circumstances, there is no benefit.

b) Deemed Payments

An employee deemed to receive imputed interest is also deemed to have paid an equivalent amount pursuant to a legal obligation.[76] Hence, any interest imputed on a loan or indebtedness used for the purpose of earning income (for example, the purchase of shares) is deductible as interest expense.[77]

---

75   *ITA*, above note 2, subs 80.4(3).
76   *Ibid*, s 80.5.
77   *Ibid*, subpara 20(1)(c)(i).

7) Forgiveness of Loan

Where an employer forgives a loan to an employee, the principal amount of the loan is included in the employee's income at the time that the employer forgives the loan.[78] An imputed interest benefit is not included in income in the year that the employer forgives the loan.[79]

8) Stock Option Plans

a) Timing and Valuation

The taxation of stock options raises special problems of timing and valuation. Assume, for example, that an employer grants its corporate executive an option to purchase 1000 shares of its stock at $10 a share at any time in the next three years. The shares trade at $12 on the day that the employer grants the option. The shares are non-transferable. The executive can exercise the options only if he is an employee of the corporation when he triggers the options. The executive exercises the option in Year 2 when the shares are trading at $50 a share and sells the shares in Year 3 for $60 a share. The executive makes an overall profit of $50,000.

There are three questions: (1) should we treat all of the gain as employment compensation? (2) when should we tax the profit? and (3) how much of the profit, if any, should we tax?

We can break down the $50,000 profit into at least three components:

- Year 1 profit on the day the option is granted: $2,000
- Year 2 profit when the option is exercised: $38,000
- Year 3 profit when the shares are sold: $10,000

The common law rule is that stock option benefits are taxable in the year in which the option is granted.[80] This is so regardless that the taxpayer has not sold the stock and realized a gain. The option represents compensation for personal service and accretion of wealth, albeit only on paper. Hence, any benefit should be taxable as employment income.

The second question is more troublesome and raises issues of timing and value. To be sure, the executive theoretically increases his net wealth in Year 1 when he acquires a contractual right of $12,000 value. At that time, however, there are several uncertainties. The options have

---

78 *Ibid*, subs 6(15).
79 *Ibid*, para 80.4(3)(b). See also IT-421R2, above note 64 at para 11.
80 See *Abbott v Philbin*, [1961] AC 352 (HL); *Commissioner v Lobue*, 351 US 243 (1956).

value but only if the executive continues as an employee with the corporation. The price of the stock may decline before he exercises the options. It is also difficult to value benefits from unexercised options, particularly where the company restricts the right to dispose of the underlying shares ("golden handcuffs").

Of course, we can tax the employee immediately on the $2,000 gain and then allow for retroactive adjustments for price declines, etc., or discount the value of the benefit to take the uncertainties into account. Both of these choices create uncertainty and are prone to valuation disputes. Alternatively, we can delay taxation until the employee exercises the options and crystallizes his profit of $40,000.

There is a trade-off in both solutions. If we delay the tax, the taxpayer defers his liability and benefits therefrom. If we tax the employee in Year 1, we must discount the value of the benefits for risk and uncertainty, which will likely stimulate litigation.

The third question raises separate policy issues. Clearly, the final $10,000 gain derives from holding the shares that the taxpayer acquires in Year 2. This portion of the gain derives from the taxpayer's investment decision to hold the shares rather than from his continued employment. Thus, we tax this amount as a gain from the sale of capital assets and not as employment compensation.

b) The Statutory Scheme

Section 7 addresses the problems of timing and valuation. The basic rule is simple: option benefits are taxable if they derive from employment because they are in effect an alternative to cash compensation. The statutory scheme, however, is more complex, because the rules also serve other economic objectives, such as equity, ownership in Canadian corporations and employee equity participation.

We must answer three questions:

1) Does the option benefit derive from employment?
2) When is the benefit taxable?
3) What is the value of the benefit?

i)   "By Virtue of Employment"

An employee is taxable on stock option benefits only if she derives the benefits by virtue of employment.[81] Subject to tax treaty provisions, non-residents are also taxable on stock options in respect of employment in Canada, regardless of where they exercise the options.[82] Stock

---

81   *ITA*, above note 2, subs 7(5).
82   *Hale v Canada*, [1992] 2 CTC 379 (FCA).

options issued for other considerations (for example, as a gift or in return for guaranteeing a loan) are not a benefit from employment.[83]

ii) Timing

The benefit from a stock option arises when the employee acquires his shares at a price less than their value. We determine the time of acquisition by reference to general principles of commercial practice, as modified by statute. For example, a federal corporation may not issue shares until they are fully paid for in money or in property.[84] Thus, under federal corporate law, a taxpayer cannot acquire shares in a corporation until he pays for the shares. In some other jurisdictions, however, shares may be purchased and paid for at different times on an installment basis. In these circumstances, the employee acquires his shares when the contract is made, even though he does not pay for shares until a later date.

iii) Valuation

The value of the benefit is determined when the employee acquires his shares or exercises the option.[85] The benefit is equal to the difference between the cost of the option to the employee, any amount that he pays for the shares, and the value of the shares at the time when he acquires them from the plan.[86] For example, assume that an individual acquires 100 shares at a cost of $10 per share when the shares have a value of $15 per share and that he pays $1 per share for the option. The value of the taxable benefit is $4 per share or $400. At a tax rate of 50 percent, the net cost of the benefit is $200. The individual would be in the same financial position if the employer paid him an additional $400.

"Value" means "fair market value."[87] In the case of publicly traded securities, stock market prices are usually indicative of fair market value of non-control block shares. The valuation of shares of private corporations is more difficult. Shares of private corporations are generally valued by reference to estimated future cash flows and the adjusted

---

83   *Busby*, above note 47 (options granted by virtue of taxpayer's "special" relationship with principal shareholder and for guaranteeing corporation's loans were not taxable as employment income). See also Interpretation Bulletin IT-113R4, "Benefits to Employees: Stock Options" (7 August 1996).

84   *Canada Business Corporations Act*, RSC 1985, c C-44, subs 25(3); see also *Business Corporations Act*, RSO 1990, c B.16, subs 23(3).

85   *Steen v Canada*, [1988] 1 CTC 256 (FCA), aff'g [1986] 2 CTC 394 (TD).

86   *ITA*, above note 2, para 7(1)(a).

87   See, for example, *Steen v Canada*, above note 85.

net value of assets. The *pro rata* value of the corporation may be adjusted to reflect a discount for minority interests and lack of liquidity.

iv) Options Issued by Canadian-Controlled Private Corporations

There are special rules that apply to Canadian-controlled private corporations (CCPCs). These rules are essentially incentive provisions to promote equity participation in Canadian corporations.

A taxpayer's taxable benefit from shares that she acquires from a CCPC's stock plan in an arm's length transaction is reduced if she holds the shares for at least two years.[88] The employee may defer recognition of any benefit that she derives from the stock options until she disposes of the shares. This rule delays the point of income recognition and defers the tax payable. The longer the employee holds on to the shares, the greater the value of the tax deferral. When the employee disposes of the shares, she is taxable on only 50 percent of the value of the benefit derived.[89]

An employee who disposes of her shares in a CCPC within two years from the date that she acquires them is usually taxable on the full value of any benefit derived in the year that the employee disposes of the shares.[90] An exchange of options or of shares as a consequence of an amalgamation or a share-for-share exchange is not a disposition for the purposes of the two-year rule.[91] The Act deems shares that are identical properties to be disposed of in the order they are acquired.[92]

The following illustrates the difference between the two different types of stock option plans:

> **Example**
> Assume that an employee acquires shares in the following circumstances:
>
> *Case (A): General Rules*
> Shares with a fair market value (FMV) of $100 for $76.
>
> *Case (B): CCPC*
> Shares with FMV of $100 for $76 from a CCPC and holds the shares for two years.

---

88   *ITA*, above note 2, subs 7(1.1) and para 110(1)(d.1). This is so whether the shares are issued by the employer corporation or by another CCPC with which the employer does not deal at arm's length.

89   See *ibid*, subs 7(1.1) and para 110(1)(d.1).

90   *Ibid*, subpara 110(1)(d.1)(ii). But see Interpretation Bulletin IT-113R4, above note 83 at para 19.

91   *ITA*, *ibid*, subss 7(1.4) & 7(1.5).

92   *Ibid*, subs 7(1.3).

Then:	(A) General Rules	(B) CCPC
Acquisition of shares:		
FMV at acquisition	$100	–
Cost of acquisition	(76)	76
Stock option benefit	24	nil
Adjusted cost base (ACB) of shares:		
Cost of acquisition	$76	$76
Add:		
Stock option benefit	24	–
ACB of shares	$100	$76
Disposition of shares:		
Sale price	$100	$100
ACB	(100)	(76)
Capital gain	–	–
Stock option benefit	–	24
50% deduction	–	(12)
Net		$12
Inclusions in income:		
Upon acquisition	$24	$–
Upon disposition	–	12
Total	$24	$12

v) Adjusted Cost Base of Shares

The inclusion of stock option benefits in income would lead to double taxation if the full gain was taxed again when the employee disposes of his shares. Hence, to prevent double taxation, the full value of any benefit included in the employee's income is added to the cost base of the shares acquired.[93] Thus, any subsequent gain or loss on the disposition of the shares is calculated by reference to the adjusted cost base of the shares. For example, where an employee of a public company acquires shares at $12 per share when the shares have a market value of $18 per share, the full benefit of $6 is added to the cost base of his shares. Hence, the adjusted cost base of the shares increases to $18. If the employee sells the shares for $35 per share, he will have a capital gain of $17 per share.

---

93   *Ibid*, para 53(1)(j).

9) Counselling Benefits

Employer-provided counselling services for employees are not taxable as benefits from employment if the counselling is in respect of:[94]

- The employee's (or related individual's) physical or mental health;
- Re-employment for employees whose employment has been terminated; or
- Retirement.

These exclusions from employment income are accommodations for hardship cases and are intended to facilitate re-employment.

10) Directors' Fees

A director of a corporation holds an "office."[95] Directors' fees are taxable as income from an office.[96] Where a director's fees are paid directly to a third party or are turned over by the director to a third party (for example, to a partnership of which she is a member), the CRA administratively permits the fees to be taxable as the income of the ultimate recipient and not the director.[97]

E. DEDUCTIONS FROM EMPLOYMENT INCOME

Employment income is generally taxable on a "gross" basis without deductions. Subsection 8(2) limits the deduction of expenses from employment income to those that the Act specifically authorizes. As we shall see later, the Act taxes business income on a "net" basis—that is, net of deductions. Because of this difference in the treatment of deductions, most individuals would prefer to be considered as independent contractors for tax purposes.

1) Salesperson's Expenses

A salesperson may deduct expenses from employment income if he is:[98]

---

94   *Ibid*, subpara 6(1)(a)(iv).
95   *Ibid*, subs 248(1).
96   *Ibid*, subs 5(1) and para 6(1)(c).
97   See Interpretation Bulletin IT-377R, "Director's, Executor's and Juror's Fees" (27 January 1989) and rulings document 2006-0193141 E5.
98   *ITA*, above note 2, para 8(1)(f) and subs 8(9).

- Employed to sell property or negotiate contracts;
- Required to pay his business expenses;
- Ordinarily required to carry out his duties away from the employer's regular place of business;
- Remunerated, at least in part, by commissions related to the volume of sales; and
- Not in receipt of a tax-free allowance for travelling expenses that is excluded from income.[99]

The employee must file a prescribed form where the employer certifies that the employee has satisfied the above conditions.[100]

The deduction is limited to the commission income that he receives in the year. The employee must file a prescribed form where the employer certifies that the employee has satisfied all the above conditions.[101]

2) Capital Cost Allowance

A salesperson may also deduct capital cost allowance (CCA) and interest expense in respect of a motor vehicle or aircraft that she uses in the performance of employment-related duties.[102] The claim for CCA and interest expense is not limited to commission income and may be used to reduce income from other sources. The expenses claimed must be reasonable in the circumstances.[103]

3) Travelling Expenses

Employees who:

- Are ordinarily required to carry on their employment duties away from their employer's regular place of business,
- Are required to pay their own travelling expenses, and
- Do not receive a tax-free allowance,

---

99 *Ibid*, subpara 6(1)(b)(v). *Cossette v MNR* (1955), 13 Tax ABC 170 (where the allowance is unreasonably low, the taxpayer may include the allowance in income and deduct his actual expenses.)
100 *Ibid*, subs 8(10).
101 *Laliberté v MNR* (1953), 9 Tax ABC 145 (travelling salesman allowed to deduct rent for sample rooms); *Sherman v MNR*, [1970] Tax ABC 618 (advertising expenses of securities salesman allowed as deduction).
102 *ITA*, above note 2, para 8(1)(j); *ITA Regulations*, above note 70, s 1100(1).
103 *ITA*, *ibid*, s 67. *Niessen v MNR* (1960), 60 DTC 489 (TAB) (claim for CCA on Cadillac disallowed as excessive).

are allowed to deduct their travelling expense[104] to the extent that they are not reimbursed by their employer.[105] In this context, "ordinarily" means as a matter of regular occurrence.[106] The deduction is available to all employees and is not restricted to commissioned salespeople.

A salesperson who claims a deduction for expenses under paragraph 8(1)(f), however, cannot also claim travelling expenses under paragraph 8(1)(h). The salesperson may, however, claim the deduction under whichever of the two provisions is most advantageous to him or her.

a) Inadequate Compensation

An employee who is not fully reimbursed for her employment-related expenses may be able to claim the shortfall as an expense deduction. For example, an employee who spends 30 cents a kilometre to run a motor vehicle and is reimbursed only 20 cents a kilometre may claim an expense deduction equal to 10 cents per kilometre travelled on the employer's business if she can establish that the allowance was unreasonably low.[107]

b) Requirement of Travel

Deductibility of travelling expenses depends upon the employee being required to travel away from his or her employer's place of business. This requirement need not be expressly stated in the employment contract, but may be implied from the surrounding circumstances, such as employer expectations, industry practice, etc.[108] The employer must, however, certify that the employee meets all of the statutory requirements.[109]

---

104 *ITA, ibid*, paras 8(1)(h) or (h.1).
105 *Ibid*, subparas 6(1)(b)(v), (vi) & (vii).
106 *Canada v Healy*, [1978] CTC 355 (FCTD), rev'd [1979] CTC 44 (FCA) (jockey club employee not "ordinarily" reporting for work at Fort Erie but spending one third of his time there); *Canada v Patterson*, [1982] CTC 371 (FCTD) (school principal who made fifty-six trips to other schools "ordinarily" required to carry out duties in different places; expenses deductible).
107 *Peters v MNR*, [1986] 2 CTC 2221 (TCC). But see *Gauvin v MNR* (1979), 79 DTC 696 (TRB) and *Hudema v Canada*, [1994] CTC 42 (FCTD) and Interpretation Bulletin IT-522R, "Vehicle, Travel and Sales Expenses of Employees" (29 March 1996).
108 *Moore v MNR*, [1987] 1 CTC 319 (FCTD) (principal would have received unfavourable performance reviews had she not attended meetings; expenses allowed); *Rozen v Canada*, [1986] 1 CTC 50 (FCTD) (requirement to use automobile in course of employment implied term of contract); *Canada v Cival*, [1983] CTC 153 (FCA) (deduction denied where taxpayer not required to use own car under contract of employment).
109 *ITA*, above note 2, subs 8(10).

4) Motor Vehicles and Aircraft

Subject to the restrictions in respect of travelling expenses, an employee may also deduct motor vehicle and aircraft expenses incurred in the course of employment.[110] Any interest paid on money borrowed to purchase, and capital cost allowance resulting from the ownership of, a motor vehicle or aircraft is deductible to the extent that the vehicle or aircraft is used in the course of employment.[111]

5) Meals

An employee may claim 50 percent of meal expenses as part of travel costs if he consumes the meal while away for at least 12 hours from the municipality in which his employer is located.[112]

6) Legal Expenses

An employee can deduct legal expenses that he pays to collect an amount owed to him if the amount would, if received, be taxable as income from employment. Legal expenses subsequently reimbursed are taxable as employment income under paragraph 6(1)(j) except to the extent that they were previously included in income or reduced the legal expense deduction.[113]

Legal expenses associated with establishing a right to a pensions benefit or retiring allowance (including payments for wrongful dismissal) are also deductible.[114]

7) Musicians

An employed musician who must furnish her own musical instruments may deduct amounts that she pays on account of the maintenance,

---

110 *Ibid*, paras 8(1)(f) and (h).
111 *Ibid*, paras 8(1)(j) and subs 8(9).
112 *Ibid*, subs 8(4) and s 67.1.
113 *Ibid*, para 8(1)(b). See, for example, *Loo v Canada*, 2004 FCA 249 (plaintiff one of fifty-five BC lawyers suing their employer, the federal Department of Justice, because they are paid less than Justice lawyers in Toronto; legal fees deductible; not relevant to determine whether claim is well founded in law or likely to succeed).
114 *ITA, ibid*, para 60(o.1). See, for example, *Atkinson v Canada*, 2004 TCC 445 (Informal Procedure) (police officer allowed to deduct legal fees of $32,226.49 since he would have lost his job and pension had he not successfully defended the criminal charges made against him).

nsurance or rental of such instruments.[115] Where the musician owns the instrument used in employment, she is also entitled to depreciate it at a rate of 20 percent on a declining balance basis.[116]

8) Canadian Residents Employed Overseas

As a general rule, Canadian residents are taxable on their global income regardless of where they earn the income.[117] Residence-based taxation ensures that individuals are taxed on an equal basis on their ability to pay tax on income without reference to its geographic source. This promotes horizontal equity.

Some residents employed outside Canada, however, are eligible for special tax credits on their overseas employment income. These concessions are provided for "competitive reasons" to allow Canadian employers to compete for international contracts by reducing their net payroll costs. The tax credits put Canadian employers on a competitive footing with foreign companies that receive similar tax subsidies from their governments. Thus, we trade off equity for economic competitiveness.

The overseas employment tax credit has three constraints. A Canadian resident is entitled to the credit only if:[118]

- He is employed by a "specified employer";[119]
- His employment-related duties are performed outside Canada for a period of more than six consecutive months; and
- The employer is engaged in the construction, exploration, engineering or agricultural business, or in a prescribed activity.

The tax credit is equal to 80 percent of the employee's net overseas earnings up to a maximum of $80,000 annually. The credit is prorated over the number of days the employee works abroad in a year and is applied against the taxes that he or she would otherwise pay.

9) Other Deductions

Section 8 also lists other deductions from employment income. Here are a few of the major deductions:

---

115 *ITA, ibid*, para 8(1)(p).
116 *Income Tax Regulations*, above note 70, s 1100(1)(a)(viii).
117 *ITA*, above note 2, subs 2(1); s 3.
118 *Ibid*, subs 122.3(1).
119 *Ibid*, para 122.3(2).

Type of Expense	Statutory Reference
• Annual professional membership dues required to maintain professional status.	subpara. 8(1)(i)(i)*
• Costs of supplies consumed in the performance of duties of employment.	subpara. 8(1)(i)(iii)
• Employment expenses of artists	para. 8(1)(q)
• Trade union or association annual dues	subpara. 8(1)(i)(iv)
• Annual union dues	subpara. 8(1)(i)(v)
• Expenses of railway company employees employed away from ordinary place of residence	para. 8(1)(e); IC 73-21R8

* *Lucas v MNR*, [1987] 2 CTC 23, 87 DTC 5277 (FCTD).

F. LIMITATIONS ON DEDUCTIONS

1) Subsection 8(2)

The deductibility of an employment expense depends on two principal criteria:

1) Authority for the deduction, and
2) Reasonableness of the amount claimed.[120]

Subsection 8(2) tells us that the deduction must be specifically authorized. There are no deductions from employment income under general commercial principles.

The reasonableness of an expense is always a question of fact taking into account comparables within business and industry.

2) Food and Entertainment

The Act restricts the deduction of these expenditures to 50 percent of the amount actually paid.[121]

G. CONCLUSION

The tax provisions dealing with employment income affect millions of employees. Since employment income is the largest source of public revenues, the CRA is ever vigilant in taxing such income. We have seen,

---

120 *Ibid*, s 67.
121 *Ibid*, subs 67.1(1).

however, that even this small area of tax law is complex and subject to inconsistent legislation and judicial interpretation. The inconsistency detracts from the equitable treatment of employees. The taxation of relocation benefits, for example, produces inconsistent results for employees who move to new locations.

The presumption against the non-deductibility of employment expenses is understandable in the interests of administrative convenience. It does, however, place an unfair burden on employees who incur employment-related expenses that are not enumerated in the Act. As we will see in subsequent chapters, the substantial differences between the generous treatment of business expenses and the strict regulation of employment income are a powerful incentive for individuals to recharacterize income from one source into the other. Classification may be the beginning of wisdom but it also makes tax law that much more complex.

FURTHER READINGS

ATIYAH, PATRICK. *Vicarious Liability in the Law of Torts* (London: Butterworths, 1967).

HANSEN, BRIAN, VERN KRISHNA, & JAMES RENDALL, EDS. "The Taxation of Employees" in *Canadian Taxation* (Toronto: De Boo, 1981) at 187.

KRISHNA, VERN. "The Scope of Employment Benefits" (1994) Can Curr Tax C-55.

KHAN, AN. "Who Is a Servant?" (1979) 53 Austl L J 832.

CHAPTER 7

BUSINESS AND PROPERTY INCOME

All income for tax purposes is calculated by source. In this chapter we look at three sources: business income, investment income and capital gains. We distinguish between the three sources of income so that we apply the proper rules to each.

The general feature of business income is activity (a combination of labour and capital); capital gains and losses arise from the disposition of property; and investment (property) income is the passive yield from property. There are, however, a myriad of statutory rules that modify each of the three sources.

Although most of the rules in subdivision (b) apply to both business and property income, the two sources of income are distinct. There are some rules that apply only to business and others that apply only to property. Hence, we start with the distinction between "business" and "property" and then move to "capital gains."

A. THE MEANING OF "BUSINESS"

The Act does not define "business." Subsection 248(1) merely says that "business" includes a profession, calling, trade, manufacture or under-taking of any kind whatever, and, for most purposes, also includes an adventure or concern in the nature of trade.[1]

---

1   *Income Tax Act*, RSC 1985, c 1 (5th Supp) [*ITA*], subs 248(1) "business"; see s 253 for an extended meaning of "carrying on business" as it relates to non-residents.

Generally, "business" refers to activity—whether economic, industrial, commercial or financial. The traditional common law definition of business is "anything which occupies the time and attention and labour of a man for the purpose of profit."[2] As the English Court of Appeal said in *Erichsen v Last*:[3]

> I do not think there is any principle of law which lays down what carrying on of trade is. There are a multitude of incidents which together make the carrying on [of] a trade, but I know of no one distinguishing incident which makes a practice a carrying on of trade, and another practice not a carrying on of trade. If I may use the expression, it is a compound fact made up of a variety of incidents.

A "trade" is the business of selling goods, with a view to profit, that the trader has either manufactured or purchased.[4]

The quintessential characteristics of business are activity, enterprise, entrepreneurship, commercial risk and the pursuit of profit. "Business" implies activity and profit motive.[5] The pursuit of profit differentiates a trade or business from a hobby or pastime. Thus, the first question to determine is whether the taxpayer undertakes the activity in pursuit of profit or as a personal endeavour or hobby. Pursuit of profit, and not its actual realization, is the key element in distinguishing between commercial ventures and hobbies.

Paragraph 18(1)(a) restates the necessity of the profit motive test in a negative way: a taxpayer is not entitled to deduct an expense unless she incurs the expenditure for the purpose of gaining or producing income from a business or property.

The purpose of the pursuit of profit distinguishes between commercial and personal activities. Hence, one looks to see if there are indicia of commerciality or badges of trade. The test has relevance only if there is some personal or hobby element to the taxpayer's activity. It

---

2   *Stewart v Canada*, 2002 SCC 46 [*Stewart*]; see also *Smith v Anderson* (1880), 15 Ch D 247 at 258 (Eng CA); *Terminal Dock and Warehouse Co v MNR*, [1968] 2 Ex CR 78, [1968] CTC 78 (Ex Ct), aff'd (1968), 68 DTC 5316 (SCC).

3   (1881), 4 TC 422 at 423 (Eng CA).

4   *Grainger & Son v Gough*, [1896] AC 325 (HL).

5   See, for example, *Fleming v MNR*, [1987] 2 CTC 2113 (TCC) (university professors did not have expectation of profit in publishing research); *Shaker v MNR*, [1987] 2 CTC 2156 (TCC) (keen desire; talent and determination did not necessitate reasonable expectation of profit in an undertaking); *Kusick v MNR* (1987), [1988] 1 CTC 2052 (TCC) (taxpayer changed type of business, obviously realized no chance of profits); *Ianson v MNR* (1987), [1988] 1 CTC 2088 (TCC) (horse racing carried on as hobby); *Issacharoff v MNR* (1987), [1988] 1 CTC 2006 (TCC).

has no relevance if the activity is clearly commercial. If the activity is clearly commercial (for example, a law practice), it is irrelevant whether it actually generates income or loss. It is not for the revenue authorities to determine *ex post* whether the taxpayer had a reasonable expectation of profit (REOP) in the pursuit of a commercial venture.[6] If the activity is not a personal endeavour or hobby, the next question is whether the source of commercial income is business or property income.[7]

If a venture has both commercial and personal elements, one must determine if the commercial element is sufficient to characterize the income as a source of income for the purposes of the Act.[8] Thus, we look to see if there are sufficient commercial indicia, such as adequate financing, time devoted to activity, or industry norms.

The profit motive test is crucial to the integrity of the tax system. It draws the line between providing limitless tax subsidies for personal pursuits with minimal economic flavour and economic enterprises conducted on a commercial basis for profit. Taxpayers should not expect other taxpayers to subsidize their personal hobbies. On the other hand, the test should not be so stringent that it discourages entrepreneurial activities.

The term "business" is not the same as REOP. In *Stewart v Canada* (*Stewart*), the Supreme Court effectively overruled the REOP test in commercial contexts:

> In our view, the reasonable expectation of profit analysis cannot be maintained as an independent source test. To do so would run contrary to the principle that courts should avoid judicial innovation and rule-making in tax law . . . . In addition, the reasonable expectation of profit test is imprecise, causing an unfortunate degree of uncertainty for taxpayers. As well, the nature of the test has encouraged a hindsight assessment of the business judgment of taxpayers in order to deny losses incurred in bona fide, albeit unsuccessful, commercial ventures [*per* Iacobucci and Bastarache JJ].[9]

Stewart did not completely abolish the REOP test but rather confined it to cases where there is some personal element to the activity in question.[10]

---

6   As the Supreme Court of Canada said in *Stewart*, above note 2 at para 53: "With respect, in our view, courts have erred in the past in applying the REOP test to activities such as law practices and restaurants where there exists no such personal element."

7   See *Stewart, ibid.*

8   *Ibid.*

9   *Ibid* at para 4.

10 See *Nadoryk v Canada*, 2003 FCA 458.

B. THE MEANING OF "PROPERTY"

Investment (property) income is the *yield* from property. For example: shares yield dividends, bonds yield interest, intellectual property yields royalties, real property yields rent. The Act defines "property" to include virtually every type of economic interest:[11]

> "[P]roperty" means property of any kind whatever whether real or personal, immovable or movable, tangible or intangible, or corporeal or incorporeal and, without restricting the generality of the foregoing, includes
> (a) a right of any kind whatever, a share or a chose in action,
> (b) unless a contrary intention is evident, money,
> (c) a timber resource property, and
> (d) the work in progress of a business that is a profession.

A right of property includes the right to possess, use, lend, alienate, consume or otherwise possess it to the exclusion of others.[12] Thus, a right of property represents a bundle of distinct rights. For example, the right of ownership is a right distinct from the right of possession. One can own without possessing and possess without owning.

There is, however, one important exclusion: "income from property" does *not* include a capital gain from the property itself; "loss from property" does not include a capital loss from the property.[13] Gains and losses from selling a property are a separate source of income to which completely different rules apply.[14]

---

11 · *ITA*, above note 1, subs 248(1) "property"; see also *Fasken Estate v MNR*, [1948] CTC 265 (Ex Ct); *Jones v Skinner* (1835), 5 LJ Ch 87 at 90: "It is well-known, that the word 'property' is the most comprehensive of all the terms that can be used, inasmuch as it is indicative and descriptive of every possible interest the party can have." See also *Manrell v Canada*, 2003 FCA 128 (in the context of non-competition payments).

12   *Western Electric Co v MNR*, [1969] CTC 274 at 289 (Ex Ct), aff'd [1971] CTC 96 (SCC) (amounts paid to appellant claimed not to be rentals, royalties or otherwise for the use of property; Court determined that payments equivalent to royalties under treaty); *Canada v St John Shipbuilding & Dry Dock Co*, [1980] CTC 352 (FCA), leave to appeal to SCC refused (1981), 34 NR 348 (lump sums paid for computerized information not related to use, sales or benefit derived; not within classes of property in treaty).

13   *ITA*, above note 1, subs 9(3).

14   See Subdivision c, *ibid*.

C. BUSINESS INCOME VS. CAPITAL GAINS

The importance of characterization on account of income or capital is crucial. Capital gains are taxed at lower effective tax rates than business income. In some cases, capital gains are completely exempt from tax.[15]

The Act does not define "capital gain" or "income." The purported definitions in paragraphs 39(1)(a) and (b) of the Act are circular and of minimal practical value. The distinction between "capital gains" and "income" derives essentially from the case law.

Business income is the gain from trading. Property income is the periodic yield of an investment itself. Capital gains derive from realization of the investment. The distinction is often put in the form of an analogy.[16]

> The fundamental relation of "capital" to "income" has been much discussed by economists, the former being likened to the tree or the land, the latter to the fruit or the crop; the former depicted as a reservoir supplied from springs, the latter as the outlet stream, to be measured by its flow during a period of time.

The tree is the capital that produces yield (the fruit). Income is the profit that derives when we sell the fruit in a trading transaction. A gain from the sale of the tree itself is capital gain. For example:

- A building is capital; rent derived from the building is income;
- Shares are capital; dividends on the shares are income; and
- Bonds are capital; interest payments on the bonds are income.

Thus, an investment in property represents capital, and the flow from the investment represents income. We saw earlier that the flow of income may be business income or property income.

Capital gains derive from a disposition of "capital property" or the underlying investment. Income gains derive from a sale of trading assets or as the yield from investments. Thus, the key to determining whether we have an income gain or a capital gain is in identifying whether we have sold trading assets or sold an investment.

---

15 See, for example, the exemption for principal residences and shares of small business corporations.
16 *Eisner v Macomber*, 252 US 189 at 206 (1920).

1) The Meaning of "Capital Property" or "Investment"

The fundamental question in the structure of capital gains transactions is: what is a "capital property" or "investment"? How do we recognize investments (the sale of which yields a capital gain) and trading assets (the sale of which yields business income)? This characterization is more problematic than it appears at first blush. For example, consider the following judicial statement:[17]

> It is quite a well-settled principle that where the owner of an ordinary investment chooses to realize it, and obtains a greater price for it than he originally acquired it at, the enhanced price is not profit . . . . But it is equally well established that enhanced values obtained from realisation or conversion of securities may be so assessable, where what is done is not merely a realisation or change of investment, but an act done in what is truly the carrying on, or carrying out, of a business.

The statement merely leads us to the next question: how do we know when a person is trading or investing?

The distinction between business income and capital gains cannot rest upon the taxpayer's desire to make a profit. Everyone wants to make a profit, whether they are trading or investing. Trading implies a profit-making scheme to earn income by buying and selling property. Investment implies acquiring and holding an asset for its potential yield, but with the possibility that the investment will, at some time, be sold for a profit. The distinction depends upon the taxpayer's intention at the time he purchases the property.

2) Taxpayer Intention

An "investment" is property that one acquires with the intention of holding or using it to produce income. Thus, in tax law, an investment is a means to an end. Where a taxpayer acquires property with an intention to trade — that is, to purchase and resell the property at a profit — any gain or loss from trading is business income (loss). Hence, the distinction between an investment and trading inventory depends not upon the nature of the property, but upon the intention with which the taxpayer acquires it.

For example, suppose A registers an Internet domain name for $100 and later sells it to B for $1,000. The characterization of the $900 gain depends upon A's intention at the time A registered the name.

---

17   *Californian Copper Syndicate Ltd v Harris* (1904), 5 Tax Cas 159 at 165–66 (Scot Ex Ct 2d Div).

If A's regular practice is to acquire and sell domain names, then the gain is business income. If, however, A acquires the name to use for her website and sells it to B when her plans change, the gain is a capital gain. The taxpayer's intention at the time he acquires the asset is the capital issue. The taxpayer's conduct, rather than any *ex post facto* declarations, usually provides the key to his intentions. There is, however, no single factor to evaluate a taxpayer's intentions. We look at the circumstances of each transaction and balance multiple indicia to determine the taxpayer's intention. Some judges say: "a common sense appreciation of *all* the guiding features will provide the ultimate answer."[18] This may be satisfactory in judicial decision making, but is not very helpful for taxpayers who must make business and tax filing decisions.

In addition to looking at a taxpayer's primary intention for the purpose of characterizing income or gain, we also look to see if the taxpayer had a secondary intention to trade. Where a taxpayer has a *secondary* intention to trade, any gain or loss resulting from the trade is business income (loss).[19] As with intention, secondary intention to trade is also a question of fact and the trier of fact may draw inferences from the taxpayer's conduct.[20] The determination is on a balance of probabilities.[21] Hence, taxpayer credibility is always in issue. Indeed, courts often use secondary intention as a surrogate for determining credibility.

A taxpayer has a secondary intention to trade if the possibility of early resale at a profit was a *motivating* consideration at the time that she acquired the property. Thus, the critical times are just before, and the moment that, the taxpayer enters into a binding agreement to

---

18 *BP Australia Ltd v Commissioner of Taxation of the Commonwealth of Australia*, [1966] AC 224 at 264 (PC), Lord Pearce, approved by the SCC in *Canada v Johns-Manville Canada Inc*, [1985] 2 SCR 46 at 56 (thorough analysis of law; purchase of land to allow expansion of mining pit so that slope could be maintained at safe angle was an operational expense); see also *Canadian General Electric Co v Canada*, [1987] 1 CTC 180 (FCA) (heavy water production "know-how" and licence sold; amount received was income because sales replaced taxpayer's business); *Paco Corp v Canada*, [1980] CTC 409 (FCTD) (losses for demonstration plant constituted operating expense; determined by taxpayer's intention).

19 *Bayridge Estates Ltd v MNR*, [1959] CTC 158 (Ex Ct) (profit one of motives in sale of raw land); *Fogel v MNR*, [1959] CTC 227 (Ex Ct) (bylaws necessitated abandonment of building plans; subsequent sale for profit found to have been alternative intention); *Regal Heights Ltd v MNR*, [1960] SCR 902 (plans for shopping centre frustrated and parcels of land sold; profits of highly speculative venture constituted income).

20 *Reicher v MNR*, [1975] CTC 659 (FCA).

21 *Factory Carpet Ltd v Canada*, [1985] 2 CTC 267 (FCTD) [*Factory Carpet*].

purchase the property in question.[22] Although motive to trade or invest is a subjective criterion, we determine its absence or presence by inference from objective evidence—that is, the taxpayer's conduct and the circumstances surrounding the particular transaction.[23]

"Business" includes an adventure in the nature of trade—generally an isolated transaction. A gain or loss that results from a taxpayer's response to a changing investment climate, however, is not an adventure in the nature of trade. An intention at the time of acquiring an asset that one will sell the asset if the purchase proves unprofitable merely indicates prudent planning. It does not imply a secondary intention to engage in business or an adventure in the nature of trade.

There is a difference, however, between a taxpayer who responds to a changing investment climate and a taxpayer who actively contemplates the potential of profit on resale at the time that he invests. Where the potential of profit is a motivating consideration, it may suggest a secondary intention to engage in an adventure in the nature of trade.[24]

a)   Determining Taxpayer Intention

A taxpayer's intention, whether primary or secondary, is always a question of fact. We look at various criteria as aids in determining intention. No single criterion is conclusive. The following, however, are particularly relevant: (1) number of similar transactions, (2) nature of the asset, (3) related activity, (4) corporate objects and powers, and (5) degree of organization.

i)   Number of Similar Transactions

Repetitive behaviour may suggest trading. Evidence that the taxpayer engaged in similar transactions to the one at issue provides equivocal,

---

22   *Dickson v MNR*, [1977] CTC 64 (FCA) (resolution to sell land dated 1964 but agreement dated 1967; purchaser's financial plight at date of signing agreement relevant to intention); *Racine v MNR*, [1965] CTC 150 (Ex Ct) (to constitute "secondary intention," purchaser must have possibility of reselling as operating motivation for acquisition at moment of purchase).

23   *Reicher v MNR* (1975), 76 DTC 6001 at 6004, Le Dain JA (FCA): "The issue on this appeal is whether at the time they acquired the property the appellant . . . had a secondary intention, as an operating motivation for such acquisition, to sell the property at a profit should a suitable opportunity present itself."

See also *Hiwako Investments Ltd v MNR*, [1978] CTC 378 (FCA) [*Hiwako Investments*] (whether or not the onus is on taxpayer to disprove minister's stated assumption that taxpayer primarily motivated by intention to trade); *Kit-Win Holdings (1973) Ltd v Canada*, [1981] CTC 43 (FCTD) (minister did not precisely allege exclusive motivation to develop property for profit).

24   *Hiwako Investments*, ibid at 383.

but potentially prejudicial, proof he is a trader and engages in a business. All other things being equal (although they rarely are), the greater the number of similar past transactions, the greater the likelihood that the gain or loss is business income or loss.

The converse, however, does not apply with equal force. Merely because a transaction is an isolated event does not mean that it is not business income or loss. As the Exchequer Court stated:[25]

> while it is recognized that, as a general rule, an isolated transaction of purchase and sale outside the course of the taxpayer's ordinary business does not constitute the carrying on of a trade or business so as to render the profit therefrom liable to the income tax . . . it is also established that the fact that a transaction is an isolated one does not exclude it from the category of trading or business transactions of such a nature as to attract income tax to the profit therefrom.

A gain from an isolated transaction can give rise to business income or loss if the transaction is either closely related to the taxpayer's ordinary business activities or the property disposed of is a "trading" property.[26] Lord President Clyde put it succinctly:[27]

> A single plunge may be enough provided it is shown to the satisfaction of the Court that the plunge is made in the waters of trade.

ii) *Nature of Asset*

The nature of the asset can be important in characterizing any gain or loss from its disposition. Land, for example, particularly raw land, is viewed suspiciously as a trading asset, rather than an investment asset, particularly if coupled with development. This attitude also extends to the sale of shares of corporations incorporated solely for the purpose of holding raw land.[28] In contrast, share transactions are generally on account of capital unless there is a pattern of regular trading. As the Supreme Court observed:[29]

> a person who puts money into a business enterprise by the purchase of the shares of a company on an isolated occasion, and not as a

---

25 *Atlantic Sugar Refineries Ltd v MNR* (1948), 49 DTC 507 at 511 (Ex Ct), aff'd [1949] SCR 706 [*Atlantic Sugar*].

26 *MNR v Taylor*, [1956] CTC 189 (Ex Ct).

27 *Balgownie Land Trust Ltd v IRC* (1929), 14 Tax Cas 684 at 691 (Scot).

28 *Fraser v MNR*, [1964] SCR 657; see also *Mould v MNR*, (1986), 86 DTC 6087 at 6089 (FCTD) (156 acres of land sole asset of corporation: " . . . the acquisition of the shares was merely a method of obtaining an interest in the land").

29 *Irrigation Industries Ltd v MNR*, [1962] SCR 346 at 351 [*Irrigation Industries*].

part of his regular business, cannot be said to have engaged in an adventure in the nature of trade merely because the purchase was speculative in that, at that time, he did not intend to hold the shares indefinitely, but intended, if possible, to sell them at a profit as soon as he reasonably could. I think that there must be clearer indications of "trade" than this before it can be said that there has been an adventure in the nature of trade.

Thus, a purchase of shares with an intention to resell at a profit is not, *by itself*, likely to result in the characterization of any gain or loss from their sale as resulting from an adventure in the nature of trade. An isolated transaction in shares, however, can give rise to business income or loss if there are other factors that indicate an intention to trade.[30] A "quick flip" of shares may suggest a trading intention unless it can be explained on other grounds. For example, an isolated transaction in speculative "penny shares" may give rise to business income or loss if the taxpayer is acting like a promoter. *A fortiori*, speculative and highly leveraged trading in high risk, non-yielding, shares and options may be seen as trading in securities.[31]

An expectation of profit is not, by itself, sufficient to characterize a transaction as an adventure in the nature of trade. Certain types of assets, though, and typically commodities (for example, copper or pork bellies) that cannot possibly provide any investment yield, are usually "trading assets." As Lord Carmont stated:

> this means that, although in certain cases it is important to know whether a venture is isolated or not, that information is really superfluous in many cases where *the commodity itself* stamps the transaction as a trading venture, and the profits and gains are plainly income liable to tax.[32]

In contrast, assets with a *potential*, even if a somewhat remote possibility, of yielding income, are generally "investment assets" and

---

30   *Osler Hammond & Nanton Ltd v MNR*, [1963] SCR 432 (investment dealer sold shares arranged for during underwriting); *Hill-Clarke-Francis Ltd v MNR*, [1963] SCR 452 (lumber dealer purchased all outstanding shares of supplier; Court looked at intention at time of acquisition and sale of shares).

31   See, for example, *Oakside Corporation Ltd v MNR*, [1991] 1 CTC 2132 (TCC).

32   *IRC v Reinhold* (1953), 34 Tax Cas 389 at 392 (Scot) [emphasis added]; see also *Rutledge v CIR* (1929), 14 Tax Cas 490 (Scot Ct of Sess) (isolated transaction in toilet paper characterized as adventure in nature of trade); *IRC v Fraser* (1942), 27 Tax Cas 502 (Scot) (isolated transaction in whiskey gave rise to funds taxable as business income); *MNR v Taylor*, [1956] CTC 189 (Ex Ct) (isolated transaction in lead).

profits resulting from transactions in these types of assets are usually, though not inevitably, characterized as capital gains. Corporate shares in particular enjoy this status. Corporate shares tend to be viewed as investment assets because they have the *potential* to yield dividends. As the Supreme Court said in *Irrigation Industries Ltd v MNR*:

> the nature of the property in question here is shares issued from the treasury of a corporation and we have not been referred to any reported case in which profit from one isolated purchase and sale of shares, by a person not engaged in the business of trading in securities, has been claimed to be taxable . . . . *Corporate shares are in a different position because they constitute something the purchase of which is, in itself, an investment.* They are not, in themselves, articles of commerce, but represent an interest in a corporation which is itself created for the purpose of doing business. Their acquisition is a well recognized method of investing capital in a business enterprise.[33]

Microsoft is an example of a company that only began paying dividends after thirty years of operation.

The converse is equally true. It is generally difficult, but by no means impossible, for a taxpayer to establish that she was engaged in a speculative venture or an adventure in the nature of trade in trading shares.[34] Thus, share losses are seen as capital transactions.

Assets other than "trading assets" and "investment assets" fall into some middle ground in which the nature of the asset does not play as important a role as the taxpayer's conduct in relation to the asset. Real estate, other than vacant land, falls into this middle ground.

To summarize:

- By itself, nothing conclusive can be determined from the fact that a transaction is an isolated one in the taxpayer's experience;
- If there are other factors indicative of trade, a profit from an isolated transaction will be taxable as ordinary income resulting from an adventure in the nature of trade;
- Even if there are no other business attributes, a transaction may still give rise to business income if the asset traded is of a trading, and not of an investment nature; and

---

33 *Irrigation Industries*, above note 29 at 352 (gain from speculative mining shares purchased with short-term loan on account of capital) [emphasis added].

34 *Becker v Canada*, [1983] CTC 11 (FCA) (purchase of shares in business with intention of transforming it into profitable enterprise); *Factory Carpet*, above note 21 (purchase of shares with substantial deductible non-capital losses with intention of revamping and reselling business, therefore trading).

- If the asset in question is an investment asset (e.g., corporate shares), and there are no other factors indicative of trading, the transaction will usually (not inevitably) be viewed as a capital transaction. This is so even though the investment asset is acquired for the purpose of resale at a profit.

iii) Related Activity

A taxpayer's profits and losses from transactions that are closely related to his other business activities are usually business income or losses.[35] It is very difficult for a taxpayer to maintain successfully that a profit arising out of a transaction connected in any manner with ordinary business activity is a capital gain. As Thorson P said:

> they were transactions in the same commodity as that which it had to purchase for its ordinary purposes. In my view, they were of the same character and nature as trading and business operations as those of its business in its ordinary course, even though they involved a departure from such course.[36]

There is a rebuttable presumption that a transaction connected with a taxpayer's usual business is intrinsically part of that business. It is not easy, however, to rebut the presumption. Actual use of the property as an investment asset over some period of time, or a plausible explanation for selling the investment, may be sufficient to rebut the presumption.

iv) Corporate Objects and Powers

Corporate objects and powers are less significant now than they were a hundred years ago. A corporation has the capacity, rights, powers and privileges of a natural person.[37] Thus, unless specifically restricted

---

35   See generally: *Smith v MNR* (1955), 12 Tax ABC 166 (mortgage discounting closely related to taxpayer's business as realtor; treated as trading since so related); *Darius v MNR*, [1971] Tax ABC 889, aff'd (1974), 74 DTC 6260 (FCTD) (shareholder in construction company sold land parcels in her own name to achieve better tax result than company able to achieve); *Morrison v MNR* (1927), 1 DTC 113 (Ex Ct) (taxpayer with skill and knowledge in trade acquired through experience, who then traded privately in the same commodity, was carrying on a business); *Boivin v MNR* (1970), 70 DTC 1364 (TAB) (a dozen property "flips" by wife on direction of building contractor husband motivated by profit and deemed "trading"); *Everlease (Ontario) Ltd v MNR*, [1968] Tax ABC 162 (building sold to cover lack of funds was trade due to owner's close association with real estate developers and managers).

36   *Atlantic Sugar*, above note 25 at 513 (Ex Ct).

37   See, for example, *Business Corporations Act*, RSO 1990, c B.16, s 15.

by its articles of incorporation, a corporation may engage in any business other than those from which it is specifically precluded by statute. A corporation may restrict its scope of business activities by specifying the restrictions in its articles of incorporation or other constating documents.[38] For tax purposes, characterization of corporate income depends upon the business that the corporation actually conducts and not on any restrictions in its incorporating documents.[39]

v)   Degree of Organization

Where a taxpayer deals with property in much the same way as a dealer would with similar property, any resulting profit is likely business income. Thus, a transaction, albeit isolated and unrelated to the taxpayer's ordinary business activity, may have the stamp of business purpose if it is organized and carried on in the manner of a trader. As Lord Clyde said in *IRC v Livingston*:

> I think the test, which must be used to determine whether a venture such as we are now considering is, or is not, "in the nature of 'trade,'" is whether the operations involved in it are of·the same kind, and carried on in the same way, as those which are characteristic of ordinary trading in the line of business in which the venture was made.[40]

If a taxpayer walks and quacks like a duck, it will be considered a duck.

For example, a taxpayer who purchases undeveloped land that he subdivides and sells, behaves as a developer would in the normal course of business. In the absence of a convincing explanation, the taxpayer's profits would constitute income from business.[41]

3) Electing Capital Gains

To reduce the uncertainty associated with the troublesome question of whether a gain is on account of income or capital, the Act allows

---

38   See, for example, *Canada Business Corporations Act*, RSC 1985, c 44, para 6(1)(f), and Ontario *Business Corporations Act*, *ibid*, subss 3(2) and 17(2).
39   *Sutton Lumber & Trading Co v MNR*, [1953] 2 SCR 77.
40   *IRC v Livingston* (1927), 11 Tax Cas 538 at 542 (Scot).
41   See, for example, *Moluch v MNR* (1966), 66 DTC 5463 at 5468 (Ex Ct), where the court observed: "Moreover I am unable to distinguish what the appellant did after his decision to subdivide had been reached from what a person engaged in the business of land development would do once he had acquired a parcel of property." See also Interpretation Bulletin IT-218R, "Profit, Capital Gains and Losses from the Sale of Real Estate, Including Farmland and Inherited Land and Conversion of Real Estate from Capital Property to Inventory and Vice Versa" (16 September 1986).

taxpayers to elect "guaranteed" capital gains or capital loss treatment on a disposition of certain types of properties.[42] The following rules apply:

- The election is available only upon the disposition of a "Canadian security."
- To qualify as a "Canadian security," the issuer of the security must be a Canadian resident, and the security must be either equity or debt. Warrants and options do not qualify as "Canadian securities."[43]
- Once a taxpayer elects to have a gain deemed a capital gain, all subsequent dispositions of "Canadian securities" by the taxpayer are similarly characterized. Hence, all losses would also be considered capital losses.[44]
- The election is not available to a trader or dealer in securities.[45]
- The election must be made on a prescribed form and filed together with the tax return for the year.

Traders and dealers in securities cannot use the election. Of course, whether a person is a trader or dealer is a question of fact to be determined by the taxpayer's intentions and conduct. A person who participates in the promotion or underwriting of securities is a trader or dealer.[46] Corporate "insiders" who trade for a quick profit are generally "traders."

D. BUSINESS VS. INVESTMENT INCOME

Having drawn a line between "business income" and "capital gains," we now further refine the process and distinguish between business income and investment income. The characterization of income as resulting from business or investments (more technically, income from property) is also a question of fact.[47]

Since most businesses use property to generate income, it is not particularly helpful to ask whether the income derives from the *use* of

---

42   ITA, above note 1, subss 39(4), 39(4.1) and 39(6).
43   Ibid, subs 39(6); Income Tax Regulations, CRC, c 945, s 6200.
44   ITA, ibid, subs 39(4).
45   Ibid, subs 39(5).
46   Interpretation Bulletin IT-479R, "Transactions in Securities" (29 February 1984).
47   Canadian Marconi Co v Canada, [1986] 2 SCR 522 at 532 [Canadian Marconi], Wilson J: "It is trite law that the characterization of income as income from a business or income from property must be made from an examination of the taxpayer's whole course of conduct viewed in the light of surrounding circumstances."

property. The critical question is: does the income flow *from* property or *from* business? The subtlety of this distinction causes difficulties in characterizing these two sources of income. There is no bright-line test that clearly answers the question.

In many, perhaps most, cases the distinction between business income and property income does not affect the end result. A taxpayer's income for a taxation year from a source that is business *or* property is her profit therefrom for the year.[48] We calculate income from both of these sources according to the same commercial and statutory rules. There are, however, circumstances in which the distinction between the two is critical. For example:

- The attribution rules that apply to prevent income splitting between spouses apply only to income from property and do not apply to business income;[49]
- A Canadian-controlled private corporation is eligible for special tax credits on its active business income that substantially reduce the effective tax rate on such income;[50]
- A special Part IV tax applies to income from property that a private corporation earns.

Income from property is the passive investment yield on an asset. Rent, dividends, interest and royalties are typical examples. We earn the yield on the investment by a relatively passive process. For example, where an individual invests in land, stocks, bonds or intangible property,[51] and collects investment income therefrom without doing much more than holding the property, the income is investment income or income *from* property.

In contrast, business income implies activity in the earning process. Business generates from the *use* of property as part of a process that combines labour and capital. For example, a taxpayer may *invest* in bonds and clip the coupons to earn the interest income therefrom; alternatively, he may actively *trade* in bonds to earn a profit from trading activities. In the first case, the earnings derive from a passive process and are investment income; in the second case, the income is from business.[52]

---

48   *ITA*, above note 1, subs 9(1).
49   *Ibid*, s 74.1.
50   *Ibid*, subs 125(1).
51   Such as copyrights or trademarks.
52   It is important to note that profits from an isolated trade may be business income. The phrase "adventure in the nature of trade" implies an isolated transaction: see *ITA*, above note 1, subs 248(1) "business."

The line between income from business and investment income is unclear. What is the level of activity beyond which a passive holding becomes an active process of earning income?[53] When does dawn turn into day?

1) Real Estate

Income that derives from passive ownership of real estate is investment income. Income that flows from the use of real estate as an asset in a commercial endeavour is business income.[54]

The critical test in distinguishing an investment in real estate from a real estate business is the level of services provided as a supplement to the rental of the real property.[55] The greater the level of services that one provides as an adjunct to the rental of real estate, the greater the likelihood that the income therefrom is business income.[56] The distinction does not rest on any single criterion but upon an assessment of the aggregate level of activity associated with the generation of the income. One factor may outweigh several others, but it is always a facts and circumstances test.

Here, as elsewhere in the law, it is easy to characterize at either extreme of the spectrum. It is clear, for example, that a hotel rents its guests more than a room, whereas a tenant in an apartment usually rents only space with minimal services. The distinction is less clear, however, between a full service apartment that provides extensive an-

---

53   *Canadian Marconi*, above note 47 ($18 million invested yielded interest that was included in manufacturing and processing profits); *Wertman v MNR* (1964), 64 DTC 5158 at 5165 (Ex Ct) (concerning rent from apartment units: "the concepts of income from property and income from business are not mutually exclusive but blend completely"); *Walsh v MNR*, [1965] CTC 478 (Ex Ct) (ordinary janitorial services did not convert property to business, as would maid, linen, laundry and breakfast services); *Burri v Canada*, [1985] 2 CTC 42 (FCTD) (services provided by owners incidental to the making of revenue from property through the earning of rent).

54   *Martin v MNR*, [1948] CTC 189 at 193 (Ex Ct).

55   The phrase "mere [sic] investment" has sometimes been used to describe a passive investment that gives rise to income from property. See, for example, *Marks v MNR* (1962), 30 Tax ABC 155.

56   *Fry v Salisbury House Estate Ltd*, [1930] AC 432 at 470 (HL) (management company operated elevators, provided porters, security guards, heating and cleaning at extra charge; property ownership, not trade); see also *Crofts v Sywell Aerodrome Ltd*, [1942] 1 KB 317 (CA) (activities, though varied and extensive, consisted of exercise and exploitation of property rights of aerodrome); *Malenfant v MNR*, [1992] 2 CTC 2431 (TCC) (income from hotel and motel rooms was income from rental property as services provided were only those required to maintain rooms).

cillary services and a hotel that makes minimal provision beyond accommodation. The provision of maid, linen, laundry and food services, for example, suggests business. In contrast, routine and necessary ancillary services, such as heating, cleaning and snow removal, are seen as mere adjuncts to the ownership of property. In either case, time spent on managing the property is not the determining factor.[57]

2) Investments

The characterization of income from investments raises even more subtle distinctions. The issue is particularly important for Canadian corporations because of the special rules in respect of the small business deduction, the manufacturing and processing credit and the refundable dividend tax on investment income under Part IV of the Act.

a) Integration Test

An "active business" is "any business carried on by the taxpayer other than a specified investment business or a personal services business"[58] and for some purposes "includes an adventure or concern in the nature of trade."[59]

"Investment income" is "income for the year from a source . . . that is property."

Thus, the characterization of a taxpayer's income from short-term investments involves two steps:

1) Determine whether the taxpayer's investments are an integral part of his or her business activities. If they are, income from the investments is business income; and

2) If they are not, determine whether the taxpayer's investment activities constitute a separate business. If they do, the income from those activities is business income. If the investment activity does not constitute a separate business, the income from those activities is income from property.

b) "Employed and Risked" Test

A taxpayer's investments are considered to be an integral part of a business if her funds are "employed and risked" in the business.[60] Is the

---

57   See, for example, the comments of Thurlow J in *Wertman v MNR*, above note 53 at 5167.

58   *ITA*, above note 1, subs 248(1) "active business."

59   *Ibid*, subs 125(7) "active business."

60   See *Canada v Ensite Ltd*, [1986] 2 SCR 509 at 518 (property yielding interest must be linked to some "definite obligation or liability of the business"); *Bank*

making of investments a part of the mode of conducting the business? If the answer is yes, then the income from the investments is part of the income of the business.

Business income from investments represents the fruit derived from a fund "employed and risked" in the taxpayer's business. For example, the temporary investment of working capital constitutes an intrinsic part of the business.

c) Separate Business Test

Where a taxpayer's investments are not an integral part of his business operations, the question arises whether the investment activities constitute a separate business.[61] The answer to this question depends upon:

- The number and value of transactions;
- The time devoted to investment activities;
- The relationship between the taxpayer's investment income and his total income; and
- The relationship between the value of the taxpayer's investment and the total value of his assets.

Line Ltd v CIR (1974), 49 Tax Cas 307 (Scot Ct of Sess) (no actual risk or employment of reserve funds in the company's business of owning, operating and replacing ships). In Canada v Marsh & McLennan Ltd, [1983] CTC 231 (FCA), for example, the taxpayer, an insurance broker, temporarily invested its insurance premiums in short-term paper. The taxpayer could do so because of the lag between the time that it received a premium from its customer and the time that it remitted the premium to the customer's insurer. The taxpayer's business involved two dimensions: brokerage and investment. The two activities were so interdependent that its investments were an integral part of its business; hence, its investment income was income from a business and *not* income from property. See also the speech of Lord Mersey in *Liverpool & London & Globe Insurance Co v Bennett* (1913), 6 Tax Cas 327 at 379–80 (HL).

61   *Canadian Marconi*, above note 47. The taxpayer, a manufacturer of electronic equipment, divested itself of its broadcasting division and found itself with surplus funds of approximately $20 million. While awaiting a suitable opportunity to invest in another business, the taxpayer invested these surplus funds in short-term, interest-bearing securities. During the period under assessment, the taxpayer earned substantial interest income (approximately $5 million) on which it claimed the manufacturing and processing credit on the basis that its income from its short-term investments represented "business income" and, therefore, "active business income." In deciding in favour of the taxpayer, the Supreme Court applied the presumption that income that a corporate taxpayer earns is business income. The facts fell short of supporting the minister's contention that he rebutted the presumption. See also *Colonial Realty Services Ltd v MNR*, [1987] 1 CTC 2343 (TCC) (excess funds placed in investment certificates; no corporate activity or circumstances converted the yield to active business income).

Is the taxpayer merely managing personal investments or carrying on an investment business? The greater the amount of time devoted to, and the greater the value of, investment activities as compared to business activities, the more likely it is that the investment segment constitutes a separate business.

E. STATUTORY INCLUSIONS

Income from business or property is the "profit" therefrom. Although profit is generally determined according to accounting principles and commercial practice, the Act does not rely completely upon such principles and practice in the measurement of income for tax purposes. In certain circumstances, the Act specifies that certain amounts are to be included in income for tax purposes, regardless of the manner in which the particular item is treated in accounting practice. The purpose of the specific inclusions is to:

- Make timing adjustments;
- Modify the common law concept of income; and
- Clarify uncertain issues in accounting practice.

1) Timing Adjustments

We calculate "profit" from business or property on an accrual basis of accounting. Paragraph 12(1)(b) of the Act reinforces this concept and requires a taxpayer to include in income in a year any receivables on account of goods sold or services rendered in the year, regardless of when the amounts are due or actually collected. An amount is considered "receivable" when the taxpayer completes the sale or service, so that his right to receive the amount is perfected.

Generally accepted concepts of accrual accounting require inclusion in income only of amounts that have been earned. Unearned revenue is a liability and not income. For tax purposes, however, paragraph 12(1)(a) modifies the general accounting rule: *all* receipts, whether earned or unearned, are included in income for the year. Thus, a taxpayer must include in income an amount received on account of services to be rendered in the future. The taxpayer may, however, claim a reserve against unearned income.[62] Although it appears that we arrive at the same result as accrual accounting "profit," there are restrictions on the use of reserves.

---

62   *ITA*, above note 1, para 20(1)(m).

2) Modification of Common Law

a) Interest Income

"Interest" is the return or material consideration given for the use of money belonging to another person. Interest must be referable to a principal sum of money or an obligation to pay money.[63]

Interest may vary with the gross revenues or profits of the borrower.[64] However, amounts payable as a percentage of profit are less likely to constitute interest.[65] Profit percentage arrangements are more usually associated with a partnership relationship between the parties.[66]

Payments on account of interest are generally for the use of money over a period. Thus, in business and commerce, interest is merely the equivalent of a "rental" charge for the use of someone else's money. The courts, however, determined interest as an expenditure on account of capital. To overcome the judicial characterization of interest as a payment on account of capital, the Act specifically provides for the treatment of interest as an income or expense item.

i) Receivable

There are several ways to account for interest income for tax purposes—the cash basis, modified cash basis, receivable basis, accrual basis and modified accrual basis. Different rules apply to individuals, corporations and partnerships.

For tax purposes, the term "receivable" means *legally* receivable and not "receivable" in the sense that one uses it in accounting.[67] Thus, the word has a narrower meaning for tax purposes than it has in general accounting.

An amount is "receivable" for tax purposes only when the taxpayer has a clear legal right to it. The right must be legally enforceable. For

---

63   *Reference re s 6 of Farm Security Act 1944 (Saskatchewan)*, [1947] SCR 394 at 411, aff'd [1949] AC 110 (PC); *Canada v Melford Developments Inc*, [1982] 2 SCR 504; see also *Halsbury's Laws of England*, 4th ed, vol 32 (London: Butterworths, 1980) at 53, where "interest" is defined as "the return or compensation for the use or retention by one person of a sum of money belonging to or owed to another. Interest accrues from day to day even if payable only at intervals." The CRA generally accepts these criteria in defining interest. See Interpretation Bulletin IT-533, "Interest Deductibility and Related Issues" (31 October 2003) at para 1.

64   *Pooley v Driver* (1876), 5 Ch D 459 (CA); *Cox v Hickman* (1860), 11 ER 431 (HL); see *Partnerships Act*, RSO 1990, c P.5, para 3(1)(d).

65   See, for example, *Balaji Apartments Ltd v Manufacturers Life Insurance Co* (1979), 25 OR (2d) 275 (HCJ).

66   See, for example, *Sedgwick v MNR*, [1962] CTC 400 (Ex Ct).

67   *MNR v J Colford Contracting Co*, [1962] SCR viii.

example, assume a taxpayer buys a bond for $1,000 on 1 December, and the bond pays interest at a rate of 12 percent per year payable at the end of May and November of each year. By 31 December, the taxpayer will have earned 1/12 of his annual interest income. In accrual accounting, the taxpayer is considered to have earned $10 in the month of December even though he may not have received payment. The $10 would be accrued as a receivable for general accounting purposes. For tax purposes, however, the $10 is not "receivable" because there is no legal obligation on the issuer of the bond to pay the interest as at 31 December. The legal obligation to pay the interest will arise on the date stipulated in the bond contract.

ii) Consistency

A taxpayer who selects a particular method of reporting interest income for a particular property must conform to that method from year to year. Although a taxpayer is required to account for interest income on a consistent basis from year to year, there is no requirement that the taxpayer follow the same basis for reporting interest income from all sources. For example, a taxpayer may report interest income from Canada Savings Bonds on a cash basis and, in the same year, report interest income from a mortgage on a receivable basis.[68] Paragraph 12(1)(c) merely requires that interest from the *same source* be reported on a consistent basis—that is, interest from the same debtor on the same type of obligation.

iii) Annual Reporting

As a general rule, an individual may report interest income on a cash or accrual basis.[69] Thus, an individual can use cash basis reporting to defer the recognition of income.

There are, however, special restrictions in respect of income from "investment contracts," which must be reported annually, regardless of whether the income has been paid out in the year.[70] The rule prevents prolonged deferral of tax on such income.

An "investment contract" is a debt such as a note, bond, debenture or guaranteed investment contract, but does not include the following:[71]

- Salary deferral arrangements;

---

68   *Industrial Mortgage & Trust Co v MNR*, [1958] CTC 106 (Ex Ct); see also Interpretation Bulletin IT-396R, "Interest Income" (29 May 1984).

69   *ITA*, above note 1, para 12(1)(c).

70   *Ibid*, subs 12(4).

71   *Ibid*, subs 12(11) "investment contract."

- Income bonds and debentures;
- Retirement compensation arrangements;
- Employee benefit plans;
- Small business development bonds;
- Small business bonds; or
- Debt obligations in respect of which investment income is otherwise included in income at least annually.

iv) Blended Payments

A taxpayer is not obliged to charge interest on money loaned to another.[72] Interest, however, may be blended into principal, in which case it must be segregated and included in income for tax purposes.[73] A blended payment is a single payment in which interest and principal are blended into one amount on repayment of a loan.[74] Whether a payment is blended is a question of fact that depends upon the terms of the contract.

Interest and principal may also be blended by issuing debt at a discount and redeeming it at its face value upon maturity. Strip coupon bonds, for example, do not stipulate any interest rate or amount on their face, but are issued at a discount from their face value. The discount rate is a direct function of the prevailing interest rate. The redemption value is, in effect, a blended payment which, on maturity, must be broken down into interest and principal components.[75]

b) Discounts

i)   Rate Adjustments

It is important to distinguish between effective and nominal interest yields. Debt instruments are sometimes issued at a discount to their face value. The discount plus the "coupon rate" (i.e., the nominal rate of interest on the face of the instrument) combine to produce the overall "effective" rate of return or "yield" of the instrument. Thus, debt issued at a discount effectively raises its rate of interest. For example, if a corporation issues a one-year $1,000 bond with a nominal rate of

---

72 *MNR v Groulx*, [1966] CTC 115 (Ex Ct), aff'd [1967] CTC 422 (SCC). Note, however, that the recipient of an interest-free loan may be taxable on the benefit imputed on the loan; see s. 80.4, *ibid*.
73 *Ibid*, subs 16(1).
74 See, generally, Interpretation Bulletin IT-265R3 "Payments of Income and Capital Combined" (7 October 1991) (now archived by the CRA as being out of date).
75 *O'Neil v MNR* (1991), 91 DTC 692 (TCC); see also *Beck v Lord Howard de Walden*, [1940] TR 143; *Lomax v Peter Dixon & Son Ltd*, [1943] 1 KB 671.

interest of 10 percent at $960, the effective rate of interest or yield to the bondholder is 14 percent ($100 interest plus $40 discount). Hence, discounting the issue price of a bond is simply another way of changing the effective rate of interest on the bond.

The common law, however, considers the discount on a bond as a capital gain.[76] Hence, the common law rules are an incentive to convert interest income into capital gains. The Minister of Finance described the difficulties of this interpretation in the budget speech of 20 December 1960:

> Unfortunately, increasing use is deliberately being made of a device to pay bondholders the equivalent of interest in a form that is tax-free. If a borrower issues a one-year $100 bond for, say, $96 and the bond bears a coupon rate of 1 per cent, the bondholder will receive $4 more than he paid for it when the bond matures at the end of the year. This excess over purchase price, plus the $1 in interest, will give the lender a 5.2 per cent return on his investment but it has been found difficult to collect tax on more than the $1 designated as interest.

The Act changes the common law rule in various ways, depending upon the tax status of the issuer of the bond.

Where a tax-exempt organization, a non-resident person not carrying on business in Canada or a governmental body issues a bond at a "deep discount," the *entire* discount is income in the hands of the first taxable Canadian resident to hold the bond.[77] A bond has a "deep discount" if the effective rate of interest on the bond exceeds the nominal rate by more than one-third.

Where a taxable entity issues a bond at a discount, a purchaser of the bond can treat the difference between the issue price and its par value as a capital gain. If the discount is a "deep discount," the taxable entity issuing the bond can deduct only one-half of the discount as interest expense. If the discount is "shallow" (i.e., the effective rate of interest does *not* exceed the nominal rate by more than one-third and it is not issued at less than 97 percent of its maturity value), the taxable entity can deduct the entire discount.[78]

---

76   *Wood v MNR*, [1969] SCR 330.
77   *ITA*, above note 1, subs 16(3).
78   *Ibid*, para 20(1)(f).

Example

Assume: A municipality issues bonds with a face value of $1,000 (coupon rate of 4.5 percent, maturity five years) at a price of $930.

Then:

Nominal rate	4.50%
Effective rate (yield)	(6.14)
Difference	1.64%

Since 6.14 percent is more than $4/3 \times 4.50\%$, the entire discount of $70 per bond is income in the hands of the first Canadian resident, taxable owner of the bond.

Example

	Shallow Discount	Deep Discount
Issue price of bond	$990	$960
Nominal rate of interest	8%	8%
Effective rate of interest	10%	12%
Discount on bond	10	40
Amount deductible by issuer	$10	$20

3) Variations from Accounting Practice

a) Payments Based on Production or Use of Property

The sales price of a property may be fixed at the time the parties enter into the agreement of purchase and sale. Alternatively, the price may be determined by reference to a formula based upon production from, or use of, the property. For example, a taxpayer may sell land containing sand for a fixed amount of $15,000 or on the basis that the purchaser shall pay 5 cents for every ton of sand extracted from the land. The fixed payment of $15,000 may be characterized as on account of capital. In the latter case, the sale price is dependent upon the quantity of sand taken from the land, and the total price is not determined until all of the sand is extracted. The payments would be considered income.

Paragraph 12(1)(g) provides that a taxpayer must include in income all amounts that he receives and that depend upon the use of, or production from, property. In the above example, if the purchaser of the land extracts 300,000 tons, he will pay $15,000 to the seller, which will be taxed as income. This rule prevents taxpayers from converting what would otherwise be fully taxable rent or royalty income into capital.

Examples:

- A sells land containing 300,000 tons of sand for $15,000. The purchase price is payable at a rate of $5,000 per year for three years.
  » Paragraph 12(1)(g) does *not* apply to the transaction. The payments are not related to the "use of" or "production from" property.
- B sells land containing sand to X. The sale price is determined at 5 cents per ton of sand extracted over the next three years. X extracts 300,000 tons and pays the vendor $15,000.
  » Paragraph 12(1)(g) applies; the $15,000 is income to B.
- C sells land containing sand to Y. The sale price is determined at 5 cents per ton of sand extracted in the next three years, provided that the total price cannot exceed $10,000. Y extracts 300,000 tons and pays C $10,000.
  » Paragraph 12(1)(g) applies; the $10,000 is income to C. The payment is based upon production from property.
- D sells land containing sand to Z. The sale price is determined at 5 cents per ton of sand extracted in the next three years but *not to be less than* $10,000. In fact, Y extracts 300,000 tons and pays $15,000.
  » Paragraph 12(1)(g) does *not* apply to the $10,000 since this amount is not dependent upon production; $5,000 is included in D's income by paragraph 12(1)(g).

b) Stock Dividends

Dividends are income from property in the hands of a passive investor and income from business in the hands of a taxpayer who is in the investment business. For most tax purposes, a "dividend" includes stock dividends.[79]

For accounting purposes, a stock dividend is simply the capitalization of retained earnings into share capital. It represents the transformation of one type of equity capital (retained earnings) into another type (share capital). A stock dividend does not have any income effect in accounting.

For tax purposes, stock dividends are included in income under section 12. But the tax treatment of dividend income, whether on account of investments or from business, is complicated by the potential of double taxation of such income. Thus, there is a special regime for the taxation of dividends that depends on:

- The status of the recipient;

---

79   *Ibid*, subs 248(1) "dividend."

- The source of the dividend; and
- The nature of the payer corporation.

c) Inducement Payments

An "inducement payment" is an economic incentive intended to lead or persuade a person to perform a particular action or decision. Examples include government subsidies to business to locate in a particular place and landlord inducements to tenants to sign a lease in a shopping plaza. An inducement may be on account of capital or on account of income.

For tax purposes, however, an inducement receipt, whether from a governmental or private organization, is taxable as income.[80] This is so whether the payment is a grant, subsidy, forgivable loan, deduction from tax or other allowance. A taxpayer may, however, elect to treat an inducement payment as a reduction in the cost or capital cost of any property that he or she acquires with the payment.[81] The effect of such an election is that it allows the taxpayer to defer recognition of the income until such time as he disposes of the property.

4) Other Inclusions in Income

Item	Statutory Reference
Amounts received for goods and services to be rendered in the future	subpara 12(1)(a)(i)
Amounts received for deposits on returnable items	subpara 12(1)(a)(ii)
Amounts received for property sold or services rendered, due in a future tax year	para 12(1)(b)
Amounts received as interest (or in lieu of interest) if not previously included	para 12(1)(c)
Amount deducted in preceding year as a reserve for doubtful debts	para 12(1)(d)
Amounts deducted in preceding year as reserve for guarantee	paras 12(1)(d.1); 20(1)(l.1)
Amount deducted in preceding year as a reserve for:	subpara 12(1)(e)(i)
• deposits on returnable containers	subpara 20(1)(m)(iv)

---

80   *Ibid*, para 12(1)(x).
81   *Ibid*, subss 53(2.1) and 13(7.4).

Item	Statutory Reference
• goods delivered and services performed after end of year	subparas 20(1)(m)(i) & (ii); subs 20(6)
• a manufacturer's warranty	para 20(1)(m.1)
• prepaid rent	subpara 20(1)(m)(iii)
• policies of an insurer	para 20(7)(c)
Amount deducted in preceding year as unpaid amounts	subpara 12(1)(e)(ii)
Insurance proceeds used to repair depreciable property	para 12(1)(f)
Amounts received based on production or use of property disposed	para 12(1)(g) ss 12(2.01)
Amount deducted in preceding year for quadrennial survey	para 12(1)(h)
Recovered bad debts, previously deducted	para 12(1)(i)
Dividends from corporations resident in Canada and other corporations	paras 12(1)(j) & (k)
Income from partnership	para 12(1)(l)
Income from trusts	para 12(1)(m)
Benefits from profit-sharing plan and employee trust to employer	paras 12(1)(n)
Net amounts received from employee benefit plan	para 12(1)(n.1)
Royalties paid or payable to government authority	paras 12(1)(o), 12(1)(x.2)
Amount received under *Western Grain Stabilization Act*	para 12(1)(p)
Amount deducted for employment tax	para 12(1)(q)
Cost of inventory at year-end representing an allowance for depreciation	para 12(1)(r)
Reinsurer must include maximum amount which insurer may claim as reserve	s 18(9.02)
Amount deducted as investment tax credit if not previously included	para 12(1)(t)
Government of Canada grant for home insulation or energy income conversion	para 12(1)(u)
Forfeited salary deferral amounts	para 12(1)(n.2)
Amounts received from retirement compensation arrangement	para 12(1)(n.3)

Item	Statutory Reference
Amount of negative balance arrived at in scientific research deduction	para 12(1)(v)
Benefit received from non-interest bearing or low interest loan by virtue of services performed by corporation carrying on a personal services business	para 12(1)(w)
Inducement or assistance payments	para 12(1)(x); *French Shoes Ltd v MNR*, [1986] 2 CTC 132 (FCTD)
Cash bonus on Canada Savings Bonds	s 12.1
Certain amount in respect of fuel tax rebates under *Excise Tax Act*	para 12(1)(x.1)
Automobile provided to partner	para 12(1)(y)
Amateur athlete trust payments	para 12(1)(z)
Proceeds of a right to receive production	s 12(i)(g.1)
Debts for disposition of eligible capital property written off and later recovered	s. 12(1)(i.1)
Amounts from foreign corporations, foreign trusts & foreign investment entities	s 12(1)(k)
Amounts paid to foreign governments for oil & gas production	s 12(1)(o.1)
Amounts received as beneficiary of Qualifying Environmental Trust	s 12(1)(z.1)
Amounts received as consideration from the disposition of a Qualifying Environmental Trust	s. 12(1)(z.2)
Certain amounts related to debt forgiveness	s 12(1)(z.3)
Amounts related to eligible funeral arrangements	s 12(1)(z.4)
Refund of amounts for anti-dumping duties previously deducted	s 12(1)(z.6)

FURTHER READINGS

General

DURNFORD, JOHN. "The Distinction between Income from Business and Income from Property and the Concept of Carrying on Business" (1991) 39 Can Tax J 1131.

HARRIS, EDWIN C. "Timing of Income and Expense Items" (1975) Corp Mgmt Tax Conf 84.

Measurement of Income

ARNOLD, BRIAN J. "Timing and Income Taxation: The Principles of Income Management for Tax Purposes" (1983) 35 Can Tax Found 133.

General Deductions

BROOKS, NEIL. "The Principles Underlying the Deduction of Business Expenses" in Brian Hansen, Vern Krishna, & James Rendall, eds, *Canadian Taxation* (Toronto: Richard De Boo, 1981) ch 5.

Interest

ARNOLD, BRIAN J, & GORDON D DIXON. "Rubbing Salt into the Wound: The Denial of the Interest Deduction after the Loss of a Source of Income" (1991) 39 Can Tax J 1473.

BALE, GORDON. "The Interest Deduction Dilemma" (1973) Can Tax J 317.

KRISHNA, VERN. "Interest Deductibility: More Form over Substance" (1993) Can Curr Tax C-17.

————. "More Uncertainty on Deduction of Interest Expenses" [Case Comment: *Attaie v Canada (MNR)*, T-1319-85 (1987) (TCC)] (1987–89) 2 Can Curr Tax J-59.

Capital Cost Allowance

HUGGETT, DONALD R, ED. "Capital Cost Allowances" (1974) 11 Can Tax N 71.

LOUIS, DAVID. *Canada's Best Real Estate Tax Shelters* (Willowdale, ON: Hume, 1985).

MACDONALD, RC. "Capital Cost Allowances" (1973) 47 Cost and Management 43.

MATHESON, DAVID I. "Acquisition and Disposition of Depreciable Assets" (1969) 17 Can Tax J 277.

CHAPTER 8

BUSINESS AND PROPERTY DEDUCTIONS

A. DEDUCTIONS

1) General Comment

We saw earlier that income from an office or employment is taxable on a gross basis. In contrast, income from business and property is taxable on a net basis. Thus, we need to determine which expenses are deductible from business and property revenues in order to calculate net profit for tax purposes.

The calculation of net profit is a question of law. Nevertheless, we start by looking to the taxpayer's financial statements. We determine net profit according to commercial and accounting principles to the extent that they do not conflict with the Act or judicial decisions. The court in *Royal Trust* explained the scheme for the deductibility of expenses as follows:

> Thus, it may be stated categorically that in a case under the *Income Tax Act* the first matter to be determined in deciding whether an outlay or expense is outside the prohibition of . . . [paragraph 18(1)(a)] of the Act is whether it was made or incurred by the taxpayer in accordance with the ordinary principles of commercial trading or well accepted principles of business practice. If it was not, that is the end of the matter. But if it was, then the outlay or expense is properly deductible unless it falls outside the expressed exception of . . . [paragraph 18(1)(a)] and, therefore, within its prohibition.[1]

---

1   *Royal Trust Co v MNR* (1957), 57 DTC 1055 at 1060 (Ex Ct).

Figure 8.1 Overview of Structure

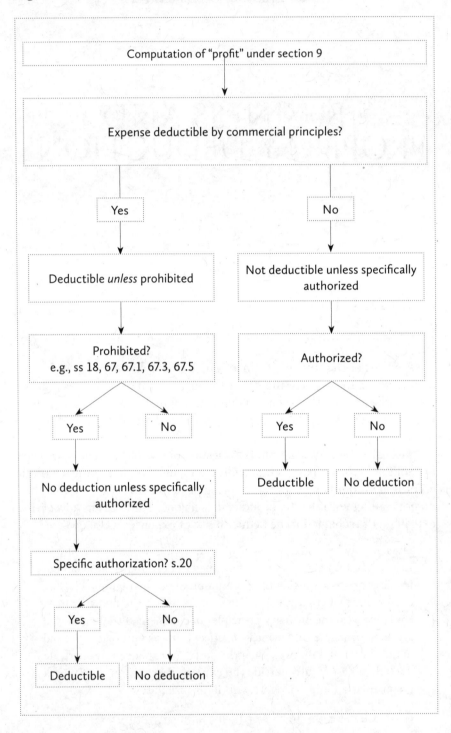

2) General Rules

To be deductible from revenue, in computing net profit, an expenditure must satisfy six basic tests. It must:

* Be incurred for the purpose of earning income;
* Be of an income nature and not a capital expenditure;
* Be reasonable in amount;
* Not be a personal expenditure;
* Not be expressly prohibited by the Act; and
* Not constitute "abusive" tax avoidance.

Apart from these six tests, there is no blanket public policy prohibition on the deductibility of expenses.[2]

The above criteria serve purposes that are different from those that generally accepted accounting and commercial principles serve. For example, the requirement that an expenditure should be reasonable in amount is not an accounting rule, but a constraint to protect the government's taxable base. The prohibition against the deductibility of expenses that the statute specifically proscribes allows the legislator to use it to foster socio-economic and public policies. The anti-abuse rule is intended as a broad "catch-all" clause for expenses that the legislator did not proscribe more specifically.

3) Purpose of Expenditure

An expenditure is deductible as an expense in computing income only if one incurs it for the purpose of earning income.[3] It is the purpose, and not the result, of the expenditure that determines deductibility. Thus, an expense for the purpose of earning income from a business is deductible, regardless of whether it actually produces income. For example, if a taxpayer incurs advertising expenses for the purpose of promoting sales, failure of the advertising program to stimulate sales does *not* disqualify the expenditure as a deductible expense.[4]

---

2   *65302 British Columbia Ltd v Canada*, [1999] 3 SCR 804 [*65302 BC Ltd*].

3   *Income Tax Act*, RSC 1985, c 1 (5th Supp) [*ITA*], para 18(1)(a). This rule does
    little more than reinforce subs 9(1), which states that the income from a
    business or property is the profit therefrom. To constitute an "expense," the
    taxpayer must be under an obligation to pay money to someone. An obligation
    to do something that may entail an expenditure in the future is *not* an expense;
    see *Canada v Burnco Industries Ltd*, [1984] CTC 337 (FCA).

4   See *BC Electric Railway Co v MNR*, [1958] CTC 21 (SCC) [*BC Electric Railway*]
    (payments made by taxpayer to enable it to become more profitable not deduct-

The essential limitation in paragraph 18(1)(a) is that the taxpayer must incur the outlay or expense "for the purpose" of gaining or producing income "from the business." Thus, the purpose must be that of gaining or producing income from the business in which the taxpayer engages. *A fortiori*, the business must exist at the time that the taxpayer incurs the expenditure.

4) Primary Purpose

Income-earning purpose is a question of fact. We can break down expenditures into deductible and non-deductible portions.[5] An expenditure does not have to be wholly and exclusively expended for business purposes in order to be deductible.[6] The focus is on the *primary* purpose of the expenditure. For example, a lawyer who travels from Toronto to Paris for a business meeting can deduct her travel expenses for the trip, even though she remains there for the weekend for personal reasons. The lawyer may also deduct any *incremental* expenditures (such as additional hotel and meal charges) associated with the personal portion of her visit if the expenses are part of the cost of waiting for meetings to resume on Monday. The personal component is secondary to the primary business purpose of the visit.

5) Legal Fees and Criminal Charges

We use the primary purpose test to evaluate the deductibility of legal fees. For tax purposes, an individual's business income is his net profit from the business—revenues less expenses to earn income. Thus, a taxpayer can deduct legal fees in the normal course of business.

Legal fees on account of criminal charges pose a more challenging problem in tax law. Although courts look at accounting and commercial principles to determine business practice, determining net profit is

---

ible even though made for purpose of producing income on account of capital; case departing from previous law; see editorial note at [1958] CTC 21.

5   *Consumer's Gas Co of Toronto v MNR* (1955), 13 Tax ABC 429 (taxpayer obtained gas export permit to improve business; permit and fees for securing permit capital in nature; remainder of fees referable to particular business difficulties, not assets); *KVP Co v MNR*, [1957] CTC 275 (Ex Ct) (extensive aerial surveys required by province to preserve timber cutting rights; current expense to the extent of previous average survey expense).

6   Considerable care should be taken in reading English cases on the deductibility of expenses incurred for business and personal purposes. Under the English statute, an expenditure must be *wholly and exclusively* for business purposes if it is to be deductible; see *Mallalieu v Drummond*, [1983] 2 AC 861 (HL).

essentially a question of law. One starts by asking whether the taxpayer would have incurred the particular expense "but for" the pursuit of business income. Would the need to incur the expense exist apart from the business?

Thus, characterising criminal charges as business or personal is the key to determining deductibility of legal fees, most of which occur in the context of white collar crimes. However, white-collar crimes vary considerably. Typically, such charges arise out of corporate or personal conduct in the context of illegal combines, price fixing, securities violations, insider trading, unlawful conspiracy to lessen competition, accounting fraud and income tax evasion. Some day we may see prosecutions for bribery and corruption of domestic and foreign government officials.

Regardless of the context of the offence, the critical element in determining deductibility of legal fees is the primary purpose of the conduct that led to the charges. If the primary purpose of the activity is to earn business income, the expense is deductible unless the expenditure is on account of capital. To be sure, all criminal charges against individuals also have some personal consequences—psychological problems, loss of job, financial problems, reputation implications, jail, etc. The key decision, however, is to determine which of the two—business or personal—is the primary reason for the charges.

If the primary purpose of incurring legal defence costs is to preserve and maintain the business, the fees are deductible even if there is a secondary personal element for the expenditures. This is essentially a question of fact in each case. The ultimate outcome of the criminal charges—guilty or not guilty verdict—is entirely irrelevant in assessing the deductibility of legal fees.

Businesses are taxable on their income, whether or not the income flows from unlawful practices. Hence, they should deduct their legal fees even if they arise from illegal commercial operations that generate taxable income. In this context, legal fees are simply "working expenses"—one incurs them in the process of earning business income. For example, legal fees in defending violations of competition laws are usually deductible because of the close nexus between the alleged criminal act and the earning of business income through anti-competitive acts. Tax law is neutral and does not morally judge corporate behaviour.

In contrast, legal fees to defend charges of income tax evasion are not deductible. Tax evasion is not a normal or ordinary incident of carrying on business. The evasion occurs after the income-earning process is complete. In *Thiele Drywall Inc v Canada*, for example, the taxpayer falsely recorded payments that it made to certain individuals as reimbursements for expenses instead of income for services.[7] Mis-characterizing service payments as reimbursements is not part of the process of earning business income. The Tax Court disallowed the taxpayer's claim for legal fees because of the underlying nature of the offence.

The issue of deducting legal fees cuts close to the bone if the defendant is a lawyer who faces potential disbarment from his law society. Legal fees to avoid disbarment, or secure reinstatement, as a lawyer may be deductible if they are directly on account of current expenses and not on account of securing a capital asset—the licence to practice. It is easier to defend the deduction of fees to prevent disbarment because the expenses are in respect of protecting an asset that the lawyer already has and uses directly to produce business income. Fees to defend personal charges—for example, sexual harassment—that may lead to disbarment by the law society are less likely to be deductible. The potential of disbarment is not sufficiently close to the primary purpose of the expenditure, namely, the defence of the sexual harassment allegations.

B. CURRENT EXPENSE OR CAPITAL EXPENDITURE

1) General Principles

The income tax is a tax on realized income. Hence, we start by asking whether an expenditure is on account of income or capital. Only expenditures on account of income are deductible. Expenditures on account of capital are not deductible for tax purposes.[8] Paragraph 18(1)(b) merely reinforces the accounting concept that income represents the excess of revenues over expenses over a specified period.

Thus, the calculation of net profit is all about purpose and timing. To be deductible as an expense: (1) one must incur the expenditure for the purpose of gaining or producing income from a business or property, and (2) the expense must be relevant to the current period. These two requirements are interrelated:[9]

> Since the main purpose of every business undertaking is presumably to make a profit, any expenditure made "for the purpose of gaining or producing income" comes within the terms of [paragraph 18(1)(a)], whether it be classified as an income expense or a capital outlay.

---

7   *Thiele Drywall Inc v Canada*, [1996] 3 CTC 2208 (TCC).
8   *ITA*, above note 3, para 18(1)(b).
9   *BC Electric Railway*, above note 4.

Once it is determined that a particular expenditure is one made for the purpose of gaining or producing income, in order to compute income tax liability it must next be determined whether such disbursement is an income expense or a capital outlay.

The concept of income is essentially one of timing: the matching of revenues and expenses in a particular time period.

Expenditures that benefit more than one accounting period are capital outlays for accounting purposes. For example, expenditures on long-enduring assets, such as goodwill, incorporation fees, patents and trademarks, are typically expenses of a capital nature. The distinction between current expenses and capital expenditures is at the heart of the measurement of income.[10]

For tax and accounting purposes, we measure income for a finite period of time—usually annually. Thus, we match revenues and expenses for a year. Expenditures that benefit subsequent fiscal periods are not current expenses, but capital outlays. As a statement of principle, this is straightforward enough. But how does one in law distinguish an expenditure that benefits the current period from one that benefits the future?

2) Mixed Law and Fact

The characterization of expenditures as current expenses or capital outlays is a question of mixed law and fact.[11] The determination of the question depends not upon the nature of property acquired[12] but upon the nature of the expenditure: what did the taxpayer expend the payment for?

There is no single definitive or conclusive test for determining whether an expenditure is of a capital or revenue nature.[13] There are several legal principles that distinguish between capital and revenue

---

10 *Canderel Ltd v Canada*, [1998] 1 SCR 147 (Tenant Inducement Payments constituted running expenses that could be deducted entirely in the year in which they were incurred; in attempting to assess a taxpayer's profit for tax purposes, the test is which method of accounting best depicts the reality of the financial situation of the particular taxpayer.)

11 *Canada v Johns-Manville Canada Inc*, [1985] 2 SCR 46 [*Johns-Manville*]; applied in *Gifford v Canada*, [2004] 1 SCR 411 (financial advisor paid departing colleague $100,000 for his client list—that is to say, goodwill with clients—and a non-compete agreement; payment on account of capital, thus interest on associated loan not deductible).

12 *Golden Horse Shoe (New) Ltd v Thurgood*, [1934] 1 KB 548 at 563 (CA).

13 *BP Australia Ltd v Commissioner of Taxation of the Commonwealth of Australia*, [1966] AC 224 (PC from Austl) [*BP Australia*].

expenditures. One applies them flexibly to particular factual situations.[14] A test that may be useful in one set of circumstances may not be relevant in another.[15] One test, however, has general acceptance:

> . . . where an expenditure is made, not only once and for all, but with a view to bringing into existence an asset or an advantage for the enduring benefit of a trade, I think that there is very good reason (in the absence of special circumstances leading to an opposite conclusion) for treating such an expenditure as properly attributable not to revenue but to capital.[16]

The primary focus here is on the purpose of the expenditure, not on the physical attributes of the particular property. The *purpose*, rather than the result, of an expenditure determines whether it is a capital outlay or a current expense.[17] Does one incur the expenditure for the purpose of bringing into existence an asset of enduring value? The

---

14 *Johns-Manville*, above note 11; *BP Australia, ibid* (deductibility of amount paid to gas stations to secure monopoly of station, that is to say, that it sell only BP gas in furtherance of marketing reorganization plan), approved by the Supreme Court of Canada in *MNR v Algoma Central Railway*, [1968] SCR 447 (Court agreed with test enunciated in *BP Australia*, then decided without reasons); see also *Bowater Power Co v MNR* (1971), 71 DTC 5469 at 5480 (FCTD):

> The solution, therefore, depends on what the expenditure is calculated to effect from a practical and business point of view, rather than upon the juristic classification of the legal rights, if any, secured, employed or exhausted in the process. The question of deductibility of expenses, must also, therefore, be considered from the standpoint of the company or its operations, as a practical matter.

15 *Commissioner of Taxes v Nchanga Consolidated Copper Mines Ltd*, [1964] AC 948 at 959 (PC), Lord Radcliffe.

16 *British Insulated & Helsby Cables v Atherton*, [1926] AC 205 at 213–14 (HL).

17 *Hinton v Maden & Ireland Ltd* (1959), 38 Tax Cas 391 (HL) (replacement cost of knives and lasts in shoe manufacturing machinery characterized as capital; equipment essential to functioning of plant); *MacMillan Bloedel (Alberni) Ltd v MNR*, [1973] CTC 295 (FCTD) (although fan belts and oil were operating costs deductible in maintaining fleet of trucks, tires lasting a year were not; tires comprising 10–15 percent of value of truck; truck purchased intact not in individual parts); *Oxford Shopping Centres Ltd v Canada*, [1980] CTC 7 (FCTD), aff'd [1981] CTC 128 (FCA) ("once and for all" payment by taxpayer to municipality to assist with road changes deductible); see also *Johns-Manville Corp v MNR* (1981), 82 DTC 6054 at 6057 (FCA) in which the court stated:

> I recognize that the regular recurrence of the acquisitions is relevant in determining whether the outlays for the lots are income or capital in nature. But it is in no way decisive. As Dixon J. (as he then was) put it in *Sun Newspapers Limited v The Federal Commissioner of Taxation* (1938), 61 C.L.R. 337 at page 362 ([Aust HC]), "recurrence is not a test, it is no more than a consideration, the weight of which depends upon the nature of the expenditure."

physical characteristics of the product of the expenditure do not deter-mine its nature. For example, for General Motors the cost of manufac-turing an automobile is an expense if it sells the automobile in the year, but is on account of capital if it is not sold and remains in inventory at the end of the year. The recurrence of the expenditure is irrelevant.

Thus, annual expenditures are on account of capital if they are in-tended to bring into existence assets of enduring value — that is, if the assets have a life longer than a year. Conversely, a one-time expendi-ture is a current expense if one intends to consume the entire benefit of the expenditure in one fiscal period.

a) Enduring Benefit

What is an "enduring benefit"? The test refers to benefits that endure in the sense that some assets have a life longer than one year. Benefits that accrue from saving payments over a number of years are not ne-cessarily a capital asset. In *Anglo-Persian Oil Co Ltd v Dale*, Rowlatt J explained the distinction as follows:

> . . . a benefit which endures, in the way that fixed capital endures;
> not a benefit that endures in the sense that for a good number of years
> it relieves you of a revenue payment. It means a thing which endures
> in the way that fixed capital endures. It is not always an actual asset,
> but it endures in the way that getting rid of a lease or getting rid of
> onerous capital assets . . . endures.[18]

The explanation is not entirely satisfactory. Note that Rowlatt J uses the word "endures" seven times to explain "enduring," which suggests the difficulty of defining the concept.

One can also derive an enduring benefit from discharging a liability:

> [T]he disposition of a source of liability may be equivalent to the
> acquisition of a source of profit — an extension perhaps, but not an
> exception, to the principle that in some sense or other an asset of a
> capital nature, tangible or intangible, positive or negative, must be
> shown to be acquired.[19]

The "enduring benefit" test is difficult to apply. To be sure, it pro-vides an answer in self-evident cases. Common sense and accounting principles tell us that a taxpayer who purchases a building for rental purposes cannot write off its entire cost in the year that he acquires it,

---

18   *Anglo-Persian Oil Co Ltd v Dale* (1931), 16 Tax Cas 253 at 262 (CA), approved by
   Lord Wilberforce in *Tucker v Granada Motorway Services Ltd*, [1979] STC 393 at
   396 (HL).

19   *Commissioners of Inland Revenue v Charron Co* (1968), 45 Tax Cas 18 at 75 (HL).

and that the purchase price is a capital expenditure that has enduring benefits over many years. It is equally clear that the costs of heating the building are period costs and should be charged as current expenses against revenues in each year for the purpose of determining net profit. But what of the in-between cases? Consider the following:

- A taxpayer expends $20,000 on advertising the building for rent;[20]
- A taxpayer spends $40,000 on lobbying against rent control legislation;[21]
- A taxpayer installs a concrete lining in the basement of the building to protect it against an oil nuisance created by a nearby refinery.[22]

Each of these cases involve subtle distinctions that are not as easy to resolve. Some judges are quite candid about the difficulty of characterizing expenditures. As Sir Wilfred Greene MR said:

> . . . there have been . . . many cases where this matter of capital or income has been debated. There have been many cases which fall upon the borderline: indeed, in many cases it is almost true to say that the spin of a coin would decide the matter almost as satisfactorily as an attempt to find reasons.[23]

The Master of the Rolls speaks as a judge. A tax lawyer who decides such questions on a "spin of the coin" should increase her liability insurance.

b) Direct vs. Indirect Consequences

We should not interpret "enduring" literally but in its commercial context. Many current expenses have enduring benefits in the sense that advantages that accrue from the expenditure continue for a long time. For example, a payment to be rid of an incompetent employee is a current expense even though the payment will, hopefully, have enduring beneficial consequences.[24] An oil change is of enduring benefit to the life of an automobile. Nevertheless, routine maintenance is a current expense even though it enhances the long-term life of an asset.

---

20. *MNR v Tower Investment Inc*, [1972] CTC 182 (TAB) (court allowed deferral of deduction, in effect, matching expense to period when most of the resulting revenue would accrue).

21 *Morgan v Tate & Lyle Ltd*, [1955] AC 21 (HL) (expenditure on propaganda campaign to prevent nationalization of sugar refining industry was current expense); *Boarland v Kramat Pulai Ltd* (1953), 35 Tax Cas 1 (cost of pamphlet circulated to shareholders, critical of government policy not wholly on account of trade).

22 *Midland Empire Packing Co v Commissioner*, 14 TC 635 (1950) (US) (concrete lining essentially a repair; deductible as expense).

23 *IRC v British Salmson Aero Engines Ltd* (1938), 22 Tax Cas 29 at 43 (CA).

24 *Mitchell v BW Noble Ltd* (1927), 11 Tax Cas 372 (CA) (payment to get rid of a director was a revenue expense).

i)   Goodwill

Expenditures on account of the development or acquisition of goodwill are difficult to classify. In *MNR v Algoma Central Railway*,[25] for example, the taxpayer expended funds to obtain a geological survey of the mineral potential of the area through which the railway operated. The expenditure was a once-and-for-all cost intended to stimulate its railway traffic by attracting developers to engage in mining the area. There were two issues: (1) did the expenditures bring into existence an asset of enduring value? and (2) was enduring value to be tested by looking to the immediate or ultimate consequences of the expenditures? The Exchequer Court held that the direct consequences of the expenditures did not bring into existence an asset of an enduring nature; the expenses were deductible as a current expense.

Clearly, purchased goodwill is an asset of enduring value, and the purchase price is a capital outlay.[26] For example, if one were to purchase the Coca Cola Company, there would be considerable goodwill in the brand name. In contrast, routine institutional advertising by Coca Cola that generates goodwill is a current deductible expense. In both of these situations, however, we can clearly and directly trace the funds to the end use.

It is the intermediate case, where one expends funds to protect an existing asset, that presents the most difficulties. In *Canada Starch Co v MNR*,[27] for example, the taxpayer spent $80,000 to develop a new brand name, "Viva." When faced with opposition to its registration as a trademark on the grounds that "Viva" was confusing with another registered trademark, the taxpayer paid $15,000 in return for withdrawal of the opposition to registration. Jackett P described the difference between acquiring and developing assets as follows:[28]

- An expenditure for the acquisition or creation of a business entity, structure or organization, for the earning of profit, or for an addition to such entity, structure or organization, is an expenditure on account of capital; and
- An expenditure in the process of operation of a profit-making entity, structure or organization is an expenditure on revenue account.

---

25   *MNR v Algoma Central Railway*, above note 14.
26   See, for example, *Gifford v Canada*, above note 11.
27   *Canada Starch Co v MNR* (1968), 68 DTC 5320 (Ex Ct) [*Canada Starch*]; *Border Chemical Co v MNR*, [1987] 2 CTC 183 (FCTD) (legal fees to defend a taxpayer's senior officials against criminal prosecution not deductible as expenses if cost incurred to prevent damage to taxpayer's goodwill).
28   *Canada Starch*, ibid at 5323.

Since the taxpayer's expenditures *in* the course of its operations that gave rise to the trademark were current expenses, the $15,000 payment was part of the process of the registration of an asset that already existed. Therefore, the expenditure was deductible as an expense.

On the general question of expenditures on account of promotion, advertising and goodwill, Jackett P said:

> [I]n my view, the advertising expenses for launching the new product in this case were expenses on revenue account. I expressed a similar view in *Algoma Central Railway v MNR* . . . a decision that was upheld on appeal. As I indicated there, "According to my understanding of commercial principles . . . advertising expenses paid out while a business is operating, and directed to attract customers to a business, are current expenses." Similarly, in my view, expenses of other measures taken by a businessman with a view to introducing particular products to the market—such as market surveys and industrial design studies—are also current expenses. They also are expenses laid out while the business is operating as part of the process of inducing the buying public to buy the goods being sold.
>
> It remains to consider expenses incurred by a businessman, during the course of introducing new products to the market, to obtain the additional protection for his trade mark that is made available by trade mark legislation. A new mark adopted and used in the course of marketing a product gradually acquires the protection of the laws against passing off (assuming that it is, in fact, distinctive). This is something that is an incidental result of ordinary trading operations. Additional expenditure to acquire the additional protection made available by statute law seems to me to be equally incidental to ordinary trading operations. It follows that, in my view, the fees paid to the trade mark lawyers and to the trade mark office are deductible. In this case, no submission was presented to me as to any principle whereby I should distinguish between the ordinary cost of acquiring trade mark registration and the $15,000 payment that, in this case, was necessary in the judgment of the appellant to obtain registration of the trade mark . . . and I have been able to conceive of no such principle.[29]

c) Preservation of Capital Assets

The distinction between a current expense and capital expenditure is even more blurred when the question arises in the context of expenditures to maintain or preserve capital assets already in existence. Is an expenditure that one incurs for the protection or maintenance of

---

29　*Ibid* at 3324–325.

a capital asset a capital expenditure? The answer depends more upon the *type* of property on which one incurs the expenditure than on any clear-cut, black-letter rule.

i) Legal Expenses

The deductibility of legal expenses for protecting a capital asset is unclear. The weight of the cases is against deductibility. In an early case, *Dominion Natural Gas Co v MNR*,[30] for example, the Supreme Court held that legal expenses incurred in successfully protecting the taxpayer's gas franchise were capital outlays and not deductible from income. In reaching his decision, Duff CJC enlarged Lord Cave's test (bringing into existence an asset of enduring benefit to the business) as follows:[31]

> The expenditure was incurred "once and for all" and it was incurred for the purpose and with the effect of procuring for the company "the advantage of an enduring benefit."

In contrast to a decision of the English court in the same year,[32] the Court did not accept that the expenses were incidental to the ordinary course of the taxpayer's business. Thus, the Court put up a two-step hurdle to establish that an expenditure is current and deductible.

The stature of *Dominion Natural Gas Co v MNR*, however, has been eroded by subsequent decisions. In *MNR v Kellogg Co of Canada*,[33] for

---

30   [1941] SCR 19.

31   *Ibid* at 24.

32   See *Southern v Borax Consolidated Ltd*, [1940] 4 All ER 412 at 416 and 420, Lawrence J:

> In my opinion, the principle which is to be deducted from the cases is that where a sum of money is laid out for the acquisition or the improvement of a fixed capital asset it is attributable to capital, but *if no alteration is made* in the fixed capital asset by the payment, then it is properly attributable to revenue, being in substance a matter of maintenance, the maintenance of the capital structure or the capital assets of the company . . . .
>
> It appears to me that the legal expenses which were incurred . . . did not create any new asset at all but were expenses which were incurred in the ordinary course of maintaining the assets of the company, and the fact that it was maintaining the title and not the value of the company's business does not, in my opinion, make it any different. [Emphasis added.]

See also *Mitchell v BW Noble Ltd*, above note 24 at 421:

> The object (of the expenditure) . . . was that of preserving the status and reputation of the company which the directors felt might be imperilled . . . to avoid that and to preserve the status and divided-earning power of the company seems to me a purpose which is well within the ordinary purpose of the trade.

33   *MNR v Kellogg Co of Canada*, [1942] CTC 51 (Ex Ct), aff'd [1943] CTC 1 (SCC).

example, the taxpayer successfully deducted substantial legal fees incurred in defending an allegation of trademark infringement. The Supreme Court distinguished its earlier decision in *Dominion Natural Gas Co v MNR* on the basis that the trademark action in *MNR v Kellogg Co of Canada* was neither a right of property nor an exclusive right. The Court held the expenses to be ordinary legal expenses and deductible in the ordinary course of business.[34]

In *Evans v MNR*,[35] the taxpayer, who was entitled to one-third of an estate left to her by her husband and by her father, incurred legal fees when her right to the income of the estate was challenged. Once again, the Supreme Court held that the legal fees were a current expense and were not paid on account of capital. Cartwright J, speaking for the majority of the Court, distinguished *Dominion Natural Gas Co v MNR* on the basis that the legal fees in that case were "expenses to preserve a capital asset in a capital aspect." In the Court's opinion, Mrs Evans' right to the income of the estate was not a capital asset.

Thus, the distinction between a capital expenditure and an expense comes down to whether one incurs the expenditure to preserve a capital asset in a capital aspect or in a revenue aspect. But what is the distinction between "a capital aspect" and "a revenue aspect"?[36] This test does not likely add anything to the other tests. Ultimately, the resolution of the entire question depends on the facts and circumstances. As the Privy Council said in *BP Australia Ltd v Commissioner of Taxation of Commonwealth of Australia*:

> [T]he solution to the problem is not to be found by any rigid test or description. It has to be derived from many aspects of the whole set of circumstances, some of which may point in one direction, some in the other. One consideration may point so clearly that it domin-

---

34   *MNR v Kellogg Co of Canada, ibid*, in which the learned Chief Justice said at 3:

> The right upon which the (taxpayer) relied was not a right of property, or an exclusive right of any description, but the right (in common with all other members of the public) to describe their goods in the manner in which they were described.

35   *Evans v MNR*, [1960] SCR 391; see also *Farmer's Mutual Petroleums Ltd v MNR*, [1966] CTC 283 (Ex Ct), aff'd [1967] CTC 396 (SCC) (legal expenses incurred in defending title to mineral rights were capital outlays); *BC Power Corp v MNR* [1966] CTC 451 (Ex Ct) (legal expenses incurred in preserving right to shares that had purportedly been expropriated by a provincial government were non-deductible capital expenditures).

36   See, for example, *Jager Homes Ltd v MNR*, [1988] 1 CTC 215 (FCA) (legal fees to defend action to wind up company on capital account and not deductible as current expense).

ates other and vaguer indications in the contrary direction. It is a commonsense appreciation of all the guiding features which must provide the ultimate answer.[37]

ii) Repairs, Maintenance and Alterations

The dividing line between capital expenditures and current expenses due to routine maintenance and repairs is also unclear. Here too, the underlying principle is easy to state, but difficult to apply. An expenditure in one fiscal period that enhances, substantially improves, enlarges or prolongs the life of an asset beyond the period is a capital outlay. In contrast, an expenditure that merely maintains an asset or restores it to its original condition is a deductible current expense.

It is easy to identify the correct answer in polar cases when one does not really need an answer. It is the grey areas in between that cause the problems and litigation. For example, it is clear that the extension of an existing building by adding new floor space is a capital expenditure; it brings into existence an asset of enduring value. It is equally clear that routine maintenance of an existing building, for example, performance of minor repairs, replacement of light bulbs, cleaning and maintenance of heating and ventilation systems are current expenses.

Between these extremes, however, there are cases that cause considerable difficulty. One must distinguish each expenditure *in the context of the taxpayer's activities*. For example, a taxpayer who expends money to restore a decrepit and rundown building incurs capital expenditures, even though routine deductible maintenance by the previous owner would have prevented the building from deteriorating to a decrepit state. Similarly, a business that regularly expends funds to change the oil in its fleet of automobiles incurs current expenses. Neglecting to change the oil in its automobiles may, at a later date, involve substantial costs by way of engine replacements that would result in capital outlays.[38]

iii) "Repair" vs. "Renewal"

"Repair" and "renew" do not necessarily imply different meanings. "Repair" means "restoration by renewal or replacement of subsidiary parts of a whole." "Renewal" means "reconstruction of the entirety, meaning

---

37   *BP Australia*, above note 13 at 264–65, cited with approval by the SCC in *Johns-Manville*, above note 11.

38   *Better Plumbing Co v MNR* (1952), 6 Tax ABC 177; see also *Glenco Investment Corp v MNR*, [1967] CTC 243 (Ex Ct) (cost of plumbing and electrical installations in a warehouse acquired and converted into a commercial building suitable for rental was capital outlay).

by the entirety, not necessarily of the whole."[39] The Privy Council considered the relationship between repairs and renewals in *Rhodesia Railways Ltd v Bechuanaland Collector of Income Tax*:

> The periodical renewal by sections, of the rails and sleepers of a railway line as they wear out through use, is in no sense a reconstruction of the whole railway and is an ordinary incident of railway administration. The fact that the wear, although continuous, is not and cannot be made good annually, does not render the work of renewal when it comes to being effected, necessarily a capital charge. The expenditure here in question was incurred in consequence of the rails having been worn out in earning the income of the previous years on which tax had been paid without deduction in respect of such wear, and represented the cost of restoring them to a state in which they could continue to earn income. It did not result in the creation of any new asset; it was incurred to maintain the appellant's existing line in a state to earn revenue.[40]

iv) Replacements

Renewal costs which go beyond financing the replacement of worn-out parts and transforming one asset into another are capital expenditures. In *Highland Railway Co v Balderston*, the taxpayer was not allowed to deduct the costs of replacing iron rails with steel rails as a current expense. The Lord President of the Scottish Court of Exchequer said:[41]

> [T]hen when we come to the question of the alteration of the main line itself, it must be kept in view that this is not a mere relaying of the line after the old fashion; it is not taking away rails that are worn out o[r] partially worn out, and renewing them in whole or in part along with the whole line. That would not alter the character of the line; it would not affect the nature of the heritable property possessed by the Company. But what has been done is to substitute one kind of rail for another, steel rails for iron rails.

In other words, steel rails are a different asset from iron rails, although either may be used for the same purpose — transporting trains.

---

39   *Lurcott v Wakely*, [1911] 1 KB 905 (CA).
40   *Rhodesia Railways Ltd v Bechuanaland Collector of Income Tax*, [1933] AC 368 at 374 (PC).
41   *Highland Railway Co v Balderston* (1889), 2 Tax Cas 485 at 488; see also *Tank Truck Transport Ltd v MNR* (1965), 65 DTC 405 (TAB) (replacement of twelve cast iron tanks with stainless steel tanks held to be capital outlay).

The deductibility of replacement costs as a current expense depends on the magnitude of the replacement in the context of the complete unit of which it forms a part. The replacement of small parts in an automobile is routine maintenance; replacement of the entire engine is a capital outlay. The test in each case is: Are the expenditures on account of repair of the larger property by replacement of a component, or on account of replacement of an entire unit, complete in itself?[42] The question is often pragmatically resolved by comparing the cost of replacement with the cost of ordinary repairs in the context of the total unit of which the replacement is a part. The higher the cost of replacement compared to the costs of the total unit, the greater the likelihood that the costs are on account of capital.

d) Discharge of Obligations

A payment to eliminate an enduring disadvantage or an onerous obligation may have enduring benefits and constitute a capital expenditure. Here too, the polar cases are clear. A *surrogatum* payment to discharge a revenue expense (for example, a payment to dismiss an unsatisfactory employee) is deductible as a current expense.[43] Similarly, a payment to discharge a capital liability is a capital expenditure.[44] The intermediate cases are not as clear. The emphasis is on the permanency of the advantage secured by discharging the liability.[45]

---

42 *MNR v Vancouver Tugboat Co*, [1957] CTC 178 (Ex Ct) ($42,000 replacement of tugboat engine held to be replacement of substantial part of the whole, hence capital outlay); *Canada Steamship Lines Ltd v MNR*, [1966] CTC 255 (Ex Ct) (cost of replacing boiler in ship held to be capital expenditure).

43 *Mitchell v BW Noble Ltd*, above note 24 (payment to secure retirement of director whose conduct likely to damage taxpayer's business was revenue payment).

44 *Countess Warwick Steamship Co Ltd v Ogg*, [1924] 2 KB 292 (payment to secure cancellation of contract to acquire capital asset was capital expense).

45 *Whitehead (Inspector of Taxes) v Tubbs (Elastics) Ltd*, [1984] STC 1 at 3 (CA) (payment to secure release from onerous term in loan agreement, which significantly limited taxpayer's power to borrow, constituted capital payment), Oliver LJ:

> Here the advantage sought to be achieved was one which was permanent in the sense that the company was relieved, for the balance of the loan period, of the disadvantages arising from the restrictions and relieved of restrictions attributable to a non-recurring transaction. One cannot separate the payment made from the origins of the restrictions in respect of which it was made. In effect these restrictions — and whether they were contained in the agreement or the debenture is really immaterial, for they clearly went and were intended to go hand-in-hand — were the price or premium paid by the company for the loan, and the loan, it is not in dispute, was clearly a transaction of a capital nature.

202 INCOME TAX LAW

e) Factual Ambiguity

As the above discussion illustrates, the characterization of expenditures is factual in the context of broadly defined legal principles. At the very least, the process is uncertain and ambiguous. We resolve factual ambiguity in the taxpayer's favour.[46] As Estey J, speaking for a unanimous Supreme Court, stated:

> Such a determination is, furthermore, consistent with another basic concept in tax law, that where the taxing statute is not explicit, reasonable uncertainty or factual ambiguity resulting from lack of explicitness in the statute should be resolved in favour of the taxpayer.[47]

f) Summary

There is no single test that one can apply to all circumstances. There are, however, three broad criteria that offer a useful starting point in determining whether an expenditure is on account of capital or revenue:

1) The character of the advantage or the duration of the benefit (the more enduring the benefit the more likely that the expenditure is on account of capital);

2) Recurrence and frequency of the expenditure (the more frequent the expenditure the less enduring the benefit); and

3) Identification of the payment as a *surrogatum* for expenditures that would be on account of capital or revenue (a substitute for a capital expenditure is more likely a capital expenditure).

C. UNREASONABLE EXPENSES

A taxpayer may deduct an expense only to the extent that it is reasonable in amount. This rule, which relates to the amount of the expense, prevents taxpayers from artificially reducing their income through unreasonable expenses.

What is "reasonable" is a question of fact. One determines "reasonable" by comparing the expense in question with amounts paid in similar circumstances in comparable businesses. In *Doug Burns Excavation Contractor Ltd v MNR*,[48] for example, the Tax Court disallowed the taxpayer's deduction for a bonus of $100,000 that it paid to the president's wife who worked as a clerk in the office.

---

46 *Johns-Manville*, above note 11.
47 *Ibid* at 5384.
48 [1983] CTC 2566 (TCC).

D. EXPRESS PROHIBITIONS (LEVIES, FINES AND PENALTIES)

An expense is deductible if it is incurred for the purposes of gaining or producing income. Thus, a taxpayer may deduct expenses incurred for illegal acts to the extent that he incurs them to earn income. However, this principle does not extend to the deduction of fines and penalties.

A taxpayer cannot deduct a fine or penalty imposed by law in any jurisdiction, including a foreign jurisdiction. The prohibition overturns the decision of the Supreme Court in *65302 British Columbia Ltd v Canada*,[49] which held that fines and penalties incurred for the purpose of gaining or producing income are deductible expenses under paragraph 18(1)(a).

The rationale of the prohibition is that allowing the deduction of fines and penalties diminishes their ability to deter taxpayers from engaging in illegal activities, and thus is contrary to public policy objectives. However, the Act leaves open the door for the deduction of prescribed fines where it would be inconsistent with public policy to deny their deductibility.[50]

E. ILLEGAL PAYMENTS

Corrupting government officials is a cost of doing business in certain countries. Indeed, it is impossible to do business in some countries—for example, India, Nigeria and Afghanistan—without paying bribes to government officials. We distinguish, however, between bribing domestic and foreign officials. Bribing domestic officials is absolutely illegal in Canada. Corruption of foreign officials may be legal or illegal depending upon the circumstances and the nature of the payment. Some forms of foreign bribery are acceptable, while others are not.

The *Corruption of Foreign Public Officials Act*[51] features three primary offences: bribery of foreign public officials, money laundering,

---

49   In *65302 BC Ltd*, above note 2, an over-quota levy imposed on an egg-producing poultry farm by the BC Egg Marketing Board was an allowable deduction pursuant to subs 9(1) and para 18(1)(a) of the Act, above note 3. The levy was incurred as part of the taxpayer's day-to-day operations. Furthermore, the business decision to produce over-quota was a deliberate decision made in order to realize income. Since the fine was imposed to remove the profit of over-quota production, it was allowable as a deductible current expense.

50   See, for example, *Income Tax Regulations*, CRC, c 945, s 7309, which prescribes fines under the *Excise Tax Act*.

51   SC 1998, c 34.

and possession of proceeds from money laundering and bribery. Aiding, abetting and counselling such activities are also criminal offences.

The core offence, which covers individuals and corporations, is the bribery of foreign public officials at any level of government, whether international, national or local. A "bribe"—in German, "Schmiergeld" or lubrication money—is an offer or promise, either explicitly or implicitly, to give undue pecuniary or other advantage, directly or through intermediaries, in order to obtain or retain business or other improper advantage. The offence extends to all businesses, professions and trades, regardless of where they are situated or practiced. For example, it is an offence to bribe a foreign public official to obtain a contract to build an embassy in Canada.

The essence of the offence is the corruption of foreign public officials to get them to act or refrain from acting in the performance of their public duties. For example, it would be an offence to pay a foreign prime minister to secure an open-bid contract to build a football stadium in his country. Similarly, payments to foreign tax officials to obtain undue or favourable tax concessions enacted for the purposes of conferring an advantage are bribery.

However, all bribes are not equally offensive in law. Business must go on according to the local culture. In certain societies "grease," "commissions," "facilitation fees," "agency fees" and "baksheesh" are essential to doing business. Many governments control the issuance of licences to produce, manufacture or distribute products that sometimes assure the recipient of a monopoly or protected market. Civil servants and ministers grant such licences and, in the process, may supplement their income. No bribe, no licence. Canadian companies that participate, directly or indirectly, in any such bidding process can be prosecuted.

Not all payments to expedite performance by foreign officials are bribes. For example, "facilitation" payments to get officials to perform acts of a "routine nature" within the scope of their public duties are not bribes under the statute. Thus, one can pay foreign officials to perform functions that they are supposed to be performing as part of their job—issuance of a permit, licence or visa to which one is entitled—without breaking the law.

For example, it is routine, indeed expected, that one must pay customs officials in some countries to ensure that there is no delay in unloading perishable food off a ship. Judges in some countries also expect supplemental consideration to release their judgments in a timely manner. Similarly, it would not be considered socially offensive to pay a tax official to issue an assessment or clearance certificate to which one would normally be entitled upon completion of certain transactions.

The real difficulty is in determining when grease crosses the line from being a facilitation payment and becomes an illegal act. The distinction is important in at least four legal aspects. First, and most obvious, bribery of foreign officials is a criminal act and carries a maximum term of imprisonment of five years. Lawyers must give opinions on the character of payments to corporations and their auditors.

Second, the offence carries a fine that is entirely in the discretion of the judge. The Act does not stipulate any maximum amount.

Third, bribes are not deductible as expenses for income tax purposes even if the taxpayer pays them solely for the purposes of conducting business and there is no alternative but to pay if one is to secure the contract (section 67.5(1)). Further, there is no limitation period and the tax authorities can reassess the taxpayer at any time (section 67.5(2)).

Fourth, in the event that the taxpayer is prosecuted and convicted, the amount of the (unlimited) fine is not deductible for tax purposes. Thus, both the bribe and the fine are payable with after-tax dollars.

Canada has not prosecuted anyone under these provisions in recent years. Nevertheless, Canadian corporations with international operations must abide by the rules even if they are doing business through a foreign subsidiary corporation.

F. PERSONAL AND LIVING EXPENSES

1) General Comment

A taxpayer cannot deduct personal or living expenses in computing income from business or property.[52] To be deductible, an expense must be incurred for the purpose of earning income.[53] The Act allows a taxpayer

---

52   ITA, above note 3, para 18(1)(h) and subs 248(1) "personal or living expenses." The prohibition does not cover travelling expenses (including the full cost of meals and lodging) incurred on a business trip. "Personal or living expenses" include expenses incurred to maintain a property where the property is not maintained in connection with a business that is being carried on for profit or with a reasonable expectation of profit. They also include expenses incurred for purchasing a life insurance policy, the proceeds of which are payable to the taxpayer, or to a person related to the taxpayer.

53   Paragraph 18(1)(h), ibid, was originally implemented as para 2(2)(e) of c 55, SC 1919, which amended s 3 of the Income War Tax Act, 1917. In response to a question in the House regarding the purpose of this section, asked by a questioner who noted that it was already "quite evident that no one has the right to deduct his personal and living expenses from income before he declares it for the purposes of this Act," the Minister of Finance stated that the section was "just to

to deduct expenses incurred during "for profit" activities and prohibits the deduction of expenses incurred during "for pleasure" activities or on account of capital. The distinction between profit, pleasure and capital expenses involves difficult classification problems. Characterization involves drawing a line between categories. The line that divides deductible and non-deductible expenses should provide an accurate measure of income that is both equitable and can be administered easily.

The distinction between profit and pleasure expenses is blurred and, indeed, sometimes meaningless because it is impossible to quantify profit and pleasure at discrete intervals. Nevertheless, the distinction is important for tax purposes and taxpayers are routinely asked to determine which of the two objectives, profit or pleasure, is the predominant motive for an expenditure. The distinction between the two determines whether a taxpayer pays a dollar or 50 cents on the dollar for a particular expense. The courts are equally uncomfortable with these distinctions and often rely more upon compilations of deductible and non-deductible lists, rather than on principled formulations based upon tax policy.

Expenses can be put on a continuum. At one extreme are those expenses that are of a purely business nature, and there is no serious issue of their deductibility. For example, a taxpayer who pays salaries, rent, utilities and operating expenses on account of his business is entitled to deduct the expenditures (subject only to quantum limitations) as routine business expenses.[54] At the other end of the continuum, we find expenses that are of a purely personal nature. Hence, for example, a taxpayer is not generally entitled to deduct her personal meals, clothing, cosmetics, personal grooming and the everyday costs of living. The difficulty of determining deductibility, however, is in the middle where the expenditure is clearly neither one nor the other, but has attributes both of business and personal. It is in this grey area that one must determine which attributes predominate.

Expenditures in the grey zone of deductibility can be broken down into two broad categories: (1) the "special costs" of a person engaged in business, such as child care and commuting, and (2) "personal gratification costs" that give pleasure in the pursuit of profit or bring about profit in the pursuit of pleasure for example, travel and entertainment. Tax law deals quite easily with both of these categories of expenditures in the case of employed persons. Employees are prohibited from de-

---

make it clear that deduction must not be made" and to "make it perfectly clear that the full net income must be assessed" (Commons Debates, 24 June 1919).
54 Ibid, s 9.

ducting any expenses unless the deduction is specifically authorized by the statute.[55] Thus, we tax employees based on their gross income with minimal deductions. We justify this rule on the basis of revenue considerations and administrative simplicity, without much concern for an accurate measure of net income.

The problem, however, is not so easily resolved in the case of business expenditures, where the rule is the converse: a taxpayer is entitled to deduct any expense incurred for the purpose of earning income unless the deduction is specifically *prohibited*. This inverse burden leads to tension between employed persons and those engaged in business and it raises the issue of equitable treatment of taxpayers who are similarly situated. Thus, individuals generally prefer independent contractor status for tax purposes and employee status under labour laws. This allows them the best of both worlds, maximum tax deductions and maximum protection in the workplace.

2) Purpose Test

We determine the purpose of an expenditure by looking for the predominant reason for which one incurs the expenditure. This is a positive test and quite different from asking the converse: "what would happen if the taxpayer did *not* incur the expense?" The purpose test is not the "but for" test. The test for deductibility is *not*: "but for this expense, could the taxpayer have earned his income?" Such a broad test would completely obliterate the distinction between business and personal expenses and negate the value of the purpose test.

For example, how should we classify child care expenses, the classic hybrid of "for profit" and "for pleasure" expenditures? In a conventional family setting with infant children, both parents cannot go out to work without some provision for the children. This raises two questions. Are the expenses incurred:

1) Primarily and predominantly for the purpose of allowing the parent (usually the mother) to engage in business? and
2) As a basic function of family life and, hence, of a personal nature?

In *Smith v Commissioner* (*Smith*),[56] for example, the United States Board of Tax Appeals denied the taxpayer a deduction for babysitting expenses on the theory that allowing such a deduction would extend the deduction to all consumption expenditures (such as food, shelter,

---

55   *Ibid*, subs 8(2).
56   *Smith v Commissioner* (1939), 40 BTA 1038, aff'd 113 F 2d 114 (US 2d Cir 1940).

clothing and recreation) that allow taxpayers to carry on their day-to-day activities. The board was concerned with opening the floodgates for the deduction of all personal expenditures, however tenuous their connection with the income-earning process:

> The fee to the doctor, but for whose healing service, the earner of the family income could not leave his sickbed; the cost of the labourer's raiment, for how can the world proceed about its business unclothed; the very home which gives us shelter and rest and the food which provides energy, might all by an extension of the same proposition be construed as necessary to the operation of business and to the creation of income. Yet these are the very essence of those "personal" expenses the deductibility of which is expressly denied.[57]

There is, however, an important distinction between expenses incurred primarily for personal purposes and expenses incurred predominantly for the purpose of earning income, but which have only incidental and ancillary personal elements. The difficulty lies in drawing the line between the two.

It is clear that certain expenditures are common to everyone, whether they are employed, engaged in a business or unemployed. The basic personal expenditures for food, shelter, clothing and the everyday necessities of life are clearly not deductible, regardless of one's working status. One does not incur such expenditures primarily for the purposes of earning income.

Child care expenses, however, pose a different conceptual problem. Child care expenses are a basic family consumption expenditure if we begin from the premise that one parent must stay at home to look after the child. Then, any child care expenses are primarily of a personal nature. The business aspect of the expenditure on account of child care arises if, and only if, the previously stay-at-home parent decides to enter the commercial marketplace and engage in business. Thus, one's perspective on child care expenses depends on where one starts the analysis. To be sure, the short answer is that the Act has a detailed statutory framework for the deduction of child care expenses and, hence, cannot deduct such expenses under the general provisions[58] because of the prescribed scheme.[59] But that response merely avoids the difficult question. Apart from specific statutory provisions, the theoretically correct answer is surely that the incremental cost of a

---

57   *Ibid* at 1038–39.
58   *ITA*, above note 3, s 9.
59   *Ibid*, s 63.

hybrid profit/pleasure expenditure is deductible for tax purposes if the primary and predominant motive for incurring the expenditure is to earn business income.

The deductibility of child care expenses also raises equity issues if some taxpayers get tax-free child care while others are denied the same treatment. An employer, for example, can deduct the cost of child care that it provides at its facilities if it incurs the expenses for the purposes of earning business income. Since the employer requires and needs the services of all of its employees (some of whom have young children), the cost of providing child care on its premises is directly related to the employees' services. Parents with young children who are being well taken care of on the employer's premises are likely to work longer, and with less anxiety, than parents who need to dash off to rescue their children at pre-determined hours from daycare services. The same can be said of nanny care.[60] Thus, a person who pays for child care services to get to her business is not entitled to deduct the cost, or her employer can deduct the same cost to obtain her services.

The supposed logic of this disparate treatment is that the employer incurs the cost *after* his employees are on the business premises, whilst the parent incurs her child care expenses to get *to* the employer's premises. This invites arbitrage in salary negotiations. The obvious behavioural response is that one should (if possible) engage in salary arbitrage: negotiate a lower salary with on-site child care, rather than a higher salary with nanny care paid with after-tax dollars.

The question in *Smith*[61] was essentially whether the differential in child care expenses (or any part thereof) should be allowed as business expenses incurred for the purposes of earning income. The answer, based on the floodgates theory that allowing such expenses would open the door to allowing every other personal expense as a deduction (the "but for" test as the yardstick for determining deductibility), was not entirely satisfactory. There is a difference between expenses that are incurred, regardless of whether one works or not (basic food, personal clothing, shelter, etc.), and the incremental expenses associated only with the process of earning income.

Scott v Canada[62] recognizes this distinction in allowing a "foot and transit courier" to deduct the cost of his incremental food and water required to perform his job. The taxpayer travelled 150 kilometres a day carrying a backpack that weighed between 20–50 pounds. He worked

---

60   See *Symes v Canada*, [1993] 4 SCR 695.
61   *Smith v Commissioner*, above note 56.
62   *Scott v Canada*, [1998] 4 CTC 103 (FCA).

on foot and public transportation 10 hours per day, 5 days per week, 52 weeks per year. He consumed an *extra* meal per day for which he sought to deduct $11 ($8 for extra food and $3 for extra bottled water and juice) as business expenses. Since the taxpayer incurred expenses on account of food and beverages, the CRA denied his deduction for the incremental expenses. The Federal Court, quite rightly, refused to deny the deduction for the expenses simply on the grounds that such expenses have always been considered "personal" and, therefore, must continue to be so.[63] Instead, the court allowed the taxpayer to deduct his *incremental* food and drink expenses because the extra consumption was the direct result of his efforts to earn income. The incremental food and drink were the equivalent of the incremental gas that a person uses in his automobile for business purposes.[64]

The court, also quite rightly, rejected arguments that the deduction for food and beverage expenses would open the floodgates to a myriad of claims for deductions for personal expenses. The floodgates argument, always a concern for tax administrators, is an argument of last resort to preserve the status quo. The deduction "should in no way be interpreted as providing a basis to challenge all traditional prohibitions on the deduction of food and beverages as a business expense under the Act." The deduction for food and beverages is already tightly controlled under subsection 67.1(1) of the Act, which limits the deduction for such expenses to a maximum of 50 percent of the amount expended, even if one incurs the expense entirely for business purposes. Thus, it is unlikely that the floodgates will open on account of food and beverage expenses incurred for business purposes.

The question remains, however, as to how far the courts will go in permitting the deduction of other personal costs that are incurred

---

63   See, for example, Iacobucci J's comment in *Symes v Canada*, above note 60 at para 47:

> This appeal presents a particular expense which has been traditionally characterized as personal in nature. If, in coming to a decision, this Court stated that since such expenses have always been personal they must now be personal, the conclusion could be easily and deservedly attacked. For this reason, proper analysis of this question demands that the relationship between child care expenses and business income be examined more critically, in order to determine whether that relationship can be sufficient to justify the former's deductibility.

64   In *Scott v Canada*, above note 62, McDonald J stated at para 10:

> This result takes into account the different methods by which the same job is done and puts all couriers on an equal footing. Arguably, it also recognizes and encourages [rather than discourages as a prohibition on this expense would] new environmentally responsible ways of producing income.

solely and incrementally for the purposes of earning business income. Can the mortician deduct his sombre clothing, the lawyer her navy suit, the accountant his white shirt, the actress her designer clothes?

To summarize: Characterizing business expenses involves three questions: (1) what is the need that the expense meets? (2) would the need exist apart from the business? and (3) is the need intrinsic to the business? The answers to these questions are essentially questions of fact.[65]

> If a need exists even in the absence of business activity, and irrespective of whether the need was or might have been satisfied by an expenditure to a third party or by the opportunity cost of personal labour, then an expense to meet the need would traditionally be viewed as a personal expense. Expenses which can be identified in this way are expenses which are incurred by a taxpayer in order to relieve the taxpayer from personal duties and to make the taxpayer available to the business.
>
> Traditionally, expenses that simply make the taxpayer *available* to the business are not considered business expenses since the taxpayer is expected to be available to the business as a *quid pro quo* for business income received.

The needs test based upon primary objective should, in the absence of specific statutory provisions, provide an unequivocal answer. But it does not. The expense must also be *intrinsic* to the business. Why? In *Symes v Canada*, for example, the taxpayer's child care expenses met the needs test. The taxpayer could not operate her business without being present on the premises. The Supreme Court, however, said that the expenses merely made her *available* to practice her profession, rather than for any purpose intrinsic to the operation of the business itself. The expenses got her to her business, but they were not an integral part of the business. But having got to her place of business, the expenses would have been deductible by the business.

3) Type of Expenditure

Given the subjective nature of the purpose test, many courts look to the nature of an expenditure to determine its purpose. Is the expenditure

---

65   *Symes v Canada*, above note 60 at para 80 [emphasis added]:

> In another case, the arguments might be differently balanced, since the existence of a business purpose within the meaning of s. 18(1)(a) *is a question of fact*, and that the relative weight to be given to the factors analyzed will vary from case to case . . . . It can be difficult to weigh the personal and business elements at play.

of a type that is ordinarily and usually a direct expenditure in the pursuit of business, or one that is primarily personal and only tenuously related to business? Consider the distinction between a businessperson who entertains an out-of-town client at home for $100 and one who takes a client out for dinner to a restaurant for $400. Expenses of entertaining at home are usually personal, even though one devotes the entire discussion to business matters. This is because home entertainment is ordinarily and usually a personal affair. In contrast, $200 of the cost of the dinner in the restaurant would be deductible as a business expense, even if most of the evening was spent discussing personal affairs. Entertaining in restaurants is ordinarily and usually associated with business, and expenses in respect thereof are usually "business expenses."[66]

The distinction between business and personal expenses sometimes also depends upon the taxpayer's discretionary power to incur the expense. For example, Thorson P denied a deduction for commuting expenses on the basis that:

---

66   *Vuicic v MNR* (1960), 24 Tax ABC 253 (tavern keeper not allowed to deduct capital cost allowance in respect of $7,000 boat); *Brown v MNR* (1950), 1 Tax ABC 373 (special clothing required by radio technician posted in north not deductible); *No 431 v MNR* (1957), 17 Tax ABC 300 (salary paid to physician's housekeeper entirely personal or living expense notwithstanding housekeeper's answering physician's telephone); *Macquistan v MNR* (1965), 38 Tax ABC 23 (babysitter employed by physician in order to permit her to carry on practice was personal expense); *Nadon v MNR* (1965), 40 Tax ABC 33 (housekeeper engaged during illness of taxpayer's wife not deductible); *Lawlor v MNR*, [1970] Tax ABC 369 (lawyer not entitled to deduct cost of babysitters employed to permit business entertaining); *Cree v MNR*, [1978] CTC 2472 (TRB) (auto racing not carried on with reasonable expectation of profit; losses not deductible); *Hume v MNR*, [1980] CTC 2645 (TRB) ("hobby" investor denied deduction for cost of investment periodicals); *Warden v MNR*, [1981] CTC 2379 (TRB) (high school principal denied deduction of losses from farming and other operations since no expectation of profit); *Peters v MNR*, [1981] CTC 2451 (TRB) (bank employee denied deduction of losses from bee keeping and sheep raising); *White v MNR*, [1981] CTC 2456 (TRB) (taxpayer's losses from breeding and racing quarter horses disallowed for lack of reasonable expectation of profit); *Beyer v MNR*, [1978] CTC 2026 (TRB) (car racing losses not deductible); *Payette v MNR*, [1978] CTC 2223 (TRB) (writing and publication of books without reasonable expectation of profit; outlays not deductible); *Fluet v MNR*, [1978] CTC 2902 (TRB) (bank manager's cost and maintenance of guard dog for family protection not deductible); *Merchant v MNR*, [1980] CTC 2336 (TRB) (expenses incurred in attempt to secure leadership of Saskatchewan Liberal Party not deductible); *Symes v Canada*, [1991] 2 CTC 1 (FCA), aff'd [1993] 4 SCR 695 (lawyer's nanny expenses not deductible).

The personal and living expenses referred to . . . are those over which the taxpayer has a large amount of personal control, depending upon the scale of living which he may choose. Such expenses would probably not be deductible even if there were no provision in the statute relating to the matter, for if personal and living expenses were deductible from income and only the balance left for taxation purposes, the amount of net or taxable income would depend upon the taxpayer's own choice as to the scale of living that he might adopt and in many cases there would be no taxable income at all. It is obvious that the determination of what the taxable income of a taxpayer shall be cannot depend upon or be left to the taxpayer's own choice as to whether his personal and living expenses shall be up to the extent of his income or not.[67]

The rationale that personal expenses should not be deducted because they are within the discretion of the taxpayer is not persuasive. Most expenses, including business expenses, are ultimately within the taxpayer's discretion. A simpler explanation is sufficient: personal expenses are not deductible against business income because they are not incurred primarily and predominantly for business purposes and, as such, they are not relevant in determining income from business.

4) Business vs. Personal Expenditures

The concept of source of income is an intrinsic part of the Canadian income tax system.[68] The distinguishing feature of the source concept is the pursuit of profit. In order to determine whether a particular activity constitutes a source of income, the taxpayer must show that he carries on the activity in pursuit of profit. Thus, the characterization of income as being from a commercial activity is the first step in determining business or property income.

A hobby for personal pleasure is not a source of income. An amateur photographer, for example, who exhibits her works for pleasure, but never sells any, cannot claim expense deductions for her materials and supplies. There is no theoretical reason, however, why hobby sales would not be income even though expenses are not deductible. Tax law does not demand symmetry of income and expenses.

The law presumes that an activity in pursuit of profit that does not involve any personal or hobby element—such as, the practice of law—is a commercial venture and, as such, a source of income.[69] The

---

67   *Samson v MNR* (1943), 2 DTC 610 at 616–17 (Ex Ct).
68   See Chapter 4 and *Stewart v Canada*, 2002 SCC 46 at para 5 [*Stewart*].
69   *Stewart*, ibid.

only question that remains is whether the source is income from business or income from property.

If the activity is clearly commercial, there is no need to further analyze the taxpayer's business decisions even if subsequently they are seen as unsound and unprofitable. After all, many business people make bad commercial decisions. They should not be penalized by the tax system on an *ex-post* analysis of their commercial decisions. The objective is to determine the commercial nature of the taxpayer's activity and not his business acumen with hindsight.[70]

Where there are mixed personal and commercial elements to an activity, one must determine which elements predominate. Does the taxpayer carry on the activity in a sufficiently commercial manner to constitute a source of income? In these circumstances, one must evaluate the commercial content of the undertaking by looking at the taxpayer's expectation of profit and mode of operation. For example, a serious photographer may conduct her activities with the commercial hallmarks of a professional. If in an objective analysis of the evidence it is clear that her predominant intention is to derive profit from her activities, the income has a source and expenses to earn the income are deductible if they otherwise satisfy the Act.

Thus, the characterization of income and expenses involves two distinct steps. First, one must determine whether the taxpayer's undertaking is for profit or for personal purposes. If the taxpayer undertakes the activity primarily for profit, it is a source of income. The second step is to determine whether the source of income is from business or from property. The traditional common law definition of "business" is anything that occupies the time, attention and labour of a person for the purpose of profit.[71] Business income generally requires a higher level of taxpayer activity than property income. Nevertheless, regardless of the level of taxpayer activity, any commercial undertaking in pursuit of profit is a source of income, either from business or property.

A commercial activity is one that the taxpayer undertakes for profit. We determine the taxpayer's intention by looking at objective evidence to support her intentions. The taxpayer must establish that her predominant intention is to make a profit from the activity and that she carries on the activity in accordance with objective standards of business behaviour. Thus, one looks at:

1) The taxpayer's profit and loss experience in past years;

---

70   See *Stewart, ibid* at para 55.

71   *Smith v Anderson* (1880), 15 Ch D 247 at 258 (CA); *Terminal Dock and Warehouse Co v MNR*, [1968] 2 Ex CR 78, aff'd (1968), 68 DTC 5316.

2)   The taxpayer's training and expertise in the field of her activities;
3)   The taxpayer's intended course of action; and
4)   The financial viability of the venture to show a profit.

This list is not exhaustive and the factors to be taken into account in determining intention will differ according to the facts and circumstances of each case. Thus, having a reasonable expectation in the financial viability of the venture to show a profit is only one factor in evaluating the taxpayer's intention. A reasonable expectation of profit is not the only factor and it is not conclusive.

5) Statutory Exceptions

Some expenses that may be, at least in part, personal expenses are, nevertheless, deductible under specific statutory provisions. For example, moving expenses,[72] child care expenses,[73] and tuition fees[74] are all expenditures that are deductible from income or creditable against taxes in narrowly defined circumstances. The justification for the deductibility of these expenses for tax purposes is usually social or economic policy considerations; for example, mobility of labour, access to labour markets and investment in human capital and resources.

G. ABUSIVE TAX AVOIDANCE

A taxpayer seeking to deduct expenses from income must be mindful of the general anti-avoidance rule (GAAR). GAAR applies to "abusive" income tax avoidance transactions and arrangements. The thrust of the rule is that the CRA can ignore an offensive "avoidance transaction" and redetermine its income tax consequences in certain circumstances.[75]

An "avoidance transaction" is any transaction or series of transactions that gives rise to a tax benefit, unless the transaction is one that is undertaken for *bona fide* purposes other than that of obtaining a tax benefit. The Act defines a "tax benefit" to include, *inter alia*, any transaction to avoid taxes! But even a tax-motivated transaction is not an "avoidance transaction" if it does not misuse the Act, regulations, *Income Tax Application Rules* (ITARs) or tax treaties.[76]

---

72   *ITA*, above note 3, s 62.
73   *Ibid*, s 63.
74   *Ibid*, s 118.5.
75   *Ibid*, s 245.
76   *Ibid*, subs 245(4).

H. EXEMPT INCOME

An expense to earn exempt income is not deductible for tax purposes.[77] Generally, "exempt income" is any income that is not included in computing income under Part I of the Act.[78] Thus, one cannot offset expenditures to earn exempt income against other taxable income.

I. SPECIFIC DEDUCTIONS

The starting point in computing income from business or property is to determine the *net* profit therefrom according to generally accepted commercial principles. In addition to the deductions allowed according to commercial and accounting principles, the Act also specifically authorizes the deduction of certain expenses. The rationale for this specific list of deductions varies: some of the rules regulate deductions that might otherwise be governed by unclear or flexible accounting principles (e.g., reserves); some (e.g., capital cost allowances) replace broad accounting rules with more specific and detailed tax rules; some (e.g., restrictions on financing passenger motor vehicles) reflect a concern that the tax system should not subsidize personal expenditures; and some incorporate political and cultural value judgments (e.g., restrictions on advertising in non-Canadian periodicals). There is no single thread that connects these deductions. Each has its own rationale.

J. RESERVES AND CONTINGENT LIABILITIES

1) General Scheme

As a general rule, a taxpayer cannot deduct a reserve or a contingent liability.[79] A reserve is an appropriation, rather than an expense that one incurs for the purpose of earning income. As we will see, however, there are many exceptions to the rule.

The term "reserve" has a much broader meaning in tax law than it does in accounting. For accounting purposes, a "reserve" denotes an appropriation of income from retained earnings. Such appropriation

---

77   *Ibid*, para 18(1)(c).
78   *Ibid*, subs 248(1) "exempt income."
79   *Ibid*, para 18(1)(e); Interpretation Bulletin IT-215R Archived, "Reserves, Contingent Accounts and Sinking Funds" (12 January 1981), as amended by Special Release dated 30 November 1989.

may be pursuant to a contractual stipulation (for example, pursuant to a trust indenture) or at the discretion of the taxpayer.[80] For tax purposes, however, a "reserve" generally refers to an amount that one sets aside for future use. One must distinguish between reserves and unpaid liabilities. A "reserve" represents an amount set aside as a provision against a future uncertain event. A liability is a known and existing obligation.[81] Thus, an obligation is a liability for tax purposes only if all of the conditions precedent to create the liability have been satisfied.[82]

A contingent liability is a potential liability that depends upon an event that may or may not happen.[83] Thus, contingent liabilities are not immediate liabilities, but have the potential of becoming real on the happening of some event.

Generally, a taxpayer may claim a reserve in a year only if the Act specifically authorizes the deduction. A reserve that a taxpayer claims in a particular year is added back into his or her income in the following year. The taxpayer may then claim a new reserve according to the terms and conditions of the authorizing provisions. One must annually justify the deduction of a reserve.

2) Deductible Reserves

Deduction Allowed For	ITA Reference	To Be Included in Income in Following Year
Reserve for doubtful debts	20(1)(l)	12(1)(d)
Reserve for goods delivered and services performed after end of year	20(1)(m)(i), (ii)	12(1)(e)(i)
Reserve for deposits on returnable containers	20(1)(m)(iv)	12(1)(e)(i)
Manufacturer's warranty reserve	20(1)(m.1)	12(1)(e)(i)
Reserves for amounts not due on instalment sales contracts	20(1)(n)	12(1)(e)(ii)
Reserve for quadrennial survey	20(1)(o)	12(1)(h)
Prepaid rents	20(1)(m)(iii)	12(1)(e)(i)

---

80 *CICA Handbook* (Toronto: Canadian Institute of Chartered Accountants, 2010–) s 3260.01.

81 *No 297 v MNR* (1955), 14 Tax ABC 100 (amount set aside by taxpayer for employee bonuses not a reserve since liability to pay definite).

82 *Kerr Farms Ltd v MNR*, [1971] Tax ABC 804 (conditions precedent outstanding; accrued employee bonuses not liabilities).

83 See *Winter v Inland Revenue Commissioners* (1961), [1963] AC 235 at 262 (HL), Lord Guest. See also *Wawang Forest Products Ltd v R*, 2001 DTC 5212 (FCA). (A legal obligation to pay does not become contingent because of delay.)

3) Doubtful Debts

A taxpayer may deduct a reasonable amount for doubtful trade accounts if the amounts receivable in respect of the accounts were included in income, either in the year in which the reserve is sought or in a previous year.

A reserve calculated for financial statement purposes is not necessarily the amount deductible for tax purposes. Whether the collectibility of a debt is sufficiently "doubtful" to justify a reserve is a question of fact. This requires specific analysis of each account. As a matter of practice, however, the CRA does accept reserves calculated as a percentage of doubtful accounts, provided that the taxpayer can support the percentage by reference to his actual loss experienced. A reserve computed as a simple percentage of the taxpayer's total accounts receivable is not acceptable for tax purposes.

The factors usually taken into account in determining the collectibility of an account receivable are as follows:[84]

- History and age of the overdue account;
- The debtor's financial position;
- Past experience in respect of the debtor's bad debts;
- General business conditions;
- Specific business conditions in the debtor's industry;
- Specific business conditions in the debtor's locality; and
- Changes in sales and accounts receivable as compared with previous years.

A taxpayer who claims a reserve for doubtful accounts in one year must include the amount in income in the following year.[85] The taxpayer can then make a fresh evaluation of the collectibility of accounts receivable and deduct a new reserve in the current year. Thus, unlike an accounting practice that permits incremental additions to, and subtractions from, the previous year's reserve, we deduct the *entire* amount of the reserve in the year in which we claim it. This amount is then added to income in the following year, a new amount is deducted, and so on. This scheme allows the CRA to challenge the entire reserve in the year that the taxpayer claims it, without any risk that a portion of the reserve is statute-barred. Under accounting practices, it is arguable that only the incremental portion is current. The base of the reserve could be statute-barred.[86]

A taxpayer may also deduct her actual bad debts.[87] Thus, the initial claim for a reserve is a tentative one that is added back to income in the

---

84   *No 81 v MNR* (1953), 53 DTC 98 at 105.
85   *ITA*, above note 3, para 12(1)(d).
86   *Ibid*, subs 152(4).
87   *Ibid*, para 20(1)(p).

following year. The taxpayer may either collect the amount in a subsequent year or claim a write-off for actual bad debts. An amount written off that is subsequently collected by the taxpayer is brought back into income in the year of collection.[88]

Example

Assume:

Year	Accounts Receivable (year end)	Reserve for Doubtful Debts	Bad Debts Deducted	Bad Debts Recovered
1	$100,000	$10,000	–	–
2	$120,000	$12,000	$6,000	–
3	$150,000	$15,000	$4,000	$5,000

Then, the *net* deduction from income in each year is determined as follows:

Year 1

Reserve for doubtful debts	$ 10,000
Net deduction (Year 1)	$ 10,000

Year 2

Reserve for doubtful debts	$ 12,000
Bad debts deducted	6,000
	18,000
Less: reserve deducted (Year 1)	(10,000)
Net deduction (Year 2)	$ 8,000

Year 3

Reserve for doubtful debts	$ 15,000
Bad debts deducted	4,000
	19,000
Less: reserve deducted (Year 2)	(12,000)
Bad debts recovered	(5,000)
Net deduction (Year 3)	$ 2,000

a) Future Goods and Services

Payments on account of goods to be delivered or services to be rendered in the future are included in income in the year the taxpayer receives the payment.[89] This rule overrides the generally accepted accounting principle that we recognize income when it is realized and not when it is received. A taxpayer can, however, deduct a reasonable amount in

88   *Ibid*, para 12(1)(i).
89   *Ibid*, para 12(1)(a) & (b). This is a variation from accounting principles, which do not recognize income until it is earned.

respect of goods that will be delivered, or services that will be rendered, in a subsequent year.[90] This reserve is available only in computing income from a business and *not* in computing income from property.

A taxpayer can also deduct a reserve for deposits that may be refundable (excluding deposits on bottles), prepaid rent for the use of land or chattels, and for amounts that are receivable but not yet due.[91]

Both paragraphs 20(1)(m) and 20(1)(n) refer to the deduction of a reasonable amount as a reserve. What is "reasonable" is a question of fact depending upon the circumstances. A reasonable reserve is not necessarily equal to the amount included in income under paragraph 12(1)(a). For example, a taxpayer who sells tokens that are redeemable for products must include the proceeds from the tokens in income. If all the tokens have not been redeemed at the end of the taxation year, the taxpayer may claim a reserve equal to the value of the tokens that he expects will be redeemed by customers. Where, however, the history of the taxpayer's business indicates that some of the tokens sold will never be redeemed, the reserve must be reduced by the amount of the tokens that he does not expect to be redeemed.

b) Amounts Not Due

In calculating income from a *business*, a taxpayer may deduct a reserve for the purchase price of property sold that is not due until some time after the end of the year.[92]

4) Limitations on Reserves

The Act limits reserves in various circumstances. The following illustrate some of the limits. Note the general limitation in paragraph 20(8)(b), which restricts the reserve to a three-year period.

a) Food, Drink and Transportation

Where a taxpayer claims a reserve in respect of food, drink or transportation to be delivered or provided after the end of the year, the reserve cannot exceed the revenue from these sources included in income for the year.[93]

---

90   *Ibid*, para 20(1)(m).
91   *Ibid*, paras 20(1)(m) & (n).
92   *Ibid*, para 20(1)(n); *Home Provisioners (Manitoba) Ltd v MNR*, [1958] CTC 334 (Ex Ct) (absolute assignment of right to receive instalment payments precluded right to claim reserve).
93   *ITA*, *ibid*, subs 20(6).

Example

Assume:

Transportation tickets issued in year	$60,000
Tickets unused at the end of the year	$10,000

Then:

The reserve under paragraph 20(1)(m) and subsection 20(6) is $10,000 unless experi-
ence indicates that a portion of the tickets will never be redeemed. If experience
indicates, for example, that 5 percent of all tickets issued are never redeemed, a
reasonable reserve would be computed as follows:

Tickets unused at the end of the year	$10,000
Tickets that will not be redeemed [5% × $60,000]	(3,000)
Reasonable reserve	$7,000

b) Non-Residents

A taxpayer who gives up her Canadian residency and does not carry on
business in Canada cannot deduct a reserve in respect of unrealized
receivables. Thus, since a reserve that a taxpayer claims in one year is
added to her income in the following year, the taxpayer cannot avoid
tax simply by giving up Canadian residence.[94]

c) Guarantees, Indemnities and Warranties

Where a taxpayer sells property or services and provides a guarantee,
indemnity or warranty for those goods or services, the cost of the guarantee is usually included in the sale price. The taxpayer cannot claim
a reserve in respect of the expected liabilities under the guarantees,
indemnities or warranties.[95]

K. INTEREST EXPENSE

1) General Comment

The cost of financing is an important decision for businesses and investors. If one starts with the simple financial premise that interest represents the rental cost of the use of money over time, interest expense
should be deductible if one incurs it to earn income. The Act allows a
taxpayer to deduct interest on money borrowed to earn income from

---

94   *Ibid*, subs 20(8); paras 20(1)(n) and 12(1)(e).
95   *Ibid*, subs 20(7). For obvious reasons, taxpayers computing income on a cash
      basis are not entitled to claim a reserve under para 20(1)(m).

business or property.[96] However, the provisions have been technically parsed with requirements that generate substantial litigation.

The trouble began with a Supreme Court decision that held that interest is an expenditure on account of capital. The Court held that a tax deduction for interest on borrowed money would in fairness require a similar deduction for the *imputed* cost of equity capital:

> . . . *in the absence of an express statutory allowance*, interest payable on capital indebtedness is not deductible as an income expense. If a company has not the money capital to commence business, why should it be allowed to deduct the interest on borrowed money? The company setting up with its own contributed capital would, on such a principle, be entitled to interest on its capital before taxable income was reached, but the income statutes give no countenance to such a deduction.[97]

The decision in *Canada Safeway Ltd v MNR* (*Canada Safeway*) was wrong. Without specific authority, tax law does not allow for the deduction of imputed or notional costs. Nevertheless, the law stands: without specific statutory authority, interest expense is a capital expenditure for tax purposes and, therefore, not deductible.[98]

Paragraph 20(1)(c) allows one to deduct interest in the pursuit of certain "for profit" activities. The object of section 20(1)(c)(i) is to create an incentive to accumulate income-producing capital by allowing taxpayers to deduct interest costs associated with its acquisition. This is seen as desirable because it creates wealth and increases the income tax base.[99] Parliament formulated this provision specifically to overrule *Canada Safeway*'s denial of the deduction of interest as an expense. Paragraph 20(1)(c) is not an anti-avoidance provision, and one should not interpret it as such without precise and specific language.[100]

2) Tax Arbitrage

Financing decisions depend upon risk, reward, security and taxes. Two characteristics of the Canadian income tax system have a particularly important influence on financing transactions. First, there are the statu-

---

96 *Ibid*, para 20(1)(c).
97 *Canada Safeway Ltd v MNR*, [1957] SCR 717 at 727 [emphasis added].
98 *ITA*, above note 3, para 18(1)(b).
99 *Ludco Enterprises Ltd v Canada*, [2001] 2 SCR 1082 at para 63.
100 *Neuman v Canada (MNR)*, [1998] 1 SCR 770 at para 63: "We should not be quick to embellish [a] provision . . . when it is open for the legislator to be precise and specific with respect to any mischief to be avoided."

tory distinctions between the various sources of income and expenses. Interest on money that one borrows for business and investment purposes is generally deductible for tax purposes. Interest on debt to earn exempt income or capital gains is not deductible.

Second, there is the distinction between debt and equity capital. Debt represents borrowed capital that creates a liability to repay according to a pre-determined schedule. Equity is capital that one invests in exchange for an ownership interest. There is generally no fixed timetable to repay equity capital to the enterprise's owners.[101] Interest on borrowed money is an expense of earning profits. For tax purposes, dividends on shareholder equity are a distribution of profits to the owners *after* they earn the profits. Hence, dividends are not deductible as an expense of obtaining financing. These two features of the tax system—strict segregation of income by source and the distinction between debt and equity capital—materially affect Canadian corporate financing decisions as taxpayers arbitrage to reduce taxes and maximize their economic returns.

Dividend income is double taxed: first, in the corporation that pays tax on the income from which it pays dividends; second, in the hands of the shareholder who receives the dividend. Double taxation is unfair and distorts tax structures.

Since interest is generally deductible only when one incurs it in the pursuit of "for profit" activities and is not deductible when one uses debt "for pleasure" or for consumption, individuals have an incentive to tax arbitrage, that is, convert non-deductible personal interest into deductible business expenses by arranging transactions to attach the interest to their "for profit" activities. For example, a lawyer with cash savings might borrow an equal amount to invest in the capital of his law firm and then use the savings to buy a home.[102]

Even "for profit" activities promote tax arbitrage. For example, one might use loans on which interest is fully deductible to produce income that is taxed at a lower rate. Thus, an investor might deduct interest expense taxed at 46 percent to earn Canadian-source dividend income taxed at 31 percent. With only slightly greater sophistication, an investor might borrow to earn business income, which is fully taxable, and convert the end-profit into a capital gain, only one-half of which

---

101 There may be some exceptions in the case of redeemable preferred shares, etc. These types of shares, however, more closely resemble debt capital with an equity flavour, rather than pure equity capital.

102 See, for example, *Singleton v Canada*, [1999] 3 CTC 450 (FCA), aff'd [2001] 2 SCR 1046. See also *Ludco Enterprises Ltd v Canada*, above note 99.

is taxable. Tax arbitrage is merely an economic response to differential tax rates.

3) Statutory Requirements

"Interest" is compensation for the use of a sum of money belonging or owed to another.[103] It represents a legal obligation that one calculates by reference to the principal sum owing. The obligation to pay interest may arise from an express agreement, by legal implication, or by statute. Thus, in effect, interest expense represents the rental cost for debt capital.

Paragraph 20(1)(c)[104] allows a taxpayer to deduct interest if the interest:

- Is paid or payable in the year;
- Arises from a legal obligation;
- Is payable on borrowed money that is used for the purpose of earning income (other than exempt income) from a business or property; and
- Is reasonable in amount.

The paragraph overcomes the common law restriction that interest is a capital expenditure. The provision, however, restricts the deductibility of interest to money that one uses in "for profit" activities and denies the deduction for funds used in "for pleasure" activities. Also, it limits the deductibility of interest to money *used for the purpose* of earning income from business or property. Thus, it confines the deduction to specific sources of income.

If a payment blends capital and interest, the interest component is deductible if it otherwise satisfies the paragraph.[105] Where an interest rate is established in a market of lenders and borrowers acting at arm's length from each other, it is generally a reasonable rate.[106]

4) Legal Obligation

The determination of what is interest is essentially a question of law. The main criterion is that interest represents payment for the use of debt capital. Hence, one calculates interest by reference to a principal

---

103 *Reference re s 6 of Farm Security Act 1944 (Saskatchewan)*, [1947] SCR 394 at 411, aff'd [1949] AC 110 (PC).
104 *ITA*, above note 3, para 20(1)(c).
105 *Ibid*, subs 16(1).
106 See *Mohammad v Canada* (1997), 97 DTC 5503 at 5509 (FCA); *Irving Oil Ltd v Canada*, [1991] 1 CTC 350 at 359 (FCA).

sum. Some courts have grafted an additional precondition that interest must accrue daily.[107] This requirement, however, serves no particular policy and is an unnecessary appendage. There are many financial instruments that pay interest only if the instrument is held for a minimum period.

Interest is deductible only if the lender has legal rights to enforce payment of the amounts due. Thus, deductibility depends upon an unconditional and legally enforceable obligation to pay interest. The obligation must be actual and not contingent. If there is no legal obligation to pay the interest, paragraph 18(1)(e) prevents its deduction.

5) Use of Money

Paragraph 20(1)(c) allows a taxpayer to deduct an amount paid or payable in respect of the year "pursuant to a legal obligation to pay interest on borrowed money *used for the purpose of* earning income from a business or property . . . or a reasonable amount in respect thereof" (emphasis added). The phrase "used for the purpose of" incorporates two separate tests: use and purpose. One applies these tests to distinguish between "for profit" and "for pleasure" activities.

A taxpayer may deduct interest as an expense only if she uses the borrowed money for earning income from a business or investment property. Interest is not deductible for the purposes of earning capital gains, which are a separate source of income.[108] Thus, a taxpayer who borrows to buy shares can deduct interest if she reasonably expects that the shares will pay dividends. The amount of dividends expected or received is not determinative.[109] However, the taxpayer is not entitled to a deduction if she expects to earn only capital gains when she sells the shares.

---

107 *Ontario (AG) v Barfried Enterprises Ltd*, [1963] SCR 570.

108 See, for example, *Ludmer v MNR*, [1993] 2 CTC 2494 (TCC) [*Ludmer*] (interest on money used to purchase shares not deductible if *income* from shares cannot yield profit); *Ludco Enterprises Ltd v Canada*, [1999] 3 CTC 601 (FCA) [*Ludco Enterprises*]; *Hastings v MNR*, [1988] 2 CTC 2001 (TCC) (interest expense on commodities trades not deductible); *Canada v Stirling*, [1985] 1 CTC 275 (FCA) (interest and safekeeping charges for purchase of gold bullion not deductible in determining capital gain); *Canada v Canadian Pacific Ltd*, [1977] CTC 606 (FCA) (deduction of interest under old subs 8(3) only allowable where corporation subject to Part I tax); *Birmingham Corp v Barnes*, [1935] AC 292 (clarification of capital costs for laying tramway lines where expenditure contributed to by another party).

109 *Ludco Enterprises*, *ibid* at para 59.

The use test traces the direct flow of funds to determine how one applies the borrowed money. It is the actual, and not the alleged, uses of borrowed money that determines the deductibility of interest payable on the funds.[110] In *Sinha v MNR*,[111] for example, a student borrowed from the Canada Student Loan Plan at a low rate of interest and reinvested the borrowed funds at a higher rate. The board rejected the minister's argument that the purpose of the borrowing was personal and allowed the taxpayer to deduct his interest expense since he actually used the borrowed money for investment purposes.

6) Purpose of Borrowing

The second test of interest deductibility is that the taxpayer must use the funds for the purpose of earning income from business or property. The taxpayer must have a *bona fide* intention to use the borrowed money for an income-earning purpose. However, earning income from business or property need not be the primary or dominant purpose for borrowing. Absent a sham or window dressing, the taxpayer's ancillary purpose to earn income from these sources satisfies the requisite purpose.[112] Actual realization of income is irrelevant. The purpose test is concerned solely with intention.[113]

> Eligibility for the deduction is contingent on the use of borrowed money for the purpose of earning income . . . it is not the purpose of the borrowing itself which is relevant. What is relevant, rather, is the taxpayer's purpose in using the borrowed money in a particular manner . . . . Consequently, the focus of the inquiry must be centred on *the use to which the taxpayer put the borrowed funds.*

Similarly, in *Shell Canada Ltd v Canada*, the Supreme Court said:[114]

> The issue is the use to which the borrowed funds are put. It is irrelevant why the borrowing arrangement was structured the way that it was or, indeed, why the funds were borrowed at all.

For example, a taxpayer who borrows money at a given rate of interest and then lends the money at less than his borrowing cost cannot be said to be using the money for the purpose of earning income. The absence of an intention to earn income makes the interest non-deduct-

---

110 *Bronfman Trust v Canada* (1987), 87 DTC 5059 (SCC) [*Bronfman Trust*].
111 *Sinha v MNR*, [1981] CTC 2599, 81 DTC 465 (TRB).
112 *Ludco Enterprises Ltd v Canada*, above note 108 at para 51.
113 *Bronfman Trust*, above note 110 at 5064 [emphasis added].
114 *Shell Canada Ltd v Canada*, [1999] 3 SCR 622 at para 47 [*Shell Canada*].

ible. There may be limited circumstances, however, where a person borrows money and lends it at a lower rate for the purpose of helping a major customer survive economic hardship. The indirect purpose of such transactions is acceptable for tax deduction.

We determine the purpose of borrowing by tracing the direct and immediate use of the borrowed funds into the income-earning process.[115] Interest is deductible only if there is a sufficiently direct link between the borrowed money and the current eligible use.[116] It also does not necessarily matter if the borrowed funds are commingled with funds used for another purpose, provided that the borrowed funds can in fact be traced to a current eligible use.[117] The deduction is not available where the link between the borrowed money and an eligible use is merely indirect. In *Singleton v Canada*, for example, the taxpayer, a partner in a law firm, withdrew $300,000 from his capital account in the firm to purchase his home, which he registered in the name of his wife. By pre-arrangement, on the same day, he borrowed an identical amount from the bank and replenished his capital account in the firm. The taxpayer could deduct his interest on the bank borrowing because the funds were directly traceable to the business. Tax minimization, as a motive, is not a bar to the deduction of an expense. Taxpayers can arrange their affairs for the sole purpose of achieving favourable tax results.[118] Tax avoidance is not offensive, per se. Absent statutory language, business transactions do not require an independent business purpose.[119] However, they cannot abuse the provisions of the Act.

Thus, the form of borrowing, not its economic substance, determines the deductibility of interest expense. Interest on debt that only indirectly earns income is not deductible for tax purposes. In *Bronfman Trust v Canada* (*Bronfman Trust*),[120] for example, the settlor created a trust in favour of his daughter under which she would receive 50 percent of its income and such additional allocations as the trustees in their discretion might decide. The trust invested its capital in income-earning securities.

---

115 *Singleton v Canada*, above note 102 (SCC).

116 *Tennant v MNR*, [1996] 1 SCR 305.

117 *Shell Canada*, above note 114.

118 See *Neuman v Canada (MNR)*, above note 100 at para 63: "The *ITA* has many specific anti-avoidance provisions and rules governing the treatment of non-arm's length transactions. We should not be quick to embellish the provision at issue here when it is open for the legislator to be precise and specific with respect to any mischief to be avoided."

119 *Stubart Investments Ltd v Canada*, [1984] 1 SCR 536; *Neuman v MNR*, *ibid* at para 39: "Taxpayers can arrange their affairs in a particular way for the sole purpose of deliberately availing themselves of tax reduction devices in the *ITA*."

120 *Bronfman Trust*, above note 110.

When the trustees decided to make a capital distribution of $2 million to the beneficiary, they chose to borrow the funds rather than liquidate capital to make the payment. The decision to borrow was based on business reasons. It was financially inexpedient to liquidate any portion of the trust's investments at that time. By borrowing money for the capital distribution, the trustees preserved the income-yielding capacity of the trust's investments. The Supreme Court held that the economic substance of the underlying transactions did not justify deduction of the interest on the borrowing. Chief Justice Dickson said:

> In my view, the text of the Act requires tracing the use of borrowed funds to a specific eligible use, its obviously restricted purpose being the encouragement of taxpayers to augment their income-producing potential. This, in my view, precludes the allowance of a deduction for interest paid on borrowed funds which indirectly preserve income-earning property but which are not directly "used for the purpose of earning income from . . . property."[121]

This principle applies equally to all taxpayers, including corporations, trusts and individuals.[122]

While transforming funds into a different currency may change its legal form and relative value, it does not change its substance—it remains money. Hence, there is no change in current use:[123]

> The mere fact that an exchange had to occur before usable money was produced is not particularly significant. Except where the borrower is a money trader, borrowed money can rarely itself produce income. It must always be exchanged for something, whether it be machinery or goods, which then produces income. The necessity of such an exchange does not mean the eventual production of income is an indirect use of the borrowed money.

7) Expectation of Income

The deductibility of interest depends upon the intention of the borrower at the time that she invests the funds. The investment in business or property must have the potential to yield "income." "Income" means gross income, not net income. Thus, it is not necessary to make a taxable profit in order to deduct the interest expense. It is sufficient

---

121 *Bronfman Trust, ibid* at 5067.
122 *Ibid.*
123 *Shell Canada*, above note 114, McLachlin J.

that the taxpayer had a reasonable expectation at the time that she invested of earning an amount that would come into income for taxation purposes.[124] It is also irrelevant whether the invested funds actually produce income.[125] For example, interest on borrowed funds invested in a business venture that loses money is deductible if the taxpayer had a reasonable, albeit frustrated, expectation of earning some income.

The intention must be to earn income from business or property and not from capital gains. Income from capital gains is not income from property.[126] Thus, interest expenses solely to earn capital gains are not deductible in computing income from business or property.[127]

8) Current Use

It is the current, and not the original, use of funds that determines the deductibility of interest expense. As Jackett P said in *Trans-Prairie Pipelines Ltd v MNR*:

> . . . interest should be deductible for the years in which the borrowed capital is employed in the business rather than that it should be deductible for the life of a loan as long as its first use was in the business.[128]

Similarly, in *Bronfman Trust*:

> . . . a taxpayer who uses or intends to use borrowed money for an ineligible purpose, but later uses the funds to earn non-exempt income from a business or property, ought not to be deprived of the deduction for the current, eligible use.[129]

---

124 *Ludco Enterprises*, above note 108 at para 61.
125 See *Lessard v MNR*, [1993] 1 CTC 2176 (TCC) (interest on funds used to acquire shares deductible even though taxpayer was sole shareholder, because shares constituted a potential source of income).
126 *ITA*, above note 3, subs 9(3). See *Ludmer v MNR*, [1993] 2 CTC 2494 (TCC), aff'd (*sub nom Ludco Enterprises Ltd v Canada*) [1994] 1 CTC 368 (FCTD), aff'd (*sub nom Ludco Enterprises Ltd v Canada*) [1999] 3 CTC 601 (FCA), rev'd 2001 SCC 62; *Hugill v Canada*, [1995] 2 CTC 16 (FCA).
127 *Bronfman Trust*, above note 110 at 5067 ("The fact that the loan may have prevented capital losses cannot assist the taxpayer in obtaining a deduction from income which is limited to use of borrowed money for the purpose of earning income.") See also *Mandryk v MNR*, [1992] 1 CTC 317 (FCA) (taxpayer not entitled to deduct interest expense to honour personal guarantees of corporate indebtedness).
128 *Trans-Prairie Pipelines Ltd v MNR* (1970), 70 DTC 6351 at 6354 (Ex Ct); approved by SCC in *Bronfman Trust*, above note 110.
129 *Bronfman Trust*, *ibid* at 5065.

Hence, change of use can affect deductibility. For example, if a taxpayer initially borrows money to invest in bonds, and later sells the bonds and uses the money to take a vacation, the interest expense ceases to qualify as a deduction from the date that he changes use of the borrowing.[130] Conversely, interest on funds initially borrowed for personal purposes and later used for business purposes qualifies for deduction as of the date of change of use. For example, a taxpayer who borrows money to purchase a residential cottage for personal use, and then sells the cottage and uses the proceeds to buy shares, can deduct the interest on the borrowed funds as of the date of the share purchase.

9) Reloaned Funds

Where an individual borrows money and then lends the money to his corporation, the deductibility of the interest paid by the individual depends upon the purpose of the lending.

Where an individual borrows at a commercial rate of interest and loans at a lower rate, she cannot generally be borrowing for the purpose of earning income. Hence, any interest payable on the funds is *prima facie* not deductible. The CRA, does, however allow a deduction to the extent that the individual actually earns income. In certain cases, there is a full deduction of the interest expense even though the individual loans the funds at a lower rate than the cost of her borrowing.[131]

10) Exempt Income

Interest expense is deductible only if one incurs it to earn income from business or property and the income is taxable. Interest expense is not deductible if the taxpayer uses the funds to earn income that is exempt or to acquire a life insurance policy.[132]

130　*ITA*, above note 3, subpara 20(1)(c)(i).

131　See Interpretation Bulletin IT-533 "Interest Deductibility and Related Issues" (31 October 2003) and *Canadian Helicopters Ltd v Canada*, 2002 FCA 30.

132　See *ITA*, above note 3, para 20(1)(c). "Exempt income" is defined as property received or acquired by a person in such circumstances that it is, because of any provision in Part I, not included in computing the person's income, but does not include a dividend on a share or a support amount. See para 248(1) "exempt income."

11) Compound Interest

A taxpayer can deduct interest on interest—that is, compound interest—if she meets all of the other conditions of deductibility.[133] Compound interest, however, is deductible only when it is paid and not when it is merely payable.

12) Bond Discounts

A bond is a legal obligation that acknowledges debt. Typically, the debt obligation entitles its owner to periodic payments and, eventually, on a stated date the principal (face value) of the debt. A bond has a nominal interest rate, which is the rate that the contract specifies in relation to the face value of the debt. For example, assume that a corporation issues bonds with a face value of $1,000. The stated or nominal interest rate is 8 percent payable annually and the bond matures in 25 years. Thus, the purchaser of the bond can expect interest payments of $80 at the end of each year and a lump sum of $1,000 at the end of 25 years. The nominal rate of interest is 8 percent. If the market rate of interest is also 8 percent, the present value of the bond is exactly equal to its face value ($1,000).

Present value of future income stream is:		
$80 per year × present value* of annuity (10.6748)	=	$854
$1,000 × present value** of future sum	=	146
Total present value of bond		$1,000

* Present value of a future annuity at 8 percent for 25 years equals 10.6748.

** Present value of a future amount at 8 percent for 25 years equals 0.1460.

The present value of the bond depends upon the annual cash flow ($80), the discount rate (8 percent), the number of years outstanding (25) and the face value of the principal amount ($1,000) payable at the end of the contract. The price that an investor will be willing to pay for the bond today is $1,000—that is, an amount equal to the present value of its future cash flows. This is entirely logical as the nominal contractual interest rate is exactly equal to the market rate of interest.

Now assume that the market rate of interest rises to 10 percent. The nominal contractual rate of interest remains at 8 percent. The present value of the bond falls to $818.

---

133 *Ibid*, para 20(1)(d).

Present value of income stream is:

$80 per year × present value* of annuity (9.0770)	=	$726
$1,000 × present value** of future sum	=	92
Total present value of bond		$818

* Present value of a future annuity at 10 percent for 25 years equals 9.0770.

** Present value of a future amount at 10 percent for 25 years equals 0.0923.

If a new investor buys the bond for $818, her annual yield is $80/$818 or 9.78 percent. In addition, the investor will realize a gain of $182, that is, $1,000 minus $818 if she holds the bond to maturity. The combination of the interest yield and the gain provides an effective annual yield of 10 percent over the life of the bond. Thus, the increase in the market rate of interest causes the capital value of the bond to fall, which raises the effective rate of interest to current market levels.

It is arguable in law that, for tax purposes, the gain of $182 is an "appreciation gain" that results from holding the asset to maturity. In economic terms, however, what we really have is an increase in the interest income that the bondholder earns to reflect the change in the market rate of interest. It is entirely irrelevant to a bondholder who holds to maturity whether she earns 10 percent annually on a face value of $1,000 or 8 percent annually on a discounted value of $818 plus a lump sum gain upon maturity. In either case, the bondholder's effective yield to maturity is 10 percent. This is the substantive economic result in efficient capital markets.

A discount is the amount by which the face or nominal value of a debt obligation exceeds its issue or selling price. In the above example, the bond discount is $182. A bond can be discounted upon its issue, or later in accordance with market fluctuations in interest rates. A corporation can, for example, choose to issue a $1,000 face value bond for $818 in order to increase the effective interest rate for the bondholder.

Since we tax capital gains at a lower rate than interest income, applying purely legal principles, the bondholder could effectively convert $182 of interest income into capital gains if the corporation issues the bond at an initial discount of that amount. In these circumstances, form would prevail over economic substance.

The capital value of a bond also fluctuates with the time remaining to maturity. Continuing with the above example, assume that the $1,000 bond has a nominal rate of 8 percent and 20 years remaining to maturity. If the market rate of interest is 10 percent, the bond has a capital value of $830.

Present value of income stream is:		
$80 per year × present value* of annuity (8.5136)	=	$681
$1,000 × present value** of future sum (0.1486)	=	149
Total present value of bond		$830

* Present value of a future annuity at 10 percent for 20 years equals 8.5136.

** Present value of a future amount at 10 percent for 20 years equals 0.1486.

The value of the bond has increased from $818 to $830 in five years because the bond is that much closer to maturity and the eventual pay-out of the face value of $1,000. At a price of $830 the bond has an effective yield of 10 percent. Once again, the effective yield comprises two components: the annual interest yield of 80/830 = 9.64 percent and the capital gain of $170 over the next 20 years.

The Act has special rules to prevent taxpayers from transforming fully taxable income into capital gains. In effect, the statute looks through the legal form of the initial issuance of a bond to its economic substance.[134] Where an issuer floats an obligation at a price of at least 97 percent of its principal amount and the obligation does not yield an amount in excess of 4/3 of the nominal interest rate, the entire amount of the discount is deductible in computing income. In contrast, where the issuer floats a bond for an amount less than 97 percent of its face amount, or its yield exceeds 4/3 of its nominal interest rate, only 50 percent of the discount is deductible in computing income.

In the above example, the discounted price of the bond is less than 97 percent of its face value but the effective yield does not exceed 4/3 of the nominal interest rate.[135] Hence, the issuer can deduct only 50 percent of the discount as interest expense.

A discount on a debt obligation that does not normally stipulate an interest rate (for example, strip coupon bonds) is considered interest if the discount is reasonable in the circumstances.

13) Refinancing

The Act deems a taxpayer who borrows money to repay money that he previously borrowed to incur the second borrowing for the same purposes as the original borrowing.[136]

---

134 *Ibid*, para 20(1)(f).

135 The effective interest rate of 10 percent, 4/3 of 8 percent = 10.67 percent.

136 ITA, above note 3, subs 20(3); see also Advance Tax Ruling ATR04 "Exchange of Interest Rates SS. 9(1)/Para.18(1)(a)" (29 November 1985) (archived).

14) Existence of Source

Interest on borrowed money must be traceable to a current eligible use in order for the expense to be deductible. An essential requirement for the deduction of interest is that the source of income to which the interest expense relates must continue to exist.[137] For example, a taxpayer who finances the purchase of shares may claim any directly related interest expense as a deduction only if he continues to hold the original investment or substituted securities. This is so even if the security declines in value or becomes worthless.

Section 20.1 does, however, allow one to deduct interest in certain circumstances even where borrowed money ceases to be used to earn income because the source of the income no longer exists.[138]

15) Accrued Interest

The purchaser of a debt obligation (other than an income bond, income debenture, small business development bond or small business bond) can deduct accrued interest (that is, interest earned but not paid) to the date of the purchase to the extent that he includes the amount as interest in computing income for the year. At the same time, the vendor of the debt includes the accrued interest in computing its income.[139]

16) Financing Costs

A taxpayer can deduct expenses that she incurs in issuing shares or in borrowing money for the purpose of earning income from a business or

---

137 *Emerson v Canada*, [1986] 1 CTC 422 (FCA), leave to appeal to SCC refused, [1986] SCCA No 187 (taxpayer not allowed to deduct interest on money used to purchase shares after selling shares at loss); see also *Deschenes v MNR*, [1979] CTC 2690 (TRB); *Alexander v MNR*, [1983] CTC 2516 (TRB); *Lyons v MNR*, [1984] CTC 2690 (TCC); *McKay v MNR*, [1984] CTC 2805 (TCC); *Botkin v MNR*, [1989] 2 CTC 2110 (TCC); *MNR v Malik*, [1989] 1 CTC 316 (FCTD); *Dockman v MNR*, [1990] 2 CTC 2229 (TCC); *Kornelow v MNR*, [1991] 1 CTC 2403 (TCC).

138 See Department of Finance examples in its technical notes to the section.

139 *ITA*, above note 3, subs 20(14); Interpretation Bulletin IT-410R "Debt Obligations: Accrued Interest on Transfer" (4 September 1984) (archived). This rule only operates where there has been an assignment or transfer of title; evidence of registration of title would likely be necessary. See *Hill v MNR*, [1981] CTC 2120 (TRB) ("bond flip": interest payment for carrying cost of bonds not deductible); *Smye v MNR*, [1980] CTC 2372(TRB) (purchase of bonds plus accrued interest; upon sale, taxpayer deducted price for accrued interest from investment yield of bond).

property.[140] Such financing expenses, which typically include legal and accounting fees, printing costs, commissions, etc., would otherwise be caught by the prohibition against deducting expenses not directly related to the income-earning process.[141] These expenses are deductible on a rateable basis over a five-year period.

17) Capitalizing Interest

In certain circumstances, a taxpayer may prefer not to write off interest expense against current operations. For example, there may be little advantage in taking a deduction for interest expense on money borrowed to construct an asset if the asset is not producing income. Where the deduction of interest would merely create a loss that the taxpayer cannot use within the time limits allowed for carryover of losses,[142] the taxpayer may prefer to treat the interest charges as part of the cost of the asset. He can then write off the total cost of the asset when it begins to produce income. In other words, the taxpayer may prefer to treat interest costs as a capital expenditure rather than as a current expense. This aspect is now less of a concern since the loss carryover extends to twenty years.

a) Depreciable Property
A taxpayer who acquires depreciable property with borrowed money may elect to capitalize the interest charges.[143] The taxpayer may capitalize only those costs that would otherwise have been deductible as interest expense or as an expense of borrowing money. Interest expense to earn exempt income is not deductible and cannot be capitalized. Second, the election is available not only in respect of costs the taxpayer incurs in the year that she acquires the asset but also costs that she incurs in the three immediately preceding taxation years. The extension of the election to the three preceding years recognizes that large undertakings extend over many years and that money may be borrowed, and expenses incurred, prior to the period in which the money is actually used for its intended purpose of constructing a capital asset.

---

140 *ITA, ibid*, para 20(1)(e).
141 *Montreal Light, Heat & Power Consolidated v MNR*, [1944] CTC 94 (PC); *Canada v Royal Trust Corp of Canada*, [1983] CTC 159 (FCA) (whether or not payment constitutes "commission" is a question of fact).
142 See *ITA*, above note 3, para 111(1)(a) (limitation period in respect of non-capital losses).
143 *Ibid*, s 21. Special restrictions on "soft costs" are discussed in Section K(17)(e), below in this chapter; see subs 18(3.1).

b) Election

The election must be made for the taxation year in which:

* The depreciable property is acquired; or
* The money borrowed has been used for exploration, development or the acquisition of property.

A taxpayer cannot elect to capitalize interest in anticipation of the acquisition of depreciable property or the use of borrowed money for exploration or development. The taxpayer can elect only after acquiring the property or expending the funds. Upon election, however, it becomes effective for the borrowing costs and interest of the current and the three preceding years.

A taxpayer may elect under subsection 21(1) only for the taxation year in which he acquires the depreciable property. Where the taxpayer erects a building or other structure, he is considered to acquire it at any time to the extent of the construction costs at that time. Hence, a taxpayer must file a separate election for each taxation year in respect of the interest expense related to that year.[144]

The election does not have to be made in respect of the full amount of the costs of borrowing; a taxpayer may elect to capitalize only part of the interest charges and deduct the remainder as a current expense.

The portion of the interest that the taxpayer capitalizes is added to the capital cost of the depreciable property that she acquires. Thus, the capitalized cost will eventually be written off through capital cost allowances. The adjusted cost base of the property will also be increased for the purpose of determining capital gains upon disposition of the property.[145]

c) Reassessment

Where the taxpayer elects to capitalize interest charges that would otherwise have been deductible in preceding years, the minister must reassess the taxpayer for those taxation years. Having made the election, the taxpayer may continue to capitalize interest in succeeding years if in each of those succeeding years, she capitalizes the *entire* amount of the interest on the property.

---

144 This election is explained in the CRA's Interpretation Bulletin IT-121R3 "Election to Capitalize Cost of Borrowed Money" (6 May 1988) (archived).

145 *ITA*, above note 3, s 54 "adjusted cost base."

d) Compound Interest

A taxpayer can also capitalize compound interest and the expense of raising money. For example, a taxpayer may pay a commitment fee to a financier before it advances the necessary funds. The commitment fee, or standby interest, may be capitalized as part of the cost of borrowed money.[146]

e) "Soft Costs"

"Soft costs" (such as interest expense, mortgage fees, property taxes or commitment fees) incurred in respect of the construction, renovation or alteration of a building, are not deductible as current expenses during construction, and must be added to the cost of the building.[147] Similarly, "soft costs" in respect of land subjacent to a building under construction must be capitalized. The restriction on the deduction of these expenses only applies in respect of outlays incurred before completion of construction, renovation or alteration of the building.

The scope of the prohibition against writing off soft costs as current expenses is very broad. Included in interest expenses are expenses incurred on borrowed money used to finance working capital if it can reasonably be considered that the borrowed money freed up other funds for the construction of the building. In other words, "indirect financing" is caught by the prohibition.[148]

18) Limitations on Deduction

A taxpayer cannot deduct carrying charges (interest and property taxes) in respect of vacant land to the extent that the expenses exceed income from the land.[149] Thus, carrying charges on land are deductible only to the extent of the taxpayer's net revenues from the land. The purpose of this rule is to discourage speculation in real estate.

Land that one uses in the course of a business is exempt from the limitation in respect of carrying charges for land. However, the exemption from the rule does not apply to property developers whose business is the sale or development of land, or to land that is held, but not used, in a business.

---

146 *Sherritt Gordon Mines Ltd v MNR*, [1968] CTC 262 (Ex Ct).
147 ITA, above note 3, subs 18(3.1). This rule does not apply to capital cost allowance, landscaping costs, disability related modifications to buildings under para 20(1)(gg) and soft costs deductible under subs 20(29).
148 *Ibid*, subs 18(3.2).
149 *Ibid*, subs 18(2).

L. CAPITAL COST ALLOWANCE

1) General Comment

We saw earlier that a taxpayer cannot deduct expenditures on account of capital outlays, depreciation, obsolescence or depletion.[150] The prohibition against the deduction of depreciation and similar expenses flies in the face of accounting principles. The Act does, however, allow for the deduction of capital cost allowance (CCA) in lieu of such expenses.

In computing income from a business or property, a taxpayer may deduct[151] "such part of the capital cost to the taxpayer of property, or such amount in respect of the capital cost to the taxpayer of property, if any, as is allowed by regulation." Thus, a taxpayer cannot deduct depreciation calculated for financial statement purposes, but may claim a deduction for CCA, according to prescribed rules.[152]

The basic concept underlying the capital cost allowance system is straightforward: CCA is a deduction from income that is intended to allocate the approximate cost of capital assets over their useful lives. Thus, in a sense, the CCA system is nothing more than statutory depreciation at pre-determined rates.

The technical application of the CCA system is, however, extremely complex because the government uses the system as an instrument of social, economic and political policy. For example, the system sometimes stimulates investment through accelerated capital cost allowance; in other circumstances, the CCA system discourages particular types of investment by denying or restricting the allowance on those investments. For example, prior to 1988, the statute allowed for a rapid write-off of the cost of Canadian films. A taxpayer could claim 100 percent of the cost of film ownership in one year. This was intended to encourage the development of Canadian culture. In 1988, the CCA rate was reduced to a 30 percent write-off so as to discourage the use of films as tax shelters by high-income taxpayers. In both cases, the CCA rate did not relate to the life of films.

---

150 *Ibid*, para 18(1)(b).
151 *Ibid*, para 20(1)(a); *Income Tax Regulations*, above note 50, Pt. XI (ss 1100–107). The phrase "capital cost allowance" refers to an allowance in respect of the capital cost of depreciable property.
152 See, generally, *eBay Canada Ltd v MNR*, 2007 FC 930, additional reasons 2008 FC 180, aff'd 2008 FCA 348 (describes eBay's activities outside the United States relevant to demand requirements under s 231.2 of the *ITA*, above note 3).

2) Structure

a) Classification

We must answer three basic questions in respect of the CCA system:

1) Is the capital property depreciable capital property?
2) To which class of assets does the property belong?
3) What is the rate of depreciation applicable to the particular class?

An asset is eligible for CCA only if it is described in one of the classes listed in the regulations. The classes list most tangible assets that are expected to depreciate over time. The list also includes intangible assets with limited lives (such as patents and limited life franchises).[153]

CCA allows a taxpayer to deduct the actual cost of depreciable assets over a period of time.[154] The statute prescribes the rate at which a taxpayer can claim CCA on an asset. The rate is the same for all taxpayers with similar assets performing similar activities. The rates generally allow for generous write-offs. The deduction for tax purposes in the early years of an asset's life usually exceeds the comparable depreciation allowed on the asset for accounting and financial statement purposes. Thus, in part at least, the CCA system compensates taxpayers for the effects of inflation on asset replacement costs. It also creates deferred tax accounting problems because of the difference between tax and accounting depreciation.

b) Permissive

The deduction of CCA is permissive: a taxpayer *may* claim CCA in a particular taxation year. The amount of CCA that a taxpayer may deduct in any year, however, is subject to prescribed upper limits. Thus, taxpayers have some flexibility in determining the amount of income they will recognize for tax purposes in any year.

c) General Structure

The general structure of the CCA system is as follows:

- A taxpayer can deduct CCA within the terms of the Act and the regulations.

---

153 *Income Tax Regulations*, above note 50, Part XI (ss 1100–107); Schedule II.
154 Interpretation Bulletin IT-285R2, "Capital Cost Allowance: General Comments" (31 March 1994).

- The regulations group eligible assets into prescribed classes that have approximately similar lives.
- The balance in each class at any point in time is its undepreciated capital cost (UCC).
- The UCC of each class is increased by acquisitions in that class.
- Each class is subject to a *maximum* percentage rate of CCA.
- The balance is reduced by dispositions and by the deduction of amounts of CCA claimed.
- A taxpayer may deduct a portion or all the allowance prescribed, or forgo the claim in a particular year and postpone amortization of the class of assets to later years.
- CCA can be claimed only when assets are available for use.
- The diminishing balance method, rather than the straight-line method,[155] is used in computing the annual allowance for most classes of assets. Each year, the specified rate is applied to the UCC remaining in the class after deduction of amounts previously allowed.
- The balance remaining to be depreciated diminishes until the taxpayer acquires new assets of the class.
- Proceeds from the disposition of assets reduce the balance of the class, up to a maximum equal to the cost of the asset.
- On disposal of assets, CCA previously taken is "recaptured" to the extent that the proceeds of disposition exceed the UCC of the group of assets in the particular class.
- The UCC of a class can never be a negative amount. If the proceeds from a disposition of assets exceed the UCC of the class and, therefore, reduce it below zero, the excess amount is immediately recaptured into income.
- Where the proceeds of disposition of an asset exceed its original capital cost, the excess is a capital gain.
- Upon disposal of *all* the assets in a particular class, any remaining balance of UCC for the class is deductible in the year as a "terminal loss."
- There can be no capital loss on the disposition of depreciable property.

The following example illustrates these relationships.

---

155 The straight-line method may be used in a few situations; for example, depreciation of Class 13 leasehold interests.

Example

Assume:

In Year 1 a taxpayer acquires one tangible asset to which the following data applies:

Capital cost	$10,000
CCA claimed	2,000

In Year 2 the taxpayer disposes of the asset, which is the only asset in its class. Assume, alternatively, that the taxpayer receives the following amounts:

Example (A)	$11,000
Example (B)	$9,000
Example (C)	$6,000

Then:	(A)	(B)	(C)
Capital cost	$10,000	$10,000	$10,000
CCA claimed	(2,000)	(2,000)	(2,000
Undepreciated capital cost	$8,000	$8,000	$8,000
CCA recaptured	$2,000	$1,000	–
Capital gain	$1,000	–	–
Terminal loss	–	–	$(2,000)

3) Depreciable Property

Capital cost allowance is claimable only on depreciable property of a prescribed class.[156] "Depreciable property" is defined as "property acquired by the taxpayer in respect of which the taxpayer has been allowed, or . . . [is] entitled to, 'capital cost allowance.'"[157] This definition is not very helpful.

The Act sets out certain properties that are excluded from the prescribed classes. For example, the following properties are *not* eligible for capital cost allowance:

- Property, the cost of which is deductible as an ordinary expense.[158]
- Property that is "described in" or is part of, the taxpayer's inventory.[159]
- Property not acquired for the purpose of gaining or producing income.[160]

---

156 *Income Tax Regulations*, above note 50, s 1100(1)(a).
157 *ITA*, above note 3, subs 248(1) "depreciable property" and para 13(21) "depreciable property."
158 *Income Tax Regulations*, above note 50, s 1102(1)(a).
159 *Ibid*, s 1102(1)(b). See Chapter 4 for distinction between income from business on sale of inventory and capital gains on sale of capital assets. See also Interpretation Bulletins IT-128R, "CCA : Depreciable Property" (21 May 1985) and IT-102R2, "Conversion of Property, Other than Real Property, from or to Inventory" (22 July 1985).
160 *Income Tax Regulations*, *ibid*, s 1102(1)(c).

- Property for which the taxpayer is entitled to a deduction for scientific research.[161]
- Property that is a yacht, camp, lodge, golf course or facility if any part of the maintenance costs are not deductible because of subparagraph 18(1)(l)(i).[162]
- Certain works of art created by non-residents.[163]
- Land.[164]
- Animals, trees and plants, radium, intangible assets, rights of way.[165]
- Property situated outside of Canada that belongs to a non-resident.[166]

A taxpayer may claim CCA on depreciable property of a prescribed class. Schedule II describes the principal classes of property.

4) Capital Cost of Property

a) General Comment
Capital cost allowance is based on the "capital cost" of an asset. One determines the capital cost of a property by calculating its laid-down acquisition cost.[167] Thus, the capital cost of an asset includes any legal, accounting, engineering or other fees that the taxpayer incurs to acquire the property.

"Cost" refers to the actual cost of the property to the taxpayer, whether paid in money or some other property. Where the value of the consideration paid is not readily apparent (such as when payment is made by the issuance of shares), the taxpayer should obtain an appraisal to determine the capital cost of the property.[168]

Where a corporation acquires an asset in exchange for treasury shares in an arm's length transaction, the contract price will usually pre-

---

161 *Ibid*, s 1102(1)(d).
162 *Ibid*, s 1102(1)(f).
163 *Ibid*, s 1102(1)(e).
164 *Ibid*, s 1102(2).
165 *Ibid*, Schedule II, Class 8, subpara (i).
166 *Ibid*, s 1102(3).
167 ITA, above note 3, para 20(1)(a); Interpretation Bulletin IT-285R2, "Capital Cost Allowance: General Comments" (31 March 1994) at paras 8–12; see also Ross M Skinner, *Accounting Principles: A Canadian Viewpoint* (Toronto: Canadian Institute of Chartered Accountants, 1972) at 5: "The recorded cost of a tangible capital asset should include all costs necessary to put the asset in a position to render service."
168 *Craddock v Zevo Finance Co*, [1944] 1 All ER 566, aff'd [1946] 1 All ER 523n (HL) (price paid by company *prima facie* nominal value of shares but contrary may be established in appropriate cases).

vail. Under most Canadian corporate statutes, the contract price must be added to the appropriate stated capital account of the corporation.

"Cost" means the entire laid-down cost of equipment even though certain expensive parts of the equipment might require frequent replacement.[169] The cost of property paid for in foreign currency is its Canadian dollar equivalent as at the date of acquisition.[170]

5) Undepreciated Capital Cost (UCC)

The starting point in calculating CCA is to determine the capital cost of each depreciable property. The regulations group depreciable properties into classes with similar life expectations. When we deduct CCA from the capital cost of property, the residue is the "undepreciated capital cost" (UCC) of the property.[171] Thus, UCC represents the as yet undepreciated cost of the class of assets. In accounting terms, this is equivalent to the net book value of the asset.

We determine a taxpayer's UCC of a class of depreciable property by adding the following:[172]

- The capital cost depreciable property of the class;
- Government assistance repaid by the taxpayer subsequent to the disposition of property in respect of the acquisition of which she received assistance;
- Any amount recaptured in respect of the class; and
- Repayment of contributions and allowances the taxpayer received and that were previously deducted from the capital cost of that class.

Next, we deduct the aggregate of:

- The total CCA and terminal losses that the taxpayer has claimed for property of the class;
- The proceeds of disposition of any property of the class disposed of (the deduction not to exceed the capital cost of the property); and

---

169 *MacMillan Bloedel (Alberni) Ltd v MNR*, above note 17 (taxpayer claimed cost of tires for logging equipment as current expense; practice held contrary to generally accepted accounting principles); see also *Cockshutt Farm Equipment of Canada Ltd v MNR* (1966), 41 Tax ABC 386 ("capital cost to the taxpayer" means actual, factual or historical cost of depreciable property at time of acquisition).

170 Interpretation Bulletin IT-285R2, above note 167.

171 *ITA*, above note 3, para 13(21) "undepreciated capital cost"; *Income Tax Regulations*, above note 50, s 1100(1)(a); see *ITA*, *ibid*, subss 248(1) and 13(21).

172 *ITA*, *ibid*, para 13(21) "undepreciated capital cost"; *Income Tax Regulations*, *ibid*, s 1100(1)(a).

- Government assistance received, or that the taxpayer is entitled to receive, as well as investment tax credits claimed, subsequent to the disposition by the taxpayer of the property to which such assistance or tax credit related.

For the purpose of calculating CCA in a year an asset is acquired, only one-half of the net additions to the class is generally added to the UCC balance.[173] The remaining half is added to the UCC after calculating CCA for the year of acquisition. The effect of this rule is that CCA on a newly acquired asset may be claimed at only one-half of the normal rate in the year of acquisition.

Example

Alpha Ltd acquires one Class 8 asset (depreciable at 20 percent) for $40,000 in Year 1, its first year of operation. In Year 2, Alpha disposes of the asset for $34,000 and acquires another Class 8 asset for $50,000. Assuming that Alpha claims the maximum CCA in each year, the UCC of the class at the end of Year 2 is as follows:

		Class 8
Opening UCC		$ NIL
Add:		
50% of net additions	20,000	
Balance before CCA		$20,000
CCA claimed		
($20,000 × 20%)		(4,000)
Balance before adjustment		16,000
Add:		
Remaining 50% of net additions		20,000
UCC at the end of Year 1		36,000
Add:		
Additions in Year 2	$50,000	
Dispositions in Year 2	(34,000)	
Net additions	$16,000	
50% × $16,000		8,000
Balance before CCA		44,000
CCA claimed		
($44,000 × 20%)		(8,800)
Balance before adjustment		35,200
Add:		
Remaining 50% of net additions		8,000
UCC at the end of Year 2		$43,200

---

173 *Income Tax Regulations, ibid,* s 1100(2). There are limited exceptions to this rule.

6) Adjustments on Disposition of Assets

The theory underlying the CCA system is that the taxpayer should write off the cost of depreciable property over its useful life by applying pre-determined rates of depreciation. Subsequent events may show, however, that the taxpayer claimed insufficient or excessive CCA over a period of time. This may occur where the taxpayer voluntarily claims less than the maximum CCA allowable, or where the maximum rate applicable to a class of assets is, for policy reasons, either too restrictive or too gener-ous. Thus, the UCC of depreciable property may be higher or lower than its fair market value.

a) Terminal Losses

Where a taxpayer disposes of the property of a class for less than its UCC, he suffers a shortfall in the depreciation claimed on the particu-lar class and is entitled to recoup the amount of the shortfall through a "terminal loss" claim. However, the taxpayer can claim a terminal loss only if he disposes of all the property of a class and owns no property of the class at the end of the taxation year.

Where a taxpayer is eligible for a terminal loss, he must claim the loss in the year, or lose it forever. Thus, unlike a claim for CCA, the claim for a terminal loss is not permissive.

Example

Assume: Beta Ltd. has an undepreciated capital cost (UCC) Class 8 balance of $45,000 at the beginning of Year 1. During the year it acquires another Class 8 asset at a cost of $10,000. In Year 2, Beta Ltd. disposes of all of its Class 8 assets for $38,000. Assuming that it claims the maximum CCA in each year, Beta's terminal loss is determined as follows:

Opening UCC (Year 1)	$45,000
Add:	
50% of net additions	5,000
Balance before CCA	50,000
CCA claimed (Year 1) (20% × $50,000)	(10,000)
Balance before adjustment	40,000
Add:	
Remaining 50% of net additions	5,000
UCC at the end of Year 1	45,000
Subtract:	
Proceeds of disposition (Year 2)	(38,000)
Balance in class (Year 2)	7,000
Terminal loss claimed (Year 2)	(7,000)
UCC at the end of Year 2	NIL

b) Recapture

Just as a taxpayer may claim too little CCA on a class of assets, it is also possible that he may have been allowed too much CCA. This may occur, for example, where the rate for a particular class of assets is deliberately set high in order to encourage economic activity in a particular sector. Thus, a sale of the assets of a class at fair market value may show that the assets were "over-depreciated" in the past. The Act "recaptures" any over-depreciated amount into income.[174]

i) Negative Balance

As noted earlier, the UCC of a class of assets is calculated by adding certain amounts and deducting others. Where a class has a negative balance at the end of the year, the amount of the balance is recaptured into income for that year[175] and added back to the UCC of the class. This brings the asset balance of that particular class back to nil.[176]

Recapture of CCA represents an adjustment for excessive claims of depreciation in earlier fiscal periods. In most cases, however, one can reduce the amount of CCA subject to recapture in any taxation year by acquiring additional property of the same class during the taxation year. Thus, it is usually possible to manipulate the amount of recapture recognized in a particular year by timing new acquisitions of depreciable capital assets.[177] However, this does not apply to cases where similar properties must be segregated — for example, rental properties that have a cost of $50,000 or more.[178]

ii) Limited to Capital Cost

Recapture of CCA represents a clawback of excessive depreciation. Thus, the Act limits recapture to the capital cost of the particular depreciable property in the class. Proceeds of disposition in excess of the capital cost of an asset do not give rise to recapture of CCA. Rather, the excess of proceeds of disposition over the capital cost of an asset is a capital gain.[179] The distinction is important because recapture of

---

174 *ITA*, above note 3, para 13(21) "undepreciated capital cost"; see also para 13(21.1)(a); *Canada v Malloney's Studio*, [1979] 2 SCR 326 (house demolished prior to sale of land; no part of proceeds from sale of land apportionable to demolished building).

175 *ITA*, *ibid*, subs 13(1).

176 *Ibid*, subpara 13(21); Interpretation Bulletin IT-220R2, "Capital Cost Allowance: Proceeds of Disposition of Depreciable Property" (25 May 1990).

177 *ITA*, *ibid*, subpara 13(21) "undepreciated capital cost."

178 *Income Tax Regulations*, above note 50, ss 1101(5b) and 1101(1ac).

179 *ITA*, above note 3, subpara 13(21)F "undepreciated capital cost." Note: this rule does not apply to timber resource properties.

CCA is fully taxable as income, whereas only one-half of capital gains are taxable.

Example		
Assume:		
Capital cost of asset		$10,000
CCA claimed		(5,000)
UCC of class		$5,000
Proceeds of disposition (net)		$8,000
Then:		
UCC before disposition		$5,000
Deduct *lesser* of:		
(i) Net proceeds	$8,000	
(ii) Capital cost	$10,000	
Lesser amount		(8,000)
Recapture of CCA		(3,000)

iii) Deferral

A taxpayer can defer the recapture of CCA. For example, a taxpayer who receives proceeds of disposition by way of insurance compensation for stolen or lost property (or by way of compensation for expropriated property) can elect to defer recognition of any recapture if she replaces the property with more expensive property.[180] This election is also available upon disposition of a "former business property."[181]

A "replacement property" is a property that the taxpayer acquires for the same or similar use as the property being replaced. A replacement property need only be a substitute for the original property; it need only be capable of being put to a similar use. It does *not* have to be an identical property.[182]

To obtain the benefit of the deferral, the taxpayer must make an election when filing a return for the year in which she acquires the replacement property. Upon election, part of the proceeds of disposition of the former property are, in effect, transferred from the year in which the disposition occurs to the year in which the replacement property is acquired.

---

180 *Ibid*, subs 13(4).
181 *Ibid*, subss 13(4) and 248(1) "former business property."
182 *Ibid*, subs 13(4.1).

An election to defer recapture of CCA is also an automatic election to defer any capital gain triggered on the disposition.[183]

7) First Year Half-Rate Rule

The Act limits in the first year the capital cost allowance on assets acquired during the year to one-half the allowance that is otherwise deductible.[184] This rule prevents tax avoidance by discouraging taxpayers from acquiring property at the end of a year in order to claim the full year's allowance. For example, a taxpayer might otherwise buy an asset on 31 December and claim CCA for the full year.[185]

The Act excludes from the UCC of a class one-half of the net additions of property of that class in the year. The one-half that is excluded is then added back to the UCC of the class, after one determines the CCA claim.

8) Works of Art

The CCA system also serves non-accounting cost allocation purposes, such as social and cultural policy objectives. Thus, a taxpayer may claim CCA on certain types of works of art created by Canadian artists, including:[186]

- Prints, etchings, drawings and paintings that cost more than $200; and
- Hand-woven tapestries and carpets that cost more than $215 per square metre.

However, a taxpayer *cannot* claim CCA on other types of works of art, such as:

---

183 *Ibid*, subs 44(4); Interpretation Bulletin IT-259R4, "Exchanges of Property" (23 September 2003); *Korenowsky v MNR* (1964), 35 Tax ABC 86 (delay beyond specified periods precludes deferral).

184 *Income Tax Regulations*, above note 50, s 1100(2). This rule applies only to acquisitions made subsequent to 12 November 1981. For acquisitions made prior to that date, the taxpayer was able to claim the full allowance in the year of acquisition. As to when a taxpayer acquires property, see *MNR v Wardean Drilling Ltd*, [1969] CTC 265 (Ex Ct).

185 *Hewlett Packard (Canada) Ltd v Canada*, 2004 FCA 240 (each year HP bought a new fleet of cars from Ford to replace the old fleet. In order to maximize its CCA, HP bought the new fleets just before, and sold the old fleets just after, its fiscal year-end. The minister argued HP was doubling up on CCA. The court disagreed and allowed CCA on the old fleet since HP retained both legal and beneficial interest until after fiscal year-end of each year).

186 *Income Tax Regulations*, above note 50, s 1102(1)(e).

- Antique furniture more than 100 years old that costs more than $1,000;
- Prints, etchings, drawings, paintings and carpets that are not the work of Canadian artists; and
- Engravings, lithographs, etchings, woodcuts or charts made before 1900.

M. ELIGIBLE CAPITAL PROPERTY

1) General Comment

The CCA system deals for the most part with capital expenditures for tangible capital property. There is a different regime in respect of capital expenditures on intangible capital assets—such as goodwill, franchises, customer lists and incorporation fees—that have an infinite life. We refer to these assets as "eligible capital property."

Expenditures on account of eligible capital property are deductible in computing business income. The deductibility of such expenditures is, however, subject to stringent limits. Only three-quarters of such expenditures are deductible. The maximum rate of write-off is 7 percent per year on a declining balance basis. Similarly, the Act includes 75 percent of the proceeds from the disposition of an eligible property in income, but only for amounts that exceed the taxpayer's "cumulative eligible capital account."[187] Thus, the regime draws on features from both the capital gains and the CCA systems.

The general tax structure of eligible capital expenditures centres around the operation of a notional account, the "cumulative eligible capital amount." This account functions as follows:

- 75 percent of outlays on account of eligible capital expenditures are included in the taxpayer's "cumulative eligible capital" account;[188] and
- 75 percent of the proceeds of disposition from eligible capital properties are credited to the "cumulative eligible capital" account.[189]

The balance in the "cumulative eligible capital" account at the end of the year can be amortized against business income at a maximum rate of 7 percent per year on a declining balance basis.[190] Any negative balance in the account as at the end of the year is recaptured and included in the

---

187 *ITA*, above note 3, para 20(1)(b), s 14.
188 *Ibid*, para 14(5) "cumulative eligible capital."
189 *Ibid*.
190 *Ibid*, para 20(1)(b).

taxpayer's income for the year.[191] Thus, the tax structure for eligible capital property is a hybrid between the CCA rules (declining balance, fixed rate, recapture, etc.) and the capital gains rules.

2) Eligible Capital Expenditures

An eligible capital expenditure is a capital expenditure of an intangible nature that a taxpayer incurs to earn income from a business, but one that is not deductible under any other provision of the Act. The Act specifically excludes the following expenditures from "eligible capital expenditures":[192]

- An outlay otherwise deductible in computing income or deductible under some provision of the Act, other than paragraph 20(1)(b);
- Outlays made specifically non-deductible by some provision of the Act, other than paragraph 18(1)(b);
- An outlay made to earn exempt income;
- The cost of tangible property or an interest therein, or the right to acquire the same;[193]
- The cost of intangible property that is depreciable property, or an interest therein; for example, leasehold interests, patents and franchises with a limited life, all of which costs would be deductible under the CCA provisions;
- The cost of property that would otherwise be deductible in computing a taxpayer's business income, or an interest therein, or the right to acquire the same;
- An amount paid to a creditor in settlement of a debt;
- An amount paid to a person in his or her capacity as a shareholder of the corporation;
- The cost, or part of the cost, of an interest in a trust, or a right to acquire the same;
- The cost, or part of the cost, of an interest in a partnership, or a right to acquire the same; and
- The cost or part of the cost of a share, bond, etc., or a right to acquire the same.

a) "Eligible Capital Amount"
"Eligible capital amount" is three-quarters of the proceeds of the disposition of property (as adjusted by a formula) that would represent an

---

191 Ibid, subs 14(1).

192 Ibid, para 14(5) "eligible capital expenditures."

193 In most cases, a deduction in respect of tangible property would be available under the CCA provisions.

eligible capital expenditure to the purchaser. That is, if the purchaser has made an eligible capital expenditure, the vendor is in receipt of an eligible capital amount equal to three-quarters of that expenditure, less any outlays and expenses incurred on disposition.[194]

b)   "Eligible Capital Property"

"Eligible capital property" is any property that, if sold, would require the inclusion, in computing the taxpayer's income, of three-quarters of the proceeds under subsection 14(1).

c)   Characterization of Expenditures and Receipts

Amounts that a taxpayer incurs or receives on the purchase and sale of property are not necessarily characterized as mirror images of each other. In *Samoth Financial Corp v Canada*,[195] for example, the taxpayer acquired the exclusive right to sell Century 21 franchises in Canada to licensed real estate brokers. The taxpayer paid $100,000 for this right. The taxpayer acted as a trader in selling the Century 21 franchises, but maintained that the receipts from those sales were on account of eligible capital property. The Federal Court of Appeal held the receipts from the sale of the franchises to be on account of business income and not on account of capital. Hence, not being on account of capital, the receipts could not constitute amounts received on account of eligible capital property. Although the purchase of the franchises might have been on account of eligible capital property, the sale of the franchises did not necessarily require a mirror image characterization of the proceeds of sale. In Mahoney J's words:

> In applying the so-called "mirror image rule" . . . the face to be seen in the mirror by the [taxpayer] is not that of the actual purchaser of one of its franchises acquiring a capital asset but its own face, that of a trader in franchises.[196]

3)   Goodwill

"Goodwill" is an asset. It has been described as "the probability that the old customers will resort to the old place."[197] In other words, it is the advantage that accrues to a person as a result of a reputation. The reputation may rest on honest dealing, hard work or advertising.[198] In finan-

---

194 *Ibid*, subpara 14(5) "cumulative eligible capital"; subs 14(1).
195 *Samoth Financial Corp v Canada* (1986), 86 DTC 6335 (FCA).
196 *Ibid* at 6335.
197 *Cruttwell v Lye* (1810), 34 ER 129 at 134.
198 *Trego v Hunt*, [1896] AC 7 (HL).

cial terms, goodwill means a premium sales price on the disposition of a business. The premium compensates for the "excess" earning power of the business because of its goodwill. Accountants define goodwill as:

> an intangible asset of a business when the business has value in excess of the sum of its net identifiable assets . . . . It has been said to fall into the three classes of commercial, industrial, and financial goodwill, which are the consequences of favourable attitudes on the part of customers, employees, and creditors, respectively. As to its value, the most common explanations emphasize the present value of expected future earnings in excess of the return required to induce investment.[199]

"Goodwill" is also defined in terms of excess earning power over the "normal" rate of return of a business. For example, in *Dominion Dairies v MNR*:

> [G]oodwill can be viewed as the purchase of earning power in excess of a normal return on the investment . . . . This advantage evidences itself in the form of earnings in an amount greater than that expected in a typical firm in the industry with a similar capital investment.[200]

The tax system treats purchased goodwill differently from expenditures incurred in building up goodwill. A taxpayer who expends money on advertising, customer relations, employee relations, etc., may write off the expenditures on a current basis, even though the expenditures cultivate an asset. Where, however, a taxpayer purchases goodwill built up through such expenditures, the cost is an "eligible capital expenditure," which can only be amortized in the manner described.

4) Recapture of Negative Balances

Generally speaking, where, at the end of a taxation year, the amounts required to be deducted from a taxpayer's pool of expenditures in respect of eligible capital property exceed the amounts required to be added to the pool, the excess ("negative balance") must be included in the taxpayer's income for the year.

Where an individual's cumulative eligible capital has a negative balance at the end of a taxation year, the amount that must be included in income is limited to that portion of the negative balance that represents the recapture of previous deductions claimed in respect of eligible cap-

---

199 CICA, *Terminology for Accountants* (Toronto: CICA, 1976)..
200 *Dominion Dairies Ltd v MNR* (1966), 66 DTC 5028 at 5033–34 (Ex Ct).

ital property. The remainder of the negative balance is either deemed (in the case of qualified farm property) or electible (in the case of other properties) as capital gains and, therefore, may be eligible for the capital gains exemption (see Chapter 9).

Comprehensive Example: Computation of Net Income for Tax Purposes

Assume:

A taxable Canadian corporation with 30 June as its year-end provides the following statement of income for its 2011 taxation year:

Income Statement—2011

Revenue		$2,000,000
Costs of goods sold:		
Inventory—opening	$300,000	
Purchases	800,000	
Cost of goods available	1,100,000	
Inventory—closing	(200,000)	(900,000)
Gross profit		$1,100,000
General, administrative and selling expenses:		
Depreciation and amortization	$120,000	
Accounting & legal	15,000	
Commission	80,000	
Donations	30,000	
Bad debts	25,000	
Rental	120,000	
Salary, wages and fringe	250,000	
Interest	35,000	
Insurance	5,000	
Travel (airline)	20,000	
Utilities	45,000	
General	100,000	(845,000)
Income before under-noted items		$255,000
Other income:		
Dividends	$20,000	
Interest	15,000	
Receipt on disposal of investment	50,000	85,000
Income before income tax expense		$340,000
Current	$30,000	
Deferred	140,000	(170,000)
Net income		$170,000

Comprehensive Example: Computation of Net Income for Tax Purposes

Additional information on the above income statement is as follows:

(a) The $50,000 receipt on disposal of investment was the result of the sale of some securities that were acquired in 1974 at a cost of $5,000, resulting in a capital gain of $45,000.

(b) The interest income was derived from the accounts receivable for late payments.

(c) The $20,000 dividends were received from shares that are held for investment purposes.

(d) Included in the general expenses of $100,000 is $5,000 paid as an entrance fee to a social club. In addition, $50,000 was accrued as bonus to be paid to the two senior executives of the company. As of 10 August 2011, the bonus accruals of 2009 and 2010 taxation years of $30,000 and $35,000, respectively, remained unpaid.

(e) Interest expense includes $8,500 of interest paid for late instalments of corporate tax.

(f) The $25,000 bad debts expense was determined for accounting purposes. For income tax purposes, a reserve for bad debts of $35,000 was made at the end of the preceding year; $10,000 was determined to be bad in 2011 and was written off: $4,000 has been collected in 2011 from the accounts written off in previous years; and a reserve for bad debts at the end of the 2011 taxation year was determined to be $50,000.

(g) The maximum CCA that could be claimed for the year is $100,000. The balance of the cumulative eligible capital account is $64,285 before amortization.

(h) Donations are made up of the following payments:

(i) Canadian Red Cross	$10,000
(ii) Federal political parties	$15,000
(iii) United Nations	$5,000

Then:

Determination of 2011 Net Income for Tax Purposes

Net income per financial statements		$170,000
Add:		
Income tax expense	$170,000	
Taxable capital gain	22,500	
Entrance fee	5,000	
Accrued bonus (2010)	35,000	
Interest on late instalment	8,500	
Bad debts	25,000	
Reserve (2010)	35,000	
Bad debts recovered	4,000	
Depreciation and amortization	120,000	
Donations and political contributions	30,000	455,000
		$625,000

Comprehensive Example: Computation of Net Income for Tax Purposes		
Less:		
Gain on investment	$50,000	
Bad debts	10,000	
Reserve (2011)	50,000	
CCA	100,000	
CEC deduction at 7%	4,500	(214,500)
Net income for tax purposes		$410,500

FURTHER READINGS

Characterization of Income

Durnford, John W. "Profits on the Sale of Shares: Capital Gains or Business Income—A Fresh Look at Irrigation Industries" (1987) 35 Can Tax J 837.

———. "The Distinction between Income from Business and Income from Property, and the Concept of Carrying on Business" (1991) 39 Can Tax J 1131.

Krishna, Vern. "Characterization of 'Income from Business' and 'Income from Property'" (1984) 1 Can Curr Tax C-37.

Interest Income

Ulmer, John M. "Taxation of Interest Income" (1990) 42 Can Tax Found 8:1.

General Deductions

Brooks, Neil. "The Principles Underlying the Deduction of Business Expenses" in Brian Hansen, Vern Krishna, & James Rendall, eds, *Canadian Taxation* (Don Mills, ON: Richard De Boo, 1981) ch 5.

Interest

Krishna, Vern. "Interest Deductibility: More Form over Substance" (1993) Can Curr Tax C-17.

———. "More Uncertainty on Deduction of Interest Expenses" [Case Comment: *Attaie v Canada (MNR)*, T-1319-85 (1987) (TCC)] (1987–89) 2 Can Curr Tax J-59.

———. "Is There a Choice of Methods in Accounting for Interest Expenses?" (1984) 1 Can Curr Tax C-21.

———. "Interest Expenses" (1983) 17:7 CGA Magazine 39.

———. "Deducting Interest Expenses" (1983) 17:11 CGA Magazine 21.

CHAPTER 9

CAPITAL GAINS
AND LOSSES

A. GENERAL COMMENT

Capital gains are a separate and distinct source of income. A taxpayer must include 50 percent of capital gains in income and may deduct therefrom 50 percent of capital losses.[1] There is no separate tax on capital gains. Capital gains and losses merely expand or contract the taxable base to which we apply the normal tax rates. Thus, capital gains and losses are a separate source of realized income subject to lower effective tax rates.

The "preference" for capital gains adds enormous complexity to the Act. Quite apart from the understandable preference of taxpayers to characterize income as capital gains, the Act further complicates the structure by creating numerous subcategories of capital properties, each of which has special rules and exemptions.

Our tax law has always "preferred" capital gains over other forms of income. The capital gains preference debate is now long in the tooth, and we are no closer to resolving the issue today than we were when capital gains were first excluded from income.

Why should we treat capital gains preferentially? First, there is an intuitive notion that the appreciation of capital is not what we normally consider as "income." There is a clear split between the courts and policymakers on this issue. For example, in 1872, long before the development of the Haig-Simons formulation of income, the United States

---

1   *Income Tax Act*, RSC 1985, c 1 (5th Supp) [*ITA*], s 38.

Supreme Court stated that "the mere fact that property has advanced in value between the date of its acquisition and sale does not authorize the imposition of the tax on the amount of the advance. Mere advance in value in no sense constitutes the gains, profits, or income . . . . It constitutes and can be treated merely as increase of capital."[2]

Similarly, in 1923, United States Treasury Secretary, Andrew Mellon, said he "believed it would be sounder taxation policy generally not to recognize either capital gain or capital loss for purposes of income tax."

The Carter Commission (1967) clearly favoured the theory that "a buck is a buck" regardless of its source. In Canada today one can say that there are no clearly defined objectives of capital gains taxation, and that our policies, both of taxation and preference, are an amalgam of intuition, political ideology, and competitive economic considerations.[3]

A capital gain derives from an increase in the capital value of an asset. This raises two distinct issues: (1) when should we tax the increase? and (2) how much of the increase should we tax? An increase in the value of capital reflects the increase in the discounted future cash income from the underlying investment. In the case of stocks, for example, the increment in stock values is either the enhancement in anticipated future cash flows or a reduction in the discount factor. Since we tax dividends from earnings, we must also tax capital gains to the extent that they represent undistributed earnings. However, although there are some similarities between dividends and capital gains, there are also significant differences with respect to timing, bunching and inflation.

Second, we can justify the capital gains preference as relief from the "bunching" of accrued property appreciation. Capital gains usually result from appreciation that builds up over an extended period. The gain one realizes usually extends beyond one fiscal year. The realization principle of income recognition is a rule of administrative convenience. For example, if one buys shares in Year 1 for $20 and sells the shares in Year 5 for $120, the realized gain of $100 reflects the unrealized accrual of gains over five years. Since the personal tax rate structure is progressive,[4] we would penalize the investor with a higher marginal tax rate if we taxed the entire gain in his income in Year 5. This might be unfair to the investor.

Taxing only one-half of a gain is a rough-and-ready (palm tree) way of mitigating the effect of progressive rates on "bunched" income.

---

2   *Gray v Darlington*, 82 US 63 at 66 (1872). This position was altered by the passage of the 16th Amendment in 1913.

3   See Stanley Surrey, "Definitional Problems in Capital Gain Taxation" (1956) 69 Harv L Rev 985; Walter Blum, "A Handy Summary of the Capital Gains Arguments" (1957) 35 Taxes 247.

4   See Chapter 1.

The United States Supreme Court recognized this in *Burnet v Harmel*,[5] where it held that the purpose of the capital gains preference was to "relieve the taxpayer from . . . excessive tax burdens on gains resulting from a conversion of capital investments, and to remove the deterrent effect of those burdens on such conversions."

Of course, bunching has no effect at all on an investor whose marginal rate of tax in each of the five preceding years would have been in the top tax bracket even without the capital gain. Such an investor derives a windfall from the preference. Also, one can always relieve against the bunching effect by allowing the investor to spread back the tax on his entire gain at the average rate that would have applied had the investor accrued the gain annually over the five-year period. This is a complicated averaging mechanism to the bunching problem. In the end, averaging may, accidentally, yield the same approximate result as simply reducing the overall effective rate to 50 percent.

Third, the preference mitigates the "lock-in" effect of the realization rule, and makes it less costly for investors to switch investments when it is in their economic interest to do so. The "lock-in" effect stems from the realization principle. In the above example, the investor with an unrealized gain of $100 in Year 5 may identify a better economic investment with a higher potential yield. If she sells the initial investment, however, the investor will trigger tax of, say, 40 percent, which would leave her with only $60 to reinvest. This effectively reduces the net rate of return on the new investment, and makes it less desirable. Thus, the investor might choose not to sell the original investment and defer the tax that would otherwise be payable. Usually, she could defer the tax until the later of her or her spouse's death.[6] If the investor can defer the tax for 30 years, and the interest rate is 8 percent, the future value of the $40 tax that would be payable if she sells today is $403.[7] Thus, the investor can multiply her tax saving ten times simply by not selling and locking herself into the original investment.

Lock-in restricts the mobility of capital and reduces its efficiency. To liquidate a poorly performing investment and reinvest in another venture, the return on the new investment must be sufficient to pay for the capital gains tax bite on the old investment. The investor will liquidate the initial investment only if the return on the new opportunity is sufficiently higher to offset the tax bite on the old asset. Otherwise, it is better to lock in to the initial investment. The capital gains preference

---

5   287 US 103 at 106 (1932).
6   *ITA*, above note 1, subss 70(5) & (6).
7   Future value = $40 × 10.063 (see Appendix A).

reduces the deterrence effect of lock-in and allows capital to flow to a more efficient use.

To be sure, if capital gains tax restricts the mobility of capital, one can remove the problem by allowing the investor a complete rollover of taxes if he invests the proceeds in other capital investments. As we will see, we allow many such rollovers for in-kind exchanges of property. The important point is that the capital gains bunching problem derives essentially from the realization principle, which is a rule of administrative convenience. The preference is a politically and administratively convenient, perhaps even optimum, solution to a vexing problem.

That said, however, there is another vexing aspect of capital gains, namely, inflation. Unlike dividends and interest income, which are taxed annually, capital gains are taxable only when we realize them. Suppose you buy a stock for $100 and sell it in a year for $140. If the capital gains tax rate is 40 percent, the tax on the gain is $16. But the gain of $40 is illusory to the extent that inflation reduces its economic value. If inflation is 10 percent, the real economic gain in the year is only $30. This means that the effective tax rate of $16 on the economic gain of $30 is really 53 percent. Hence, we increase tax rates indirectly in periods of high inflation. This doubly affects the taxpayer. The longer the holding period and the more serious the inflation rate, the higher the effective capital gains tax rate. Thus, at the very least, we should index capital gains so as not to tax illusory gains.

B. SEGREGATION BY SUB-SOURCE

We bring capital gains into income according to the rules in section 3. Paragraph 3(b) includes the following gains in income:

- *Net* taxable capital gains from dispositions of property other than listed personal property (LPP); and
- Taxable *net* gains from dispositions of LPP.

"Net" refers to the excess of gains over losses. Capital losses are generally deductible only against capital gains. One cannot use any excess of capital losses over capital gains to reduce income from other sources.[8] There is only one exception to this rule: one may apply business investment losses (a special type of capital gain) against "ordinary" income.

The scheme of section 3 in respect of capital gains and losses is as follows:

---

8   See *ITA*, above note 1, paras 3(d)–(f).

Taxable capital gains from property other than listed personal property	XXX	
Add: taxable *net* gain from listed personal property	XXX	
		XXX
Exceeds:		
The amount, if any, by which allowable capital losses from property other than listed personal property *exceeds* allowable business investment losses	XXX	(XXX)
Amount included in income		(XXX)

C. CAPITAL PROPERTY

A capital gain or loss arises only when a taxpayer disposes of capital property. The Act defines "capital property" as property, the disposition of which gives rise to a capital gain or loss.[9] This circular definitional structure is not helpful. Thus, with the exception of specific items, the characterization of a gain or loss as being on account of income or capital is determined by reference to common law principles.[10]

1) Exclusions from Capital Gains

The Act specifically excludes the following properties from property that can give rise to a capital gain:[11]

- Property the disposition of which gives rise to income from a business, a property, or an adventure in the nature of trade;[12]
- Eligible capital property;
- Depreciable property;
- Cultural property disposed of pursuant to the *Cultural Property Export and Import Act*;[13]
- Canadian and foreign resource properties, which include mineral, oil and gas rights;
- Insurance policies, including life insurance policies within the meaning of section 138, except for a taxpayer's deemed interest in a related segregated fund trust;

---

9   *Ibid*, para 54 "capital property" (b).
10 The CRA does not give advance rulings on the characterization of gains—see Information Circular 70-6R5 "Advance Income Tax Ruling" (17 May 2002).
11 *ITA*, above note 1, para 39(1)(a).
12 *Ibid*, s 248(1) "business."
13 RSC 1985, c C-51.

- Timber resource properties; and
- An interest of a beneficiary under a qualifying environmental trust.

Note, however, that the disposition of a cultural property can give rise to a capital loss.[14]

To summarize: a capital gain or loss is a gain or loss that arises from the disposition of property *to the extent that* it is not ordinary income or loss and does not arise from the disposition of one of the special types of property listed above. Thus, generally, a capital gain or loss arises from the disposition of an investment acquired for the purpose of producing income, rather than as a trading asset.

2) Types of Capital Property

We use the terms "capital gain" and "capital loss" in a broad sense to denote a gain or loss from the disposition of a capital property. There are, however, different types of capital properties, which give rise to different types of capital gains and losses. The Act subdivides capital properties into four categories:

- Personal-use property;[15]
- Listed personal property;[16]
- "Business investment" property;[17] and
- Other capital properties.

The gain or loss from each of these subcategories of capital property is calculated separately and according to detailed specific rules.

D. COMPUTATION OF GAIN OR LOSS

A capital gain is the difference between the "proceeds of disposition" (POD) from capital property and the sum of its "adjusted cost base" (ACB) and the expenses of disposition:[18]

$$\text{Capital Gain} = \text{POD} - (\text{ACB} + \text{Expenses})$$

---

14   Interpretation Bulletin IT-407R4, "Dispositions of Cultural Property to Designated Canadian Institutions" (7 November 1996 Consolidated).

15   *ITA*, above note 1, s 54 "personal-use property."

16   *Ibid*, s 54 "listed personal property."

17   *Ibid*, para 39(1)(c); Interpretation Bulletin IT-484R2, "Business Investment Losses" (28 November 1996).

18   *ITA*, *ibid*, para 40(1)(a).

For present purposes, we assume that "proceeds of disposition" means selling price and "adjusted cost base" means the cost of property. We discuss the technical meaning of these terms later.

Example

Assume: A taxpayer sells a capital property for $10,000 that he purchased for $6,000 and incurs expenses of $800 in selling the property.

Then:

Selling price		10,000
Less: cost (ACB)	$6,000	
Selling expenses	800	(6,800)
Capital gain		$3,200

The taxpayer's taxable capital gain is $1,600; that is, the capital gain times the inclusion rate ($3,200 × 50%).

A taxpayer's capital loss from a disposition of property is the amount by which the "adjusted cost base" and selling expenses exceed the "proceeds of disposition."[19]

Example

Assume: T sells a capital property that cost $16,000 for cash proceeds of $2,000; T also incurs $80 as expenses of sale.

Then:

Proceeds of Sale		$2,000
Less: Cost (ACB)	$16,000	
Selling expenses	80	(16,080)
Capital loss		$(14,080)

T's allowable capital loss is $7,040—the capital loss times the inclusion rate ($14,080 × 50%).

---

1) Reserves

The Act generally recognizes capital gains and losses only when the taxpayer realizes the gain or loss. The taxable event that gives rise to a gain or loss is the disposition of the property. A taxpayer may, however, dispose of property and not be paid the full price upon its sale. In these circumstances, the taxpayer realizes a capital gain, but does not collect the cash at the time of the transaction. To impose tax on uncollected gains might be a hardship for some taxpayers. Thus, subject to certain restrictions, the Act allows a taxpayer to defer recognition of a portion of the gain on uncollected proceeds.

---

19   *Ibid*, para 40(1)(b).

Where a taxpayer deducts a reserve in one year, she must bring the amount deducted into income in the following year. The taxpayer can then claim a further reserve in each of the following years to the extent that part of the proceeds of sale remain outstanding at the end of the year.[20] However, the reserve cannot exceed the amount of the reserve claimed in the immediately preceding year in respect of the property. Thus, if a taxpayer claims less than the maximum allowed in one year, she cannot claim a larger reserve in respect of the same property in the next year.[21]

a)   Limitations

The maximum reserve that a taxpayer may claim in a year is limited to the *lesser* of two amounts:[22]

1)   A "reasonable" amount; and
2)   An amount determined by reference to a formula.

i)   "A Reasonable Reserve"

A reserve is reasonable if it is proportional to the amount that is not payable to the taxpayer until after the end of the taxation year. Thus, one may calculate a reserve as follows:

$$\frac{\text{Capital gain} \times (\text{Amount not payable until after the end of the year})}{(\text{Total proceeds})}$$

However, a taxpayer is free to choose any other "reasonable" method.[23]

Example

Assume: In Year 1, T sold a capital property (with an ACB of $63,000) in an arm's length transaction for $100,000, payable $20,000 on completion of the sale and $20,000 per year for the next four years. Expenses of selling the property came to $7,000.

Then:

Proceeds of sale		$100,000
Less: Cost (ACB)	$63,000	
Selling expenses	7,000	(70,000)
Capital gain		$30,000
Less: Reasonable reserve (see below)		(24,000)
Capital gain recognized in Year 1		$6,000

---

20   *Ibid*, subpara 40(1)(a)(iii); see also the various restrictions on claiming reserves in subs 40(2).
21   *Ibid*, subpara 40(1)(a)(ii).
22   *Ibid*, subpara 40(1)(a)(iii).
23   *Canada v Ennisclare Corp*, [1984] CTC 286 (FCA).

Example

A "reasonable" reserve may be calculated as follows:

Year	Calculation	Reserve	Capital Gain Recognized
1	$30,000 × $\frac{\$80,000}{100,000}$ =	$24,000	$6,000
2	30,000 × $\frac{60,000}{100,000}$ =	$18,000	$6,000
3	30,000 × $\frac{40,000}{100,000}$ =	$12,000	$6,000
4	30,000 × $\frac{20,000}{100,000}$ =	$ 6,000	$6,000
5		NIL	$6,000
Total capital gain recognized			$30,000

ii) Maximum Reserve

A taxpayer cannot claim a reserve for more than five years. This limitation ensures that the cumulative amount of capital gain recognized is *not less* than 20 percent of the total gain times the number of taxation years that have elapsed since the disposition. Thus, the taxpayer must include at least one-fifth of the gain in each year, regardless whether he receives any proceeds in the year.

iii) Special Reserves

The Act extends the maximum five-year limitation to ten years if he transfers property to his child and the property is:[24]

• Land and depreciable property used in a family farm or fishing business;
• A share in a family farm or family fishing corporation;
• An interest in a family farm or family fishing partnership; or
• A share in a small business corporation.

2) Selling Expenses

A taxpayer can deduct expenses incurred in disposing of a capital property. Only expenses that one incurs in connection with the actual disposition of capital property are deductible in calculating a capital gain or loss. Expenses that one incurs for the purposes of earning income from a capital property are not deductible in calculating the amount of a capital gain or loss.

---

24   *ITA*, above note 1, subs 40(1.1).

Expenses that one incurs in enhancing capital property into a saleable condition and expenses connected directly with the disposition of the property are also deductible from the proceeds of disposition. For example, fixing-up expenses, finder's fees, sales commissions, broker's fees, surveyor's fees, transfer taxes, title registration fees, and legal expenses that relate to the disposition are deductible.

E. DISPOSITIONS

A capital gain arises when a taxpayer disposes of capital property—that is, when he legally alienates his rights in the property. In certain circumstances, however, the Act deems a taxpayer to dispose of property even though he does not physically or legally alienate his property rights.[25]

1) "Property"

"Property" includes real and personal property (whether corporeal or incorporeal, movable or immovable, tangible or intangible), shares, choses in action and timber resource properties. Indeed, the term comprises virtually every possible interest a person may have.[26]

2) "Disposition"

The concept of "disposition" is a central element in the capital gains system. A "disposition" is any event that is an alienation of property or a loss of ownership. The alienation may occur by a voluntary or involuntary action on the owner's part.

A "disposition" includes any event, voluntary or involuntary, that implies a loss of ownership. The words "disposed of" embrace every event by which property ceases to be available to the taxpayer for use in producing income, either because the property ceases to be physically accessible to the taxpayer or because it ceases to exist.[27] Thus,

---

25   See, for example, *ibid*, s 45 (deemed disposition on change of use of property); subs 50(1) (deemed disposition of bad debt); subs 70(5) (deemed disposition on death).

26   *Re Lunness* (1919), 46 OLR 320 (SCAD). See *Manrell v Canada*, 2003 FCA 128 for a detailed analysis of the meaning of property in the context of non-competition agreements.

27   See, generally, *Victory Hotels Ltd v MNR*, [1962] CTC 614 (Ex Ct) (determination of disposition when documentation conflicting); *MNR v Wardean Drilling Ltd*, [1969] CTC 265 (Ex Ct) (asset paid for in 1963, delivered in 1964; deductible in 1964, when all incidents of title passed); *Canada v Cie immobilière BCN Ltée*,

"disposition" has a broader meaning than "sale."[28] There is, however, one important exception: a transfer of legal title of property to a "bare trustee" is not a disposition if there is no change in beneficial ownership.[29]

In the simplest case, the proceeds from a disposition of property are equal to the consideration that the taxpayer receives for the property. In certain cases, the Act deems the amount of proceeds—for example, when the taxpayer gifts the property.

A "disposition"[30] also includes any event entitling a taxpayer to "proceeds of disposition,"[31] including proceeds from:

- The sale price of property;
- Compensation for stolen property;
- Compensation for property lost or destroyed;
- Compensation for expropriated property (including any interest penalty or damages that are part of the expropriation award);[32]

[1979] 1 SCR 865 (meaning of "disposed of"); *Lord Elgin Hotel Ltd v MNR* (1964), 64 DTC 637, appeal quashed [1969] CTC 24 (Ex Ct) (winding-up of company and distribution of shares constituted "disposition" of hotel); *Canada v Malloney's Studio Ltd*, [1979] 2 SCR 326 (demolition of building constituted disposition of building even though taxpayer did not receive proceeds of disposition); see also *Rose v Federal Commissioner of Taxation* (1951), 84 CLR 118 (HCA); *Gorton v Federal Commissioner of Taxation* (1965), 113 CLR 604 (HCA); *Henty House Pty Ltd (In Voluntary Liquidation) v Federal Commissioner of Taxation*, [1953] HCA 54 at para 7, where the Australian High Court commented upon the meaning of the term "disposition" as follows:

> The entire expression "disposed of, lost or destroyed" is apt to embrace every event by which property ceases to be available to the taxpayer for use for the purpose of producing assessable income, either because it ceases to be his, or because it ceases to be physically accessible to him, or because it ceases to exist . . . the words "is disposed of" are wide enough to cover all forms of alienation . . . and they should be understood as meaning no less than "becomes alienated from the taxpayer," whether it is by him or by another that the act of alienation is done.

28 *Olympia & York Developments Ltd v MNR*, [1980] CTC 265 (FCTD) (instalment contract; transfer of possession but not title constituted "disposition," although no "sale" until later); *Canada v Imperial General Properties Ltd*, [1985] 1 CTC 40 (FCA), leave to appeal to SCC refused (1985), 16 DLR (4th) 615 (sale complete when conditions precedent satisfied); *Attis v MNR*, [1984] CTC 3013 (TCC) (minister entitled to fix proceeds of disposition by reference to sale price).

29 *ITA*, above note 1, para 248(1) "disposition" (e).

30 *Ibid*, subs 248(1) "disposition."

31 *Ibid*, s 54 "proceeds of disposition."

32 *ER Fisher Ltd v MNR*, [1986] 2 CTC 114 (FCTD) (interest paid pursuant to *Expropriation Act*, as penalty, because Crown's offer inappropriate, constituted "proceeds of disposition"); *Sani Sport Inc v MNR*, [1987] 1 CTC 411 (FCTD), aff'd

- Compensation for damaged property (unless funds have been expended in repairing the damage within a reasonable time);
- Mortgage settlements upon foreclosure of mortgaged property (including reductions in the liability of a taxpayer to a mortgagee as a result of the sale of mortgaged property);
- The principal amount of a debtor's claim that has been extinguished as a result of a mortgage foreclosure or conditional sales repossession;[33]
- A winding-up (or redemption) dividend, to the extent that it does not exceed the corporation's pre-1972 capital surplus on hand;
- Redemptions, acquisitions or cancellations of shares, bonds and other securities;
- Settlements or cancellations of any debt owing to a taxpayer;
- Conversion of shares on an amalgamation;
- Expiry of options to acquire or dispose of property; and
- Transfers of property to or by a trust (including transfers to an RRSP, DPSP, EPSP or RRIF, even if the transfer does not involve a change of beneficial ownership).

However, a "disposition" does *not* include any of the following:[34]

- Transfers of property to, or by, a creditor for securing or releasing a debt;
- Issuance by a corporation of its own bonds or debentures;
- Transfer of property without change in beneficial ownership (except transfer by resident trust to non-resident trust or transfer to a trust governed by RRSP, DPSP, EPSP or RRIF);
- Issuance by a corporation of its own shares;
- Cancellations of inter-company shareholdings on an amalgamation;
- Amounts that represent a deemed dividend on a winding-up or share redemption; and
- Amounts deemed to be dividends paid to a non-resident person in a non-arm's length sale of shares of one Canadian corporation to another Canadian corporation.[35]

[1990] 2 CTC 15 (FCA) [*Sani Sport*] (amount paid as damages for loss of business opportunity included in proceeds of disposition).

33   See *ITA*, above note 1, s 79.

34   *Ibid*, s 54 "proceeds of disposition"; subs 248(1) "disposition."

35   The underlying sale of shares is a disposition and the proceeds are reduced by the amount of the deemed dividend.

3) Foreign Currencies

Gains and losses in foreign currency transactions are taxable according to the usual rules, either as income gains (or losses) or as capital gains (or losses). Thus, the first step is to determine whether a gain or loss is on account of income or capital. The characterization of the currency gain or loss usually follows the transaction from which it results.[36] Hence, gains and losses from business transactions are income items; gains and losses from transactions in capital assets are capital gains and losses. A foreign exchange loss is not per se an "outlay or expense" for the purposes of determining a capital gain or loss.[37]

A taxpayer determines the cost of his capital property in Canadian dollars as of the time that he acquires it. Thus, the capital cost of a property to a taxpayer is its actual, factual cost.

4) Deemed Dispositions

The Act deems certain transactions and events to be dispositions of property, which triggers deemed proceeds of disposition.

a)   Change in Use of Property

i)   Personal to Commercial
A taxpayer who acquires property for personal use is deemed to have disposed of the property for proceeds equal to its fair market value if she begins to use the property for commercial purposes.[38] For example, assume a taxpayer who owns and lives in a house that cost $100,000 begins to rent out the house at a time when its fair market value is $170,000. The act of renting out the house is a change in its use. The Act deems the taxpayer to have disposed of, and immediately reacquired, the house for $170,000. Thus, the taxpayer realizes a capital gain of $70,000 even though she does not receive any funds from the change of use.

Where a taxpayer changes the use of property from personal to commercial, she may elect to ignore the change in use for income tax purposes. The effect of such an election is that the Act deems the taxpayer not to have begun to use the property for commercial purposes.[39] The taxpayer may rescind the election at any time.

---

36   *Tip Top Tailors v MNR*, [1957] SCR 703.
37   *Avis Immobilier GMBH v Canada*, [1994] 1 CTC 2204 (TCC), aff'd on appeal (1996), 97 DTC 5002 (FCA), leave to appeal to SCC refused, [1997] SCCA No 29.
38   *ITA*, above note 1, para 45(1)(a).
39   *Ibid*, subs 45(2).

The election allows the taxpayer to defer any capital gain arising by virtue of a change in the use of the property and defer payment of tax until such time as she disposes of the property or rescinds the election. During the tenure of the election the taxpayer cannot claim capital cost allowance on the property.[40]

ii) Commercial to Personal

The Act also deems a taxpayer who acquires property for commercial purposes to have disposed of the property at its fair market value if she begins to use it for personal purposes.[41] In the above example, if the taxpayer changes back the use of the house from commercial to personal use at a time when the fair market value of the house is $200,000, the change of use will trigger a capital gain of $30,000. This rule does not apply where the taxpayer changes the use of property from commercial use to a principal residence if she elects in writing.[42]

b) Leaving Canada

The Act deems a taxpayer who ceases to be resident in Canada to dispose of certain properties immediately before giving up residence. The deemed disposition may give rise to a capital gain, resulting in a "departure tax."[43]

The following properties are not subject to the departure tax:

Description	Reference
• Where the taxpayer is an individual, real or immovable property situated in Canada, a Canadian resource property or a timber resource property.	subpara 128.1(4)(b)(i)
• Where the taxpayer is an individual, capital property used, eligible capital property in respect of and inventory described in the business carried on by the individual in Canada through a permanent establishment.	subpara 128.1(4)(b)(ii)

---

40   *Income Tax Regulations*, CRC, c 945, s 1102(1)(c) (excludes from depreciable property any property not acquired by taxpayer for the purpose of gaining or producing income).

41   *ITA*, above note 1, para 45(1)(a); *Woods v MNR*, [1978] CTC 2802 (TRB) (capital gain on deemed disposition in respect of taxpayer's dwelling when he occupied it after renting it out for nine years); *Leib v MNR*, [1984] CTC 2324 (TCC) (change in use of principal residence deemed to be disposition despite taxpayer not receiving funds).

42   *ITA, ibid*, subss 45(3) & (4).

43   *Ibid*, para 128.1(4)(b); *Davis v Canada*, [1978] CTC 536 (FCTD), aff'd [1980] CTC 88 (FCA).

Description	Reference
• Where the taxpayer is an individual, an excluded right or interest defined in subs 128.1(10) as including payments under certain pension plans, deferred income arrangements, retiring allowances, death benefits, unemployment insurance benefits and options under stock option plans.	subpara 128.1(4)(b)(iii)
• Where the taxpayer is an individual other than a trust and during the preceding 10 years was resident in Canada for a total of 60 months or less, property that the taxpayer owned when he last became resident in Canada or that was acquired by the taxpayer by inheritance or bequest after he last became resident in Canada.	subpara 128.1(4)(b)(iv)

Resident taxpayers may elect to defer or trigger accrued gains on their capital property.

c) Options

i) Nature

An option is a contractual right that gives its holder the power to buy or sell property at some time in the future at a fixed or otherwise determinable price.[44] An option is a "property" for income tax purposes[45] and can be sold, exercised or allowed to expire.

ii) Characterization on Issuance

The issuance of an option may be an income transaction or a capital transaction.[46] The usual tests in characterizing gains as income gains or capital gains also apply to options. The determination depends upon the taxpayer's intention to invest or trade in the property on which the option is granted.[47] Where the optionor does not grant the option in the course of his business, any consideration for the option is a capital gain.

iii) Granting of Options

The Act deems a taxpayer who grants an option in respect of a capital property to have disposed of the property at that time.[48] The ad-

---

44   See, generally, *Day v MNR* (1971), 71 DTC 723 (TAB), for discussion on meaning of option.

45   *ITA*, above note 1, subs 248(1) "property"; *Day v MNR*, *ibid.*

46   See *Western Leaseholds Ltd v MNR*, [1960] SCR 10 (revenues from granting mineral rights options were income); *Hill Clark Francis Ltd v MNR*, [1963] SCR 452.

47   *Cook v MNR*, [1987] 1 CTC 377 (FCTD); see also *Day v MNR*, above note 44 (meaning of "option").

48   *ITA*, above note 1, subs 49(1).

justed cost base of the option is nil. Thus, the issuance of an option for valuable consideration triggers a capital gain in the year in which the taxpayer issues it. This rule does not apply to options to buy or sell a principal residence, options that a corporation issues to acquire its bonds, debentures or equity capital, or options that a trust grants to acquire units of the trust. Special rules apply to employee stock options.

Where a taxpayer grants a call option (an option to purchase property), the granting of the option is a disposition of property. The statute deems the adjusted cost base of the property to be nil. The taxpayer must report the gain on the option in the year that he grants it.[49]

If the option is exercised, the granting of the option is retrospectively deemed not to have been a disposition of property.[50] Thus, upon the exercise of the option the earlier transaction is, in effect, retrospectively cancelled for tax purposes. The grantor then includes the price of the option in the proceeds of disposition from the property that he sells pursuant to the option.[51]

Thus, the price of the option increases the proceeds of disposition. The purchaser includes the cost of the option in the adjusted cost base of the property that he acquires.[52] The grantor can retrospectively adjust the tax return for the year in which the grantor issued the option, and recalculate the earlier option gain.[53]

Example

Assume: In Year 1, Alpha Ltd grants T an option to purchase a parcel of land for $400,000. T pays $15,000 for the option, which

1. Effect on Alpha Ltd upon issuance of option:

Proceeds of disposition	$15,000
ACB (deemed)	NIL
Capital gain	$15,000

2. Effect on Alpha Ltd upon exercise of option:

Proceeds from sale of land	$400,000
Add: proceeds from option	15,000
Total proceeds of disposition	415,000
ACB of land	(50,000)
Capital gain	$365,000

---

49   Ibid.
50   Ibid, subs 49(3).
51   Ibid, para 49(3)(a).
52   Ibid, para 49(3)(b).
53   Ibid, subs 49(4).

Alpha Ltd may file an amended return in Year 5 to retroactively reduce its capital gain in Year 1 to nil.

3. Adjusted cost base of land to purchaser (T):

Exercise price	$400,000
Option price	15,000
ACB	$415,000

Where a taxpayer issues a put option (an option to sell property), any consideration that he receives for the option is considered as proceeds of disposition in the year of issuance.[54] Where the option is subsequently exercised by the grantee, the Act deems the granting and exercise of the option not to have taken place. Instead, the grantor's and grantee's proceeds of disposition and cost of the property are adjusted for the price of the option.[55]

d) Bad Debts

Where a taxpayer establishes that his account receivable from a disposition of capital property has become uncollectible, the taxpayer can elect to be deemed to have disposed of the debt.[56] A taxpayer can deduct bad debts arising from the sale of capital property only when he actually establishes the debt to be bad.

A taxpayer cannot reserve for doubtful accounts in respect of debts created from dispositions of capital property. Similarly, a taxpayer who establishes that a corporation in which he holds shares has become bankrupt or is subject to a winding-up order can elect to be deemed to have disposed of any shares.[57] The taxpayer can then claim a capital loss even though he has not disposed of the shares. Where the taxpayer makes the election, he is deemed to have disposed of the bad debt or the shares for nil proceeds at the end of the year, and to have then acquired it for a cost of nil.

Since a taxpayer who disposes of a bad debt can elect to do so for nil proceeds and to reacquire it for the same amount, any recovery on account of a debt previously written off will give rise to a capital gain.[58]

---

54   *Ibid*, subs 49(1).
55   *Ibid*, subs 49(3.1).
56   *Ibid*, subs 50(1).
57   *Ibid*, para 50(1)(b).
58   See also subpara 40(2)(g)(ii), *ibid*.

e) Death

Upon a taxpayer's death, she is deemed to have disposed of all her capital properties immediately before death.[59] The disposition gives rise to deemed proceeds of disposition. The amount of the proceeds depends upon the type of capital property and the date of death.

i) Depreciable Capital Property

The Act deems a taxpayer to dispose of his depreciable property at its fair market value.[60] Thus, the deceased's executor must include the full amount of any gain accrued on depreciable property as proceeds of disposition. At the same time, the beneficiary who inherits property is deemed to acquire the property at an amount equal to the deceased's (deemed) proceeds of disposition (fair market value).[61]

ii) Other Capital Property

Capital properties other than depreciable properties are also deemed to be disposed of immediately before death for proceeds equal to the fair market value of the property.[62]

f) Trusts

To discourage indefinite accumulations of property in trusts, the Act provides for periodic deemed dispositions of all property held in trust. A trust is deemed to dispose of all of its capital property on the twenty-first anniversary of the day on which the trust was created.[63]

5) Involuntary Dispositions

A taxpayer may involuntarily dispose of his property — for example, the property may be stolen or expropriated. In these circumstances, it may be a hardship for the taxpayer to pay tax on any proceeds received. Thus, the Act allows a taxpayer who involuntarily disposes of property to elect to defer any capital gain from the disposition,[64] provided that he replaces the property with a substitute property before the end of the later of the second taxation year or twenty-four months.[65] She must

---

59 *Ibid*, para 70(5)(a).
60 *Ibid*.
61 *Ibid*, para 70(5)(b).
62 *Ibid*, para 70(5)(a).
63 *Ibid*, subss 104(4), (5), (5.3)–(5.8).
64 *Ibid*, sub 44(1).
65 Interpretation Bulletin IT-259-R4, "Exchanges of Property" (23 September 2003); *ITA*, *ibid*, para 44(1)(c).

acquire a capital property to replace the former property. A business asset must be replaced with a business asset.

The deferral is available in respect of the following types of receipts:[66]

- Compensation for property[67] that has been lost or destroyed;
- Compensation for property that is stolen;
- Compensation for property that is expropriated under statutory authority; or
- Sale proceeds from property sold under the duress of an intention to expropriate under statutory authority.

F. ADJUSTED COST BASE

The capital cost of a property is the amount that the taxpayer pays, including the amount of any liabilities that he assumes, for the property. The "adjusted cost base" of a property means:[68]

- Where the property is depreciable property, its capital cost; and
- Where the property is any other property, the cost of the property as adjusted by section 53.

The Act does not define either "capital cost" or "cost." Hence, we interpret them according to their commercial usage.

"Cost" refers to the price that the taxpayer gives up in order to acquire the property.[69] It includes incidental acquisition costs such as brokerage, legal, accounting, engineering and valuation fees. Carrying costs (such as interest expense) for the unpaid price of property are not part of the "cost" of the asset for purposes of the capital gains rules.[70]

There are special rules for determining the adjusted cost base of properties that a taxpayer owned at the start of the "new system" on

---

66   ITA, ibid, subs 44(1).
67   Sani Sport, above note 32 (FCA) (compensation for property includes damages suffered by business loss).
68   ITA, above note 1, s 54 "adjusted cost base."
69   Canada v Stirling, [1985] 1 FC 342 (CA) (interest expense on unpaid portion of price of gold bullion, and safekeeping charges, not part of cost of bullion).
70   Canada v Stirling, ibid at 343 (FC); see also Canada v CP Ltd, [1977] CTC 606 (FCA) (taxpayer not entitled to CCA on perishable product or expenditures in respect of property not owned); Canada v Consumer's Gas Co, [1984] CTC 83 (FCA) (taxpayer to add cost of pipelines to UCC without reduction for reimbursement); Birmingham Corp v Barnes, [1935] AC 292 (HL) (deductibility of grant received and renewal costs in determination of "actual cost" to build tramway).

1 January 1972. These rules are set out in the *Income Tax Application Rules* (ITARs).[71]

1) Deemed Adjusted Cost Base

There are numerous provisions that *deem* the cost of a property to be a certain amount. Note that whenever the Act deems a disposition of property for deemed proceeds, it also deems a reacquisition of the property at a deemed cost base. Thus, every capital property always has an adjusted cost base at any given point in time.

a) Change of Use

Where a taxpayer changes the use of a capital property from business to personal use, or vice versa, he is deemed to have acquired the property for the new purpose at a cost equal to its fair market value at the time of the change in use.[72] Thus, despite the absence of a market transaction, there is a carryover of basis from the business use to the personal use.

Similarly, where a taxpayer changes the proportions of business and personal use of a capital property, the taxpayer may be deemed to have acquired the portion of the property subject to the new use at a cost proportional to its fair market value at that time.[73]

b) Identical Properties

The cost of identical properties is their weighted average cost at any time.[74] A new average is to be determined each time another identical property is acquired and added to the pool. The cost of identical capital properties (other than depreciable property or an interest in a partnership) owned by a taxpayer on 31 December 1971, is also the weighted average cost of the properties.[75] Note, however, that this calculation is made separately from the one for identical properties acquired after 31 December 1971. In effect, a taxpayer must maintain two separate pools of identical properties: one for pre-1972 properties and the other for post-1971 properties.

---

71   RSC 1985, c 2 (5th Supp) [*ITAR*].
72   *ITA*, above note 1, s 45.
73   *Ibid*, para 45(1)(c).
74   *Ibid*, s 47.
75   *ITAR*, above note 71, s 26(8).

c) Becoming a Canadian Resident

A taxpayer who becomes resident in Canada is deemed to acquire each property that he owns at that time at its fair market value.[76] This rule does not apply to "taxable Canadian property."[77]

d) Options

When a taxpayer exercises an option to acquire property, the adjusted cost base of the property to the purchaser includes the cost of the option.[78] Upon exercise, the option and the property acquired are unified into one cost basis on their joint market values.

e) Conversions

Where a taxpayer acquires shares of a corporation in exchange for convertible shares, bonds, debentures or notes issued by the corporation, and the acquisition is made without any cash consideration, the taxpayer's cost of the shares is deemed to be the adjusted cost base of the convertible property immediately before the exchange.[79]

f) Non-Arm's Length Transactions

Where a taxpayer acquires property in a non-arm's length transaction at an amount greater than its fair market value, he is deemed to acquire the property at its fair market value at the time.[80] If he acquires the property at less than its fair market value, the adjusted cost base of the property is his actual cost.

g) Prizes

A taxpayer who wins a prize in a lottery is deemed to acquire the property at a cost equal to its fair market value at the time of winning the prize.[81] A lottery prize is exempt from tax.

h) Dividends in Kind

A taxpayer who receives a dividend in kind (other than a stock dividend) is deemed to acquire the property at its fair market value.[82]

---

76   *ITA*, above note 1, para 128.1(1)(c).
77   *Ibid*, subs 248(1) and para 128.1(1)(b).
78   *Ibid*, subs 49(3).
79   *Ibid*, s 51.
80   *Ibid*, para 69(1)(a).
81   *Ibid*, subs 52(4); see *Rumack v MNR*, [1984] CTC 2382 (TCC); [1992] 1 CTC 57 (FCA).
82   *ITA*, *ibid*, subs 52(2).

i) Stock Dividends

A stock dividend includes any dividend paid by the issuance of shares of any class of a corporation.[83]

The value of a stock dividend is the amount by which the corporation increases its paid-up capital by virtue of paying the dividend.[84] In the case of a stock dividend that does not qualify as a "dividend," the cost is nil.[85] The cost of stock dividends that a taxpayer receives will affect the adjusted cost base of all other identical shares that she owns.[86]

2) Adjustments to Cost Base

We determine the cost base of a property by reference to commercial principles and statutory deeming provisions. The cost base, which is adjusted for various events and transactions, is a point in time determination. There are two types of adjustments—*additions* to the cost base[87] and *deductions* from the cost base.[88]

Generally, a taxpayer adds to the cost base of property when he receives an amount that either has previously borne, or was exempt from, tax. The additions to the adjusted cost base of property prevent double taxation of the same amount. For example, where an employee is taxed on a stock option benefit that is included in her employment income, the value of the benefit is added to the cost base of her shares.[89] Without this addition, the taxpayer would be taxed again on the same gain when she sells the shares.

Conversely, a taxpayer deducts from the cost base of property when he has previously received an amount free of tax.

a) Acquisition of Land

A taxpayer may not deduct interest on debt relating to the acquisition of vacant land to the extent that the expense exceeds any income from the land.[90] Alternatively, the taxpayer may add the disallowed carrying charges to the cost base of the land.[91]

---

83   See *ibid*, subs 248(1) "dividend."
84   See *ibid*, para 248(1)(c) "amount."
85   *Ibid*, para 52(3)(a.1).
86   *Ibid*, s 47.
87   *Ibid*, subs 53(1).
88   *Ibid*, subs 53(2).
89   *Ibid*, para 53(1)(j).
90   *Ibid*, subs 18(2).
91   *Ibid*, subpara 53(1)(h)(i).

b) Stock Dividends and Options

Stock dividends have an adjusted cost base equal to the aggregate of the value of the dividend and any amount included in the taxpayer's income as a shareholder benefit.[92]

Where an employee acquires shares of a corporation under an employee stock option plan, the employee is deemed to receive a "stock option" benefit under section 7. The amount of the benefit is added to the adjusted cost base of the shares acquired.[93]

3) Negative Adjusted Cost Base

As a rule, the adjusted cost base of a property at the time that it is disposed of cannot be less than nil.[94] If at any time the deductions from the cost of property exceed its adjusted cost, the adjusted cost base of the property becomes a negative amount. The Act then deems the negative amount to be a capital gain from the disposition of the property, which is then immediately added to the cost of the property, thereby raising its adjusted cost base to nil.

Example

Assume: A taxpayer owns a capital property with an adjusted cost base of $2,000. During the year, the cost base is adjusted by subsection 53(1) additions of $300 and subsection 53(2) deductions of $2,700.

Then the taxpayer's adjusted cost base is calculated as follows:

Cost of property	$2,000
Subsection 53(1) additions	300
	2,300
Subsection 53(2) deductions	(2,700)
Deemed capital gain	(400)
Paragraph 53(1)(a) addition	400
ACB of property	$NIL

4) Part Dispositions

Where a taxpayer disposes of only a part of a capital property, one calculates the adjusted cost base of that part by taking a "reasonable" proportion of the cost base of the part to the whole. The adjusted cost base of the part of the property that was disposed of is then deducted from

92   *Ibid*, subss 52(3), 15(1.1), and 248(1) "stock dividend."
93   *Ibid*, para 53(1)(j).
94   *Ibid*, subs 54 "adjusted cost base" (d).

the adjusted cost base of the whole property.[95] The balance becomes the cost base of the remaining part.[96]

G. PERSONAL-USE PROPERTY

"Personal-use property" is a subset source of capital property. Personal-use property includes:[97]

- Property that a taxpayer owns that he uses primarily for his personal use or enjoyment; or
  - » the enjoyment of a person related to him; or
  - » if the taxpayer is a trust, a beneficiary under the trust or any person related[98] to the beneficiary.
- A debt owing to a taxpayer in respect of the disposition of personal-use property; and
- An option to acquire property that would, if it were acquired, be personal-use property of a taxpayer or a person related to him or her.

Cars, boats, furniture, clothing and residences are common examples of personal-use property.

A taxpayer cannot claim a capital loss on personal use property.

1) Listed Personal Property (LPP)

"Listed personal property," a further subset of personal-use property, is property specifically listed in the Act and includes:[99]

- Prints, etchings, drawings, paintings, sculptures or other similar works of art;
- Jewellery;
- Rare folios, rare manuscripts or rare books;
- Stamps; and
- Coins.

An interest in, or right to, any of these items is also listed personal property. Listed personal property items are assets that one acquires for dual purposes—personal consumption and investment value. Hence,

---

95 *Ibid*, para 53(2)(d).
96 *Ibid*, s 43; there are special rules governing partial dispositions of personal-use property.
97 *Ibid*, s 54 "personal-use property."
98 See *ibid*, subs 251(2).
99 *Ibid*, s 54 "listed personal property."

gains from listed personal property are taxable; losses are deductible, but only against gains from listed personal property.[100]

2) Computational Rules

To minimize record keeping for low-value items of personal-use property, the Act deems the minimum adjusted cost base and proceeds of disposition of personal-use property to be $1,000.[101] Consequently, if both the actual cost and the actual proceeds on disposition of an item of personal-use property are less than $1,000, the transaction does not give rise to any capital gain or capital loss. Thus, taxpayers do not need to keep a detailed record of low-value transactions.

Example

A taxpayer purchases and then sells personal-use property for the amounts indicated. The gain or loss in each case is calculated as follows:

	A	B	C
Proceeds of disposition	$900	$1,200	$2,000
Cost	(600)*	(600)*	(1,500)
Capital gain	$NIL	$200	$500

* Deemed to be $1,000

A special rule applies to exclude from the $1,000 minimum any property—typically art—that a taxpayer acquires with the intention of "flipping" to a charity. The purpose of the exclusion is to discourage bogus "art flips" to charities.[102]

3) Bad Debts

Where a taxpayer establishes that a debt owing to him from a sale of personal-use property has become a bad debt, he may offset any prior capital gain that he recognized on the sale of the property by recognizing a capital loss when the debt becomes bad.[103]

---

100 See para 3(b), *ibid*, which includes net LPP gains in income.
101 *Ibid*, subs 46(1).
102 *Ibid*, subs 46(5).
103 *Ibid*, subs 50(2).

Example

Assume: A taxpayer sells personal-use property with an ACB of $9,000 for proceeds of $10,000 in Year 1. The taxpayer receives $6,000 cash and accepts a note for $4,000. In Year 3, the debtor defaults on the note and the debt is established to have become bad.

Then:

Year 1: Proceeds of disposition	$10,000
ACB of property	(9,000)
Capital gain	$1,000
Year 3: Deemed proceeds of debt	$3,000
ACB of debt	(4,000)
Capital loss	$(1,000)

4) Part Dispositions

To prevent taxpayers from taking unfair advantage of the deemed minimum $1,000 adjusted cost base and proceeds of disposition rules by selling sets of property in bits and pieces, a special rule requires that the $1,000 be allocated whenever the various parts of a personal-use property are sold individually or when a set of personal-use property is sold piecemeal. The $1,000 amount is allocated in the following proportion:

$$\frac{\$1,000 \times (\text{Adjusted cost base of part disposed})}{(\text{Adjusted cost base of the whole property})}$$

The deemed cost and deemed proceeds of disposition rules are then applied in relation to the part of the personal-use property that has been disposed of on the basis of this reduced amount.[104]

The second aspect of this rule applies to dispositions of a set of personal-use properties that have an aggregate fair market value in excess of $1,000 and would ordinarily be disposed of together. If a set of personal-use properties is sold in more than one transaction to the same person, or to a group of persons who do not deal with each other at arm's length, the set is deemed to be a single property and the $1,000 amount is proportionally reduced.[105]

---

104 *Ibid*, subs 46(2). Note that these allocation rules apply only when a taxpayer disposes of a part of a personal-use property and retains another part. Accordingly, upon the disposition of the final remaining part, no allocation is required, since the taxpayer would not be retaining another part.

105 *Ibid*, subs 46(3).

5) Capital Losses

Capital losses arising from a disposition of personal-use property (other than listed personal property) are deemed to be nil. Capital losses on LPP can be offset only against capital gains on LPP. Any remaining balance can be carried back three years and carried forward seven years; in each of those years, the LPP loss can be offset only against LPP gains.[106]

H. IDENTICAL PROPERTIES

Where a taxpayer acquires a capital property identical to other properties that she owns, the cost of each of the properties is calculated by taking the weighted average of their adjusted cost bases. The weighted average cost of properties must be recalculated each time the taxpayer acquires another property identical to property already owned by the taxpayer.[107] The weighted average cost of identical properties is determined by dividing the aggregate of their adjusted cost bases by the number of properties owned.

Example

A taxpayer owns 100 common shares of XYZ Co., which she acquired at a cost of $20 per share. The taxpayer acquires a further 200 shares of the same class and kind of the same corporation at $30 per share.

The weighted average cost of the shares is calculated as follows:

100 shares × $20/share	$2,000
200 shares × $30/share	6,000
300	$8,000
Weighted average cost per share ($8,000/300)	$26.67

Properties owned by a taxpayer as at 31 December 1971 are segregated in a separate pool from identical properties acquired by the taxpayer after that date. In other words, a weighted average cost is calculated for identical properties owned on 31 December 1971, and a separate average cost is calculated for properties acquired subsequently. A disposition of identical properties is always deemed to be made first out of the pre-1972 pool.[108]

---

106 *Ibid*, subs 41(2).
107 *Ibid*, s 47 and para 3(b).
108 *ITAR*, above note 71, ss 26(8)–(8.3).

Whether property acquired by a taxpayer is "identical" to property already owned by her is a question of fact. Corporate shares of the same class and with the same rights are identical properties, notwithstanding that they may be physically identifiable as separate properties by virtue of their serial numbers.

Bonds and debt obligations issued by a corporation are considered similar to other debts issued by the debtor if they are identical in respect of their legal and equitable rights. This is so even if the principal amounts are different.[109]

Land can never be an identical property even if the lots are adjoining lots and of the same size and quality. Each plot of land is unique.

I. LOSSES DEEMED TO BE NIL

The Act deems certain capital losses to be nil. The general thrust of these deeming provisions is to prevent a taxpayer from creating or accelerating an "artificial" capital loss by structuring transactions within a group of related economic entities. Sometimes the non-recognition of the capital loss is permanent; at other times the amount of the capital loss that is deemed to be nil is added to the cost base of some other property owned by the taxpayer, so that there will be a corresponding reduction in the capital gain (or increase in the capital loss) on the disposition of the other property.

1) Dispositions between Affiliated Persons

The stop-loss and affiliated person rules deny losses that taxpayers trigger between themselves and their spouses and common-law partners, corporations under common control, partnerships and members of partnerships who, either alone or together with other affiliated persons, are generally entitled to more than half of the partnership's earnings. They also apply to trusts and any beneficiaries who, either alone or together with certain other affiliated persons, are entitled to more than half of the trust's income or capital.

There are essentially three distinct conditions that trigger the rules. First, a person must dispose of a property at a loss. Certain types of dispositions—such as deemed losses that occur as a result of migration from Canada—do not trigger the rules.

---

109 *ITA*, above note 1, subs 248(12).

Second, the person who disposes of the property or someone affiliated with the person must, within a 61-day window that centres on the date of the disposition, acquire that same property or what is referred to as a "substituted property."

Third, the disposing person or a person affiliated with that person must own the property or substituted property in question on the 61st day of that same period.

In these circumstances, the rules apply to deny the loss to the disposing person.[110] There are, however, other consequences depending upon the identity of the disposing person.

If the disposing person is an individual, the loss is added to the tax cost (ACB) of the property or substituted property that is in the hands of the acquirer. In effect the loss can be passed from the individual to another person. If, however, the disposing person is a trust, partnership or corporation, the loss remains with the disposing party and is effectively suspended, thereby preventing such losses from moving from that trust, corporation or partnership to another person. The trust, corporation or partnership may subsequently claim the loss, generally when either the property is subsequently sold to a non-affiliated person or the parties break their affiliated connection.

For example, assume that Jane is the sole shareholder of her corporation. Jane owns a parcel of land that is capital property. The fair market value of the land is $100,000 but its ACB is $275,000. Jane wishes to trigger the loss to offset against her capital gains in the same year. She disposes of the land to her corporation, triggering a capital loss of $175,000. Since Jane and her corporation are affiliated persons, the stop-loss rules apply. The Act denies Jane the loss and adds it to the ACB of the land, which the corporation now owns.[111] If the corporation subsequently sells the land for $100,000 in a non-affiliated transaction, it can recognize a capital loss of $175,000. In effect, the individual's loss passes to the corporation upon the subsequent sale.

If the corporation had initially owned the land and sold it to Jane, the corporation could not claim the $175,000 loss.[112] Further, since the disposing person is a corporation, there is no ACB adjustment in this case and the loss is suspended. The corporation can claim the loss when Jane sells the land in a non-affiliated transaction.

---

110 *Ibid*, subpara 40(2)(g)(i) and para 40(3.4)(a).
111 *Ibid*, subpara 40(2)(g)(i).
112 *Ibid*, para 40(3.4)(a).

2) Lotteries

A taxpayer who does not win a lottery cannot claim a capital loss in respect of the cost of the ticket.[113]

3) Superficial Losses

An individual cannot claim a "superficial loss."[114] A superficial loss arises when an individual, or certain affiliated parties,[115] disposes of property and replaces it with "substituted property" within a period of 61 days.[116] This prevents individuals from claiming paper losses for tax purposes. For the purpose of this rule, the 61-day period commences 30 days before, and ends 30 days after, the day of disposition of the property. This rule also applies to property that certain affiliated persons may acquire during the 61 days. For example, it applies to property acquired by the individual, his spouse or common law partner.

The taxpayer can, however, increase the cost base of the "substituted property" by the amount of his superficial loss.[117] Consequently, when he disposes of the "substituted property," he can reduce any gain on the property. Alternatively, the taxpayer can increase the actual loss by the amount of his superficial loss.

4) Disposition of a Debt

A capital loss from a disposition, whether actual or deemed, of a debt is deemed to be nil unless the taxpayer acquired the debt for the purpose of gaining or producing income from a business or property (other than exempt income), or as consideration for the disposition of capital property to an arm's length person.[118]

5) Disposition of Personal-Use Property

A taxpayer's loss from a disposition of personal-use property is deemed to be nil unless the property qualifies as listed personal property or is a PUP debt referred to in subsection 50(2).[119] The non-recognition of the loss is permanent.

---

113 *Ibid*, para 40(2)(f).
114 *Ibid*, subpara 40(2)(g)(i).
115 *Ibid*, subs 251.1(1).
116 *Ibid*, s 54 "superficial loss."
117 *Ibid*, para 53(1)(f).
118 *Ibid*, subpara 40(2)(g)(ii).
119 *Ibid*, subpara 40(2)(g)(iii).

J. PRINCIPAL RESIDENCE

A Canadian resident is not taxable on a capital gain from his principal residence.[120] The entire amount of the gain is tax exempt, regardless of the value of the property sold. Thus, the principal residence exemption is one of the generous exemptions in the Act.

1) Meaning of "Principal Residence"

There are several requirements to qualify a property as a "principal residence." Generally, these requirements address four separate criteria:[121]

1) The type of property:
   * the property must be a housing unit, a leasehold interest in a housing unit or a share in a co-operative housing corporation;[122]
2) Owner occupation:
   * the property must be owned by the taxpayer; and
   * the property must be "occupied" by the taxpayer during the year;[123]
3) The period of ownership:
   * the property must be ordinarily inhabited at some time during the year by the taxpayer, her spouse, former spouse, common law partner, former common law partner or child; or
   * if the property was acquired for the purpose of gaining or producing income and the use changes to that of a principal residence, an election can be made under subsection 45(3) to prevent the deemed disposal and reacquisition in subsection 45(1) from operating;
4) Designation on tax return:
   * the property must be designated by the taxpayer as her sole principal residence for the year.

The residence does not have to be in Canada to be eligible for the exemption.

A principal residence includes the land under and adjacent to the housing unit. Any adjacent land must contribute to the taxpayer's use and enjoyment of the housing unit as a residence. The statute deems

---

120 *Ibid*, para 40(2)(b).
121 *Ibid*, s 54 "principal residence."
122 *Flanagan v MNR*, [1989] 2 CTC 2395 (TCC) (van, trailer or mobile home can qualify as housing unit eligible for exemption).
123 *Ennist v MNR*, [1985] 2 CTC 2398 (TCC) (24-hour occupancy of condominium not sufficient to satisfy requirement that residence be "ordinarily inhabited").

land up to half a hectare as part of the principal residence. Where the total area of land exceeds half a hectare,[124] the excess land does not qualify as a principal residence unless the taxpayer can establish that the excess is necessary for his use and enjoyment of the housing unit as a residence.[125]

The principal residence exemption is anomalous and regressive because there is no dollar limit to the exemption. Nevertheless, it is a sacred cow. Given that the Act restricts the exemption by the physical dimensions of the residence and land, and not by its value, it is obviously advantageous to own as much land as possible as part of the residence. For example, a residence located on half a hectare of land in, say, Rosedale (Toronto) is obviously much more valuable than one on half a hectare in Moose Jaw (Saskatchewan).

Strictly speaking, a property does not qualify as a principal residence for a particular year unless the taxpayer designates it as such in her income tax return for the year in which she disposes of it. The CRA does not, however, call for the designation unless the taxpayer makes a taxable capital gain on the disposition of the principal residence after deducting the exempt portion of the gain.

2) Exempt Gains

The exempt portion of a capital gain realized on the disposition of a principal residence is determined by the following formula:[126]

$$\left(1 + \frac{\begin{array}{c}\text{Number of taxation years ending after the}\\\text{acquisition date for which the property was}\\\text{the taxpayer's principal residence and during}\\\text{which the taxpayer was resident in Canada}\end{array}}{\begin{array}{c}\text{Number of taxation years ending after the}\\\text{acquisition date during which the taxpayer}\\\text{owned the property}\end{array}}\right) \times \text{Capital gain realized}$$

3) Limits on Exemptions

The general rule is that a family unit living together can together designate only one principal residence per year. For the purpose of this rule,

---

124 Approximately 1.25 acres.
125 *Canada v Yates*, [1986] 2 CTC 46 (FCA) (minimum lot size can be used to determine amount of land necessary for use and enjoyment).
126 *ITA*, above note 1, para 40(2)(b).

a "family unit" comprises: the taxpayer, her spouse or common-law partner, children under the age of eighteen who are not married or living in a common-law partnership.[127]

a) Two Exempt Residences

The "1+" in the numerator of the fraction, used to determine the exempt portion of the gain, allows a taxpayer to claim an exemption in respect of two principal residences in the same year. Such a situation typically arises when a taxpayer sells his principal residence during the course of the year and purchases another residence in the same year. In these circumstances the taxpayer would own and occupy two residences in the same year, both of which could be eligible for the principal residence exemption.

Example: Where the taxpayer owns more than one residence

A taxpayer purchased a house in Year 1 and lived in it until he sold it on 28 February Year 4. He purchased a second house on 1 February Year 4 and moved into it on 1 March Year 4, living there until he sold it on 1 October Year 4. He purchased a third house on 30 September Year 4, and moved into it on 1 November Year 4.

First House

Designated as principal residence for Years 1–3	3 years
Exempt portion of capital gain on its sale	1 + 3 years
Therefore, any capital gain is exempt.	4 years

Second House

Designated as principal residence for Year 4	1 year
Exempt portion of capital gain on its sale	1 + 1 years
Hence, any capital gain is also exempt.	1 year

If the third house was also sold in Year 4, the taxpayer could not take advantage of the principal residence exemption on both the second and third houses. This is because only one of these houses could be designated as a principal residence for Year 4. In these circumstances, however, the taxpayer may choose which house to designate for exemption. Alternatively, the taxpayer could arrange to have the closing on the third house delayed until January Year 5.

---

b) Extended Family Unit

Where the taxpayer claiming the principal residence exemption is an unmarried person or an individual under eighteen years of age, the concept of the family unit is extended to include the taxpayer's mother, father and unmarried brothers and sisters under eighteen years of age.[128]

---

127 *Ibid*, s 54 "principal residence."
128 *Ibid*, s 54 "principal residence" (c).

c)   "Ordinarily Inhabited"

The principal residence exemption is available only if the residence was ordinarily occupied by the taxpayer, his spouse, former spouse, common-law partner, former common-law partner, or child.

Whether a residence was "ordinarily inhabited" during the taxation year by the taxpayer (or by certain related persons) depends upon the circumstances of each case. Generally, the CRA is quite generous in its interpretation of what constitutes habitation of a residence. For example, it will accept seasonal occupation of a vacation house (such as a cottage or ski chalet) as sufficient to qualify the premises for the principal residence exemption. The CRA goes even further: it will accept a seasonal residence as eligible for the exemption even where the taxpayer rents out the premises for incidental rental income. That is, provided that the rental is not a commercial or business enterprise, the taxpayer may occupy the premises for a limited portion of the season, rent it out for the remainder of the year, and still claim the exemption.

4)   Change in Use Elections

a)   Personal to Income-Earning Use

We saw earlier that a taxpayer who changes the use of capital property from personal to income-earning use may elect under subsection 45(2) to have the change in use ignored for income tax purposes. The effect of the election is that the taxpayer is deemed not to have changed the use of the property from personal to business and not to have disposed of the property at its fair market value at that time.

The "change in use" election is particularly useful in respect of a principal residence. The election has two effects:

1)   It allows the property to retain its status as a principal residence for four years (or possibly longer in the case of a work relocation) after the year in which the taxpayer moves out of the property;[129] and

2)   The election deems the taxpayer not to have changed his use of the property.

Where an individual elects under subsection 45(3), she may designate the property as a principal residence up to four years even though the property is used to earn income. Hence, if the taxpayer changes use of the property again and resumes habitation of the premises, the second change will not give rise to a deemed disposition; the taxpayer

---

129   See *ibid*, subs 45(2), subpara 54 "principal residence" (b)(i) and para 54 "adjusted cost base" (d).

will be considered never to have changed the use of the property in the first place. Thus there will be no income tax consequences when the taxpayer moves back into the property. This is because during the tenure of the election the taxpayer is deemed to be using the property for her own personal use (whether or not the property still qualifies as a principal residence); when the taxpayer moves back into the property, she will actually be using it for her own personal use.

An election under subsection 45(2) can be made only in respect of a change of use that occurs when the taxpayer moves out of the property, that is, when the taxpayer changes the use from personal to earning income. A taxpayer who does not make an election on moving out of the residence cannot avoid the resultant deemed disposition, and related tax consequences, on moving back into the property at a later date.

The election continues in effect for up to four years after the year in which the taxpayer moved out or until it is rescinded by the taxpayer, at which time the taxpayer is deemed to have disposed of the property.

K. SHARES OF SMALL BUSINESS CORPORATIONS

Capital gains from the disposition of shares of a "qualified small business corporation" are exempt from tax up to a maximum of $750,000. A "qualified small business corporation" (QSBC) is a Canadian-controlled private corporation:[130]

> that uses all or most of its assets in an active business carried on primarily in Canada and the assets of which, throughout a period of 24 months immediately preceding the disposition of shares, have not been owned by any person other than the individual who claims the exemption, or by a person or partnership related to him or her.

This exemption encourages risk-taking and stimulates investment in small businesses in Canada by providing an economic stimulus to equity participation and the development of Canadian business enterprises. As the Minister of Finance said when he introduced the exemption in 1985, it is intended to "unleash [the] full entrepreneurial dynamism of individual Canadians."[131]

The exemption depends on three factors:

---

130 *Ibid*, subs 125(7) "Canadian-controlled private corporation"; subs 248(1) "active business," "small business corporation."

131 Budget speech, *House of Commons Debates* (23 May 1985) at 5014.

- The taxpayer's residence;
- The type of capital property that gives rise to the gain; and
- The net cumulative amount of investment income and financing expenses in the year in which the gain is realized.

The gain is generally restricted to individuals who are resident in Canada.[132] The exemption may not be claimed by a trust, but because a trust is treated as a conduit, it may flow through its capital gains to its beneficiaries by making a special designation.

The exemption applies only to "qualified" small business corporation shares.[133] The qualifications concern the control of the corporation, the fair market value of the assets that are attributable to use in an active business, and the carrying on of the active business primarily in Canada. These restrictions target the exemption to restrict the benefits to activities that are likely to stimulate the Canadian economy.

L. CAPITAL LOSSES

A taxpayer's income for a taxation year is determined by aggregating income from each source on a separate basis. As a general rule, capital losses can be used only to offset capital gains.[134] Unused capital losses may, however, be carried forward indefinitely and applied against capital gains in future years; they may also be carried back three years and applied against capital gains reported in those years.[135]

1) Current Year Losses

a) Listed Personal Property Losses
Capital gains and losses from listed personal property (LPP) are calculated separately from capital gains and losses on all other types of capital properties. A taxpayer is required to include his "taxable *net* gain" for the year from dispositions of LPP with his capital gains.[136] Losses from dispositions of LPP are deductible, but only to the extent of gains for the same year from dispositions of LPP. In other words, if LPP losses exceed LPP gains, the excess cannot be deducted in computing the taxpayer's income for that year, even if he has other net taxable capital

---

132 *ITA*, above note 1, subs 110.6(5).
133 *Ibid*, subs 110.6(1) "qualified small business corporation share."
134 *Ibid*, para 3(b).
135 *Ibid*, para 111(1)(b).
136 *Ibid*, para 3(b); s 41.

gains from dispositions of other types of capital property. LPP losses may not be deducted from capital gains on non-LPP.

b) Allowable Capital Losses

A taxpayer may also deduct her allowable capital losses (net of allowable business investment losses) from dispositions of property for the year to the extent of her taxable capital gains from dispositions of property and her taxable net gain from dispositions of listed personal property.

The effect of these rules is that a taxpayer may deduct her allowable capital losses realized on property (other than LPP) from her taxable net gains on listed personal property.

c) Allowable Business Investment Losses (ABIL)

A business investment loss is a special type of capital loss that receives preferential treatment for income tax purposes. A business investment loss arises on the disposition of shares or debt of a "small business corporation."[137] An allowable business investment loss is 50 percent of a business investment loss.[138]

Unlike ordinary capital losses, which may be deducted only against capital gains, an allowable business investment loss may be deducted against income from any source. Thus, an allowable business investment loss may be deducted from business or property income.

A taxpayer's deduction for business investment losses is restricted if he has previously claimed the capital gains exemption.[139]

A business investment loss arises upon the disposition of the shares or debt of a corporation that qualified as a small business corporation at any time within the preceding twelve months.[140] The disposition of the shares or debt may be triggered either by an actual disposition (for example, sale or transfer) or through a deemed disposition.[141]

i)   "Small Business Corporation"

A "small business corporation" is a Canadian-controlled private corporation that uses all or substantially all (as measured by fair market value) of its assets in an active business in Canada.[142] A corporation may also qualify as a small business corporation if all, or substantially

---

137 *Ibid*, para 39(1)(c).
138 *Ibid*, para 38(c).
139 *Ibid*, subs 39(9).
140 *Ibid*, subs 248(1) "small business corporation."
141 See, for example, subs 50(1), *ibid*.
142 *Ibid*, subs 248(1) "small business corporation."

all, of its assets are invested in shares of another small business corporation with which it is connected.

ii) Deemed Disposition

A taxpayer is deemed to have disposed of his shares of a small business corporation if:

- The corporation is insolvent or bankrupt, or
- At year-end, the corporation is insolvent, the fair market value of its shares is nil, the corporation (or any corporation that it controls) does not carry on business and it is reasonable to expect that the corporation will be wound up or dissolved.

The term "insolvent" is not defined, but it is reasonable to expect that it has the usual meaning of insolvency, namely, the inability to pay liabilities as they come due.

2) Unused Losses

Capital losses that are not deductible in the year in which they are sustained may be "carried over" and deducted in other years.

a) LPP Loss Carryovers

Where a taxpayer's losses for a year from LPP exceed his gains for the year from dispositions of LPP, the excess is the "listed personal property loss" for that year.[143] A listed personal property loss for a particular year can be deducted, in computing the "net gain," only from dispositions of listed personal property for the three preceding and the seven succeeding years.[144]

b) Net Capital Loss Carryovers

Allowable capital losses from dispositions of property other than listed personal property that are not deductible in computing a taxpayer's income in the year in which they are sustained, become part of the taxpayer's "net capital loss."[145] A taxpayer's net capital loss for a year may be carried back and deducted in computing her taxable income for the three preceding years. Also, subject to certain limitations, the loss may be carried forward indefinitely.[146] In either case, net capital losses

---

143 *Ibid*, subs 41(3).
144 *Ibid*, para 41(2)(b).
145 *Ibid*, subs 111(8) "net capital loss."
146 *Ibid*, para 111(1)(b).

may be deducted against only the excess of taxable gains over allowable capital losses of other years.

i)   Change of Corporate Control
A net capital loss from an earlier year cannot be deducted by a corporation if, before the end of the year, control of the corporation changes hands and a person who did not control it at the time when the net capital loss was sustained acquires the corporation. This rule does not generally affect the deductibility of capital losses sustained *in the year* in which the new person or persons acquires control. Note, however, that subsection 249(4) deems the acquired corporation's year to end immediately before the change of control. Thereafter, the loss carryover restrictions in subsection 111(4) apply.[147]

ii)   Death
Where a taxpayer dies with unclaimed net capital losses, the losses may be applied as follows:[148]

• Against the taxpayer's net taxable capital gains for the year of death, and
• Against the taxpayer's other sources of income in the year of death or in the immediately preceding year, to the extent that the losses exceed the taxpayer's lifetime capital gains exemption.[149]

Thus, exemptions claimed in respect of capital gains during a taxpayer's lifetime reduce the taxpayer's unused net capital losses on death.

M. VALUATION DAY

The concept of Valuation Day value is fundamental to the structure of the transitional rules for capital gains. The Valuation Day value of a capital property is its value at the beginning of the new system, when capital gains were first subjected to tax. The "V-Day value" of a property is its fair market value on Valuation Day, which was 22 December 1971 for publicly-traded shares or securities and 31 December 1971 for all other capital property.[150]

---

147   *Ibid*, para 111(4).
148   *Ibid*, para 111(2).
149   The capital gains exemption is discussed in Chapter 12.
150   *ITAR*, above note 71, s 24.

N. ANTI-AVOIDANCE PROVISIONS

There are several anti-avoidance provisions that are intended to prevent or discourage taxpayers from artificially converting fully taxable income into income that is either non-taxable or taxable at a lower rate. Some of these provisions are quite specific and narrow in scope. For example, the rules in respect of "superficial losses" are directed squarely at preventing the creation of capital losses by transferring and reacquiring properties.[151] The following additional provisions should be noted:

Subs 55(2)	Specific provision to prevent "capital gains strips"
Subs 110.6(7)	Intended to prevent conversion of taxable capital gains of corporations into exempt capital gains of individuals
Subss 110.6(8), (9)	Intended to prevent the conversion of dividend income into exempt capital gains of individuals
S 245	General anti-avoidance provision
S 84.1	Designed to prevent surplus stripping
Part II.1 Tax	Prevents conversion of proceeds of disposition into exempt capital gains

FURTHER READINGS

EWENS, DOUGLAS S. "The Capital Gains Exemption and the Butterfly" (1986) 34 Can Tax J 914.

SHEPPARD, ANTHONY F. "Capital Gains: Twenty Years Later a Buck Is Still Not a Buck" in Neil Brooks, *The Quest for Tax Reform: The Royal Commission on Taxation Twenty Years Later* (Toronto: Carswell, 1988).

WILLIAMSON, W GORDON. "Transfers of Assets to and from a Canadian Corporation" (1986) 38 Can Tax Found 12.

WISE, RICHARD M. "Fair Market Determinations: A Few More Requirements" (1983) 31 Can Tax J 337.

151　*ITA*, above note 1, subpara 40(2)(g)(i), s. 54 "superficial loss."

OTHER INCOME AND DEDUCTIONS

A. GENERAL COMMENT

Anglo-Canadian tax law insists upon income having a source. The source theory does not, however, conveniently embrace all receipts. To this point, we have examined the rules governing the computation of income from the following specifically identified sources — office, employment, business, property and capital gains. There are certain types of income that one cannot conveniently identify as originating from, or relating to, these named sources. These are loosely categorized as "other sources" of income, a grouping that comprises various receipts and allowances that do not have a common link.

The taxable base should be broad and inclusive if we use it as the measure of a taxpayer's ability to pay. Section 56 of the Act brings into income a variety of receipts that one may not necessarily include through one of the named sources of income. It is, however, important to note the opening words of section 56: "*Without restricting the generality of section 3, there shall* be included in computing the income of a taxpayer for a taxation year" [emphasis added]. Section 56 does not curtail the scope of section 3. Income from a source inside or outside Canada — that is, income from *any* source regardless of location — is included in section 3.

Section 56 contains a long list of items. In this chapter we look only at some of the more significant items, including:

- Pension benefits;

- Death benefits;
- Support payments;
- Indirect payments;
- Retiring allowances;
- Scholarships, bursaries and fellowships;
- Research grants;
- Prizes; and
- Social assistance payments.

B. PENSION BENEFITS

In theory, pension benefits accrue gradually as the employee's pension grows through employer contributions and investment earnings. For most tax purposes, however, pension income is taxable when the taxpayer receives his pension.

Employer contributions to employee registered pension plans are not taxable as employment-source income.[1] Within specified limits, employees can also deduct contributions to a registered pension fund or plan.[2]

Pension benefits from a pension plan (not including benefits from an employee benefit plan) are taxable upon their withdrawal from the plan and are included in income in the year that the taxpayer receives payment.[3]

An employee must include all pension benefits in income as she receives them. This is so whether the payments are under a registered or unregistered plan, lump sum, or periodic. Pensions and supplementary pensions received under the *Old Age Security Act* and the *Canada Pension Plan* are also taxable as income.[4]

Registration of pension plans is of importance only in determining the deductibility of contributions to a plan; it has no bearing on the taxability of receipts out of a plan. All pensions to taxpayers resident in Canada are taxable.

---

1   *Income Tax Act*, RSC 1985, c 1 (5th Supp) [*ITA*], subpara 6(1)(a)(i); subs 248(1) "superannuation or pension benefit."

2   *Ibid*, para 8(1)(m).

3   *Ibid*, subpara 56(1)(a)(i); *Muller v MNR* (1960), 26 Tax ABC 295 (pension does not have to be related to an office or employment to be taxed).

4   Equivalent payments under Quebec plans are also included in the taxpayer's income.

Hence, in the absence of special provisions in a tax treaty,[5] a foreign taxpayer who takes up residence in Canada becomes liable to tax on his pension income. This is so even though the taxpayer may not have been entitled to a deduction at the time that he contributed to the pension plan.[6]

C. DEATH BENEFITS

Payment on account of a death benefit is included in income in the year of receipt. A "death benefit" is a payment made upon the death of an employee in recognition of service in an office or employment. A death benefit to an employee's spouse or common law partner is tax-free to a maximum of $10,000.[7]

D. SUPPORT PAYMENTS

The statutory provisions in respect of spousal support payments are divided into two segments: (1) receipts included in income under subdivision d; (2) deductions permitted under subdivision e. The inclusion and deduction provisions are mirror images of each other.[8] A payment that is deductible by the payer is required to be included in income by the payee. A payment that is taxable to the recipient may be deducted by the payer. These provisions are discussed further under "Other Deductions."

E. RETIRING ALLOWANCES

At common law, a retiring allowance for the loss of employment is compensation for the loss of a source of income, rather than compensation from a source of income. If the common law doctrine prevailed, taxpay-

5   See, for example, Article XVIII in the *Canada-US Tax Treaty*, as amended by the 5th Protocol, which provides relief for cross-border pensions connected to RSP limits.
6   *Canada v Herman*, [1978] CTC 442 (FCTD).
7   *ITA*, above note 1, subpara 56(1)(a)(iii), subs 248(1) "death benefit."
8   *Ibid*, para 56(1)(b), s 56.1; para 60(b), s 60.1. See *Thibaudeau v MNR*, [1995] 2 SCR 627 (para 56(1)(b)) does not impose a burden on recipient so as to attract s 15 of the *Charter*.

ers could quite easily structure their remuneration to avoid taxation. The Act, however, specifically brings retiring allowances into income.[9]

The Act defines a "retiring allowance" as a payment in recognition of long service, compensation for loss of an office or employment or damages for wrongful dismissal.[10]

A payment pursuant to the terms of an employment contract is generally not a retiring allowance; it is remuneration.[11] In exceptional circumstances, a contractual payment to an employee upon termination of employment may be considered a "retiring allowance" if the payment is in recognition of the length of the employee's service to the company. There is generally an element of gratuitousness in the making of the payment, even though it may result from a threat of litigation.

F. SCHOLARSHIPS, BURSARIES AND FELLOWSHIPS

Scholarships, fellowships, bursaries and prizes for achievement are included in income.[12] There is an exemption, however, for individuals entitled to the education credit in the year or the immediately preceding year and for scholarships for elementary and high school students.[13]

The terms "scholarship," "fellowship" and "bursary" are often used interchangeably to mean financial assistance to selected students pursuing further education. A "prize for achievement" is an award for accomplishment. The phrase does not necessarily imply an award for victory in a competition or contest.[14] An award is only considered a "prize" if the winner of the prize is aware of the existence of, and enters, the contest.[15]

G. RESEARCH GRANTS

Tax law is about distinguishing between sources of income. Thus, we distinguish a fellowship, scholarship or bursary from a research grant. A research grant is a sum of money given to a person to defray expenses

---

9   ITA, *ibid*, subpara 56(1)(a)(ii).
10   *Ibid*, subs 248(1) "retiring allowance."
11   *Ibid*, para 6(3)(b).
12   *Ibid*, para 56(1)(n), subs 56(3).
13   *Ibid*, subs 56(3).
14   *Canada v Savage* (1983), 83 DTC 5409 at 5415 (SCC), Dickson J.
15   *Canada v McLaughlin*, [1978] CTC 602 (FCTD).

in connection with a research project. Research grants sometimes include remuneration for the researcher.

"Research" generally involves a critical or scientific inquiry aimed at discovering new facts and exploring the potential for their practical application. Usually, the terms of the grant will establish that the primary purpose of the grant is the carrying out of research.

An individual is taxable on a research grant only if he receives it directly. A payment of funds to the taxpayer's educational or research institution to finance research by the taxpayer is not taxable to the researcher.[16]

Research-related expenses are deductible from a research grant to the extent of the total value of the grant.

A taxpayer who must travel to conduct her research may deduct travelling expenses (including the full amount expended for meals and lodging) incurred in the carrying out of the research. A researcher who resides temporarily in a place while engaged in research is "sojourning" rather than travelling. Amounts paid for meals and lodging while sojourning in a place are considered personal and living expenses. It is not clear how long a stay in a place converts a traveller into a sojourner.[17]

H. PRIZES

A prize for achievement is an award for accomplishment. Prizes are taxable as income in the year received[18] only if the prize is for achievement in a field of endeavour ordinarily carried on by the taxpayer. Thus, prizes won in games of chance or for athletic achievement are not taxable.[19] The Act also exempts certain prescribed prizes of recognition by the general public for particularly meritorious endeavours.[20]

I. SOCIAL ASSISTANCE PAYMENTS

Although most social assistance payments are not taxable, they must initially be included in income.[21] The taxpayer may then claim a deduction

---

16   *ITA*, above note 1, para 56(1)(o).
17   *Ibid*, subpara 56(1)(o)(i); Interpretation Bulletin IT-75R4, "Scholarships, Fellowships, Bursaries, Prizes, Research Grants and Financial Assistance" (18 June 2003).
18   *ITA*, *ibid*, para 56(1)(n).
19   *Canada v Savage*, above note 14 at 545.
20   *Income Tax Regulations*, CRC c 945, s 7700.
21   *ITA*, above note 1, para 56(1)(u).

for the same amount in determining taxable income.[22] Thus, although the net effect is that social assistance payments are not taxable, the inclusion of social assistance payments in a taxpayer's income may have other consequences. For example, it may reduce the amount of other tax incentives, such as refundable tax credits, to which the taxpayer might otherwise be entitled.

The trend in recent Canadian tax legislation is to shift the tax burden of social welfare payments to the payer with the highest rate of tax in a family. Thus, the Act includes social assistance payments in the income threshold tests of the spouse with the higher marginal tax rate. This, in effect, restricts a family's access to any other income-tested tax incentives.

J. OTHER SELECTED INCLUSIONS

Other Inclusions in Income	Statutory Reference	Comment
Amounts paid for benefit of taxpayer and/or children in tax-payer's custody	56.1	
Unemployment insurance benefits	56(1)(a)(iv)	
Transitional assistance benefit	56(1)(a)(v)	received by employees of automotive industry covered by the 1965 Canada-US pact on automotive products
Prescribed benefit under government assistance program to extent not already included in income	56(1)(a)(vi)	
Annuity payments	56(1)(d), (d.2)	
Amount received from the disposition of an income-averaging annuity contract	56(1)(e), (f); 61(4) ("income-averaging annuity contract")	
Benefits under a supplementary unemployment benefit plan	56(1)(g); 145	
Benefits received under an RRSP or a RRIF	56(1)(h); 146	
Home buyers' plan	56(1)(h.1); 146.01	

---

22   *Ibid*, para 110(1)(f).

Other Inclusions in Income	Statutory Reference	Comment
Benefits from a deferred profit-sharing plan	56(1)(i); 147	
Amount received from the disposition of an interest in a life insurance policy	56(1)(j); 148(1), (1.1)	
Legal costs awarded by a court on an appeal for tax assessment, interest or penalties, and costs reimbursed from a decision of the Canada Employment and Immigration Commission or under the *Unemployment Insurance Act* or *Canada Pension Plan*	56(1)(l)	provided costs of the appeal or decision are deductible under para 60(o)
Reimbursement of legal expenses paid to collect or establish right to a retiring allowance or pension benefit	56(1)(l.1)	
Amount received from an RESP	56(1)(q); 146.1	
Home insulation or conversion grants	56(1)(s); Regs. 5500, 5501	
Benefits from an RRIF	56(1)(t); 146.3	
Workers' compensation	56(1)(v)	
Amounts received from some other person's salary deferral arrangement	56(1)(w)	amount included in income to the extent that it was not included in the other person's income
Proceeds from disposition of an interest in a RCA	56(1)(y)	
Value of benefits received or enjoyed in respect of workshops, seminars, training programs, etc.	56(1)(aa)	received by reason of membership in a registered national arts service organization

K. OTHER DEDUCTIONS

1) General Comment

Just as the *Income Tax Act* includes in income various miscellaneous receipts that are not directly attributable to a particular source, it also allows for the deduction of certain expenses that are not directly related to a particular source of income. These "other deductions" constitute an open category of expenses, each with its own rationale and underlying policies.

Personal expenses may become deductible by virtue of their intimate connection with a business. For example, meals and entertainment, travelling expenses and the cost of special wardrobes in specialized professions have an aura of business expenditures. These types of expenditures pose problems because it is not easy to draw the line between personal and business, and the connection between the expenditure and the business purposes may be tenuous. Take, for example, personal clothing. A professional lawyer or accountant is expected to dress in an appropriate manner suitable for his environment in the business workplace. Thus, the cost of a business suit or dress is closely connected by convention and culture with the earning of business income. Nevertheless, expenditures on account of clothing are generally considered to be primarily personal expenses and, hence, not deductible for tax purposes.

There comes a point, however, when clothing serves only a limited and specialized purpose, and the expenditure is primarily on account of business. For example, an actor may require special-effects clothing; a doctor or surgeon may require special tunics; an auto mechanic special overalls. In these cases, the clothing is considered business-related because of its restricted use outside of the workplace.

2) Spousal and Child Support

"Spouse" includes common-law partners and same-sex (homosexual/gay/lesbian) partners. A "common-law partner" is an individual who cohabits with the taxpayer in a conjugal relationship—see subsection 248(1).

a) General Comment
The expenses of supporting one's family are personal expenses that one does not incur for the purposes of earning income. Hence, absent statutory authority, one would not be entitled to deduct support payments from income. However, it is entirely tenable, from an economic perspective, that the recipient should be taxable on support, since such payments are an accretion to wealth.

The characterization of receipts of income does not depend on the character of the expenditure to the payer. The tax consequences to the recipient and the payer are determined independently. For example, where an individual takes her family to a restaurant, the cost of the meal is a personal, non-deductible expense. The amount spent, however, is taxable to the owner of the restaurant as business income.

We vary from this theoretical norm for several reasons. We allow a spouse to deduct support payments because we recognize such payments as extraordinary expenses that reduce the payer's ability to pay. Indeed, without tax relief, some spouses would find that their tax equalled, or even exceeded, their income after making support payments. Assume, for example, that an individual earns $100,000 and pays support of $35,000. Without a deduction for the support, his tax of approximately $36,000 would exceed the support payments. Thus, we justify the deduction for spousal support because it affects the taxpayer's ability to pay.

The support provisions also impact federal and provincial revenues. Since the payer usually has a higher marginal tax rate than the payee, the deduction for spousal support allows spouses to shift down on the rate schedule. This obviously has revenue consequences. For example, a deduction of $35,000 of spousal support has a net after-tax cost of $17,500 if the payer has a 50 percent tax rate. The treasury makes up part of the revenue loss by taxing the other spouse on the support. If this spouse has a marginal rate of 25 percent, however, the tax cost to him is only $8,750. Thus, the treasury picks up the net loss of revenue because of the difference in marginal rates.

The statutory provisions in respect of spousal support are mirror images of each other.[23] A payment that is deductible by the payer is taxable to the payee. A payment that is taxable to the recipient is deductible to the payer. Thus, read together, the rules concern the choice of taxable person rather than the definition of income or expense. In effect, one spouse is merely a conduit or pass-through for gross income that legally belongs to the other spouse by virtue of divorce settlement or decree.

An individual who is living separate and apart from her spouse or former spouse[24] because of the breakdown of their marriage can deduct spousal support payments if the payments are:[25]

- Pursuant to an order of a competent tribunal or a written agreement;
- In the nature of an allowance;

---

23   *ITA*, above note 1, paras 56(1)(b) and 60(b). *Thibaudeau v MNR*, above note 8 (para 56(1)(b) is not unconstitutional under s 15 of the *Canadian Charter of Rights and Freedoms*, Part I of the *Constitution Act, 1982*, being Schedule B to the *Canada Act 1982* (UK), 1982, c 11); see also Interpretation Bulletin IT-530R, "Support Payments" (17 July 2003).

24   See *ITA*, *ibid*, subs 252(3) for extended meaning of "spouse."

25   *Ibid*, paras 60(b) and 56.1(4) "support amount."

- Payable on a periodic basis; and
- For the maintenance of the recipient and/or the children.

The Act limits the deduction to situations where the payer and the payee are living separate and apart from each other. It is a question of fact whether individuals are living separate and apart from each other. In certain circumstances, persons living under a common roof may be living apart from each other.[26]

The default rule is that support payments are considered child support and, therefore, are neither deductible nor taxable if the order or agreement is silent as to their character.[27] A payment is spousal support only if the order or agreement clearly identifies it as being *solely* for the support of the spouse or former spouse.[28]

b) Order or Written Agreement

i) *Payments Prior to Agreement*

A payment is deductible only if it is pursuant to an order of a competent tribunal or a written agreement. The CRA does not accept anything less than a decree from a competent tribunal. Amounts that a taxpayer pays before the court order requires him to do so, or before the spouse enters into a written agreement, are deductible[29] only if the order or

---

26 *Sanford v Canada*, [2001] 1 CTC 2273 (TCC), aff'd 2002 FCA 381. *Rushton v Rushton* (1968), 66 WWR 764 (BCSC) ("separate" means having withdrawn from marriage with intent to destroy bond; "apart" means physically separate); *Rousell v Rousell* (1969), 69 WWR 568 (Sask QB) (essence of evidence of separation being cessation of marital relationship); *Galbraith v Galbraith* (1969), 69 WWR 390 (Man CA) (examination of law on cruelty as grounds for separation though couple living in same dwelling); *MNR v Longchamps* (1986), 86 DTC 1694 at 1695 (TCC) ("the termination of all rapport between a husband and his wife of the kind evidenced in this appeal is certainly in my opinion within the meaning that must be attributed to the expression, 'living apart'"; "there was no communication between them, no socializing whatsoever, each attending to his or her own affairs without consultation between them"); *Boos v MNR* (1961), 27 Tax ABC 283 (husband so withdrawn and separated from wife and children as to be in desertion, though still occupying same home).
27 *ITA*, above note 1, para 56(1)(b).
28 *Ibid*, subs 56.1(4) "child support amount."
29 See Interpretation Bulletin IT-530R, above note 23; *Hardtman v MNR*, [1977] CTC 358 (FCTD) (although court able to distinguish between sham and equitable maintenance, even prior to any agreement, court without such equitable jurisdiction); *Pezet v MNR*, [1974] CTC 2315 (TRB) (no retroactivity of deductibility where payments made prior to agreement, unless legislation provides otherwise); *Gagné v MNR*, [1976] CTC 2163 (TRB) (husband's letter listing expenses that he would pay did not constitute "agreement," since no evidence of consent); *Brooks v MNR*, [1977] CTC 2048 (TRB) (amounts paid prior to

agreement incorporates the payments. The parties must ensure that they have an order or agreement before the end of the year following the payments.[30]

ii) Written Agreement

A "written agreement" is a document signed by both parties to the agreement. It is not enough that the parties exchange correspondence with each other or that their lawyers or accountants exchange correspondence and discuss draft agreements.[31] The CRA will not accept anything less than a clear-cut "written agreement" signed by both parties. An exchange of correspondence may, however, crystallize into a "written agreement" in the same way that one can enter into a contract through an exchange of letters.[32]

iii) Paid under an Agreement

A payment is made under an order or agreement if it complies with the legal obligation created in the agreement.[33] Thus, only those amounts that are actually set out in the court order or written agreement are deductible by the payer and taxable to the payee. Voluntary payments in excess of the agreed-upon amounts are not "made under" the order or agreement. Conversely, payments that are made under a court order or agreement are taxable as income to the recipient even though the order or agreement might stipulate that the amounts are to be paid on a "tax-free" basis.[34]

---

agreement and order not deductible; even amount of arrears paid pursuant to order not deductible).

30 *ITA*, above note 1, subs 60.1(3).

31 *Feinstein v Canada*, [1979] CTC 329 (FCTD) (agreement destroyed by fire in attorney's office; payments not deductible in these exceptional circumstances); *Chamberland v MNR*, [1981] CTC 2302 (TRB) (agreement in principle, signed by one spouse is insufficient even if payments actually made); *Ardley v MNR*, [1980] CTC 2126 (TRB) (legal fees for separation agreement paid, but no proof of execution of agreement); *Hardy v MNR*, [1978] CTC 3120 (TRB) (and cases cited therein) (payments made pursuant to a written agreement that the payer refused to sign not deductible); *Andrychuck v MNR*, [1986] 2 CTC 2214 (TCC) (informal correspondence between spouses does not constitute "written agreement"; wife's letter requesting $300 support per month insufficient); *Jacoby v MNR*, [1981] CTC 2935 (TRB) (unsigned written agreement insufficient); *Jaskot v MNR*, [1992] 1 CTC 2145 (TCC) (increase in support payments not deductible as only written evidence in correspondence of recipient's solicitor).

32 *Burgess v MNR*, [1991] 1 CTC 163 (FCTD).

33 *Canada v Sills*, [1985] 1 CTC 49 (FCA).

34 *Canada v Sigglekow*, [1985] 2 CTC 251, additional reasons at (1985), 85 DTC 5594 (FCTD).

c) "Allowance"

An allowance is a pre-determined sum of money that the recipient can use for her own benefit. The amount must be:[35]

- Limited and pre-determined;
- Paid on account of maintenance; and
- At the complete discretion of the person to whom it is paid.

In addition, subsection 56.1(4) requires that the recipient have complete discretion over the money paid to her. Amounts over which the recipient does not have discretion do not qualify as spousal support.

d) Payable on a Periodic Basis

A recurring problem in interpreting support agreements is the distinction between support payments and property settlements. Spousal support is deductible by the payer, and taxable to the payee, but only if it is payable on a periodic basis. Thus, the obligation to pay support is an annual charge against one spouse's pre-tax income, and entails a redirection of that income to his spouse. The amount payable on a periodic basis is deductible even if the payment is a lump sum, whether in arrears or in advance.[36]

The Act confines the deduction to support expenses. There is no deduction for property settlements. Property settlements are capital divisions between spouses. Thus, capital payments to extinguish support are not deductible as an expense.[37] For example, the present value of an agreement to pay 60 monthly payments of $1,000 is equal to a lump sum of $49,272 if we assume an interest rate of 8 percent. The lump sum and the periodic payments are mathematically equal present-value amounts at that rate. Nevertheless, the lump sum is not deductible for tax purposes because it is the capitalized value of the annual expenses.[38] Thus, legal form prevails over economic substance.

"Periodic" means recurring at fixed or regular intervals. The payment must be payable on a periodic basis and the periodicity requirement must be in the court order or the written agreement.[39] It is not enough that the taxpayer actually pays on a periodic basis. The statutory

---

35   *Gagnon v Canada*, [1986] 1 SCR 264 ($360 paid to spouse pursuant to divorce decree, for purpose of paying two mortgages and interest was "allowance"); *Canada v Pascoe*, [1975] CTC 656 (FCA).

36   See *Ostrowski v Canada*, 2002 FCA 299.

37   There are other provisions that allow for tax-free capital settlements: see, for example, *ITA*, above note 1, subs 73(1).

38   *MNR v Armstrong*, [1956] SCR 446.

39   *ITA*, above note 1, para 60(b).

requirement is that the payment be *payable* on a periodic basis, not that it is actually paid periodically.[40] Thus, the obligation to pay at periodic intervals must not be left to the discretion of the payer.[41]

Although some of the earlier jurisprudence interpreted "periodic" to mean that payments be on at least a monthly basis, the CRA is now more flexible. Even annual payments sometimes qualify as periodic.[42] It would, however, be quite unusual for payments that recur less frequently than annually to qualify as periodic payments.

Support is usually paid in cash and recognizes the spouse's legal obligations. It is paid at regular intervals and, in most cases, continues for a stipulated period or until the recipient spouse's death. Thus, the deduction and inclusion regime is appropriate for spousal support, because the payments are of an income nature and the spouse merely acts as the conduit for his legal obligations.

In contrast, property settlements are usually executed over a brief period and may include non-cash assets. Property settlements are not contingent upon subsequent events such as remarriage. A spouse is entitled to a share of the marital property, even if she remarries immediately after the settlement. The deduction inclusion system is inappropriate for capital settlements.

Difficulties arise because complex and sizable agreements have elements of both spousal support and property settlements. There is also the danger of lump-sum property settlements masquerading as spousal support because of the advantage to the paying spouse (normally the husband), who will usually have the higher marginal rate. Thus, the use of inappropriate language in an agreement can effectively convert spousal support into a property settlement.

An allowance for spousal support is a limited, pre-determined sum of money that one pays to enable the recipient to provide for certain kinds of expenses. Its amount is determined in advance and, once paid, it is at the complete discretion of the recipient. A lump-sum payment

---

40   *Canada v Sills*, above note 33 (lump-sum payments for arrears of periodic alimony characterized as periodic notwithstanding tardiness and manner of payment); *James v Canada*, [1985] 1 CTC 239 (FCTD) (recipient taxable on payments made pursuant to order even though payments were late and amounts less than specified in order).

41   *Jones v Ogle* (1872), 8 Ch App 192 at 198 (in construction of will, partnership profits did not come within meaning of "periodical payment in the nature of income"); *No 427 v MNR* (1957), 57 DTC 291 (TAB) (single $5,000 payment, which was one of several of increasing value to be paid over twelve years, was periodic in nature).

42   *Hanlin v Canada*, [1985] 1 CTC 54 (FCTD) (three annual payments held to be part of series of payments payable on periodic basis).

also represents a limited, pre-determined sum of money. Thus, the distinction between an allowance and a lump-sum payment blurs if the lump-sum payment is also payable in equal instalments on a periodic basis.

The problem is essentially one of formal legal characterization, rather than underlying economic substance. One must distinguish between where support stops and property settlement begins. For example, what is the economic distinction between spousal support of $1,000 per month, payable for 10 years (despite remarriage and a property settlement) and one that pays one spouse her share of $120,000 at a rate of $1,000 per month over 10 years? What if the spousal support is front-end loaded; that is, one spouse receives an allowance of $1,500 per month for the first five years and only $500 per month for the last five years? What if the front-end load is $1,800 per month for five years and $200 per month for the last five years? At what point does the spousal support convert into a property settlement?

i)   Periodic vs. Lump Sum Payments

The distinction between lump-sum amounts and periodic allowances reflects the underlying difference between income and capital. The *Income Tax Act* taxes income, not capital. Similarly, one may deduct expenses but not capital expenditures. A lump sum payable in instalments is a capital amount and is neither deductible nor taxable. An obligation to pay a lump sum is a finite capital debt. The debt is assignable by the creditor and survives his life. Hence, the debt can pass to the estate. The critical element in determining the deductibility of maintenance payments (as opposed to capital settlements) is whether the payments were payable on a periodic basis. Thus, lump sum payments, whether in arrears or in advance, may be deductible if they are on account of maintenance.[43]

The following are some of the relevant criteria in distinguishing between spousal support and property settlements.[44]

Indicia	Spousal Support	Property Settlement
Frequency of payments	Weekly, monthly, annually	More than annually
Ratio of payment in relation to income and living standards	Low Small percentage of annual income of payer	High In excess of annual income of payer

43   See, for example, *Ostrowski v Canada*, above note 37.
44   See, generally, *McKimmon v Canada*, [1990] 1 CTC 109 (FCA).

Indicia	Spousal Support	Property Settlement
Interest payments prior to due date	None	Yes
Acceleration by payee as penalty on default	No	Yes
Prepayment at option of payer	No	Yes
Amount allows for significant capital accumulation by recipient	No	Yes
Liability to pay is for definite and fixed time	No	Yes
Payments for indefinite period or until some identifiable family event (e.g., age of child)	Yes	No
Assignability of payments	No	Yes
Survival of obligation to pay after death of payer	No	Yes
Release from future obligations to pay	No	Yes

a. Frequency of Payments

Periodicity implies an obligation to pay at fixed intervals and not at variable times. Moreover, the payments should be payable on a reasonably regular basis—whether weekly, monthly or quarterly. Payments made at intervals of greater than one year would rarely be allowances on account of maintenance.

b. Amount Paid in Relation to Living Standards

Spousal support is for maintenance, and not for the accumulation of capital. Thus, a payment that is a very substantial portion of the payer's income is unlikely an allowance for maintenance. On the other hand, a payment that merely maintains the recipient's standard of living is an allowance for maintenance.

There is no hard-and-fast rule as to what constitutes maintenance. The answer depends upon the lifestyle of the parties and their standard of living. The courts have denied taxpayers deductions for educational expenses, medical expenses, camping expenses, hospital insurance premiums and life insurance premiums.[45]

---

45 *Urichuk v Canada*, [1993] 1 CTC 226 (FCA) (characterization in separation agreement of instalment payments as additional maintenance does not prevent a contrary finding); *Golightly v MNR*, [1970] Tax ABC 161 (various payments, including insurance, university room and board, tuition and medical insurance paid directly to institution pursuant to separation agreement were not "maintenance"); *Ivey v MNR*, [1982] CTC 2034 (TRB) (payments of school fees, summer camp fees and medical expenses for child with cystic fibrosis outside meaning of "maintenance"); *Shaw v MNR*, [1978] CTC 3230 (TRB) (payment by tax-

c. Interest

Maintenance payments do not typically bear interest. Payments that bear interest are more likely lump-sum settlements payable by instalments.

d. Acceleration Clauses

Pre-payment and acceleration clauses are generally associated with lump-sum capital settlements. An acceleration clause in a settlement contract suggests that the debt is a non-deductible capital obligation.

e. Accumulation of Capital

The quantum of payments is important: maintenance payments are for the recipient's living costs. They are not intended to allow for an accumulation of capital over a short period of time. It is accepted, however, that modest payments on account of capital accumulation may qualify as maintenance. For example, blended monthly mortgage principal and interest payments allow for a modest accumulation of capital over time. Mortgage costs are a normal living expense.

f. Term of Payments

Spousal support is either payable for an indefinite or unspecified period of time. Where time is specified, the payments generally relate to a significant event in the life of the parties. For example, spousal support payments may depend upon the coming of age of a child, because one anticipates such an event to cause a material change in the recipient's needs. In contrast, a lump sum generally represents a finite debt between the parties, and payments on account thereof are expected to continue for a fixed and specified term.

g. Assignment of Obligation

Maintenance allowances are typically personal and non-assignable. They are not assignable to third parties, and terminate upon the death of the recipient. In contrast, lump sum capital settlements are assignable debts, and form part of the recipient's estate.

h. Release from Future Obligations

An agreement that releases the payer from all future obligations to pay maintenance is a lump-sum settlement. The consideration for the release from future maintenance is the capitalized present value of the payments that would have been made on account of future maintenance. The capital payment may be in cash, or the payer may assume a liability (such as a mortgage) on the recipient's behalf. For example,

---

payer of spouse's income tax on maintenance payments and spouse's moving expenses not "alimony" or "maintenance"); *Evans v MNR*, [1960] SCR 391 (car payments made for spouse not "maintenance" although car highly useful).

one spouse may assume a mortgage on the other spouse's property in exchange for his release from further liability for maintenance.

ii) Rollovers

Capital settlements between spouses and ex-spouses are subject to a different tax regime than are periodic payments. Section 73 allows an individual two choices when transferring capital property to her spouse or ex-spouse. The spouse may:

1) Rollover the property to the other spouse on a tax-free basis, or
2) Elect to realize any capital gain accrued up to the date of the transfer.

In either case, the recipient takes the property at a cost equal to the transferor's proceeds of disposition. If the transferor elects a rollover, the recipient assumes the property at the transferor's cost; if the transferor realizes a capital gain, the recipient acquires the property at its fair market value.

iii) Arrears

Payments payable on a periodic basis do not change in character merely because they are not made on time. The test for deductibility is whether the payments are *payable* on a periodic basis, not whether they are actually paid on a periodic schedule.[46] Thus, payments on account of arrears are deductible and taxable if they are identifiable under the terms of the agreement.[47]

e) Child Support

Child support payments made under a written agreement or court order on or after 1 May 1997 are not deductible by the payer. Similarly, such child support is not taxable to the recipient.[48]

Child support means any support the court order or written agreement does not identify as being *solely* for the support of the taxpayer's spouse or former spouse. For example, where an agreement provides for a global support amount for the spouse and children, the entire amount is child support and, therefore, not deductible and not taxable. Similarly, if a court order or written agreement provides for the payment of amounts to a third party, the entire amount is child support if the order or agreement does not clearly specify otherwise.

---

46   *Canada v Pascoe*, above note 35.
47   *Canada v Sills*, above note 33.
48   Interpretation Bulletin IT-530R, above note 23.

The term "children" has the same meaning that the term "child" has in other provisions of the Act.[49] For the purposes of paragraphs 56(1)(b) and 60(b), the payer must be the legal parent of a child of the recipient.[50]

Where a payer must make both spousal and child support payments, the presumption is that the payments go first towards child support and then for spousal support. Thus, in the event that the payer defaults, the recipient receives the payments first on a non-taxable basis. The payer cannot deduct any portion on account of spousal support until the payer fully satisfies his child support obligations.

f) Third-Party Payments

It is usual to structure spousal support to make payments tax-deductible to the payer and taxable to the recipient. In most cases, this allows taxpayers to rate-shift and reduce their overall tax obligations. As noted above, payments are deductible if they are paid on a periodic basis by a person to her spouse or former spouse.

There are circumstances, however, when it is financially prudent to pay some or all of the support payments directly to a third party for the benefit of the spouse or children. Subsection 60.1(1) deems amounts that otherwise qualify for deduction to be deductible even if they are paid directly to a third party. The provision also ensures that the parties can take into account third-party amounts payable for child support in determining the deduction for spousal support.

Third-party support payments are deductible where the payments are:[51]

- Paid pursuant to either a judicial order of a competent tribunal or a written agreement that stipulates that subsections 56.1(2) and 60.1(2) apply;
- For the maintenance of the payer's spouse, former spouse, an individual of the opposite sex who is the legal parent of a child of the taxpayer, and/or children;
- Incurred at a time when the payer and the recipient were living separate and apart; and
- In respect of support expenses incurred either in the year or in the preceding taxation year.

---

49   *ITA*, above note 1, subs 252(1).
50   *Ibid*, subs 56.1(4) "child support amount."
51   *Ibid*, subs 60.1(2).

Subsection 60.1(2) deems such payments to be payable on a periodic basis.[52] There are additional requirements if the payment to a third party is in respect of mortgage payments on the family home. In these circumstances a payment is deductible only if:[53]

- The payer does not reside in the family home;
- The payment is not in respect of the purchase of tangible property; and
- The payment for principal and interest is not in excess of 20 percent of the original amount of the loan incurred to finance the home.

In order for a third-party payment to be deductible, the judicial order or written agreement must *specifically* provide that subsections 60.1(2) and 56.1(2) of the Act apply to the payments. Failure to enumerate the.subsections in the terms of settlement disqualifies the payments for deduction. Some courts[54] have blunted the severity of this harsh approach and accepted an oblique reference in the minutes of settlement as sufficient to satisfy the statutory requirement. It is better, however, to specify in the minutes of settlement that the subsections apply.

i)   Deemed Allowance

The Act deems spousal support payments paid to a third party to have been paid as an allowance. Such payments are deductible by the payer and taxable in the hands of the person for whose benefit the payments are made.

Typically, third-party payments are made on account of, for example, medical and dental bills, mortgage payments, tuition fees, household utilities, camp fees and condominium maintenance fees. Of these expenses, mortgage fees, utilities and tangible property associated with medical, dental or educational requirements can easily be made tax-deductible.

It is less clear, however, whether condominium maintenance expenses (common area charges) paid directly to the condominium corporation are deductible for tax purposes. Expenditures incurred on account of the family home are deductible in respect of the acquisition or improvement of the home to the extent that they do not exceed 20 percent of the original cost of financing the home. Condominium fees

---

52   See also Interpretation Bulletin IT-530R, above note 23.

53   *ITA*, above note 1, subs 60.1(2).

54   See, for example, *Cottrell v MNR*, [1990] 2 CTC 2031 (TCC) (payments deductible where minutes of settlement referred to payments in issue); *Bishop v MNR*, [1993] 1 CTC 2333 (TCC) (payment of support arrears to welfare authorities neither taxable nor deductible; payment constituted discharge of indebtedness).

cannot be considered to qualify as either an acquisition or an improvement cost. Hence, it is generally better to include condominium fees as part of the negotiated allowance that is paid directly to the spouse.

ii) Prior Payments

Support payments made prior to obtaining a judicial order or entering into a written agreement are also tax-deductible if the order or agreement specifically so provides.[55] In effect, the order or agreement can retroactively render the payments deductible even though they were not paid under the order or agreement.

3) Child Care Expenses

a) General Comment

Child care is probably the single biggest impediment for women who wish to continue their career as professionals. There are two distinct aspects of the problem: first, many mothers want to stay home with young children during their formative years; second, the cost of child care to pursue a part-time or full professional career can be a disincentive. Whether we lose women professionals for personal family life choices or inadequate incentives, society ultimately bears the social and financial costs.

What is the most effective, efficient and fair manner of retaining the services of professional women? There are no easy answers. Ultimately, tax law must be a compromise between competing values: social, political and revenue costs.

Child care is a basic function of family life. Expenses for child care have escalated as more mothers go out of the home to work. However, unlike some personal expenses, such as food and shelter that one incurs whether one works or not, child care has a strong element of business purpose. If a mother cannot work without bringing in child care and the family needs income, any incremental cash that the family pays for such care is clearly income related.

The income tax system addresses the issue of child care expenses, but it does so ineffectively and inadequately. The fundamental principle for the deductibility of business expenses is that the taxpayer should incur the expenses primarily for the purpose of earning income. The existence of business purpose is a question of fact.

The present regime of child care deductions and benefits is a haphazard conglomerate of rules that are not particularly effective or suited

---

55   *ITA*, above note 1, subs 60.1(3).

to the needs of the new economy. In the aggregate, they provide minimal accommodation for women who wish to pursue their professional careers.

There are many circumstances where parents, particularly women, incur child care expenses primarily and predominantly for the purpose of allowing them to work, either as employees or in business. Indeed, in many families, both parents must work to survive. While all parents must care for their children, parents who work outside the home as employees or engage in business incur incremental child care expenses that can be linked directly and solely to the purpose of earning income. Hence, child care expenses could be deductible as business expenses under conventional tax principles. But for the child care expense, the mother (in most cases) could not work and earn income.

However, courts are careful with "but for" analysis in determining the purpose of expenditures for fear of opening the floodgates to all manner of deductions, however tenuous their connection with the income-earning process. The fear of floodgates still prevails. Nevertheless, the Supreme Court in *Symes v Canada* was prepared to examine the issue of child care expenses afresh and more critically and did not reject the "but for" test. Indeed, it is more than likely that the Court would have allowed the deduction under general tax principles were it not for the statutory fly (section 63) in the ointment.

Section 63 of *Income Tax Act* specifically details the terms and conditions under which employees and professionals may deduct child care expenses. The rules are technical, narrowly circumscribed and permit unrealistically low deductions—$7,000 for children under the age of 7 and $4,000 for a child between 7 and 16 years of age. The provision purports to be relieving and permissive. In fact, it impedes deduction for professionals under the more general "but for" business purpose test. The Supreme Court ruled the section to be a complete code in itself that, in effect, precludes deductibility under any other general provisions of the statute—a variation of *inclusio unius est exclusio alterius* (the inclusion of one implies the exclusion of others).

To be sure, the government has legitimate concerns about the deductibility of child care expenses and the potential revenue loss to the public treasury. However, we need to balance the potential tax cost against the enormous hidden costs to society in educating professionals for 8 to 10 years at public expense and then losing their services. Losing the services of female family physicians, for example, further constrains supply of medical services just when Canada's aging population is increasing its demands on the public healthcare system. If the government is concerned with long waiting times for access to family physicians, it might consider enhancing tax incentives to increase the supply of medical services.

Working women are caught between a rock and a hard place. The courts say that the statutory provisions dealing with child care are a complete code and, therefore, individuals cannot deduct such expenses under the general principles of tax law. Meanwhile, taxpayers cannot challenge the inadequacy of the code because it is complete and within the purview of Parliament. Thus, the statutory rules that purport to help working mothers are a boomerang that penalizes professional women.

b) The Statutory Rules

The Act provides a measure of tax relief to parents who incur child care expenses so that they may pursue financial gain outside of the home.[56] The deduction is strictly controlled. The limits and constraints on the deduction are tight and, in most cases, permit only the lower income parent to make a claim.

The taxpayer must incur the expenses to permit one parent (or a supporting person of the child) to pursue employment, business, research or educational activities. The maximum yearly deduction is the least of:

- The amount actually paid for child care;
- Two-thirds of the taxpayer's earned income for the year; and
- $7,000 for each eligible child under 7 years of age, $4,000 for each child between 7 and 16 years of age at the end of the year, and $10,000 for children for whom one can claim a disability credit.

The deduction for child care expenses is usually available only to working mothers. Only in extremely rare situations may a father claim a deduction for child care expenses.

i) Definition of "Child Care Expense"

The Act defines "child care expense" restrictively. One must satisfy the following additional conditions to qualify an expenditure as a "child care expense":[57]

- The child care services must be provided in Canada;[58]

---

56   Ibid, s 63; see also Interpretation Bulletin IT-495R3, "Child Care Expenses" (11 May 2005).
57   ITA, ibid, subs 63(3) "child care expense."
58   However, s 64.1, ibid, allows individuals who are absent from Canada, but still resident in Canada for tax purposes, to deduct payments for child care services

- The services must be provided by a Canadian resident (other than the child's parents) for whom the taxpayer or his spouse does not claim a dependency credit; and
- The person providing the service must not be under 18 years of age if she is related to either the taxpayer or his spouse.

Advertising expenses, agency placement fees and transportation expenses to locate, interview or bring to Canada a caregiver also qualify as "child care expenses."

Subsection 63(4) provides another exception to the "in Canada" rule for child care services. Where a taxpayer resides in Canada near the Canada-US border, the child care services may be provided in the United States rather than in Canada. However, the US facility must be closer to the Canadian taxpayer's place of residence by a reasonably accessible route than any place in Canada where such child care services are available.

ii)   Claim by Lower-Income Parent
In two-parent families, child care expenses are generally deductible only by the spouse with the lower income. The purpose of this restriction is to target the deduction for women. In exceptional circumstances, the higher-income spouse is entitled to the child care deduction.[59]

iii)   Claim by Higher-Income Parent
The higher-income parent may make a claim for child care expenses, but only if the other parent:[60]

- Attends full-time at a designated educational institution;
- Is certified to be mentally or physically ill and incapable of looking after children;
- Is certified to be mentally or physically ill to the extent that she is confined to a bed or wheelchair, or is a patient in a hospital for a period of at least two weeks in the year;
- Is imprisoned for at least two weeks in the year; or
- Is living apart from the taxpayer at the end of the year and for a period of at least ninety days that began in the year by reason of marriage breakdown.

In any of these circumstances the amount deductible by the higher-income parent is restricted to the *least* of the following amounts:

---

provided outside of Canada.
59   *Ibid*, subss 63(1) & (2).
60   *Ibid*, para 63(2)(b).

- The aggregate of
  - » $7,000 per eligible child under 7 years of age (or $10,000 if the child is eligible for disability tax credit) for whom child care expenses have been paid; and
  - » $4,000 per other eligible child over 6 and under 16 years of age (or over 15 years of age with physical or mental impairment) for whom child care expenses were incurred;
- Two-thirds of the taxpayer's "earned income" for the year;
- The number of weeks the taxpayer was eligible to make the claim multiplied by the total periodic child care expenses incurred with respect to an eligible child.

Subsection 63(3) defines "periodic child care expense" to mean 1/40 of the $4,000, $7,000 and $10,000 amounts as $100, $175 and $250 (respectively) weekly.

iv) Nil Income
In most cases where a husband and wife have child care expenses, the child care expenses are deductible by the spouse with the lower income. The Act deems a taxpayer with no income to have income of zero.[61] The rationale of this rule is to prevent the sole breadwinner in a single income family from claiming child care expenses.[62]

4) Moving Expenses

a) General Comment
Moving expenses also have a dual flavour of personal and business-related expenditures. Under the common law, if an employer transferred his employee from one location to another and paid the moving expenses, the expenses were deductible to the employer and were not taxable to the employee. The employee could not, however, take a deduction for moving expenses if he paid for his own move.

Mobility of labour is an important and necessary part of the Canadian economy. Labour mobility reduces unemployment and increases productive capacity. Given the size of the country, taxpayers often incur substantial moving expenses in connection with employer-related

---

61   Ibid, para 3(f).
62   Paragraph 3(f), ibid, was enacted after court decisions held that where one spouse had no income at all, the spouse with income could deduct the child-care expenses since there was only one income. See Fiset v MNR, [1988] 1 CTC 2335 (TCC); McLaren v MNR, [1988] 1 CTC 2371 (TCC); See Fromstein v Canada, [1993] 2 CTC 2214 (TCC) concerning the same issue, after the enactment of para 3(f).

relocations. The statutory deduction for moving expenses in section 62 recognizes the importance of labour mobility. The deduction also recognizes that employees who pay their own expenses and are not re-imbursed by their employers should be placed on an equal footing with self-employed persons who move to a new work location.

The Act generally regards employment-related moving expenses as a cost of earning income and permits the deduction of such expenses if the taxpayer:[63]

- Commences employment in Canada;
- Commences business in Canada; or
- Commences full-time studies at a post-secondary educational institution.

An individual may deduct her moving expenses in the year of the move *or any subsequent year* to the extent that she has employment or business income at a new work location against which she can apply the moving expenses.[64]

Moving expenses are not deductible against investment income.[65]

b) Eligibility for Deduction

An individual who moves to a place in Canada for the purpose of employment, or to carry on a business, may deduct moving expenses if she satisfies three conditions:[66]

- Both the old residence and the new residence are in Canada;
- The new residence is at least 40 km closer to the new employment or business location than was the old residence;[67] and
- The move is related to the commencement of the business, employment or studies.[68]

Students may deduct expenses of moving into or out of Canada. The change in the taxpayer's residence must be by reason of the commencement of her business, employment or studies.

---

63 See ITA, *ibid*, subs 248(1) "eligible relocation"; see also Interpretation Bulletin IT-178R3, "Moving Expenses" (consolidated).

64 *Moodie v Canada*, 2004 TCC 462 (Informal Procedure).

65 *Schultz v MNR*, [1988] 2 CTC 293 (FCTD).

66 ITA, above note 1, subs 62(1); subs 248(1) "eligible relocation."

67 Now see TCC decision in *Nagy v Canada*, 2007 TCC 394 (Informal Procedure); *Giannakopoulos v Canada* [1995] 2 CTC 316 (FCA); *Cameron v MNR*, [1993] 1 CTC 2745 (TCC) (40 kms is measured "as the crow flies"); *Haines v MNR*, [1984] CTC 2422 (TCC) (distance to be measured in straight line).

68 *Kubryk v MNR*, [1987] 1 CTC 2125 (TCC).

c) Definition of "Moving Expenses"

The Act does not define "moving expenses." Thus, expenses that fall within the common understanding of "moving expenses" are deductible. One looks at the economic substance of the expenditure to determine whether it constitutes a "moving expense." The Act specifically includes the following as deductible "moving expenses":[69]

- Travelling costs, including reasonable expenses for meals and lodging, incurred in the course of the move;
- Movers' costs, including storage charges;
- The cost of meals and lodging either near the old residence or near the new residence, for a period not exceeding fifteen days;
- The cost of cancelling a lease;
- Selling costs[70] to dispose of the old residence;
- Legal expenses, registration, and land transfer taxes in respect of the acquisition of a new residence in the new location, if the taxpayer sells the old residence;
- Interest, property taxes, insurance premiums, and the cost of heating and utilities in respect of the old residence, to the extent of the lesser of $5,000 and the total of such expenses; and
- The cost of revising legal documents to reflect the address of the new residence, of replacing drivers' licences and non-commercial vehicle permits, and of connecting or disconnecting utilities.

Expenditures not listed above are also deductible as "moving expenses" if they qualify under the general understanding of that phrase.

However, the following expenditures are not deductible:[71]

- Expenses reimbursed to the taxpayer by the employer;
- Expenses paid directly by the individual's employer;
- Expenses that are deductible under any other section of the Act;
- Expenses in excess of the individual's income in the year of the move from employment or business at the new location; and
- Where the taxpayer is a student, any expenses in excess of the taxable portion of scholarships, fellowships, bursaries and research grants.

Moving expenses are generally deductible only in the year in which the move occurs. Expenses in excess of the deductible limit for a year may, however, be carried over and deducted against income in the following year. To be deductible in the year following the move, the

---

69   *ITA*, above note 1, subs 62(3).
70   *Collin v MNR*, [1990] 2 CTC 92 (FCTD) (lump sum paid by vendor to reduce purchaser's effective mortgage rate constituted "cost of selling property").
71   *ITA*, above note 1, subs 62(1).

expenses must not have been deductible in the year in which the individual incurred them. Thus, deductible moving expenses that are not claimed by the taxpayer in the year of the move are forever lost.[72]

Example

Horace Rumpole graduated from the University of Ottawa in Year 1 and found a job as an accountant in Vancouver. He commenced his job on 1 November Year 1 at a starting salary of $30,000 per year, payable monthly on the last day of the month.

As part of his contract of employment, his new employers reimbursed Horace $2,000 to defray the cost of his otherwise deductible moving expenses to Vancouver.

On 1 October Year 1 Horace moved out of his Ottawa apartment and into a hotel, where he stayed for seven days. As a consequence of his move to Vancouver, Horace incurred the following expenditures:

Lease cancellation costs on his apartment in Ottawa	$400
Hotel and meal expenses in Ottawa and Vancouver (21 days)	$2,100
Airfare and ground transportation	$600
Movers' charges	$3,500
Storage charges	$600
Legal fees re: acquisition of house in Vancouver	$1,400
Airfare for house hunting trip in September Year 1 and associated living costs	$850

Unfortunately for Horace, there was a fire in his mover's premises in Vancouver, where his furniture and belongings were being stored. The storage company did not carry sufficient insurance, and Horace's goods, worth $7,000, were destroyed.

The maximum deduction available to Horace for Year 1 is calculated as follows:

Eligible moving expenses under subsection 62(3):

Lease cancellation costs	$400
15 days hotel and meal expenses: 15/21 × $2,100	$1,500
Airfare and ground transportation	$600
Movers' charges:	$3,500
Storage charges	$600
	$6,600
Reimbursed amount	(2,000)
Net moving expenses	$4,600
Income at new job: 2/12 × $30,000	$5,000
Maximum deduction	$4,600

---

72   *Ibid*, para 62(1)(b).

Example, continued

Note:

1. The legal fees ($1,400) for the acquisition of the new house in Vancouver are not deductible as moving expenses, because the taxpayer did not dispose of a residence at his old location: paragraph 62(3)(f).
2. The "income at new job" limits deductibility of expenses: paragraph 62(1)(c). Horace worked for November and December, Year 1, for 2/12 of his annual salary.

5) Other Selected Deductions

Other deductions to be found in various sections of the Act or in income tax rulings include the following:

Type of Deduction	Statutory References
Capital element of each annuity payment, if paid under a contract, will or trust	para 60(a)
Support payments	para 60(b); IT-530R
Repayment of support payments	para 60(c.2); IT-530R
Annual interest accruing on succession duties, inheritance taxes or estate taxes	para 60(d); IT-533
Premium or payment under registered retirement savings plan	para 60(i); IT-124R6
Transfer of superannuation benefits	para 60(j); IT-528
Transfer of surplus under a defined benefit provision of a registered pension plan	para 60(j.01)
Certain payments to registered pension plan	para 60(j.02)
Repayment under prescribed statutory provision of pension benefits included in income	para 60(j.03), 60(j.04)
Transfer of retiring allowances	para 60(j.1); IT-337R4
Transfer to a spousal RRSP	para 60(j.2)
Transfer of refund of a premium under a registered retirement savings plan	para 60(l); IT-528
Estate tax applicable to property to which the taxpayer is the successor	para 60(m)
Succession duties payable on property to which the taxpayer is the successor	para 60(m.1)
Amount of overpayment of pension or benefits received by the taxpayer to the extent repaid by her	para 60(n)
Amount in respect of fees or expenses in the preparation, institution or prosecution of an objection or an appeal regarding certain decisions	para 60(o); IT-99R5
Amount in respect of legal fees to collect or establish a right to pension benefits	para 60(o.1); IT-99R5

Type of Deduction	Statutory References
Refund of income payments in an arm's length transaction	para 60(q); IT-340R
Repayment in respect of a policy loan under a life insurance policy, to the extent the amount was included in income and not otherwise deductible	para 60(s)
Certain amount included in income in respect of a retirement compensation arrangement	para 60(t)
Amount included in income as proceeds from a disposition of an interest in a retirement compensation arrangement	para 60(u)
Contribution to a provincial pension plan	para 60(v)
Repayment of unemployment insurance benefit to the extent not otherwise deductible	para 60(v.1)
Tax on old age security benefits	para 60(w)
Refund of undeducted additional voluntary contributions to a registered pension plan in respect of services rendered	para 60.2
Payments made as consideration for an income-averaging annuity contract	subs 61(1)
Moving expenses	s 62
Child care expenses	s 63
Disability supports deduction	ss 64 and 64.1; IT-519R2

FURTHER READINGS

BENOTTO, MARY LOU. "An Income Tax Checklist" in The Law Society of Upper Canada, *Special Lectures 1993: Family Law: Roles, Fairness and Equality* (Toronto: The Law Society of Upper Canada, 1993) 297.

BITTKER, BORIS. "A Comprehensive Tax Base as a Goal of Income Tax Reform" (1967) 80 Harv L Rev 925.

BOWMAN, STEPHEN W, ET AL. "The Taxability of Child Support Payments and the *Charter of Rights and Freedoms*" (1994) 42 Can Tax J 907.

DURNFORD, JOHN W, & STEPHEN J TROOPE. "Spousal Support in Family Law and Alimony in the Law of Taxation" (1994) 42 Can Tax J 1.

HARRIS, PETER H. "Tax Treatment of Civil Litigation and Damage Awards, Alimony and Maintenance Payments" (1985) 6 Advocate's Q 346.

SANDLER, DANIEL. "Family Law and the Family Jewels" (1991) 39 Can Tax J 513.

DAMAGES

A. GENERAL COMMENT

Civil litigation—generally a fight over money damages—is a long journey. At the end of the journey—which can last ten to fifteen years—the only real concern that the exhausted plaintiff and defendant have in common is the amount that they take out of, or put into, their pockets net of costs, legal fees and taxes. The tax treatment of damage awards has a significant effect on the ultimate cost of financial recovery or indemnity.

The only thing that one can say with any certainty about damage awards is that some are taxable and others are not. Taxation depends upon how we characterize the award, which in turn depends upon the underlying cause of action. If damages are income, the next step is to determine the source and type of income and the applicable tax rate.

To determine the nature of damages we start by looking at the purpose of the award. Broadly speaking, damages in lieu of income that would otherwise have been taxable retain their character as such and are taxable. Damages on account of capital are not taxable. However, as we shall see, damages on account of income can sometimes be crystallized into capital receipts.

B. THE CAUSE OF ACTION

The first stage is framing the cause of action and the claim for damages in the pleadings. Counsel rarely considers tax issues at this stage because she is focusing on establishing liability. However, the pleadings can affect the court's ultimate characterization of damages.

The second stage is to identify the components of the award and the methodology that the trial judge uses for each component. Typically, damage awards break down into general damages, special damages, punitive damages (if any), pre-judgment and post-judgment interest. Each of these components has different tax consequences.

The third stage is the actual calculation of the amount of damages. This step is most likely to cause subsequent disputes with the tax authorities. One needs a yardstick to calculate losses. The most obvious choice is earnings lost because of the wrong done. Thus, we determine the quantum of damages by capitalizing the stream of lost earnings resulting from the actionable event.

We determine the taxability of damages by ascertaining the nature of the settled interest. In certain cases, we crystallize an income stream of lost profits into a lump sum non-taxable capital amount. For example, we might award a lump sum to compensate for the loss of a rental property by looking at the monthly rental income that the property was producing for the landlord. The damages that substitute for the rental income would be taxable as income. If, however, the entire building is destroyed, the capitalized lump sum value of the potential rental cash stream is in the nature of capital. There is no universal formula for characterization in tax law.[1] In *London & Thames Haven Oil Wharves Ltd v Attwooll*, for example:

> Judges have from time to time been careful to say that no clear and comprehensive rule can be formulated, and no clear line of demarcation can be drawn, by reference to which it can be determined in every case whether the sum received should be regarded as a capital receipt or as a revenue receipt to be taken into account in arriving at the profit or gains of the recipient's trade. Each case must be considered on its own facts.[2]

---

1   See, for example, the 4:3 split decision of the Supreme Court of Canada in *Tsiaprailis v Canada*, 2005 SCC 8 [*Tsiaprailis*]. In Rulings Directorate document 2005—0121521E5, the CRA acknowledges that it will respect the *Tsiaprailis* decision distinguishing between settlement payments related to past and future benefits based on the *surrogatum* principle—future related liability will be on capital account, past liabilities will be on account of income.

2   [1966] 3 All ER 145 at 149, rev'd [1967] 2 All ER 124 (CA) [*London & Thames*].

Does the award compensate the plaintiff or punish the defendant? If the damage award compensates the plaintiff, what is the nature of the compensation?

C. LITIGATION CONSIDERATIONS

1) Where a settlement agreement does not clearly delineate and allocate damage amounts to different heads, the minister or the court may reasonably allocate the sums among the heads.[3]

2) The minister or the court may rely on the taxpayer's pleadings and briefs to determine the true nature of the damage payment.[4]

3) A court does not have to entertain inconsistent legal positions in the initial litigation and in a subsequent tax case. Thus, initial pleadings can lock in the taxpayer's position in a subsequent tax case.

4) Taxpayers should lead evidence to refute unfavourable assumptions that the minister makes regarding the characterization of damage payments. The evidence will usually be in the initial pleadings and/or minutes of settlement.

5) Settlement agreements bind the parties, but not the CRA. However, the CRA is more likely to accept a settlement that provides a reasonable allocation between the various heads of damages. A good faith settlement agreement that shows bona fide arm's length negotiations in an adversarial proceeding is persuasive.

6) The trial court's reasoning is crucial to the characterization of damages for tax purposes. A tax court is more likely to characterize a trial judgment for damages as taxable if it does not explicitly link the damages to non-taxable heads of the award.

7) A plaintiff should seek to have sums of damages identified in relation to specific non-taxable causes of action during the initial proceedings.[5]

8) A taxpayer who disagrees with his opponent's characterization of damages in litigation should object in writing at the earliest opportunity.[6]

---

3   *Tsiaprailis,* above note 1.
4   *Bourgault Industries Ltd v Canada,* 2006 TCC 449, aff'd 2007 FCA 373.
5   *Valley Equipment Ltd v Canada,* 2006 TCC 510, aff'd 2008 FCA 65.
6   *Boerson v Canada,* 2007 TCC 671.

D. BREACH OF CONTRACT

Damages for breach of contract are usually premised on the economic value of the bargain or "expectation interest": the principle of compensation. Thus, damages should restore the plaintiff to the financial position she would have enjoyed had the defendant performed the contract.[7] Exemplary or punitive damages in contract cases are the exception.[8]

1) The *Surrogatum* Principle

The general principle is that damages in lieu of receipts that would otherwise have been taxable to the taxpayer are taxable as income. Diplock LJ stated the principle as follows:

> Where, pursuant to a legal right, a trader receives from another person, compensation for the trader's failure to receive a sum of money which, if it had been received, would have been credited to the amount of profits (if any) arising in any year from the trade carried on by him at the time when the compensation is so received, the compensation

---

7 *Livingstone v Rawyards Coal Co* (1880), [1879–80] 5 App Cas 25 at 39 (HL), Lord Blackburn (damages represent "that sum of money which will put the party who has been injured, or who has suffered, in the same position as he would have been in if he had not sustained the wrong for which he is now getting his compensation or reparation"); see Harry Street, *Principles of the Law of Damages* (London: Sweet & Maxwell, 1962) at 3; *Yetton v Eastwoods Froy Ltd*, [1967] 1 WLR 104 at 115 (QB), Blain J; Anthony Ogus, *The Law of Damages* (London: Butterworths, 1973) at 17–21 and 283–38; *Victoria Laundry (Windsor) Ltd v Newman Industries Ltd*, [1949] 2 KB 528 at 539 (CA), Asquith LJ (damages for late delivery of boiler deemed foreseeable business losses); *Robinson v Harman* (1848), 1 Exch Rep 850 at 855, Parke B (tenant knew lessee did not have title to property leased; damages assessed at entire amount of loss notwithstanding); *Koufos v C Czarnikow Ltd*, [1969] 1 AC 350 at 400 (HL), Lord Morris (sugar cargo depreciated as market price dropped while ship dallying en route; ship owner expected to have contemplated such result); *British Westinghouse Electric and Manufacturing Co v Underground Electric Railways Co of London*, [1912] AC 673 at 689 (HL), Viscount Haldane LC (measure of damages where defective turbines replaced and replacement turbines achieved greater efficiency than the ones in question).

8 *Addis v Gramophone Co Ltd*, [1909] AC 488 (HL) (although discredited by wrongful dismissal, employee not able to claim compensation for injured feelings or lack of notice); *Dobson v Winton & Robbins Ltd*, [1959] SCR 775 (vendor suing on contract of sale of land entitled to specific performance or damages equal to decrease in price eventually received plus interest). See however *Jarvis v Swan Tours Ltd* (1972), [1973] 1 QB 233 (CA) (damages awarded against travel agent when plaintiff's holiday failed to meet advertised description).

is to be treated for income tax purposes in the same way as that sum of money would have been treated if it had been received instead of the compensation. The rule is applicable whatever the source of the legal right of the trader to recover the compensation. It may arise [1] from a primary obligation under a contract, such as a contract of insurance; [2] from a secondary obligation arising out of nonperformance of a contract, such as a right to damages, either liquidated, as under the demurrage clause in a charter party, or unliquidated; [3] from an obligation to pay damages for tort . . . ; [4] from a statutory obligation; [5] or in any other way in which legal obligations arise.[9]

Thus, one must determine the character of damages as taxable income or non-taxable capital based on the legal right settled and not upon the method that one uses to calculate the award. We usually compute damages by reference to the profit lost through non-performance of the contract.

However, the fact that one uses lost profits as the yardstick to calculate damages does not conclusively determine their taxability. For example, assume that A has a contract with B that will render him a profit of $10,000 per year for the next 15 years. If B does not perform the contract, A will lose $150,000 in profits. Ignoring problems of mitigation, etc., A would usually be entitled to the present value of that amount, which at a discount rate of 8 percent is $85,595. The taxability of the lump sum would depend upon the nature of the settled interest.

Compensation for total destruction of an entire business is a capital payment even if one determines the capitalized value by discounting the future lost profits of the business. Thus, taxable profits may transform into non-taxable capital receipts when we crystallize an income stream into a lump-sum capital amount.

---

9   *London & Thames*, above note 2 at 134 (CA). See also *Schwartz v Canada*, [1994] 2 CTC 99 (FCA), rev'd [1996] 1 SCR 254 (*surrogatum* principle also applies to employment contracts, whether anticipatory or otherwise). See also *Bueti v Canada*, 2007 FCA 294; *Eaton v Canada*, 2007 TCC 555, aff'd 2008 FCA 162 (*surrogatum* principle applies to compensation awarded by the Canadian Human Rights Tribunal in the form of lost wages); *Goff Construction Ltd v Canada*, 2008 TCC 322 (General Procedure), aff'd 2009 FCA 60 (*surrogatum* principle applies to settlement payments made to settle a negligence action. The *surrogatum* principle should not be applied in a vacuum.); *RCI Environnement Inc c Canada*, 2007 TCC 647 (*surrogatum* principle applies to compensation received for reduction of capital by surrender of a non-competition agreement. The TCC's decision has been appealed to the FCA); *Cloutier-Hunt v Canada*, 2007 TCC 345 (*surrogatum* applies to interest payments made pursuant to a Canadian Human Rights Tribunal award).

In *Bueti v Canada*,[10] for example, the Federal Court of Appeal relied on a lease termination agreement between the taxpayer and a tenant to determine whether the payment in relation thereto was taxable to the taxpayer. As the termination agreement did not refer to any payments as being on account of capital, the court held that the payment was taxable on account of lost income. The court relied on the termination agreement rather than the judgment or settlement agreement.

Similarly, in *Boerson v Canada*,[11] a settlement agreement between a debtor and creditor was silent as to allocation of the payment between interest and principal. The debtor treated the payment as interest and sent the creditor a T5 slip. The creditor's lawyer immediately sent a letter to the debtor indicating that the creditor was treating the payment as a non-taxable return of principal. The court applied debtor/creditor law to determine that the creditor had the right to make the allocation. The letter from the creditor's lawyer made the allocation clear.

a) Global Payments

A global payment covering several different heads of damages—for example, loss of earnings and payment on account of capital—should be broken down and distributed into its taxable and non-taxable segments. The allocation is easy where a court awards damages because of litigation and the judgment sets out the various heads of damages. An amount paid in settlement of a cause of action is more difficult to allocate and one should allocate amounts during negotiation of the settlement.

b) Capital Receipts

Payments on account of capital are not taxable. This is so whether the payment is on account of judicially assessed damages or pursuant to a settlement. For example, a payment to compensate the plaintiff for the destruction of the entire structure of her income-earning apparatus is a capital receipt.

c) Judgments

i) Non-Performance

Damages for non-performance of a service contract may be taxable as income or non-taxable capital receipts. The distinction depends upon the degree of dislocation of the business. If the rights and advantages that are lost on cancellation of a contract destroy or materially cripple the whole

---

10   *Bueti, ibid.*
11   *Boerson v Canada*, above note 6.

structure of the business, compensation secured in a judgment or settlement is for the loss of a capital asset and not a revenue receipt.[12]

> The sum received by a commercial firm as compensation for the loss sustained by the cancellation of a trading contract or the premature termination of an agency agreement may, in the recipient's hands, be regarded either as a capital receipt or as a trading receipt forming part of the trading profit. It may be difficult to formulate a general principle by reference to which in all cases the correct decision will be arrived at since in each case the question comes to be one of circumstance and degree.

In *Van Den Berghs Ltd v Clark*,[13] for example, the taxpayer entered into an agreement with its competitor that provided for, among other things, profit-sharing, joint arrangements, control of supply and restrictions on entering into other pooling arrangements. The parties terminated the contract following a dispute between them and the taxpayer received compensation for cancellation of its future rights under the contract. The compensation was on account of a non-taxable capital receipt because the cancelled agreements related to the whole structure of the profit-making apparatus and affected the whole conduct of the business.[14]

2) Employment Damages

a) Wrongful Dismissal

i) Nature of Claim
Damages for wrongful dismissal are in substance a payment in lieu of notice of termination. Thus, where a contract is terminable on notice,

---

12   *IRC v Fleming & Co (Machinery) Ltd* (1951), 33 Tax Cas 57 at 63 (Scot).

13   *Van Den Berghs Ltd v Clark*, [1935] AC 431 (HL). See also *Transocean Offshore Ltd v Canada*, 2004 TCC 454 (General Procedure), aff'd 2005 FCA 104, leave to appeal to SCC refused, [2005] SCCA No 235 (Canadian corporation paid non-resident corporation $40 million in damages to compensate for the repudiation of a contract. *Surrogatum* principle applies: damages taxable since paid in lieu of rent which would have been taxable under *Income Tax Act*, RSC 1985, c 1 (5th Supp) [*ITA*], Part XIII, para. 212(1)(d)).

14   *Van Den Berghs Ltd v Clark*, ibid at 442; see also *Barr, Crombie & Co v CIR* (1945), 26 Tax Cas 406 (Scot) at 411, Lord Normand LP:

> In the present case, virtually the whole assets of the appellant company consisted in this agreement. When the agreement was surrendered or abandoned practically nothing remained of the company's business. It was forced to reduce its staff and to transfer into other premises, and it really started a new trading life. Its trading existence as practised up to that time had ceased with the liquidation of the shipping company.

damages for lost earnings are restricted to the amount payable during the period of notice.[15]

ii) Statutory Rules

Damages for wrongful dismissal are "retiring allowances"[16] and taxable as "other income" and not as employment income,[17] whether the taxpayer receives the damages pursuant to a judgment or in settlement of litigation. In either case, the taxpayer must include the full amount of the payment in her income in the year that she receives it. As with employment income, however, the payer must report damage payments and withhold tax at the prescribed rates.[18] Paragraph 212(1)(j.1) requires a withholding tax of 25 percent of any amount paid to non-residents.

iii) Blended Payments

Where the damage award represents compensation for lost earnings during the period for which the employer should have given notice and also for mental suffering, one might argue that the mental suffering component is not taxable as a "retiring allowance" since it is not in respect of loss of office or employment.[19] The better view, however, is that the entire award is in respect of a loss of office or employment. The earnings component compensates for lack of notice and the mental anguish component compensates for the manner in which the employee lost his employment.[20] Thus, although one head of the award goes to time and the other goes to the method of termination, both arise from the same cause of action. They are in respect of improper loss of office or employment.[21]

---

15   *British Guiana Credit Corp v Da Silva*, [1965] 1 WLR 248 at 259 (PC).
16   *ITA*, above note 13, s 248(1) "retiring allowance."
17   *Ibid*, subpara 56(1)(a)(ii).
18   *Ibid*, para 153(1)(c).
19   *Specht v Canada*, [1975] CTC 126 (FCTD).
20   See, for example, the reasoning in *Canada v Savage*, [1983] 2 SCR 428.
21   *Young v MNR*, [1986] 2 CTC 2111 (TCC). As Linden J said in *Brown v Waterloo Regional Board of Commissioners of Police* (1982), 37 OR (2d) 277 at 288–89 (HCJ), rev'd in part (1983), 43 OR (2d) 113 (CA):

> The aim of aggravated damages is to "soothe a plaintiff whose feelings have been wounded by the quality of the defendant's misbehavior." They are a "balm for mental distress" which is brought about by the wrongful "character of the defendant's wrongdoing." There must be evidence of damage of this type to the plaintiff. Aggravated damages are not meant to punish the defendant. (See Cooper-Stephenson and Saunders, *Personal Injury Damages in Canada* (1981) at 55; *Robitaille et al. v. Vancouver Hockey Club Ltd.* (1979), 19 BCLR 158 at 183, Esson J.; varied 124 DLR (3d) 228, 16 CCLT 225, 30 BCLR 286 (C.A.)) In sum, though based on the quality of the defendant's conduct, aggravated damages are compensatory in purpose.

b) Signing Bonuses

An amount paid to an employee on account of a contractually agreed settlement (such as a "signing bonus") is taxable as income regardless of whether the employer makes the payment pursuant to a legal agreement entered into before, during, or immediately after employment.[22]

c) Arbitration Awards

Arbitration awards for breach of a collective agreement are taxable as employment income if the employer pays the amount as compensation for lost wages or other taxable benefits.[23] The gross amount of the award is income even if the employee receives only the net amount after deductions for income tax, CPP, EI, etc. Section 110.2 permits a taxpayer to spread a lump-sum award over the number of years to which the payment relates.

d) Employment Insurance Benefits [Paragraph 6(1)(f)]

Insurance payouts for disability benefits are often the product of settlements that combine past and future amounts. In *Tsiaprailis v Canada*,[24] for example, the insurer settled for a lump-sum payment of $105,000 in lieu of past benefits and 75 percent of the present value of the insured's future benefits, plus interest, costs and disbursements. The majority of the Supreme Court (per Charron J) applied the *surrogatum* principle to the "arrears portion" of the award.

The *surrogatum* principle provides that amounts on account, or in lieu, of otherwise taxable amounts are also taxable. Thus, the determinative issue is: what is the payout intended to replace? Employment and litigation counsel should factor in the tax consequences of negotiated settlements to determine the portion of the "in lieu" amount attributable to past taxable amounts and future non-taxable amounts.

Canadian law seems to have recognized the need for something like aggravated damages in contract law by awarding damages, not only for financial losses, but also for any mental suffering incurred by the plaintiff in appropriate cases. (See *Pilon v Peugeot Canada Ltd* (1980), 29 OR (2d) 711, 114 DLR (3d) 378, 12 BLR 227, for example.) The purpose behind allowing such damages is to compensate for hurt feelings, anxiety and stress caused by certain types of contractual breach, where they are in contemplation of the parties. Where the conduct of a defendant that violates a contract is particularly callous, the likelihood of mental suffering would be more foreseeable to him.

22   *ITA*, above note 13, subs 6(3); *Greiner v MNR*, [1984] CTC 92 (FCA).
23   *Vincent v MNR*, [1988] 2 CTC 2075 (TCC) (damage award restoring taxpayer to position he would have been in had wages set out in collective agreement for working on day of rest been paid); *Merrins v MNR*, [1995] 1 CTC 111 (FCTD) (amount received on settlement of grievance from lay-off is retiring allowance).
24   *Tsiaprailis*, above note 1.

3) Breach of Warranty of Authority

a) Nature of Claim

An agent is liable for breach of warranty of authority for misrepresenting his authority to a person who suffers damage by acting on the strength of the misrepresentation. The law imposes the obligation because "a person, professing to contract as an agent for another, impliedly, if not expressly, undertakes to or promises the person who enters into such contract, upon the faith of the professed agent being duly authorized, that the authority which he professes to have does in point of fact exist."[25]

b) Damage Principles

We determine damages for breach of warranty of authority according to the usual contract rule: compensate the injured party and restore the person to the position she would have enjoyed had the authority claimed by the professed agent truly vested in her.[26]

The taxation of damages for breach of warranty of authority also follows the usual *surrogatum* rule: damages that substitute for amounts that would have been taxable are taxable. Thus, here too, characterization for tax purposes depends upon the anterior determination as to the nature of the receipts that the damage award is intended to replace and not upon the method of calculating the amount.

In *Canada v Manley*,[27] for example, the taxpayer received damages of $587,400 in lieu of a finder's fee to which he would have been entitled if the professed agent with whom he was dealing had the authority that he claimed to have. Since the finder's fee would have constituted "profit" from an adventure in the nature of trade, the damages in lieu thereof were also taxable as income from a business.[28]

Thus, at least in contract and agency, tax law usually applies the *surrogatum* principle to damage awards. In both cases, it is easy to justify the principle because the law almost invariably relates the damages to an income-earning and profit-making process.

---

25 *Collen v Wright* (1857), 8 E & B 647 at 657 (Ex Ch).
26 See, for example, *Manley v Levy* (1974), [1975] 2 SCR 70 (action for commission payment turned on credibility of witnesses); *Re National Coffee Palace Co* (1883), 24 Ch D 367 (CA) (broker purchased shares from wrong company; purchaser repudiated; outstanding purchase price exacted from broker by liquidator).
27 *Canada v Manley*, [1985] 1 CTC 186 (FCA).
28 *Ibid* at 191.

4) Tort Damages

a) General Principles

Tort damages are more complex than damages in contract and agency. Tort damages are generally taxable based on the same principles that apply to other damages. Compensation for income receipts are taxable as income; compensation for capital receipts is exempt. However, there are important differences in principle for torts that involve damage to business or investments and torts that concern personal injuries or fatal accidents.

b) Business or Investments

Compensation for injury to business or property depends upon the nature of the hole that the damage award fills. Damages for injury to a business resulting in a loss of profits are taxable as income; compensation for destruction of an entire business is a non-taxable capital receipt. This rule applies regardless of the method that one uses to estimate the loss of profits. Lord Clyde illustrated the principle as follows:

> Suppose someone who chartered one of the Appellant's vessels breached the charter and exposed himself to a claim of damages . . . there could, I imagine, be no doubt that the damages recovered would properly enter the Appellant's profit and loss account for the year. The reason would be that the breach of the charter was an injury inflicted on the Appellant's trading, making (so to speak) a hole in the Appellant's profits, and damages recovered could not be reasonably or appropriately put . . . to any other purpose than to fill that hole. Suppose on the other hand, that one of the taxpayer's vessels was negligently run down and sunk by a vessel belonging to some other shipowner, and the Appellant recovered as damage the value of the sunken vessel, I imagine that there could be no doubt that the damages so recovered could not enter the Appellant's profit and loss account because the destruction of the vessel would be an injury inflicted, not on the Appellant's trading, but on the capital assets of the Appellant's trade, making (so to speak) a hole in them, and the damages could therefore . . . only be used to fill that hole.[29]

Here too, there is no bright-line test to determine when compensation for lost earnings constitutes income or the capitalized value of earnings. It is a question of fact in each case.

---

29   *Burmah SS Co Ltd v IRC* (1930), 16 Tax Cas 67 (Scot) at 71–72 (contract damages for late delivery of ship included in income as being on account of lost profits).

c) Depreciable Property
The Act includes compensation for damages to depreciable property in the taxpayer's income to the extent that he expends the money to repair the damage.[30] In effect, inclusion of the compensation in, and deduction of the repair costs from, income constitute a "wash transaction." This in effect means that the net tax effect is neutral.

d) Capital Property
Damages for total loss or destruction of capital property are "proceeds of disposition" and go towards determining the capital gain or loss on the disposition of the property.[31] Thus, total loss or destruction of property is equivalent to a sale of the property.

e) Eligible Capital Property
Compensation for damage to eligible capital property (for example, goodwill) is usually an eligible capital amount. If, however, the damage is so severe as to destroy the substrata of the taxpayer's business, any compensation for such damage is a capital receipt.[32]

f) Personal Injuries
Income tax considerations are also relevant to damages for torts involving personal injuries. Here, the underlying principles are more elusive. There are two points in time when we can consider the issue of taxability:

1) At trial when we determine liability and assess damages; and
2) When the plaintiff receives payment of the award.

i) Determination of Settlement
We do not take tax factors into account in determining the amount that a defendant pays to the plaintiff in a personal injury case.[33] The theory is that we are compensating the plaintiff for the loss of his earning capacity and not for lost earnings. It does not matter that we determine the value of the plaintiff's capacity by direct mathematical reference to the plaintiff's lost earnings. We arrive at this result by asserting our conclusion. Dickson J explained the rule as follows:

---

30 *ITA*, above note 13, para 12(1)(f).
31 *Ibid*, s 54 "proceeds of disposition"; subs 248(1) "disposition."
32 See Interpretation Bulletin IT-273R2 "Government Assistance" (13 September 2000).
33 *Andrews v Grand & Toy Alberta Ltd* (1978), 83 DLR (3d) 452 (SCC) [*Andrews*] (plaintiff awarded $69,981 for prospective loss of earnings determined by discounting at 7 percent the sum of $564 (monthly earnings) over a period of 30.81 years (estimated working life)).

. . . an award for prospective income should be calculated with no deduction for tax which might have been attracted had it been earned over the working life of the plaintiff. This results from the fact that it is earning capacity and not lost earnings that is the subject of compensation. For the same reason, no consideration should be taken of the amount by which the income from the award will be reduced by payment of taxes on the interest, dividends, or capital gain. A capital sum is appropriate to replace the lost capital asset of earning capacity. Tax on income is irrelevant either to decrease the sum for taxes the victim would have paid on income from his job, or to increase it for taxes he will now have to pay on income from the award.[34]

Thus, damage awards for personal injuries can be substantial where the tortfeasor renders a person who has a normal life expectancy incapable of working. In these circumstances, we capitalize the plaintiff's pretax earnings to determine the value of his lost earning capacity.

ii) *Taxation of Settlement*
A plaintiff is not taxable on damages for personal injuries. This is so regardless of whether she is paid special damages for loss of earnings up to trial or general damages for loss of prospective earnings.[35] Thus, the damages compensate for capacity even though one measures them by reference to earnings.[36] The *surrogatum* principle does not apply in respect of damages for personal injuries. Our courts are reluctant to penalize the plaintiff by reducing her award through tax discounts. Instead, they shift the higher cost to the defendant, which, in many cases, is an insurance company.

g) Fatal Accidents
The theory of tort damages is quite different, however, with respect to fatal accidents. Here, we typically determine damages under fatal accident statutes on a net of tax basis by capitalizing the deceased's net take-home pay. Justice De Grandpré explained this rule as follows:

---

34   *Andrews, ibid* at 474.

35   *Cirella v Canada*, [1978] CTC 1 (FCTD).

36   See *Graham v Baker* (1961), 106 CLR 340; see also *Groves v United Pacific Transport Pty Ltd*, [1965] Qd R 62 where Gibbs J observed at 65:

> Although it is usual and convenient in an action for damages for personal injuries to say that an amount is awarded for loss of wages or other earnings, the damages are really awarded for the impairment of the plaintiff's earning capacity that has resulted from his injuries. This is so even if an amount is separately quantified and described as special damages for loss of earnings up to the time of trial. Damages for personal injuries are not rightly described as damages for loss of income.

It seems to me that what the widow and the child have lost in this case is the support payments made by the deceased, support payments which could only come out of funds left after deducting the cost of maintaining the husband, including the amount of tax payable on his income. I cannot see how this pecuniary loss could be evaluated on any other basis than the take-home pay, that is the net pay after deductions on many items, including income tax.[37]

The above rule places the beneficiary in the same financial position that she would have enjoyed had the deceased lived and continued to earn income. It is, however, not possible to reconcile the rule with the theory in non-fatal personal injury settlements. The difference in results is perverse. Nevertheless, the capacity theory does not apply in the context of fatal accident cases.[38]

h) Investment Income

Interest and dividends on investments acquired with a damage award are generally taxable as income from property.[39] Similarly, taxable capital gains realized on property acquired with the proceeds of a damage award are also included in income. We make an exception, however, for personal injury awards paid to, or on behalf of, persons under the age of twenty-one. Interest and property income received from, or accrued on, the investment of a personal injury award is exempt from tax until the end of the taxation year in which the injured person attains the age of twenty-one. Taxable capital gains from dispositions of property acquired with the proceeds of damage awards or settlements are also exempt from tax if the injured person was less than twenty-one years of age at any time in the year.[40] Amounts earned from the reinvestment of exempt income are also exempt.[41]

---

37   *Keizer v Hanna*, [1978] 2 SCR 342 at 371; see also *Andrews*, above note 33 at 474 [DTC], Dickson J:

> In contrast with the situation in personal injury cases, awards under the Fatal Accident Acts should reflect tax considerations, since they are to compensate dependants for the loss of support payments made by the deceased. These support payments could only come out of take-home pay, and the payments from the award will only be received net of taxes.

38   *Keizer v Hanna*, *ibid* at 372, Grandpré J ("I cannot consider that the deceased here was a capital asset").

39   *ITA*, above note 13, paras 12(1)(c) and (k).

40   *Ibid*, para 81(1)(g.1). In his 21st year, the injured person can elect to recognize any accrued capital gains; see s 81(5).

41   *Ibid*, para 81(1)(g.2).

The purpose of this exception is to provide relief for young persons who have suffered personal injuries. It is unclear why the plight of young injured persons warrants preferential treatment over older persons in similar circumstances.

i) Interest on Special Damages
The law crystallizes tort damages as at the time of the tortious act. In determining the amount of damages, it is usual to break down the award into two components: (1) special damages up to the date of trial; and (2) general damages for future losses. The CRA excludes interest on special damages from income.[42]

FURTHER READINGS

BOWMAN, DGH. "Tax Treatment of Payments Made in the Context of Litigation" in The Law Society of Upper Canada, *Special Lectures 1986: Income Tax for the General Practitioner* (Don Mills, ON: De Boo, 1986) 96.

KRISHNA, VERN. "Characterization of Wrongful Dismissal Awards for Income Tax" (1977) 23 McGill LJ 43.

McDONNELL, THOMAS E. "Deductibility of Legal Expenses Incurred to Recover Damages for Wrongful Dismissal" [Case Comment *Lyonde v MNR*, [1988] 2 CTC 2032 (TCC)] (1988) 36 Can Tax J 697.

MORGAN, MA. "Compensatory Payments Made in a Litigation Context: Tax Treatment to the Recipient" in The Law Society of Upper Canada, *Special Lectures 1986: Income Tax for the General Practitioner* (Don Mills, ON: De Boo, 1986) 109.

---

42 See Interpretation Bulletin IT-365R2, "Damages, Settlements and Similar Receipts" (8 May 1987).

FROM NET INCOME TO TAXABLE INCOME

A. GENERAL COMMENT

Up to this point, we have looked at the rules for calculating net income. Now, we look at the rules that determine "taxable income," which is the base to which we apply tax rates.[1] In the next chapter we will review the computation of the tax payable on taxable income.

Taxpayers are taxable on their taxable income. Canadian residents are taxable on their worldwide taxable income for the year.[2] Subject to treaty provisions, non-residents are taxable only on their Canadian source taxable income during a taxation year.[3] The tax payable by a taxpayer is equal to his tax base multiplied by the appropriate tax rates.

Taxable income is net income, as adjusted for social policy, and economic and equity considerations. Thus, taxable income moves us a further step away from the concept of economic net income.

Equally important, we use the concept of taxable income to ameliorate the adverse effects of calculating taxes on a calendar year or fifty-two week basis by permitting for carryover of losses.

There are two controversial issues in designing an appropriate structure to determine the taxable base:

---

1   *Income Tax Act*, RSC 1985, c 1 (5th Supp) [*ITA*], subs 2(2); Div C (ss. 110–14.2).
2   *Ibid*, subs 2(1).
3   *Ibid*, subs 2(3). A non-resident's taxable income is determined by reference to the rules in Div D (ss 115–16).

1) What relief, if any, should we provide for individual and personal circumstances?
2) Should the relief take the form of a deduction from income or a credit against taxes payable?

1) "Taxable Income"

"Taxable income" is the mathematical measure of the taxable base. A resident's "taxable income" is her net income plus or minus the adjustments in Division C of the *Income Tax Act*.

We saw earlier that income for tax purposes is a taxpayer's net realized economic gains from a source recognized in law. However, income, which for tax purposes represents the net realized increment in wealth, is not always the best measure of a taxpayer's ability to pay tax. We now look at some of the adjustments that the tax system makes for individual circumstances. Also, we see, once again, how the system affects behaviour by providing incentives for particular activities — for example, charitable giving.

Taxable income is a fairer measure of a taxpayer's ability to pay tax than net income. In the case of individuals, for example, it is easy to see that taxpayers who have the same amount of net realized income may not have equal capacity to pay tax. For example, consider two individuals, each of whom earns $50,000: an unmarried person with no dependants and a married person with a family of six, one of whom is seriously ill and requires expensive care. The individuals have different capacity to pay tax.

Should we allow the individual with substantial financial responsibilities a measure of tax relief to ease the burden of his responsibilities? Should the amount of relief be related to his income, or should it be a blanket amount, regardless of the particular circumstances? If relief is income-tested, should we test it by reference to the individual's income or her family income? How do we determine "family" for the purposes of income testing? These are difficult and, sometimes, controversial questions for which we do not have absolute answers. Nevertheless, they are questions that require rigorous analysis.

2) Deduction or Credit?

The first policy issue is whether we should provide relief for persons in different financial circumstances through tax deductions or tax credits.

A tax deduction is a reduction of income in computing taxable income. The net saving from a deduction is the amount deducted, multiplied by the taxpayer's marginal tax rate. For example, a deduction of $1,000 reduces tax by $450 if the taxpayer's marginal rate is 45 percent, and by $300 if his rate is 30 percent. Thus, the higher the marginal tax rate, the more valuable the deduction to the individual and the greater the revenue loss to the public treasury. Deductions provide an accurate measure in determining an individual's net increment to wealth.

A tax credit also reduces the tax that would otherwise be payable by the taxpayer. However, the savings resulting from a tax credit are fixed, regardless of the taxpayer's marginal tax rate. For example, a tax credit of $500 reduces tax by that amount, no matter whether the taxpayer's marginal tax rate is 45 percent or 30 percent. Hence, tax credits have an equal distributive impact. However, unless refundable, a tax credit is of value only to those taxpayers who would otherwise have to pay tax. A tax credit does not assist a taxpayer who does not have any tax payable. We use tax credits to accommodate personal circumstances that might affect a taxpayer's ability to pay tax.

We subtract a tax credit directly from the amount of tax payable, rather than from income. Thus, each individual achieves the same saving regardless of his income level or marginal tax rate. For example, the basic tax credit applies to all individuals regardless of their income level. Hence, a person earning $100,000 per year receives exactly the same basic credit as a person earning $30,000 per year.

Governments can also use "refundable" tax credits for the purpose of furthering a particular tax policy objective. This type of tax credit will entitle the taxpayer to a tax credit even where no taxes are payable. Hence, an individual could receive money even though he paid no tax. We use refundable credits to implement income redistribution social policies.

B. CHARITABLE DONATIONS

1) General Comment

The tax system has financial incentives for taxpayers—particularly high-income taxpayers—who contribute to charitable, philanthropic and public service organizations. These incentives encourage private financial support of philanthropic activities considered beneficial to society. We justify the incentives based on social policy. Since all economic rules affect behaviour, charitable deductions and credits are vulnerable to misuse. They are a substantial cost to the federal and provincial treasuries, and, therefore, require strict control.

The nature and extent of the incentives depend upon two principal criteria: (1) the type of taxpayer, and (2) the amount of the donation.

2) Individuals

An individual can claim a tax credit for charitable donations. The rate at which she may claim the credit depends upon the amount donated. The credits are linked to the lowest and highest marginal tax brackets: 15 percent credit on the first $200 of gifts; 29 percent on any excess to a maximum of 75 percent of the individual's net income in the year.[4] For a high-rate taxpayer, the combined provincial-federal rate is equivalent to approximately 45 percent.

3) Corporations

A corporation can deduct its charitable donations. Gifts to charitable (and certain other organizations) are deductible by a corporation up to an annual maximum of 75 percent of its income for the year.[5] Donations in excess of 75 percent of net income may be carried forward for five years and deducted to the extent that they were not deducted in a previous year.

There are two substantive criteria for determining deductibility of a donation:

1) Is the contribution a gift? and
2) Was the gift to a registered charity or other public service organization?

a) What Constitutes a Gift?

The common law does not define "gift" in precise terms. As Deane J said:

> The word "gift" . . . is intended to bear the meaning which it bears as a matter of ordinary language. . . . [I]t is not to be assumed that its ambit can properly be defined, with a lawyer's or logician's precision, by reference to a number of unqualified propositions or tests.[6]

At common law, a "gift"[7] is a voluntary and gratuitous transfer of property from one person to another; it may be conditional but, once

---

4   *Ibid*, subs 118.1(3).
5   *Ibid*, para 110.1(1)(a).
6   *Leary v Federal Commissioner of Taxation* (1980), 32 ALR 221 at 241 (FCA).
7   "Gift" is defined in *Halsbury's Laws of England*, 4th ed, vol 20, §1 as follows:

> A gift *inter vivos* may be defined shortly as the transfer of any property from one person to another gratuitously while the donor is alive and not in expectation of death . . . .

the condition is satisfied, it is not revocable. A gift requires a transfer:[8]

- By way of benefaction;[9]
- Without exchange for material reward or advantage; and
- Without contractual obligation.

Thus, the essence of a gift is that it is a transfer without *quid pro quo*, a contribution motivated by detached and disinterested generosity that does not confer monetary advantage on the donor.[10]

Subsection 248(30) modifies the common law meaning of "gift" for tax purposes to include donations that confer an advantage[11] on the donor, provided that the value of the donated property exceeds the value of the advantage that the donor receives. Thus, a person does not make a gift if he receives valuable consideration equal to his "donation."[12] For

---

In *Black's Law Dictionary*, 4th ed (St Paul, MN: West, 1968), "gift" is defined as:

[a]   voluntary transfer of personal property without consideration.
and:
[b]   parting by owner with property without pecuniary consideration . . . .

The *Shorter Oxford Dictionary* defines "giving" as:

. . . [a] transfer of property in a thing, voluntarily and without any valuable consideration . . . .

See also *Commissioner of Taxation of the Commonwealth v McPhail* (1968), 41 ALJR 346 at 348 (HCA), where Owen J said:

. . . but it is, I think, clear that to constitute a "gift," it must appear that the property transferred was transferred voluntarily and not as the result of a contractual obligation to transfer it and that no advantage of a material character was received by the transferor by way of return . . . .

This definition was approved by the Federal Court in *Canada v Zandstra*, [1974] CTC 503 (FCTD).

8   *Leary v Federal Commissioner of Taxation*, above note 6 at 243 (quoted with approval by the Federal Court of Appeal in *MNR v McBurney*, [1985] 2 CTC 214 (FCA), leave to appeal to SCC refused (1986), 65 NR 320n (SCC)).
9   *Collector of Imposts (Vic) v Cuming Campbell Investment Pty Ltd* (1940), 63 CLR 619 at 642 (HCA), Dixon J (transfer by way of benefaction being "essential idea" of gift). Some courts speak of a "detached and disinterested generosity"; see, for example, *Commissioner v LoBue*, 351 US 243 at 246 (1956) (gift of affection, respect, admiration, charity or like impulses); *Robertson v US*, 343 US 711 at 714 (1952); *Commissioner v Duberstein*, 363 US 278 at 285 (1960); see also *Savoy Overseers v Art Union of London*, [1896] AC 296 at 308 and 312 (HL), Lord McNaghten (charitable donation made where donor not looking "for any return in the shape of direct personal advantage"); *Collector of Imposts (Vic) v Cuming Campbell Investments Pty Ltd*, ibid at 641.
10   *Tite v MNR*, [1986] 2 CTC 2343 (TCC).
11   *ITA*, above note 1, para 248(31)(a).
12   *Tite v MNR*, above note 10 (taxpayer's claim for charitable donation denied where evidence demonstrated that payment to acquire print equal to value of work).

example, payment for a dinner organized by a charity may involve both charitable and non-charitable elements.[13] Regardless of the form and documentation of the arrangements, it is the substance of the contribution that determines whether the taxpayer makes a gift or a disguised payment for services. There is, however, no litmus paper test: one looks to the substance of the contribution.[14]

Although a payment pursuant to a contractual obligation to the donee is not a gift, the absence of a contractual obligation does not necessarily imply that the payment is a gift. Also, a contractual obligation between the donor and a third party does not necessarily deprive a payment of its character as a gift. For example, a contract between A and B that each will contribute an equal amount to a registered charity does not *per se* disqualify their contributions as gifts.

b) Blended Payments

Blended contributions should be broken down into their component parts. For example, the admission price to a charity event may cover the costs of goods and services (such as food and entertainment) and a premium intended as a gift.[15] Similarly, a global payment to a charity that offers both religious and secular education might comprise a payment for tuition fees and a gift for charitable purposes. The tuition component is a personal expenditure; the gift for charitable purposes is deductible as a donation. The allocation between the deductible and the non-deductible portions should be reasonable.[16]

c) Eligible Organizations

The following organizations are eligible for donations, subject to the extent of the annual maximum limit:[17]

---

13 *Canada v Burns*, [1988] 1 CTC 201 (FCTD) (taxpayer's payments to amateur athletic association not "gifts" because taxpayer expected and received benefit in return for payments).

14 See, for example, *Commissioner v Duberstein*, above note 9 at 289, Brennan J:

> Decision of the issue presented in these cases must be based ultimately on the application of the fact-finding tribunal's experience with the mainsprings of human conduct to the totality of the facts of each case. The non-technical nature of the statutory standard, the close relationship of it to the data of practical human experience, and the multiplicity of relevant factual elements, with their various combinations, creating the necessity of ascribing the proper force to each, confirm us in our conclusion that primary weight in this area must be given to the conclusions of the trier of fact.

15 *Aspinall v MNR*, [1970] Tax ABC 1073.

16 *MNR v McBurney*, above note 8.

17 *ITA*, above note 1, para 110.1(1)(a).

- Registered charities;
- Registered Canadian amateur athletic associations that promote amateur sports on a national basis;
- Resident housing corporations that provide low-cost housing accommodations for the aged;
- Canadian municipalities;
- The United Nations and its agencies;
- Prescribed foreign universities that admit Canadian students;[18] and
- Certain foreign charitable organizations to which the federal government has contributed in the year or in the preceding year.

The deduction is available only if the taxpayer provides receipts that disclose prescribed information.[19]

d) Charities

A "charity" can be either a charitable organization or charitable foundation.[20] A "charitable organization" is one that devotes all its resources to charitable activities that it carries on itself.[21] A "charitable foundation" is a trust or corporation that operates exclusively for charitable purposes.[22]

Although the definition of "charitable organization" in subsection 149.1(1) focuses on "activities," it is really the purpose of the activities that determines charitable status.[23]

An organization qualifies as a charity under section 149.1 of the *Income Tax Act* if:[24]

1) Its purposes are charitable, and the purposes define the scope of the activities that it engages in, and
2) It devotes all of its resources to these activities.[25]

Income Tax Special Purposes Commissioners v Pemsel (*Pemsel*)[26] lists four types of trusts:

---

18   *Income Tax Regulations*, CRC, c 945, s 3503.
19   *Ibid*, s 3501 and subs 110.2(2).
20   *ITA*, above note 1, subs 149.1(1) "charity."
21   *Ibid*, subs 149.1(1) "charitable organization."
22   *Ibid*, "charitable foundation."
23   *AYSA Amateur Youth Soccer Association v Canada (Revenue Agency)*, 2007 SCC 42.
24   *Vancouver Society of Immigrant and Visible Minority Women v Canada (MNR)*, [1999] 1 SCR 10.
25   Unless the organization falls within the specific exemptions of *ITA*, above note 1, subss 149.1(6.1) & (6.2).
26   *Income Tax Special Purposes Commissioners v Pemsel*, [1891] AC 531 at 583 (HL). These categories are well accepted in Canadian law; see *Towle Estate v MNR*, [1967] SCR 133 at 141.

1) Trusts for the relief of poverty;
2) Trusts for the advancement of education;
3) Trusts for the advancement of religion; and
4) Trusts for other purposes beneficial to the community.

In addition, the organization must also have a charitable purpose that is within "the spirit and intendment" of the preamble to the *Charitable Uses Act*, 1601.[27]

At first blush, the fourth division appears to be a broad and inclusive category for all sorts of beneficent activities. In fact, it is not easy to qualify under this division because of the requirement that the charitable purpose must also meet the spirit and intendment of the *Charitable Uses Act*, a statute enacted in 1601. Stated in modern English, but reflecting social perceptions of a bygone era, the statute's list of charitable purposes is as follows:[28]

> The relief of aged, impotent, and poor people; the maintenance of sick and maimed soldiers and mariners, schools of learning, free schools, and scholars in universities; the repair of bridges, ports, havens, causeways, churches, seabanks, and highways; the education and preferment of orphans; the relief, stock, or maintenance of houses of correction; marriage of poor maids; supportation, aid, and help of young tradesmen, handicraftsmen, and persons decayed; the relief or redemption of prisoners or captives; and the aid or ease of any poor inhabitants concerning payment of fifteens, setting out of soldiers, and other taxes.

Only activities that are beneficial to the community *and* that come within the spirit and intendment of the above preamble are recognized as "charitable."[29]

The CRA applies the tests rigidly, without accommodation or adaptation to the nuances of modern Canadian society and oblivious to Lord Wilberforce's admonition that "the law of charity is a moving subject."[30]

---

27   (UK), 43 Eliz I, c 4.
28   Justice Slade in *McGovern v AG*, [1982] Ch 321 at 332.
29   See, for example, *National Anti-Vivisection Society v IRC*, [1948] AC 31 (HL) (main object political; unclear whether public benefit advanced if such scientific research curtailed); *Re Strakosch*, [1949] Ch 529 (CA) (gift must be beneficial to community in way law regards as charitable).
30   *Scottish Burial Reform and Cremation Society Ltd v Glasgow Corporation*, [1968] AC 138 at 154 (HL).

The preamble should not be read literally, but in the context of contemporary society.[31] As Lord Upjohn put it:

> This so-called fourth class is incapable of further definition and can to-day hardly be regarded as more than a portmanteau to receive those objects which enlightened opinion would regard as qualifying for consideration under the second heading.[32]

It is clear, however, that despite some relaxation of the rules for registration, the basic focus remains: are the activities of a public character or are they "member-oriented"?[33]

Vancouver Society of Immigrant and Visible Minority Women v MNR[34] sets out the test to assess whether an organization's purposes are beneficial in a way the law regards as charitable. In assessing an organization's purposes, one must:

1) Consider the trend of decisions that establish certain objects as charitable under this heading, and determine whether, by reasonable extension or analogy, the facts fit within the earlier decisions;[35]
2) Examine certain accepted anomalies to see whether they fairly cover the objects under consideration; and
3) Ask whether, consistent with the declared objects, the income and property in question can be applied for purposes clearly falling outside the scope of charity.

Under the *Pemsel* test, an organization is not "charitable" if its activities are illegal or contrary to public policy. However, there must be a definite and somehow officially declared and implemented policy for an activity to be considered "contrary to public policy." An entity should not be denied charitable status merely because its objects are politically controversial.[36]

---

31   See, for example, *Native Communications Society of British Columbia v MNR*, [1986] 2 CTC 170 (FCA); *Vancouver Regional FreeNet Assn v Canada (MNR)*, [1996] 3 FC 880 (CA) (non-profit network establishing a free community computer that would provide free access to information on the Internet granted charitable organization status).

32   *Scottish Burial Reform and Cremation Society Ltd v Glasgow Corporation*, above note 30 at 150.

33   *Seventh Division, Pacific Northwest Region, National Model Railroad Association v MNR*, [1989] 1 CTC 300 (FCA).

34   *Vancouver Society of Immigrant and Visible Minority Women v MNR*, above note 24.

35   See also *Vancouver Regional FreeNet Assn v Canada (MNR)*, above note 31 (the provision of free access to information and to a means of communication was a type of purpose similar to those that had been held to be charitable in previous caselaw).

36   *Everywoman's Health Care Society v MNR* (1991), [1992] 2 FC 52 (CA) (abortion counselling and medical services registered as a charity). See also *Canadian Magen*

i)   Tax-Exempt Status

A registered charity is a tax-exempt organization. The tax subsidy in respect of registered charities is double-barrelled: the charity is tax-exempt and its benefactors obtain a tax deduction or credit.

The tax exemption is justifiable on the basis that it encourages private organizations to engage in philanthropic activities that would otherwise fall to the public sector. The subsidy is expensive, however, and the Act has stringent registration and annual accounting requirements.

ii)   Political Activities

An organization is not a charity if its main or principal object is political.[37] For example, tenants and ratepayer groups that merely lobby governments to act in support of societal change do not qualify as charitable organizations if their primary focus is political activity.[38] Similarly, anti-pornography groups that are, in effect, "political" organizations lobbying for legislative change under the guise of education do not qualify as charitable organizations.[39]

However, charities that engage in non-partisan political activities that are only "ancillary and incidental" to their charitable purposes or activities can maintain registration as tax-exempt organizations.[40] For example, a charity can use mass mailings or media campaigns to influence public opinion or government policy. More active involvement in partisan political activities, however, endangers a charity's registration.[41]

The following activities are "political":[42]

David Adom for Israel v Canada (MNR), 2002 FCA 323 (medical and ambulance services offered in occupied territory not registered as a charity on other grounds).

37   Re Patriotic Acre Fund, [1951] 2 DLR 624 at 633 (Sask CA): "[T]he Court has no means of judging whether a proposed change in the law will or will not be for the public benefit and therefore cannot say that a gift to secure the change is a charitable gift."

38   NDG Neighbourhood Association v MNR, [1988] 2 CTC 14 (FCA) (tenants' association denied registration as charity).

39   Positive Action Against Pornography v MNR, [1988] 1 CTC 232 (FCA).

40   ITA, above note 1, subs 149.1(6.1).

41   Ibid, para 149.1(6.1)(c); Action des Chrétiens pour l'Abolition de la Torture (L'ACAT) c Canada, 2002 FCA 499, leave to appeal to SCC refused, 2003 CSCR no 73 (SCC) (exercise of moral pressure on governments held to be a political rather than charitable purpose); Alliance for Life v MNR, [1999] 3 CTC 1 (FCA) (pro-life organization did not qualify for exemption under subs 149.1(6.2) because materials were political and not ancillary and incidental to their charitable activities); Human Life International in Canada Inc v Canada (MNR), [1998] 3 FC 202 (CA), leave to appeal to SCC refused, [1998] SCCA No 246 (minister allowed to revoke organization's charitable status as the organization was primarily concerned with swaying public opinion).

42   McGovern v AG, above note 28.

- The furthering of the interests of a particular political party;
- The procuring of changes to the laws of the country;
- The procuring of changes to the laws of a foreign country;
- The procuring of a reversal of government policy or of particular decisions of governmental authorities in the country; or
- The procuring of a reversal of government policy or of particular decisions of governmental authorities in a foreign country.

4) Valuation

a) Fair Market Value

Once we determine that a contribution to an eligible organization qualifies as a gift, the next task is to attach a value to it. We generally value gifts at their fair market value at the time that the donor transfers the property to the donee. The fair market value of an asset is its exchange value.[43] Where there is a regular and efficient market for the asset (for example, widely-held shares on a stock exchange), its trading price is probably the best, though not necessarily the only, measure of its fair market value.[44] Where there is no efficient market for the asset, it is necessary to determine fair market value through other criteria, such as, earnings value, liquidation value, replacement value, etc.

The "fair market value" of an asset for tax purposes is the highest price that it "might reasonably be expected to bring if sold by the owner in the normal method applicable to the asset in question, in the ordinary course of business in a market not exposed to any undue stresses, and composed of willing buyers and sellers dealing at arm's length and under no compulsion to buy or sell."[45] Thus, the focus of fair market value is on an efficient, normal and knowledgeable market.

b) Expert Evidence

As noted above, the best and usually most accurate measure of a property's value is its fair market value at the time that the taxpayer donates it to the charity. We can determine fair market value with precision if there is an active and open market for the property. For example, one can determine the value of publicly traded shares by reference to the trading price of a share at a particular time on a particular day.

Where there is no active market, however, one must rely upon the opinion of experts to determine the value of the property. A non-arm's

---

43   See, generally, *Mann Estate v British Columbia (Minister of Finance)*, [1972] 5 WWR 23 (BCSC), aff'd [1973] 4 WWR 223 (BCCA), aff'd [1974] 2 WWR 574 (SCC).
44   *Ibid* at 27 (BCSC).
45   *Henderson v MNR*, [1973] CTC 636 at 644 (FCTD), aff'd [1975] CTC 485 (FCA).

length expert opinion can be a reliable guide to value, but only if the expert is truly independent.

Valuation is a sophisticated art that calls for the expertise and judgment of people trained in its discipline. It is also an art that is vulnerable to manipulation and one should consider carefully the expert testimony of professional valuators. Expert evidence should, in Lord Wilberforce's words, "be, and should be seen to be, the independent product of the expert, uninfluenced as to form or content by the exigencies of litigation."[46] Unfortunately, some experts have a propensity for moulding their opinions to identify with, and accommodate, their client's positions. To quote Adrian Keane in the *Modern Law of Evidence*:

> [T]he danger is particularly acute in the case of opinions expressed by expert witnesses, of whom it has been said, not without some sarcasm, "it is quite often surprising to see with what facility and to what extent, their views can be made to correspond with the wishes or the interests of the parties who call them."[47]

Similarly, Professor Bonbright:

> few, if any, appraisers can take an unbiased position when they take the witness stand under an engagement from one of the contesting parties . . . a court must choose between the tremendous errors implicit in a capitalization of audited reported earnings, and the tremendous errors implicit in a capitalization of prejudiced prophecies.[48]

C. LOSSES

1) General Comment

We measure income for a period of time—a fiscal year, which is the calendar year for individuals and partnerships and any fifty-three-week period for corporations.

The fiscal year as the unit of time to measure income is inherently problematic, particularly for taxpayers whose incomes fluctuate. For example, a taxpayer who earns income in one year and suffers an equal loss in the next faces financial hardship as a result of paying tax in the first year without any relief in the second. Consider the following:

---

46   *Whitehouse v Jordan*, [1981] 1 WLR 246 at 256–57 (HL).
47   Adrian Keane, *Modern Law of Evidence* (Abingdon, UK: Professional Books, 1985) at 377.
48   James C Bonbright, *Valuation of Property* (New York: McGraw-Hill, 1937) vol. 1 at 251.

Taxpayer	Year 1	Year 2	Year 3	Total
A	$120,000	$(40,000)	$(80,000)	NIL
B	(80,000)	120,000	(40,000)	NIL
C	(40,000)	(80,000)	120,000	NIL

The economic well-being of all three taxpayers is identical over the three-year span. There are, however, important differences if we tax the three taxpayers annually. Taxpayer A must pay tax on income of $120,000 in Year 1, Taxpayer B in Year 2, and Taxpayer C in Year 3. We cannot accurately measure a taxpayer's income until the end of his economic existence. On the other hand, a tax system cannot wait until he dies, or in the case of a business enterprise, until it ceases.

Thus, without provisions to allow for the shifting of losses from one tax year to another, taxpayers could end up paying tax on illusory income. The *Income Tax Act* allows taxpayers to offset losses from one source against income from other sources in the same year.[49] There are, however, several restrictions. For example, capital losses may be offset only against capital gains; listed personal property losses may be used only against listed personal property gains.[50] Losses from a decline in value of household durables (for example, cars, furniture) are personal losses, which the Act disallows.[51] Where a taxpayer does not use her losses in the year in which they occur, she may, within certain limits, use them to offset income in other years.[52]

2) Types of Losses

The complexity of the tax loss rules is attributable to three factors. First, economic losses are forced to fit into the annual accounting requirement. Second, in the absence of consolidated corporate reporting, we must confine losses within corporate entities and restrict any spillover between corporations within an economic group. Third, given the compartmentalized structure of the Act, the characterization of losses is as important as the characterization of income. There are different rules for each type of loss. Some losses (such as non-capital losses) are more valuable to a taxpayer than others (such as capital losses) because the

---

49   *ITA*, above note 1, s 3.
50   *Ibid*, para 3(b); subs 41(2).
51   *Ibid*, subpara 40(2)(g)(iii).
52   *Burleigh v Canada*, 2004 TCC 197 (General Procedure) (losses can be carried forward/back whether or not they were reported in an income tax return in the year they were incurred).

entire loss may be written off against all sources of income. But capital losses do not expire and have a longer shelf life than non-capital losses.

Thus, the first step in determining the tax treatment of a loss is to determine its nature and character. There are five major categories of losses:

1) Non-capital losses,
2) Capital losses,
3) Restricted farm losses,
4) Farm losses, or
5) Limited partnership losses.

We subdivide capital losses into four subcategories:

1) General,
2) Personal-use property losses,
3) Listed personal property losses, and
4) Business investment losses.

Generally, a taxpayer's loss from a source first offsets other sources of income for the purpose of calculating income for the current year. Losses that we cannot use in the current year to reduce income from other sources may be carried back or forward to other years and deducted in computing the taxpayer's taxable income for those years. Thus, current year losses are deductible in the computation of net income. Losses carried over to other years (whether prior or subsequent) are deductible only in the computation of taxable income.

a) Non-Capital Losses

A non-capital loss (which we loosely refer to as a "business loss") is deductible from income in any of the three taxation years preceding, and the twenty taxation years following, the year in which we incur the loss.[53] Thus, we can use non-capital losses to offset income over a period of twenty-four years: the year of the loss, three years prior, and twenty years subsequent, to the loss.

We initially apply a taxpayer's losses from non-capital sources against income in the current year. The residue less any portion that is a farm loss becomes the taxpayer's non-capital loss. There are special rules for farm losses.[54]

A taxpayer cannot increase his non-capital loss by the deductions permitted under subdivision e of Division B (sections 60–66.8). These deductions may, however, reduce other income in the year. For example,

---

53   *ITA*, above note 1, para 111(1)(a).
54   *Ibid*, para 111(1)(d).

an individual who suffers a business loss in a particular year cannot increase his loss carryforward by including in the non-capital loss any amounts paid as support. If, however, the individual was also employed in the same year, he could use any support payments to reduce or eliminate his employment income and carry forward the business loss.

A taxpayer must deduct his non-capital losses in the order in which the taxpayer incurs them.[55] A loss is generally deductible only by the taxpayer who incurs it. For example, where an individual incurs a non-capital loss, the loss cannot be claimed by another taxpayer to whom he sells the business. Similarly, a sole proprietor cannot transfer the losses of the proprietorship on selling his business to a corporation. This is so even if the individual owns all of the corporation's shares.

Since a corporation is a legal entity, any losses that it incurs belong to it. It is only in very rare circumstances that another corporation can use its losses. Note, however, that even though a corporation owns its losses, a change of control of the corporation may extinguish its non-capital losses.[56]

b) Net Capital Losses

A taxpayer may offset his allowable capital losses against taxable capital gains. However, listed personal property losses may only offset gains on listed personal property.[57]

A taxpayer's "net capital loss" is made up of:[58]

- The excess of its allowable capital losses over taxable capital gains, and
- Any unutilized allowable business investment losses previously included in its non-capital losses in respect of which the carryover period expired in the year.

Net capital losses have an unlimited shelf life. They may also be carried back three years. However, net capital losses may be applied only against capital gains in other years.[59]

---

55 *Ibid*, subpara 111(3)(b)(i).
56 *Ibid*, subs 111(5).
57 *Ibid*, para 3(b).
58 *Ibid*, subs 111(8) "net capital loss." The taxpayer's net capital loss is also reduced as required by s 80 (debt forgiveness). Capital losses that also qualify as "allowable business investment losses" are initially treated as non-capital losses and may be written off against income from any source. If they cannot be used as non-capital losses within the carryforward period, they are added to net capital losses and may be carried forward indefinitely.
59 *Ibid*, para 111(1)(b).

c) Farm Losses

There are three types of farm losses:

1) Business farm losses;
2) Restricted farm losses; and
3) Hobby farm losses.

The Act controls farming losses strictly because of the propensity of "gentlemen farmers" to offset such losses against their professional income. Business farm losses are subject to the rules generally applicable to business losses.[60]

A taxpayer's "farm loss" is the excess of her losses from farming and fishing over any income from these sources.[61] A taxpayer may carry back her farm losses three years and forward twenty years and apply the losses against income from any source.[62]

A "restricted farm loss" is a farming loss suffered by a taxpayer who carries on business with an expectation of profit, but whose *chief* source of income is neither farming nor a combination of farming and some other source of income.[63]

A taxpayer cannot deduct more than $8,750 in any year for such "farming losses."[64] Any loss in excess of this limit becomes the taxpayer's "restricted farm loss" for the year. The taxpayer can carry forward her restricted farm loss to future years.[65]

As with business losses, a restricted farm loss may be carried back three years and forward twenty years.[66] The amount of a restricted farm

---

60   *Ibid*, para 111(1)(d) and subs 111(8) "farm loss"; *Brown v Canada*, [1975] CTC 611 (FCTD). In both *Kroeker v Canada*, 2002 FCA 392, and *Taylor v Canada*, 2002 FCA 425 farming losses were fully deductible even though taxpayers had full time jobs; sufficient time, labour and capital were devoted to farm.

61   *ITA, ibid*, subs 111(8) "farm loss." For the meaning of "farm loss," see *Moldowan v Canada*, [1978] 1 SCR 480 (three classes of farmers; tests for "chief source of income"); *Graham v Canada*, [1983] CTC 370 (FCTD), aff'd [1985] 1 CTC 380 (FCA), leave to appeal to SCC refused (1985), 62 NR 103n (SCC) (although Hydro employee, taxpayer's main preoccupation farming); *Hadley v Canada*, [1985] 1 CTC 62 (FCTD) (sizable investment in farming made employment more a source of investment finance; losses allowed); *Bender v MNR*, [1986] 1 CTC 2437 (TCC) (four-pronged test for deductibility of farm losses); *Croutch v MNR*, [1986] 2 CTC 246 (FCTD) (no reasonable expectation of profit from horse breeding operation).

62   *ITA, ibid*, para 111(1)(d).

63   *Moldowan v Canada*, above note 61.

64   *ITA*, above note 1, subs 31(1).

65   *Ibid*, subs 31(1.1).

66   *Ibid*, para 111(1)(c).

loss that is deductible in any year is limited to the amount of the tax-payer's income from farming for the year.[67]

A hobby farm loss is a loss from a farming operation that is conducted without a profit motive or a reasonable expectation of profit.[68] Hobby farm losses are not deductible at all since they are not income from a source.[69]

d) Allowable Business Investment Losses

A "business investment loss" is a special type of capital loss—a hybrid[70] that is deductible from income from *any* source.

A "business investment loss" is a loss that a taxpayer incurs on a disposition of capital property under the following conditions:[71]

- The capital property is a share of a "small business corporation" or a debt owed to the taxpayer by such a corporation;
- Where the taxpayer is a corporation and the capital property is a debt, the debtor corporation is at arm's length from the taxpayer; and
- The shares or debt are, unless subsection 50(1) applies, disposed of to a person dealing with the taxpayer at arm's length.

An allowable business investment loss has features of both business and capital losses: it results from a disposition of capital property, but it may be used to offset income from any source.[72] Any unused portion of an allowable business investment loss is a non-capital loss. Thus, one can apply unused allowable business losses against income from any source.

However, since an unused allowable business loss is treated as a non-capital loss, it has a limited life. It may be carried back three years and carried forward for only twenty years.[73] In contrast, net capital losses may be carried back three years and carried forward indefinitely. An allowable business loss that is not used within the twenty-year carryforward period applicable to non-capital losses reverts to a net

---

67   *Ibid.*

68   *Sobon v Canada*, 2004 TCC 2 (Informal Procedure), rev'd 2006 FCA 247 (taxpayer not entitled to deduct farm losses in excess of $8,750 per year; ostrich farm sustained losses in all ten years of its operation and could not generate a profit as it was currently run).

69   See the guidelines that the Supreme Court set out in *Stewart v Canada*, 2002 SCC 46 and *Walls v Canada*, 2002 SCC 47.

70   ITA, above note 1, para 39(1)(c); subs 111(8) "non-capital loss."

71   *Ibid*, para 39(1)(c); see also subs 248(1) "small business corporation."

72   *Ibid*, s 3.

73   *Ibid*, para 111(1)(a), subs 111(8) "non-capital loss."

capital loss.[74] Thereafter, it may be carried forward indefinitely but applied only against taxable capital gains. Hence, its hybrid character.

e) Limited Partnership Losses

A taxpayer may carry forward limited partnership losses indefinitely and apply them against income from any source. The Act restricts the deduction for limited partnership losses, however, to the amount that the taxpayer is "at risk" in the partnership in the year.[75]

3) Change of Corporate Control

a) General Comment

There are special rules to discourage taxpayers from trading in "loss companies" — that is, corporations with accumulated losses purchased and sold primarily for the sake of tax, rather than business, advantages. The Act streams the carryforward of losses when control of a corporation changes hands.[76] In the absence of these rules, a taxpayer could purchase a "loss company" solely for its losses, inject a new profitable business into it and shelter the profits of the new business from tax.

b) *De Jure* Control

"Control" implies ownership of sufficient shares to carry with them the ability to cast a majority of the votes on election of a board of directors. Thus, at common-law, control means *de jure* and not *de facto* control. As Jackett P said in *Buckerfield's Ltd v MNR*:[77]

> [M]any approaches might conceivably be adopted in applying the word "control" in a statute such as the *Income Tax Act* . . .
>
> It might, for example, refer to control by "management," where management and the Board of Directors are separate, or it might refer to control by the Board of Directors. The kind of control exercised by management officials of the Board of Directors is, however, clearly not intended by [s. 256] when it contemplates control of one corporation by another as well as control of a corporation by individuals . . . . The word "control" might conceivably refer to *de facto* control by one or more shareholders whether or not they hold a majority of the shares. I am of the view, however, that in [s. 256 of] the *Income Tax*

---

74   *Ibid*, subs 111(8) "net capital loss."
75   *Ibid*, para 111(1)(e).
76   *Ibid*, subs 111(4) & 111(5).
77   *Buckerfield's Ltd v MNR*, [1964] CTC 504 at 507 (Ex Ct); *Duha Printers (Western) Ltd v Canada*, [1998] 1 SCR 795.

Act, the word "controlled" contemplates the right or control that rests in ownership of such a number of shares as carries with it the right to a majority of the votes in the election of the Board of Directors.

The lack of power to elect a majority of the board of directors, however, does not necessarily imply a lack of control; control can also be determined by other tests, such as the power to wind up the corporation.[78]

c) Statutory Exceptions

There are circumstances, however, in which the Act deems control of a corporation not to have changed. For example, the Act deems a person who acquires shares of a corporation not to have acquired control by virtue of the acquisition, redemption or cancellation of shares, if immediately before such transaction she was related to the acquired corporation.[79]

d) Restrictions on Losses

The Act stringently controls the use of accumulated losses following a change of corporate control. The rules limit transfers of losses between unrelated corporate taxpayers and discourage business arrangements that are nothing more than "loss-trading" or "loss-offset" transactions. For example, in a typical "loss-trading" transaction, a taxpayer might sell property with an accrued gain using an intermediary corporation with accumulated losses as a conduit. Any gain from the transaction could then be offset against the intermediary's losses to reduce taxable income. With some exceptions, the loss-transfer rules do not allow for migration of losses between corporations.

e) Non-Capital Losses

A corporation may carry forward its non-capital and farm losses following a change of control if it satisfies two conditions: prior year's losses are deductible against income from the *same* business, but only if the corporation that sustained the loss continues to carry on that same business for profit or with a reasonable expectation of profit. The corporation must carry on the acquired business with a reasonable expectation of profit throughout the year following the time of its acquisition.[80]

---

78   *Imperial General Properties Ltd v MNR*, [1985] 2 SCR 288.
79   ITA, above note 1, para 256(7)(a).
80   *Ibid*, subpara 111(5)(a)(i).

f) Deemed Year-End

A corporation is deemed to have a year-end immediately before its control changes hands.[81] Any losses incurred in the year in which control changes are subject to the restrictions on loss carryovers. Thus, a change of corporate control can speed up the timetable for the use of losses.

g) Capital Losses

The restrictions on capital losses are even more stringent than for non-capital losses. Net capital losses for preceding years may not be deducted in computing its income for the year of change of control or in any subsequent year. Further, losses incurred in years subsequent to the change of control cannot be carried back to offset income earned in the years prior to the change of control.[82]

Following a change of corporate control, the Act deems a corporation to have realized any losses accrued on its non-depreciable capital properties.[83] The corporation may not deduct its net capital losses for preceding years and in the year of the change of control in computing its income in any subsequent year. The Act also reduces the adjusted cost base of the non-depreciable capital properties by the amount of the capital loss.[84] The purpose of these rules is to make it less attractive to trade in corporations that are pregnant with capital losses.

D. CAPITAL GAINS EXEMPTION

1) Purpose

Canada enacted a capital gains exemption in 1985. The exemption is intended to encourage risk-taking and to stimulate investment in small businesses while assisting farmers and fishers and broadening the participation of individuals in the equity markets.

Capital gains from dispositions of shares of farm and fishing properties and qualified small business corporations are exempt from tax to a maximum of $750,000 during an individual's lifetime. At a tax rate of 50 percent, the full exemption for taxable capital gains of $375,000 is worth $187,500 in tax savings.

---

81 *Ibid*, subs 249(4).
82 *Ibid*, subs 111(4).
83 *Ibid*, para 111(4)(d). Other provisions, such as subs 111(5.1), apply to properties such as depreciable property.
84 *Ibid*, para 53(2)(b.2).

The exemption is generous. Here we see the tension between competing values. We tax capital gains on the theory of fairness. But we reduce the amount taxable to 50 percent. Then, we exempt some gains for certain taxpayers on the theory of economic incentives.

2) Structure

The $750,000 lifetime capital gains exemption is available in respect of three broad categories of capital properties:

1) "Qualified farm property,"[85]
2) Shares of qualified small business corporations,[86] and
3) Qualified fishing property.[87]

An individual's exemption depends upon three principal factors:

1) The individual's residence;
2) The type of capital property that gives rise to the gain; and
3) The net cumulative amount of the individual's investment income and financing expenses in the year in which she realizes the gain.

These three factors determine who is eligible for the exemption and how much of the gain the individual may shelter from tax in a particular year.

3) Eligible Taxpayers

a) Residents

Only individuals resident in Canada may claim the exemption. An individual can claim the exemption if she is resident in Canada:

- throughout the year; or
- for part of the year, if the individual was resident in Canada throughout the year preceding, or the year following the year in which she realized the gain.[88]

A trust cannot claim the exemption. A trust may, however, flow through its capital gain to its beneficiaries by making a special designation.[89] A

---

85   *Ibid*, subs 110.6(1) "qualified farm property."
86   *Ibid*, subs 110.6(2.1).
87   *Ibid*, subs 110.6(1) "qualified fishing property."
88   *Ibid*, subs 110.6(5).
89   *Ibid*, subss 104(21) & 104(21.2).

spouse trust may claim a deduction in respect of its eligible taxable capital gains in the year in which the spouse dies.[90]

b) Deemed Residents

For the purposes of the exemption, the Act deems an individual who was resident in Canada at any time in a taxation year to have been resident in Canada throughout the year if he was resident in Canada throughout either the year immediately preceding, or the year immediately following, the taxation year.[91] Thus, a person who becomes a non-resident in a particular year can claim the exemption if he was resident in Canada throughout the year immediately preceding it.

An immigrant may claim the exemption on becoming resident in Canada if she remains a resident throughout the following year.

4) Farm or Fishing Property

The general purpose of the farm and fishing property rules is to limit the exemption to taxpayers engaged in the business of farming for a minimum stipulated period of time and to circumstances in which farming constitutes the taxpayer's main source of income.

a) "Qualified Farm Property"

A taxpayer is entitled to the exemption in respect of "qualified farm property." The phrase "qualified farm property" refers to farm property held personally or through a partnership or family farm corporation.

More specifically, an individual's "qualified farm property" includes any real property that has been used by:[92]

- The individual;
- Her spouse or common-law partner;
- Her child or parent;
- The individual's family farm corporation in which she owns shares; or
- A family farm partnership in which she has an interest.

The property must have been used to carry on the business of farming in Canada. The business may be, or may have been, carried on by the individual who owns the farm property, his spouse or children, his family farm corporation or his family farm partnership in which he, or

---

90   *Ibid*, subs 110.6(12), paras 104(4)(a) & (a.1).
91   *Ibid*, subs 110.6(5).
92   *Ibid*, subs 110.6(1) "qualified farm property."

his spouse, children or parents have an interest. For the purposes of these rules, grandchildren qualify as children.[93]

5) Small Business Corporation Shares

The exemption is also available in respect of capital gains that a taxpayer realizes from the disposition of qualified small business corporation (QSBC) shares.

The Act defines a QSBC as:[94]

- A share of the capital stock of a small business corporation that is a Canadian-controlled private corporation, in which all or most of the fair market value of the assets is attributable to assets used principally in an active business carried on primarily in Canada;
- A Canadian-controlled private corporation in which the assets, throughout a period of 24 months immediately preceding the corporation's disposition, have not been owned by any person other than the individual claiming the exemption, or by a person or partnership related to the individual; and
- Throughout a period of 24 months preceding the disposition more than 50 percent of the fair market value of the assets were used principally in an active business primarily in Canada.

Shareholders of newly incorporated small business corporations can, however, claim the exemption, even where the corporation has existed for less than 24 months. Thus, a sole proprietor can dispose of his active business by transferring all of the business to a corporation and then selling the shares of the corporation rather than the assets of the business.[95]

There is a risk that the CRA may attack a quick flip of shares after a rollover to a corporation as an income transaction that is not eligible for the capital gains exemption.[96]

6) Anti-Avoidance Rules

The capital gains exemption is a generous tax preference. Thus, taxpayers have an incentive to convert income that is fully taxable into non-taxable capital gains. There are several anti-avoidance provisions

---

93   *Ibid*, para 110.6(1) "child."
94   *Ibid*, subs 248(1); see also subs 110.6(1) "qualified small business corporation share."
95   *Ibid*, s 54.2.
96   See, for example, *Fraser v MNR*, [1964] SCR 657.

in place in anticipation of such manoeuvres. Some of the provisions are very specific, while others are broad provisions that cast a wide net. Indeed, in some cases, the net has been cast so widely that it is impossible to determine the types of transactions it might catch.

The primary focus of the anti-avoidance provisions, however, is the prevention of three types of tax avoidance:

1) Conversion of capital gains earned by corporations into capital gains earned by individuals (Type A);
2) Conversion of taxable dividend income into capital gains (Type B); and
3) Disproportionate allocations of gains between taxpayers.

a) Type A Conversions

Only individuals can claim the exemption in respect of capital gains. Consequently, there is every incentive to convert potential corporate capital gains into gains attributable to individual shareholders.

An individual cannot claim the exemption for a gain realized as a consequence of a corporation or partnership's acquisition of property at a price that is significantly less than its fair market value.[97] For example, where a corporation disposes of a property by transferring it to another corporation for less than its fair market value, any capital gain from a sale of the shares of either corporation is not eligible for the exemption if the dispositions of property are part of a series of transactions. This rule applies where the transformed gain results from a "series of transactions or events."[98] It is not necessary to establish any intention or purpose on the part of the taxpayer to transform the gain. The events must, however, be sufficiently connected to constitute a "series of transactions."

b) Type B Conversions

The second category of anti-avoidance provisions is concerned with the conversion of dividend income into capital gains. In the simplest case, a corporation can enhance the value of its shares by restricting the dividend payout on the shares. In these circumstances, the CRA may deny the taxpayer's claim for an exemption in respect of the gain from a disposition of the shares.[99]

---

97 *ITA*, above note 1, para 110.6(7)(b).
98 See *ibid*, subs 248(10) (defining "series of transactions").
99 *Ibid*, subs 110.6(8).

More specifically, an individual may not claim the capital gains exemption in respect of gains realized on shares where:[100]

- It is reasonable to conclude that a significant part of the gain is attributable to non-payment of dividends on the shares; or
- The dividends paid in the year or in any preceding taxation year were less than 90 percent of the average annual rate of return on the shares for that year.

The individual need not have an intention to convert dividend income into capital gains. It is sufficient that there is a causal connection between significant enhancement in the value of the shares and inadequacy of the payment of dividends. The onus is then on the individual to provide an alternative explanation for the enhanced value of the shares.

The average annual rate of return on a share is the rate of return that a "knowledgeable and prudent investor" would expect to receive on such a share.[101] In determining the rate, any delay, postponement or failure to pay dividends in respect of the shares should be ignored. Variations in the amount of dividends payable from year to year should also be ignored.

Finally, the return is to be determined on the assumption that the shares may only be disposed of for proceeds equal to their issue price. These assumptions are intended to provide a nearly mechanical formula for determining a rate of return, without regard to all the factual financial nuances that might otherwise influence the return on shares.

E. CONCLUSION

Taxable income is net income adjusted for various policy considerations, such as encouraging philanthropy and providing economic incentives. Most important, however, the loss-carryover provisions adjust for the consequences of using an artificial timeline—fifty-two weeks—for calculating tax payable.

---

100 *Ibid.*
101 *Ibid*, subs 110.6(9).

FURTHER READINGS

General

McQUILLAN, PETER E. "Computation of Income for Tax Purposes" (1992) 44 Can Tax Found 5:27.

Charitable Donations, Medical Expenses, etc.

BALE, GORDON. "Construing a Taxing Statute or Tilting at Windmills: Charitable Donation Deduction and the *Charter of Rights and Freedoms*" (1985) 19 ETR 55.

KRISHNA, VERN. "Charitable Donations: What is a Charitable Purpose?" (1986) 1 Can Curr Tax C-159.

———. "Charitable Donations: What Constitutes a 'Gift'?" (1985) 1 Can Curr Tax J-107.

ZWEIBEL, ELLEN B. "Looking the Gift Horse in the Mouth: An Examination of Charitable Gifts Which Benefit the Donor" (1986) 31 McGill LJ 417.

Capital Gains Exemption

STACK, THOMAS J. "Capital Gains and Losses on Shares of Private Corporations" (1987) 39 Can Tax Found 17:1.

TEMPLETON, WENDY. "Anti-Avoidance and the Capital Gains Exemption" (1986) 34 Can Tax J 203.

———. "The Taxation of Corporate Reorganizations: Anti-Avoidance and the Capital Gains Exemption" (1986) 34 Can Tax J 203.

———. "The Taxation of Corporate Reorganizations: Anti-Avoidance and the Capital Gains Exemptions: Part 2" (1986) 34 Can Tax J 446.

PART IV

HOW MUCH TAX?

COMPUTATION OF TAX: INDIVIDUALS

A. INTRODUCTION

We·turn now to the first step in determining how much tax is payable. The formula is simple:

$$\text{Tax Payable} = \text{Tax Income} \times \text{Tax Rate}$$

To this point, we have focused on calculating income and taxable income; that is, the taxable base upon which we calculate the tax payable. The next step is to apply tax rates to the taxable base and, finally, adjust for tax credits.

Setting an appropriate tax rate is a complex matter involving economic models as well as political and international considerations. First, and most obvious, we must set the rate at a level that generates sufficient government revenues. There is no consensus, however, on the ultimate impact of tax rates on the total revenue collected. One's intuitive response is that raising tax rates increases overall revenues. There is, however, a countervailing force: high tax rates promote tax avoidance and aggressive tax planning. They can also reduce incentives to earn income. High tax rates may sometimes actually reduce total government revenues. A taxpayer who can retain only 15 cents of every dollar of income is not as motivated to work as one who can keep 85 cents of each dollar.

Second, we must harmonize individual, trust, and corporate rates to keep the tax system reasonably neutral among different forms of organization. For example, if the corporate tax rate is substantially lower than individual rates, there is an incentive to incorporate and accumulate income in the corporation.

Third, our rates—particularly corporate rates—must be internationally competitive. For example, Canadian corporate tax rates must take into account rates in the United States, our largest trading partner, or risk losing business and investments if our rates are substantially higher.

Fourth, political considerations affect the tension between individual and corporate rates. Individuals vote; corporations do not.

Determining the tax payable is a multi-step process and involves more than applying a single rate to taxable income. Once we determine the basic tax by applying a tax rate to taxable income, there are various credits, surtaxes and reductions.

Division E of the *Income Tax Act* (*ITA*) has three parts—rules that apply to: individuals, corporations and all taxpayers. As we will see, the computation of tax takes into account several rates and credits in balancing the competing demands of revenue generation, fairness and equity, economic efficiency and political survival.

Rate comparisons—particularly between countries—can be deceptive. The nominal tax rate is only the starting point of comparison. The nominal tax rate is adjusted by tax credits (federal and provincial), surcharges and general rate reductions. The effective tax rate is the actual total tax payable divided by net income—that is, the amount that the taxpayer actually pays to governments. It is the effective rate that drives tax planning.

B. BASIC TAX RATE

1) Federal

Section 117 of the *ITA* sets out the federal tax rates applicable to individuals. There are four basic rate steps: 15, 22, 26 and 29 percent (2011). The amounts to which these rates apply are indexed to account for inflation.

2) Provincial

The rates in section 117 are the federal rates. In addition to federal tax, Canadian residents are also liable for provincial income tax. Provinces that have a tax collection agreement with the federal government ("participating provinces") may elect to calculate their income taxes using one of two methods: the "tax on tax" method or the "tax on income" method.

The "tax on tax" method calculates the provincial income tax by applying the provincial rate of tax to the federal tax payable. This method is inflexible and limits the ability of the provinces to raise revenues and determine their tax policies. In response to the provinces' desire for more control over how their income taxes are levied, the federal government introduced the "tax on income."[1]

The "tax on income" method calculates the provincial income tax by reference to taxable income, rather than to federal tax payable. As such, it allows the provinces to determine their income tax brackets and rates and create their own distinct block of non-refundable tax credits,[2] which allows the provinces greater flexibility in setting tax policy. However, in order to ensure a common tax base, the provinces and the federal government use a common definition of "taxable income."

All of the participating provinces have adopted the new tax on income method. Quebec is the only province that does not have a tax collection agreement with the federal government. It also calculates the provincial income tax by reference to "taxable income."

Apart from the indexing of tax brackets for inflation, the basic rate schedule is fairly stable; the nominal rates are not usually altered from year to year. Instead, governments increase or decrease the effective rate of taxes by imposing or removing surtaxes, or by allowing for special tax credits.

The combined federal/provincial rates vary between provinces. In 2011, for example, the combined top marginal rate is 39 percent in Alberta, 43.7 percent in British Columbia, and 46.4 percent in Ontario.

C. TAX CREDITS

An individual's tax payable is adjustable by personal and other tax credits. A tax credit reduces the effective tax that would otherwise be payable by the individual. Tax credits depend on:

1) Status;
2) Source of income;

---

1   See, generally, the Department of Finance's *Federal Administration of Provincial Taxes*, October 1998. Report prepared by the Federal-Provincial Committee on Taxation for presentation to Ministers of Finance, online: www.fin.gc.ca/fapt/fapt3e.html.

2   Subject to restrictions on minimums; see *ibid* at Design and Operation.

3) Type of expenditure; and
4) Location of source of income.

Tax credits serve various purposes: fairness, social justice, elimination of double tax and social policies. A tax credit reduces the individual's tax by an amount that is fixed, without reference to his marginal rate of tax. Thus, tax credits generally benefit all eligible taxpayers equally.

The value of the benefit does not increase as marginal rates rise. For example, a taxpayer can claim a credit for:

- Personal tax credits;
- Pension income;
- Dividends from taxable Canadian corporations;
- Tuition and education;
- Medical expenses;
- Charitable donations;
- Eligible children;
- Overseas employment;
- Foreign taxes;
- Children;
- Public transit;
- Children's fitness; or
- Adoption.

We calculate these according to a formula that applies a percentage (usually the lowest marginal tax rate) to the aggregate of the claimable amounts. The credits are indexed and, as such, are partially adjusted each year to reflect inflationary increases measured by the CPI.

Some of the credits are refundable — that is, the individual receives a cash refund if the credits exceed her income for the year. Others are non-refundable, and the taxpayer loses the credit if she cannot deduct it from tax otherwise payable for the year.

Tax credits are available at both the federal and provincial levels. Each province has the flexibility (subject to some restrictions) to choose which tax credits it will offer and to set the amount of those credits. Thus, tax credits vary from province to province. The federal tax credits are as follows.

1) Personal Tax Credits

A taxpayer can claim tax credits on account of:

- Single status;
- Spousal and common-law partner status;

- Equivalent-to-spouse status;
- Dependants; and
- Age.

These credits are not refundable. References to spouse in this chapter include, where appropriate, common-law partners.

See Appendix B for amounts.

a) Method of Calculation

An individual claims a credit by aggregating the dollar value of all the amounts that he can claim, and multiplying this value by the "appropriate percentage" for the year.[3] The "appropriate percentage" for a taxation year is the lowest marginal tax rate applicable in the particular year.[4]

Provinces determine their own unique income tax brackets and rates and create their own distinct block of non-refundable tax credits.[5] As a result, provincial tax credits are often different than the federal tax credits. Provinces are not required to follow any federal increases in a credit except in the case of expenditure-based credits. For expenditure-based credits (e.g., CPP, EI, tuition fees, medical expenses, charitable donations), provinces may increase credits beyond the level of the gross federal credit, but they cannot reduce them below the federal level.

b) Single Status

Every individual is entitled to their personal claim,[6] multiplied by the "appropriate percentage." This credit effectively eliminates individuals with minimal incomes from the tax roster.

c) Spousal Status

An individual who supports her spouse or a common-law partner can claim an additional amount as a tax credit.

A person is "married" if he undergoes a form of marriage recognized by the laws of Canada and is not a widow or widower, or divorced.[7] Subsection 252(3) expands the meaning of "spouse" to include individuals of the opposite sex who are party to a void or voidable marriage.

---

3   *Income Tax Act*, RSC 1985, c 1 (5th Supp) [*ITA*], subs 118(1).
4   *Ibid*, subs 248(1) "appropriate percentage"; subs 117(2).
5   See, generally, the Department of Finance's *Federal Administration of Provincial Taxes*, above note 1.
6   *ITA*, above note 3, para 118(1)(c).
7   *Canada v Scheller*, [1975] CTC 601 (FCTD); *McPhee v MNR*, [1980] CTC 2042 (TRB); *Canada v Taylor Estate*, [1984] CTC 244 (FCTD).

d) Wholly-Dependent Persons

A person who is not entitled to the spousal status credit but who supports a person who depends upon him can claim the credit for a wholly-dependent person (also referred to as the "equivalent-to-spouse credit").[8] The amount claimable under this provision is equivalent to the amount that a married person whose spouse does not earn more than the total threshold amount can claim.

The equivalent-to-spouse credit is available only to an individual who maintains (either alone or jointly with another person), and lives in, a self-contained domestic establishment and actually supports therein the dependent person. For example, a single parent supporting a child would qualify for the credit under this provision.

There are two additional qualifications for the claim on account of wholly-dependent persons. First, except where the claim is in respect of the taxpayer's child, the credit is available only in respect of dependants who reside in Canada.[9] A taxpayer is not entitled to the credit in respect of foreign resident dependants.

Second, except in the case of a claim for a parent or grandparent, a taxpayer cannot claim an amount in respect of a dependant who is 18 years of age or older, unless the person's dependency is because of mental or physical infirmity.[10]

e) Dependants

A taxpayer may also claim an amount in respect of individuals who depend upon him for support. The claim depends upon five criteria:[11]

1) Dependency;
2) Relationship between the persons;
3) Residence;
4) Age; and
5) Mental or physical infirmity of dependant.

i) Dependency

Whether an individual is dependent on a taxpayer is a question of fact. In the event that a person partially depends on two or more taxpayers, their aggregate claim in respect of the dependant cannot exceed the maximum amount that would be deductible in respect of a claim by one taxpayer. Where the supporting individuals cannot agree on the

---

8   *ITA*, above note 3, para 118(1)(b).
9   *Ibid*, cl 118(1)(b)(ii)(A).
10   *Ibid*, cl 118(1)(b)(ii)(D).
11   *Ibid*, para 118(1)(d).

portion of the total that each will deduct, the minister may allocate the amount between them.

ii) Relationship

The term "dependant" in respect of a taxpayer or his or her spouse means:[12]

- Their children or grandchildren;
- Their nieces or nephews, if resident in Canada;
- Their brothers or sisters, if resident in Canada; and
- Their parents, grandparents, aunts or uncles, if resident in Canada.

iii) Residence

Except in respect of a claim for the taxpayer's, or his or her spouse's, children or grandchildren, the dependency deduction is available only for the support of dependants who reside in Canada. The CRA is concerned with bogus dependency claims from foreign countries.

iv) Age

The infirm dependent deduction is available only in respect of dependants over the age of 18.

v) Mental or Physical Infirmity

A taxpayer can claim the dependency deduction for individuals over the age of 18, but only if they depend upon her because of mental or physical infirmity.[13]

f) Age

An individual who is 65 years of age or older can claim an additional amount.

2) Pension Income

Pension income credits provide some relief from inflation, particularly for individuals who have to live on fixed incomes. The credit depends on two factors: the source of the pension and the recipient's age.

An individual who is 65 years of age or older may claim a credit in respect of his pension income by applying the appropriate percentage to the lesser of $1,000 and his "qualified pension income" for the year.[14]

---

12   *Ibid*, subs 118(6).
13   *Ibid*, subpara 118(1)(d)(ii).
14   *Ibid*, para 118(3)(a).

"Pension income" includes:[15]

- Life annuity payments out of a superannuation or pension fund;
- Annuity payments out of registered retirement savings plans;
- Payments out of registered retirement income funds;
- Payments out of deferred profit-sharing plans; and
- Accrued income on an annuity or life insurance policy included in income.

3) Tuition Fees

Tuition fees on account of education are generally personal and capital expenditures. Thus, an individual could not, without specific authorization, claim a deduction or a credit for tuition fees. For social policy reasons, however, we allow individuals a tax credit for tuition fees paid to certain educational institutions.

There are two different sets of conditions that regulate the credit for tuition fees: (1) students attending educational institutions in Canada; and (2) students attending educational institutions outside Canada. The rules in respect of the former category are considerably less stringent than those in respect of the latter.

a) Institutions in Canada
A student may claim a credit for fees paid to attend:[16]

- A post-secondary educational institution; or
- An institution certified by the Minister of Human Resources Development to provide courses that furnish or improve occupational skills.

We determine the credit by applying the "appropriate percentage" to the eligible tuition fees paid in the year. The credit is available only if the total fees exceed $100.

b) Deemed Residence
A student who is deemed to be a resident of Canada[17] can claim the credit even if she attends an educational institution outside Canada. The credit is available on the same terms and conditions as if the student were attending an institution in Canada.[18]

---

15   *Ibid*, subs 118(7) "pension income."
16   *Ibid*, para 118.5(1)(a).
17   *Ibid*, s 250.
18   *Ibid*, subs 118.5(2).

c) Transfer of Unused Credits

A student can transfer his tuition tax credit to his spouse.[19] Where a student is unmarried, or a married student's spouse does not claim a personal tax credit for him or her, the education and tuition tax credit may be transferred to the student's parents or grandparents.[20]

The maximum amount the student can transfer each year is $5,000 minus the amount he uses that year.

d) Fees Paid by Employer

Tuition fees paid by a student's employer are also creditable by the student, but only to the extent that the student includes the fees in income. The employer may deduct the fees as a business expense if it pays the fees for business purposes.[21]

e) "Tuition Fees"

Tuition fees include:

- Admission fees;
- Charges for the use of a library, or laboratory fees;
- Exemption fees;
- Examination fees;
- Application fees;
- Confirmation fees;
- Charges for a certificate, diploma or degree;
- Membership or seminar fees specifically related to an academic program and its administration;
- Mandatory computer service fees; and
- Academic fees.

Fees for student activities (whether social or athletic), medical care fees, transportation and parking charges, board and lodging, equipment costs of a capital nature, and initiation or entrance fees to professional organizations are not creditable for tax purposes.

f) Books

Although the cost of books does not usually qualify as a tuition fee, a student may claim a credit for such costs if he is enrolled in a correspondence course and the cost of the books is an integral part of the fee paid for the course.

---

19   *Ibid*, s 118.8.
20   *Ibid*, s 118.9.
21   *Ibid*, s 9.

g) Period Covered by Fees

Only tuition fees paid in respect of a particular year[22] are creditable in that year. Fees paid to cover tuition for an academic session that straddles the calendar year are eligible for the tax credit only for the year to which they relate. For example, where the academic year is from September in one year to May of the next year, the tuition tax credit must be allocated so that the portion from September to December is claimable in one year and the portion from January to May is claimable in the subsequent year.

h) Educational Institutions outside Canada

A full-time student enrolled at a university outside Canada can claim a credit by applying the "appropriate percentage" to the amount of eligible tuition fees paid in respect of the year to the university.[23]

The qualifications to claim the tuition fee credit for attending a university outside Canada are considerably more stringent than those for institutions in Canada. The credit is available only if the student satisfies the following conditions:

- The student attends a course that is of not less than thirteen consecutive weeks' duration;
- The program of study leads to a degree (not a diploma) from the institution;
- The institution that the student attends is a university, not a college or other educational institution; and
- The student attends on a full-time basis.

Students are considered in "full-time attendance" at a university if the institution regards them to be full-time students for academic purposes. A certificate from a university stating that a student was in full-time attendance in a particular academic year or semester is acceptable for tax purposes. Hence, a student who holds a full-time job and takes a full course load at a university is considered to be in full-time attendance at the educational institution for tax purposes.

The CRA interprets the thirteen consecutive weeks' attendance requirement quite liberally. For example, a student satisfies the requirement if she drops out of the course before completing the program of studies, the particular academic term falls a little short of thirteen weeks, or the term is broken by official holidays.

---

22   *Ibid*, subs 118.5(1).
23   *Ibid*, para 118.5(1)(b).

4) Education Credit

In addition to the tuition fee credit, a student can also claim an "education credit" for attending at a designated educational institution, if he enrolls in a qualifying educational program at that institution.[24] As with the other tax credits, we determine the education tax credit by applying the "appropriate percentage" for the year to the number of months of full-time attendance at the institution, multiplied by $400.

5) Medical Expenses

Medical expenditures are personal expenses and, therefore, would usually be non-deductible for tax purposes. The Act does, however, provide some relief for "extraordinary" medical expenses over a minimum threshold limit to reflect the burden of such expenditures on one's ability to pay. The Act attempts, with limited success, to balance the social policy of providing relief for extraordinary medical expenses with stringent revenue constraints.

a) Computation of Credit

We determine the medical expense credit by applying the "appropriate percentage" to the sum of the taxpayer's medical expenses in excess of a threshold amount.[25] The credit applies to the lesser of the threshold amount and 3 percent of the individual's income from the year.

b) Meaning of "Medical Expenses"

A taxpayer may deduct medical expenses incurred on behalf of:[26]

- Herself;
- Her spouse;
- Children, or her spouse's children if they depend on the taxpayer for support; or
- Her, or her spouse's or common-law partner's, children, grandchildren, parents, grandparents, brothers, sisters, uncles, aunts, nieces, or nephews who reside in Canada and depend on her for support.

The taxpayer must support her claim for the credit by filing receipts with the return for the year.

"Medical expenses" means expenses paid to a medical practitioner, dentist, nurse or public or licensed private hospital. At first glance, the

---

24   *Ibid*, s 118.6.
25   *Ibid*, subs 118.2(1).
26   *Ibid*, subss 118.2(2), 118(6).

phrase "medical expenses" appears to include any expenditures that an individual may incur as a consequence of disability or illness. In fact, the phrase is circumscribed by several restrictive conditions. The list of eligible medical expenses is regularly reviewed and expanded in light of new medical technologies.

An individual must satisfy all of the requirements before he can claim the credit.[27] Recently, the courts have become a little more liberal in their interpretation of the provisions following the Supreme Court of Canada's guidelines that the *Income Tax Act* should be read in context and that ambiguous provisions should be interpreted according to the "object and spirit" of the rule.[28] See, for example, Judge Bowman's comments in *Radage v Canada*:[29] "The court must, while recognizing the narrowness of the tests . . . construe the provisions liberally, humanely and compassionately and not narrowly and technically."[30]

D. DIVIDEND TAX CREDIT

Corporate income is potentially vulnerable to double taxation, once at the corporate level and again at the shareholder level. The statute provides partial relief through the dividend tax credit. An individual who receives a taxable dividend from a taxable Canadian corporation must include 125 percent of the dividend in income.[31] In other words, the cash value of the dividend is "grossed-up" by 25 percent. In theory, the gross-up reflects the underlying corporate tax (at an assumed rate of 20 percent) that the corporation paid on its income. The individual may, however, claim a dividend tax credit against the amount of federal tax that the gross-up imputes to the corporation.[32]

This two-step process of "grossing up" taxable dividends, followed by a tax credit, is a structural device that prevents, at least, to a limited extent, double taxation of corporate income. The tax credit integrates

---

27 See, for example, *Witthuhn v MNR* (1957), 17 Tax ABC 33 (board denied claim for medical expenses for amounts paid to attendant to look after infirm spouse; taxpayer claimed expenses on basis that spouse was confined to bed or wheelchair; spouse in fact did not own wheelchair, but instead sat in a special rocking chair; claim denied as rocking chair not a "wheelchair").

28 *Stubart Investments Ltd v Canada*, [1984] 1 SCR 536; see Chapter 2.

29 *Radage v Canada*, 96 DTC 1615 at 1625 (TCC).

30 See also *Crockart v Canada*, [1999] 2 CTC 2409 (TCC) (meaning of a "hospital bed").

31 *ITA*, above note 3, para 82(1)(b).

32 *Ibid*, s 121.

the tax paid by Canadian corporations with the tax paid by shareholders on dividends.

E. OVERSEAS EMPLOYMENT TAX CREDIT

As a rule, Canadian residents are liable for tax on their worldwide income.[33] We refer to this as a system of full tax liability. However, an individual employed on an overseas contract may be entitled to a special tax credit. The credit is available only in limited circumstances, but it is extremely generous. The credit allows Canadian businesses employing Canadian workers to compete in international markets with other countries that offer similar tax relief to their residents. Thus, we trade off tax equity against international competitiveness.

The credit is available only to an individual who is employed by a specified employer, and then only if the employee works overseas for a period of at least six consecutive months in certain approved activities. Thus the statute limits the credit in four ways:[34]

- The taxpayer must work for a "specified employer";
- The employer must engage in an approved activity;
- The employee must work abroad for more than six consecutive months; and
- The amount of the credit is subject to a ceiling.

Also, the credit is not available where the specified employer and the non-resident firm are not at arm's length and Canadian residents hold less than 10 percent of the interests.

A "specified employer" is generally an employer resident in Canada.[35] The employer must engage in an approved activity such as construction, exploration for and exploitation of natural resources or an agricultural project.

The amount of the credit is subject to a ceiling.[36] The credit is equal to that portion of the tax otherwise payable that is the lesser of $80,000 and 80 percent of the employee's net overseas employment income of her total income.

---

33 *Ibid*, subs 2(1); see also Chapter 3.
34 *Ibid*, subs 122.3(1); Interpretation Bulletin IT-497R4, "Overseas Employment Tax Credit" (14 May 2004).
35 *ITA*, *ibid*, subs 122.3(2) "specified employer."
36 *Ibid*, para 122.3(1)(c) & (d).

F. ALTERNATIVE MINIMUM TAX

High-income taxpayers may be subject to an "alternative minimum tax" (AMT), even though they do not have any taxable income.[37]

The alternative minimum tax applies only to individuals and to certain trusts; it does not apply to corporations. AMT is an alternative tax. Generally, a taxpayer's "adjusted taxable income" for the alternative minimum tax is her regular taxable income plus certain add backs in respect of tax preference items.[38] These tax preference items are deductions that might be used to shelter income.

In computing "adjusted taxable income" for AMT purposes, a taxpayer is entitled to a basic exemption of $40,000.[39]

The federal alternative minimum tax is payable at a flat rate of 56 percent on "adjusted taxable income." The taxpayer pays the higher of the amount and the regular federal tax. Combined with a provincial tax rate of approximately 40 percent, the AMT is about 22 percent.

---

37   *Ibid*, subss 127.5–127.55.
38   *Ibid*, s 127.52.
39   *Ibid*, s 127.53.

COMPUTATION OF TAX: CORPORATIONS

The rules that deal with the computation of tax payable by corporations are more detailed and complex than the rules that apply to individuals. This is because corporate taxation depends upon numerous variables: (1) type and size of the corporation; (2) ownership structure; (3) type and source of income; and (4) amount of income earned in a year.

A. GENERAL TAX RATE

The general basic rate of federal tax payable by a corporation is 38 percent (2011).[1] A general rate reduction reduces the federal tax.[2] The general rate reduction does not apply to the income upon which a Canadian-controlled private corporation (CCPC) claims the small business deduction.[3] In 2011, the general rate reduction was 11.5 percent. By 2012, the net federal tax is expected to drop to 15 percent.

---

1   *Income Tax Act*, RSC 1985, c 1 (5th Supp) [*ITA*], para 123(1)(a).
2   *Ibid*, s 123.4(1).
3   *Ibid*, subs 123.4(2).

B. TAX ADJUSTMENTS

Few, if any, corporations actually pay tax at the basic rate. The adjustments to the basic corporate tax include the following:

- Provincial tax credit;
- Foreign tax credit;
- Small business deduction;
- Manufacturing and processing profits deduction;
- Logging tax deduction;
- Investment tax credit; and
- Political contributions credit.

Also, the Act taxes certain types of corporations at special rates because of their special status.[4]

C. PROVINCIAL TAX CREDIT

A corporation can claim a tax credit of 10 percent of its taxable income earned in a province.[5] The provincial tax credit vacates part of the tax field to the provinces so that they may levy a corporate tax of their own.

The provincial tax credit applies only to a corporation's "taxable income earned . . . in a province." We determine this amount by allocating the corporation's total taxable income to its "permanent establishment[s]" in the provinces.[6] The calculation of a corporation's provincial tax credit involves four steps:

1) Determine whether the corporation has a "permanent establishment" in one or more provinces;
2) Allocate the taxable income of the corporation to the various provinces in accordance with the prescribed formulae;
3) Calculate the provincial tax abatement as 10 percent of the amount of "taxable income earned" in the provinces; and
4) Deduct the provincial tax abatement from the corporation's "tax otherwise payable."

The Act does not define "tax otherwise payable." It means the tax that is payable after the deduction of all permissible deductions.

---

4 For example, investment corporations are subject to the special rules in *ibid*, s 130.
5 *Ibid*, s 124(1).
6 *Income Tax Regulations*, CRC, c 945, ss 401 & 402.

1) "Permanent Establishment"

A "permanent establishment" is a fixed place of business of a corporation. A fixed place of business includes:[7]

- An office;
- A branch;
- A mine;
- An oil well;
- A farm;
- Timberland;
- A factory;
- A workshop; or
- A warehouse.

Where a corporation does not have a fixed place of business, the term "permanent establishment" means the principal place in which the corporation conducts its business.[8]

2) Computation of Provincial Tax Credit

The provincial tax credit is 10 percent of its total taxable income allocated to the provinces in which the corporation has permanent establishments. This amount is deducted from the federal tax otherwise payable.

The provincial tax credit applies only to taxable income that a corporation earns in a province. It does not apply to taxable income that it earns in a foreign jurisdiction. Foreign-source income that a corporation earns is taxable at the full corporate tax rate. The corporation may, however, claim foreign tax credits.

D. SMALL BUSINESS DEDUCTION

A CCPC that earns active business income in Canada can claim an annual tax credit (the "small business deduction") equal to 17 percent of the first $500,000 of its active business income.[9] Thus, in effect, a CCPC pays federal tax at a rate of 11 percent on the first $500,000 of its business income (2011).

---

7   *Ibid*, s 400(2).
8   *Ibid*, s 400(2)(a).
9   *ITA*, above note 1, s 125.

	%
Basic federal rate	38.00
Less provincial abatement	(10.00)
Federal rate	28.00
Small business deduction	(17.00)
Total federal tax	11.00

FURTHER READINGS

DART, ROBERT J. "A Critique of an Advance Corporate Tax System for Canada" (1990) 38 Can Tax J 1245.

ERLICHMAN, HARRY. "Profitable Donations: What Price Culture?" (1992) 11:2 Philanthropist 3.

SHERBANIUK, DOUGLAS J. "Future Trends in Tax Policy: Focus on the Alternative Minimum Tax and the Corporate Income Tax Discussion Papers" in The Law Society of Upper Canada, *Special Lectures 1986: Income Tax for the General Practitioner* (Don Mills, ON: De Boo, 1986) 425.

SMITH, ROGER S. "Rates of Personal Income Tax: The Carter Commission Revisited" (1987) 35 Can Tax J 1226, and in W Neil Brooks, ed, *The Quest for Tax Reform* (Toronto: Carswell, 1988) at 173.

TREMBLAY, RICHARD G. "Foreign Tax Credit Planning" (1993) Corp Mgmt Tax Conf 3:1.

CHAPTER 15

TAX CREDITS

A. GENERAL COMMENT

Canadian residents are subject to full tax liability on their worldwide income. Hence, a taxpayer may be subject to double taxation to a foreign government for income taxed at source, and to Canada on the basis of residence. A resident taxpayer may, however, claim a credit against Canadian tax for taxes paid to a foreign government.[1] The foreign tax credit, which one calculates separately in respect of each country, relieves juridical double taxation, but does not provide any relief from economic double taxation.[2] For example, if company A in Canada owns 5 percent of company B in the United States, income that company B earns is taxable in the United States. The foreign tax credit merely provides relief from the tax on any dividends that company B pays to A, and not on the underlying US corporate tax.

The tax credit is available only in respect of obligatory taxes paid to a foreign government. Discretionary foreign taxes levied by a foreign government that would not have been imposed if the taxpayer were not entitled to a Canadian foreign tax credit are not eligible for credit in Canada.[3] The rationale for this rule is that the Canadian government does not want to finance foreign governments by encouraging them to

---

1   *Income Tax Act*, RSC 1985, c 1 (5th Supp) [*ITA*], s 126.
2   *Ibid*, subs 126(6).
3   *Ibid*, subs 126(4).

levy taxes on Canadians resident in their country in the expectation that the taxpayers will receive a rebate for the tax under Canadian tax law.

The foreign tax credit rules deal with three different circumstances:

- Foreign taxes paid by a resident on non-business income;
- Foreign taxes paid by a resident on business income; and
- Taxes paid by non-residents in respect of certain capital gains.

B. NON-BUSINESS-INCOME TAX

A resident taxpayer may deduct from "tax otherwise payable" under Part I an amount equal to the non-business-income taxes[4] that it pays to a foreign jurisdiction. The tax credit cannot exceed the amount of Canadian tax that would have been payable on the foreign income had the taxpayer earned the income in Canada.[5]

"Non-business-income tax" generally means taxes paid to a foreign jurisdiction, whether a foreign country or a subdivision of a foreign country. It does not include:[6]

- Amounts included in calculating the taxpayer's "business income tax" (the credit for business income taxes is calculated separately);[7]
- Taxes in respect of which the taxpayer has already taken a deduction in computing income;[8]
- Taxes attributable to income eligible for the overseas employment tax credit;[9]
- Taxes payable to a foreign country based solely on the taxpayer being a citizen of that country if the taxes are attributable to income earned in Canada;[10]

---

4   *Ibid*, subs 126(7) "non-business-income tax."
5   This is the effect of the formula in *ibid*, subs 126(1).
6   *Ibid*, subs 126(7) "non-business-income tax."
7   *Ibid*, subs 126(7) (a) "non-business-income tax."
8   *Ibid*, subs 20(11) (deduction for tax in excess of 15 percent paid to foreign government on income from property, other than real property); subs 20(12) (deduction for tax paid to foreign government in respect of income from business or property, other than, where the taxpayer is a corporation, from shares of a foreign affiliate, to the extent of the "non-business-income" tax paid by taxpayer); subs 104(22.3) (recalculation of trust's foreign tax); subs 126(7) "non-business-income tax" (b) & (c).
9   See *ibid*, subs 122.3(1).
10   *Ibid*, subs 126(7) "non-business-income tax" (d); for example, a US citizen who pays US tax on employment income earned in Canada is not entitled to the foreign tax credit for the US taxes.

- Taxes relating to an amount that is refunded to any person or partnership;[11]
- Taxes reasonably attributable to a taxable capital gain for which the taxpayer or a spouse has claimed a deduction;[12]
- Taxes reasonably attributable to a loan received or receivable by the taxpayer;[13] and
- Taxes relating to an amount that was exempt by treaty.[14]

The credit is available only for foreign taxes that the taxpayer actually pays for the year. Hence, tax refunded by a foreign government in a subsequent year because of a loss carryback necessitates a recalculation of the foreign tax credit for the year to which the refund applies.[15]

The foreign tax credit is subject to a limit calculated according to the following formula:

$$\frac{\text{(Amount of foreign non-business income)}}{\text{(Income from all sources)}} \times \text{Canadian tax otherwise payable}$$

The effect of this formula is that the credit rate for foreign taxes cannot be higher than the tax rate that the taxpayer would pay if it earned the income in Canada.[16]

C. BUSINESS-INCOME TAX

The credit for foreign business income tax is for the benefit of Canadian resident taxpayers who have branch operations in foreign countries.

"[B]usiness-income tax" means tax paid by the taxpayer that may reasonably be regarded as a tax in respect of the income of the taxpayer from any business carried on by him in a foreign country.[17]

As with the tax credit for non-business-income tax, the tax credit for business-income taxes must be calculated separately for each country in which the taxpayer carries on business.

---

11 *Ibid*, subs 126(7) "non-business-income tax" (e); some countries, such as Brazil, refund taxes withheld from payments to foreigners to the local payer; the purpose of these refunds is to subsidize domestic operations and borrowings.

12 *Ibid*, subs 126(7) "non-business-income tax" (g); s 110.6.

13 *Ibid*, subs 126(7) "non-business-income tax" (h); subs 33.1(1).

14 *Ibid*, subs 126(7) "non-business-income tax" (i); subpara 110(1)(f)(i).

15 *Icanda Ltd v MNR*, [1972] CTC 163 (FCTD).

16 ITA, above note 1, para 126(1)(b).

17 *Ibid*, subs 126(7) "business-income tax."

Business-income taxes paid to a foreign jurisdiction may exceed the amount that the taxpayer can claim as a credit against Canadian taxes. Any excess may be carried forward as an "unused foreign tax credit" for ten years and carried back for three years.[18] The foreign tax credit in respect of the current year must be claimed before any unused credits from other years.[19]

The credit in respect of business-income tax is limited to the amount of tax that would have been payable on a comparable amount of income earned in Canada.[20] Non-business-income tax credits are to be deducted before business-income tax credits.[21]

D. EMPLOYEES OF INTERNATIONAL ORGANIZATIONS

Employees of international organizations are usually exempt from income tax levied by the country in which they are stationed. Some of these organizations (for example, the United Nations) impose a levy upon their employees for the purpose of defraying the expenses of the organization. The levy is calculated in the same manner as an income tax.

Since a Canadian resident working abroad is subject to Canadian income tax on his worldwide income, the imposition of this additional levy constitutes double taxation of the income. To prevent double taxation, Canadian residents employed by international agencies are allowed either a deduction or a credit for foreign income.

An employee of a prescribed international organization may deduct his employment income in calculating taxable income.[22]

Employees of other international organizations may claim a tax credit for foreign taxes paid to the organization.[23]

---

18   *Ibid*, para 126(2)(a), subs 126(7) "unused foreign tax credit."
19   *Ibid*, subs 126(2.3).
20   *Ibid*, para 126(2)(b), subs 126(2.1).
21   *Ibid*, para 126(2)(c).
22   *Ibid*, subpara 110(1)(f)(iii).
23   *Ibid*, subs 126(3).

E. POLITICAL CONTRIBUTIONS CREDIT

Contributions to political parties and to candidates for political office are not deductible from income for tax purposes.[24] The Act does, however, allow a credit for political contributions against tax payable.[25] The purpose of the credit is to encourage taxpayers to support the democratic process.

The credit is available in respect of contributions to a "registered party" or to an "officially nominated candidate" in a federal election. Some of the provinces also allow for a credit against provincial taxes for contributions to provincial political parties and officially nominated candidates in provincial elections.

---

24   *Ibid*, para 18(1)(n); *Stasiuk v Canada*, [1986] 2 CTC 346 (FCTD) (taxpayer denied deduction for amounts expended on publicizing her political views).

25   *ITA*, *ibid*, subs 127(3).

PART V

CORPORATIONS

CHAPTER 16

BASIC PRINCIPLES

A. GENERAL COMMENT

Up to this point, we have looked at the rules in respect of the computation of net income, taxable income and tax payable. Most of the rules apply to all taxpayers, including individuals, corporations and trusts. We turn our attention now to the rules that apply specifically to corporations and their shareholders.

The complexity of corporate taxation derives from the division of economic and legal ownership. In terms of economic relationships, the shareholders of a corporation own its assets, whilst corporate profits and losses accrue to their benefit or detriment. Thus, in economic terms, the income and losses of the corporation reflect upon the shareholder's financial stake in the corporation.

In corporate law, however, a corporation and its shareholders are separate legal entities. Thus, shareholders do not have a direct legal interest in the assets of the corporation, but have a legal interest in the corporation's equity.

This distinction between the economic and the legal relationships between the shareholders of a corporation and the corporate entity works well in corporate law. The corporation, which is a statutory entity, allows shareholders to limit their personal liability for corporate debts. Thus, for most corporate purposes, a creditor of a corporation cannot attach personal liability to its shareholders.

Tax law generally follows the corporate model that a corporation is a separate taxpayer in its own right.[1] However, the legal distinction between a corporation and its shareholders gives rise to difficult problems. Tax law cannot focus solely on the legal relationship and completely ignore the economic relationship between a corporation and its shareholders. Thus, although the corporation and its shareholders are separate taxpayers, we shall see many tax rules that reach through the corporation to its shareholders.

For most purposes, we calculate the income of a corporation in a manner similar to that of an individual. Of course, a corporation cannot claim personal tax credits and dependency deductions. But apart from these distinct circumstances, we determine the net income and taxable income of a corporation according to the general rules described in the preceding chapters.

There are, however, two important differences in the taxation of individuals and corporations. First, most individuals (at least those who are employees) file their income taxes on a cash basis. Corporations may not use cash basis accounting and must use the accrual basis. This requirement is implicit in section 9.

Second, individuals who are employees must report their income on a calendar-year basis.[2] In contrast, corporations may select their fiscal year on any twelve-month basis.[3]

B. THE CORPORATE ENTITY

1) Separate Legal Entity

A corporation is a "person" and, therefore, a "taxpayer."[4] The defining attribute of a corporation is that it is a legal entity distinct from its shareholders.

Thus, unlike a partnership, which is a relationship between persons carrying on business in common with a view to profit,[5] a corporation has a legal existence separate and apart from its shareholders.

Since a corporation is a separate entity, its property, assets and liabilities belong to, or flow from, the corporation. This is so even if it has only one shareholder who owns all of its issued and outstanding shares.

---

1   *Income Tax Act*, RSC 1985, c 1 (5th Supp) [*ITA*], subs 248(1) "person," "taxpayer."
2   *Ibid*, para 249(1)(b).
3   *Ibid*, para 249(1)(a) and subs 249.1(1).
4   *Ibid*, subs 248(1) "person," "taxpayer."
5   See, for example, *Partnerships Act*, RSO 1990, c P.5, s 2.

The "one person company" is no less a separate legal identity than a publicly-held corporation.

2) The *Salomon* Doctrine

Salomon v Salomon & Co[6] is the *locus classicus* upholding the principle that a corporation has a legal identity that is distinct from its shareholders. Salomon incorporated a company to which he sold his unincorporated shoe manufacturing business in return for all but six of its issued shares and £10,000 of secured debentures. When the company fell upon hard times and was wound up a year later, the unsecured creditors, alleging that the company was a mere alias or agent of its principal shareholder, claimed that Salomon was personally liable to indemnify their claims. The House of Lords held that the parties had complied with all of the requirements of the corporate statute authorizing the creation of the company, that the corporation was not a sham, and that Salomon had not acted fraudulently. As a secured creditor of the corporation, Salomon ranked ahead of its unsecured creditors. As Lord Macnaghten said,

> The company attains maturity on its birth. There is no period of minority — no interval of incapacity . . . . The company is, at law, a different person altogether from the subscribers to the memorandum; and, though it may be that after incorporation the business is precisely the same as it was before, the same persons are managers, and the same hands receive the profits, the company is not in law the agent of the subscribers or trustee for them. Nor are the subscribers, as members liable, in any shape or form, except to the extent and in the manner provided by the Act.[7]

3) Parent and Subsidiary

The principle that a corporation is a legal entity separate from its shareholders also applies to the relationship between a parent company and its subsidiary. Thus, in the absence of a specific statutory provision to the contrary, a parent corporation and its subsidiary are separate and distinct legal entities. This is so even where the parent owns all the

---

6   *Salomon v Salomon & Co*, [1897] AC 22 (HL).
7   *Ibid* at 51. Although Mr. Salomon had not committed any fraud on his creditors, it was found that he had sold his business to his company at an extravagant price. As Lord Macnaghten stated, the price "represented the sanguine expectations of a fond owner rather than anything that can be called a businesslike or reasonable estimate of value" (at 49).

shares of its subsidiary and the two are, in effect, one economic entity.[8] This characteristic has important tax implications as we move profits up the chain from a subsidiary to its parent, as it creates the potential for double taxation.

4) Multiple Relationships

Another important consequence of the doctrine of separate corporate personality is that an individual can have multiple relationships with a corporation.[9] For example, an individual may own shares in the corporation, be employed by it, be its director or have a debtor/creditor relationship with the corporation. Each of these relationships give rise to different sources of income.

5) Piercing the Corporate Veil

In limited circumstances, the law disregards a corporation's separate legal existence and lifts its veil to reach through the entity to its individual members. Piercing the corporate veil ignores legal ownership in favour of economic ownership.

a) Common Law Piercing

We usually ignore a corporation's separate legal personality if one uses it to defeat public convenience, justify wrong, protect fraud or defend crime.[10] As Lord Denning said in *Littlewoods Mail Order Stores Ltd v McGregor*:

> The doctrine laid down in *Salomon* has to be watched very carefully. It has often been supposed to cast a veil over the personality of a limited company through which the courts cannot see. But that is not true. The courts can and often do draw aside the veil. They can, and often do pull off the mask. They look to see what really lies behind.[11]

---

8   *Aluminum Co of Canada v Toronto*, [1944] SCR 267 (SCC); *Barnes v Saskatchewan Co-operative Wheat Producers Ltd*, [1946] 1 WWR 97 at 113 (Sask CA), aff'd [1947] SCR 241; *Ebbw Vale Urban District Council v South Wales Traffic Licensing Authority*, [1951] 2 KB 366 (CA), Cohen LJ (under ordinary rules of law, parent and wholly-owned subsidiary are distinct legal entities; in absence of agency contract between companies, one cannot be said to be agent of other).

9   *Lee v Lee's Air Farming Ltd* (1960), [1961] AC 12 (PC).

10   See John W Durnford, "The Corporate Veil in Tax Law" (1979) 27 Can Tax J 282; Ivan R Feltham, "Lifting the Corporate Veil" in The Law Society of Upper Canada, *Special Lectures 1968: Developments in Company Law* (Don Mills, ON: De Boo, 1968) 305.

11   *Littlewoods Mail Order Stores Ltd v McGregor*, [1969] 3 All ER 855 at 860 (CA).

The principle that one can pierce the veil for the protection of public convenience, prevention of wrong, avoidance of fraud or prevention of crime applies equally in corporate and tax law. There is no separate doctrine for corporate piercing.[12]

b) Statutory Piercing

The legislature can, to use Lord Devlin's phrase, also forge a sledgehammer capable of cracking open the corporate shell. Indeed, tax law uses the sledgehammer frequently. For example:

Statutory Reference	Item	Comment
Subs 256(2.1) discretionary anti-avoidance provision	Associated corporations	The minister has discretionary power to deem two or more corporations to be associated with each other. Associated corporations are, in effect, treated as one corporation for the purpose of certain tax deductions and credits, such as the small business deduction.
S 227.1	Liability of directors for failure of corporation to remit taxes	Directors may be personally liable for certain taxes that the corporation failed to deduct, withhold, remit or pay.
Para 18(1)(p); subs. 125(7) ("personal services business")	Personal services income	In determining whether a business is a "personal service business," the relationship between the "incorporated employee" and the person to whom services are rendered is examined as if the corporation did not exist.
Para 251.1	Affiliated persons	To prevent recognition of losses where certain types of property are transferred within an economic group or family-affiliated persons.

6) Personal Liability of Shareholders

We use limited liability companies to attract capital investment without exposing shareholders to unlimited liability for their corporate debts. Although we can pierce the corporate veil to attach personal liability to shareholders, we do so only in clearly convincing cases of fraud, shams

---

12 *Consolidated-Bathurst Ltd v Canada* (1985), 85 DTC 5120 at 5124 (FCTD) additional reasons at [1985] 1 CTC 351 (FCTD), var'd (1986), 87 DTC 5001 (FCA).

and outrageously offensive conduct. Shareholders can, however, be personally liable for corporate tax.

For example, section 160 prevents a taxpayer from rendering herself judgment-proof by transferring property to persons with whom she does not deal at arm's length. The section applies when a corporation pays dividends to a person with whom it does not deal at arm's length (such as an owner/manager or relative) and the corporation at that time is liable for tax. The section is a strict liability provision. It does not require any intent to avoid taxes on the part of the transferor or any knowledge by the transferee that the corporation paid its dividend when its past tax years were open to potential reassessment.

C. GENERAL STRUCTURE OF CORPORATE TAXATION

The rules dealing with corporate taxation are more complex than the rules of individual taxation. There are two principal reasons for the increased complexity: the potential for double taxation of corporate income and the use of corporations to defer personal taxes. For example:

- Since a corporation is a taxpayer separate and distinct from its shareholders, corporate income is potentially subject to double taxation, once at the corporate level and again in the individual shareholder's hands.
- Since each corporation in a related group of corporations (e.g., parent and subsidiary) is a separate taxpayer, dividends among related corporations are subject to multiple taxation if they are taxed in each of the corporations.
- Since corporations and shareholders are separate taxpayers, individuals can use corporations to defer their personal taxes if the corporate tax rate is lower than the individual rate.
- Since corporations and shareholders are separate taxpayers, one can use corporations to park corporate income in offshore subsidiaries in low tax countries or tax havens and defer the Canadian tax until the subsidiary repatriates its profits to Canada.

Corporate taxation is also complicated because the law must manoeuvre between two different contexts: the legal doctrine that a corporation is a separate legal entity and the economic reality that there is a close interest between the corporation and its shareholders. As a separate legal entity, the rate of tax that applies to the corporation is quite independent of any rate that applies to individuals. Since, however, the corporation and its shareholders have an economic relationship, the tax rate that we apply to corporations has a direct bearing on its shareholders. If a corporation is overtaxed, its shareholders suffer economic harm. If a corporation is undertaxed, the shareholders reap the rewards.

1) Why Tax Corporations?

Double taxation of corporate income results from the taxation of corporations as separate taxable entities. Thus, the first question is whether we should have a corporate tax. What if we simply attributed income on an annual basis to the corporation's individual shareholders, regardless of whether the corporation actually paid out its income as dividends? Under this scheme, the corporation would merely be a conduit for its shareholders, in much the same way as a partnership is for its partners, or a trust is for its beneficiaries. By adjusting the tax rate on dividends, we could raise the same total revenues as we do under the dual regime of corporate and shareholder taxation.

After all is said and done, only individuals ultimately bear the burden of tax. Artificial entities do not really "pay" tax—they are merely legal conduits for individuals, who bear the real economic burden of taxation. As the Carter Commission said:[13]

> Equity and neutrality would best be achieved under a tax system in which there were no taxes on organizations as such, and all individuals and families holding interests in organizations were taxed on the accrued net gains from such interests on the same basis as all other net gains . . . .

Although theoretically appealing, the concept of notionally flowing through corporate income to individual shareholders would create some practical problems. Notional flow-through of corporate income that would be taxed in the hands of individuals could create severe liquidity problems for taxpayers if the corporation did not actually pay cash dividends. Shareholders might be compelled to sell portions of their shareholdings to raise the necessary funds to pay their tax liabilities. This could have a significant effect on capital markets.

There would also be difficulties with corporate control if individual shareholders had to sell a portion of their shareholdings in order to raise cash for their tax bills. Corporate control could change from the liquidation of shares, and family-owned businesses, in particular, would be vulnerable.

---

13 *Report of the Royal Commission on Taxation*, vol 4 (Ottawa: Queen's Printer, 1966) at 4 (Chair: KM Carter).

Private corporations might encounter difficulties in finding a suitable market for their shares, which would need to be valued annually if they were to be sold.

Also, non-residents would escape the income tax under Part I of the Act and pay only the substantially lower withholding tax (generally 5–15 percent) on dividends under Part XIII as modified by Canada's bilateral tax treaties.

The Carter Commission accepted these difficulties as sufficient justification for a separate corporate tax:[14]

> Although we can see no grounds in principle for taxing corporations and other organizations, we have reluctantly reached the conclusion that there are good and sufficient reasons for continuing to collect a tax from them.

Hence, the rationale for the structure of our corporate tax model is clearer if we accept the proposition that corporate income should not notionally flow through and be taxed in the hands of individual shareholders on an annual basis. In the absence of a flow-through of income to shareholders, we must tax corporate income annually if we are to prevent tax deferral. If corporate income is not taxed at its full rate, there would be incentive to accumulate income in the corporation in order to defer any tax that would otherwise be payable if it were paid out to shareholders. Thus, the prevention of tax deferral is an important reason for levying an annual tax on corporate income.

2) What is the Ideal Tax Rate?

If we have a separate corporate tax, what is the ideal tax rate? The problem now assumes additional dimensions.

The corporate tax rate determines the extent to which one can defer tax by using the corporate form to conduct business. A corporate tax rate lower than individual rates invites deferral. Assume, for example, that the corporate tax rate is 25 percent and that the top marginal rate for individuals is 50 percent. If an individual can shift $200,000 income into his corporation and invest the tax savings ($50,000) at 8 percent per year, the tax saved will be worth $233,000 in 20 years. Thus, each dollar of tax savings accumulates to 4.7 times its value in 20 years. If the taxpayer could do this annually for 20 years, the tax savings for each year would accumulate to $2,521,000.

---

14   *Ibid.*

If the individual sold his shares in the twentieth year, the value of the tax savings would transform into a taxable capital gain of $1,260,500.[15] If the capital gains tax rate is 23 percent, the taxpayer, in addition to the tax deferral advantage, saves 27 percent of $2,521,000, or $680,670. Thus, the taxpayer would benefit from tax deferral benefit and shifting his tax rate to a lower amount.

We could eliminate the tax deferral advantage by making the corporate tax rate equal to the highest marginal rate for individuals. If we did, the tax system would be substantially neutral at the top end, and businesses could make their decisions based on non-tax criteria. There would be no tax deferral advantage to earning income through a corporation.

A corporate rate equal to the top individual tax rate (approximately 45 percent) would also remove business and economic incentives from those who presently obtain special low rates of taxation—for example, small businesses. Thus, any gain in tax neutrality between different types of taxpayers would carry with it the cost of lost tax incentives for certain sectors of the economy. There would also be international trade consequences if Canadian rates were higher than our trading partners.

Several factors determine the corporate tax rate, but the desirability of having competitive international tax rates plays a pre-eminent role. Canadian corporations must compete internationally, and the tax rates of our principal trading partners have a significant influence on the structure of Canadian corporate taxation.

There are also other questions:

- Should there be special incentives for domestic investment over foreign investment?
- Should the corporate tax system favour Canadian corporations that earn income within Canada over Canadian corporations that earn income in foreign countries?
- Should there be special tax incentives for foreign corporations that come into Canada to do business in Canada?

The "ideal" corporate tax rate must take into account competitive tax rates and Canada's obligations under its tax and trade treaties.

3) Double Taxation

One can argue that in an ideal world corporate tax should be nothing more than a withholding tax for individuals who ultimately bear the real economic burden of taxation. In fact, one of the most acute problems of

---

15   0.5 × $2,521,000.

the corporate tax system is the potential for "double taxation" of corporate income. Typically, we tax corporate income at the corporate level when the corporation earns the income, and again at the shareholder level, when the corporation pays a dividend.

. Where a corporation earns income and distributes it to shareholders who are individuals, both the corporation and the individuals pay tax on the distributed income. The problem of "double taxation" is compounded where there is a chain of corporations, and income passes through the chain to the ultimate individual shareholder. In these circumstances, the double tax problem becomes a multiple taxation problem.

The Canadian corporate tax system is a compromise that attempts to reconcile two different problems. First, we cannot easily deem corporate income to flow through annually on a notional basis to individual shareholders without distorting the capital markets and corporate control. Second, treating the corporation as a separate entity raises the potential of double taxation of corporate income paid out to shareholders, and tax deferral on income that the corporation retains. In the absence of some form of notional flow-through of corporate income to shareholders, corporate income must bear its own tax annually. Otherwise, there would be an incentive to accumulate income in the corporation in order to defer any tax that would be payable if it paid out the income to shareholders. Thus, preventing undue tax deferral is also an important reason for taxing corporate income annually.

We could eliminate the double taxation problem by levying tax on corporate income at a rate equal to the top marginal rate of tax applicable to individuals and allowing the corporation a deduction for dividends that it pays to shareholders. Such a system would, in effect, treat the corporation as a conduit for its shareholders and impose a corporate tax only on retained earnings. There would be no tax on distributed earnings. In fact, this is the method that we apply to the taxation of trusts.

The conduit approach, however, does not work as well with corporations. Non-residents own a much larger percentage of corporate shares than trust interests. Also, under Canada's tax treaties, the withholding tax rate on dividend payments to non-residents is substantially lower than the rate payable by domestic shareholders. Hence, any such system would create a clear advantage for non-residents over residents, or would require complete renegotiation of Canada's treaties, which would have other adverse consequences.

Alternatively, we could tax the corporation on its income and completely eliminate the tax on dividends. This would, in effect, eliminate double taxation of corporate income. The problem with this approach, however, is that it would necessitate a corporate tax rate that is at least equal to the top marginal rate of individual taxation. Otherwise, high-income taxpayers would pay a lower rate of tax on their corporate income than they would on their personal income.

There are two difficulties with eliminating the tax on dividends: (1) the high tax on corporate income would be unfair to lower income individuals and tax-exempt shareholders earning corporate income, and (2) the high rate of corporate tax may not be competitive in international markets. A corporate tax rate that is significantly higher than the rate applicable in the United States, for example, would have severe economic repercussions for Canada.

Given the limitations associated with each of the above alternatives, we search for a compromise that relieves double taxation and prevents the tax deferral of corporate income. There is no perfect solution, and each country adopts a method that suits its own economic and political preferences.

The Canadian tax system provides some relief against double/multiple taxation of corporate and shareholder income. The nature of the relief varies depending upon whether the corporate/shareholder relationship is between:

- Corporation and individual;
- Domestic corporation and domestic corporation;
- Domestic corporation and foreign corporation; or
- Individual and foreign corporation.

4) Tax Integration

Should corporate and individual taxes be fully integrated to prevent double taxation and, if so, how? There are three basic models that countries use to relieve corporate double taxation:

- The classical method;
- The imputation model; or
- The advance corporate tax model.

a) The Classical Method

Under the classical method (for example, the US system), taxable corporations are taxed first at the corporate level and then again at the shareholder level if, and when, the corporation distributes its income to shareholders. This method clearly results in unequivocal double taxation of corporate income. The US provides relief, however, to certain types of corporations (for example, corporations with fewer than

408 INCOME TAX LAW

75 shareholders and limited liability companies) by treating them as conduits for their shareholders. Thus, under this system, depending on the type of corporation, some corporate income is subject to deliberate double taxation and other corporate income is not.

b) The Imputation Model

Under the imputation system, corporate income is taxed to the corporation, but the corporation's taxes are subsequently credited or imputed to the shareholder when it pays dividends to individual shareholders. Thus, the shareholder obtains relief for the corporation's taxes. In a full imputation system, corporate and individual taxes are "integrated" and all income that flows through the corporation to its shareholder is taxed only once.

For example, under the imputation model, an individual who receives a dividend from a corporation "grosses up" the cash value of the dividend to a value that is notionally equivalent to the corporation's pre-tax income. The amount of the gross-up is simply a mathematical function of the underlying corporate tax rate. For example, where a corporation earns $100 of income and pays tax of 50 percent on the income, it has $50 to distribute to its shareholders. Assuming that the corporation pays a dividend of $50 to an individual shareholder, the shareholder grosses up the dividend by multiplying it by 2 and includes $100 in income. The amount included is equal to the corporation's pre-tax income. Thus, assuming that the corporation has previously paid 50 percent tax on its income, the shareholder calculates her personal tax liability on the equivalent of the corporation's pre-tax income of $100.

The individual then pays tax at her rate on the equivalent of the corporation's *pre-tax* income of $100 and receives a credit for taxes ($50) equal to that paid by the corporation. The underlying principle of the imputation model is that the corporation's taxes are imputed to its shareholders as if they had paid them, and the shareholders claim a tax credit equal to the gross-up value of the dividends. The following illustrates a full imputation model.

Imputation Model			
Individual's Tax Bracket	26%	39%	44%
Corporate income	$100	$100	$100
Less: Corporate tax @ 50%	(50)	(50)	(50)
Net Income paid as dividend	50	50	50
Add: Dividend gross up of 100%	50	50	50
Taxable amount of dividend	$100	$ 100	$100

Imputation Model			
Individual tax	$26	$39	$44
Less: Tax credit	(50)	(50)	(50)
Net refund	24	11	6
Add: Cash dividend	50	50	50
Total cash received by individual	$74	$61	$56

In the example, the corporate tax of $50 that we impute to the individual is fully integrated with the personal tax. The amount that the individual retains is exactly equal to the amount that the shareholder would have paid if she had earned the income directly rather than through the corporation. At 44 percent, for example, the shareholder retains $56 net after she pays all corporate and personal taxes.

The example below compares the classical, full imputation, and partial imputation models. In each case we assume that the corporate tax rate is 50 percent, that the shareholder has a personal tax rate of 44 percent, and that partial imputation is at 50 percent. Then, assuming that the corporation earns $100 and pays out all of its after-tax income as dividends, the combined cost to the corporation and the shareholder in each case is as follows:

Classical Method, Full and Partial Imputation Models			
Tax	Classical Method	50% Imputation	100% Imputation
Corporate Tax			
Net Income	$100	$100	$100
Less: Corporate tax @ 50%	(50)	(50)	(50)
Net income after tax	$50	$50	50
Shareholder Tax			
Dividend received	$50	$50	$50
Add: Dividend gross-up	0	25	50
Taxable amount of dividend	$50	$75	$100.
Individual Tax @ 44%	$22	$33	$44
Less: Credit for corporate tax	(0)	(25)	(50)
Shareholder tax	$22	$8	$(6)
Corporate and shareholder tax	$72	$58	$44

The classical method is clearly the most expensive for taxpayers and results in a combined tax of $72 on income of $100. In contrast, full imputation results in a tax of $44 on $100 of income, which, in the example, is exactly equal to the tax that the shareholder would have paid had she earned the income directly rather than through a corporation.

Hence, other things being equal, one would expect a country with a classical system of corporate taxation (e.g., the United States), to have a lower corporate tax rate than a country with a full imputation system.

Subject to one proviso, the full integration of corporate and personal taxes is equitable, neutral, eliminates double taxation and tax deferral. In the example, the shareholder pays 44 percent tax, whether he earns the income through a corporation or personally. A full imputation system integrates the corporate and personal tax. To achieve this result, however, the corporate tax rate must be at least equal to the top personal rate, so there is no systemic incentive to defer taxes by retaining income in the corporation.

If the corporate tax rate is lower than personal tax rates, there is an incentive to retain earnings in the corporation in order to defer the higher personal tax payable on dividends. Such a bias also creates an ancillary distortion: earnings retained in the corporation will usually cause the value of the corporation's shares to increase, so that, when disposed of, they will give rise to capital gains. Since capital gains are usually taxable at preferred rates, an additional distortion builds in to the system. Thus, one must structure the imputation model in the context of corporate and personal tax rates and other systemic tax preferences. Since corporate tax rates are substantially influenced by international considerations, it is not always easy to implement an efficient full imputation system.

The imputation model is also not without its conceptual problems. One of the difficulties of the full imputation model is that the shareholder receives a credit for taxes that the corporation notionally pays even though the corporation may not actually have paid any tax on the income in the year. For example, a corporation may earn $100 income but pay no tax on it because it can reduce its taxable income to zero through fast write-offs of expenditures, such as capital cost allowance, research and development costs, depletion allowances, or other tax incentives or preferences. The model, however, allows the shareholder a tax credit for the tax supposedly paid by the corporation. Thus, the imputation model is premised on an assumption that may not be, and rarely is, valid. Tracking the actual amount of tax paid by each corporation and tracing it to its dividends leads to another tax model.

c) The Advance Corporate Tax Model

The Advance Corporate Tax (ACT) model is essentially a variation of the imputation model. But unlike the imputation model, which involves a credit for corporate taxes on a notional basis, the ACT model involves tracking the actual taxes and dividends paid by a corporation. Under this model, where a corporation pays taxes, it establishes a "Taxes Payable" account. When it pays a dividend to its shareholders, it withholds tax on behalf of the shareholder and claims the tax withheld from the shareholder as a credit to reduce its Taxes Payable account.

The essence of the ACT system is that it relies on a direct dividend tax credit, rather than a notional credit as under the imputation model. The tax withheld on distribution to shareholders is equal to the amount of tax that the corporation actually paid. The limitation of the system is that it creates an incentive to distribute income. Otherwise, corporate income is double taxed if the corporation does not pay enough dividends to cover its full tax liability. The pressure to pay dividends prevents corporate capital accumulation.

5) Tax Rates

a) General Rates
Canadian corporate tax rates depend on four principal factors:

- The type of corporation,
- The source of income,
- The timing of distribution to shareholders, and
- The relationship between the corporation and its shareholders.

The federal corporate tax rate starts at 38 percent of taxable income.[16] This rate is reduced by 10 percent of the corporation's taxable income earned in the year in a province.[17] Then there is a general rate reduction (for non-CCPCs) of 13 percent (2012). Thus, the general federal corporate rate of tax on taxable income earned in Canada is 15 percent. There are other reductions depending upon the nature of income. See, for example, the general rate reduction or the reduction for CCPCs.

The 10 percent reduction in the federal corporate tax rate from 38 percent to 28 percent in effect vacates an area of the income tax field to the provinces to allow them to levy their own corporate income taxes. The provinces levy corporate taxes at varying rates that generally exceed 10 percent. We obtain the actual total tax on corporate income by adding the applicable provincial rate to the federal rate. For example, where a province levies corporate tax at 14 percent, the combined federal-provincial corporate tax is 33 percent. In fact, the effective rate of federal tax on corporate income depends on various factors that can

---

16   *ITA*, above note 1, subs 123(1).
17   *Ibid*, subs 124(1). The basic rate of federal tax is subject to various adjustments in the form of tax credits and surtaxes.

increase or decrease the nominal rate. For example, some corporations receive tax credits for certain types of income.

b) Flat Rate

The basic federal corporate tax is a flat rate. Because the tax is applied at a flat rate, the average rate of tax that a corporation pays is usually the same as its marginal rate. Thus, with some exceptions, discussed below, the rate of tax that a corporation pays on its "top dollar" is the same as the rate that it pays on its first dollar of taxable income. This characteristic of the corporate tax structure is extremely important when considering the interplay between the tax that a corporation pays and the tax that its shareholders pay. It might, for example, influence the decision as to how much an owner-manager should extract from a corporation by way of salary (deductible to the corporation) or dividends (not deductible), which would be taxable to the individual at progressive marginal rates.

c) Special Rates

Although the corporate tax is a flat rate, it is important to note that there are, in fact, several different flat rates. The rate applicable to a particular corporation depends upon the type of corporation, the amount that it earns in the year, the source and type of its income, and its shareholdings. Each of these factors plays a role in determining the rate at which a corporation is taxable.[18] For example, in 2009 the federal tax rate on the first $500,000 of active business income earned by a Canadian-controlled private corporation (CCPC) was 11 percent.[19]

	%
Basic federal rate	38.00
Federal abatement	(10.00)
	28.00
Small business deduction	(17.00)
Small business rate	11.00

6) Taxation of Shareholders

When a corporation pays dividends, its shareholders may also be liable for tax on their dividend income. The taxation of shareholders depends upon the following:

---

18   See, for example, *ibid*, ss 125 & 125.1.
19   The "small business deduction" rates are adjusted periodically.

- Type of shareholders (corporate or individual),
- Status of the payer corporation (Canadian or foreign),
- Size of shareholdings (controlling shareholder or portfolio investor),
- Type of dividend (taxable or capital), and
- Source of income from which the dividend is paid (active or passive).

A complicating feature of the corporate tax system is the potential for double taxation of income in the corporation and again in the hands of its shareholders. The Act does, however, provide some relief from double taxation. For example, dividends between taxable Canadian corporations flow through tax-free of the Part I tax.[20] Individuals who receive dividends from taxable Canadian corporations can claim a dividend tax credit,[21] which reduces the net rate on such income. The extent of the relief from double taxation of corporate income depends upon the status of the payer corporation and the source and amount of its income.

D. TYPES OF CORPORATIONS

1) Canadian Corporations

A Canadian corporation is a corporation that is resident in or incorporated in Canada.[22] There is no requirement that the corporation be owned by Canadian residents or by Canadian citizens.[23] The Act deems any corporation incorporated in Canada after 26 April 1965 to be resident in Canada.[24] A corporation incorporated in Canada before 27 April 1965 that has either become a resident of Canada or carried on business in Canada after that date is also a resident of Canada.[25]

2) Taxable Canadian Corporations

A taxable Canadian corporation is a Canadian corporation that is not exempt from Part I tax, except pursuant to paragraph 149(1)(t).[26]

---

20   *Ibid*, subs 112(1).
21   *Ibid*, s 121.
22   *Ibid*, subs 89(1) "Canadian corporation."
23   *Ibid*, para 250(4)(a).
24   *Ibid*.
25   *Ibid*, para 250(4)(c).
26   *Ibid*, subs 89(1) "taxable Canadian corporation."

3) Public Corporations

Generally, public corporations are corporations with widely dispersed shareholdings that are listed on a stock exchange in Canada.

More specifically, a "public corporation" is a corporation that is resident in Canada that has:[27]

- Its shares listed on a designated stock exchange in Canada;[28]
- Elected to become a public corporation and has complied with certain prescribed conditions; or
- Been designated by the minister to be a public corporation and has complied with certain prescribed conditions.

4) Private Corporations

The Act defines private corporation status by applying a negative test to the definition of a public corporation. Thus, a private corporation is a corporation that is:[29]

- Resident in Canada,
- Not a public corporation, and
- Not controlled by one or more public corporations or prescribed Federal Crown corporations or any combination of the two.[30]

We determine whether a corporation is controlled by a public corporation on the basis of the *de jure* test.

5) Canadian-Controlled Private Corporations

A Canadian-controlled private corporation (CCPC) is a private "Canadian corporation" that is not controlled by non-residents, by a public corporation, or by any combination of non-residents and public corporations.[31] The definition of CCPC does not require control by Canadian residents, but lack of control by non-residents. For example, a private

---

27   *Ibid*, "public corporation."
28   *Income Tax Regulations*, CRC, c 945, s 3200: prescribed stock exchanges include Tiers 1 and 2 of the TSX Venture Exchange (also known as Tiers 1 and 2 of the Canadian Venture Exchange), the Montreal Stock Exchange and the Toronto Stock Exchange. Over-the-counter trading of shares, which is done through Tier 3 of the TSX Venture Exchange, does not qualify a corporation as a public corporation.
29   *ITA*, above note 1, subs 89(1) "private corporation."
30   See *Income Tax Regulations*, above note 28, s 7100.
31   *ITA*, above note 1, subs 125(7) "Canadian-controlled private corporation." See *Silicon Graphics Ltd v Canada*, 2002 FCA 260.

corporation that is owned 50 percent by non-residents and 50 percent by residents qualifies as a CCPC.

"Control" means both legal and factual control—that is, the amount of shareholdings and *de facto* influence.[32]

The *de jure* (legal) test is essentially numerical. One adds up the shares that non-residents and public corporations own to determine if they exceed 50 percent.

6) Other Corporations

A corporation may be neither a private corporation nor a public corporation. Thus, the mere fact that a corporation does not qualify as a public corporation does not automatically make it a "private corporation." For example, a resident unlisted subsidiary of a public corporation is neither a public nor a private corporation. In contrast, a resident subsidiary of a non-resident corporation whose shares are widely held may qualify as a private corporation.

7) Special Status Corporations

Certain types of corporations carrying on business in Canada are subject to special rules. There are various reasons for granting corporations special status. The Act treats certain investment-type corporations as financial intermediaries for their shareholders and integrates the tax at the corporate and individual levels. In other cases, corporations, such as credit unions and co-operative organizations, are accommodated by special provisions that take into account the special needs of the businesses that these entities conduct.

8) Exempt Corporations

Certain corporations are completely exempt from tax. There are two types of exempt corporations:

- Those exempt from tax by virtue of their status *per se* (e.g., a municipality in Canada or a municipal or public body performing a function of government in Canada);[33] or

---

32   See *ITA, ibid*, subs 256(5.1); *Mimetix Pharmaceuticals Inc v Canada* (2001), 2001 DTC 1026 (TCC [General Procedure]), aff'd 2003 FCA 106.

33   *ITA, ibid*, paras 149(1)(c), (d), (d.1) to (d.6) and (e).

- Those exempt from tax by virtue of a particular status and additional tests (e.g., a registered charity is exempt from tax on its income if it complies with certain rules in respect of its activities).[34]

E. CORPORATE FINANCE

The conventional sources of corporate funding are:

- Share capital,
- Debt capital,
- Retained cash earnings,
- Off-balance-sheet financial instruments (warrants, options, leases, etc.), and
- Government grants and subsidies.

The choice of financing depends upon the type of corporation, its size, its access to capital markets, and the residence of its shareholders.

Small private businesses generally issue shares and debt. They can also use internally generated cash and apply for government grants. Publicly listed corporations with access to sophisticated capital markets may issue derivatives, such as rights and warrants.

There are two major factors in determining the financial structure of a corporation:

1) Access to funds, and
2) The cost of funds.

Market and tax considerations influence the cost of funds. Thus, where a corporation has a choice between alternative sources of funding, its decision to opt for one source over another—or to balance between different sources of funds—will depend upon income tax considerations. For example, a corporation may determine the ratio of its debt to equity capital by tax considerations such as the residence of its shareholders, which determines the withholding tax rate, or the thin capitalization rules,[35] which determine the deductibility of interest.

1) General Characteristics of Debt and Share Capital

The capital structure of most private corporations essentially comprises two elements: equity and debt. Equity, in turn, comprises two subcategories: share capital and retained earnings.

---

34   *Ibid*, para 149(1)(f); see, generally, s 149.1.
35   *Ibid*, subs 18(4).

a) Share Capital

Share capital represents an ownership interest in the corporation. The rights, restrictions, terms, and conditions attached to corporate shares determine the nature of the interest. A corporation is not obliged to redeem its common shares or pay a dividend on the shares. In the absence of any special provisions, all shares of a corporation are presumed to be equal.[36] The issue price of shares is usually its stated capital. For tax purposes, the stated capital is the starting point of determining paid-up capital (PUC).

Share capital has two fundamental tax characteristics:

- A corporation can return the PUC of shares to its shareholders tax-free; and
- Dividends are not deductible from income and must be paid with after-tax dollars.

These two characteristics affect the corporate financial structure of most enterprises.

b) Debt Capital

Debt generally arises from a contractual obligation whereby one person lends money to another on terms and conditions negotiated between the parties. The characteristics of corporate debt are as follows:

- Debt does not represent ownership in a corporation, but merely creates a relationship of debtor and creditor between the lender and the corporation;
- Corporate creditors generally rank ahead of shareholders in any claims to the corporation's assets;
- Debt may be secured by corporate assets; and
- Interest on business debt is generally deductible for tax purposes.

c) Hybrid Capital

Certain financial instruments have characteristics of both debt and share capital. Owing to the significant tax differences in the treatment of debt and equity capital, corporations often devise hybrid instruments that allow them the best of both worlds. For example, payments on debt are generally deductible for tax purposes; payments can be discretionary and, in this sense, resemble dividends on share capital. From the corporation's perspective, it is attractive to issue a hybrid instrument that has the corporate characteristics of share capital, but

---

36 *Canada Business Corporations Act*, RSC 1985, c C-44 [*CBCA*], subs 24(3); Ontario *Business Corporations Act*, RSO 1990, c B.16 [*OBCA*], subs 22(3).

that can be classified as debt for tax purposes. The tax authorities are understandably concerned about such instruments. There are complex rules to minimize their use. These rules circumscribe the use of hybrids, such as, "taxable preferred shares," "term preferred shares" and "income bonds."

2) Corporate Law

Neither the *Canada Business Corporations Act*[37] (*CBCA*) nor the *Business Corporations Act* of Ontario[38] (*OBCA*) defines "capital." Generally, "capital" refers to proceeds from the sale of capital stock and represents money that the shareholder pays for an undivided interest in the assets of a corporation.[39]

Thus, in corporate law, the term "capital" means the share capital of a corporation. This is a narrower meaning than "equity capital," which means corporate share capital and retained earnings—the total nominal equity interest of shareholders.

The concept of capital in tax law derives from corporate law. A corporation's share capital for tax purposes—technically, its paid-up capital (PUC)—is its "stated capital" for the purposes of corporate law, as adjusted by specific provisions of the Act.

In corporate law, the concept of "stated capital" has two distinct purposes:

1) Protection of creditors, and
2) Protection of shareholders.

Corporate creditors look to a corporation's stated capital as a measure of security—the pool from which the corporation will pay its debts. Hence, creditors are interested in the capital structure of the corporation—its debt to equity relationships—to which they loan money. Creditors want to ensure that the corporation does not dissipate its capital through unauthorized corporate withdrawals that will endanger its solvency.[40]

Stated capital also measures the limits of the shareholders' exposure for corporate debts. Most corporate statutes limit a shareholder's maximum exposure for corporate liabilities to his contribution to the corporation's stated capital.

---

37   *Ibid.*
38   Above note 36.
39   *Toronto v Consumers' Gas Co*, [1927] 4 DLR 102 (PC from Ontario).
40   *Inrig Shoe Co, Re* (1924), 27 OWN 110 (SC); see *JMPM Enterprises Ltd v Danforth Fabrics (Humbertown) Ltd*, [1969] 1 OR 785 (HCJ) (issuance of additional shares to affect a change in control being "sale or other disposition" of control).

A corporation may not issue any shares until it receives full consideration in the form of money, property or past services in return for the shares. If past services constitute the consideration for issued shares, the fair value of those services must not be less than the money the corporation would have received had it issued the shares for cash.[41]

A corporation may also issue shares for non-cash property. The value of the property cannot be less than the cash consideration the corporation would have received had it issued its shares for money.[42]

The concept of "stated capital" is important in corporate law and is also the springboard for determining PUC for tax purposes.

Stated capital is the amount of money that a shareholder "commits" to the corporation and, in most cases, represents the shareholder's maximum liability to corporate creditors. Thus, in a sense, it is the financial measure of the limits of liability of shareholders and represents to creditors the amount of funds or assets that shareholders have invested in the corporation.

3) Tax Aspects of Equity Financing

Three fundamental tax characteristics determine corporate capital structures:

1) Corporations pay dividends with after-tax dollars. Dividends are not deductible from income for tax purposes.
2) Corporations can return their capital (PUC) to shareholders on a tax-free basis.
3) Inter-corporate dividends between public Canadian companies are essentially tax-free.

a) Paid-Up Capital (PUC)

The concept of PUC is unique to tax law. Since the *Income Tax Act* levies a tax on income—not on capital—we distinguish between corporate income and capital.

"PUC" measures capital for tax purposes and is the amount that a corporation can return to its shareholders on a tax-free basis. Payments to shareholders in excess of the PUC of their shares are taxable as income.

The PUC of a share starts off equal to its stated capital for corporate purposes. For example, where a corporation issues shares for $100 per share, both its stated capital and PUC are $100. PUC does not necessarily

---

41   *CBCA*, above note 36, subs 25(3); *OBCA*, above note 36, subs 23(3).
42   *CBCA*, *ibid*, subs 25(3); *OBCA*, *ibid*, subs 23(3).

change when one sells shares. PUC is a share-specific attribute. Adjustments to PUC appear only on the corporation's books. We determine PUC as at a point in time.

In contrast, the cost (adjusted cost base) of a share is a feature unique to the shareholder. It has no effect on the corporation. In the above example, the cost of the shares to the purchaser is $100.

However, stated capital and PUC can diverge because of subsequent adjustments for tax purposes that do not affect the corporation's financial records. Thus, PUC for tax purposes may differ from stated capital for financial accounting purposes. It can also vary from the cost base of the shares if one sells the shares. In the above example, if the shareholder sells her shares for $150 per share, the cost base of each share to the new purchaser is $150. Thus, the initial shareholder derives a gain of $50. The new price has no effect on the company's books and records. The PUC of each share remains $100. PUC and stated capital of the shares are unchanged by the shareholder transactions.

PUC can change for tax purposes without affecting stated capital for corporate purposes. For example, the PUC of a class of shares may change in certain non-arm's length sales, transfers of property to a Canadian corporation, amalgamations and in non-arm's length purchases of shares from non-residents. Thus, a corporation's PUC for tax purposes can be quite different from its stated capital for financial accounting purposes.

b) Adjustments to PUC

At the outset of corporate life, the PUC of a share for tax purposes is equal to its stated capital for corporate purposes. The two measures of capital can, however, diverge because of subsequent adjustments for tax purposes. For example, one might adjust the PUC of a class of shares for transactions under any of the following provisions of the *Income Tax Act*:

- Subsections 66.3(2) and (4) (flow-through shares);
- Sections 84.1 and 84.2 (non-arm's length sales);
- Section 85 (transfer of property to a corporation);
- Subsection 87(9) (amalgamation);
- Subsection 192(4.1) (designation by corporation); and
- Section 212.1 (non-arm's length purchase of shares from non-resident).

Thus, a corporation's PUC for tax purposes may be quite different from its stated capital for financial accounting purposes.

c) Share Redemptions

Where a corporation redeems shares for an amount in excess of their PUC, the excess is deemed to be a dividend.[43] For example, assume that the stated capital and PUC of a share are $100, and the shareholder's adjusted cost base is $150. If the corporation redeems the share for $180, the shareholder is deemed to receive a dividend of $80.

Cash paid on redemption	$180
PUC	100
Deemed dividend	$80

At the same time, the Act deems the shareholder to dispose of her share and to derive proceeds of disposition, which may trigger a capital gain. In order to prevent double taxation, however, the Act reduces the shareholder's proceeds of disposition by the amount of the deemed dividend — that is, $80.

Cash paid on redemption	$180
Less: deemed dividend	(80)
Proceeds of disposition	$100
Less: adjusted cost base	(150)
Capital loss	$(50)

Thus, the shareholder is deemed to receive a dividend of $80 and suffers a capital loss of $50 — that is, an economic net gain of $30. The treatment of the dividend and capital loss for tax purposes, however, is quite different. The shareholder obtains a tax credit on the dividend if the corporation that redeems the share is a Canadian corporation.[44] Only one-half of the capital loss of $50 is deductible for tax purposes, and then only against the shareholder's capital gains. If the shareholder does not have any capital gains, the tax bite can exceed the economic gain.

The Act deems the capital loss of $50 to be nil if the taxpayer is affiliated with the corporation immediately after the redemption. In such a case, we add the amount of the denied loss proportionately (based on relative fair market value) to the ACB of any other shares that the shareholder owns. The purpose of this stop-loss rule is to prevent the shareholder from recognizing his loss where he remains a part of an economic group of affiliated persons.[45]

---

43   *ITA*, above note 1, subs 84(3).
44   *Ibid*, s 121.
45   *Ibid*, subs 40(3.6) and para. 53(2)(f.2).

d) Taxable Preferred Shares

One of the fundamental structural characteristics of the corporate tax system is that corporations pay dividends with after-tax earnings. In contrast, interest expense is generally deductible for tax purposes and comes out of pre-tax earnings. On the other side of the coin, dividends generally flow on a tax-free basis between taxable Canadian corporations,[46] whereas interest income is taxable. Thus, the system has a built-in structural bias. A taxable corporation prefers dividend income to interest income, but prefers to pay interest expense instead of dividends on its financings.

In most cases, the opposing economic interests of creditor and debtor corporations in arm's length relationships will cause the parties to arrive at the most appropriate and market-efficient solution for corporate financing needs. Typically, there is a rate differential between interest charged on debt obligations and dividends on shares. The differential takes into account their disparate income tax treatment, which affects the cost of capital. The market model breaks down, however, if one of the parties to the financing transaction is not a taxable entity or has large accumulated losses.

We justify the tax-free flows of inter-corporate dividends on two bases: (1) the dividends are paid out of previously taxed profits to an entity that has an economic interest in the payer; and (2) the dividends will eventually be taxed again when paid out to individual shareholders. Thus, the disparity between dividend and interest income is premised on the prevention of double taxation of the same income within an economic unit of corporations.

The disparate tax treatment of dividend and interest income creates other problems, however, because of hybrid equities with the features and characteristics of both—instruments that look like shares, but that have all the important characteristics of debt, such as a fixed and pre-determined life. These so-called "shares" are usually underwritten by guarantees and have a specific term. Hence, they are known as "term preferred shares."

Term preferred shares are equity instruments with preferences that one usually associates with preferred shares. The difference between ordinary and term preferred shares is that the latter have a limited term and are usually supported by guarantees for repayment. This type of financial instrument is most attractive when the borrower (for example, a taxable corporation) does not need and cannot use, an interest deduction because it does not have sufficient taxable income to absorb the deduction. (The taxable corporation may not be able to utilize the

---

46   See *ibid*, subs 112(1).

interest deduction because it has, for example, accumulated losses, low profit margins or accelerated write-offs.) In these circumstances, the corporation can usually negotiate more favourable borrowing terms on a hybrid, rather than a conventional debt, instrument if the corporation pays the lending institution in the form of tax-free dividends.

Similarly, even if both the lender and the borrower are taxable entities, there can be a tax advantage if the borrower's tax rate is lower than that of the lending institution. The net result of this tax-driven financial arbitrage is that otherwise profitable enterprises (but without taxable income because of available tax write-offs) can transform what are, in effect, payments on debt-type instruments into tax-free dividends in exchange for a lower borrowing cost.

Part VI.1 of the Act levies a special tax to be paid by a corporation that has paid taxable dividends on taxable preferred shares. The tax is, in effect, a refundable tax on large corporations that use after-tax financing. The tax is imposed at three different rates as follows:[47]

Rate	Application
50%	Taxable dividends (other than excluded dividends) on "short-term" preferred shares in excess of dividend allowance;
40%	Where issuing corporation makes an election at the time of issue and where the terms of the shares so provide; and
25%	In all other cases where taxable dividends are paid on taxable preferred shares.

The rate of 50 percent is intended to approximate the amount of tax that would be paid on an equivalent amount of interest if we assume a 33.3 percent rate of corporate tax. The underlying rationale of these rates is to ensure that sufficient income tax is paid at the corporate level to recover the tax benefit given to the recipient corporation for the inter-corporate dividend deduction or to individuals for the dividend tax credit.

i) Meaning of "Taxable Preferred Shares"
A share is a taxable preferred share if:

- The shareholder is entitled to a fixed annual dividend, as and when directors of the issuing corporation declare it;
- The shareholder is entitled to a fixed entitlement if the corporation winds-up or redeems its shares;
- It has any preference to dividends in relation to any other share; or
- It is convertible into a share that would be a taxable preferred share.

---

47   *Ibid*, subs 191.1(1)(a), effective from 2003.

A "taxable preferred share" does not include prescribed shares or shares issued by a corporation in financial difficulty.[48]

The definition of taxable preferred shares is comprehensive enough to include shares that are considered to be "common shares" in most other circumstances. Given the broad definition of "taxable preferred share," the term encompasses ordinary "common shares" that have rights, conditions, privileges or restrictions attached to them that fall within the definition. For example, it is not unusual to see so-called "common shares" that may be redeemable at a pre-determined ("fixed") amount. Such a share is caught within the definition of "taxable preferred share" for the purposes of the special taxes.

ii) Tax on Preferred Shares

The Part VI.1 tax on dividends on taxable preferred shares is, in effect, a refundable tax. The tax is structured to prevent taxable corporations that do not have taxable income from using after-tax financial instruments to pay tax-free dividends to taxable lending institutions.

A corporation pays the tax on its taxable dividends on taxable preferred shares, but can claim a refund of the tax in certain circumstances. The refund is in the form of a deduction from income in an amount equal to three times the tax paid.[49] The tax is fully refundable only if the corporation that pays the dividend has sufficient income against which it can use the deduction. Thus, the payer corporation cannot use its Part VI.1 tax to reduce income if it does not have any income that is subject to tax.

iii) Exemptions

There are several exemptions from the special tax on taxable preferred shares.

a. "Substantial Interest"

There are exemptions in respect of substantial interest shareholdings that are, essentially, dividends received by a related party or those received by a shareholder who owns at least 25 percent of the votes and of the value of the capital stock of the paying corporation.[50] A dividend paid to a shareholder with a substantial interest in the corporation is an "excluded dividend" for the purposes of the tax.[51]

---

48   The concept of "financial difficulty" is itself defined in paragraph (e) of the definition of "term preferred share" in subsection 248(1), *ibid.*

49   *Ibid*, para 110(1)(k).

50   *Ibid*, subs 191(1) & (2).

51   *Ibid*, subss 191(1) & 191.1(1).

b. "Dividend Allowance"
The Part VI.1 tax applies only to dividends paid in excess of the corporation's dividend allowance. The dividend allowance is set at $500,000, which must be shared among associated corporations.[52] The allowance is reduced on a dollar-for-dollar basis by preferred share dividends paid in the preceding year in excess of $1,000,000.[53] Thus, small corporations may issue taxable preferred shares without getting caught by the tax.

c. Financial Intermediaries
There are also some special exemptions in respect of dividends that financial intermediary corporations pay and receive and certain deemed dividends that arise on corporate reorganizations.[54]

4) Debt Financing

Debt is often the primary source of capitalization of a small business corporation in the early stages of its life. There are advantages to using debt to capitalize a small business corporation. If one structures the loan properly, interest on the debt is deductible for tax purposes. The owner of the business can also secure the debt and rank ahead of other creditors to the extent of the security.[55]

Thus, an individual can start an enterprise with a small amount of share capital and contribute the balance of the capital by way of a secured shareholder loan. External lenders (for example, banks) will, however, usually require the owner/shareholder to provide a personal guarantee for borrowed funds.

There are several factors to be taken into account in selecting an appropriate method of debt financing. One must consider, for example, the cost of capital, its availability, and the risk exposure of the enterprise. No single formula applies to every corporation. Each corporation must take into account the terms and conditions attached to its debt financing in the context of the economic climate at the particular time.

Debt financing falls into one of two broad categories: long-term or short-term. One uses long-term debt, typically with a maturity of fifteen to twenty years, to finance the purchase of assets that have a long life. Shorter term debt financing is appropriate only for short-term needs.

---

52 *Ibid*, subs 191.1(3); s 256(1) "associated corporations."
53 *Ibid*, subs 191.1(2).
54 *Ibid*, subs 191(1).
55 Except against banks and lending institutions.

a) Discounts and Premiums

Corporations can issue debt obligations at face value, at a discount, or at a premium from their face value. A discount or premium generally reflects economic adjustments to the nominal rate of interest to bring it into line with the effective market rate applicable at the time that the obligation is issued.

A bond's premium or discount may be on account of interest or capital. What is the "true nature" of the discount or premium? Does the debt obligation have a commercial rate of interest? Does the bonus or discount vary with the length of time that the loan funds are outstanding, the extent of capital at risk and the nature of the financial operation? For example, discounts on financial market instruments, such as treasury bills, bankers' acceptances and call loans, are in substance interest. The discount is the economic reward for simply holding the principal sum of the instrument for a period of time. For example, a treasury bill that is issued at 95 and matures at par (100) in one year has an effective interest rate of 5.3 percent.[56]

Discounts on debt obligations are deductible from income.[57] Where an obligation is issued at a price that is equal to at least 97 percent of its principal amount and it does not yield an amount in excess of 4/3 of the nominal interest rate, the entire amount of the discount is deductible in computing income.

Where, however, a bond is issued for an amount that is less than 97 percent of its face amount, for a yield in excess of 4/3 of its nominal interest rate, only one-half of the discount is deductible in computing income for tax purposes.

b) Interest

The Act does not define the term "interest." "Interest" is the return or consideration for the use or retention by one person of a sum of money belonging to or owed to another.[58] It is in effect a payment for the use of property (money).

i) Source of Income

One of the requirements for the deduction of interest is the existence of the source of income to which the interest expense relates.[59] For ex-

---

56   $5/95 \times 100$.

57   *ITA*, above note 1, para 20(1)(f).

58   *Reference re s 6 of Farm Security Act, 1944 (Saskatchewan)*, [1947] SCR 394 at 411, aff'd (*sub nom AG Saskatchewan v AG Canada*) [1949] AC 110 (PC); *Riches v Westminster Bank Ltd*, [1947] AC 390 (HL); see also Chapter 8.

59   *Emerson v Canada*, [1986] 1 CTC 422 (FCA), leave to appeal to SCC refused, [1986] SCCA No 187 (taxpayer not allowed to deduct interest on money used to

ample, a taxpayer who finances the purchase of investment securities may claim any directly related interest expense as a deduction. The deduction is available so long as the taxpayer continues to hold the original investment or substituted securities. This is so even if the security declines in value or becomes worthless.

The deduction may also be claimed, however, in certain circumstances if the investment is sold and the funds are used for another eligible purpose.

Interest on money used to acquire income-earning property may be deductible even if one disposes of the property. The conditions for continued deductibility are:[60]

- The borrowed money must have been used for the purpose of earning income from capital property (other than real or immovable property or depreciable property); and
- The property must have been disposed of at its fair market value.

ii) Accrued Interest

A taxpayer who purchases a debt obligation (other than an income bond, income debenture, small business development bond or small business bond) can deduct interest accrued on the debt to the date of the purchase. The deduction is restricted to the extent that the amount is included as interest in computing income for the year. The accrued interest paid to the vendor of the debt obligation is included in computing the vendor's income.[61] Alternatively, the purchasing taxpayer may choose to capitalize the interest.

iii) Expenses of Issuing Debt

A taxpayer can deduct expenses incurred in borrowing money for the purpose of earning income from a business or property.[62] In the absence of specific authorization, financing expenses (which typically include legal and accounting fees, printing costs, commissions, etc.) would be caught by the prohibition against deducting expenses not directly

---

purchase shares after shares sold at loss); *Bronfman Trust v Canada*, [1987] 1 SCR 32, [1987] 1 CTC 117, 87 DTC 5059 (SCC) (interest not deductible where principal borrowed to make capital distribution to trust beneficiary).

60   *ITA*, above note 1, subs 20.1(1).

61   *Ibid*, subs 20(14); Interpretation Bulletin IT-410R, "Debt Obligations: Accrued Interest on Transfer" (4 September 1984) archived by CRA. This rule only operates where there has been an assignment or transfer of title. Evidence of registration of title would likely be necessary; see *Hill v MNR*, [1981] CTC 2120 (TRB); *Smye v MNR*, [1980] CTC 2372 (TRB); *Canada v Antosko*, [1994] 2 SCR 312.

62   *ITA*, *ibid*, para 20(1)(e).

related to the income-earning process.[63] Financing expenses are deductible on a rateable basis over a five-year period.

iv) Lump Sum Payments

Interest may be paid lump sum at the end of the term of a loan.[64]

5) Hybrid Debt

Just as a corporation can issue hybrid share capital (that is, share capital with substantial debt characteristics), so also can it issue hybrid debt—debt capital with all of the characteristics of equity. There are two advantages of hybrid debt: (1) in the absence of special rules, payments on debt are generally deductible for tax purposes; and (2) payments can be discretionary and, in this sense, resemble dividends on share capital. There are special rules that control the deductibility of interest on hybrid debt capital.

a)   Income Bonds and Debentures

An income bond or debenture is a hybrid that pays interest or dividends only when and to the extent that the issuing corporation makes a profit.[65] This allows its issuer the flexibility of making interest or dividend payments only if it is in a profitable position and able to do so. Thus, an income bond or debenture resembles share capital. An "income bond" or "income debenture" is an instrument that does not, in any circumstances, exceed a term of five years, and is issued:[66]

- As part of a proposal or arrangement with creditors that is approved under the *Bankruptcy Act* and *Insolvency Act*;
- At a time when all or substantially all of its assets were under the control of a receiver, or similar person; or
- At a time when the issuing corporation or a resident non-arm's length corporation was in default, or reasonably expected to be in default, on a debt obligation.

The proceeds of the issue must be used in a business that is carried on immediately before its issue by the issuing corporation, or by a

---

63   *Montreal Light, Heat & Power Consolidated v MNR*, [1944] CTC 94 (PC); *see Canada v Royal Trust Corp of Canada*, [1983] CTC 159 (FCA) (payment was commission for services rendered therefore qualified as an eligible capital expenditure).

64   *Lomax v Peter Dixon & Son Ltd*, [1943] 1 KB 671 (CA).

65   *ITA*, above note 1, subs 248(1) "income bond."

66   *Ibid.*

corporation with which it does not deal at arm's length. The Act deems interest or dividends paid by a resident corporation on an income bond or debenture to be dividends[67] and, therefore, not deductible from income for tax purposes.

i)   Financial Difficulty

Interest on income bonds that a resident corporation issues to afford relief from financial difficulty is deductible and is not deemed to be a dividend.[68]

ii)   Taxable as Dividends

Payments on income bonds or debentures that are deemed to be dividends are taxable as such in the recipient's hands. Thus, in the case of individuals, the dividend is treated as a taxable dividend subject to the usual gross-up and dividend tax credit rules.[69] Where the recipient is a corporation, the dividend may be deductible as an inter-corporate dividend under section 112 of the Act. The dividend may also be subject to the refundable tax under Part IV if the recipient is a private corporation.

b)   Convertible Debt

A convertible debt is debt that is convertible into equity. Convertible debt allows the lender the best of two worlds: the security of debt capital and the growth potential of share capital. The corporation that issues convertible debt also benefits in that it can deduct interest payments on the debt. As a trade-off for the convertibility feature, interest on convertible debt is usually lower than that on conventional debt.

6)   Leases

A lease is a contractual arrangement whereby one of the parties (the "lessor") grants to another party ("the lessee") the use, possession and enjoyment of an asset for a period of time in consideration of rental payments. Thus, a lease payment represents rental for the use of property. The terms and conditions of a lease can be tailored to meet the financial needs of the lessor and the lessee. Almost any asset that can be purchased can be leased. The most common forms of leases in business, however, deal with automobiles, furniture, equipment and real property.

Leasing is "off-balance sheet" financing. The popularity of leasing assets is attributable to the financial advantage of keeping debt off the

---

67   *Ibid*, subs 15(3).
68   *Ibid*, para 18(1)(g).
69   *Ibid*, para 82(1)(b), s 121.

balance sheet, which allows for a more favourable debt to equity ratio. Also, leasing does not drain the cash flow of an enterprise in the same way as a purchase of assets.

a) Tax Treatment

Leasing brings to the fore the entire form versus substance debate in tax law. This in turn raises difficult issues of whether we should look at legal versus economic substance in determining the character of a "lease." Consider the following situations:

1) X agrees to lease a small office for fifty-five years. In exchange for the long lease, the landlord gives X a fixed rental price of $10,000 per year. The agreement is clearly a rental for the use of the office for fifty-five years.

2) Y buys an office for $123,860 (the present value of $10,000 annually over fifty-five years at 8 percent) and finances the purchase through a ten-year mortgage at 8 percent. The agreement is clearly for the purchase of real property. Y can claim capital cost allowance on the property and can deduct the mortgage interest for business purposes.

3) Z leases an office for $10,000 per year (as in case 1 above) but also negotiates an option to purchase the property at the end of fifty-five years for $1. Until that time, the landlord retains full legal title to the property, but Z pays all of the maintenance, taxes and utilities for the office. The form of the transaction is clearly hybrid. Z does not have title but has all the costs of ownership. The agreement looks like a lease, but, in economic substance, it more closely resembles an outright purchase.

The income tax considerations of leasing depend upon three principal factors:

1) The nature of the agreement;
2) The tax status of the lessee and the lessor; and
3) The type of property leased.

The leasing rules apply only to property leases. The capital cost allowance rules apply to purchases of property. Thus, the distinction between a lease and purchase is critical.

In the absence of specific tax rules, the characterization of a contractual arrangement depends upon the law of the jurisdiction that regulates the contract. One determines the nature of an acquisition by reference to the normal incidents of ownership of property: title (actual or constructive), possession, use and risk. In Quebec, the matter is determined by reference to the *Civil Code*.

Payments for the use of leased property may represent rental payments or instalments on account of its purchase price. Payments on account of rent are deductible as a current expense in the computation of income.[70] Payments on account of the purchase of depreciable property are capital costs and eligible for capital cost allowance.[71] The distinction between these two types of payments is blurred, however, where the contract provides for a lease with an option to purchase the property. In such cases, we determine whether the true nature of the contract is a lease or an installment purchase.

A lease option agreement that is a pure financing arrangement, is, in effect, a transaction that is a purchase of an asset: the lease is merely the vehicle to finance the purchase. In contrast, a "genuine" lease-option agreement is, in both substance and form, a rental agreement, but one which allows the lessee the privilege of changing her mind and purchasing the asset at a later date. There is no bright-line test to distinguish between these two types of agreements. Obviously, they both involve the same arrangements; namely, periodic payments with an option to purchase the asset at a later date. The two arrangements, however, have substantially different legal and tax results.

For example, in a "financial lease," it is quite usual for the lessee to assume the responsibility for paying the expenses of the leased property, such as taxes, insurance, maintenance, etc. The obligation to pay these expenses, which are normally associated with the ownership rather than the rental of property, does not, in and by itself, necessarily imply that the transaction is, in substance, a purchase. Such an obligation is only one factor that one evaluates to determine the character of a particular contract. The fact that the lessee assumes the expenses does not necessarily render the contract something other than a true lease.

FURTHER READINGS

The Corporate Entity

Krishna, Vern. "Blowing Hot and Cold at the Same Time" (1994) 5 Can Curr Tax 7.

Ross, David W. "Incorporation and Capitalization of a Private Corporation" (1987) 39 Can Tax Found 11:1.

---

70   *Ibid*, s 9.
71   *Ibid*, para 20(1)(a).

Structure of Corporate Taxation

CUMMING, PETER. *The Taxation of Business Enterprises* (North York, ON: York University, Osgoode Hall Law School, 1992–1993).

Types of Corporations

MACKNIGHT, ROBIN J. "What's in a Name?: Classifying Partnerships, Associations and Limited Liability Companies for Income Tax Purposes" (1993) Corp Mgmt Tax Conf 21:1.

General

EDGAR, TIM. "The Classification of Corporate Securities for Income Tax Purposes" (1990) 38 Can Tax J 1141.

General Characteristics of Debt and Share Capital

ASHTON, RK. "Does the Tax System Favour Incorporation?" (1987) Brit Tax Rev 256.

Corporate Law Aspects of Equity Financing

KRISHNA, VERN. "Income Splitting Corporate Structures" (1994) Can Curr Tax C-45.

———. "Corporate Share Capital Structures and Income Splitting" (1991) Can Curr Tax C-71.

———. "Common Law Piercing of the Corporate Veil to Reach Individual Shareholders" (1985) 1 Can Curr Tax J-101.

KRISHNA, VERN, & ANTHONY VANDUZER. "Corporate Share Capital Structures and Income Splitting: *McClurg v Canada*" (1993) 21 Can Bus LJ 335.

Tax Aspects of Debt Financing

ARNOLD, BRIAN J. "Is Interest a Capital Expense?" (1992) 40 Can Tax J 533.

LOVELAND, NORMAN C. "Income Tax Aspects of Borrowing and Lending" in The Law Society of Upper Canada, *Special Lectures 1986: Income Tax for the General Practitioner* (Don Mills, ON: De Boo, 1986) 289.

CORPORATE BUSINESS INCOME

A. GENERAL COMMENTS

There are various types of corporations: private, public, exempt, conduit, investment, etc. The scheme of taxation in respect of each of these types of corporations is different and takes into account their special circumstances and policy considerations. We look at the rules for the taxation of investment income that private corporations earn in Chapter 18. In this chapter we look at the taxation of the business income of private corporations.

B. THE STATUTORY SCHEME

The scheme for the taxation of corporate business income is different from the taxation of investment income because the underlying policies of the two are quite different. The statutory scheme for private corporations reflects three distinct policies:

1) High income taxpayers should not be able to defer tax on investment income by holding their investments in personal holding corporations;
2) Corporate income should not be taxed more than once; and
3) We can use the income tax system to support "small businesses" through tax incentives.

There are three factors that determine the taxation of corporate business income:

1) The type of corporation;
2) The type of income; and
3) The source of the income.

C. TAX INTEGRATION

"Integration" means that the amount of tax that a taxpayer pays on income should be the same, regardless whether he earns the income through a proprietorship, partnership or a corporation. We integrate corporate and shareholder taxes by crediting corporate taxes against personal shareholder taxes. The shareholder receives a credit at the personal level for taxes that the corporation notionally paid at the corporate level. These two features "integrate" the amount of tax payable by corporations and their shareholders.

The theoretical tax integration model for business income implies three assumptions:

- The combined federal and provincial corporate tax is 20 percent on business income;
- Dividends to individual shareholders are taxable at a grossed-up value to take into account the corporate tax previously paid; and
- Individual shareholders pay tax at 40 percent and receive a tax credit equal to the amount of the tax previously paid by the corporation.

If all of these assumptions apply, the tax payable by the corporation and its shareholder on its business income would be exactly equal to the amount of tax that would have been paid by the individual shareholder if he had earned the income directly. In other words, the corporate tax would fully "integrate" with the individual's tax. The following example illustrates the theoretical framework of tax integration.

Example: Theoretical Model of Integration	
Assume:	
Federal corporate tax rate	12%
Provincial corporate tax rate	8%
Combined federal/provincial tax rate	20%
Shareholder federal/provincial marginal rate	40%
Dividend gross-up	25%
Active business income	$100

Example: Theoretical Model of Integration

Then:

Corporate Tax:

Business income	$100
Corporate tax	(20)
Net income paid as dividend	$80

Shareholder Tax:

Dividend received	$80
Gross-up for corporate tax	20
Amount taxable	$100

Tax thereon:

Federal/provincial tax	$40
Credit for corporate taxes	(20)
Net tax payable	$20
Net cash ($80 dividend less $20 tax)	$60
Amount retained if income earned personally	$60
Tax differential	0

The theory is perfect. Life, however, is not theoretical. Neither the federal government nor any province fully satisfies the model. There is always some over- or under-integration of corporate/shareholder taxes because:

- The combined rate of the federal/provincial corporate tax is rarely, if ever, exactly equal to 20 percent in any province. Each province levies tax independently of the federal government and sets its own corporate tax rates, regardless of the federal government's theoretical assumptions.
- Federal and provincial governments sometimes impose surtaxes, which effectively increase the basic tax rates. This immediately distorts the underlying assumption that the federal rate is 12 percent. In addition, provincial surtaxes can introduce additional distortions.
- The corporation may have a fiscal year that does not coincide with the calendar year. Thus, assumptions made about corporate tax rates on a fiscal year basis do not necessarily coincide with actual tax rates applicable to individuals who are taxable on a calendar year basis.
- The low rate of tax applies only up to $500,000 of income.
- The combined marginal tax rate of individuals in the top bracket usually exceeds the theoretical 40 percent.

Each of these factors can distort tax integration and result in double taxation of corporate income.

1) Limits on Integration

The tax incentives for "small business" are an important part of the Canadian tax system. There are two forms of incentives: low rates of tax on business income and partial integration of corporate and shareholder taxes. But the incentives have a cost. They are, in effect, "tax expenditures." Hence, the system seeks to restrict the incentives to a manageable cost. The low tax rate is available only to Canadian-controlled private corporations (CCPCs) on active business income earned in Canada.

The basic rate of federal tax on a CCPC's active business income is 11 percent on the first $500,000 of income, compared with 16.5 percent for other corporations. Assuming a provincial tax rate of approximately 4.5 percent (Ontario 2011), the total rate of tax on the first $500,000 of income is about 16 percent. This rate of tax is available only to CCPCs that earn active business income in Canada.

The dividend tax credit is premised on the assumption that the corporation paid tax at a rate of 20 percent. Thus, even in the theoretical model, there is a penalty of double taxation for doing business through a corporation if income exceeds $500,000.

Basic rate	38%
Provincial abatement	(10%)
	28%
Small business deduction	(17%)
Total federal	11%
Provincial tax	5%
Combined federal/provincial	16%

2) Canadian-Controlled Private Corporations

A CCPC is a private corporation resident in Canada and that is not controlled—directly or indirectly—by non-resident persons, by public corporations or by any combination of non-residents and public corporations.[1]

---

1   *Income Tax Act*, RSC 1985, c 1 (5th Supp) [*ITA*], subs 125(7) "Canadian-controlled private corporation"; Interpretation Bulletin IT-458R2, "Canadian-Controlled Private Corporation" (31 May 2000).

3) Active Business Income

"Active business" includes any business other than a "specified investment business" or a "personal service business." It also includes income
from an adventure or concern in the nature of trade.[2]

"Business" includes "a profession, calling, trade, manufacture or
undertaking of any kind whatever."[3] The adjective "active" is expansive.
For example, in *Canada v Cadboro Bay Holdings Ltd*:

> [A]ny quantum of business activity that gives rise to income in a tax-
> ation year for a private corporation in Canada is sufficient to make
> mandatory the characterization of such income as income from an
> "active business carried on in Canada."[4]

a) Presumptions

There is a rebuttable presumption that corporate income derives from
business. In *Canadian Marconi Co v Canada*, for example, Wilson J said:

> It is frequently stated in both the English and Canadian case law that
> there is in the case of a corporate taxpayer a rebuttable presumption
> that income received from or generated by an activity done in pursuit
> of an object set out in the corporation's constating documents is in-
> come from a business.
>
> . . .
>
> The question whether particular income is income from busi-
> ness or property remains a question of fact in every case. However,
> the fact that a particular taxpayer is a corporation is a very relevant
> matter to be considered because of the existence of the presumption
> and its implications in terms of the evidentiary burden resting on
> the appellant.[5]

The presumption, coupled with the generous judicial interpretation of
"active," gives an expansive meaning to the phrase "active business."

The presumption is not ironclad, however, and should be read in the
context of the statutory structure for the taxation of corporate income.
Business income is taxed quite differently from investment income.
The judicial presumption should not be read to negate the statutory
scheme for the taxation of business and investment income.

---

2   *Ibid*, subs 125(7) "active business carried on by a corporation."
3   *Ibid*, subs 248(1) "business."
4   *Canada v Cadboro Bay Holdings Ltd* (1977), 77 DTC 5115 at 5123 (FCTD).
5   *Canadian Marconi Co v Canada* (1986), 86 DTC 6526 at 6528 & 6529 (SCC).

b) Business vs. Investment Income

The distinction between investment income and business income depends upon activity and proportionality, including:[6]

- Activity associated with the generation of the income;
- Number and value of transactions;
- Relationship between the income in question and total income; and
- Relationship between the value of the assets producing the income in question and total assets.

The greater the volume of activity and the value of transactions, and the closer the relationship between the income earned and the total income and assets of the taxpayer, the greater the likelihood that the income is "business income."

Business income is "active business income," unless it derives from a "specified investment business" or a "personal service business."[7]

A "specified investment business" is a business that derives its income principally from investments and property. Thus, it includes a business whose principal purpose is to earn income from interest, dividends, royalties, rents, etc.[8]

c) Incidental Business Income

Incidental business income, such as income from investment of surplus cash, rental of excess space, interest on accounts receivable and certain investment income from associated corporations is active business income.[9] Active business income does not, however, include income from property from a source in Canada.[10]

---

6   *Ibid.*

7   *ITA*, above note 1, subs 125(7) "active business carried on by a corporation," "personal services business," "specified investment business."

8   *Ibid*, subs 125(7) "specified investment business" and subs 129(4) "income or loss."

9   *Ibid*, subs 125(7) ("income of the corporation for the year from an active business"); *Canada v Marsh & McLennan Ltd*, [1983] CTC 231 (FCA), leave to appeal to SCC refused (1984), 52 NR 231 (meaning of what is ancillary, incidental or subsidiary to active business); *Canada v Ensite Ltd*, [1983] CTC 296 (FCA), aff'd [1986] 2 SCR 509 (test is whether property employed and risked in business; property used to fulfil a mandatory condition precedent to trade was property used or held in the business); *Alamar Farms Ltd v Canada*, [1993] 1 CTC 2682 (TCC) (rental payments from surface leases and royalty income was incidental to taxpayer's principal activity of farming and, therefore, active business income). See also subs 129(6) (investment income from associated corporation deemed to be active business income).

10   *ITA, ibid*, subs 129(4) "income or loss."

For example, cash and short-term liquid investments that are an integral part of a business are business assets and generate business income.[11] The critical element is whether the corporation depends and relies upon the investments for the operation of its business.[12] A business that engages in the lending of money under security of mortgages, investing in securities and the renting of property can qualify as an active business.[13]

D. THE SMALL BUSINESS DEDUCTION

The small business deduction is limited by three parameters:

1) The corporation's active business income;
2) The corporation's Canadian source taxable income; and
3) An overall limit of $500,000.

These restrictions ensure that only small corporate businesses with Canadian-source active business income can claim the deduction. The small business deduction is not available to proprietorships and partnerships, regardless of their size.

Subsection 125(1) limits a corporation's small business deduction in any year to 17 percent of the *least* of its:[14]

• Net Canadian active business income for the taxation year;
• Taxable income for the taxation year less 10/3 of its foreign non-business income tax credit and three times its foreign business income tax credit; and
• Business limit, which is $500,000 unless the corporation is associated with another corporation.

These three limiting factors restrict the availability of the small business deduction to the active business income of "small" Canadian corporations.

Each of the three limits to the small business deduction plays a different role. The first confines the deduction to "active business income" and excludes investment income and income from a personal service business.[15]

---

11 *Irving Garber Sales Canada Ltd v MNR*, [1992] 2 CTC 261 (FCTD).
12 *Majestic Tool & Mold Ltd v Canada*, [1993] 2 CTC 2813 (TCC) (interest from term deposits was active business income).
13 *Canada v Rockmore Investments Ltd*, [1976] CTC 291 (FCA).
14 *ITA*, above note 1, subs 125(1).
15 *Ibid*, para 125(1)(a); subs 125(7) "active business carried on by a corporation."

The second limitation confines the small business deduction to domestic source income. Thus, a CCPC cannot claim the deduction on foreign income that has not been taxed in Canada and on account of which it claims a foreign tax credit.[16]

The corporation's taxable income is reduced by ten-thirds of its foreign non-business income tax credit. The factor (10/3) is based on the assumption that the corporation paid a tax of 30 percent on its foreign non-business income. For example, assume that a corporation earns $100 foreign non-business income on which it pays $30 tax. Then, 10/3 × $30 = $100, which is the amount that the corporation deducts from its taxable income. Similarly, the multiplication factor of three times assumes that the corporation paid foreign tax at a rate of 33.3 percent on its foreign business income.

The third restriction limits the annual deduction to a maximum of $500,000[17] so as to restrict the deduction to "small" businesses. The overall limit also curtails the revenue loss from this initiative.

E. ASSOCIATED CORPORATIONS

The small business deduction is an obvious incentive for taxpayers to set up multiple corporations solely for the purpose of multiplying the deduction. Thus, a special set of rules controls artificial multiplication of the deduction by restricting the maximum amount that a group of associated corporations can claim.[18] Corporations can be associated with each other because of inter-related shareholdings[19] or through ministerial discretion.[20]

Where two or more Canadian-controlled private corporations are "associated" with each other, the maximum of their aggregate claim is $500,000. Income subject to this preferential tax rate will be allocated between associated corporations based on their allocation of the business limit. The group must file an agreement allocating the annual business limit among the associated corporations. They must file the

---

16   *Ibid*, para 125(1)(b).
17   *Ibid*, para 125(1)(c); subss 125(2) & (3) (business limit of $400,000 to be allocated among group of associated corporations).
18   *Ibid*, subs 125(2).
19   *Ibid*, subs 256(1).
20   *Ibid*, subs 256(2.1); see, generally, Interpretation Bulletin IT-64R4, "Corporations: Association and Control" (14 August 2001).

agreement annually with the minister.[21] The allocation may be in any amount that the group agrees upon.[22]

1) Inter-Related Shareholdings

Corporations are associated with each other if they are subject to common control and common ownership of shares by a person or a related group of persons. The central element underlying "association" is control, whether *de jure* or *de facto*. There are five basic rules to determine corporate association, and several anti-avoidance rules to prevent taxpayers from circumventing the basic rules.

a) Control of One Corporation by Another

Two corporations are associated with each other in a taxation year if, at any time in the year, one of the corporations controls (directly, indirectly or in any manner whatever) the other.[23]

De Jure control is generally manifested through voting rights. Thus, 50 percent plus 1 of voting power is usually sufficient to secure control for most corporate purposes. Control may, however, also exist by virtue of other factors. For example, the power to wind up a corporation and appropriate the majority of its assets may be effective control.[24]

b) Control of Corporations by Same Person

A corporation is associated with another corporation in a taxation year, if at any time in the year, the same person or group of persons control both corporations.[25]

c) Cross-Ownership of Shares

A corporation is associated with another corporation in a taxation year, if at any time in the year, each of the corporations is controlled (directly, indirectly or in any manner whatever) by one person, and the person who controls one of the corporations is related to the person who controls the other, and either one of those persons owns, in respect of each

---

21 *ITA*, *ibid*, subs 125(3).
22 *Ibid*, subs 125(3).
23 *Ibid*, para 256(1)(a).
24 *Canada v Imperial General Properties Ltd* (1985), 85 DTC 5500 at 5503 (SCC) (in interpreting subs 256(1), "the court is not limited to a highly technical and narrow interpretation of the legal rights attached to the shares of a corporation").
25 *ITA*, above note 1, para 256(1)(b).

corporation, not less than 25 percent of the issued shares of any class (other than a specified class) of the capital stock thereof.[26]

d) Group Control and Cross-Ownership
A corporation is associated with another corporation in a taxation year if, at any time in the year, one of the corporations is controlled (directly, indirectly or in any manner whatever) by one person and that person is related to each member of a group of persons that controls the other corporation, and that person owns not less than 25 percent of the issued shares of any class (other than a specified class) of the capital stock of the other corporation.[27]

e) Control by Related Group and Cross-Ownership
A corporation is associated with another corporation in a taxation year if, at any time in the year, each of the corporations is controlled (directly, indirectly or in any manner whatever) by a related group and each of the members of one of the related groups is related to *all* of the members of the other related group, and one or more persons who are members of both related groups owns not less than 25 percent of the issued shares of any class (other than a specified class) of the capital stock of each corporation.[28]

2) Specified Class of Shares

The 25 percent cross-ownership rules do not apply to shares of a "specified class." "Specified shares" are generally non-voting preferred shares that confer minimal shareholder power.

3) Association with Third Corporation

Two otherwise unassociated corporations are associated with each other if they are both associated with the same third corporation.[29] For example, if Alpha Limited is associated with Beta Limited and Gamma Limited, then Beta Limited and Gamma Limited are also associated with each other. This rule does not apply for the purposes of the small business deduction if the third corporation does not claim the deduction. For example, the third corporation may not claim the deduction either because it explicitly elects not to do so or because it does not

---

26   *Ibid*, para 256(1)(c).
27   *Ibid*, para 256(1)(d).
28   *Ibid*, para 256(1)(e).
29   *Ibid*, subs 256(2).

qualify for the deduction because it is not a "Canadian-controlled private corporation."

F. CORPORATE CONTROL

There are two forms of corporate control: *de jure* and *de facto*. The word "control" without any qualifier means *de jure* control. The Act uses the phrase "controlled, directly or indirectly in any manner whatever" to describe *de facto* control. Either form can result in corporations being associated with each other.

1) *De Jure* Control

a) Voting Power

Generally, *de jure* corporate control means the ownership of a sufficient number of shares to be able to elect a majority of the board of directors of a corporation.[30] Thus, *de jure* control is the legal power to manage a corporation's affairs and the power to exercise corporate control in the long run.[31]

This test does not always provide a clear answer. For example, where a corporation's shareholdings are divided equally between two shareholders, neither has the power to elect a majority of the directors, and the corporation may not be legally controlled by either person.

b) Appropriation of Assets

The lack of power to elect a majority of the board of directors is not always determinative of *de jure* corporate control. Control may be inferred from some other form of corporate power, for example, the power to wind up a corporation and appropriate its assets.[32]

c) "Group of Persons"

For the purposes of determining whether a corporation is controlled by a group of persons, "group" means any two or more persons each of whom owns the corporation's shares.[33]

The existence of a group of persons does not depend upon common links between the persons, the size of the collectivity or a common

---

30   *Buckerfield's Ltd v MNR*, [1964] CTC 504 (Ex Ct).
31   *Donald Applicators Ltd v MNR*, [1969] CTC 98 (Ex Ct), aff'd [1971] CTC 402 (SCC).
32   *Canada v Imperial General Properties Ltd*, above note 24.
33   *ITA*, above note 1, para 256(1.2)(a).

intention to obtain a tax benefit. Ownership of shares in the corporation by two or more persons is sufficient to constitute a group.

d) Market Value Control

A corporation may be controlled by virtue of a person owning more than 50 percent of the fair market value of its shares, even though the shares do not represent majority voting power in the corporation.

A corporation is deemed to be controlled by another corporation, person or a group of persons where the "controller" owns:[34]

- Shares that represent more than 50 percent of the fair market value of all of the corporation's issued and outstanding shares; or
- Common shares that represent more than 50 percent of the fair market value of all of the corporation's issued and outstanding common shares.

This test is based on the premise that the fair market value of an individual's shareholdings in a corporation may be as relevant an indication of real power as a test based on the legal ability of shareholders to elect a majority of the corporation's board of directors.

e) Holding Corporations

A shareholder of a holding corporation that has a subsidiary is considered to have an equity ownership in the subsidiary corporation.[35] The Act "looks through" the holding corporation and attributes ownership of the subsidiary's shares directly to the shareholder of the holding corporation. The attributed ownership of the shares is in the proportion that the fair market value of the holding corporation's shares owned by the shareholder is to the fair market value of all of the issued and outstanding shares of the holding corporation at that time. The fair market value of the shares is determined on the assumption that all of the outstanding shares are non-voting.[36]

f) Partnerships

A similar "look through" rule also applies to shares owned by a partnership. A member of a partnership that owns shares of a corporation is considered to directly own the proportionate interest in those shares.[37] Where the income and loss of the partnership for its fiscal period is nil,

34   Ibid, para 256(1.2)(c).
35   Ibid, para 256(1.2)(d).
36   Ibid, para 256(1.2)(g).
37   Ibid, para 256(1.2)(e).

the proportion is calculated on the assumption that the partnership's income is $1,000,000 in that period.

g) Trusts

Under trust law, a trustee is the legal owner of shares held in trust by the trustee. For tax purposes, corporate shares owned by a trust are considered to be owned by the beneficiaries of the trust and, in some cases, by the person from whom the trust property was received.[38]

i) Testamentary Trusts

Where, in a testamentary trust, some of the beneficiaries are entitled to all of the income of the trust prior to the death of one of them or all of them, and no other person is entitled to any capital of the trust before that time, the shares are deemed to be owned by the beneficiaries before that time.[39] If the trust is a discretionary trust, all of the discretionary beneficiaries are deemed to own the shares.[40]

ii) Other Trusts

Where the trust is not a testamentary trust, each beneficiary is deemed to own a proportion of the shares based upon the fair market value of the interest in the trust.[41] If the trust is a discretionary trust, all of the discretionary beneficiaries are deemed to own the shares.[42]

iii) Reversionary Trusts

Where a trust is a "reversionary" trust, the person from whom the trust receives the property is also deemed to own the shares.[43] The result of these rules is that it is entirely possible that the Act can deem more than one person to own the same shares at the same time.

h) Attribution Rules

Where the shares of a corporation are owned (or deemed to be owned) by a child who is under eighteen years of age, the shares are considered to be owned by the child's parents.[44] This rule does not apply if the child manages the business and affairs of the corporation without sig-

---

38 *Ibid*, para 256(1.2)(f).
39 *Ibid*, cl 256(1.2)(f)(i)(B).
40 *Ibid*, cl 256(1.2)(f)(i)(A).
41 *Ibid*, subpara 256(1.2)(f)(iii).
42 *Ibid*, subpara 256(1.2)(f)(ii).
43 *Ibid*, subpara 256(1.2)(f)(iv).
44 *Ibid*, subs 256(1.3).

nificant influence by the parents. The shares may be attributed to either parent, depending upon the purpose of the determination.

i) Options and Rights

A person who has an option or a right to acquire or to control the voting rights of shares is treated as if she owned those shares.[45] This rule does not apply where the option or right is not exercisable until the death, bankruptcy or permanent disability of a designated individual. Thus, an option or right that is triggered under a shareholders' agreement may be exempt from the deeming provision, provided that the option or right is exercisable only upon the death, bankruptcy or permanent disability of the individual designated in the agreement.

Similarly, where a person has a right to cause a corporation to redeem, acquire or cancel its shares owned by other shareholders, he or she is deemed to be in the same position in relation to the control of the incorporation and ownership of its shares as if the shares had already been redeemed, acquired or cancelled by the corporation.[46]

j) Tax Avoidance

There is a broad anti-avoidance rule to catch cases that may escape through the net of the specific rules described above. This applies where two or more corporations are associated with each other and one of the main reasons for the separate existence of the corporations in a taxation year is to reduce the amount of tax that would otherwise have to be paid.[47]

For example, where two parts of what could reasonably be considered to be one business (for example, manufacturing and sales of a single product line) are carried out by two corporations each of which is controlled by different persons, the two separate corporations may be deemed to be associated with each other for the purposes of the small business deduction. If they are associated, the two corporations may claim only one small business deduction in respect of the income generated by both businesses.

To avoid association under this rule, it is necessary for the taxpayer to establish, in effect, that *none* of the main reasons for the existence of multiple corporations is to reduce the amount of tax that would otherwise be payable.[48] The intention of the corporations is inferred from

---

45 *Ibid*, para 256(1.4)(a).
46 *Ibid*, para 256(1.4)(b).
47 *Ibid*, subs 256(2.1).
48 See *Maritime Forwarding Ltd v Canada*, [1988] 1 CTC 186 (FCTD) (incorporating to reduce leasing costs not sustainable as main reason for creation of multiple corporations); *Kencar Enterprises Ltd v MNR*, [1987] 2 CTC 246 (FCTD)

those by whom it is managed and controlled. The taxpayer must establish that the separate existence of the corporations was dictated solely by business expediency and not by tax considerations.[49]

2) *De Facto* Control

The *de facto* test focuses on the influence, as opposed to the power, that a person or group of persons may have on a corporation. It is premised on the theory that there is more to control than mere legal power as expressed in voting rights.

Although the purpose of the *de facto* test is to prevent artificial manipulation of the associated corporation rules, it does not provide any greater certainty than the more traditional common law doctrines. Thus, the *de facto* test merely substitutes statutory uncertainty for judicial uncertainty.[50]

a) "Directly or Indirectly in Any Manner Whatever"

A corporation is associated with another corporation if the two corporations are controlled "directly or indirectly in any manner whatever" by the same person or by persons with common and related interests.[51] A corporation is considered to be "controlled, directly or indirectly in any manner whatever" by a person where the person has any direct or indirect influence that, if exercised, would result in control in fact of the corporation.[52]

The critical test in each case is to determine whether a person or group of persons ("the controller") has the requisite direct or indirect influence over the affairs of a corporation. The controlling person may be another corporation, an individual or a group of persons. For example, a corporation may be controlled by a person who owns less than 50 percent of the voting shares of the corporation if the remaining shares are widely distributed among other persons (such as employees)

("minister's direction could only be challenged by establishing that none of the main reasons for the separate existence of the corporations was to reduce the amount of tax payable").

49 *Doris Trucking Co v MNR*, [1968] CTC 303 (Ex Ct).

50 See, generally, *Multiview Inc v Canada*, [1997] 3 CTC 2962 (TCC) (relevance of absence of casting vote); *Silicon Graphics Ltd v Canada*, 2002 FCA 260 (*de facto* control and power to effect significant change in board of directors); *Mimetix Pharmaceuticals Inc v Canada*, 2003 FCA 106 (non-residents had significant power—hence, *de facto* control).

51 *ITA*, above note 1, subs 256(5.1).

52 *Ibid*, subs 256(5.1).

who could reasonably be considered to be amenable to the wishes of the person with "influence."

i) Influence

The test does not require the "controller" to have any legally-enforceable right or power over the corporation. It is sufficient that the controller have influence, whether direct or indirect, over the affairs of the corporation.

Further, the test uses the presence of potential influence, and does not depend upon the actual exercise of influence in a particular case. In other words, the "controller" does not have to actually exercise influence over the affairs of the corporation; the controller merely has to have sufficient influence that, if exercised, could result in control in fact of the corporation.

ii) Exceptions

A person may have influence over another by virtue of a legal arrangement between them that governs the manner in which a business is carried on by a corporation. Provided that the corporation and the "controller" are dealing with each other at arm's length, the *de facto* control test does not apply where the controller's influence derives only from an agreement or arrangement, the main purpose of which is to govern the business relationship between the corporation and the controller. For example, where a franchise agreement or lease gives the franchisor or lessor some power to regulate the products sold by the corporation or the hours during which it conducts its business, the power does not, in and of itself, result in the franchisor or lessor having *de facto* control over the corporation.

G. PERSONAL SERVICES BUSINESS INCOME

A personal services business is a business in which a major shareholder of a corporation provides services through the corporation in circumstances where the shareholder would normally provide the services as an employee. Thus, in effect, the shareholder is an "incorporated employee." Employment income is taxed at progressive marginal rates.[53] Corporate income is taxed at a flat rate.[54] Since the corporate tax rate on active business income that a Canadian-controlled private corporation

---

53   *Ibid*, s 117; see also Chapters 6 and 14.
54   *Ibid*, s 123.

earns is approximately 16 percent (combined federal and provincial rates), there is a considerable advantage in converting employment income (which is taxed at about 45 percent at the high end) into business income. A common technique of converting employment income into business income was to use a corporation to render personal services.

The Act taxes personal services business income (PSBI) on a gross income basis, with only minimal deductions. Thus, the Act taxes PSBI on the same basis as employment income. Neither is eligible for the small business deduction. PSBI is taxable at the full federal corporate rate of 28 percent, without any refund of tax on dividends. In computing PSBI, a corporation generally can deduct only salaries and benefits paid to the "incorporated employee."[55]

There is no clear cut answer in every case to determine whether corporate income is active business income or PSBI. For example, the CRA accepts that self-employed real estate agents who incorporate to provide real estate services are independent contractors and not "incorporated employees." Thus, their income is eligible for the small business deduction. In contrast, the CRA will not extend independent contractor status to corporate directors who provide management services on an exclusive contract basis.

PSBI does not include:[56]

1) The income of a corporation that throughout the year employs more than five full-time employees;[57] or
2) Amounts that a corporation receives from its associated corporation.

H. PROFESSIONAL CORPORATIONS

Under various provincial corporate statutes (for example, the *Business Corporations Act* of Ontario (*OBCA*)), lawyers, accountants and doctors can incorporate their practices in professional corporations (PCs) and obtain significant tax advantages. However, shareholders of PCs cannot limit their liability for negligence or malpractice and remain jointly and severally liable for all professional liability claims against them. This makes the choice of form of practice an important decision. Large law and accounting partnerships are better off practising as limited liability partnerships (LLPs) in order to limit personal malpractice exposure. On

---

55 *Ibid*, para 18(1)(p).
56 *Ibid*, subs 125(7) "personal services business" (c) & (d).
57 *Hughes & Co Holdings Ltd v MNR*, [1994] 2 CTC 170 (FCTD) (more than five employees means at least six employees). The employees must be full-time employees.

the other hand, sole proprietors and smaller partnerships of two to four partners may be better off practising as PCs for the tax advantages.

The difference between the tax payable by incorporated and un-incorporated law and accounting practices is significant. Since individuals pay tax on their business income at progressive marginal tax rates, the top tax rate is about 45 percent in Ontario. In contrast, the federal corporate rate of tax is about 11 percent (approximately 16 percent combined federal and provincial rates) on the first $500,000 of professional income. The percentage point spread allows professionals to defer tax if they leave their income in the corporation. Since partners must share the $500,000 limit between themselves, the real benefits of incorporation accrue only to sole practitioners and small partnerships.

A PC cannot carry on any business other than the practice of the profession of its shareholders. All of the shareholders of the PC must be members of the same profession: lawyers in the case of law firms, accountants in the case of accounting firms, etc. There can be no multi-disciplinary practices in a PC. A PC may, however, carry on any ancillary activities and can invest its surplus funds, including any cash saved from its deferred tax.

FURTHER READINGS

General

ANDERSSON, KRISTA. "Implications of Integrating Corporate and Share-holder Taxes" (1991) 50 Tax Notes 1523.

SHINDER, BERNARD. "The Taxation of Small Business: An Historical and Technical Overview" (1984) 32 Can Tax J 1.

Canadian-Controlled Private Corporations

LEWIN, RICHARD. "Income Tax Planning and the Rules of Association" (1987) 39 Can Tax Found 32:1.

NATHANSON, DAVID C. "Active Versus Passive Once Again: Active Business Income and Investment Income of Canadian-Controlled Private Corporations" (1981) 33 Can Tax Found 908.

Corporate Control

HALPERN, JACK V. "Determination of Control for the Purposes of Being a 'CCPC'" (1990) 38 Can Tax J 942.

MOSKOWITZ, EVELYN P. "Dealing at Arm's Length: A Question of Fact" (1987) 39 Can Tax Found 33:1.

Personal Services Business Income

KRISHNA, VERN. "Personal Services Business Income" (1983) 17:10 CGA Magazine 31.

Small Business Corporations

WARD, DAVID A, & JOHN M ULMER. "Corporate Taxation: Shares Eligible for the Capital Gains Exemption" (1986) 5 Legal Alert 81.

Other

BROWN, CATHARINE A. "Spouse Trusts" (1986) 38 Can Tax Found 37.

TREMBLAY, RICHARD. "Active Business Income" (1990–92) Can Curr Tax P-45.

CHAPTER 18

CORPORATE INVESTMENT INCOME

A. GENERAL COMMENT

The corporate tax on investment income depends upon the type of corporation. Public corporations pay tax at normal rates. The taxation of income by a private corporation earns depends upon the source of its income.

B. TAX OBJECTIVES

The rules in respect of the taxation of corporate investment income serve two objectives: (1) to "integrate" the amount of tax that a corporation pays on its investment income with the tax that its individual shareholders pay; and (2) to discourage individuals from deferring tax by placing their investments in private holding companies.

"Integration" means that an individual should pay the same amount of tax on investment income, regardless of whether she earns the income personally or indirectly through a corporation. We achieve integration by synchronizing the corporate tax rate with the effective rate of tax that an individual pays on corporate investment income.

We implement the second objective by initially taxing corporate investment income at a high rate to prevent tax deferral. Thus, we tax the income (other than taxable dividends) that a Canadian-controlled private corporation earns at the full corporate rate. Then, we refund a portion of the tax to the corporation when it pays out taxable dividends to its shareholders. The initial tax blunts any tax deferral advantage. The tax refund to the corporation when it pays out dividends reduces the net effective rate of tax to a level that approximately equals the rate that an individual would pay on such income if she earned it directly.

C. TYPES OF INVESTMENT INCOME

There are three basic categories of investment income:

* Dividends;
* Rent, interest, royalties, etc.; and
* Capital gains.

Full taxation followed by a tax refund applies to all three forms of investment income. But since we tax each of the three forms of investment income differently, the mathematical adjustments to integrate each type of investment income are slightly different.

D. DIVIDEND INCOME

All corporate income is potentially subject to double taxation, first at the corporate level, then again to the shareholders. The tax system provides some relief by partially imputing corporate taxes to shareholders. But the relief is neither complete nor perfect. The tax rules in respect of inter-corporate dividends between private corporations do, however, substantially eliminate double taxation while preventing tax deferral. There is a separate regime for dividends from public corporations.

Generally, the tax relief for private corporations operates as follows. A corporation includes in its income all taxable dividends that it receives from other corporations.[1] In computing its taxable income, however, a corporation may deduct taxable dividends that it receives from:[2]

* A "taxable Canadian corporation"; or
* A resident corporation that it controls.

The effect of this two-step structure is that dividends between Canadian corporations flow through free of Part I tax and are not subject to double taxation.

---

1   *Income Tax Act*, RSC 1985, c 1 (5th Supp) [*ITA*], paras 12(1)(j) & (k).
2   *Ibid*, subs 112(1); dividends from non-resident investment corporations may not be deducted.

454 INCOME TAX LAW

The basic structure for the taxation of inter-corporate dividends prevents multiple taxation of income passing through several different corporations. Including taxable dividends in income and then deducting these dividends in calculating taxable income effectively exempts inter-corporate dividends from Part I tax.

Without more control, however, taxpayers could defer taxes if the corporate tax rate is lower than personal tax rates. Individuals in high tax brackets could earn their dividend income in a holding company and defer personal taxes until the company paid out its income. A special tax under Part IV of the Act on the dividend income of private corporations prevents tax deferral by high-income individuals. The Part IV tax on dividend income is fully refundable to the corporation when it pays taxable dividends to shareholders so that there is no double taxation.[3]

1) Theoretical Model

The underlying theory of the Part IV tax is to:

1) Prevent tax deferral through the use of holding companies; and
2) "Integrate" the personal and corporate tax on investment income.

We achieve these objectives through a three-part mechanism:

1) the Part IV tax on portfolio dividend income;
2) a dividend refund to the corporation; and
3) a dividend gross-up and tax imputation credit for individuals.

Since inter-corporate dividends flow tax-free, an individual could defer personal taxes by placing his investments in a holding company. The Part IV corporate tax, which is fully refundable, prevents tax deferral.

An individual who receives a dividend from a taxable Canadian corporation is taxable on 125 percent of the dividend. For example, a cash dividend of $100 is taxable as $125. In theory, the 25 percent "gross-up" accounts for corporate taxes that the corporation paid on its income. The individual may claim a federal tax credit equal to two-thirds of the "gross-up" of 25 percent included in income.[4] The grossing-up of the dividend in income followed by a dividend tax credit "integrates" the total tax paid by the individual with the tax paid by the corporation. Thus, in theory and under certain assumptions, the combined effect of

---

3   *Ibid*, subs 129(1).
4   *Ibid*, s 121. In addition, most provinces also provide a dividend tax credit, which varies between provinces.

the Part IV tax and the dividend tax credit should prevent tax deferral and integrate corporate and shareholder taxes.

The following example illustrates the theory of integration of corporate and personal taxes on dividend income in a private corporation. Note, the model depends upon at least four assumptions: the corporate tax rate, the dividend gross-up rate, federal-provincial tax rates, and the Part IV refund rate.

Example

Portfolio Dividends: Theoretical Model

Assume that Harry Smith owns all the shares of Smith Ltd, which receives a dividend of $10,000 from the Royal Bank of Canada. The corporation flows through the $10,000 as a dividend to Harry Smith. Assume a combined (federal and provincial) tax rate of 40 percent for both personal and corporate tax.

Corporate Tax:

Net income from portfolio dividends	$10,000
Less: Inter-corporate dividends (subs. 112(1))	(10,000)
Taxable income	NIL
Part I tax	NIL
Part IV tax on dividends @ 33.3%	3,333
Net income after tax	6,667
Refund of Part IV tax on payment of dividend	3,333
Amount available for dividend	$10,000

Shareholder Tax:

Dividend income	$10,000
Gross-up of dividend by 25% (para. 82(1)(b))	2,500
Taxable amount	$12,500
Federal/provincial tax @ 40% (assumed)	$5,000
Federal/provincial dividend tax credit*	2,500
Net tax payable	$2,500
Income retained	$7,500
Effective Tax Rate on Income	25%

* Assuming the federal credit is ²/₃ of the gross-up and the provincial credit is ¹/₃ of the gross-up.

In the model, the Part IV tax washes out when the corporation pays dividends. In the above example, Harry Smith, with a combined federal/provincial tax rate of 40 percent, pays $2,500 tax on a dividend of $10,000, regardless of whether he receives the dividend directly or through a holding corporation. Thus, in theory at least, the tax on portfolio dividends that a private corporation earns integrates perfectly with the personal tax system.

2) Actual Rates

The theoretical model may or may not apply as we move away from its underlying assumptions. For example, the rates of corporate and personal taxes go up and down. Also, the provinces vary their effective rates and move off the model. The example below compares a "pure" integration model with an assumed top marginal rate of 31.33 percent on dividend income.

Example Portfolio Dividends: Theory vs. Actual	Integration Model	Actual Taxes (Assumed rates)
Corporate Tax:		
Portfolio dividends	$10,000	$10,000
Part IV tax payable	3,333	3,333
Net income after tax	$6,667	$6,667
Refund of tax on payment of dividend	3,333	3,333
Amount available for dividend	$10,000	$10,000
Shareholder Tax:		
Dividend income	$10,000	$10,000
Gross-up of dividend	2,500	2,500
Taxable amount	$12,500	$12,500
Federal/provincial tax @ 40%	$5,000	
Dividend tax credit	2,500	
Tax thereon at top marginal rates (31.33% in Ontario)		$3,133
Net tax payable	$2,500	$3,133
Income retained	$7,500	$6,867
Effective Tax Rate on Dividend	25%	31%

As federal and provincial taxes fluctuate, the effective tax rate on dividends varies from the theoretical norm. In the above example, the effective rate of tax on dividends is 31 percent, which closely approximates the amount of the Part IV tax.

3) Part IV Tax

a) Rationale
The Part IV tax is an anti-deferral mechanism. It attempts to place an individual who holds portfolio investments through a holding company in the same position as a person who holds portfolio investments directly. Thus, in theory, the income tax effects of owning portfolio

investments are neutral regardless of the vehicle selected to hold the investments.

b) Application

The Part IV tax, which is a fully refundable tax, applies to only two types of corporations:[5]

1) Private corporations; and
2) "Subject corporations."

A "subject corporation" is a corporation (other than a private corporation) that resides in Canada and is controlled directly or indirectly in any manner by, or for the benefit of, an individual or a related group of individuals.[6] An individual or a related group of individuals is considered to be in control of a corporation if they control its shares indirectly through another corporation, partnership or trust.[7]

c) Taxable Dividends

A private corporation is subject to Part IV tax on taxable dividends that it receives from:

- Non-connected[8] Canadian corporations resident in Canada, if the dividends are deductible in computing the recipient's taxable income;[9]
- Foreign affiliates;[10] and
- Connected private corporations in proportion to the dividend refund obtained by the payer corporation.[11]

For the purpose of determining its liability for Part IV tax, a corporation may deduct its non-capital losses and farm losses for the current year[12] and its non-capital and farm loss carryover.[13] A corporation has the option of deducting its loss carryovers to reduce its Part IV tax or in calculating its taxable income.

---

5   *Ibid*, para 186(1)(b).
6   *Ibid*, subs 186(3) "subject corporation."
7   See *ibid*, s 104, subs 186(6), para 251(5)(a) and subs 256(6.1).
8   *Ibid*, subs 186(4).
9   *Ibid*, subpara 186(1)(a).
10   *Ibid*, subss 186(1) and 186(3) "assessable dividend."
11   *Ibid*, para 186(1)(b). This provision ensures that, until such time as dividends are paid out to individuals or non-connected corporations, the payer corporation's tax refund is matched with the payee corporation's liability to Part IV tax.
12   *Ibid*, para 186(1)(c).
13   *Ibid*, para 186(1)(d).

d) Connected Corporations

The critical factor in determining the liability of a corporation for Part IV tax is its relationship with the corporation from which it receives a dividend (the "payer" corporation). If the payer and recipient corporations are not connected with each other, the recipient corporation is liable to Part IV tax on its taxable dividends from the payer. If the corporations are connected, the recipient corporation is liable for Part IV tax, but only if the payer corporation gets a dividend refund as a consequence of paying the dividend.

A payer and a recipient corporation are "connected" with each other if:

- The recipient corporation controls the payer; or
- The recipient corporation owns more than 10 percent of the issued fully-voting shares of the payer and the fair market value of all the shares owned by the recipient exceeds 10 percent of the fair market value of all issued shares of the payer.[14]

Thus, a private corporation that receives a taxable dividend is not subject to Part IV tax if it owns more than 10 percent of the votes and value of the payer corporation, unless the payer obtains a dividend refund in respect of the dividend.

e) Excluded Dividends

We saw earlier that inter-corporate dividends generally flow tax-free between corporations. There are certain dividends, however, that do not flow on a tax-free basis between corporations. For example, subsections 112(2.2) and (2.4) deny the inter-corporate dividend deduction on certain "guaranteed" shares and "collateralized preferred shares" that have security guarantees to protect any loss on the shares. In these circumstances, since the corporation is fully taxable under Part I on the dividends, Part IV does not apply. Paragraph 186(1)(a) also excludes from Part IV tax any taxable dividends received from a connected corporation.

f) Interest Income

The following example illustrates the theoretical operation of the Part IV tax on interest income.

---

14   *Ibid*, subs 186(4).

Example (Theoretical Model)

Assume: A private corporation receives $1,000 interest income. The corporation pays Part I tax at a rate of 40 percent and pays a dividend to its sole shareholder, an individual with a marginal tax rate of 40 percent. The dividend refund is assumed at 33.3 percent. The "Corporate" column shows how the income would be treated if originally earned by a corporation and the "Personal" column shows how it would be treated if originally earned by an individual.

Then:

	Corporate	Personal
Tax effect on corporation:		
Interest income	$1,000	
Corporate Part I tax 40%	400	
Net income after tax	600	
Refund of tax on payment of dividend	200	
Available for dividend	$800	
Effective corporate tax rate	20%	
Tax effect on individual:		
Interest income earned directly by individual		$1,000
Dividend received	$800	
Gross-up @ 25% (equal to corporate tax)	200	
Taxable amount	$1,000	$1,000
Tax thereon:		
Personal tax before dividend tax credit 40%	$400	$400
Dividend tax credit (equal to corporate tax)	200	NIL
Tax payable	$200	$400
Net income retained by individual	$600	$600
Effective individual tax rate	20%	40%
Combined corporate/personal tax rate	40%	40%

E. OTHER INVESTMENT INCOME

"Other investment income" is investment income other than portfolio dividends; it includes taxable capital gains, income from property and income from a "specified investment business."[15]

---

15   *Ibid*, subs 125(7) "specified investment business."

1) Tax Integration

There are similar rules that deal with other forms of investment income, such as interest income, rents, royalties and taxable capital gains,[16] that also neutralize the use of holding companies. Thus, an individual who places investments in a holding company does not, in theory, enjoy any tax advantage over an individual who holds her investments directly. But in the case of investment income other than dividends, the rules apply only to income that a Canadian-controlled private corporation earns.

The structure for the taxation of investment income earned by a Canadian-controlled private corporation involves four steps:

1) A Canadian-controlled private corporation is initially taxed on its investment income at the full federal corporate tax rate of 38 percent;
2) When the corporation pays a dividend, it receives a refund, but only for a portion of the taxes that it previously paid on that income;[17]
3) When the dividend is paid to an individual, the "grossed-up" value of the dividend is included in the individual's income;[18]
4) The individual may then claim a dividend tax credit to adjust for the net amount of corporate tax that was notionally paid on his behalf by the corporation.[19]

Once again, the purpose of the structure is to prevent tax deferral and to eliminate double taxation of corporate investment income.

2) "Investment Income"

There are two types of investment income: "aggregate investment income" and "foreign investment income."

a) Aggregate Investment Income
"Aggregate investment income" comprises:[20]

- The excess of taxable capital gains over allowable capital losses to the extent that such gains and losses are from sources in Canada that relates to a period that the corporation was a CCPC; and
- Net property income (including income from a "specified investment business") from Canadian sources.

---

16 *Ibid.*
17 The refund is processed through an account described as the refundable dividend tax on hand account (RDTOH); *ibid*, subs 129(3).
18 *Ibid*, para 82(1)(b).
19 *Ibid*, s 121.
20 *Ibid*, subs 129(4) "aggregate investment income."

i) Presumptions

Investment income does not include income from a business.[21] The distinction between investment income and business income is essentially a question of fact.[22] In the case of corporate taxpayers, however, there is a rebuttable presumption that income earned in the pursuit of the corporation's objects (as stated in its constating documents) is income from a business.[23] Although the question is open,[24] there does not appear to be any compelling reason why the presumption would not also apply to corporations that do not require objects clauses in their constating documents.

Thus, depending upon the rigidity with which one applies the presumption, corporations have some flexibility in characterizing the source of their income as flowing from business or investments. The presumption should not, however, be applied in such a manner as to destroy the legislative scheme distinguishing between active business income and investment income.[25]

ii) Specified Investment Business

A "specified investment business" is a business whose principal or main purpose is to derive income from property.[26] Such income includes dividends, interest, rents and royalties. A "specified investment business" does not include the business of leasing personal property, but it does include the business of leasing real property. The principal purpose test is an annual test.

There are two important exceptions to the meaning of specified investment business. A business that employs more than five full-time employees throughout the year is not a "specified investment business." Thus, a "specified investment business" includes any business with less than six full-time employees whose principal purpose is to earn income from property or the leasing of real property.

In certain circumstances, a business that derives income from property can be an active business even if it does not have more than five full-time employees. For example, a business that derives administrative services from its associated corporation can be an active business if it would have employed more than five employees had the associated corporation not provided those services.

21 See Chapter 17.
22 *Canadian Marconi Co v Canada*, [1986] 2 CTC 465 at 470 (SCC).
23 *Ibid* at 468.
24 *Ibid* at 470.
25 *Canada v Ensite Ltd*, [1986] 2 CTC 459 at 464 (SCC).
26 ITA, above note 1, subs 125(7) "specified investment business."

b) Foreign Investment Income

We calculate "foreign investment income" in the same way as "aggregate investment income," except that it takes into account only income earned from non-Canadian sources.[27] "Foreign investment income" does not include any income or loss from property that an active business uses incidentally.[28]

3) Refund of Tax

The original theoretical model for the refund of taxes on investment income was based on the assumption that the top individual tax rate was 40 percent. As the provinces increased their tax rates, however, it became attractive to hold investments through a CCPC. To address the disparity between theoretical and actual provincial rates, section 123.3 imposes an additional refundable tax of 6.67 percent. Thus, the total amount refundable is now 26.67 percent.

The theoretical scheme of the refundable tax is as follows: we assume that a Canadian-controlled private corporation pays tax on its investment income at 46.67 percent; when it pays out dividends, it receives a refund of 26.67 percent on its Canadian investment income. (This is the "refundable portion" of its Part I tax.[29]) Also assume that the shareholder includes the grossed-up value (125 percent) of the cash dividend in income and claims a dividend tax credit equal to the value of the dividend gross-up. Then, corporate and personal taxes are "integrated" if the individual's marginal tax rate is 46.67 percent. Thus, the tax burden is neutral, whether the shareholder receives the investment income directly or through a holding company.

4) Capital Gains

There is one significant difference between the tax structure in respect of corporate capital gains and other sources of investment income. Only 50 percent of capital gains are included in income as taxable capital gains, and only 50 percent of capital losses are allowed as a deduction from taxable capital gains. The non-taxable portion (50 percent of the capital gain) goes into a special account called the "Capital Dividend

---

27   *Ibid*, subs 129(4) "foreign investment income."
28   See *Aqua-Gem Investments Ltd v MNR*, [1986] 1 CTC 2528 (TCC) (interest from short-term investments was income "incident to" taxpayer's business).
29   *ITA*, above note 1, subs 129(1); subpara 129(3)(a)(ii).

Account,"[30] which the corporation can pay out tax-free to shareholders and does not affect the adjusted cost base of the shares.[31] Thus, capital gains earned through a corporation are treated in a similar manner to gains earned directly by an individual.

The following example illustrates the flow-through of capital gains through a corporation. (The theoretical model assumes a combined corporate/personal tax of 27 percent on capital gains.)

Example (Theoretical Model)

Assume: A private corporation earns $1,000 capital gains. The corporation pays a dividend to its sole shareholder, an individual with a marginal tax rate of 40 percent. The corporation pays Part I tax at a rate of 46.67 percent. The dividend refund is assumed at 33.3 percent.

Then:

	Corporate	Personal
Tax effect on corporation:		
Capital gains	$1,000	
Tax-free portion of gain (50%)	500	
Taxable capital gain	500	
Corporate Part I tax (46.67%)	233	
Net income after tax	267	
Refund of tax on payment of dividend	133	
Available for dividend	$400	
Effective corporate tax rate on gain	10%	
Tax effect on individual:		
Capital gains realized directly by individual		$1,000
Taxable dividend received	$400	–
Gross-up @ 25% (equal to corporate tax)	100	–
Taxable amount	$500	$500
Tax thereon:		
Personal tax before dividend tax credit (40%)	$200	$200
Dividend tax credit (equal to corporate tax)	(100)	–
Tax payable	$100	$200
Capital dividend (tax free)	$500	
Net income retained by individual	$800	$800
Effective personal tax rate	10%	20%
Combined corporate/personal tax rate	20%	20%

---

30   *Ibid*, subs 89(1) "capital dividend account."
31   *Ibid*, subs 83(2).

5) Capital Dividends

The non-taxable portion of capital gains is credited to an account called the "Capital Dividend Account."[32] A dividend paid out of the "Capital Dividend Account" is tax-free to the shareholder and does not affect the adjusted cost base of the shares.[33] It is important to track the balance of the capital dividend account. Part III of the Act imposes a 60 percent tax upon amounts that a taxpayer elects in excess of the CDA balance.

6) Refundable Dividend Tax on Hand

The refundable dividend tax on hand (RDTOH) account is a notional account used to calculate a corporation's entitlement to a tax refund.

The refundable tax in respect of portfolio dividend income is available to all private corporations. For non-portfolio dividend income, however, the refund is available only in respect of the investment income of a corporation that was a Canadian-controlled private corporation throughout the taxation year.[34]

The tax refund is equal to one-third of taxable dividends paid by the corporation, subject to a maximum equal to the corporation's RDTOH.[35] The refund can be applied against other corporate taxes payable by the corporation.

The balance in the RDTOH account at the end of a particular year is reduced in the following year by the amount of dividend refunds to which the corporation has become entitled as a result of the payment of taxable dividends to its shareholders.[36]

FURTHER READINGS

General

PROVENZANO, LOUIS J. "The Impact of Escalating Provincial Tax Rates on an Owner-manager's Decision to Earn Investment and Active Business Income Directly or through a Corporation" (1993) 45 Can Tax Found 33:1.

---

32   *Ibid*, subs 89(1) "capital dividend account."
33   *Ibid*, subs 83(2).
34   *Ibid*, para 129(3)(a).
35   *Ibid*, subs 129(1).
36   *Ibid*, para 129(3)(c).

Dividends

McCALLUM, J THOMAS. "Taxation of Portfolio Dividends" (1995) 5 Can
  Curr Tax 67.

Other Investment Income

BROADHURST, DAVID G. "Income Tax Treatment of Investment Corporations and Nonresident-Owned Investment Corporations" (1985)
  37 Can Tax Found 44.

Other

DURNFORD, JOHN W. "Profits on the Sale of Shares: Capital Gains or
  Business Income? A Fresh Look at Irrigation Industries" (1987) 35
  Can Tax J 837.

WILLIAMSON, GORDON. "Transfer of Assets to and from a Canadian
  Corporation" (1986) 38 Can Tax Found 12:1.

PART VI

TAX AVOIDANCE

GENERAL
ANTI-AVOIDANCE RULE

Lawyers use the law as shoemakers use leather: rubbing it, pressing it, and stretching it with their teeth, all to the end of making it fit for their purposes.

—Louis XII of France

A. GENERAL COMMENT

Individuals have sought to avoid taxes for as long as kings and governments have levied them. Just as rulers—whether democractic or autocratic—are creative in devising taxes, individuals are innovative in avoiding them. We see tax planning 6,000 years ago in Mesopotamia when a king imposed fines on his citizens who swam across the local river to avoid the toll tax on the local bridge. The king responded immediately by making swimming across the river illegal—the first tax anti-avoidance rule in history.

It is a fundamental principle of Anglo-Canadian law that a taxpayer is entitled to arrange his affairs to minimize tax.[1] This principle, generally known as the *Westminster* principle, is the foundation for tax avoidance—the reduction of tax payable by lawful means. Thus, we

---

1   See Explanatory Notes (1988) to GAAR tabled with the *Income Tax Act* legislation at 464, quoted *per curiam* in *Canada Trustco Mortgage Co v Canada*, 2005 SCC 54 at para 30 [*Canada Trustco*].

start with the premise that the avoidance of tax is perfectly legitimate. As Learned Hand J said:[2]

> Over and over again courts have said that there is nothing sinister in so arranging one's affairs as to keep taxes as low as possible. Everybody does so, rich or poor; and all do right, for nobody owes any public duty to pay more than the law demands: taxes are enforced exactions, not voluntary contributions. To demand more in the name of morals is mere cant.

However, statutory restrictions narrow the scope of legitimate tax planning. Thus, one must distinguish between acceptable tax mitigation and "abusive" tax avoidance.

Tax provisions to control avoidance vary in scope and intensity. Some are narrow and specific to certain types of transactions;[3] others are broad and stated as general principles. The General Anti-Avoidance Rule (GAAR)[4], a broadly stated statement of principle of statutory construction that affects both domestic and international tax planning, is the apex of all anti-avoidance measures.

Although a person is entitled to arrange her affairs so as to reduce tax, this right is subject to a proviso that the arrangement constitutes lawful tax mitigation. What constitutes lawful tax mitigation? The answer to this seemingly simple question is fraught with uncertainty. By definition, all tax planning involves tax minimization. But at what point does one cross over from acceptable tax mitigation to unacceptable tax avoidance?

Tax mitigation that is not subject to GAAR is "lawful." Tax avoidance that is caught by GAAR is "unlawful." The distinction between what is "lawful" and "unlawful" depends upon taxpayer motive, the rationale of the particular statutory provision(s) and the underlying structure of the Act. We see this in the decisions of the Supreme Court: *Canada Trustco Mortgage Co v Canada (Canada Trustco)*,[5] *Mathew v Canada*[6] and *Lipson v Canada*.[7]

Judicial attitudes towards tax planning reflect a society's social, political and economic values. Thus, case law reflects the ebb and flow of judicial tolerance towards tax avoidance: the tolerance of the *Westminster*

---

2   *Commissioner of Internal Revenue v Newman*, 159 F 2d 848 at 850–51 (2d Cir 1947).

3   See, for example, the "superficial loss" provisions in the *Income Tax Act*, RSC 1985, c 1 (5th Supp) [*ITA*], subpara 40(2)(g)(i).

4   *Ibid*, s 245.

5   *Canada Trustco*, above note 1.

6   *Mathew v Canada*, 2005 SCC 55.

7   *Lipson v Canada*, 2009 SCC 1 [*Lipson*].

principle in the heyday of *laissez-faire* economics; the hardening of attitudes after the Second World War and a lessening tolerance towards arrangements that curtailed public revenues. For example, we see the beginning of the change in sentiment towards tax avoidance in Lord Greene's speech in *Lord Howard de Walden v IRC*:

> For years a battle of manoeuvre has been waged between the Legislature and those who are minded to throw the burden of taxation off their own shoulders on to those of their fellow-subjects. In that battle the Legislature has often been worsted by the skill, determination and resourcefulness of its opponents, of whom the present appellant has not been the least successful. It would not shock us in the least to find that the Legislature has determined to put an end to the struggle by imposing the severest of penalties. It scarcely lies in the mouth of the taxpayer who plays with fire to complain of burnt fingers.[8]

And a year later in Viscount Simon's speech in *Latilla v IRC*:

> [T]here is, of course, no doubt that they are within their legal rights, but that is no reason why their efforts, or those of the professional gentlemen who assist them in the matter, should be regarded as a commendable exercise of ingenuity or as a discharge of the duties of good citizenship.[9]

Then, Lord Denning's moral tone in his characteristically terse style: "The avoidance of tax may be lawful, but it is not yet a virtue."[10]

B. TAXPAYERS' RIGHTS

A taxpayer is entitled to arrange his affairs so as to attract the minimum amount of tax. We identify this principle with Lord Tomlin's speech in the House of Lords in *IRC v Duke of Westminster*:

---

8 *Lord Howard de Walden v IRC*, [1942] 1 KB 389 at 397 (CA) (taxpayer who transferred assets to a foreign Canadian company liable for income tax and surtax as he had the "power to enjoy" these assets within the meaning of the *Finance Act*).

9 *Latilla v IRC*, [1943] AC 377 at 381 (HL) (taxpayer unsuccessfully attempted to reduce British income tax by transferring profit to capital; transaction within s 18 of the *Finance Act*).

10 *Re Weston's Settlements; Weston v Weston*, [1969] 1 Ch 223 at 245 (CA) (in making a determination whether to vary trusts for the purpose of avoiding or reducing tax, court may consider the expediency of such a scheme and the interests of the beneficiaries).

> Every man is entitled, if he can, to order his affairs so that the tax attaching under the appropriate Acts is less than it otherwise would be. If he succeeds in ordering them so as to secure this result . . . he cannot be compelled to pay an increased tax.[11]

Similarly, this can be seen in American tax jurisprudence. As Justice Holmes said:

> We do not speak of evasion, because, when the law draws a line, a case is on one side of it or the other, and if on the safe side is none the worse legally than a party that has availed himself to the full of what the law permits. When an act is condemned as an evasion, what is meant is that it is on the wrong side of the line indicated by the policy if not by the mere letter of the law.[12]

In retrospect, we see that the *Westminster* principle was the high watermark of judicial tolerance towards tax planning. The phrase "every man is entitled to arrange his affairs to minimize tax" is probably the best known and most frequently cited maxim of tax law. As it stands, the principle is of limited functional value. It tells us very little about how far tax planning can extend. How far can a taxpayer actually go in arranging his affairs so as to minimize tax? What are the acceptable limits of tax planning? As we shall see, the courts through judicial doctrines, and the legislature through statutory provisions, have severely curtailed taxpayer rights. Tax planning in the 21st century is much more constrained than the *Westminister* principle of the 1930s would have permitted.

· The law distinguishes between tax evasion, avoidance and mitigation. Tax evasion is the commission of an act knowingly *with the intent to deceive* so that the tax reported by the taxpayer is less than the tax payable under the law. This may occur through a deliberate omission of revenue, the fraudulent claiming of expenses or allowances or deliberate misrepresentation, concealment or withholding of material facts.[13]

Thus, tax evasion is a *mens rea* criminal offence. The Crown has the onus to prove the offence beyond a reasonable doubt based on the procedural rules of criminal law.

---

11   *IRC v Duke of Westminster*, [1936] AC 1 at 19–20 (HL). See also *Neuman v Canada (MNR)*, [1998] 1 SCR 770.

12   *Bullen v Wisconsin*, 240 US 625 at 630–31 (1916).

13   See Information Circular 73-10R3, "Tax Evasion" (13 February 1987); see also *R v Myers*, [1977] CTC 507 (Alta Dist Ct); *R v Baker* (1973), 6 NSR (2d) 38 (Co Ct); *R v Paveley*, [1976] CTC 477 (Sask CA); *R v Nicholson* (1974), 75 DTC 5095 (Ont Prov Ct); *R v Thistle*, [1974] CTC 798 (Ont Co Ct); *R v Regehr*, [1968] CTC 122 (Y CA); *R v Branch*, [1976] CTC 193 (Alta Dist Ct).

Tax avoidance is concerned with the "lawful" minimization of tax—the reduction of tax that would otherwise be payable in the absence of a tax plan. However, tax avoidance is "unlawful" if it offends prescriptive legislation.

The danger with the *Westminster* principle is that it can mislead taxpayers into believing that tax plans that merely comply with the technical provisions of the Act are acceptable. The maxim invites taxpayers to believe that they need attend only to the specific words of the Act without concern for the underlying policies and purposes of tax law. That may have been valid in the era of strict and literal interpretation of tax statutes. Purposive interpretation and broad anti-avoidance rules, however, have eroded the principle of literal interpretation, particularly in anti-avoidance legislation.

Three judicial doctrines warrant close attention:

1)   "Sham transactions";
2)   "Substance over form"; and
3)   "Economic substance" and "business purpose" tests.

1) Sham Transactions

We determine the legal effect of an arrangement by the rights and obligations that it actually creates and not merely by the wording of documentation. An arrangement that does not, in fact, create the legal rights and obligations that it purports to create is a "sham."

A "sham" is a fiction: an apparition of rights and obligations that do not really exist[14]—a transaction in which acts committed or documents executed by the parties to the transaction attempt to give to third parties the appearance of having created between the parties, legal rights and obligations that are different from those which the parties actually intended to create.[15] The sham implies that the parties

---

14   *Snook v London and West Riding Investment Ltd*, [1967] 2 QB 786 (CA) [*Snook*] (to have a sham transaction all parties must be in common agreement that the acts and documents do not create the legal rights and obligations that they appear to create); see also *IRC v Challenge Corp Ltd*, [1986] STC 548 (PC) (sham is transaction constructed to create false impression in eyes of tax authority); *Susan Hosiery Ltd v MNR*, [1969] CTC 533 (Ex Ct); *MNR v Cameron* (1972), [1974] SCR 1062; *Richardson Terminals Ltd v MNR*, [1971] CTC 42 (Ex Ct), aff'd [1972] CTC 528 (SCC); *Malka v Canada*, [1978] CTC 219 (FCTD); *Dominion Bridge Co v Canada*, [1975] CTC 263, aff'd [1977] CTC 554 (FCA).

15   This definition was adopted by the Supreme Court of Canada in *MNR v Cameron, ibid.*

to the transaction have deliberately set out to misrepresent the actual state of affairs. A sham may exist despite documentary appearance.[16]

A sham requires intention that the rights and obligations that the documentary evidence purports to create are different from the actual rights and obligations that the parties to the transaction contemplate.[17]

In *Stubart Investments Ltd v Canada* (*Stubart*),[18] the Supreme Court limited the sham doctrine to the circumstances contemplated by Lord Diplock in *Snook v London and West Riding Investment Ltd*.[19] Justice Estey said:

> . . . sham transaction: This expression comes to us from decisions in the United Kingdom, and it has been generally taken to mean (but not without ambiguity) a transaction conducted with an element of deceit so as to create an illusion calculated to lead the tax collector away from the taxpayer or the true nature of the transaction; or, simple deception whereby the taxpayer creates a façade of reality quite different from the disguised reality.[20]

Justice Estey's use of the word "deceit" in his description of "sham" did not likely narrow Lord Diplock's interpretation of the doctrine. A transaction that purports to put forward the appearance of legal rights and obligations that are different from those actually created is "deceitful" according to the common understanding of that term.

Only three years after *Stubart*, however, the Supreme Court clouded the doctrine in *Bronfman Trust v Canada* (*Bronfman Trust*).[21] The taxpayer had financed a capital payment through a bank loan and claimed a deduction for the interest expense on the loan. The CRA assessed based on the payment being on account of capital. The taxpayer argued that the expense would have been deductible if it had restructured the borrowing to make the interest payable on account of business income. For example, instead of making the payment directly on account of capital, the trust could have:

- Sold its portfolio securities to raise cash;
- Made its capital expenditure with the cash;
- Borrowed an equal amount from the bank; and

---

16   *Canada v Redpath Industries*, [1984] CTC 483 (Que Sup Ct) (must be *prima facie* evidence that tax was undisputably payable before the court will decide tax has been eroded and a sham has occurred).

17   *Snook*, above note 14 at 802.

18   *Stubart Investments Ltd v Canada* (1984), 84 DTC 6305 [*Stubart*].

19   *Snook*, above note 14.

20   *Stubart*, above note 18 at 6308.

21   *Bronfman Trust v Canada*, [1987] 1 SCR 32. See, however, *Shell Canada Ltd v Canada*, [1999] 3 SCR 622, which retreats from this approach towards tax planning.

- Used the borrowed funds to repurchase the portfolio of securities.

Had the trust executed each of these four steps in sequence, it would *actually* have created the legal rights and obligations that it purported to create, namely, borrowing to directly purchase income bearing securities. Each of the individual steps would have been a legitimate and valid commercial transaction and, hence, outside of the definition of "sham." The Supreme Court, albeit in *obiter*, observed that the restructured arrangement might be considered a sham. The Chief Justice said:

> If, for example, the Trust had sold a particular income-producing asset, made the capital allocation to the beneficiary and repurchased the same asset, all within a brief interval of time, the courts might well consider the sale and repurchase to constitute a formality or a sham designed to conceal the essence of the transaction, namely that money was borrowed and used to fund a capital allocation to the beneficiary.[22]

In *Singleton v Canada (Singleton)*,[23] the CRA referred to the *obiter* in an attempt to attack the Singleton structure of borrowing. The Supreme Court, however, deflected the CRA by characterizing the *Bronfman Trust* comments as "more musing than jurisprudence."

2) Substance vs. Form

The substance versus form argument is the single most difficult and unpredictable aspect of statutory interpretation in tax law.

It is sometimes said that the substance of a transaction determines its legal and tax consequences. This doctrine has intuitive appeal and is easy to state. It is not, however, quite so easy to define. The difficulty with the doctrine is that, despite its intuitive appeal, it does not offer any objective criteria against which we can measure particular facts. Hence, it is an unpredictable doctrine of varying scope. Lord Tomlin referred to it as the "so-called doctrine" in *IRC v Duke of Westminster*:

> [I]t is said that in revenue cases there is a doctrine that the Court may ignore the legal position and regard what is called "the substance of the matter." . . . This supposed doctrine (upon which the Commissioners apparently acted) seems to rest for its support upon a misunderstanding of language used in some earlier cases. The sooner this misunderstanding is dispelled, and the supposed doctrine given its quietus, the better it will be for all concerned, for the doctrine

---

22 *Bronfman Trust v Canada, ibid* at 55.
23 2001 SCC 61.

seems to involve substituting "the uncertain and crooked cord of discretion" for "the golden and straight metwand of the law." . . . Every man is entitled if he can to order his affairs so as that the tax attaching under the appropriate Acts is less than it otherwise would be . . . This so-called doctrine of "the substance" seems to me to be nothing more than an attempt to make a man pay and notwithstanding that he has so ordered his affairs that the amount of tax sought from him is not legally claimable.[24]

The CRA often applies the doctrine of substance over form to attack tax plans that it sees as "offensive" in some vague and unarticulated sense, but that otherwise technically comply with the Act. Thus, the doctrine becomes a camouflage for applying a motive test to tax mitigation arrangements.

3) Business Purpose

The general rule was that the motive with which a taxpayer entered into an avoidance transaction was irrelevant for the purpose of establishing the legitimacy of the transaction. As Viscount Dilhorne said:

> [T]rading transactions do not cease to be . . . merely because they are entered into in the hope of later taking advantage of the revenue law by making a claim for recovery of tax.[25]

Similarly, *per* Learned Hand J:

> [T]he rights resulting from a legal transaction otherwise valid, are not different vis-à-vis taxation, because it has been undertaken to escape taxation. That is a doctrine essential to industry and commerce in a society like our own, in which, and so far as possible, business is always shaped to the form best suited to keep down taxes.[26]

However, motive or purpose is now an important component of the statutory rules to control tax avoidance. Motive, for example, is an essential element of an "avoidance transaction" in section 245.

---

24   IRC v Duke of Westminster, above note 11 at 19–20 (HL) (employer's annual payments, under covenant, to servants not payments of salary and wages; taxpayer may arrange his affairs so as to minimize taxes).

25   FA & AB Ltd v Lupton (Inspector of Taxes), [1971] 3 All ER 948 at 954 (HL) (transactions of the taxpayers clearly joint ventures guised as share-dealing transactions intended to result in tax minimization; transactions fail).

26   Commissioner of Internal Revenue v National Carbide Corp, 167 F 2d 304 at 306 (2d Cir 1948) (creation of wholly-owned subsidiaries not necessarily invalid due to underlying motive to avoid taxation).

The traditional approach in Anglo-Canadian tax law was literal and strict interpretation of the Act. Indeed, the older cases analogize tax statutes with penal codes and frown upon purposive interpretation in the face of unambiguous language. The Supreme Court rejected any requirement for a business purpose as a stand-alone test in *Stubart*. However, the Court said that one should look at the "object and spirit" of tax legislation. Here we see the greenshoots of business purpose as it ultimately emerged in the general anti-avoidance rule.

C. THE GENERAL ANTI-AVOIDANCE RULE (GAAR)

Kings and government ought to shear, not skin their sheep.

—Robert Herrick

1) Background

There are two broad categories of tax avoidance:

1) Tax mitigation;[27] and
2) "Abusive" tax avoidance.

Tax minimization is legal and acceptable; "abusive" tax avoidance is not. Unfortunately, it is not always easy to draw the line between these two forms of tax avoidance.

The *Westminster* principle allows taxpayers to mitigate their taxes by arranging their affairs in any lawful manner. Under the principle, tax transactions and arrangements do not require a business or economic purpose. Tax saving is, in and of itself, sufficient justification to structure a transaction in a particular manner.

There is no additional requirement that transactions and arrangements should have a business or economic purpose. The Supreme Court of Canada struck down the business purpose doctrine in *Stubart*.[28] The taxpayer had transferred its profitable business to a sister corporation with accumulated tax losses. The sole objective of the arrangement was to marry the profits and the losses in the sister corporation. The taxpayer continued to operate the business, but now only as an agent of its sister corporation. Since an agent's profits belong to his principal, the arrangement allowed the taxpayer to use the accumulated losses in the

---

27   See *IRC v Challenge Corp Ltd*, above note 14.
28   *Stubart*, above note 18.

sister corporation to offset its profits. The court repudiated any requirement for a business purpose:

> I would therefore reject the proposition that a transaction may be dis-
> regarded for tax purposes solely on the basis that it was entered into
> by a taxpayer without an independent or *bona fide* business purpose.[29]

Justice Estey said that a requirement of business purpose would
deter taxpayers from participating in the very activities that the Act
sought to promote:

> Without the inducement offered by the statute, the activity may not
> be undertaken by the taxpayer for whom the induced action would
> otherwise have no *bona fide* business purpose. Thus, by imposing
> a positive requirement that there be such a *bona fide* business pur-
> pose, a taxpayer might be barred from undertaking the very activity
> Parliament wishes to encourage. At minimum, a business purpose
> requirement might inhibit the taxpayer from undertaking the speci-
> fied activity which Parliament has invited in order to attain economic
> and perhaps social policy goals.[30]

Four years after *Stubart*, however, Parliament introduced section
245, a general anti-avoidance rule to restrict tax planning and curtail
the *Westminster* principle by requiring a form of purpose in certain
circumstances.

GAAR is an amalgam of the business-purpose test in the United
States and the step transactions doctrine in the United Kingdom—a
statutory test that looks at all of the steps of a transaction or series of
transactions to determine if there is a legitimate commercial purpose.
Thus, the rule fills the vacuum that *Stubart* created.[31]

Parliament wrote GAAR because it was dissatisfied with the Supreme Court's decision in *Stubart*, which rejected both literal interpretation of the Act and the broader business purpose concept.

2) Purpose

> If not the taxpaying public or the fisc, who ultimately benefits from
> this approach? The only unequivocal beneficiary is the tax bar. The
> heavier the layers of judicial divination superimposed on the Internal
> Revenue Code, the richer tax lawyers are apt to get. The development

---

29   *Ibid* at 6322, Estey J.
30   *Ibid.*
31   *Ibid.*

of an exquisite set of intuitions about what kinds of transactions the courts "like" and "don't like" has become a large part of what tax lawyers sell.

> (Joseph Isenbergh, "Musings on Form and Substance
> in Taxation" (1982) 49 U Chicago L Rev 859 at 883

GAAR is an over-arching rule that is intended to protect the integrity of the Act by drawing a line between legitimate tax minimization and abusive tax avoidance. It is not, however, a bright line that one can easily identify and apply in a complex world with evolving business structures. As the Supreme Court acknowledged in *Canada Trustco*: "But what precisely constitutes abusive tax avoidance remains the subject of debate."[32]

The Act defines abusive tax avoidance as any transaction, or series of transactions, that gives rise to a tax benefit.[33] A "tax benefit" is any reduction, avoidance or deferral of tax or other amount payable under the Act, regulations, *Income Tax Application Rules* (*ITARs*) and tax treaties or an increase in a refund of tax or other amount under the Act.[34] Thus, without more, the rule would catch most commercial transactions and obliterate the *Westminster* principle.

Thus, GAAR is a supplementary rule to catch abusive tax avoidance where the other, more specific, anti-avoidance rules fail. Its natural consequence, intentional or otherwise, is that it creates uncertainty. The Supreme Court said, in *Canada Trustco*: "The GAAR was enacted as a provision of last resort in order to address abusive tax avoidance, it was not intended to introduce uncertainty in tax planning."[35] As applied and interpreted, however, it is impossible to escape completely from uncertainty. In *Lipson*,[36] the majority of the court readily accepted that Parliament legislated GAAR knowing that it would create widespread, serious and unpredictable effects. However, uncertainty is not sufficient to prevent the CRA from applying GAAR. Indeed, uncertainty acts as a constraint on overly aggressive tax planning. Uncertainty and the potential of professional liability are powerful brakes on excessive innovation in tax arrangements.

GAAR is not intended to catch transactions that comply with the policy of statutory provisions in the context of the Act read as a whole. The Technical Notes focus on the "object and spirit" of the Act:

---

32   *Canada Trustco*, above note 1 at para 16.
33   *ITA*, above note 3, subs 245(3).
34   *Ibid*, subs 245(1).
35   *Canada Trustco*, above note 1 at para 21.
36   *Lipson*, above note 7.

Transactions that comply with the object and spirit of other provisions of the Act read as a whole will not be affected by the application of this general anti-avoidance rule. For example, a transaction that qualifies for a tax-free rollover under an explicit provision of the Act, and that is carried out in accordance, not only with the letter of that provision but also with the spirit of the Act read as a whole, will not be subject to new section 245. However, where the transaction is part of a series of transactions designed to avoid tax and results in a misuse or abuse of the provision that allows a tax-free rollover, the rule may apply. If for example, a taxpayer, for the purpose of converting an income gain on a sale of property into a capital gain, transfers the property on a rollover basis to a shell corporation in exchange for shares in a situation where new section 54.2 of the Act does not apply and subsequently sells the shares, the new section could be expected to apply.

A transaction is not an avoidance transaction if the taxpayer undertakes it *primarily* for *bona fide* purposes other than obtaining the tax benefit. Thus, taxpayers should have substantial commercial, family or philanthropic reasons to support their transactions and tax savings should be ancillary in the overall plan.[37]

One determines the "primary purpose" of tax arrangements or transactions in an objective manner.[38] This requires a careful examination of the evidence—financial evidence, estimated tax benefits, cost of implementation, risk of loss and probability of success—when the taxpayer was arranging the transaction. This is essentially a facts and circumstances test. It is not permissible to introduce hindsight evidence of intention or purpose. The determination of primary purpose is a prospective analysis from the vantage point of the taxpayer at the time he, she or it was arranging and negotiating the transaction.[39]

The CRA uses the minister's Technical Notes and Parliamentary debates to determine the legislative intention underlying provisions of the Act.[40] Thus, the starting point in determining whether a transaction or arrangement constitutes lawful tax mitigation or tax avoidance is to ascertain the purpose of the statutory provisions used to implement the tax plan. We ascertain purpose from the statutory text of individual

---

37   *Canadian Pacific Ltd v Canada*, 2001 FCA 398, reconsideration refused 2002 FCA 98.
38   *OSFC Holdings Ltd v Canada*, 2001 FCA 260 at para 46, leave to appeal to SCC refused, [2001] SCCA No 522.
39   *Ibid.*
40   See, for example, CRA, *Technical Interpretation* (24 October 1990).

provisions read in the context of the Act read as a whole. In determining the context of the Act, however, one must also consider the specific provisions. GAAR cannot simply override specific provisions of the Act without reference to statutory context and legislative purpose. Thus, the process should follow a harmonized approach of textual, contextual and purposive analysis.

GAAR does not apply to any transaction (whether an avoidance transaction or otherwise) that does not misuse the provisions of the Act or abuse the provisions of the Act, regulations, *ITARs* or treaties when read as a whole.[41] This is the most significant constraint on what would otherwise be a boundless rule.

Thus, GAAR analysis is a multi-step process that involves:

1) A factual finding whether the taxpayer engaged in a transaction (usually obvious) or series of transactions (less obvious).
2) A factual finding that the taxpayer derived a "tax benefit" from the transaction or series of transactions through a reduction, avoidance or deferral of tax.
3) A factual finding whether the taxpayer arranged the transaction or series of transactions that gave rise to the benefit *primarily* for tax or non-tax purposes.
4) If the taxpayer derives a tax benefit from a transaction arranged primarily for tax purposes, an analysis whether the transaction (or series of transactions) misused any provisions of the Act (textual analysis).

GAAR applies if the transaction (or series of transactions) misuses a provision of the Act or abuses the provisions read as a whole (purposive analysis). The burden of establishing misuse or abuse of statutory transactions is on the minister. The benefit of any doubt goes to the taxpayer.[42]

The first three steps—existence of a transaction or series of transactions, determination of tax benefit and the primary purpose of a transaction (or series of transactions)—are essentially questions of fact. Hence, the taxpayer carries the burden to refute the minister's assumptions and facts. The determination as to whether the transaction (or series of transactions) constitutes a misuse of a specific provision or an abuse of the provisions of the Act read as a whole are questions of law and tax policy.

---

41 *ITA*, above note 3, subs 245(4).
42 See *Canada Trustco*, above note 1 at para 66 (the minister is in a better position than the taxpayer to make submissions on legislative intent).

3) The Charging Provision

Subsection 245(2) is as follows:

> Where a transaction is an avoidance transaction, the tax conse-
> quences to a person shall be determined as is reasonable in the cir-
> cumstances in order to deny a tax benefit that, but for this section,
> would result, directly or indirectly, from that transaction or from a
> series of transactions that includes that transaction.

The key terms in the charging provision are: "tax benefit," "tax consequences" and "transaction." The Act defines these terms in subsection 245(1):

- "Tax benefits" means a reduction, avoidance or deferral of tax or other
  amount payable or an increase in a refund of tax or other amount;
- "Tax consequences" to a person means the amount of income, taxable income, or taxable income earned in Canada of, tax or other
  amount payable by or refundable to the person under this *Act*, or
  any other amount that is relevant for the purposes of computing that
  amount; and
- "Transaction" includes an arrangement or event.

The existence of a tax benefit is a question of fact. The amount of the
benefit is not relevant.

a)   Recharacterization of Transactions

A taxpayer is entitled to mitigate his taxes provided that his transaction(s)
do not result in abusive tax avoidance. The CRA can recharacterize abusive "avoidance transactions" by ignoring any tax benefits derived from
the particular transaction and "as is reasonable in the circumstances."

It is important to distinguish between determination of a taxpayer's
liability because of an avoidance transaction and recharacterization of
a transaction for the purposes of determining the tax consequences of
the avoidance transaction. Subsection 245(3) does not permit the CRA
to recharacterize a transaction to determine whether it is an avoidance
transaction. Either the transaction is an avoidance transaction on its
facts or it is not. Merely because the taxpayer could have rearranged
his affairs to achieve an equivalent result at a higher tax cost does not
mean that the transaction is per se an avoidance transaction. A taxpayer is entitled to mitigate his taxes if tax mitigation is not the primary
motivation for the transaction or the Act is not misused or abused in
the process of the taxpayer's planning. It is for the trier of fact to evaluate the evidence to determine whether the transaction was primarily
tax or non-tax driven.

Thus, GAAR empowers the minister to ignore certain steps in a series of commercial transactions and recalculate the resulting tax liability without regard to those steps.

Therein lies the formidable power of GAAR: the rule empowers the minister to ignore and set aside a taxpayer's arrangements and substitute an alternative tax cost in lieu thereof.

The minister does not have the power to recharacterize a transaction for the purpose of determining that it is an "avoidance transaction." The minister can recharacterize the consequences of a transaction only after he determines that it constitutes an "avoidance transaction." Thus, within the parameters of the rule, a taxpayer may still arrange her affairs to mitigate tax.

Hence, in the face of a GAAR assessment, a taxpayer must demonstrate that her tax plan or arrangement is lawful tax mitigation in the sense that it constitutes avoidance, but avoidance that is not "abusive" of the Act. Compliance with the specific provisions of the statute or treaty is not by itself sufficient to prevent GAAR from applying to a transaction or series of transactions. One must also evaluate the purpose of the provisions in the context of the Act read as a whole.[43] Thus, in effect, GAAR is a surrogate for purposive analysis.

b) "Reasonable in the Circumstances"

What is "reasonable in the circumstances" is a question of fact. The phrase is broad enough to allow the minister to keep open the list of transactions that he may consider abusive in the future. The CRA has considerable administrative flexibility in coping with new circumstances as they arise. Thus, it can ignore the offensive steps of an avoidance transaction and determine the tax consequences as if the taxpayer had not undertaken the offensive steps.

Hence, GAAR does legislatively what the House of Lords did judicially in *Furniss v Dawson*:

> [T]he fiscal consequences of a preordained series of transactions, intended to operate as such, are generally to be ascertained by considering the result of the series as a whole, and not by dissecting the scheme and considering each individual transaction separately.[44]

However, GAAR goes further than the step transactions doctrine in *Furniss v Dawson* and looks at the "object and spirit" or the purpose of

---

43   See, for example, *Lipson*, above note 7 (technical compliance with three statutory provisions not enough to prevent GAAR from applying).

44   *Furniss (Inspector of Taxes) v Dawson*, [1984] AC 474 at 512 (HL), Lord Fraser of Tullybelton [*Furniss v Dawson*].

the Act read as a whole. This makes its potential reach longer than that of its English counterpart.

4) Avoidance Transactions

An "avoidance transaction" is any transaction, or series of transactions, that gives rise to *any* tax benefit unless the transaction may reasonably be considered to have been undertaken primarily for *bona fide* purposes other than obtaining the tax benefit. In order for a transaction not to be considered an "avoidance transaction," it must be supported by substantial reasons other than the tax benefit or savings that result from the transaction. The non-tax purpose must be primary. This is a factual inquiry.

The Act defines an "avoidance transaction" as:

> . . . any transaction
> (a) that . . . would result, directly or indirectly, in a tax benefit, unless the transaction may reasonably be considered to have been undertaken or arranged primarily for bona fide purposes other than to obtain the tax benefit; or
> (b) that is part of a series of transactions, which . . . would result, directly or indirectly, in a tax benefit, unless the transaction may reasonably be considered to have been undertaken or arranged primarily for bona fide purposes other than to obtain the tax benefit.[45]

Given the broad definition of "tax benefit," it would be difficult to characterize any financial transaction that one can implement through alternative strategies—and on which one takes professional advice—as other than tax motivated. All exchanges of goods, services and intellectual property—domestic or international—involve tax consequences. Where there is a choice, an informed taxpayer will usually seek the least costly tax route that meshes with his overall business objectives. The tax benefit of the transaction does not have to be "significant." Any tax benefit is sufficient.

a) Contextual Interpretation
GAAR requires contextual interpretation to determine whether transactions constitute abusive tax avoidance. Where an arrangement is implemented through a series of transactions or steps, one should look at

---

45   *ITA*, above note 3, subs 245(3).

the entire series to determine whether or not the resulting transactions constitute tax avoidance.[46]

b) Business Purpose

An arrangement without a business purpose is valid for tax purposes if it is undertaken *primarily* for *bona fide* purposes other than obtaining a tax benefit or saving. Thus, non-business reasons can support a commercial transaction. For example, family and financial security reasons can justify the structure of transactions: an offshore asset protection trust set up to protect one's assets is not per se an avoidance transaction even if it has incidental tax benefits. Business transactions will usually require a business purpose to avoid being characterized as avoidance arrangements. The taxpayer carries the burden of establishing his commercial purpose.

Subsection 245(3) exculpates a transaction (or series of transactions) if it "may reasonably be considered" to have been undertaken or arranged primarily for *bona fide* purposes other than to obtain a tax benefit. Where there is more than one transaction, the entire series of related transactions must be considered and not just the one transaction that gave rise to the benefit.

We determine the taxpayer's purpose in undertaking a transaction or series of transactions *objectively* based on the relevant facts and circumstances at the time the transactions occurred without the benefit of hindsight.[47]

The words "reasonably be considered" mean that purpose is tested against the circumstances surrounding the transaction and the nature of the evidence. A taxpayer's "purpose" is her intention in, or reason for, engaging in a transaction or series of transactions. The law evaluates assertions of intention and purpose in an objective manner to determine whether the asserted purpose is plausible in the circumstances.

A transaction undertaken for both tax and non-tax reasons must be carefully scrutinized to determine its *primary* purpose. This is not an easy task and requires careful evaluation of both tax and non-tax considerations to determine which dominates the transaction. What if the tax and non-tax reasons are equal considerations?

---

46   *OSFC Holdings Ltd v Canada*, above note 38 at para 45:

> Once it is determined that a series of transactions results in a tax benefit, any transaction that is part of the series may be found to be an avoidance transaction. The question is the primary purpose of each of the transactions in the series. If the primary purpose of any transaction is to obtain the tax benefit, it is an avoidance transaction.

47   *Ibid.*

In the absence of any other external evidence to support a transaction, the taxpayer's credibility may be the only basis to explain the transaction. Thus, uncorroborated but credible testimony can be sufficient proof of taxpayer intention.

5) Immunity from GAAR

GAAR applies to all avoidance transactions except those that do not misuse or abuse the Act. However, subsection 245(4) limits the scope of GAAR by providing that even tax-driven transactions are lawful if they do not violate the underlying policy of the Act, regulations, *ITARs* or tax treaties by misusing or abusing the provisions of the Act.

Determining "misuse" and "abuse" are not separate inquiries but a single, unified process involving textual, contextual and purposive interpretation. The Explanatory Notes use the phrase "exploit, misuse or frustrate" to describe misuse and abuse. The rationale of GAAR is that it applies when a literal or strict construction of the Act would defeat the "object and spirit" or underlying purpose for the particular provisions.

a) Legislative Intention
The Technical Notes explain subsection 245(4) as follows:

> Even where a transaction results, directly or indirectly, in a tax benefit and has been carried out primarily for tax purposes, section 245 will not apply if it may reasonably be considered that the transaction would not result directly or indirectly in a misuse of the provisions of the Act or an abuse having regard to the provisions of the Act read as a whole. This measure is intended to apply where a taxpayer establishes that a transaction carried out primarily for tax purposes does not, nonetheless, constitute an abuse of the Act.
>
> Subsection 245(4) recognizes that the provisions of the Act are intended to apply to transactions with real economic substance, not to transactions intended to exploit, misuse or frustrate the Act to avoid tax. It also recognizes, however, that a number of provisions of the Act either contemplate or encourage transactions that may seem to be primarily tax-motivated. The so-called "butterfly" reorganization is a good example of such transactions. It is not intended that section 245 will apply to deny the tax benefits that results from these transactions as long as they are carried out within the object and spirit of the provisions of the Act read as a whole. Nor is it intended that tax incentives expressly provided for in the legislation would be neutralized by this section.

The Technical Notes make clear that the rationale of GAAR is to look to the "real economic substance" of transactions. The Supreme Court accepted this in *Canada Trustco* but did not amplify or clarify the meaning of "real economic substance." Instead, the Court merely recognized that the provisions of the Act were intended to apply to transactions that were executed within the "object, spirit and purpose" of the provisions that are relied upon for the tax benefit. The Court said:

> The courts should not turn a blind eye to the underlying facts of a case, and become fixated on compliance with the literal meaning of the wording of the provisions of the Income Tax Act. Rather, the Courts should in all cases interpret the provisions in their proper context in light of the purposes they intend to promote.[48]

"Economic substance," "purpose" and "object and spirit" are similar concepts. The new approach simply reflects Frankfurter J's admonition that all legislation has a purpose and should be interpreted accordingly. However, the purpose of a provision does not assist in determining whether one should apply it to the economic substance or the legal form of the transaction under review.

In terms of "real economic substance," for example, what is the difference between a freehold sale of a building and a 999-year lease of the property with the option to purchase it for $1 at the end of the lease? In terms of economic substance, the lease is the same as the sale of freehold property if we value the transaction at the discounted net present value of its future cash flows. Its legal form, however, is a rental agreement until the lessee exercises the option to purchase the property for $1. It is then, and then only, that title to the property will pass from the lessor to the lessee and become a sale. However, in evaluating such a situation, subsection 245(4) should apply to its "real legal form."[49]

Subsection 245(4) applies only where the abusive nature of the transaction is clear. "The GAAR will not apply to deny a tax benefit where it may reasonably be considered that the transactions were

---

48   *Canada Trustco*, above note 1 at para 56.
49   *Ibid* at para 60:
   . . . should reject any analysis under s. 245(4) that depends entirely on "substance" viewed in isolation from the proper interpretation of specific provisions of the *Income Tax Act* or the relevant factual context of a case. However, abusive tax avoidance may be found where the relationships and transactions as expressed in the relevant documentation lack a proper basis relative to the object, spirit or purpose of the provisions that are purported to confer the tax benefit, or where they are wholly dissimilar to the relationships or transactions that are contemplated by the provisions.

carried out in a manner consistent with the object, spirit or purpose of the provisions of the Act, as interpreted textually, contextually and purposively."[50]

i) Burden of Proof

GAAR applies only if it may reasonably be considered that the trans-action under review abuses, directly or indirectly, a provision of the *Income Tax Act*, regulations, *ITAR*, a tax treaty, or any other enactment that is relevant in completing tax. The rule also applies if the taxpayer's arrangements and transactions abuse, directly or indirectly, the *Income Tax Act* read as a whole. Although there are two separate circumstances when the rule applies—misuse of a provision or abuse of the Act read as a whole—the tests apply concurrently and not sequentially. As the Supreme Court said in *Canada Trustco*:

> In effect, the analysis of misuse of the provisions and the analysis of the abuse having regard to the provisions of the Act read as a whole are inseparable.[51]

To be sure, *Canada Trustco* arose before the amendment of subsec-tion 245(4), which now sets out the application of the rule in two separ-ate paragraphs but which, at the time of the decision, was contained in a single paragraph. Nevertheless, there is nothing in the newly amended subsection that suggests anything different from the Supreme Court's analysis of the provision.

The burden of proof includes both the burden of persuasion and the burden of production.[52] The burden of proof requires the party who carries the burden to convince the factfinder to view the facts in a way that favours her. This is essentially a factual burden that the taxpayer carries in tax cases under the general common law evidentiary rules and the specific statutory provisions in the *Income Tax Act*. In the con-text of GAAR, the burden of proof is clearly on the taxpayer to re-fute that she did not derive any tax benefit and that the transaction or arrangement is not an avoidance transaction. These are questions of fact.

When we turn to the next step of the analysis, however, the burden shifts to the minister. Under this step, subsection 245(4) applies only if the taxpayer misuses specific provisions of the Act or abuses the statute read as a whole. It is for the minister to show whether the agree-

---

50   *Ibid* at para 59.
51   *Ibid* at para 39.
52   Bryan A Garner, *Black's Law Dictionary*, 8th ed (Eagan, MN: Thomson/West, 2004).

ments constitute a misuse or abuse of the statutory provisions. The textual, contextual and purposive interpretation of specific provisions of the *Income Tax Act* is essentially a question of law.

b) Abusive Transactions

GAAR does not apply to any transaction that does not misuse or abuse the Act. A "misuse" of the Act depends upon the policy of the particular provision under scrutiny. What constitutes an "abuse" of the Act as a whole is a broader question that requires contextual examination of the inter-relationship of the relevant statutory provisions. It is clear that the minister would prefer not to be constrained by the statutory language of specific provisions. This is quite clear in the Ministerial Technical Notes:

> Where a taxpayer carries out transactions primarily in order to obtain, through the application of specific provisions of the Act, a tax benefit that is not intended by such provisions and by the Act read as a whole, section 245 should apply. This would be the case even though the strict words of the relevant specific provisions may support the tax result sought by the taxpayer. Thus, where applicable, section 245 will override other provisions of the Act since, otherwise, its object and purpose would be defeated.

Fiscal legislation, however, must be interpreted according to the clear and unambiguous meaning of the language used.[53] Thus, clear language should have a clear effect. For example, paying bonuses to reduce a private corporation's active business income to its business limit is often purely tax driven. However, paying a bonus to reduce income is not abusive per se because it clearly complies with the statute. The transaction may be tax motivated, but it falls within the clear and unambiguous language of the statute that allows one to deduct reasonable salaries and bonuses.[54]

The terms "misuse" and "abuse" essentially refer to the legislative rationale that underlies specific or interrelated provisions of the Act. The Department of Finance explains these terms as follows:

> . . . the application of subsection 245(4) should involve an analysis of the object and spirit of the provisions of the Act read as a whole in the context of each particular case. An attempt to define the object and spirit of the provisions, far from being a "meaningless platitude," as

---

53   *Jabs Construction Ltd v Canada*, [1999] 3 CTC 2556 (TCC).
54   *ITA*, above note 3, ss 9 and 67.

once suggested, will be the key to a coherent solution of those cases where it is uncertain whether the proposed rule will apply.[55]

Determining whether there has been misuse or abuse involves two steps. First, one must identify the relevant policies of the particular provisions of the Act and of the Act read as a whole. The second step is to assess the facts to determine whether the avoidance transaction constituted a misuse or abuse having regard to the identified policies. However, given the complexity of the Act and the fact that the minister is in the best position to determine its underlying policies, the minister should assist the court by setting out the relevant policies. Where there is no evidence of a "clear and unambiguous" policy, the court cannot make a factual finding of misuse or abuse.[56]

i) Misuse of a Provision

An avoidance transaction that offends the underlying purpose of a specific rule is a misuse of the rule that attracts GAAR. An avoidance transaction that does not misuse a provision used to implement it may, nevertheless, be caught by GAAR if it is part of a transaction that abuses the Act as a whole.

It is important to distinguish between the purpose of a particular provision and its effect. A taxpayer can use a provision to mitigate taxes (the *Westminster* principle) if she does not offend its purpose. A transaction that is expressly permitted by the Act cannot, in and of itself, constitute misuse of the Act. For example, a transaction that takes advantage of a specific authorization to claim a deduction or offset a loss is not normally subject to GAAR.

The exclusionary rule requires an examination of the "object and spirit" of the provision under review to determine whether the taxpayer has misused its purpose in the particular circumstances. Thus, the rule implicitly applies the *Stubart* guidelines and purposive interpretation to test the validity of tax-driven transactions.

The "misuse" test in subsection 245(4) is essentially a restatement of *Stubart*'s "object and spirit" test. Hence, a transaction that was not offensive or abusive of the object and spirit of a particular provision before GAAR is not a misuse of the provision after the enactment of GAAR. The CRA has stated that:

---

55   David A Dodge, "A New More Coherent Approach to Tax Avoidance" (1988) 36 Can Tax J 1 at 21; see also Information Circulars 88-2, "General Anti-Avoidance Rule: Section 245 of the *Income Tax Act*" (21 October 1988) at para 5 and IC 88-2, "General Anti-Avoidance Rule: Supplement 1" (13 July 1990).

56   *OSFC Holdings Ltd v Canada*, above note 38 at paras 68–70.

Since the principles of statutory interpretation that Revenue Canada will follow will be similar to those followed to date, transactions that before the enactment of the general anti-avoidance rule were seen to comply with the Act in the sense mentioned will not now be seen to constitute a misuse of the provisions of the Act or an abuse of the Act read as a whole. Therefore the vast majority of transactions undertaken primarily to obtain a tax benefit that were seen to be consistent with the intention of Parliament before the amendment of section 245 will continue to be acceptable.[57]

But, as we see below, the misuse test is not as clear-cut as the CRA suggests. They also say that:

... transactions that rely on specific provisions, whether incentive provisions or otherwise, for their tax consequences, or on general rules of the Act can be negated if these consequences are *so inconsistent* with the general scheme of the Act that they cannot have been within the contemplation of Parliament.[58]

We determine the object and spirit of a provision through extrinsic evidence, including legislative history and ministerial technical notes:

In determining the intention of Parliament, Revenue Canada will take into account the words and context of any relevant provisions of the Act and the scheme of the Act read as a whole and any legislative history including the comments and examples contained in the Explanatory Notes to Legislation Relating to Income Tax issued by the Minister of Finance on June 30, 1988.[59]

ii) Abuse of the Act

GAAR does not apply to avoidance transactions consummated primarily for tax purposes if the transaction does not constitute an abuse of the Act read as a whole. "Abuse of law," essentially a civil law concept incorporated into GAAR, can be used to defeat an otherwise lawful tax arrangement that is considered offensive in terms of policy.

Immunity from GAAR is only available if the avoidance transaction does not fall within either the "misuse" or the "abuse" test.[60] A transaction that misuses a particular provision but does not abuse the Act read as a whole is caught by GAAR. Conversely, a transaction that com-

---

57   Michael Hiltz, "Section 245 of the *Income Tax Act*" (1988) 40 Can Tax Found 7:1 at 7:3.

58   Information Circular 88-2, above note 55 at para 5.

59   Hiltz, above note 57 at 7:3.

60   *ITA*, above note 3, subs 245(4).

plies with the literal and technical words of particular statutory provisions may, nevertheless, be subject to GAAR if its composite effect abuses the Act as a whole.

The abuse test in subsection 245(4) is probably the most controversial aspect of GAAR. A taxpayer must evaluate the statutory purpose of several, sometimes conflicting, provisions with no clear-cut or articulated rationale. This aspect of the Rule also gives the CRA its broadest discretionary power, particularly in the context of its advance rulings procedures. Since the CRA does not rule on questions of fact, it can quash virtually any GAAR ruling request by refusing to rule. The only small comfort that one can derive is from the CRA's public pronouncement:

> Transactions that before the enactment of the general anti-avoidance rule were seen to comply with the Act . . . will not now be seen to constitute a misuse of the provisions of the Act or an abuse of the Act read as a whole.[61]

Apart from this statement, however, the CRA does not provide any interpretational guidance to taxpayers.

iii) Burden of Proof

The burden of proof for establishing the application of GAAR depends upon whether one is interpreting a factual or legal issue. Determining whether a transaction involves a tax benefit or is an avoidance transaction is a question of fact in each case. Hence, the taxpayer carries the burden of proof to refute the minister's factual assumptions. This accords with the general rule in tax law regarding the burden of proof.[62]

Subsection 245(4) clearly excludes certain types of transactions from the category of "abusive" avoidance. Since the subsection derogates from the charging provision, it is, in effect, a relieving provision. At least that was the intention of the Department of Finance that tabled the legislation. As David A Dodge, Senior Assistant Deputy Minister, said:

> Subsection 245(4) is intended to be a relieving provision. Where a transaction does not have primarily non-tax purposes, it nonetheless escapes the application of the proposed section 245 if, on a normal construction of the Act read as a whole, it may reasonably be concluded that the transaction does not represent a misuse of the provisions of the Act or an abuse of the Act read as a whole.[63]

---

61   Hiltz, above note 57 at 7:3.
62   See *Hickman Motors Ltd v Canada*, [1997] 2 SCR 336.
63   Dodge, above note 55.

"Abuse" and "misuse" of the Act are questions of law and policy. Hence, the minister carries the burden of proof on these issues. The minister must identify the object, spirit or purposes of the underlying provisions in order to apply GAAR. The theory is that on questions of legislative intent the minister is in a better position to make submissions on the statutory scheme underlying the provisions under review.[64] The burden is on a balance of probabilities.

6) Determining the Policy of the Statute

The sole purpose of GAAR is to control abusive tax avoidance. The Act defines tax avoidance as any transaction that results in a tax benefit, unless the taxpayer undertakes the transaction primarily for *bona fide* non-tax purposes. Using this test, GAAR would catch all commercial transactions with any significant element of tax planning. Such a broad interpretation would emasculate the right of a taxpayer to plan her affairs to minimize tax (the *Westminister* principle). To avoid this absurd state of affairs, the Act exempts from GAAR transactions that do not directly or indirectly misuse its provisions or abuse the provisions of the statute read as a whole. The difficulty with these exemptions is that the first is too broad and the second too obscure. Thus, GAAR can catch virtually everything or nothing.

It is trite law that a taxpayer can plan her business affairs to minimize taxes. As Learned Hand J said: "There is nothing sinister in arranging one's affairs to keep taxes as low as possible." The general anti-avoidance rule, however, states that the minister can ignore a taxpayer's avoidance transactions if the taxpayer misuses the provisions of the *Income Tax Act* or abuses the provisions of the Act read as a whole. Thus, GAAR allows the minister to recharacterize the taxpayer's tax minimization arrangements.

Determining the underlying policy of a particular provision or the Act read as a whole is not an easy task. In many, if not most, cases it is quite difficult to obtain an authoritative reading of the "object and spirit" or purpose of particular provisions. Canada began tabling Technical Notes to explain amendments to the *Income Tax Act* in 1982. Until that time, the Department of Finance jealously guarded its legislative intentions from the public.

We must distinguish between the rule of statutory construction that requires an ambiguous provision to be interpreted according to its "object and spirit" (the purpose rule) and the application of subsection

---

64   *Canada Trustco*, above note 1 at para 65.

245(4), which limits the scope of GAAR to avoidance transactions that do not offend the policy of the Act. The rule of statutory construction is that clear and unequivocal words are to be given their ordinary, grammatical meaning in the context in which they appear. Thus, it is not necessary to determine the object and spirit of a clear and unambiguous statutory provision. The statute is read as it is written.

Subsection 245(4), however, exempts an "avoidance transaction" from GAAR if it does not misuse the particular provision or abuse the statute read as a whole. Thus, compliance with the literal language of the Act, even where that language is clear and unequivocal, is not by itself enough to immunize a transaction from GAAR. The Technical Notes (30 June 1988) make this quite clear:

> . . . a transaction structured to take advantage of technical provisions of the Act but which would be inconsistent with the overall purpose of these provisions would be seen as a misuse of these provisions. On the other hand, a transaction may be abusive having regard to the Act read as a whole even where it might be argued, on a narrow interpretation, that it does not constitute a misuse of a specific provision. Thus, in reading the Act as a whole, specific provisions will be read in the context of and in harmony with the other provisions of the Act in order to achieve a result which is consistent with the general scheme of the Act.

When is it appropriate to overlook clear and unambiguous statutory language and apply GAAR? The answer must surely be: only when the overall purpose and policy of the particular provisions is equally clear and unequivocal.

7) Extrinsic Evidence

Extrinsic evidence is admissible to determine the "object and spirit" or purpose of tax provisions. Indeed, *Stubart* mandates in strong *obiter* that ambiguous provisions be determined according to their "object and spirit." This can be done only through the admission of extrinsic evidence to determine the purpose of the provisions.[65]

8) Redetermination of Tax Liability

The minister can redetermine a taxpayer's liability under GAAR "as is reasonable in the circumstances" in order to deny him the tax benefits

---

65   See, for example, *Lehigh Cement Ltd v Canada*, 2009 TCC 237 (General Procedure) (TCC reviews published articles to determine the policy rationale of subpara 212(1)(b)(vii) withholding tax exemption).

of his avoidance transaction. "Reasonable in the circumstances" is a question of fact in each case. The Technical Notes explain the provision as follows:

> Where new subsection 245(2) applies, the tax consequences to a person are to be determined so as to deny the tax benefit on a basis that is reasonable in the circumstances. For that purpose, by virtue of new subsection 245(5), among other things:
> - all or part of any deduction in computing income, taxable income, taxable income earned in Canada or tax payable may be disallowed,
> - all or part of any deduction, income, loss or other amount may be allocated to any person,
> - a payment or other amount may be recharacterized, or
> - the tax effects that would otherwise result from the application of other provisions of the Act may be ignored.

For example, payments under a lease agreement may be characterized as proceeds of disposition of property where, having regard to the agreement as a whole, it would be reasonable to establish the tax results of that transaction as if it were a sale.

As another example, assume that, in contemplation of an arm's length sale, a taxpayer transfers an asset on a tax-free basis, under a rollover provision of the Act, to a related corporation, which subsequently sells the shares. The minister can apply subsection 245(2) if the sale to the related corporation is an avoidance transaction. The appropriate tax treatment might be to treat the taxpayer as having sold the property directly to the ultimate purchaser. Further, it might be appropriate in this situation for the minister to approve, through a determination under subsection 152(1.11), an increase in the cost base of the shares of the related corporation in order to prevent double taxation of the sale proceeds — once when the property is sold and again when the taxpayer disposes of the shares. Thus, the effect of the rollover provision would be ignored in order to allow this increased cost base.

A taxpayer can dispute, through the ordinary notice of objection and appeal procedures, not only a ministerial determination that a transaction is an avoidance transaction, but also the reasonable determination of the appropriate tax consequences.

9) Third Parties

Where the reconstruction of a taxpayer's income tax liability affects a third party, the third party may also request an adjustment to his tax liability, taking into account the amended and redetermined amounts. Subsection 245(6) is as follows:

> Where with respect to a transaction
> (a) a notice of assessment, reassessment or additional assessment involving the application of subsection (2) with respect to the transaction has been sent to a person, or
> (b) a notice of determination pursuant to subsection 152(1.11) has been sent to a person with respect to the transaction
>
> any person (other than a person referred to in paragraph (a) or (b)) shall be entitled, within 180 days after the day of mailing of the notice, to request in writing that the Minister make an assessment, reassessment or additional assessment applying subsection 245 (2) or make a determination applying subsection 152(1.11) with respect to that transaction.

a) Legislative History

The Technical Notes explain the structure of subsection 245(6):

> Under new subsection 245(6), where proposed subsection 245(2) applies with respect to a transaction and, consequently, a taxpayer has been assessed or reassessed or a determination has been made under proposed subsection 152(1.11) with respect to that person, another person is entitled to request that the Minister apply subsection 245(2) in his case in order to make adjustments of a relieving nature with respect to the same transaction.

D. SERIES OF TRANSACTIONS

> I am at one with those of your Lordships who find the complicated and stylised antics of the tax avoidance industry both unedifying and unattractive but I entirely dissent from the proposition that because there is present ... the element of a desire to mitigate or postpone the respondents' tax burdens, this fact alone demands from your Lordships a predisposition to expand the scope of the doctrine of *Ramsay* and of *Furniss v Dawson* beyond its rational basis in order to strike down a transaction which would not otherwise realistically fall within it.
> —Lord Oliver in *Craven v White*, [1988] 3 WLR 423 at 463–64 (HL)

1) General Comment

The general anti-avoidance rule applies to abusive avoidance transactions, whether undertaken individually or as part of a series of transactions. Thus, in any fact situation involving more than a single transaction, one needs to determine whether the particular transactions constitute a "series." Where a sequence of events is a series of transactions, one must then determine whether GAAR applies to the entire series as a composite.

The Act does not define the meaning of the expression "series of transactions." The expression is unclear but essential to the doctrine controlling tax avoidance. The House of Lords developed the meaning of the expression in a number of cases—most notably *Craven v White*,[66] *WT Ramsay Ltd v IRC* (*Ramsay*)[67] and *Furniss v Dawson*.[68] However, the Act adds a further gloss to the expression.[69]

The *Shorter Oxford English Dictionary* defines series as "a number of things of one kind following one another in temporal succession." In the context of GAAR, it is clear that the term "series" is not merely a sequence of events in a temporal sense. It is trite to observe that all events occur in a sequence. As Lord Oliver said in *Craven v White*:

> a series means no more than a succession of related matters—a description that applies to virtually every human activity embarked upon with a view to producing any rational result.[70]

Whether a sequence of transactions constitutes a "series" or independent transactions requires an analysis of the taxpayer's intentions and conduct. The essential question is: are the individual steps or transactions sufficiently tied or linked to constitute a series?

A series of transactions constitutes a composite when its individual components are linked or glued together through firm arrangements or understandings that each component will be completed. In other words, it is "well understood" by the parties that the entire sequence will be carried to completion. The linkage of the separate steps into a "series" results from their interdependence and the manner in which the transactions are structured. Thus, we must determine: when is a sequence of events (e.g., A to B, then B to C) considered a single composite transaction (such as A to C)?

---

66 [1988] 3 WLR 423 (HL).
67 [1982] AC 300 (HL).
68 Above note 44.
69 See *ITA*, above note 1, subs 248(10), discussed below.
70 *Craven v White*, above note 66 at 452.

2) The Common Law

a) *Floor v Davis*

We trace the origins of the step transactions doctrine in the UK to the dissenting judgment of Eveleigh LJ in *Floor v Davis*.[71] The taxpayers, who were shareholders in a corporation (A), agreed in principle to sell their shares to another corporation (B). With a view to reducing or avoiding capital gains tax that would otherwise be payable on a direct sale of the shares, the taxpayers incorporated a new corporation (C), with which they exchanged their shares in A. Corporation C, now the owner of the A shares, then sold the shares for cash to the ultimate purchaser, Corporation B. C, the new corporation, was then wound up. As a result of the reorganization of its capital, C passed on the cash that it received from B to an offshore corporation. The taxpayers would not be liable for capital gains tax if it could be shown that they had not disposed of their shares directly for cash to the ultimate purchaser of the shares.

The majority of the Court of Appeal held that each step in the sequence of transactions was properly executed and represented a genuine transaction. Eveleigh LJ dissented: the taxpayer had, in effect, disposed of his shares to the ultimate purchaser even though they were transmitted through the medium of an intermediary corporation. His Lordship considered the series of events as a composite transaction.

b) The *Ramsay* Principle

In *Ramsay*,[72] the taxpayer, a farming corporation, realized a substantial capital gain on the sale of farmland, which would have been subject to capital gains tax. To avoid the tax that would otherwise have been payable, the taxpayer embarked upon a "scheme" to create a paper capital loss to offset the capital gain on the farmland. The essence of the capital loss scheme was as follows:

- The taxpayer purchased the shares of a company and loaned it two equal amounts at a rate of 11 percent;
- The loans were made on the basis that the interest on one loan could be increased provided that there was a corresponding decrease in the interest rate charged on the other loan;
- The taxpayer reduced the interest rate on one loan to zero and increased the interest rate on the other loan to 22 percent;
- The zero interest loan was then paid in full and, as a result, the taxpayer sustained a loss in the value of the shares of the corporation;

---

71 *Floor v Davis*, [1980] AC 695 (HL), aff'g [1978] 1 Ch 295 (CA).
72 *WT Ramsay Ltd v IRC*, above note 67.

• The loss was equal to the gain realized on the other loan.

Thus, the decreasing asset was sold to create a loss; the increasing asset was sold to create a tax-exempt gain. The scheme had neither commercial justification nor business purpose. The sole purpose of the transactions was to produce a paper loss equal in amount to the capital gain that the taxpayer realized.

i)   Circular Transactions

Ramsay involved a circular transaction. The arrangements were, in Lord Oliver's words:

> An artificially contrived concatenation of individual transactions linked together with the purpose of producing an end result entirely different from that which, on the face of it, would have been achieved by each successive link.[73]

The entire arrangement constituted two transactions of a self-cancelling nature, which returned the taxpayer to his starting position. In the process, however, the taxable capital gain was eliminated by offsetting it against a paper capital loss. Lord Wilberforce described the scheme as follows:[74]

> In each case two assets appear, like "particles" in a gas chamber with opposite charges, one of which is used to create the loss, the other of which gives rise to an equivalent gain which prevents the taxpayer from supporting any real loss, and which gain is intended not to be taxable. Like the particles, these assets have a very short life. Having served their purpose they cancel each other out and disappear. At the end of the series of operations, the taxpayer's financial position is precisely as it was at the beginning, except that he has paid a fee, and certain expenses, to the promoter of the scheme.

Every step of the transactions was genuinely carried through and every transaction was exactly what it purported to be: the form of the arrangement was entirely proper; no part of the scheme was a sham. Although there was no binding arrangement that each step would be followed by the next planned step, it was well understood that the entire sequence of events would be carried through to completion. Otherwise the scheme had no value.

The composite effect of the two transactions was that the taxpayer made neither a gain nor a loss. The transactions taken together were

---

73   *Craven v White*, above note 66 at 452.
74   *WT Ramsay Ltd v IRC*, above note 67 at 322.

nothing more than a scheme to avoid taxes and the House of Lords treated it as such. Lord Wilberforce said:

> To force the courts to adopt, in relation to closely integrated situations, a step by step, dissecting, approach which the parties themselves may have negated, would be a denial rather than an affirmation of the true judicial process.[75]

ii)   *Effect on* Westminster *Principle*

Ramsay does not overrule the *Westminster* principle: it does, however, limit it to genuine cases of tax mitigation. The principle does not apply where it is plain that a particular transaction is but one step in a connected series of interdependent steps designed to produce a single composite overall result. Lord Wilberforce said of the principle:

> While obliging the court to accept documents or transactions, found to be genuine, as such, it does not compel the court to look at a document or a transaction in blinkers, isolated from any context to which it properly belongs. If it can be seen that a document or transaction was intended to have effect as part of a nexus or series of transactions, or as an ingredient of a wider transaction intended as a whole, there is nothing in the doctrine to prevent it being so regarded; to do so is not to prefer form to substance, or substance to form. It is the task of the court to ascertain the legal nature of any transaction to which it is sought to attach a tax or a tax consequence and if that emerges from a series or a combination of transactions, intended to operate as such, it is that series or combination which may be regarded.[76]

iii)   *Integrated Transactions*

In what circumstances can one aggregate separate transactions into a composite transaction? What, in effect, constitutes a "series of transactions"? The facts in *Ramsay* provide a clue to the answer: the transactions were circular, could not stand alone, were not intended to do so, and it was well understood that all of the steps had to be completed in order for the tax plan to work. In Lord Oliver's words:

> But the fact was, as was plain to see, that those transactions not only were not intended to be interrupted or to stand in isolation but could not in fact have done so in the real world. They were totally dependent upon and integrated with other transactions whose purpose, and whose only purpose, was to nullify their effects and to leave the tax-

---

75   *Ibid* at 326.
76   *Ibid* at 323–24.

payer in exactly the same position as they were before. In the one case there was actually a contractual obligation to carry the steps through to the end; in the other there was the confident expectation that they would be carried through to the end and no likelihood whatever that they would not.[77]

But *Ramsay* does not imply that all sequential steps must necessarily be aggregated into a composite transaction. A sequence is only a "series" if the component transactions cannot have an independent existence and are not intended to do so. As Lord Oliver said:

> What the case does demonstrate, as it seems to me, is that the underlying problem is simply one of the construction of the relevant statute and an analysis of the transaction or transactions which are claimed to give rise to the liability or the tax exemption. But it does not follow that because the court, when confronted with a number of factually separate but sequential steps, is not compelled, in the face of the facts, to treat them as if each of them had been effected in isolation, that all sequential steps must invariably be treated as integrated, interdependent and without individual legal effect.[78]

c) *Burmah Oil*

The House of Lords reaffirmed the *Ramsay* principle in *IRC v Burmah Oil Co Ltd (Burmah Oil)*,[79] and clarified the *Westminster* doctrine. Lord Diplock said:

> It would be disingenuous to suggest, and dangerous on the part of those who advise on elaborate tax avoidance schemes to assume, that *Ramsay*'s case did not mark a significant change in the approach adopted by this House in its judicial role to a preordained series of transactions (whether or not they include the achievement of a legitimate commercial end) into which there are inserted steps that have no commercial purpose apart from the avoidance of a liability to tax which in the absence of those particular steps would have been payable. The difference is in approach. It does not necessitate the overruling of any earlier decisions of this House; but it does involve recognizing that Lord Tomlin's oft quoted dictum in *I.R.C. v Duke of Westminster*. . . . "Every man is entitled, if he can, to order his affairs so that the tax attaching under the appropriate Acts is less than it otherwise would be," tells us little or nothing as to what methods

---

77 *Craven v White*, above note 66 at 454.
78 *Ibid.*
79 *IRC v Burmah Oil Co Ltd* (1981), 82 BTC 56 (HL) [*Burmah Oil*].

of ordering one's affairs will be recognized by the courts as effective
to lessen the tax that would attach to them if business transactions
were conducted in a straightforward way.[80]

Lord Scarman went even further:

> First, it is of the utmost importance that the business community
> (and others, including their advisers) should appreciate . . . that *Ramsay's* case marks "a significant change in the approach adopted by
> this House in its judicial role" towards tax avoidance schemes. Secondly, it is now crucial when considering any such scheme to take
> the analysis far enough to determine where the profit, gain or loss is
> really to be found.[81]

Thus, "circular" tax planning schemes solely intended to produce
self-cancelling consequences do not constitute legitimate tax mitigation. But what of schemes that are not self-cancelling but have enduring
consequences?

d) *Furniss v Dawson*

Furniss v Dawson[82] involved a tax scheme intended to mitigate the capital gains tax that would have been payable by the taxpayer had he disposed of the shares of his corporation in an open-market transaction
directly to the intended ultimate purchaser. To avoid the capital gains
tax, the taxpayer exchanged his shares for shares of an offshore investment corporation that he owned. The offshore investment corporation
then sold the shares to the ultimate purchaser, who was unconnected
to the taxpayer. Under the UK *Finance Act, 1965*, the first disposition
by way of share exchange to the offshore investment corporation was
not a disposition or acquisition for capital gains tax purposes. Further,
there would be no capital gains tax liability on the sale of the shares by
the offshore investment corporation until such time as the taxpayers
disposed of their shares in the investment corporation. Thus, *Furniss v
Dawson* involved a "linear" as opposed to a "circular" transaction.

The House of Lords applied the *Ramsay* principle, not only to self-cancelling transactions, but also to those that have "enduring legal
consequences." (The offshore investment corporation was not wound
up after it had disposed of the corporation's shares to the ultimate purchaser, but continued in existence.) Lord Brightman's speech captures
the essence of the decision:

80   *Ibid* at 58.
81   *Ibid* at 64–65.
82   *Furniss v Dawson*, above note 44.

My Lords, in my opinion the rationale of the new approach is this: in a pre-planned tax-saving scheme, no distinction is to be drawn for fiscal purposes, because none exists in reality, between (i) a series of steps which are followed through by virtue of an arrangement which falls short of a binding contract, and (ii) a like series of steps which are followed through because the participants are contractually bound to take each step *seriatim*. In a contractual case the fiscal consequences will naturally fall to be assessed in the light of the contractually agreed results . . . . The day is not saved for the taxpayer because the arrangement is unsigned or contains the words "this is not a binding contract."[83]

e) Summary of the Common Law

The English common law judicial doctrine determines the existence of a series by looking at two distinct aspects of transactions: preordination of the sequence of events and existence of a commercial or business purpose. First, there must be a preordained series of transactions that constitute a composite transaction. Second, there must be steps inserted in the sequence that have no commercial purpose other than to reduce tax payable.[84]

Under the Act, a series of transactions constitutes a composite whole when its individual components are linked or glued together through "firm" arrangements or understandings that each component will be completed. In other words, it is "well understood" that the entire sequence will be completed in a preordained sequence. This is the first leg of the two-pronged English test.

How "firm" must the understanding be in order to provide the linkage between individual transactions? Must the arrangements be "preordained" in a legal sense in order to constitute a series of transactions? The answer is clearly "No." There is no distinction between tax schemes comprised of a series of steps that are followed through by virtue of an arrangement that falls short of a binding contract and schemes that are followed through because the participants are contractually bound to take each step *seriatim*. Preordination does not depend upon strict contractual rights, but on a practical certainty that transactions will be completed as planned.

---

83   *Ibid* at 526.
84   See, for example, *Craven v White*, above note 66.

Under the statutory test a sequence of transactions is considered a "series" or composite if, at the time when the intermediate transaction is entered into:[85]

- The sequence is preordained to produce a given result;
- There is no practical likelihood that the planned events will not take place in the order ordained, so that the intermediate transaction is not even contemplated practically as having an independent life; and
- The preordained events do in fact take place.

In these circumstances, the first transaction can be linked to the last and the linked group is considered a single composite whole. Preordination of transactions implies, at the very least, an orchestrated sequence with a degree of certainty and control over the end result at the time that the intermediate steps are taken. It does not require absolute certainty as to every detail, but there should be no practical or substantial likelihood or risk that the transaction will not take place. Thus, a series of transactions is preordained, so as to constitute a single composite transaction, if there is a practical certainty when the first transaction takes place that the subsequent transactions will also take place.[86]

A composite transaction is one in which, when the first transaction is implemented, all of the essential features (not just the general nature) of the second transaction are determined by persons who have the firm intention and ability to implement the second transaction. For example, in a sale from A to B and from B to C, at the time that A sells to B, C is identified as prospective purchaser and all the main terms of the sale are agreed to in principle. There does not have to be a pre-existing contract when the scheme begins; it is sufficient that there is a practical certainty that all the steps of the various transactions will be carried through to completion.

Thus, for the purpose of determining whether a particular sequence of transactions is a series or composite, it is not necessary to satisfy the second prong of the English common law test, namely, the existence of a commercial purpose for the transactions.[87] For Canadian tax purposes, the commercial purpose test is a separate and distinct test.

---

85 *Ibid* at 462–63.

86 *Hatton v IRC*, [1992] BTC 8024 (Ch Div).

87 See *Canutilities Holdings Ltd v Canada*, 2004 FCA 234, leave to appeal to SCC refused, [2004] SCCA No 373.

f) Subsection 248(10)

The Act expands the common law concept of "series of transactions" to also include any *related* transactions or events completed in *contemplation* of the series.[88] In *OSFC Holdings Ltd v Canada (OSFC)*,[89] for example, the court included within a series subsequent related events by a third party that occurred two years later in an arm's length transaction.

The taxpayer knew of the prior series of transactions to which it was not a party. Because the taxpayer knew of the series, it took them into account in arranging their own transaction. Thus, the taxpayer's knowledge of the history of the prior series was sufficient to contaminate its own transaction even though they were not a part of the original series.

Subsection 248(10) extends the meaning of the expression "series of transactions" beyond *Furniss v Dawson*. The Department of Finance was not entirely candid about its legislative intention when it enacted the subsection. The Technical Notes to the amending bill state that the legislative intention underlying the subsection—introduced in 1986, two years before the enactment of GAAR—was to "clarify" the meaning of "series of transactions."[90]

As David A Dodge, then Senior Assistant Deputy Minister of the Department of Finance, in an article entitled "A New and More Coherent Approach to Tax Avoidance," stated:

> The step transaction doctrine, however, when completed by the business purpose test as suggested in *Burmah* and *Furniss v Dawson*, represents a coherent and orthodox approach. For that reason, this doctrine has been included in proposed section 245 in the form suggested by these cases.[91]

Under *Furniss v Dawson*, a sequence would be a "series" only if at the time of the preliminary transaction, all the important elements of subsequent transactions were settled and eventually carried out. The language of subsection 248(10), however, goes further. In *OSFC*, for example, the taxpayer was not even on the horizon when E&Y hatched its plan to maximize the recovery from disposing of the assets of the Stan-

---

88   *ITA*, above note 3, subs 248(10): "For the purposes of this Act, where there is a reference to a series of transactions or events, the series shall be deemed to include any related transactions or events completed in contemplation of the series."

89   *OSFC Holdings Ltd v Canada*, above note 38.

90   See Bill C-84, SC 1986, c 6, s 126(6): "New subsection 248(10) of the Act clarifies that a reference in the Act to a series of transactions or events includes any related transaction or event completed in contemplation of the series."

91   (1988) 36 Can Tax J 1 at 15.

dard Trust Company. Thus, as the Federal Court of Appeal found, the taxpayer was not a part of the original series under the judicial doctrine of *Furniss v Dawson*. However, the court went further in holding that subsection 248(10) more than clarifies the meaning of "series of transactions" and extended the concept to include all related transactions that the taxpayer contemplates in structuring its own arrangements.

In *Canada Trustco*, the Supreme Court curtailed the broad reading of subsection 248(10) that Justice Rothstein gave the provision in *OSFC*. In its *per curiam* decision the Supreme Court says that "in contemplation" should not be read in the sense of actual knowledge but in the broader sense of "because of" or "in relation to" the series. Thus, the phrase can be applied to events either before or after the basic avoidance transaction.

3) *Westminster* Revisited

The *Westminister* dictum is accurate in the context of tax mitigation. However, it does not apply to abusive tax avoidance, whether implemented through a single transaction or a series of transactions.[92] As Lord Diplock candidly declared in *Burmah Oil*, the principle that every taxpayer is entitled to order her affairs to minimize tax "tells us little or nothing as to what methods of ordering one's affairs will be recognized by the courts."[93]

Tax mitigation, in and of itself, is neither abusive nor offensive. The manner in which the taxpayer executes the arrangement, however, determines whether it is effective. As Lord Oliver put it:[94]

> I am at one with those of your Lordships who find the complicated and stylised antics of the tax avoidance industry both unedifying and unattractive but I entirely dissent from the proposition that because there is present . . . the element of a desire to mitigate or postpone the respondents' tax burdens, this fact alone demands from your Lordships a predisposition to expand the scope of the doctrine of *Ramsay* and of *Furnish v. Dawson* beyond its rational basis in order to strike down a transaction which would not otherwise realistically fall within it.

His Lordship tactfully distanced himself from Lord Scarman's suggestion that abusive tax avoidance schemes constitute "tax evasion":

---

92   *Ensign Tankers (Leasing) Ltd v Stokes (Inspector of Taxes)*, [1992] STC 226 (HL).
93   *Burmah Oil*, above note 79 at 64–65.
94   *Craven v White*, above note 66 at 463–64.

[T]here appears to be introduced in the speech of Lord Scarman at least, a moral dimension by which the court is to identify what he described as "unacceptable tax evasion." On the face of it this might be taken to suggest that the long accepted distinction between tax avoidance and tax evasion is to be elided and that the fiscal effect of a transaction is no longer to be judged, as *Ramsay* and *Burmah*, by the criterion of what the taxpayer has actually done, but by whether what he has done is "acceptable." It may be doubted whether this was indeed what Lord Scarman intended to suggest, but if it was, he was, I think, alone in expressing this view.[95]

Subsection 245(3) states that transactions that are primarily non-tax driven are not subject to GAAR. If, however, even one transaction that is part of a series of transactions is primarily tax driven, the entire series becomes an avoidance transaction. We must then proceed to the next step: does the avoidance transaction misuse or abuse the Act?

4) Purposive Interpretation

In the context of tax avoidance, GAAR has moved statutory construction from literal to purposive interpretation. *Lipson*[96] illustrates the limits of the *Westminster* principle and technical compliance with the rules. The underlying facts in *Lipson* were as follows. The Lipsons (Earl and Jordana) purchased a family residence. They arranged the financing of the home through a series of transactions designed to make the interest on their borrowing deductible for tax purposes.

· First, Jordana Lipson borrowed $562,500 from a bank to purchase shares in her husband's family investment corporation at their fair market value. Since Jordana used the borrowed money to purchase investment assets, the interest payable on the demand note was deductible.[97] As the sale of the shares was between spouses, subsection 73(1) deemed the sale of shares to occur at cost. Hence, the sale did not trigger any immediate capital gain or tax liability.

Second, the taxpayers obtained a mortgage from a bank for $562,500. On the same day, Jordana used funds from the mortgage loan to repay the entire share loan to the bank. The bank cancelled the demand note. The taxpayer could deduct the interest on the mortgage loan as being on account of money substituted for the initial purchase of shares, on which the interest was deductible.

---

95   *Ibid* at 507.
96   *Lipson*, above note 7.
97   *ITA*, above note 3, para 20(1)(c).

Subsection 74.1(1) of the Act attributed any dividend income (net of interest expenses to earn the dividends) on Jordana's shares to Earl, who reported the income.

The legal form of each of the individual steps in the series of transactions was proper. Specific provisions of the Act authorized or deemed the results that made the interest deductible. The taxpayers meticulously dotted all their i's and crossed all their t's.

However, the transactions had no commercial or business purpose other than the tax savings. The purpose of the "cheque shuffling" between the various parties was to convert what would otherwise be non-deductible personal interest on a home mortgage into deductible interest for tax purposes. As the trial judge (Chief Justice Bowman) said in the Tax Court of Canada:

> The overall purpose as well as the use to which each individual provision was put was to make interest on money used to buy a personal residence deductible.

The finding of fact proved to be fatal in subsequent appeals. The taxpayers attempted to arrange their affairs so as to avoid and minimize the amount of tax payable. The Lipsons conceded that the transactions were tax avoidance transactions. The important question was whether the transactions were "abusive" under the GAAR.

The Lipsons actually sought to do what the taxpayer in *Singleton*[98] had done before. In *Singleton*, a lawyer withdrew his tax-paid capital from his law partnership to purchase a home and then filled the hole created by the withdrawal of his capital with substitute bank financing. The Supreme Court of Canada upheld the validity of the taxpayer's circular financing. Each step of the series was proper and complied with the terms of the *Income Tax Act*. The Supreme Court allowed Singleton to deduct his interest on the substitute financing.

However, there are two important differences between *Singleton* and *Lipson*. First, *Singleton* involved an assessment prior to GAAR. The Supreme Court of Canada upheld the *Westminster* principle in *Singleton* and the legal form of the taxpayer's actions. The Court did not have to look at the tax avoidance aspect of the transactions or the taxpayer's motives. In contrast, *Lipson* squarely pitted the *Westminster* principle against GAAR—a taxpayer cannot avoid tax by misusing particular statutory provisions or abusing the statutory framework of the *Income Tax Act* read as a whole.

---

98   *Singleton v Canada*, above note 23.

Second, Singleton withdrew his *after-tax* capital from the law firm. He had paid his full share of tax on the money. He was merely refinancing his capital. In *Lipson* the taxpayers did not pay tax on the underlying transfer of shares.

Section 73 deems a transfer between spouses to occur at the cost base of the property. For example, if a husband sells shares that cost $10 per share to his wife for $25 per share, the transaction is deemed to occur at $10 a share and there is no capital gain. Thus, the section treats spouses as an economic unit for the purpose of timing recognition of the gain. The Lipsons were clearly within the purpose and policy of the provision.

The transferee spouse assumes the transferor's cost base of $10 a share for tax purposes. If the transferee subsequently sells the shares to a third party, the Act attributes any gain or loss to the transferor, who will have to pay tax on the gain as if he had not transferred the property in the first place. Thus, the attribution rule kicks in on the subsequent sale to a third party and prevents income splitting, regardless of the transferor's motive or economic purposes. For example, if the transferee sells the shares for $40 a share, the transferor is taxable on the entire capital gain of $30 a share. The rule is a strict liability deeming provision that preserves the separate identity of each spouse as a taxable unit.

The third deeming provision—subsection 20(3)—facilitates substitute financing. The provision ensures deductibility of interest on a loan if the taxpayer uses newly borrowed funds to discharge another loan that he used for income-earning purposes.

Thus, the taxpayers arranged their affairs using three different statutory rules to minimize their taxes. They converted what would have been non-deductible personal interest expense into deductible interest. They thought they had the *Westminster* principle on their side.

GAAR, however, is an overarching rule that looks beyond technical compliance with the Act. The essence of the rule is to determine whether an avoidance transaction undermines the purpose of specific provisions or the framework of the Act. GAAR is not an economic substance over legal form rule. It is a "misuse" and "abuse" rule.

GAAR implies purposive interpretation. The test to determine whether a transaction is an avoidance transaction is in part results-oriented and in part purpose-based. The test for whether a transaction is "abusive" is results-oriented. To be "abusive" the transaction must "*result* directly or indirectly in a misuse of the provisions" of the statute, regulations or tax treaties—that is, the result must undermine the purpose. The Supreme Court of Canada stated the principle in *Canada Trustco*:[99]

> The heart of the analysis under [GAAR] lies in a contextual and purposive interpretation of the provisions of the Act that are relied on by the taxpayer, and the application of the properly interpreted provisions of the facts of a given case. The first task is to interpret the provisions giving rise to the tax benefit to determine their objects, spirit and purpose. The next task is to determine whether the transaction falls within or frustrates that purpose. The overall inquiry thus involves a mixed question of fact and law. The textual, contextual and purposive interpretation of specific provisions of the *Income Tax Act* is essentially a question of law that the application of these provisions to the facts of a case is necessarily fact-intensive.
>
> This analysis will lead to a finding of abusive tax avoidance when a taxpayer relies on specific provisions of the *Income Tax Act* in order to achieve an outcome that those provisions seek to prevent. As well, abusive tax avoidance will occur when a transaction defeats the underlying rationale of the provisions that are relied upon. An abuse may also result from an arrangement that circumvents the application of certain provisions, such as specific anti-avoidance rules, in a manner that frustrates or defeats the object, spirit or purpose of those provisions. By contrast, abuse is not established where it is reasonable to conclude that an avoidance transaction under [GAAR] was within the object, spirit or purpose of the provisions that confer the tax benefit.

To be sure, it is not always easy to extract the object, spirit or purpose of statutory provisions because of the paucity of background materials and published policy documents. Nevertheless, it is counsel's responsibility to elicit the purpose of legislation from credible sources for the court.

The straw that broke the camel's back in *Lipson* was the income attribution rule. The purpose of the rule is to prevent income shifting from high marginal rate taxpayers to lower rate taxpayers within a family economic unit. The Lipsons undermined the rule by shifting the interest expense up to the higher tax rate spouse. The court disallowed the deduction to Mr. Lipson and, instead, allowed it to Mrs. Lipson — the lower rate taxpayer in the family unit.

Thus, purposive interpretation of the attribution rules prevailed over the specific provisions of the Act. GAAR trumped *Westminster*.

---

99   *Canada Trustco*, above note 1 at paras 44 & 45.

Form prevails over substance except in those cases where substance prevails over form.

FURTHER READINGS

Canada

ADAMS, LD. *"Craven v White*: U.K. Step-Transaction Doctrine Evolves—Canadian Planners Beware" (1988) 2:13 Can Curr Tax C-57.

ARNOLD, BRIAN J, & JAMES R WILSON. "The General Anti-Avoidance Rule: Part I" (1988) 36 Can Tax J 829.

———. "The General Anti-Avoidance Rule: Part II" (1988) 36 Can Tax J 1123.

———. "The General Anti-Avoidance Rule: Part III" (1988) 36 Can Tax J 1369.

HILTZ, MICHAEL. "Section 245 of the *Income Tax Act*" (1988) 40 Can Tax Found 7:1.

———. "Subsection 247(1) and the 1985 Amendments to the *Income Tax Act*" (1987) 39 Can Tax Found 7:1.

HOBSON, WILLIAM JA. "New Guidelines from the Supreme Court of Canada and Other Canadian Courts: A Broad Interpretation of Subsection 245(1), the Interpretation Test, and Clearer Lines of Demarcation for Tax Avoidance and Tax Evasion" (1984) 36 Can Tax Found 148.

KRISHNA, VERN. "GAAR and the Purification of Corporations for the Capital Gains Exemption (Part I)" (1993) 4 Can Curr Tax A-7.

———. "Step Transactions and the General Anti-Avoidance Rule: Part I" (July 1990) 24 CGA Magazine 34.

———. "Step Transactions and the General Anti-Avoidance Rule: Part II" (August 1990) 24 CGA Magazine 25.

———. *Tax Avoidance: The General Anti-Avoidance Rule* (Toronto: Carswell, 1990).

———. "General Anti-Avoidance Rule: An Attempt to Control Tax Abuses" (1988) CGA Magazine 16.

———. "GAAR: The Ultimate Tax Avoidance Weapon" (1988) 2:16 Can Curr Tax C-75.

————. "Deductibility of Legal and Accounting Fees in Defending Tax Evasion Charges (IT-99R3)" (1986) 1 Can Curr Tax C-129.

————. "Step Transactions: An Emerging Doctrine or an Extension of the Business Purpose Test?" (1984) 1 Can Curr Tax C-15.

————. "The Demise of the Business Purpose Test?" (1984) 1 Can Curr Tax C-43.

LaBRIE, FE. "Fraudulent Tax Transactions" (1964) 3 West Ont L Rev 48.

————. "The Role of the Courts in Tax Avoidance" (1955) 3 Can Tax J 326; (1955–56) 11 UTLJ 128.

————. "The Uncertainties of Tax Planning" (1960) 9 Chitty's LJ 114; 146; 177.

Other

OECD. "International Tax Avoidance and Evasion" (1977) 31 Bulletin of International Fiscal Documentation 11.

OECD. *International Tax Avoidance and Evasion: Four Related Studies* (Paris: OECD, 1987).

OECD. "Work on Tax Avoidance and Evasion" (1980-81) Intertax 11.

WARD, DAVID A. "Tax Avoidance: Judicial and Legislative Approaches in Other Jurisdictions" (1987) 39 Can Tax Found 8:1.

WISSELINK, MA, & BARRY BRACEWELL-MILNES, *INTERNATIONAL TAX AVOIDANCE: VOLUME A* (DEVENTER, THE NETHERLANDS: KLUWER, 1979) AT 128–34, 198–214.

PART VII

ADMINISTRATIVE PROCESSES

CHAPTER 20

FILINGS, ASSESSMENTS AND RELATED ISSUES

A. GENERAL COMMENT

A basic feature of the Canadian income tax system is that it relies heavily on taxpayers to self-assess their income on an annual basis on a prescribed form and in a prescribed manner. Filing requirements depend on a taxpayer's status. Thus, voluntary compliance and self-assessment are the foundation of the administrative structure of the Act.

The term "voluntary" is a misnomer. The tax system does not rely exclusively upon voluntary compliance. It has persuasive inducements to encourage taxpayers to disclose their income. The minister can impose penalties, make third-party demands, garnish income, seize property and prosecute through the criminal process. Indeed, as we see in this chapter, the CRA powers exceed those of most other government agencies and are subject to fewer legislative and judicial controls.

B. INCOME TAX RETURNS

1) Who Must File

Not all taxpayers must file tax returns every year: filing requirements vary according to the taxpayer's status, type of income earned and tax credits claimed. The following, however, must file income tax returns:[1]

---

1   *Income Tax Act*, RSC 1985, c 1 (5th Supp), [*ITA*], subs 150(1); Information Circu-

- Corporations (other than registered charities);
- Individuals, if they are taxable in the year;
- Individuals who have taxable capital gains or have disposed of capital property in the year; and
- Individuals who owe an amount under the Home Buyer's Plan or Lifelong Learning Plan.

In addition to income tax returns, some taxpayers must also file various information returns that report income that they pay to other taxpayers.

2) Filing Deadlines

Taxpayers must file their returns on prescribed forms. Each return is in respect of a "taxation year"[2] in accordance with the following filing times:

Taxpayer	Time Limit	Form
Individuals	30 April of the following year	T1
Deceased Persons	6 months after death*	T1
Corporations (whether or not year-end tax is payable)	6 months after fiscal year-end	T2
Trusts and estates (if tax is payable in respect of the year)	90 days from end of estate's or trust's taxation year	T3
Registered charities (Info. returns)	6 months after year-end	T3010

* This rule applies for individuals who die between 1 November and the normal filing date. Where an individual dies between 1 January and 31 October, the normal filing date (30 April) applies.

For individuals in business, the Act extends the deadline for filing from 30 April to 15 June.[3]

3) Individuals

An individual must file an income tax return in respect of a taxation year if he is taxable in the year.[4] An individual may, however, file a return even though he is not taxable in a particular year. Voluntary filing a nil return even if there is no tax payable triggers the limitation

---

lar 71-14R3, "The Tax Audit" (18 June 1984).

2   ITA, ibid, s 249.

3   Ibid, para 150(1)(d).

4   Ibid, paras 150(1)(d) and 150(1.1)(b).

period within which the CRA may assess the individual in respect of the return.[5]

It is generally prudent for an individual to file annual tax returns regardless of whether or not she believes that tax is payable for the particular year. Otherwise she may be subject to penalties if it is later established that she was liable for tax in respect of that year.[6]

4) Corporations

A corporation (other than a corporation registered as a charity) must file an income tax return within six months from the end of its taxation year.[7] The return, accompanied by financial statements and supporting schedules, is due whether or not the corporation is taxable.

5) Trusts and Estates

A trust or estate must file a return in respect of each taxation year for which taxes are payable within ninety days from the end of its taxation year.[8]

A trustee in bankruptcy, liquidator, receiver or agent acting on behalf of a person who has not filed a return must file a return on behalf of that person within the relevant time limit.[9]

6) Deceased Persons

The legal representative of a person who has died without filing an income tax return must file the deceased's return within six months from the day of death,[10] if the taxpayer dies between 1 November and the normal filing date. Where the individual dies between 1 January and 31 October, the normal filing date applies.

7) Designated Persons

The minister has additional powers. Where a person who is required to file an income tax return fails to do so, the minister may designate another person to file the return within a stipulated time.[11]

---

5   *Ibid*, subs 152(4). The prescribed form for individuals is Form T1 General. Taxpayers filing simple tax returns may in certain circumstances use Form T1 Special.
6   *Ibid*, s 162.
7   *Ibid*, para 150(1)(a).
8   *Ibid*, para 150(1)(c).
9   *Ibid*, subs 150(3).
10   *Ibid*, para 150(1)(b).
11   *Ibid*, para 150(1)(e).

8) Non-Resident Taxpayers

A non-resident who is employed in Canada, carries on business in Canada or disposes of taxable Canadian property is taxable on his Canadian source income. Non-residents must file income tax returns in the same manner as resident taxpayers.[12] Non-resident taxpayers carrying on business in Canada are exempt from withholding tax on any income that is otherwise taxable under Part I of the Act.[13]

9) Receipt of Documents

The Act deems a document mailed by first class mail (or its equivalent) to have been received by the person to whom it was sent on the day when it was mailed.[14] Courier services are generally equivalent to first class mail service. The onus rests on the taxpayer to establish the facts.[15]

C. AMENDED TAX RETURNS

1) General Rule

A taxpayer does not generally have a statutory right to amend her tax return in respect of a taxation year. As a matter of practice, however, the minister will usually accept a taxpayer's amended income tax return or supplementary information and reassess the taxpayer.

2) Voluntary Disclosure

To encourage self-assessment and voluntary disclosure of tax information, the CRA accepts voluntary disclosures of undeclared income. The CRA's policy in respect of voluntary disclosure is set out in its Information Circular:[16]

---

12 *Ibid*, subs 2(3).
13 *Ibid*, subs 215(4); *Income Tax Regulations*, CRC, c 945, s 805.
14 *ITA, ibid*, para 248(7)(a).
15 *Erroca Enterprises Ltd v MNR*, [1986] 2 CTC 2425 (TCC). See also *VIH Logging Ltd v Canada*, 2003 TCC 732 (General Procedure), aff'd 2005 FCA 36 (notice sent when courier picked up mail).
16 Information Circular 85-1R2, "Voluntary Disclosures" (23 October 1992) (Information Circular 85-IR2 was cancelled and replaced by Information Circular 00-1R "Voluntary Disclosures Program" (30 September 2002)).

If a taxpayer has never filed tax returns, and the returns are then voluntarily filed, the taxpayer will be required to pay only the tax owing on the reported incomes, with interest. If a taxpayer has given incomplete information in a return and subsequently submits the missing information, the taxpayer will be required to pay only the tax owing on the adjusted income, with interest. No prosecution will be undertaken, nor will any civil penalties, including late filing penalties, be imposed, on any amounts included in such voluntary disclosures. The identity of anyone making a voluntary disclosure will be held in confidence, as in the case with all taxpayer information.

This policy applies to corporations and individuals making voluntary disclosures if the following requirements are met:

- *Voluntary Disclosure*—The taxpayer has to initiate the voluntary disclosure. A disclosure is not considered to be voluntary if it arises when the CRA has begun audit or enforcement action.
- *Verification*—Each voluntary disclosure should include enough details to allow the facts to be verified.
- *Incomplete Disclosure*—If a disclosure is voluntary but incomplete, the disclosed information will be considered voluntary. However, the taxpayer will be subject to penalties, prosecution or both, relating to any substantial undisclosed amounts.
- *Payment*—The taxpayer must pay the total amount of any taxes and interest owing, or make acceptable arrangements for paying such amounts.
- *Procedure*—A person can make a voluntary disclosure by contacting the CRA. That person will not need to make a detailed submission on the first contact. However, the taxpayer must do so within a period of time that is mutually agreed upon. The initial contact will be considered to be the date of the voluntary disclosure.

3) Statutory Right to Amend Return

A taxpayer can carry back a deduction from one tax year to a preceding year and file an amended return only in the following circumstances:[17]

Deduction	References
Capital losses in year of death and immediately preceding year may be carried back and deducted from other income	subs 111(2)
Three-year carryback of listed personal property losses	s 41

---

17   *ITA*, above note 1, subs 152(6).

Deduction	References
Carryback of gifts made in the year of death	s 118.1
Three-year carryback of unused foreign tax credits	subs 126(2)
Three-year carryback of non-capital, net capital, restricted farm and farm losses	subs 111(1)
Three-year carryback of investment tax credits to immediately preceding year	subs 127(5)
Three-year carryback of unused Part VI tax credits	s 125.2
Carryback of RRSP premium	para 60(i), 146
Election upon disposition of property by legal representative of deceased taxpayer	subs 164(6)

Taxpayers can also file amended tax returns to adjust income in a preceding taxation year where the adjustment arises as a consequence of exercising an option contract.[18]

D. WITHHOLDING TAXES

Certain types of payments are subject to withholding taxes. For example, a person who makes a compensatory payment to a taxpayer must withhold an amount on account of the payee's potential tax liability.[19] The person must remit the withheld taxes to the Receiver General of Canada.[20]

A person may also be required to file an information return. For example, every person who pays a dividend or makes an interest or royalty payment to a resident taxpayer must file a Return of Investment Income (Form T5).[21] Similarly, a person who pays to a non-resident an amount in respect of dividends, interest, rents, royalties, management fees or support payments must also file an information return outlining the details of the payment.

A person who controls or receives income, gains or profits in a fiduciary capacity is required to file a Trust Information Return.[22]

---

18 *Ibid*, subs 49(4); see Chapter 9.
19 *Ibid*, subs 153(1); *Income Tax Regulations*, above note 13, ss 100–8 (withholding and remittance).
20 See ITA, *ibid*, subs 227(9) (failure to remit on time can result in penalty); *Electrocan Systems Ltd v MNR*, [1986] 1 CTC 269 (FCTD), aff'd (1988), [1989] 1 CTC 244 (FCA) (penalty payable even if taxpayer remits arrears before assessment issued).
21 *Income Tax Regulations*, above note 13, s 201.
22 *Ibid*, s 204; Form T3.

E. DEMAND TO FILE RETURN

The minister can demand that a person file a tax return in prescribed form and disclose prescribed information, regardless of whether the taxpayer has already filed a return or is liable for tax.[23] The minister must serve such a demand personally on the taxpayer or send it by registered mail.[24]

F. FAILURE TO FILE RETURN

1) Voluntary System

The income tax system relies heavily upon so-called "voluntary" self-assessment of taxes. There are, however, severe penalties for failure to voluntarily file and conform. The system is "voluntary" only in the sense that a taxpayer must file income tax returns without being called upon to do so by the minister. Failure to file a return, or to respond to a demand for a return, within the time limits can trigger various penalties, interest charges and even criminal prosecution.

2) Penalties

There is a two-tier penalty for failure to file a tax return.

a) First Offence
On the first offence, the penalty is calculated by reference to the amount of tax unpaid at the time when the return should have been filed. This penalty is equal to the aggregate of:[25]

- 5 percent of the tax that was unpaid at the time when the return was required to be filed; and
- 1 percent of the unpaid tax for each complete month (not exceeding a total of 12 months) between the date on which the return was required to be filed and the date on which it was actually filed.

Thus, the maximum late-filing penalty is 17 percent of the amount of tax unpaid at the time when the return was required to be filed.

---

23   *ITA*, above note 1, subs 150(2).
24   See, generally, *ibid*, subs 220(1); see also subss 244(5) & (6) (procedure for proof of service).
25   *Ibid*, subs 162(1).

b) Subsequent Offences

On a second or subsequent offence, the penalty is equal to the sum of 10 percent of the unpaid tax plus 2 percent of the unpaid tax per month (not exceeding 20 months) of default.[26]

This penalty applies if the taxpayer, at the time of the subsequent failure to file a return, was previously assessed a penalty for failure to file within the preceding three-year period and the minister has demanded a return under subsection 150(2).

c) Criminal Sanctions

Failure to file an income tax return as required by the Act is also a criminal offence that carries a minimum fine of $1,000.[27] A taxpayer can be liable for both the civil and criminal penalties for failure to file a return but only if the civil penalty is assessed before the complaint giving rise to the criminal conviction is laid.[28]

d) Trustees

A trustee or other fiduciary who fails to file a return on behalf of a person for whom the trustee is acting is liable to a penalty of $10 for each day of default,[29] subject to a maximum penalty of $50.

G. FAILURE TO PROVIDE INFORMATION

In addition to providing information on income tax returns, taxpayers may also have an obligation to provide further and supplementary information to the minister. This information is used to monitor the tax system and as a check on other taxpayers. Failure to provide the supplementary information that is required of taxpayers gives rise to civil, and in some cases criminal, penalties.

1) Failure to Complete Ownership Certificate

Where a non-resident person pays a Canadian resident interest or dividends by means of a bearer coupon or dividend warrant, the resident payee must complete an ownership certificate in prescribed form.[30]

---

26   *Ibid*, subs 162(2).
27   *Ibid*, subs 238(1).
28   *Ibid*, subs 238(3).
29   *Ibid*, subs 162(3).
30   *Ibid*, s 234.

The bank at which the coupon or dividend warrant is cashed must obtain the ownership certificate from the payee and file it with the minister on or before the 15th day of the month following the cashing of the cheque or warrant.[31]

A taxpayer who fails to complete or deliver the ownership certificate is liable to a penalty of $50 per failure.[32]

2) Failure to Provide Social Insurance or Business Number

An individual must provide her social insurance number (SIN) or business number when requested to do so by a person who must file an information return in respect of that individual. An individual who fails to provide her SIN or business number when required to do so is subject to a penalty of $100.[33]

The penalty does not apply where the individual applies for a number within 15 days of the request for the number and then subsequently provides the information within 15 days of its receipt.

The person or partnership who must supply the SIN or business number on an information return is also liable to a penalty of $100 for failure to supply the information.[34] The penalty does not apply if:

- The person or partnership made a reasonable effort to obtain the number from the individual; or
- The individual had applied for, but had not received, the number at the time when the information return was filed.

3) Failure to File Information Returns

Taxpayers are sometimes obliged to file information returns in respect of their own and other people's affairs. A taxpayer who fails to provide the information as and when required by the Act or regulations may be penalized.

The penalty depends upon the nature of the offence. Where the Act sets out a specific penalty, that penalty applies to the offence. If the Act does not specify a penalty, a general penalty equal to the greater of $100 and $25 per day (not exceeding 100 days) of default applies.[35]

---

31 *Ibid*, subs 234(2); *Income Tax Regulations*, above note 13, s 207.
32 *ITA, ibid*, subs 162(4).
33 *Ibid*, subs 162(6).
34 *Ibid*, subs 162(5).
35 *Ibid*, subs 162(7).

4) Failure to File Partnership Information

Partnerships also have an obligation to file information returns. The penalty for failure to file, which is in addition to the general penalty for non-compliance with the Act or regulations, is targeted at repeat offenders. The partnership penalties apply where:[36]

- The general penalty for failure to file information has been assessed;
- A demand for the information has been made; and
- A general penalty was imposed in respect of the partnership for a similar offence in any of the three preceding fiscal years.

The penalty is $100 per member for each month or part of a month (not exceeding 24 months) during which the failure continues.

5) Tax Shelter Information

A promoter of a tax shelter must obtain an identification number for the shelter from the minister before the promoter begins selling the shelter to the general public. This number must be provided to all purchasers who acquire an interest in the tax shelter.[37] A taxpayer who purchases an interest in a tax shelter cannot claim a deduction or a credit in respect of the shelter unless the taxpayer has an identification number.

The promoter must also file an information return that discloses:

- The name, address, and social insurance number of each person who acquires an interest in the shelter;
- The amount paid by each investor; and
- Such other information as is required by the prescribed form.

A promoter who files false or misleading information in respect of the promotion of a tax shelter is liable to a penalty.

A person who sells or accepts an investor's contribution for the purchase of a tax shelter without an officially-issued identification number is also guilty of an offence and subject to penalties. The penalty is equal to the greater of:

- $500; and
- 25 percent of the total of all amounts each of which is the consideration received or receivable from a person in respect of the tax shelter

---

36   *Ibid*, subss 162(7.1), (8) and (8.1).
37   *Ibid*, subs 237.1(7.4).

before the correct information is filed with the minister or the identification number is issued, as the case may be.

6) Failure to Furnish Foreign-Based Information

Individuals, corporations, partnerships and trusts resident or carrying on business in Canada must file information returns for the year. The return, which must disclose prescribed information regarding transactions with non-resident, non-arm's length persons, must be filed within six months from the end of the corporation's fiscal year.[38]

A separate information return must be filed in respect of each non-resident person with whom the corporation had non-arm's length dealings at any time in the year. Certain non-arm's length non-residents are exempt where the total fair market value of transactions does not exceed $1,000,000.

A corporation that fails to provide information in respect of its non-arm's length transactions with non-resident persons within the stipulated time of a demand for the information is liable to a penalty.

H. CALCULATION OF TAX LIABILITY

1) Self-Assessment Procedure

A taxpayer is responsible for determining his own income tax liability.[39] As already noted, there are penalties for failure to file a return or to fully disclose income. There are, however, no sanctions for incorrectly calculating the amount of tax that is payable if all relevant information is fully disclosed.

2) Interest

A taxpayer who incorrectly underestimates her tax liability is liable for interest on the difference between the taxpayer's estimate and the amount of tax that the minister assesses.[40] The sting of the penalty is that late payment interest charges are not deductible as an expense for tax purposes.

---

38   *Ibid*, subs 162(10); ss 233.1 and 233.4.
39   *Ibid*, s 151.
40   *Ibid*, subs 161(1).

I. ASSESSMENTS

1) General Check

Income tax returns are initially computer-processed and checked for mathematical accuracy. CRA officials also examine returns to ensure that information filed with the return conforms to the requirements of the Act. We refer to this process of agency return verification and information as an "assessment."[41]

2) Quick Assessment

The minister must examine with all due dispatch all income tax returns and assess the tax and penalties payable.[42] The minister must also notify the taxpayer of the assessment by means of a notice sent to the address shown on the return.[43]

The initial assessment (sometimes called a "quick assessment")[44] is essentially a check of mathematical accuracy and verification of supplementary documentary evidence. The quick assessment procedure, which can take between eight and twelve weeks from the date that the return is filed, results in a Notice of Assessment.

3) Ministerial Delay

The phrase "with all due dispatch" is deceptively clear. As Fournier J said in *Jolicoeur v MNR*:[45]

> There is no doubt that the Minister is bound by time limits when they are imposed by the statute, but, in my view, the words "with all due dispatch" are not to be interpreted as meaning a fixed period of time. The "with all due dispatch" time limit purports a discretion of the

---

41   *Pure Spring Co v MNR* (1946), 2 DTC 844 at 857 (Ex Ct), Thorson P ("assessment" defined as "the summation of all the factors representing tax liability, ascertained in a variety of ways, and the fixation of the total after the necessary computations have been made").

42   *ITA*, above note 1, subs 152(1).

43   *Ibid*, subs 152(2); *Scott v MNR*, [1960] CTC 402 (Ex Ct) (notice of assessment mailed to taxpayer's solicitor not proper notice); *Charron v Canada*, [1984] CTC 237 (FCTD) (no obligation on minister to serve assessment or send it by registered mail); see also s 166 (effect of irregularity in complying with Act).

44   The "quick assessment" triggers the limitation periods for reassessments under subs 152(4), *ibid*.

45   *Jolicoeur v MNR* (1960), 60 DTC 1254 at 1260 (Ex Ct).

Minister to be exercised, for the good administration of the Act, with reason, justice and legal principles.

The courts tolerate, perhaps even excessively, ministerial delays, up to fifteen months in some cases.[46] They appear, however, to draw the line at twenty-two months.[47]

4) Subsequent Changes

The minister has flexible powers against taxpayers. For example, a "quick assessment" is valid even if the minister subsequently changes it. As Thorson P said in *Provincial Paper Ltd v MNR*:

> The Minister may, therefore, properly decide to accept a taxpayer's income tax return as a correct statement of his taxable income and merely check the computations of tax in it and without any further examination or investigation fix his tax liability accordingly. If he does so it cannot be said that he has not made an assessment.
>
> It may happen that it will subsequently appear that an assessment so made is inaccurate and that a reassessment is desirable. But there is a vast difference between an assessment that has turned out to be erroneous and an act that is not an assessment at all. It is for the Minister to decide in each case what he shall do. Indeed, in the vast majority of cases he accepts the taxpayer's statement of taxable income as correct and fixes his liability accordingly. It would be fantastic to say that in such cases he has not made an assessment at all. In my opinion, he has plainly done so.[48]

5) Deemed Valid

The presumption of validity of an assessment is the single most significant rule for taxpayers. The Act deems an assessment to be valid and binding on the taxpayer even if it contains an error or defect or has been incorrectly calculated or improperly issued.[49]

---

46 *Hutterian Brethren Church of Wilson v Canada*, [1979] CTC 1, aff'd [1980] CTC 1 (FCA) (delay allowed where original assessments did not say that no tax payable; unusual circumstances; colony owed $37,000,000 in 96 actions); *Weih v MNR*, [1988] 2 CTC 2013 (TCC) (reassessment at last possible date within four-year period allowed).

47 *MNR v Appleby*, [1964] CTC 323 (Ex Ct) (where misrepresentation or fraud, court will extend time limit); *J Stollar Construction Ltd v MNR*, [1989] 1 CTC 2171 (TCC) (delay of seven years invalidated assessment, not made with "all due dispatch").

48 *Provincial Paper Ltd v MNR* (1954), 54 DTC 1199 at 1202 (Ex Ct).

49 *ITA*, above note 1, subs 152(8).

The taxpayer's only recourse to an assessment is to file a Notice of Objection and ask that a court or the CRA vary it.[50] The burden of proof rests squarely on the taxpayer to show that the assessment is wrong. Thus, a taxpayer is liable unless she can prove otherwise. This rule, from which flows the minister's ultimate power over taxpayers, is an aberration in Anglo-Canadian law and unique to tax law. The rule places an intolerable burden on taxpayers, particularly those who cannot afford high professional fees to fight the minister over an extended period of time. The rule effectively denies most individual taxpayers access to justice in tax disputes.

6) No Judicial Review

A taxpayer can appeal an assessment, but only pursuant to the procedures set out in the *Income Tax Act*.[51] The Federal Court does not have the authority to otherwise quash, review or restrain an assessment under section 18 of the *Federal Courts Act*.[52]

7) Net Worth Assessments

The minister is not bound to accept the taxpayer's income tax return. The minister may assess the amount of tax payable using whatever method is appropriate in the circumstances.[53] The minister may even issue an "arbitrary" or "net worth" assessment.

a) When Used
The minister generally uses an arbitrary assessment where the taxpayer refuses to file a tax return, files a return that is grossly inaccurate, or does not furnish any evidentiary support or documentation to allow verification of the return.[54] Notwithstanding that an assessment is "arbitrary," the minister must disclose the basis on which it is formulated.[55]

---

50 *Ibid*, subs 152(8); s 165.
51 See *ibid*, s 169.
52 RSC 1985, c F-7; *MNR v Parsons*, [1984] CTC 352 (FCA) ("legal authority" of minister challengeable only on specific grounds of "quantum" and "liability"); *Gibbs v MNR*, [1984] CTC 434 (FCTD) (motion to quash assessment dismissed).
53 ITA, above note 1, subs 152(7); *Dezura v MNR*, [1947] 3 DTC 1101 (Ex Ct); *Commercial Hotel Ltd v MNR* (1947), 3 DTC 1119 (Ex Ct).
54 *Johnston v MNR*, [1948] SCR 486. See also *Hsu v Canada*, 2001 FCA 240, leave to appeal to SCC refused, [2001] SCCA No 503; *Cheung v Canada*, 2005 TCC 83 (Informal Procedure).
55 See *Kerr v MNR*, [1989] 2 CTC 112 (FCTD) (income from earnings as prostitute and living off avails of other prostitutes assessed on net worth basis).

b) Method Applied

The minister is not statutorily constrained in the manner in which the minister issues an arbitrary assessment. In most cases, however, the minister uses the "net worth" method. This method involves determining the taxpayer's worth at the beginning and at the end of the taxation years in question. Income for the period is calculated by adding the taxpayer's non-deductible expenditures to the increase in the taxpayer's "net worth" and deducting therefrom any appreciation in the value of the taxpayer's capital assets. Having determined the total increase in the taxpayer's "net worth" between two points in time, the minister allocates the estimated net income between the taxation years in question.

Example		
Assume:		
	Year 1	Year 2
Assets	$100,000	$200,000
Liabilities	$40,000	$60,000
Personal expenditures	$30,000	
Appreciation in capital value of assets between Year 1 (Y1) and Year 2 (Y2)	$20,000	
Then: (where NW = net worth)		
Income = NW (Y2) – NW (Y1) + personal expenditures – appreciation in assets		
= $140,000 – 60,000 + 30,000 – 20,000		
Income = $90,000		

c) Deemed Valid

By its very nature, an arbitrary assessment is an estimate. The minister assesses the taxpayer on the best evidence available. Unless the taxpayer can show that the assessment is incorrect, it is valid and binding.[56] The burden of proof in the appeal of an assessment rests with the taxpayer. This is so whether or not the minister imposes a penalty based on the assessment.[57] As the Supreme Court of Canada said in *Anderson Logging Co v British Columbia*:

---

56   See, for example, *Dezura v MNR*, above note 53 at 1102. Thorson P (presumption of validity of minister's assessment: when minister invokes subs 152(7), the tax so determined subject to review by court under its appellate jurisdiction; if, on appeal, court finds that amount determined by minister is incorrect in fact, appeal must be allowed to extent of error; if court not satisfied on evidence that there has been error in amount, then appeal must be dismissed; onus of proof of error in amount of determination rests on appellant).

57   *Canada v Taylor*, [1984] CTC 436 (FCTD) (since burden of proof is on taxpayer, taxpayer must start by adducing evidence).

First, as to the contention of the point of onus. If, on an appeal to the judge of the Court of Revision, it appears that, on the true facts, the application of the pertinent enactment is doubtful, it would, on principle, seem that the Crown must fail. That seems to be necessarily involved in the principle according to which statutes imposing a burden upon the subject have, by inveterate practice, been interpreted and administered. But, as concerns the inquiry into the facts, the appellant is in the same position as any other appellant. He must show that the impeached assessment is an assessment which ought not to have been made; that is to say, he must establish facts upon which it can be affirmatively asserted that the assessment was not authorized by the taxing statute, or which bring the matter into such a state of doubt that, on the principles alluded to, the liability of the appellant must be negatived. The true facts may be established, of course, by direct evidence or by probable inference. The appellant may adduce facts constituting a *prima facie* case which remains unanswered; but in considering whether this has been done it is important not to forget, if it be so, that the facts are, in a special degree if not exclusively, within the appellant's cognizance, although this last is a consideration which, for obvious reasons, must not be pressed too far.[58]

8) Determination of Losses

A taxpayer can ask the minister to determine the amount of her non-capital losses, net capital losses, limited partnership losses, restricted farm losses or farm losses for a year.[59] The minister must make the calculations and send the taxpayer a notice of the determined amount. Thus, the taxpayer has an option in respect of disputes concerning her losses: the taxpayer can either have the amount of the loss determined immediately or wait until such time as the amount of the loss has an effect upon her tax liability in another year. As we shall see, the limitation periods applicable to these two alternatives may be quite different.[60]

9) Non-Residents

Non-residents who are employed in Canada, carry on business in Canada or dispose of taxable Canadian property are taxable in Canada on their Canadian source income and are subject to the normal assess-

---

58   *Anderson Logging Co v British Columbia* (1924), 52 DTC 1209 at 1211, aff'd [1926] AC 140 (PC).
59   *ITA*, above note 1, subs 152(1.1).
60   See *ibid*, subs 152(4).

ment procedures applicable to residents. Assessments arising from the withholding tax obligations and the liability for Part XIV tax on branch profits are, with appropriate modifications, also subject to the same procedures as those applicable to residents.[61]

J. REASSESSMENTS

The minister can also reassess a taxpayer's income. Unlike the timetable for "quick assessments," however, the power to reassess has stringent limitation periods.

The limitation periods run from the date of mailing of the notice of original assessment. Within the prescribed limitation period the minister may issue as many reassessments as the circumstances require.[62] Two criteria determine the limitation period:

1) The type of taxpayer; and
2) The nature of the transaction that triggers the reassessment.

1) General Rule

In the absence of fraud or misrepresentation, the minister may normally reassess an individual's return for a particular taxation year within three years from the date of mailing of the original notice of assessment for the year.[63] During this three-year period, the minister may reconsider any fact considered relevant to the calculation of the taxpayer's liability, interest or penalties.

2) Losses, Gifts and Tax Credits

The limitation period extends to six years in respect of claims that arise from:[64]

- An individual's death, in respect of allowable capital losses for the year immediately preceding death;
- Listed personal property losses in computing net gains from dispositions of such property for the preceding three taxation years;
- Gifts made by an individual in the year of death, carried back to the preceding taxation year;

---

61   *Ibid*, subs 219(3).
62   *Abrahams v MNR*, [1966] CTC 690 (Ex Ct).
63   *ITA*, above note 1, subs 152(4).
64   *Ibid*, para 152(4)(b) and subs 152(6).

532 INCOME TAX LAW

- Non-capital, net capital, restricted farm and farm losses that are carried back to the preceding three taxation years;
- Unused business foreign tax credits to be carried back to the preceding three taxation years;
- Investment tax credits in respect of property acquired in a year that may be carried back to the preceding three taxation years;
- Carrybacks arising from an election by an individual's estate to treat capital losses incurred by the estate in its first taxation year as losses deductible by the deceased taxpayer incurred in the year of death;
- Transactions involving a taxpayer and a non-resident person with whom the taxpayer was not dealing at arm's length;
- Carryback of RRSP premiums; or
- Transactions involving additional income tax payments to, or reimbursements from, the government of a foreign country.

A reassessment issued within the six-year limitation period may be made only on the basis of adjustments that may reasonably be regarded as relating to the deduction or credit that is to be carried back to a previous taxation year.

3) Corporations

Special rules apply to corporations: the limitation period during which the minister can assess a corporation depends on the nature of the corporation.

a) Canadian-Controlled Private Corporations (CCPCs)
A CCPC can be reassessed only during the "normal reassessment period," that is, three years after the day of mailing of the original Notice of Assessment.

b) Large Corporations and Mutual Funds
The limitation period for mutual funds and corporations other than CCCPs is four years from the mailing of the original assessment.[65]

4) Method of Giving Notice

a) Mail
Most, but not all, notices of assessment and reassessment are sent by mail. We presume a Notice of Assessment to have been mailed on the date appearing on its face. The presumption may be challenged by the

---

65 *Ibid*, para 152(3.1)(a).

submission of evidence to establish otherwise.[66] The Act also deems a Notice of Assessment to have been made on the day when it was mailed.[67]

b) Any Other Method

The minister can send a notice to a taxpayer by any method. For example, in the event of postal disruptions, the notice may be hand-delivered. The Act merely requires that the minister send the notice of assessment within the stipulated limitation periods.[68] There is no specific requirement that the taxpayer receive the assessment. Hence, a notice that is properly mailed to the taxpayer's correct address is valid even if it is lost in the mail.

5) Fraud or Misrepresentation

a) No Limitation

There is no limitation period where the taxpayer makes a misrepresentation that is attributable to neglect, carelessness or wilful default, or where the taxpayer commits a fraud in connection with his tax return.[69]

The minister has the onus to prove that the usual limitation period should not apply because of the taxpayer's neglect, carelessness, wilful default or fraud.

b) Burden of Proof

"Fraud" means a false representation that is made knowingly or without belief in its truth, or recklessly or without care as to whether it is true or false.[70]

If the minister discharges the burden of proof and has the limitation period set aside, the onus reverts to the taxpayer to show that the reassessment is incorrect.[71]

---

66 *Ibid*, subs 244(14).
67 *Ibid*, subs 244(15).
68 *Flanagan v Canada*, [1987] 2 CTC 167 (FCA) (only dispatch required, not receipt, in this case notice of assessment not sent since retained by the CRA); *Bhatti v MNR*, [1981] CTC 2555 (TRB) (notice sent to taxpayer's previous address invalid where taxpayer had notified minister of change of address).
69 *ITA*, above note 1, para 152(4)(a).
70 *Derry v Peek* (1889), 14 App Cas 337 at 374 (HL).
71 *ITA*, above note 1, subs 152(4); Interpretation Bulletin IT-241, "Reassessment Made after the Four-Year Limit" (11 August 1975); Information Circular 75-7R3, "Reassessment of a Return of Income" (9 July 1984) (archived); see also *MNR v Taylor*, [1961] CTC 211 (Ex Ct) (minister must establish misrepresentation or fraud on balance of probabilities); *MNR v Foot*, [1964] CTC 317 (Ex Ct) (statu-

Even where the minister proves that the normal reassessment period does not apply, the reassessment may be made only in respect of amounts that the taxpayer failed to include in income as a result of neglect, carelessness, wilful default or fraud. The minister may not reassess any amounts that are beyond the three-year limitation period and are not attributable to the neglect, carelessness, wilful default or fraud.[72]

c)   "Neglect, Carelessness or Wilful Default"

What constitutes neglect, carelessness or wilful default? Every error of fact is, in a sense, a misrepresentation of fact. But not every misrepresentation of fact is sufficient to set aside the statutory limitation period. The minister must go further and show on a balance of probabilities that the misrepresentation is attributable to the taxpayer's neglect, carelessness or wilful default. Thus, the minister must show something more than mere error: the minister must establish culpable negligence.

i)   Culpable Negligence

Culpable negligence implies fault. The "misrepresentation" does not have to be fraudulent: innocent misrepresentation is sufficient to extend the limitation period if the misrepresentation is attributable to the taxpayer's neglect, carelessness or wilful default. In *MNR v Bisson*, for example:

> . . . any fraud necessarily presupposes a "misrepresentation," and if the latter word covered every type of inaccurate representation, the reference to fraud in [subpara 152(4)(a)(i)] would be totally unnecessary. In my view, the fact that the legislator referred not only to "misrepresentation" but to "fraud" indicates that, by the first word, he meant innocent misrepresentations which, without being fraudulent, are still culpable in the sense that they would not have been made if the person committing them had not been negligent. I therefore conclude that a taxpayer who, without any negligence on his part, commits an error in declaring his income, does not make a misrepresentation within the meaning of [subpara 152(4)(a)(i)]. When the Minister seeks to rely on this provision to proceed with a reassessment after four years, he must therefore not only show that the

---

tory time limit set aside where misrepresentation in reported income); *MNR v Appleby*, above note 47 (minister must establish beyond a reasonable doubt that there has been a misrepresentation on the part of the taxpayer); *Roselawn Investments Ltd v MNR*, [1980] CTC 2316 (TRB) (onus on minister to establish misrepresentation or fraud in any appeal from an assessment made beyond the four-year period).

72   ITA, *ibid*, subs 152(4.01).

taxpayer committed an error in declaring his income but also that error is attributable to negligence on his part.[73]

ii) Standard of Care

The test for culpability is whether the taxpayer exercised a standard of care that a wise and prudent person would in comparable circumstances. But "wisdom is not infallibility and prudence is not perfection."[74] The minister must show more than that the taxpayer committed an error of fact. The minister must also show that the error was attributable to an unacceptable standard of care; in other words, that the taxpayer was negligent in that he or she did not exercise reasonable care:

> For the Minister to show the taxpayer has not exercised reasonable care requires, in my view, something more than simply submitting evidence that the taxpayer has made deposits to his bank accounts in amounts greater than his employment income and advising the court that he . . . does not accept the taxpayer's explanation of the source of funds. . . . It is not enough to suggest misrepresentation or fraud.[75]

A taxpayer may be negligent in misstating income because of negligence in maintaining, or failing to maintain, records. A person who does not act with sufficient care, or exercise the care of a "reasonable person," is negligent.

It is important to note, however, that a finding of "negligence" sufficient to empower the minister to reassess beyond the normal limitation period in subsection 152(4) is not, per se, enough to justify the imposition of a penalty under subsection 163(2). The latter provision requires a finding of "gross negligence."

Gross negligence involves a very high degree of negligence: indifference as to whether the law is obeyed or not.[76] In Venne v Canada, for example:

> "Gross negligence" must be taken to involve greater neglect than simply a failure to use reasonable care. It must involve a high degree of negligence tantamount to intentional acting, an indifference as to whether the law is complied with or not.[77]

---

73   MNR v Bisson (1972), 72 DTC 6374 at 6380 (FCTD).
74   Reilly Estate v Canada (1983), 84 DTC 6001 at 6018 (FCTD), Muldoon J.
75   Markakis v MNR (1986), 86 DTC 1237 at 1239 (TCC); see also Venne v Canada (1984), 84 DTC 6247 (FCTD) (taxpayer who did not read tax returns prior to signing them did not exercise reasonable care).
76   Honig v MNR, [1991] 2 CTC 279 (FCTD).
77   Venne v Canada, above note 75 at 6256.

iii) Burden of Proof

The onus rests initially on the minister to establish that the taxpayer's misrepresentation is attributable to neglect, carelessness or wilful default, or that the taxpayer has committed a fraud. If the minister successfully discharges the burden, the onus shifts to the taxpayer to establish that the reassessment is incorrect.

Where the appropriate treatment of a transaction or event is in doubt or susceptible to alternative interpretations, the taxpayer is entitled to select the interpretation that is most favourable to the taxpayer. The taxpayer does not have to adopt the interpretation that is more favourable to the revenue authorities. This is so even if a similar or identical transaction is under dispute with the CRA.[78]

6) Waiver of Limitation Period

The minister may ask a taxpayer to waive the normal limitation period so that the parties can adduce information or make representations in respect of a taxation year that, in the absence of the waiver, will become time-barred. Without a waiver, the minister would feel compelled to reassess the taxpayer, who would then have to pay the tax demanded pending resolution of the dispute.[79]

The limitation period does not apply where the taxpayer files a waiver with the CRA.[80] A taxpayer may, however, restrict the scope of the waiver and, by doing so, restrict the scope of matters that the minister can reassess.[81] The taxpayer can also revoke the waiver by giving the minister six months' notice of the revocation.[82]

K. PAYMENT OF TAX

1) Payable When Due

A taxpayer must pay forthwith the full amount of assessed taxes, together with any interest and penalties thereon. The amount outstanding must be paid whether or not the taxpayer has filed a Notice of Objection to, or appeal from, the assessment.[83] The minister may, however,

---

78   See, for example, *Regina Shoppers Mall Ltd v MNR*, [1991] 1 CTC 297 (FCA).
79   *ITA*, above note 1, s 158.
80   *Ibid*, subpara 152(4)(a)(ii).
81   *Ibid*, subs 152(4.01).
82   *Ibid*, subs 152(4.1); Form T652.
83   *Ibid*, s 158; see also *Interpretation Act*, RSC 1985, c I-21, subs 27(2) (number of days calculated by excluding first day of notice and including last day).

accept security for payment of taxes or any other amount payable under the Act.[84]

The minister's powers go further: the minister can demand payment of taxes even *before they are due* if it is suspected that the taxpayer is about to leave Canada.[85] The minister may not commence collection procedures, however, until ninety days after the assessment is issued.

2) Judgment

Where a taxpayer fails to pay her taxes within the requisite time, the minister may have the debt certified and registered in the Federal Court. Upon registration, the certificate can be used as a judgment under which execution can be issued for the amount unpaid.[86] The minister can also use the judgment to garnish any debts due to the taxpayer by a third party,[87] or to seize the taxpayer's goods and chattels.[88] As already noted, the minister may, in his discretion, accept security for unpaid taxes.[89]

3) Collection Procedure

a) Normal Procedures

As a general rule, the minister cannot "collect" on an amount assessed against a taxpayer for a period of at least ninety days after the Notice of Assessment is issued.[90] Where a taxpayer objects to a Notice of Assessment, the minister cannot collect the tax payable until ninety days after the day on which the minister mails the notice that confirms or varies the assessment.[91] If the taxpayer files a Notice of Appeal to a court, the minister cannot collect any taxes under the reassessment until the court pronounces judgment.[92]

---

84   *ITA, ibid*, subs 220(4).
85   *Ibid*, subs 226(1); Information Circular 98-1R, "Collections Policies" (15 September 2000).
86   *ITA, ibid*, s 223.
87   *Ibid*, s 224.
88   *Ibid*, s 225; *Morgan Trust Co v Dellelce*, [1985] 2 CTC 370 (Ont HCJ) (under *Execution Act*, RSO 1980, c 146, s 18, sheriff can seize judgment debtor's equitable or beneficial interest in property; that is, registered retirement savings plan); *National Trust Co v Lorenzetti* (1983), 41 OR (2d) 772 (HCJ).
89   *ITA, ibid*, subs 220(4).
90   *Ibid*, subs 225.1(1.1).
91   *Ibid*, subs 225.1(2).
92   *Ibid*, subs 225.1(3) (once a Tax Court decision has been reached against the taxpayer, the CRA can enforce collection even if the case is further appealed to the Federal Court of Appeal).

b) Limitation Periods for Collection

In *Markevich v Canada* (*Markevich*),[93] the Supreme Court of Canada held that since the *Income Tax Act* did not provide for limitation periods within its collection provisions, it is subject to the limitation provisions of general application found in section 32 of the *Crown Liability and Proceedings Act*,[94] which limit the collection of federal debts to six years.

The Court also held that the minister, in its role as an agent of a province, is also subject to the provincial limitations acts with respect to debts that arise under the provincial income tax acts. However, the court made it clear that tax debts created under the federal *Income Tax Act* were not subject to provincial limitation periods.[95] In response to the Supreme Court's decision in *Markevich*, the Act has a ten-year limitation period for the collection of federal tax debts.[96]

c) Collection in Jeopardy

The minister may collect an account immediately where there are reasonable grounds to believe that a delay would jeopardize collection.[97] To do so, however, the minister must apply to a judge for permission to proceed. The minister can apply *ex parte*.

The determination as to whether delay will jeopardize the collection of taxes from a taxpayer is made on a balance of probabilities. The minister has the burden of proof, and must show that there is a real risk that the taxpayer will dissipate her property if collection is delayed because of the appeal process. As McNair J said in *Danielson v Canada (Deputy AG)*:

> . . . the issue goes to the matter of collection jeopardy by reason of the delay normally attributable to the appeal process. The wording of [subs. 225.2(2)] would seem to indicate that *it is necessary to show that because of the passage of time involved to an appeal the taxpayer would become less able to pay the amount assessed.*
>
> In my opinion, the fact that the taxpayer was unable to pay the amount assessed at the time of the direction would not, by itself, be conclusive or determinative. Moreover, the mere suspicion or concern, that delay may jeopardize collection would not be sufficient per se. *The test of "whether it may reasonably be considered" is susceptible of being reasonably translated into the test of whether the evidence on*

93   *Markevich v Canada*, 2003 SCC 9.
94   *Crown Liability and Proceedings Act*, RSC 1985, c C-50.
95   *Markevich v Canada*, above note 93; and *Kirkwood v Canada*, 2003 FCA 481.
96   *ITA*, above note 1, subs 222(4).
97   *Ibid*, subs 225.2(2).

balance of probability is sufficient to lead to the conclusion that it is more
likely than not that collection would be jeopardized by delay.[98]

4) Fleeing Taxpayer

Where the minister suspects that a taxpayer is about to leave Canada
without settling his tax account, the minister may demand immediate
payment of all amounts that are payable by the taxpayer. The demand
is made by serving, either personally or by registered letter, a notice
on the taxpayer demanding payment of all outstanding taxes, interest
and penalties thereon for which the taxpayer is liable. In these circumstances, the minister does not have to wait for the taxpayer to act after
the notice has been served; the minister may immediately seize the
taxpayer's goods and chattels through summary execution.[99]

L. WITHHOLDING TAXES

Taxpayers who make certain types of payments must deduct tax at
source. The types of payments that require withholding at source are
generally payments of a compensatory nature, payments out of deferred income plans and payments to non-residents.[100] The taxpayer
must remit taxes withheld at source to the Receiver General of Canada.
Failure to remit taxes is a strict liability offence.[101]

1) Failure to Withhold

A person who fails to withhold taxes when required to do so may be
penalized. The penalty is determined in two tiers:[102]

1) The first failure to withhold is penalized at 10 percent of the amount
    not deducted or withheld; and
2) A second (or subsequent) failure made knowingly or under circum-
    stances amounting to gross negligence in the same calendar year is
    penalized at 20 percent.

---

98 *Danielson v Canada (Deputy AG)* (1986), 86 DTC 6518 at 6519 (FCTD) [empha-
    sis added]; see also *1853-9049 Quebec Inc v Canada*, [1987] 1 CTC 137 (FCTD)
    (mere suspicion not sufficient).

99 *ITA*, above note 1, s 226.

100 *Ibid*, subs 153(1); s. 215; *Income Tax Regulations*, above note 13, ss 100–10.

101 *R v Swendson*, [1987] 2 CTC 199 (Alta QB).

102 *ITA*, above note 1, subs 227(8).

The penalty applies if the tax is remitted after the due date, regardless whether the taxpayer pays the withheld taxes before the minister issues a penalty assessment.[103]

Where a corporation fails to deduct, withhold or remit taxes in accordance with the Act, its directors may be personally liable for the taxes, together with interest and penalties thereon.[104] Failure to withhold taxes on account of certain payments[105] to non-residents renders the payer and the non-resident jointly and severally liable for the interest payable on the penalty.[106]

2) Criminal Sanctions

Where a corporation fails to remit taxes, its directors and officers become criminally liable if they acquiesced or participated in the offence. But to be criminally liable for corporate acts, the directors and officers must have the *mens rea* to participate in the offence.

M. INSTALMENT PAYMENTS

1) General Comment

As noted above, compensatory payments to employees are subject to withholding of tax at source. The employee must file an income tax return by 30 April of the year following receipt of payment and make up any deficiency in the tax payable. Where the amount withheld at source exceeds the taxpayer's liability for taxes, the employee is entitled to a refund of the excess.[107]

2) Individuals

Individuals (other than those whose chief source of income is farming or fishing) may be required to make quarterly instalments if either no

---

103 *Electrocan Systems Ltd v MNR*, above note 20 (FCA).
104 *ITA*, above note 1, s 227.1; see *Barnett v MNR*, [1985] 2 CTC 2336 (TCC) (director/sole shareholder liable for unremitted deductions); *Beutler v MNR*, [1988] 1 CTC 2414 (TCC) (director/taxpayer did not exercise due care, skill and diligence to prevent failure to remit taxes); *Fraser Estate (Trustee) v MNR*, [1987] 1 CTC 2311 (TCC) (minority shareholder/director may be liable even if others could have prevented default).
105 *ITA, ibid*, s 215.
106 *Ibid*, subs 227(8.1).
107 *Ibid*, subs 153(1); s 164.

source deductions or an insufficient amount of such deductions have been taken from the taxpayer's income. The individual settles any deficiency in the amount payable by 30 April of the following year.[108]

The first four instalments are payable on 15 March, 15 June, 15 September and 15 December in each taxation year. The amount of each instalment is 25 percent of:

- The estimated tax payable for the year; or
- The taxpayer's "instalment base" for the immediately preceding taxation year.

The final instalment is payable by 30 April of the following year.

The CRA also uses a third method — "the no-calculation method" — to calculate instalments: the first instalment base for the first two quarterly payments and the second instalment base for the last two instalments. There are no penalties or interest if the taxpayer complies with this method.

A taxpayer's "instalment base" for the immediately preceding taxation year is, in essence, the amount of tax that was payable under Part I of the Act for that preceding year.[109]

To relieve individuals from the obligation to make quarterly payments where the tax payable is insignificant, the Act exempts individuals from making instalment payments where the federal tax payable in the year, or for each of the two preceding years, is $2,000 or less.[110] In these circumstances, the individual may pay his entire tax liability by 30 April of the following year.

3) Corporations

a) Estimated Payments

A corporation must make monthly instalments of its Part I tax over a 14- or 15-month period: one instalment on the last day of each month of its taxation year, and the final instalment, for the balance of the tax payable, by the last day of the second or third month following the end of the taxation year.[111]

We determine a corporation's monthly instalments in one of three ways:

---

108 *Ibid*, subs 156(1).
109. *Ibid*, subs 156(3), *Income Tax Regulations*, above note 13, s 5300(1).
110 *ITA*, *ibid*, subs 156.1(1).
111 *Ibid*, subs 157(1).

1) Each instalment can be 1/12 of the tax on its *estimated* taxable income for the year;
2) Each instalment can be 1/12 of its "first instalment base"; or
3) The first two instalments can be 1/12 of its "second instalment base" and the next 10 instalments can be 1/10 of its first instalment base minus the first two payments.

A corporation's "first instalment base" is its tax payable under Part I for the immediately preceding taxation year; its "second instalment base" is its tax payable under Part I for the second preceding taxation year.[112]

b) Balance Payable
The balance of any Part I tax payable is due on or before the end of the third month following its year-end, if the corporation is a Canadian-controlled private corporation throughout the current year and claimed the small business deduction in the current or preceding year.[113] For other corporations, the balance is payable within two months after the year-end.[114]

c) Exemption
A corporation need not make tax instalments for a taxation year if its federal tax payable or first instalment base is $1,000 or less.[115]

d) Failure to Remit
Failure to remit the full amount of its instalment payments on the dates due renders the corporation liable to interest at a prescribed rate on the deficiency.[116] Hence, a corporation that makes instalment payments calculated by reference to its previous year's income may be liable for interest on deficient instalments as a consequence of a subsequent reassessment of that income.[117] Subsection 161(4.1), however, absolves the corporation of interest on deficient instalments if it uses one of the prescribed methods that produces the least amount of instalments for the year.[118]

---

112 *Income Tax Regulations*, above note 13, s 5301.
113 *ITA*, above note 1, subpara 157(1)(b)(i) and subs 248(1) "balance-due day."
114 *Ibid*, subpara 157(1)(b)(ii) and subs 248(1) "balance-due day."
115 *Ibid*, subs 157(2.1).
116 *Ibid*, subs 161(2). Interest is calculated from the date when the payment was due to the date when payment was made.
117 *No 384 v MNR* (1957), 16 Tax ABC 300.
118 See *IG (Rockies) Corp v Canada*, 2005 TCC 51 (Informal Procedure).

e) Short Fiscal Periods

Special rules apply in respect of tax instalments payable by corporations with short fiscal periods. In these circumstances instalments are required only on the last day of each complete month in the short taxation year; the remainder is due on the balance due date. The instalment base is calculated by grossing up the tax payable by the ratio that 365 is of the actual number of days in the year.

N. BOOKS AND RECORDS

1) Form and Content

Every person who carries on a business or is obliged to pay, or withhold, taxes from payments made to others must keep books and records of accounts at a place of business or residence in Canada.[119] The books and records should be kept in a manner that allows the minister to determine the tax payable or the tax withheld. The minister can also specify the books and records to be maintained in any particular case.

A taxpayer is not required to keep his accounts in any particular form or adhere to any particular bookkeeping system. The taxpayer need only maintain accounts sufficient to determine the amount of income that is taxable and the amount of tax that is owing.[120] There are, however, special rules in respect of record-keeping requirements applicable to registered charities, amateur athletic associations and contributions to federal political parties and candidates.[121]

2) Retention

A taxpayer must maintain general records, books of accounts and supporting vouchers for a period of at least six years following the taxation year to which the records and documents relate.[122] The "permanent" records of a corporation (such as minutes of directors' and shareholders' meetings, share ledgers, general ledgers and special contracts and

---

119 *ITA*, above note 1, s 230; Information Circular 78-10R4, "Books and Records Retention/Destruction" (June 2005). The minister can also designate the place where the books and records are to be kept.

120 *Labbé v MNR*, [1967] Tax ABC 697; see also *Freitag v MNR* (1951), 5 Tax ABC 54; *PX Cossette & Fils Inc v MNR* (1959), 23 Tax ABC 65.

121 *ITA*, above note 1, subs 230(2); s 230.1.

122 *Income Tax Regulations*, above note 13, s 5800 and *ITA*, *ibid*, para 230(4)(b).

agreements) must be maintained for a period of at least two years after the corporation is dissolved.

Similarly, the "permanent" records of a registered charity or registered Canadian amateur athletic association must be maintained for a period of at least two years after the registration of the charity or amateur athletic association is revoked.

Records in respect of political contributions and expenditures must be maintained for a period of at least two years following the calendar year to which the records relate.

A taxpayer who objects to or appeals from a Notice of Assessment must maintain her books and records until such time as the objection or appeal is resolved or the time period for a further appeal has elapsed.[123]

3) Minister's Discretion

The statutory time periods in respect of the maintenance of books and records are all subject to the discretion of the minister, who may require a taxpayer to maintain such books and records (together with supporting documents) for whatever length of time the minister considers necessary for the administration of the Act.[124] The taxpayer must obtain permission from the minister to destroy any records or books of account prior to the prescribed time.[125]

Failure to comply with the requirements in respect of the maintenance of books and records is a criminal offence carrying a monetary penalty of between $1,000 and $25,000 and possible imprisonment for a term of up to 12 months.[126]

O. DIRECTORS' LIABILITY FOR CORPORATE TAXES

A corporation is a taxpayer in its own right. Thus, with few exceptions, we tax a corporation as a separate legal entity and it is responsible for the payment of its taxes. There are circumstances, however, when the Act pierces the corporate veil and holds shareholders and directors personally liable for corporate acts.

---

123 ITA, ibid, subs 230(6).
124 Ibid, subs 230(7).
125 Ibid, subs 230(8).
126 Ibid, subs 238(1).

There are two categories of circumstances in which directors may be personally liable for corporate taxes: (1) improper payment of dividends, and (2) failure to remit withheld taxes.

1) Improper Dividends

Directors who declare dividends that render the corporation unable to pay its taxes may be liable to the corporation for the amount of the improper payment.[127] Thus, directors can end up liable for the corporation's Part I tax liability.

2) Failure to Withhold or Remit Taxes

A director may also be personally liable for corporate acts if:

- The corporation fails to withhold taxes as required or fails to remit withheld taxes;[128]
- In his capacity as an executor or administrator, the director fails to obtain a clearance certificate before distributing corporate property;[129] or
- The director authorizes or acquiesces in the commission of an offence by the corporation.[130]

Corporate directors are jointly and severally liable with the corporation if the corporation fails to deduct, withhold or remit income tax the Act requires.[131]

a)   Withholding Taxes

i)   *Compensatory Payments*
A corporation must withhold income tax at source when it pays salary, wages and certain other types of compensatory payments.[132] We determine the amount to be withheld in accordance with rules prescribed

---

127 See, for example, *Canada Business Corporations Act*, RSC 1985, c C-44, s 42; para 118(2)(c).

128 *ITA*, above note 1, s 227.1; Information Circular 89-2R, "Director's Liability: Section 227.1 of the *Income Tax Act* and Section 323 of the *Excise Tax Act*" (27 June 1997).

129 *ITA*, *ibid*, subs 159(3).

130 *Ibid*, s 242.

131 *Ibid*, subs 227.1; *Barnett v MNR*, above note 104 (director liable for payroll deductions; corporation obliged to hold funds in trust for the Crown separate and apart from its own funds).

132 *Ibid*, subs 153(1).

under Part I of the regulations. A corporation may be civilly or criminally liable for failure to deduct or withhold income tax at source.[133]

ii) Payments to Non-Residents

A resident corporation that pays or credits an amount to a non-resident person must withhold tax on behalf of the non-resident.[134] Failure to withhold renders the corporation liable for the entire amount that should have been withheld.

iii) Trust Funds

A corporation must remit all withheld taxes to the Receiver General of Canada. Pending remittance, the moneys are held in trust for the benefit of the Crown, and are not available for the satisfaction of judgment creditors.[135] The rights of the Crown are further protected under the *Bankruptcy and Insolvency Act*.[136] The Act purports to protect from legal action any person who withholds or deducts tax at source in compliance, or intended compliance, with the withholding provisions.[137]

b) Personal Liability

The director of a corporation that does not comply with the withholding requirements can be held personally liable for the amount due by the corporation, together with interest and penalties thereon.[138]

c) Limitations

A director cannot, however, be held personally liable unless:[139]

- A certificate for the amount of the corporate tax liability has been registered in the Federal Court and execution thereof has been partially or wholly unsatisfied;
- The corporation has commenced proceedings for liquidation or dissolution and a claim for the amount of the corporate tax liability is proved within six months after commencement of such proceedings; or

---

133 *Ibid*, subs 238(1).
134 *Ibid*, s 215.
135 *Ibid*, subss 227(4) & (5).
136 RSC 1985, c B-3, ss 86 & 87. These sections effectively create a deemed trust for provable Crown claims that arise as legislated obligations.
137 *ITA*, above note 1, subs 227(1). This provision raises the constitutional question as to whether the federal government has the power to withdraw a taxpayer's right of legal action.
138 *Ibid*, subs 227.1(1).
139 *Ibid*, subs 227.1(2).

- The corporation has made an assignment (or had a bankruptcy order made against it) under the *Bankruptcy and Insolvency Act* and a claim for the amount of the corporate tax liability is proved within six months after the date of the assignment or bankruptcy order.[140]

A director of a corporation is immune from personal liability unless the minister commences proceedings against him within two years from the time when the director last ceased to be a director of the corporation.[141] To use this defence, a person must have legally ceased being a director.[142]

d) Defence of "Due Diligence"

A director of a corporation is not personally liable for the corporation's failure to withhold or remit taxes where the director has exercised "the degree of care, diligence and skill to prevent the failure that a reasonably prudent person would have exercised in comparable circumstances."[143] What constitutes the degree of care and skill that would be exercised by a reasonably prudent person in comparable circumstances is a question of fact.

i) *Objective Test*

In common law, a director must demonstrate the degree of care, skill, and diligence that could reasonably be expected from her, having regard to the director's knowledge and experience.[144] The test under the Act goes one step beyond the common law: it is objective. Thus, the obligation of directors to exercise due care and skill in supervising the corporation's

---

140 *Bankruptcy and Insolvency Act*, above note 136.
141 *ITA*, above note 1, subs 227.1(4).
142 It is insufficient to simply lose control of the corporation due to its being put into receivership or liquidation: *Kalef v Canada,* [1996] 2 CTC 1 (FCA); *Drover v Canada*, [1998] GSTC 45 (FCA).
143 *ITA*, above note 1, subs 227.1(3).
144 *Re City Equitable Fire Insurance Co*, [1925] 1 Ch 407 at 428 (CA), Romer J:

> . . . [a] director need not exhibit in the performance of his duties a greater degree of skill than may reasonably be expected from a person of his knowledge and experience. A director of a life insurance company, for instance, does not guarantee that he has the skill of an actuary or of a physician. In the words of Lindley M.R.: "If directors act within their powers, if they act with such care as is reasonably to be expected from them, having regard to their knowledge and experience, and if they act honestly for the benefit of the company they represent, they discharge both their equitable as well as their legal duty to the company" . . . . It is perhaps only another way of stating the same proposition to say that directors are not liable for mere errors of judgment.

responsibilities to withhold and remit taxes to the Crown falls some-where between the subjective standard applied in common law and the more stringent obligation imposed upon professionals. Corporate directors need exercise only the degree of care, diligence and skill that a reasonably prudent individual would have exercised in comparable circumstances.

The rather low expectation of corporate directors stems from the judicial perception of the qualifications necessary to become a director. The description in *Brazilian Rubber Plantations & Estates Ltd* reflects the expectations of directors:

> The directors of the company, Sir Arthur Aylmer, Bart., Henry Wil-liam Tugwell, Edward Barber, and Edward Henry Hancock, were all induced to become directors by Harbord or persons acting with him in the promotion of the company. Sir Arthur Aylmer was absolutely ignorant of business. He only consented to act because he was told the office would give him a little pleasant employment without his incurring any responsibility. H.W. Tugwell was partner in a firm of bankers in a good position in Bath; he was seventy-five years of age and very deaf; he was induced to join the board by representations made to him in January, 1906. Barber was a rubber broker and was told that all he would have to do would be to give an opinion as to the value of rubber when it arrived in England. Hancock was a man of business who said he was induced to join by seeing the names of Tugwell and Barber, whom he considered good men.[145]

ii)   Standard of Care

What constitutes an adequate standard of care, diligence and skill on the part of a director is a question of fact in each case. A director is not bound to give continuous attention to the affairs of the corporation.[146] It is also clear that a director is entitled to rely upon the officials of the corporation to keep her informed on corporate developments. In the absence of grounds for suspicion, a director is justified in trusting her officials to execute their duties according to corporate policies.[147]

At the very least, however, a director is expected to take positive action to ensure compliance with the remittance provisions of the Act. Passive reliance on the other directors or officers of the corporation is

---

145 *Re Brazilian Rubber Plantations & Estates Ltd*, [1911] 1 Ch 425 at 427, subsequent proceedings 103 LT 882 (CA).
146 *Re City Equitable Fire Insurance Co*, above note 144 at 429.
147 *Ibid.*

not sufficient to discharge the standard of care expected of directors.[148]
Thus, we expect the directors of a corporation to:

- Establish corporate policies in respect of accounting for income taxes, both under Part I of the Act in respect of the corporation's own tax liabilities and in respect of withholding from employees and payments to non-residents;
- Call upon the financial officers of the corporation to report upon compliance with established corporate policies;
- Obtain undertakings from senior corporate officials that corporate policies in respect of income tax and other financial matters have in fact been complied with during the relevant period;
- Wherever prudent, maintain a separate trust account for payroll deductions; and
- Exercise independent judgment and not simply rely on the other directors or officers of the corporation.[149]

Corporate directors cannot be expected to do much more.[150]

---

148 *Fraser Estate (Trustee) v MNR*, above note 104 (minority shareholder/director in corporation's manufacturing operations liable for failure to remit taxes); *Beutler v MNR*, above note 104 (failure to deposit payroll deductions in separate trust account suggested absence of "due diligence").

149 *Fraser Estate (Trustee) v MNR*, ibid; *Quantz v MNR*, [1988] 1 CTC 2276 (TCC).

150 *Re National Bank of Wales Ltd*, [1899] 2 Ch 629 at 673 (CA):

Was it his duty to test the accuracy or completeness of what he was told by the general manager and the managing director? This is a question on which opinions may differ, but we are not prepared to say that he failed in his legal duty. Business cannot be carried on upon principles of distrust. Men in responsible positions must be trusted by those above them, as well as by those below them, until there is reason to distrust them. We agree that care and prudence do not involve distrust; but for a director acting honestly himself to be held legally liable for negligence, in trusting the officers under him not to conceal from what they ought to report to him, appears to us to be laying too heavy a burden on honest businessmen . . . .

aff'd (*sub nom Dovey v Cory*) [1901] AC 477 at 492 (HL), Lord Davey:

I think the respondent was bound to give his attention to and exercise his judgment as a man of business on the matters which were brought before the board at the meetings which he attended, and it is not proved that he did not do so. But I think he was entitled to rely upon the judgment, information and advice, of the chairman and general manager, as to whose integrity, skill and competence he had no reason for suspicion.

See also *Polsinelli v Canada*, 2004 TCC 186 (General Procedure), additional reasons at 2004 TCC 720 (General Procedure) (director not liable since he had taken all reasonable measures to ensure the company complied with the *Excise Tax Act*, including the hiring of a bookkeeper and a chartered accountant to handle the company's finances).

A director who is called upon to satisfy a claim in respect of corporate tax liabilities is entitled to claim contribution from fellow directors who are also liable under the claim.[151]

iii) Accounting Systems

Each corporate director is responsible for ensuring that the corporation uses a proper and acceptable accounting system to control the withholding and remittance of source deductions.[152] Further, the director should be aware of current practices and systems in the corporation.[153] We do not expect a director to be an accounting expert or a controller. She may rely upon competent professional advice and the guidance of those who are experts in accounting and control systems. A director is not expected to personally verify the collection and remittance of all source deductions, but the failure to segregate withheld deductions may indicate a lack of prudence.[154]

iv) Trust Accounts

Taxes withheld at source are trust funds. Thus, although not absolutely necessary, it is prudent to maintain a separate trust account for collecting and remitting corporate source deductions.

Although a director is a fiduciary to the corporation, the director cannot use trust funds that belong to the government of Canada to assist the corporation in overcoming a cash shortage or financial embarrassment.[155]

v) Passive Directors

The personal liability of directors for corporate source deductions applies equally to "passive" and "nominee" directors as to those who are actively involved in the corporation's management. As a matter of administrative practice, the CRA does not distinguish between active, passive, inside and outside directors.[156]

---

151 *ITA*, above note 1, subs 227.1(7). It is questionable whether the *ITA* can constitutionally confer the power on a director to claim contribution from her fellow directors. In any event, the common law would recognize such a right.

152 *Barnett v MNR*, above note 104; *Quantz v MNR*, above note 149; *Moore v MNR*, [1988] 2 CTC 2191 (TCC) (director personally liable for unremitted payroll deductions as he did not exercise the required degree of care, diligence and skill); *Merson v MNR*, [1989] 1 CTC 2074 (TCC) (director not personally responsible for unremitted source deductions as he exercised the required degree of care and diligence and the corporation did not benefit).

153 *Fraser Estate (Trustee) v MNR*, above note 104.

154 *Barnett v MNR*, above note 104; *Beutler v MNR*, above note 104.

155 *Pilling v MNR*, [1989] 2 CTC 2037 (TCC).

156 CRA Directive CA87-67 (6 October 1987), obtainable under *Privacy Act*, RSC 1985, c P-21. See also CRA's response to Question 81 at the 1987 Annual Can-

A corporate director is not entitled to delegate responsibility, and cannot claim diminished responsibility by virtue of non-involvement in the corporation's management and affairs. In this context, there is no difference between directors of large public corporations and small private corporations: they all carry the same burden of responsibility to ensure that source deductions are properly accounted for and remitted to the Receiver General.

vi) *Administrative Policies*
Information Circular 89-2R sets out the CRA's practices in respect of assessing directors personally for source deductions:[157]

- The CRA will write to directors who may be liable to inform them that an assessment is being considered and to request an explanation of all actions taken to ensure that the corporation deducted, withheld, remitted or paid all prescribed amounts.
- A director who does not respond to the CRA's information request within the time limits set out may be assessed without further notice.
- Department of Justice lawyers will be consulted only where a due diligence defence has been raised by the director. Otherwise, a decision to issue the assessment against the director will be made by the Collections Division.

3) Clearance Certificates

A legal representative must obtain a clearance certificate from the minister before distributing any property under his possession or control.[158] The certificate should certify that all taxes, interest and penalties chargeable against or payable out of the property that is to be distributed have been paid. This requirement does not extend to a director of a corporation if the director is acting *qua* director and not *qua* executor, assignee, liquidator or administrator.[159]

---

adian Tax Conference Round Table, and Information Circular 89-2R, above note 128 at para 9 (directors who relinquish their responsibilities to co-directors, officers or employees may be held liable).

157 Information Circular 89-2R, *ibid*.

158 *ITA*, above note 1, subs 159(2).

159 *Parsons v MNR* (1983), 83 DTC 5329 at 5337 (FCTD), rev'd on other grounds, [1984] CTC 352 (FCA) (roles of the various fiduciaries mentioned in subs 159(2) described by court as follows: "An assignee is a person to whom an assignment is made and assignment means that property is transferred to another. The assignee is the recipient of that property. A liquidator is a person appointed to carry out the winding up of a company whose duty is to get in and realize the property of the company, to pay its debts and to distribute the surplus (if any)

4) Participation in Offences Committed by the Corporation

A director of a corporation may be held to be a party to, and guilty of, an offence committed by the corporation if the director directs, authorizes, assents to, acquiesces in or participates in an offence committed by the corporation. The director can be held liable even though the corporation itself is not prosecuted or convicted for the offence.[160]

There are two elements to a director's personal liability for corporate offences:[161]

1) The corporation is guilty of an offence under the Act; and
2) The director participated in some way in the commission of the offence.

Thus, mere proof that a corporation was convicted of the offence is not sufficient by itself to convict a director; the corporation must be shown to have been guilty of, and not merely to have been convicted of, the offence.[162] A director may be criminally convicted in his personal capacity only if he had the *mens rea* to commit the offence.[163]

P. PENALTIES FOR FALSE STATEMENTS OR OMISSIONS

Subsection 163(2) of the Act authorizes the minister to impose a penalty on a person who has either

- "knowingly," or
- "under circumstances amounting to gross negligence,"

made, participated, assented or acquiesced in the making of a false statement or omission in an income tax return.

---

among the shareholders. An executor is the person to whom the execution of a will is entrusted by a testator . . . an executor is bound to satisfy all claims on the estate before distributing it among the legatees and other beneficiaries. An administrator is the person to whom the property of a person dying intestate is committed for administration and whose duties with respect thereto correspond with those of an executor").

160   *ITA*, above note 1, s 242.
161   *R v Hartmann*, [1971] CTC 396 (Sask Dist Ct).
162   *R v Anisman*, [1969] 1 OR 397 (HCJ).
163   *R v Swendson*, above note 101.

1) "Knowingly"

There are three degrees of knowledge: (1) actual knowledge; (2) deliberate refraining from making inquiries; and (3) constructive knowledge.

In the first category, the taxpayer must have actual knowledge of the misstatement or omission on the return. The second category deals with a situation where a person deliberately shuts her eyes to an obvious means of knowledge — in other words, deliberately refrains from making inquiries the result of which the taxpayer might not care to know. The third category, generally referred to as "constructive knowledge," is concerned with what a taxpayer "ought to have known."[164]

2) Gross Negligence

Negligence is a failure to use reasonable care. "Gross negligence" involves something greater or worse or more reckless than simply a failure to use reasonable care. "Gross negligence" requires a greater degree of culpability or errant behaviour on the taxpayer's part than one might expect in a case of "ordinary" negligence. For example, in *Venne v Canada:*[165]

> . . . "gross negligence" . . . must involve a high degree of negligence tantamount to intentional acting, an indifference as to whether the law is complied with or not. . . . To be sure, the plaintiff did not exercise the care of a reasonable man, and . . . should have at least reviewed his tax returns before signing them. A reasonable man in doing so, having regard to other information available to him, would have been led to believe that something was amiss and would have pursued the matter further with his bookkeeper.

But the mere failure to exercise the care of a reasonable person is not enough to constitute gross negligence.

3) "Has Made"

The penalty under subsection 163(2) can be imposed only on a taxpayer who "has made" or participated in, assented to or acquiesced in the grossly negligent misstatement or omission. In other words, a taxpayer is liable only if he or she is grossly negligent or the gross negligence of

---

164 See *Taylor's Central Garages (Exeter) Ltd v Roper*, [1951] 2 TLR 284 (Div Ct), in particular Devlin J at 288–89.

165 *Venne v Canada*, above note 75 at 6256, Strayer J.

the taxpayer's agent can be directly attributed to the taxpayer. In *Udell v MNR*:

> In my view the use of the verb "made" in the context in which it is used also involves a deliberate and intentional consciousness on the part of the principal to the act done. . . .[166]

Any doubt, ambiguity or uncertainty as to whether there was deliberate or intentional consciousness on the taxpayer's part should be resolved in the taxpayer's favour:

> I take it to be a clear rule of construction that in the imposition of a tax or a duty, and still more of a penalty if there be any fair and reasonable doubt the statute is to be construed so as to give the party sought to be charged the benefit of the doubt.[167]

If the words of a penal section are capable of two interpretations, one that imposes liability and one that does not inflict a penalty, the latter interpretation should prevail.[168]

Thus, subsection 163(2) applies in two main circumstances:

1) The taxpayer is grossly negligent or knowingly makes a misstatement or omission on her return for the year; or
2) The taxpayer's agent is grossly negligent or knowingly makes a misstatement *and* the agent's action or knowledge can be directly attributed to the taxpayer.

The second alternative has two separate requirements: (1) the taxpayer's advisers must be grossly negligent in the preparation of the tax return; and (2) the taxpayer must have been privy, in one of the three senses of "knowingly," to the gross negligence and in fact acquiesced or participated in the false statement or omission.

4) Penalties for Tax Advisors and Promoters

Section 163.2 also provides civil penalties against those who knowingly, or in circumstances amounting to gross negligence, make false statements or omissions in respect of another person's tax matters. This provision is a result of recommendations from the Auditor General, the House of Commons Public Accounts Committee and the Mintz Committee.[169]

---

166 *Udell v MNR* (1969), 70 DTC 6019 at 6025 (Ex Ct), Cattanach J.
167 *Ibid* at 6026.
168 *Tuck & Sons v Priester* (1887), 19 QBD 629.
169 See, generally, Information Circular 01-1 "Third-Party Civil Penalties" (18 September 2001) for CRA's views, and Income Tax Technical News #32 (15 July 2005).

5) Tax Shelter and Other Tax Planning Arrangements

A penalty applies to an individual who plans, promotes, or sells an arrangement based on a statement that he knows, or would reasonably be expected to know, but for circumstances amounting to gross negligence, is false.[170] This provision also applies to a person who provides false information for use in an arrangement. This penalty will be the greater of $1,000 and 100 percent of the gross revenue derived by the person in respect of the arrangement. This provision applies to situations where, for example, an asset is purchased at an allegedly inflated price to circumvent GAAR. The rules are particularly strict on valuation and deem them to have been false if the value stated is not within prescribed limits.

6) Onus of Proof

a) Burden
The burden of proof rests squarely on the minister to establish that the taxpayer acted knowingly or with gross negligence in the misstatement on the income tax return. The minister must show that the taxpayer acted in circumstances amounting to gross negligence on the particular facts.[171]

b) Omissions
A mere omission or misstatement of income on a return is not *in and of itself* sufficient to establish gross negligence. Subsection 163(2) requires proof of the omission or misstatement in circumstances or conduct that are tantamount to gross negligence. Thus, there must be an act of omission or misstatement by the taxpayer or his agent, and a state of mind or conduct that justifies a finding of gross negligence. The courts are hesitant to attribute the knowledge and conduct of accountants to their clients.[172]

---

170 *ITA*, above note 1, subss 163.2(3) and 237.1(7.4).
171 *James v MNR*, [1993] 1 CTC 2126 (TCC) (minister failed to discharge the onus of proving that the penalties were appropriate). See also *ITA, ibid*, subs 163(3), which establishes the reverse onus for penalties under subs 163(2) and s 163.2.
172 See, for example, *Udell v MNR*, above note 166; *MNR v Weeks*, [1972] CTC 60 (FCTD), aff'g (1970), 70 DTC 1431 (TAB); *Oudot v MNR*, [1970] Tax ABC 915; *Apex Auto-Matic Centres Ltd v MNR*, [1971] Tax ABC 751; *Joris v MNR*, [1981] CTC 2596 (TRB) (accountant's errors in tax returns not gross negligence on the part of the taxpayer).

Q. THIRD-PARTY PENALTIES

1) Criminal Penalties

A tax advisor may be held criminally liable for actions that amount to tax evasion.[173] For example, any person who intentionally participates in the filing of a false return—such as an accountant who deducts a non-deductible expense on his client's tax return—may be subject to criminal sanctions.

In practice, the CRA invokes the criminal penalty provisions only in the most "extraordinary circumstances" since pursuing criminal penalties for all cases of egregious behaviour on the part of tax advisors is administratively difficult.[174] Not only does it take considerable time and expense to pursue criminal penalties, but it is difficult to satisfy the burden of proof ("beyond a reasonable doubt") without compelling evidence.

2) Civil Penalties

The third-party civil penalties are far more of a concern to tax advisors than the criminal penalties. Not only is the burden of proof much lower—the Crown need only prove its case on a balance of probabilities—but the financial penalties are significant.

Prior to the introduction of the third-party civil penalties, civil penalties extended only to taxpayers. Tax advisors and lawyers, on the other hand, could only be pursued under the criminal provisions. Apart from these criminal sanctions, professional bodies were wholly responsible for governing the ethical behaviour of their members. Professional bodies are not generally inclined to pursue disciplinary actions on complex tax matters that require considerable technical expertise.

Following the failure of professional bodies to regulate the ethical behaviour of their members, the government introduced third-party civil penalties. The catalyst for the establishment of third-party civil penalties was *Global Communications Ltd v Canada* (*Global*).[175] The taxpayer (a reputable Canadian corporation) and certain promoters (members of major law firms) structured an aggressive tax scheme that they should have known would fail. In the wake of *Global*, the auditor general, the House of Commons Standing Committee on Public Accounts and the Technical Committee on Business Taxation (the "Mintz Committee") all recommended the creation of civil penalties for tax advisors.

---

173 *ITA*, above note 1, s 239.
174 Roch Martin, "Recent Income Tax Developments" (2002) 40:1 Alta L Rev 19.
175 [1997] 3 CTC 2527 (TCC), aff'd (1999), 99 DTC 5377 (FCA).

a) The Provisions

The recommendations of the Mintz Committee were eventually enacted in subsections 163.2(2) and 163.2(4) of the Act. These provisions, which came into force 29 June 2000, are aimed primarily at two types of abuse. The first involves tax planners who create transactions that are unsupported by the *Income Tax Act* and result in unwarranted claims for deductions (subsection 163.2(2)). The second type of abuse involves tax preparers who create or acquiesce in the creation of unsupportable deductions in the preparation of returns (subsection 163.2(4)).

b) The Penalties

The planner penalty in subsection 163.2(3) is the greater of $1,000, and the person's "gross entitlements." The preparer penalty in subsection 163.2(5) is the greater of either $1,000, or the lesser of:

- the penalty the other person would be liable to under subsection 163(2), and
- $100,000 plus the advisor's gross compensation.

To apply the penalties the CRA must show that on a balance of probabilities that the taxpayer engaged in "culpable conduct."

Culpable conduct is active conduct or a failure to act that:

1) is tantamount to intentional conduct;
2) shows an indifference as to whether the tax legislation is complied with; or
3) shows a wilful, a reckless or wanton disregard for the law.

These criteria are subjective and, given the onus of proof in tax cases, difficult to defend against.

c) Good Faith Exception

In response to the concerns about the definition of "culpable conduct" and the eventual application of section 163.2, the Department of Finance built a few exceptions into the third-party civil penalty provisions. For example, subsection 163.2(6) provides for a "good faith" exception, which exculpates a tax preparer or advisor who, in good faith, relies on information provided by another person, or because of such reliance, fails to verify, investigate or correct the information.[176]

Thus, if a client gives false information to her tax preparer and there is no obvious reason for the tax preparer to question its legitim-

---

176 The "good faith" defence is not available where the activity is an "excluded activity" under subs 163.2(1) of the *ITA*, above note 1.

acy, the tax preparer will not be penalized for relying on this information in the preparation of the client's tax return. Likewise, a tax advisor who relies on false information supplied by a client and provides advice on structuring a transaction to minimize tax should not be subject to these penalties.

d) Penalty Assessment Process

In 2001 the CRA created the Third-Party Penalty Review Committee to further alleviate concerns that the new civil penalties might be used abusively or inconsistently by tax officials. A field auditor who encounters a situation in which civil penalties might apply must first consult with a senior audit manager before implementing a third-party penalty audit. If the auditor recommends a penalty, the Committee reviews the facts, including the third party's representations, before endorsing or rejecting the recommendation.[177]

R. TRANSFERS OF PROPERTY

1) Tax Liability

Generally, when an individual transfers property to his spouse, common law partner or to a person under eighteen years of age, the transferor and transferee become jointly and severally liable for any tax payable by the transferor at the time of transfer. The liability is limited to the amount of taxes owing and any shortfall in consideration. The purpose of the joint and several liability rules is to enable the tax authorities to take their share of any tax payable to them.

The transferee spouse (or common law partner) is not liable if the transfer is pursuant to a divorce decree or a written separation agreement if the parties are separated and living apart as a result of the breakdown of their marriage.[178]

But the rules go further: they also apply to transfers between unrelated persons who do not deal with each other at arm's length.

The first two categories of transferees (spouses and persons under eighteen years of age) are readily identifiable. Transfers to the third category (transferees not at arm's length with the transferor), however, contain hidden traps.

---

177 Canadian Tax Foundation, *Canadian Tax Highlights* 10:10 (29 October 2002), online: www.ctf.ca/ctfweb/Documents/PDF/Cdn_Tax_Highlights/2002CTH10.pdf.
178 *ITA*, above note 1, subs 160(4).

2) Non-Arm's Length

The Act does not define "arm's length." The question as to whether taxpayers are dealing with each other at arm's length is sometimes a question of law and sometimes a question of fact. Persons who are married or related to each other are generally considered not to be dealing with each other at arm's length. Persons may, however, also be considered not to be at arm's length with each other as a matter of fact.

Unrelated persons who do not deal with each other in an independent manner may act in concert. If they do, they are not at arm's length with each other. The question is one of fact and, as with many questions of fact, depends upon the credibility of the taxpayer's testimony.[179] The onus is on the taxpayer to establish the nature of the relationship between the parties.

The joint and several liability of the parties is equal to the shortfall between the value of the property transferred and any consideration received by the transferor. Any subsequent payments by the transferor first reduce the transferor's personal liability in respect of his other tax debts. It is only when those other tax debts are fully paid that further payments reduce the joint and several liability. Hence, the non-arm's length transferee can remain liable for taxes long after the transfer of property.

S. INVESTIGATIONS

1) Ministerial Powers

The income tax system relies on self-assessment. The minister does, however, have considerable audit powers to ensure that taxpayers do not use self-assessment to evade income taxes. The administrative requirements in respect of the maintenance of books and records, filing of tax and information returns and payments of taxes, interest and penalties are all directed towards persuading taxpayers to remain on the "straight and narrow" path.

The CRA also has extensive powers to conduct investigations into a taxpayer's financial affairs.[180] The scope of these powers is broad, sometimes frighteningly so in a free society. The powers are not, however, without limit: the *Canadian Charter of Rights and Freedoms* provides some restraint on the minister's statutory powers.

---

179 *Lindsay v MNR*, [1990] 1 CTC 2245 (TCC).
180 Information Circular 71-14R3, "The Tax Audit" (18 June 1984).

2) Audit and Examination

The income tax system relies primarily upon self-assessment by tax-payers and "voluntary" reporting of tax liabilities. The taxpayer initially determines his liability and submits his tax return to the CRA. The CRA checks the return for mathematical accuracy, reviews supporting documents, performs some cross checks, and issues a "quick assessment" within approximately twelve weeks of filing. Mercifully for most taxpayers, particularly employees who have income and payroll taxes withheld at source, that is the end of their annual ritual with the tax collector.

But it is not the end of the process. The CRA has substantial civil and criminal audit and investigative powers to ensure compliance with the Act. However, the line between the CRA's regulatory audit and criminal investigative powers is not always clear, which causes procedural disputes and litigation.

A civil audit under the CRA's regulatory powers is a routine process for verifying the taxpayer's financial information and examining relevant supporting documents. The purpose of the audit is to ensure regulatory compliance, mathematical accuracy and supporting data. If the CRA disagrees with the taxpayer's self-assessed income, it will reassess the taxpayer and charge interest on any deficiency in taxes.

The CRA can impose civil penalties in circumstances where it can show egregious conduct by the taxpayer in preparing her return and add up to 50 percent (plus interest) of the tax deficiency to the final bill.[181]

The CRA also has broad powers in sections 231.1 (access to records on business premises) and 231.2 (demand for information), which give them considerable latitude. Taxpayer constitutional rights are only minimally protected. In contrast, a tax investigation is a criminal examination and, therefore, subject to the tighter control that the *Charter* extends to criminal matters.

Civil audits and investigations are both relationships of opposing interests. There is, however, an important difference between the parties' interests in an audit or investigation. Although all audits between taxpayers and the tax collector are adversarial, the intensity of the adversarial relationship increases exponentially where the CRA is looking to lay criminal charges against the taxpayer because "the state is pitted against the individual in an attempt to establish culpability."[182]

---

181 *ITA*, above note 1, subs 163(2) requires that the taxpayer "knowingly, or under circumstances amounting to gross negligence" omit income.
182 *R v Jarvis*, 2002 SCC 73 at headnote.

The adversarial relationship escalates because the liberty of the subject is at stake.

An examination that starts out as a routine civil audit can turn into a criminal investigation. If this happens, the nature of the relationship between the CRA and the taxpayer also changes and the CRA's powers become subject to *Charter* restrictions. Nevertheless, the CRA may still be able to use any information that it procures during the proper exercise of its audit function in a subsequent penal investigation. The use of such information for criminal purposes does not offend either section 7 (the principles against self-incrimination) or section 8 (reasonable expectation of privacy) of the *Charter*.[183]

There are competing principles of fundamental justice. In inquiries in income tax matters, the principle that relevant evidence should be available to the trier of fact outweighs the principle against self-incrimination.

Similarly, individuals have few privacy interests under section 8 of the *Charter* in materials and records that they are obliged to keep and produce for the purposes of the Act.[184] Once an auditor has inspected or compelled the production of a document or information, the taxpayer cannot be said to have a reasonable expectation that the auditor will guard its confidentiality. Given the taxpayer's diminished expectation of privacy, the state's interest to intrude on the individual's privacy in order to advance its goals of law enforcement outweighs the individual's privacy interest in her materials and records.

The CRA may conduct an audit and an investigation concurrently. However, once it begins its investigation, the CRA can use further information that it obtains under its concurrent audit powers[185] only for the purposes of the audit and not for the purposes of the investigation.

a) Business Premises

Under section 231.1 an "authorized person"[186] is entitled to audit or examine a taxpayer's books, records or property for the purposes of an audit.[187] Such a person can enter into a taxpayer's business premises and, upon gaining entry, audit and examine all of the books, records, accounts, vouchers, letters and any other documents which may, or should, relate to the amount of tax payable under the Act.

---

183 *R v Jarvis, ibid; Canadian Charter of Rights and Freedoms*, Part I of the *Canada Act 1982* (UK), 1982, c 11 [*Charter*].
184 *R v Jarvis, ibid.*
185 *ITA*, above note 1, ss 231.1 & 231.2.
186 *Ibid*, s 231 ("authorized person" means a person authorized by the minister).
187 *Ibid*, paras 231.1(1)(a) & (b); *R v Jarvis*, above note 182.

An auditor is entitled to reasonable assistance from the owner or manager of the property or business and any other person on the premises. The auditor can demand written or oral answers in respect of any question relating to the audit or examination, and can require the owner or manager of the premises to attend at the premises.[188]

The auditor's right to obtain answers to questions is not restricted to questioning employees of the taxpayer. The auditor may question any person who is on the premises, and in certain circumstances may even question members of the taxpayer's family who are not involved in the business.

Thus, tax auditors have unfettered and unrestricted power to disrupt a business for an unlimited period of time. Other than restricting entry to a reasonable time, there are no statutory limitations on the auditor's right to scrutinize the taxpayer's books, records or documents or to question the taxpayer, the employees and members of the taxpayer's family.

b) Dwelling-House

An auditor may not enter into a taxpayer's "dwelling-house"[189] without the taxpayer's consent or the authority of a search warrant.[190] A search warrant may be issued on the minister's *ex parte* application if there are reasonable grounds for believing that entry into the dwelling-house is necessary for administrative purposes.[191]

c) Search Warrants

Section 231.3 allows the minister to make an *ex parte* application to a judge for a search warrant to enter into a taxpayer's dwelling-house. The CRA can also apply for a search warrant under the *Criminal Code*,[192] which is now the standard practice.[193]

The judge may[194] issue the warrant if she is satisfied that there are reasonable grounds to believe that an offence has been committed under the Act and that evidence of the offence is likely to be found on the premises.[195]

---

188 *ITA, ibid*, para 231.1(1)(d).
189 *Ibid*, s 231 "dwelling-house."
190 *Ibid*, subs 231.1(2).
191 *Ibid*, subs 231.1(3).
192 *Criminal Code*, RSC 1985, c C-46, s 487.
193 *R v 2821109 Canada Inc*, [1995] GSTC 67 (NBCA).
194 The judge retains discretion as to whether she will issue the warrant.
195 *ITA*, above note 1, subs 231.3(3).

The warrant must be "reasonably specific" as to its scope, and must specify the documents to be searched for and seized.[196] Typically, a CRA investigator will prepare an information setting out the details of a *prima facie* offence under section 239 of the Act. The auditor is, however, allowed to seize not only the documents or things referred to in the search warrant but also any other document or thing that the auditor believes, on reasonable grounds, affords evidence of the commission of an offence under the Act.[197] Thus, in effect, the minister has virtually unlimited powers[198] of search and seizure if entry is obtained on the authority of a search warrant. This is so even if the warrant is of limited scope.[199]

The minister must report the list of documents seized from the taxpayer to the judge, but is entitled to retain the seized items that are the subject of the investigation.[200] The Act is quite clear that the judge "shall" order retention of the seized items unless the minister waives the right to retain the seized items. Thus, there is very limited judicial control over the minister and the ministry's agents.

3) Demand for Information

The minister may demand from any person any information for any purpose related to the administration or enforcement of the Act.[201] Although on the face of it this provision appears to have very broad application, in *R v Jarvis*,[202] the Supreme Court held that this section may be used only for the purpose of an audit and not for the purposes of an investigation. The minister may also demand production of any books, letters, accounts, invoices, statements or other documents from any person. The person from whom the demand is made must respond within such "reasonable time" as is stipulated in the Notice of Demand.[203]

---

196 *Ibid*, subs 231.3(4).
197 *Ibid*, subs 231.3(5).
198 An earlier version of s 231.3, *ibid*, which did not give the judge any discretion over the issuance of the warrant, was ruled unconstitutional under s 8 of the *Charter*, above note 183, in *Baron v Canada*, [1993] 1 SCR 416.
199 See *ITA, ibid*, subs 231.3(7) (in certain circumstances, such as non-compliance with warrant, judge may order documents returned to taxpayer).
200 *Ibid*, subs 231.3(6).
201 *Ibid*, s 231.2.
202 Above note 182.
203 *ITA*, above note 1, subs 231.2(1); *Tower v Canada (MNR)*, 2003 FCA 307 (s 231.2(1) permits the minister to demand responses to questions; also, tax-accountant privilege should not be recognized); *Joseph v MNR*, [1985] 2 CTC 164 (Ont HCJ) (in case of lawyer, period of less than seven to ten days would usually not be "reasonable").

a) Defences

A taxpayer can challenge a demand for information on the basis that:

- The documents demanded are not germane or relevant to the issues between the parties;
- The minister is on a "fishing expedition" and not on a specific inquiry as to some taxpayer's liability;
- The taxpayer has not been given a reasonable time to produce the documents; or
- The documents are privileged.

A demand for information constitutes a seizure, but not an unreasonable one within section 8 of the *Charter*.[204]

b) Named Persons

The minister can make the demand only in respect of information relating to named persons and for a purpose related to the administration or enforcement of the Act.[205] The test is objective and is determined on the basis of the particular facts.

It is not necessary that the person from whom the information is sought be the person whose tax liability is under investigation. The fact that the giving of the information may disclose private transactions involving persons who are not under investigation and may not be liable for tax does not invalidate an otherwise valid demand for information.

c) "Fishing Expeditions"

The demand for information must be a genuine and serious inquiry into the tax liability of some specific person or persons. The minister cannot be on a "fishing expedition" into the affairs of an unknown group of taxpayers. For example, a taxpayer cannot be compelled to provide a random sample as a check on the general compliance of some unidentified class of taxpayers.[206]

d) Reasonable Time to Respond

The minister usually stipulates a time or date in the Notice of Demand for Information. Whether the stipulated period of time is reasonable de-

---

204 *R v McKinlay Transport Ltd*, [1990] 1 SCR 627, aff'g (1987), [1988] 1 CTC 426 (Ont CA).

205 *ITA*, above note 1, subs 231.2(2).

206 *Ibid*, subs 231.2(2) (amendment to conform to decision of Supreme Court of Canada *James Richardson & Sons Ltd v MNR*, [1984] 1 SCR 614) (a demand can only be made for information relevant to the tax liability of a person or persons if a genuine and serious inquiry into their tax liability is being conducted).

pends upon the volume and complexity of the information demanded and the ease with which the taxpayer can obtain the information.[207]

e)   Unnamed Persons

The minister may demand information in respect of unnamed persons, but only pursuant to a court order authorizing the "fishing expedition."[208] The minister may obtain the order on the basis of an *ex parte* application. The judge must be satisfied that:[209]

• The unnamed person or group of persons is ascertainable; and
• The demand is made for the purpose of compliance with the Act.

The party from whom the information is demanded may seek a review of the order within fifteen days after its service.[210]

T. INQUIRY

In addition to the power to audit a taxpayer's books of account and general records, the minister can also conduct an inquiry or private hearing into the taxpayer's affairs:[211]

> This procedure is used in Special Investigations cases where persons who are considered able to give evidence concerning transactions or practices constituting tax evasion are reluctant to furnish voluntary explanations or are so closely related to the taxpayer under examination, by family relationship or business association, that they will not, for fear of recriminations or financial loss, give information unless compelled to do so.

An inquiry or hearing under section 231.4 does not violate sections 7 or 8 of the *Charter.*[212]

---

207 *James Richardson & Sons Ltd v MNR*, [1981] CTC 229 at 249 (FCTD), aff'd [1982] CTC 239 (FCA), rev'd on other grounds [1984] 1 SCR 614.
208 *ITA*, above note 1, subss 231.2(2) & (3).
209 *Ibid*, subs 231.2(3).
210 *Ibid*, subs 231.2(5); see also *Redeemer Foundation v Canada (MNR)*, 2005 FC 1361, rev'd 2006 FCA 325.
211 *ITA*, *ibid*, s 231.4; Information Circular 73-10R3, "Tax Evasion" (13 February 1987) at para 25.
212 *Del Zotto v Canada*, [1999] 1 SCR 3.

1) Hearing Officer

The minister must apply to the Tax Court for an order appointing a hearing officer to conduct the inquiry.[213] For the purposes of the inquiry, the hearing officer has all the powers of a commissioner under the *Inquiries Act*,[214] including the right to summon witnesses, to require evidence on oath, to compel the attendance of witnesses, to engage technical specialists (accountants, engineers, etc.) and to deputize technical advisors to inquire into matters within the scope of the commission.[215]

2) Exclusion from Hearing

A person whose affairs are being investigated in the course of an inquiry is entitled to be present and represented by counsel unless the person is excluded by the hearing officer. The basis for excluding a taxpayer and his counsel from an inquiry is that the taxpayer's presence would be prejudicial to the conduct of the inquiry.[216]

U. ADVANCE TAX RULINGS

1) General Comment

An advance ruling is a written opinion from the CRA (on a fee for service basis) interpreting specific provisions of the Act in the context of transactions that the taxpayer proposes to undertake. The CRA may issue such an opinion at the request of the taxpayer on a fee-for-service basis.

The purpose of a ruling is to comfort the taxpayer on transactions that he is contemplating as described in his request for the ruling. If the department is unwilling to issue a ruling, the taxpayer can adapt the structure of the transactions in order to obtain a favourable ruling. An advance ruling on a complex transaction provides certainty for the taxpayer, but obtaining one can be a long and frustrating process.

The degree of security that the taxpayer derives depends upon two factors: his candor in setting out the facts in detail and confidence in

---

213 *ITA*, above note 1, subs 231.4(2).
214 *Inquiries Act*, RSC 1985, c I-11; *ITA*, *ibid*, subs 231.4(3).
215 *ITA*, *ibid*, subs 231.4(3); *Inquiries Act*, *ibid*, s 11.
216 *ITA*, *ibid*, subs 231.4(6).

the department's administrative policy that it will generally abide by its rulings, at least vis-à-vis the taxpayer to whom it issues the ruling.[217]

2) Procedure

The department issues rulings based on facts that the taxpayer describes in his application. Taxpayers must file requests for income tax rulings in duplicate with the applicable directorate identifying the taxpayer and the relevant District Taxation Office.

A ruling request should contain a clear statement of relevant facts, copies of all pertinent documents, and a statement of the purpose of the transaction. It is also useful to include an interpretation of the relevant statutory provisions upon which the taxpayer is relying, citations to Interpretation Bulletins and, where relevant, any case law on point.

The request should also confirm that the District Office where the taxpayer files his return is not currently considering any of the issues. The CRA rules only on prospective, not completed, transactions.

3) Discretion

The advance rulings regime is discretionary and created as administrative practice. The CRA is under no legal obligation to issue a ruling or, indeed, even be bound by an issued ruling. The department issues rulings only when it is comfortable with the facts and the nature of the transaction that is the subject of the ruling. It is entirely in the CRA's domain to determine whether it considers a proposed transaction to be "offensive" or "abusive" in the sense that it has no business purpose, is improper tax avoidance or constitutes unlawful tax mitigation.

4) Status of Rulings

Advance rulings do not bind the CRA. The department issues rulings entirely in its discretion so that business transactions may proceed with certainty. The rulings mechanism is entirely an administrative creation, not an expression of legislative authority.

As a matter of administrative practice, however, the CRA will generally adhere to its ruling in respect of the taxpayer to whom it issues it and revokes an issued ruling.

---

217 See Information Circular 70-6R5, "Advance Income Tax Rulings" (17 May 2002).

5) Technical Interpretations

A taxpayer can request a "Technical Interpretation" (TI) from the CRA. A TI explains how the department will assess a proposed transaction. The advantage of a TI is that the taxpayer can request it without identifying himself and there is no fee for the service. The disadvantage is that the department is not bound by its TIs.

V. SEARCH AND SEIZURE

The minister can enter and search any building or place and seize therefrom any document or thing that may afford evidence as to the commission of an offence under the Act. However, the minister can exercise his power of search and seizure only on the basis of a search warrant issued by a superior court or Federal Court judge.[218]

1) "Seizure"

"Seizure" is the forcible taking of possession of property. Not all seizures violate section 8 of the *Charter*, only unreasonable ones. Hence, the questions in each case are: (1) has there been a "seizure"? and (2) if so, was it reasonable in the circumstances?[219]

A demand for information constitutes a "seizure," but not an unreasonable one in the context of the administrative and regulatory scheme of the Act. On the other hand, the transmission of information by the minister to the Tax Court pursuant to subsection 176(1) is an unreasonable seizure that is protected by section 8 of the *Charter*.[220]

2) Access to Seized Information

The person from whom the documents have been seized has the right to obtain one copy of all the seized documents.[221] The minister must supply photocopies at his expense. In addition, the owner of the docu-

---

218 *ITA*, above note 1, subs 231.3(1).
219 *Hunter v Southam Inc*, [1984] 2 SCR 145 (SCC); *Thomson Newspapers Ltd v Canada (Director of Investigation & Research, Combines Investigation Branch)* (1986), 57 OR (2d) 257 (CA), aff'd [1990] 1 SCR 425; *R v McKinlay Transport Ltd*, above note 204.
220 *Gernhart v Canada* (1999), [2000] 1 CTC 192 (FCA), rev'g [1997] 2 CTC 23 (FCTD).
221 *ITA*, above note 1, subs 231.3(8).

ments is entitled to have access to the documents at all reasonable times and subject to such reasonable conditions that the minister may impose. The items to be searched for and seized do not have to be described with specific particularity in the application for the warrant. Indeed, given the nature of income tax offences which lead to search and seizure, it is probably impossible to describe in detail all of the documents sought in a search.

3) Material in "Plain View"

a) Common Law Rule
The common law recognizes the "plain view" doctrine. Thus, where, during the course of executing a legal warrant, an officer locates anything which he reasonably believes is evidence of the commission of a crime, the officer has the legal power to seize it.[222] Hence, an official may seize a document without a warrant for that specific document.

b) *Criminal Code*
The CRA also has the power to seize any material falling in "plain view" that affords evidence of any income tax offence. Section 489 of the *Criminal Code*[223] enables a person executing a warrant to seize, in addition to the material that affords evidence of an offence for which the warrant was issued, any other documentary material that she believes on reasonable grounds to afford evidence of any other offence under the Act. Since the minister has the power to seize "plain view" material, the material has the same status as any other materials seized pursuant to the warrant.

4) Constitutional Restrictions

a) Section 8 of the *Charter*
Three provisions of the *Charter*[224] determine whether, and how, constitutionally-tainted evidence may be used against a taxpayer. We must answer four separate questions:

1) Has there been a seizure?

---

222 *Ghani v Jones*, [1970] 1 QB 693 at 706 (CA), Lord Denning MR; *Chic Fashions (West Wales) Ltd v Jones*, [1968] 2 QB 299 at 313 (CA), Diplock LJ; *Reynolds v Metropolitan Police Commissioner*, [1984] 3 All ER 649 at 653, 659 and 662 (CA); *R v Shea* (1983), 1 CCC (3d) 316 at 321–22 (Ont HCJ); *Texas v Brown*, 75 L Ed (2d) 502 (1983); *R v Longtin* (1983), 5 CCC (3d) 12 at 16 (Ont CA).
223 *Criminal Code*, above note 192.
224 *Charter*, above note 183.

2) Was the seizure unreasonable?
3) Should the court provide relief against the unreasonable seizure? and
4) Should the constitutionally-tainted evidence be excluded?

Section 8 of the *Charter* reads as follows:

> Everyone has the right to be secure against unreasonable search or seizure.

The operative word in section 8 is "unreasonable." There is no personal security against search and seizure per se. The only security is that the state's search or seizure cannot be unreasonable in the particular circumstances.[225]

A "seizure" is a forcible taking of possession of property.[226] However, not every taking is a seizure for the purposes of section 8.

The determination as to what is a "reasonable" search or seizure is made in the context of section 231.3 of the *Income Tax Act*. The judge who issues the warrant must be satisfied that the minister has reasonable grounds to believe that an offence has been committed, and the executing officer must have reasonable grounds for believing that the documents seized afford evidence of the commission of an offence. These two safeguards render a properly executed search and seizure "reasonable" in the context of section 8 of the *Charter*.[227]

The underlying value that is protected by section 8 of the *Charter* is the taxpayer's interest in privacy. However, section 8 provides protection only from an unreasonable search and seizure, not from all seizures.

The test for "reasonable" search and seizure is fluid and depends upon the type of intrusion into the taxpayer's privacy (for example, demand for information vs. physical seizure of documents), the type of taxpayer (for example, individual vs. corporate), the location where the seizure is executed (for example, business premises vs. personal residence), and the context (for example, criminal vs. regulatory/administrative). As Dickson CJC said in *Hunter v Southam Inc*:

225 *Kourtessis v MNR* (1988), [1989] 1 CTC 56 (BCSC), aff'd (1989), [1990] 1 CTC 241 (BCCA), rev'd [1993] 2 SCR 53.
226 *Thomson Newspapers Ltd v Canada (Director of Investigation & Research, Combines Investigation Branch)*, above note 219 at 267 (Ont CA).
227 *Solvent Petroleums Extraction Inc v MNR*, [1988] 1 CTC 325 (FCTD), aff'd [1989] 2 CTC 177 (FCA), application for leave to appeal to SCC refused, [1989] SCCA No 278, reconsideration refused (9 July 1992), Doc 21556 (SCC).

It is clear that the meaning of "unreasonable" cannot be determined by recourse to a dictionary, nor for that matter, by reference to the rules of statutory construction. The task of expounding a constitution is crucially different from that of construing a statute. A statute defines present rights and obligations. It is easily enacted and as easily repealed. A constitution, by contrast, is drafted with an eye to the future. Its function is to provide a continuing framework for the legitimate exercise of governmental power and, when joined by a Bill or a Charter of Rights, for the unremitting protection of individual rights and liberties.[228]

Three tests determine whether a search and seizure is reasonable:[229]

1) Was the search authorized by law?
2) Is the law itself reasonable? and
3) Was the manner in which the search was carried out reasonable?

If the answer to all three questions is affirmative, the seizure is reasonable and does not impugn section 8 of the *Charter.*

The burden of proof for adducing evidence that *Charter* rights have been infringed or denied depends upon the nature of the search. If the search and seizure was conducted pursuant to a warrant, the burden rests initially with the person making the allegation of infringement, namely, the taxpayer. The burden is discharged on a balance of probabilities.[230] Where, however, the search was conducted without the authority of a warrant, the onus is on the minister to show that the search was, on a balance of probabilities, reasonable in the circumstances.[231]

b)   Section 24 of the *Charter*

If it is determined that a particular search and seizure was conducted in an "unreasonable" manner, what is to be done with any evidence that is seized as a result of the illegal search? Two provisions of the *Charter* bear on this question.

Subsection 24(1) provides as follows:

Anyone whose rights or freedoms, as guaranteed by this Charter, have been infringed or denied may apply to a court of competent jurisdiction to obtain such remedy as the court considers appropriate and just in the circumstances.

---

228 *Hunter v Southam Inc*, above note 219 at 155.
229 *R v Collins*, [1987] 1 SCR 265.
230 *Ibid.*
231 *Hunter v Southam Inc*, above note 219 at 161; see also *R v Collins, ibid.*

572 INCOME TAX LAW

This is a remedial provision that allows a court considerable, though not unlimited, latitude in devising a remedy. There is no suggestion that this provision is the exclusive remedy for *Charter* violations, but it appears to be the one that is most frequently invoked in tax cases.

Although subsection 24(1) of the *Charter* confers broad discretionary power on a court to provide relief from illegal conduct, it does not mandate the court to exclude the evidence from judicial proceedings.[232] The court may exclude evidence from a trial, but only if it is satisfied that the test in subsection 24(2) of the *Charter* is met. That subsection reads as follows:

> Where, in proceedings under subsection (1), a court concludes that evidence was obtained in a manner that infringed or denied any rights or freedoms guaranteed by this Charter, the evidence shall be excluded if it is established that, having regard to all the circumstances, the admission of it in the proceedings would bring the administration of justice into disrepute.

Unlike subsection 24(1) of the *Charter*, subsection 24(2) does not confer discretion on the judge. The judge is under a duty to admit or exclude the tainted evidence.[233] Tainted evidence is *prima facie* admissible. Here too the burden of persuasion rests on the taxpayer to show that the admission of the evidence would bring the administration of justice into disrepute.

The interpretation of subsection 24(2) is complicated by the substantial difference in the language of the English and French versions of the text. The English text uses the words "*would* bring the administration of justice into disrepute." The French version provides "*est susceptible de* déconsidérer l'administration de la justice." The difference between "would" in the English text and "could" in the French text has the effect of lowering the threshold level for excluding evidence. The Supreme Court of Canada has said that the less onerous French text better serves the purpose of the *Charter*.[234]

---

232 *R v Therens*, [1985] 1 SCR 613.
233 See *R v Collins*, above note 229.
234 *Ibid.*

W. PRIVILEGE

1) General Comment

Certain types of communication between a taxpayer and his legal advisors are privileged from disclosure. In common law, communications made by a person to legal counsel in that counsel's professional capacity are privileged, and, subject to a few exceptions, neither counsel nor the client can be compelled to disclose the contents of such communications where they were intended to be confidential.[235]

Privilege has been described as follows:

> A client (whether party or stranger) cannot be compelled, and a legal adviser (whether barrister, solicitor, the clerk or intermediate agent of either, or an interpreter) will not be allowed without the express consent of his client, to disclose oral or documentary communications passing between them in professional confidence.[236]

The claim of privilege of a communication is no longer confined to communications made in contemplation, or conduct, of litigation. Where available, it extends to all professional communications made in confidence in a professional capacity with the intent that they be kept secret.[237]

2) Rationale

The rationale for holding legal communications to be privileged from disclosure is to permit legal advice to be given untrammelled by any apprehension of disclosure. As Brougham LC said:

> The foundation of this rule is not difficult to discover. It is not (as has sometimes been said) on account of any particular importance which

---

235 See, generally, *Greenough v Gaskell* (1833), 39 ER 618 (LC); *Clergue v McKay* (1902), 3 OLR 478 (Div Ct); *Butler v Board of Trade*, [1971] 1 Ch 680; *R v Bencardino* (1973), 15 CCC (2d) 342 (Ont CA); John Henry Wigmore, *Evidence in Trials at Common Law*, by John T McNaughton, vol 8 (Boston: Little, Brown & Co, 1961) paras 2290–329 at 541–641; Charles Tilford McCormick, *McCormick's Handbook on the Law of Evidence*, 2d ed by Edward W Cleary (St Paul, MN: West, 1972) at 175 and the following; Max Radin, "The Privilege of Confidential Communication between Lawyer and Client" (1928) 16 Calif L Rev 487; Clyde C Kahrl, "The Attorney-Client Privilege" (1979) 40 Ohio St LJ 699 at 701–2; A Kenneth Pye, "Fundamentals of the Attorney-Client Privilege" (1969) 15 Prac Law 15 at 16.
236 Sidney Lovell Phipson, *Phipson on Evidence*, 10th ed by Michael V Argyle (London: Sweet & Maxwell, 1963) at 251, para 585.
237 *Alcan-Colony Contracting Ltd v MNR*, [1971] 2 OR 365 (HCJ).

the law attributes to the business of legal professors, or any particular disposition to afford them protection, though certainly it may not be very easy to discover why a like privilege has been refused to others, and especially to medical advisers.

But it is out of regard to the interests of justice, which cannot be upholden, and to the administration of justice, which cannot go on, without the aid of men skilled in jurisprudence. . . . If the privilege did not exist at all, every one would be thrown upon his own legal resources; deprived of all professional assistance, a man would not venture to consult any skillful person, or would only dare to tell his counsellor half his case.[238]

3) Waiver by Client

The solicitor-client privilege to withhold or conceal confidential communications belongs to the client. The privilege is granted to protect the interests of the client, not the interests of the solicitor. As such, the client can always renounce the claim for privilege. Privilege can also be waived through voluntary disclosure.[239]

4) Statutory Definition

For tax purposes, "privilege" means the right that a person has to refuse to disclose an oral or documentary communication on the ground that the communication is one passing between client and lawyer in a professional confidence.[240]

In general terms, the following types of documents are covered by solicitor-client privilege:

- Correspondence between a solicitor and client;
- Opinion letters; and
- Tax plans, reorganizations, agreements of purchase and sale and other agreements.

The Act deems a lawyer's accounting record (including supporting vouchers and cheques) not to be a confidential communication. A solicitor's statement of account is, however, not considered an "account-

---

238 *Greenough v Gaskell*, above note 235 at 620–21. See, however, *Canada (MNR) v Singh Lyn Ragonetti Bindal LLP*, 2005 FC 1538 (the lawyer received funds as part of an abusive scheme to remove funds from a RRSP on a tax-free basis. Federal Court ordered the release of documents notwithstanding claim of privilege).
239 *Visser v MNR*, [1989] 1 CTC 192 (PEISC).
240 *ITA*, above note 1, subs 232(1) "solicitor-client privilege."

ing record," and is subject to solicitor-client privilege.[241] We determine solicitor-client privilege by reference to the law of the province in which the matter arises.[242]

A lawyer's accounting records are specifically deemed not to be confidential communications eligible for the claim of privilege. Without this exception, it would be difficult for the CRA to conduct a thorough audit of the lawyer's own income tax returns. A detailed statement of account and computerized dockets can provide a clear trail to an auditor as to the underlying nature of a tax plan and the areas of concern. Hence, the tax lawyer's dilemma: provide detailed accounting to keep the client informed and leave a road map showing the auditor the path to areas of concern to the lawyer.

Whether a document constitutes "an accounting record" is a question of fact. Solicitors' charge sheets[243] and statements of accounts[244] are not accounting records, and therefore may be the subject of a claim of privilege. Accounting records such as ledgers, books of accounts and supporting documents cannot be privileged. Although the matter is not free from doubt, the better view is that a lawyer's trust accounts ledger is a privileged document that is not to be revealed without the client's consent.[245]

5) Procedure

Privilege is invoked by the solicitor on behalf of her client. Thus, where an official seeks to examine or seize a document in the possession of a lawyer, the lawyer may invoke the privilege on behalf of a named client.[246] Unlike the common law, where privilege may extend to the identity of a lawyer's clients, the Act specifically requires disclosure of the name of the client on whose behalf solicitor-client privilege is claimed.

Where a lawyer claims that a document is covered by solicitor-client privilege, the tax officer must place the document in a package without

---

241 *Mutual Life Assurance Co of Canada v Canada (Deputy AG)*, [1984] CTC 155 (Ont HCJ) [*Muual Life*].

242 *Canada (Deputy AG) v Brown*, [1964] CTC 483 at 486 (SCC) (extent of privilege depends upon law of province in which document situated); see also *Re Kask*, [1966] CTC 659 (BCSC) ("communication" given common law meaning); *Herman v Canada (Deputy AG)* (1979), 79 DTC 5372 (Ont CA) (decision of judge in respect of solicitor-client privilege for documents not subject to appeal).

243 *Re Evans* (1968), 68 DTC 5277 (BCSC).

244 *Mutual Life*, above note 241.

245 *Cox, Taylor, Bryant v Canada (AG)*, [1988] 2 CTC 365 (BCSC).

246 *ITA*, above note 1, subs 232(3).

inspecting, examining or making copies of it. The package must be sealed and deposited either with the sheriff of the district or county in which the seizure is made or with a custodian acceptable to both parties.[247] Where the privilege is claimed in respect of a document that the tax officer is about to inspect or examine, the lawyer must place the document in a package, seal the package and retain it until the matter is adjudicated by a judge.[248]

6) Defence to Prosecution

We have seen that the minister can examine and audit a taxpayer's business records and, where authorized, can seize any documents and records which may be required as evidence in a subsequent proceeding. Obstruction of a tax audit is a criminal offence carrying a financial penalty and the possibility of imprisonment. A lawyer who makes a good faith claim for solicitor-client privilege on behalf of a named client cannot be convicted for refusing to disclose information sought by the minister as part of a tax audit.[249]

7) Fraud and Crimes

Since the rationale for solicitor-client privilege is to promote the administration of justice through full and frank disclosure of all relevant information, it would be perverse to allow privilege to assist in the perpetration of a fraudulent or criminal act.

There is a distinction between a communication made to commit a fraud or crime and a communication made in seeking advice on the defence of past crimes or fraudulent conduct. As *McCormick on Evidence* states:

> It is settled under modern authority that the privilege does not extend to communications between attorney and client where the client's purpose is the furtherance of a future intended crime or fraud. Advice secured in aid of a legitimate defence by the client against a charge of past crimes or past misconduct, even though he is guilty, stands on a different footing and such consultations are privileged. If the privilege is to be denied on the ground of unlawful purpose, the

---

247 *Ibid*, paras 232(3)(a) & (b).
248 *Ibid*, subs 232(3.1).
249 *Ibid*, subs 232(2).

client's guilty intention is controlling, though the attorney may have acted innocently and in good faith.[250]

Thus, privilege can be lost if it is shown that the privileged relationship exists for the purpose of perpetrating a fraud or crime.

8) Third-Party Communications

Third-party communications (communications by a person other than the solicitor or the client) may also be privileged in certain circumstances. Clearly, where a lawyer retains another lawyer to act as his agent, the communications of the agent lawyer are privileged.[251] Communications by a third party acting on behalf of a client are also privileged communications if the third party is retained as the lawyer's agent.[252]

9) Accountants' Communications

The general rule is that communications between an accountant and client are not privileged.[253] Thus, an accountant's audit working papers and tax files cannot be the subject of a claim for privilege. As noted above, however, where the accountant is retained as an agent of the client's solicitor, papers prepared as part of the agency contract are in effect the solicitor's papers, and are privileged communications.[254]

FURTHER READINGS

General

CANADIAN INSTITUTE. *Dealing with Revenue Canada: Audits, Appeals, Instalments, Collections* (Toronto: Canadian Institute, 1993).

HARRIS, EDWIN C. "Civil Penalties under the *Income Tax Act*" (1988) Corp Mgmt Tax Conf 9:1.

---

250 McCormick, above note 235 at 199–200.
251 *Klassen-Bronze Ltd v MNR* (1970), 70 DTC 6361 (Ont HCJ).
252 *Re Sokolov*, [1968] CTC 414 (Man QB).
253 *Tower v Canada (MNR)*, above note 203.
254 See, for example, *Mutual Life*, above note 241 (letter from solicitors containing professional correspondence between solicitors and chartered accountants with respect to tax matters was privileged).

Income Tax Returns

TREMBLAY, RICHARD G. "Information Reporting: Transactions with Non-Residents: Revenue Canada Extends Its Reach" (1989) 2 Can Curr Tax P-57.

Withholding Taxes

BROADHURST, DAVID G. "Issues in Withholding" (1988) Corp Mgmt Tax Conf 11:1.

Calculation of Tax Liability

SMITH, DAVID W. "Recent Decisions Underline Taxpayers' Liabilities" (1987) 14:6 CBA National 28.

Assessments

CANADIAN BAR ASSOCIATION, ONTARIO BRANCH, CONTINUING LEGAL EDUCATION. *Role of the Department of Justice Counsel in Tax Disputes* (Markham, ON: Audio Archives of Canada, 1984).

Reassessments

KRISHNA, VERN. "Reassessments Based on Fraud or Misrepresentation" (1992) 3 Can Curr Tax A-25.

Payment of Tax

BARTLETT, R. "Judicial Review in Taxation: A Modern Perspective" (1987) Brit Tax Rev 10.

Notice of Objection

DIXON, GORDON D. "Just and Equitable Considerations for Applications for the Extension of Notice of Objections" (1990) 28 Alta L Rev 762.

KRISHNA, VERN. "Obtaining Extension of Time to File Notice of Objection: The Palm Tree Withers" (1987) 2 Can Curr Tax A-1.

Liability of Directors for Corporate Taxes

BOWMAN, STEPHEN W. "Director's Liability: Deficiencies in Notices of Assessments" (1991) 39 Can Tax J 1324.

———. "Director's Liability: The Outsider" (1990) 38 Can Tax J 1242.

FIEN, CY M. "Directors' Liability and Indemnifications, Section 160 Assessments, and Ordinary Course of Business Provisions" (1992) 44 Can Tax Found 53:1.

KROFT, EDWIN G. "The Liability of Directors for Unpaid Canadian Taxes" (1985) 37 Can Tax Found 30.

Privilege

IVANKOVICH, IVAN F. "A Question of Privilege: Confidential Communications and the Public Accountant" (1994) 23 Can Bus LJ 201.

MACKNIGHT, ROBIN J. "Privileges of the Taxpayer" (1991) 3 Can Curr Tax P-27.

NATHANSON, DAVID C. "The Fairness Package, the Long Reach of Section 160, and Solicitor-Client Privilege" (1991) 43 Can Tax Found 49:1.

PERRY, JOHN LILBURN. "The *Income Tax Act*: Solicitor-Client Privilege and Solicitor-Client Confidentiality" (1994) 52 Advocate 405.

ROBERTS, ROBERT A, & RUSSELL W WATSON. "Solicitor-Client Privilege from a Tax Perspective" (1993) 4 Can Curr Tax T-5.

WATSON, RUSS. "Next Case, Please: Case-by-Case Privilege Offers Some Hope for Non-Lawyer Advisors (1993) 4 Can Curr Tax P-23.

PART VIII

JUDICIAL PROCESS

CHAPTER 21

OBJECTIONS AND APPEALS

A. NOTICE OF OBJECTION

1) Limitation Periods

The Notice triggers the appeal process, which is divided into two segments, administrative and judicial. The limitation periods for filing the Notice of Objection are as follows:[1]

- Individuals and testamentary trusts: within ninety days of the date of mailing of the Notice of Assessment or within one year of taxpayer's "filing due date," whichever is later.
- All other taxpayers: within ninety days of the date of mailing of the Notice of Assessment.

2) Procedure

The procedure for filing a Notice of Objection is straightforward: the Notice must be in writing, delivered or mailed to the Chief of Appeals in a CRA Tax Services Office. The Notice must set out the reasons for the objection. The minister retains discretion, however, to accept a Notice that is not served in the proper manner.

---

1   *Income Tax Act*, RSC 1985, c 1 (5th Supplement) [*ITA*], subs 165(1); Form T400A; Information Circular 98-1R, "Collection Policies" (15 September 2000); see also *ITA*, s 169.

Figure 21.1 Overview of the Litigation Process

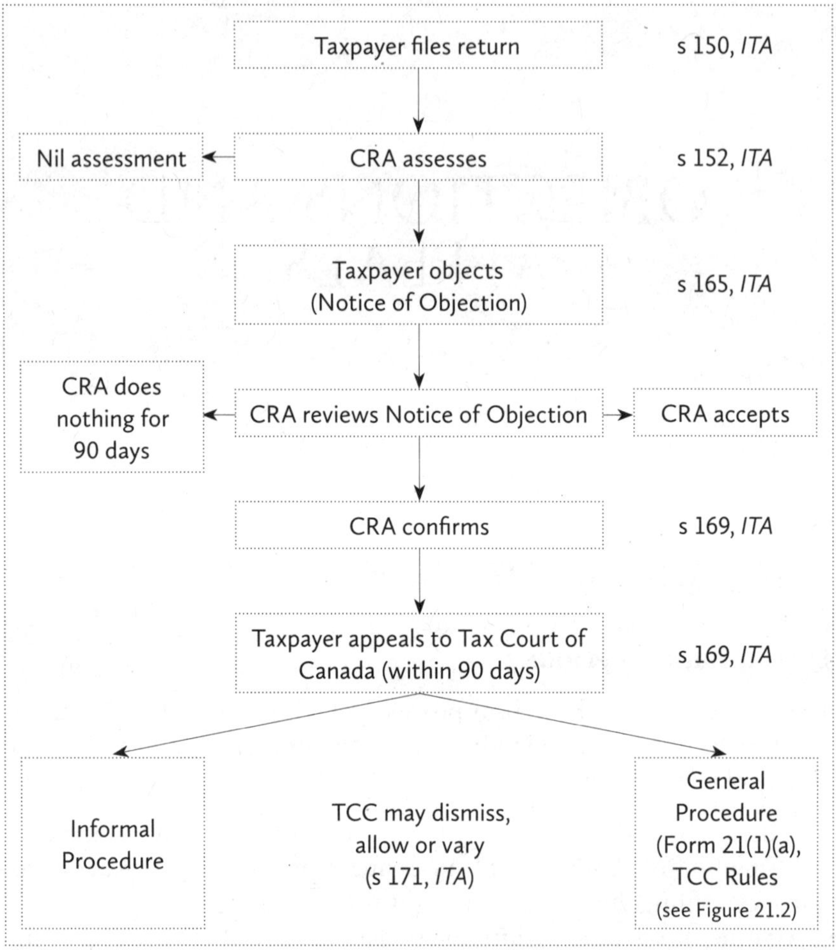

	Taxpayer files return	s 150, *ITA*
Nil assessment ←	CRA assesses	s 152, *ITA*
	Taxpayer objects (Notice of Objection)	s 165, *ITA*
CRA does nothing for 90 days ←	CRA reviews Notice of Objection → CRA accepts	
	CRA confirms	s 169, *ITA*
	Taxpayer appeals to Tax Court of Canada (within 90 days)	s 169, *ITA*
Informal Procedure	TCC may dismiss, allow or vary (s 171, *ITA*)	General Procedure (Form 21(1)(a), TCC Rules (see Figure 21.2)

A taxpayer's right of appeal depends upon the Notice being filed within the time limit. Failure to comply with the limitation period can substantially prejudice a taxpayer's rights. The CRA almost always stands on its strict and technical legal rights.[2]

Failure to meet the time limit can deprive the taxpayer of all legal rights in respect of objecting to the Notice of Assessment. A taxpayer can apply for an extension of time to file the Notice,[3] but there is no assurance that it will be granted.

---

2   See, for example, *Canadian Marconi Co v Canada*, [1989] 2 CTC 128 (FCTD), rev'd [1991] 2 CTC 352 (FCA), leave to appeal to SCC refused (1992), 90 DLR (4th) viii.

3   *ITA*, above note 1, subs 166.1.

3) Extension of Time to File

a) "Just and Equitable"

The minister has discretion to extend the time for filing a Notice of Objection in limited circumstances.

The first condition is that the minister must consider the extension "just and equitable" in the circumstances.[4] The words "just and equitable" conjure up an impression of "soft law and palm tree justice." In fact, the courts are quite reluctant to grant extensions of time. As the chairman of the Tax Review Board said in *Savary Beach Lands Ltd v MNR*:

> This Board takes the position that the granting of an extension in time under section 166.1 will be the exception rather than the rule. Human frailty will no doubt give rise on occasion to unusual circumstances, such as those before the Board this morning, wherein it is fair and reasonable to grant such an extension. However, to simply grant such extensions and imply that all applications—where the breach is but a few days—will be granted, is to make a mockery of the period of limitations set down in the Act.
>
> Therefore this Board will, in all cases, regardless of the time that passes between the limitation period in the Act and the filing of the application for extension of time, require exceptional circumstances before any such application will receive approval.[5]

b) "Exceptional Circumstances"

The second condition is that there must be "exceptional circumstances." This is a question of fact. The following examples illustrate some of the circumstances that are taken into account:

Extension Granted	
Bourdon v MNR, [1984] CTC 2654 (TCC)	Taxpayer's accountant filed Notice 42 days late.
Caouette v MNR, [1984] CTC 2447 (TCC)	Notice of Objection filed on 91st day after assessment.
Canada v Tohms, [1985] 2 CTC 130 (FCA)	Taxpayer's mental and physical condition justified extension.

---

4   *Ibid*, subs 166.1(7).
5   *Savary Beach Lands Ltd v MNR* (1972), 72 DTC 1497 at 1498 (TRB); but see *Thody v MNR*, [1983] CTC 2741 (TCC) (extension granted where delay explained and no "culpable negligence" on part of taxpayer); *Ramos v MNR*, [1983] CTC 2744 (TCC) (extension granted where taxpayer was out of country); *Graphic Specialties Ltd v MNR*, [1983] CTC 2743 (TCC) (extension granted where delay attributable to taxpayer's accountants).

Extension Granted	
Batey v MNR, [1986] 1 CTC 2439 (TCC)	Mix-up caused by incorrect application and address. Court found circumstances "just and equitable" without giving any clear reasons.
Extension Denied	
Morassutti v MNR, [1984] CTC 2401 (TCC)	Taxpayer's solicitor became aware of need to file Notice of Objection 2 weeks after expiry of 90-day period.
Tanaka v MNR, [1985] 1 CTC 2333 (TCC)	Notice of Objection filed late by accountant, who then appeared on behalf of client arguing that taxpayer should not be penalized for his mistake. Court commented on accountant's conflict of interest.
Harris v MNR, [1985] 1 CTC 2363 (TCC)	Notice filed 14 days late. Application for extension not brought for 6 months. Court attributed delay to accountant's negligence.
McGill v MNR, [1985] 2 CTC 209 (FCA)	Taxpayer wholly indifferent to proper manner of exercising his legal rights. Ignorance of law may be proper excuse in certain circumstances, but not in this case.
Aspinall v MNR, [1986] 1 CTC 2355 (TCC)	Application for extension delayed for 7 months; not brought as soon as circumstances permitted.
MNR v Pennington, [1987] 1 CTC 235 (FCA)	Notice of Objection filed 3 days late and application for extension filed 359 days after expiry of limitation period. Taxpayer not acting as soon as possible in filing application, but simply passing matter on to accountant.

c) Additional Requirements

The minister's discretion to dispense just and equitable relief is also restricted by the following additional requirements:

- The application for the extension of time for filing the Notice of Objection must be made no later than one year after the expiry of the original time limit;[6]
- The taxpayer must have been unable to act within the limitation period or had a *bona fide* intention to object to the assessment;[7] and
- The application must be brought as soon as circumstances permit.[8]

In other words, the taxpayer must have a plausible case for objecting to the assessment and act quickly and prudently to protect her interests.

---

6   *ITA* above note 1, para 166.1(7)(a).
7   *Ibid*, subpara 166.1(7)(b)(i); see also *Reid v MNR*, [1985] 2 CTC 2396 (TCC).
8   *ITA, ibid*, subpara 166.1(7)(b)(iii).

There are two separate requirements in respect of the time limits for an extension to file a Notice of Objection: the application must be brought "as soon as circumstances permit" *and*, at the very latest, no later than one year after the expiration of the original date for filing the Notice. The two time periods are conjunctive and the taxpayer must satisfy each independently of the other. Thus, the taxpayer should not wait to see if negotiations with the CRA will prove successful and then file for an extension of time if they are not. The better course is to file the application for extension immediately upon becoming aware of the expiration of the initial deadline and to continue negotiations with the CRA on a parallel track.

MNR v Pennington[9] illustrates the problems that can arise by not bringing an application for extension of time at the earliest possible opportunity. The taxpayer filed a Notice of Objection three days after the ninety-day limitation period. The CRA rejected the notice and sent the taxpayer a letter telling him that he could apply for an extension of time, and that the application must be made "as soon as possible and not later than one year" from the ninety-day limit. The taxpayer took up the matter with his accountant and asked him to attempt to negotiate a settlement of the matter in issue. When it became clear some time later that a satisfactory settlement was unlikely, the taxpayer applied for an extension of the limitation period. The Federal Court of Appeal refused the extension on the basis that the taxpayer did not act "as soon as possible" to file his application and it was not a sufficient excuse in law that he had passed the matter on to his accountant for settlement. Thurlow CJFC said:

> What the statute appears to me to require is that the taxpayer make his application as early as, under the particular circumstances, he could *reasonably be expected to get an application ready and presented*.[10]

The phrase "as soon as circumstances permit" is strictly construed, and should not be confused with the maximum time limit of one year prescribed in the statute.

4) Appeal

A taxpayer can appeal the minister's refusal to grant an extension of time to file a Notice of Objection.[11] The appeal is to the Tax Court of Canada, which has the power to grant the application on such terms as it considers just. The taxpayer must, however, satisfy all of the condi-

---

9   *MNR v Pennington* (1987), 87 DTC 5107 (FCA).
10   *Ibid* at 5109 [emphasis added].
11   *ITA*, above note 1, s 166.2.

tions in subsection 166.2(5), which places the same limits on the court's discretion as those placed on the minister.[12] The courts generally adopt a more flexible approach to extensions upon appeals.[13]

5) Disposition

The minister must consider the Notice of Objection and either confirm, vacate, or vary the assessment to which objection is made.[14] Where the minister does not confirm, vacate, or vary the assessment within ninety days of service of the Notice,[15] the taxpayer may appeal to the Tax Court without further delay.[16]

6) Refund of Taxes

A taxpayer who files a Notice of Objection or launches an appeal against an assessment can apply for a refund of the tax paid in respect thereof if another taxpayer has successfully challenged a similar assessment in court. The minister is not obliged to make the refund, but may refund the tax paid if the minister is satisfied that it would be "just and equitable" to do so.[17]

7) General Comment

The income tax system operates on the basis that a taxpayer initially assesses his own tax liability in respect of a taxation year. The tax return is then examined by the minister, who may assess, or reassess, the taxpayer in respect of the taxpayer's self-assessed liability. A taxpayer who is assessed by the minister may appeal the assessment.

The Act provides a complete code for challenging income tax assessments through the federal court system. Thus, a taxpayer can challenge

---

12   Ibid, subs 166.1(7).
13   See Carew v MNR, [1993] 1 CTC 1 (FCA) (as a matter of principle, courts are loath to let procedural technicalities stand in the way of a case being decided on its merits).
14   ITA, above note 1, subs 165(3).
15   Jolicoeur v MNR, [1960] CTC 346 (Ex Ct) (although taxpayer may appeal to Tax Court if minister does not respond within 90 days, no time limit imposed on minister to reply).
16   ITA, above note 1, s 169.
17   Ibid, subs 164(4.1).

the minister's assessment only through a tax appeal. A writ of *certiorari*[18] is not available for tax appeals.

8) Notice of Objection

The first formal step in the judicial appeal process is the Notice of Objection,[19] a formal pleading that warrants careful attention.

Although a taxpayer may negotiate with the CRA prior to filing his Notice of Objection, *all* of the taxpayer's statutory legal rights in respect of an appeal hinge upon the timely filing of the objection—that is, within the ninety-day period from the date of mailing of the notice of assessment or, in limited cases, within one year of the "filing due date." The ninety-day time limit is quite strictly enforced, and the courts will extend the time only in exceptional circumstances.[20]

9) Administrative Appeals

Typically, the Notice of Objection goes to the Appeals Branch of the CRA for administrative review. The "administrative appeal" involves discussion with, and representations to, the CRA to determine whether the Notice of Objection can be resolved on an informal basis. At this stage of the dispute, the CRA may ask the taxpayer or his representative, to supply further information by way of explanation or supplementary documentation.

18   *Federal Courts Act*, RSC 1985, c F-7; see *MNR v Parsons*, [1984] CTC 352 (FCA) (minister's assessments not to be reviewed, restrained or set aside by court in exercise of its discretion under ss 18 and 28 of *Federal Court Act*, RSC 1970, c 10 (2d Supp)).

19   *ITA*, above note 1, s 165; Information Circular 98-1R, above note 1.

20   *ITA*, ibid, ss 166.1 & 166.2; see, for example, *Morassutti v MNR*, [1984] CTC 2401 (TCC) (leave refused where taxpayer's solicitor became aware of necessity to file within two weeks of expiry of 90-day period); *Wright v MNR*, [1983] CTC 2493 (TRB) (leave refused where taxpayer missed limitation period because he would not pay his lawyer's retainer); *Horton v MNR* (1969), 69 DTC 821 (TAB) (taxpayer served notice of objection 92 days after date of assessment after learning only on last day that he had to file such notice; board rejected argument and dismissed appeal); see also *Gregg v MNR*, [1969] Tax ABC 782; *Brady-Browne v MNR* (1969), 69 DTC 797 (TAB); *Grenier v MNR* (1970), 70 DTC 1299 (TAB); *Vineland Quarries & Crushed Stone Ltd v MNR*, [1971] CTC 501 (FCTD), var'd as to costs [1971] CTC 635 (FCTD); *Paletta v MNR*, [1977] CTC 2285 (TRB).

10) Appeal to Tax Court

Where a taxpayer fails to resolve a dispute with the CRA at an administrative level, she may launch an appeal to the Tax Court. A taxpayer may appeal to the Tax Court when the minister confirms the assessment or after ninety days from the date of service of the Notice of Objection.[21]

The Tax Court of Canada has the sole power initially to hear appeals under the *Income Tax Act*. The court has two procedural tracks: informal and general. A taxpayer can use the Informal Procedure for appeals:[22]

1) Where the aggregate of all tax amounts (other than interest or provincial tax) in issue does not exceed $12,000;
2) Where the amount of the loss in issue does not exceed $24,000; or
3) Where the only amount in issue is the amount of interest assessed under the Act.

Where the disputed amounts exceed the threshold limits, the taxpayer can elect to restrict the appeal to the limits and forego any claim for the excess.

a)   Informal Procedure

The Informal Procedure is elective. Decisions of the Tax Court under the Informal Procedure cannot be appealed, but may be "judicially reviewed" by the Federal Court of Appeal. The informal track—equivalent to a Small Claims Court—provides taxpayers with a quick and inexpensive route for the settlement of tax disputes. Since approximately 70 percent of income tax appeals involve amounts of less than $12,000, the procedure is an expeditious way of processing of tax disputes.

The following rules apply to informal appeals:[23]

- The appeal must be in writing.
- The appeal should set out the reasons for the appeal and the relevant facts.
- The minister is generally required to submit a reply within 60 days from the time when the taxpayer files his notice of appeal.
- The Tax Court must hear the appeal within 180 days of the minister's reply.
- The court must issue judgment within 90 days of the hearing of the appeal.

---

21   *ITA, ibid*, subs 169(1).
22   *Tax Court of Canada Act*, RSC 1985, c T-2, subs 18(1).
23   See online: www.tcc-cci.gc.ca.

Thus, the entire appeal process is usually completed within less than a year from the date that the taxpayer files his Notice of Appeal and chooses the Informal Procedure. The taxpayer can represent himself or have an agent represent him. The agent does not have to be a lawyer.

Figure 21.2 General Procedure

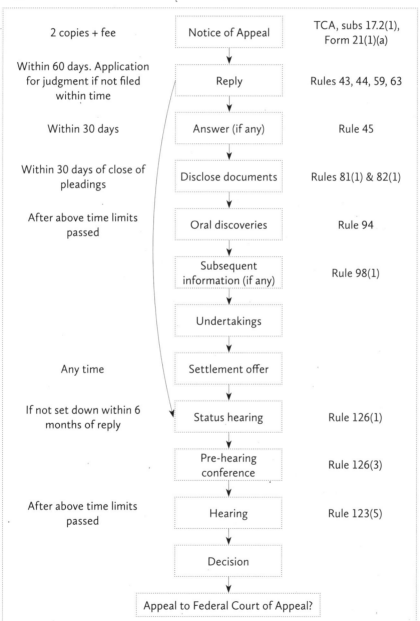

2 copies + fee	Notice of Appeal	TCA, subs 17.2(1), Form 21(1)(a)
Within 60 days. Application for judgment if not filed within time	Reply	Rules 43, 44, 59, 63
Within 30 days	Answer (if any)	Rule 45
Within 30 days of close of pleadings	Disclose documents	Rules 81(1) & 82(1)
After above time limits passed	Oral discoveries	Rule 94
	Subsequent information (if any)	Rule 98(1)
	Undertakings	
Any time	Settlement offer	
If not set down within 6 months of reply	Status hearing	Rule 126(1)
	Pre-hearing conference	Rule 126(3)
After above time limits passed	Hearing	Rule 123(5)
	Decision	
	Appeal to Federal Court of Appeal?	

b) General Procedure

The General Procedure of the Tax Court of Canada, which is formal, strictly controlled and expensive, applies where federal tax for a year exceeds $12,000.

A taxpayer can represent herself in a formal appeal or have a lawyer represent her. Non-lawyer agents are not allowed to appear before the Tax Court of Canada in a General Procedure appeal.

The General Procedure has formal rules of evidence, and decisions of the Tax Court following such an appeal have precedential value.

In contrast with the Informal Procedure, there is no pre-determined time frame for completion of the appeal in the general process. Thus, cases involving a formal appeal may extend over many years.

The following is an overview of the general and informal procedures.

	General	Informal
Representation	By self or lawyer	By self, lawyer or agent
Procedure	Similar to procedures now existing in most courts	No formal procedure required except for filing the appeal in writing
Evidence	Strict rules apply	Rules are flexible
Appeals	To the Federal Court of Appeal	Review by Federal Court of Appeal on questions of law and jurisdiction
Precedential value of case decisions	Yes	No
Time frame	No mandatory time frame for completion of an appeal	Explicit time deadlines for the CRA and the court Maximum of: • 60 days between filing of appeal and reply • 180 days between reply and hearing • 90 days between hearing and decision

11) Settlements

A taxpayer who enters into a settlement with the CRA is generally bound by the terms of the settlement, and may not appeal the same assessment. In *Smerchanski v MNR*,[24] the taxpayer, faced with the possibility of criminal proceedings on the grounds of income tax evasion, entered into a settlement just prior to the time when the right of prosecution would otherwise have been outlawed by the passage of time. Later, the taxpayer challenged the assessment, which was the basis of the settlement on the grounds that it had been obtained by duress and threat of prosecution. The Supreme Court of Canada unanimously upheld the settlement. Laskin CJC stated:

> Since it is not contested that a taxpayer may validly waive his rights of appeal against a tax assessment and that no question of public policy is involved to preclude such a waiver, the only issue of importance in this appeal is whether the tax authorities, seriously contemplating prosecution, and by indictment as in the present case, are entitled to exact a waiver of rights of appeal as a binding term of settling a clear tax liability when overtures for settlement are made by the taxpayer and, in consequence, to abandon their intention to prosecute.
>
> The threat of prosecution underlies every tax return if a false statement is knowingly made in it and, indeed, this is inscribed on the face of the tax form. It cannot be that the tax authorities must proceed to prosecution when faced with a dispute on whether there is a wilful tax evasion rather than being amenable to a settlement, be it a compromise or an uncompromising agreement for payment of what is claimed. Here there was not even such a dispute but an acknowledgement of evasion and the taxpayer's position cannot be stronger when he is a confessed evader than when he has disputed wilful evasion.
>
> I leave to one side situations where the tax authorities, having no substantial case against a taxpayer, nonetheless importune and harass him with the threat of prosecution in order to exact an unjustified settlement.[25]

12) Disposition of Appeal by Tax Court

The Tax Court can dispose of an appeal in one of four ways. It may:[26]

---

24   *Smerchanski v MNR* (1976), [1977] 2 SCR 23.
25   *Ibid* at 31. See *ITA*, above note 1, subss 165(1.2) and 169(2.2).
26   *ITA, ibid*, subs 171(1).

594 INCOME TAX LAW

1) Dismiss the appeal,
2) Vacate the assessment,
3) Vary the assessment, or
4) Refer the assessment back to the minister for further reconsideration and reassessment.

13) Appeal to the Federal Court of Appeal

A taxpayer may appeal a decision of the Tax Court of Canada under the General Procedure to the Federal Court of Appeal pursuant to the rules of the *Federal Courts Act*.[27] The Federal Court of Appeal can also judicially review Informal Procedure decisions.

a) Procedure
An appeal to the Federal Court of Appeal must be instituted within thirty days from the judgment of the Tax Court. The appeal is commenced by filing a Notice of Appeal with the Federal Court Registry and by serving all parties who are directly affected by the appeal with a true copy of the Notice.

Evidence of service must also be filed with the registry of the court.[28] The Federal Court of Appeal hears appeals with a panel of three judges.[29]

b) Direct References
The taxpayer may appeal directly to the Federal Court of Appeal where the minister:[30]

- Refuses to grant registration as a charitable organization, private or public foundation or Canadian amateur athletic association;
- Gives notice that it is proposed to revoke the registration of one of the above-listed organizations;
- Refuses to register a retirement savings plan;
- Refuses to register a profit-sharing plan;
- Revokes the registration of a profit-sharing plan;
- Refuses to issue a certificate of exemption under subsection 212(14) of the Act;
- Refuses to accept the registration of an education savings plan;
- Revokes the registration of an education savings plan;
- Refuses to accept the registration of a retirement income fund;

---

27 Above note 18, subs 27(1.1).
28 *Ibid*, subss 27(2) & (3).
29 *Ibid*, subs 16(1).
30 *Ibid*, subs 172(3).

- Refuses to register a pension plan;
- Revokes the registration of a pension plan; or
- Refuses to accept an amendment to a registered pension plan.

The Act deems the minister to have refused the registration, acceptance or issuance, as the case may be, in any of the situations listed above if the minister does not notify the applicant within 180 days after the filing of the application.[31]

The appellant must institute the appeal within a period of thirty days from the date of the minister's decision refusing the application for registration, issuance of a certificate of exemption or revocation of the registration.[32] The Federal Court of Appeal has the power to grant an extension of time beyond the thirty-day period.[33]

14) Appeal to the Supreme Court of Canada

There is no automatic right of appeal to the Supreme Court of Canada. Leave to appeal is granted only if the court is satisfied that the question being appealed involves a matter of public importance or is one that, in its opinion, it should hear for any other reason. Either the Federal Court of Appeal or the Supreme Court of Canada may grant the leave to appeal.

The Supreme Court receives approximately 600 applications for leave to appeal each year. It grants leave in approximately 12 percent of cases. The probability of having the Supreme Court hear an income tax appeal is low — about 0.2 to 0.5 percent. A panel of three judges usually decides leave applications.

An appeal to the Supreme Court of Canada must usually be brought within 30 days from the pronouncement of the judgment by the Federal Court of Appeal, or within such further time as a judge of the Federal Court of Appeal allows.

A copy of the Notice of Appeal must be filed with the Registrar of the Supreme Court, and all parties directly affected by the appeal must be served with a copy of the Notice. Evidence of service of the Notice must also be filed with the registrar of the Supreme Court.

---

31   *Ibid*, subs 172(4).
32   *Ibid*, subs 180(1).
33   *Ibid*, subs 180(1).

FURTHER READINGS

BARTLETT, R. "Judicial Review in Taxation: A Modern Perspective" (1987) Brit Tax Rev 10.

CCH CANADIAN LIMITED. *Canadian Tax Objection and Appeal Procedures*, loose-leaf (Don Mills: CCH Canadian, 1991–).

CORN, GEORGE. "Interpretation of the 'Fairness Package'" (1994) 4 Can Curr Tax A-19.

FESTERYGA, PAUL. "The Onus Issue: Who Carries the Burden of Proof in an Income Tax Appeal?" (1992) 125 CA Magazine No 734.

FRIDMAN, GHL. "No Justice for Taxpayers: The Paucity of Restitution" (1990) 19 Man LJ 303.

KRISHNA, VERN. "Obtaining Extension of Time to File Notice of Objection: The Palm Tree Withers" (1987) 2 Can Curr Tax A-1.

MCDONNELL, THOMAS E. "Administrative Matters and Appeals" in The Law Society of Upper Canada, *Special Lectures 1986: Income Tax for the General Practitioner* (Don Mills, ON: De Boo, 1986) 181.

MCMECHAN, ROBERT, & GORDON BOURGARD. *Tax Court Practice 1995* (Scarborough, ON: Carswell, 1995).

ONTARIO, MINISTRY OF REVENUE. *Ontario Tax Appeals: Practices and Procedures* (Revised) (Toronto: Ontario Ministry of Revenue, 1988).

PATERAS, BRUNO J. "Tax Evasion after the *Charter*" (1990) Meredith Memorial Lectures 435.

PETERSON, SHIRLEY D. "International Enforcement of Canadian and U.S. Tax Laws" (1993) Corp Mgmt Tax Conf.

WISE, RICHARD M. "Tax Evasion and Mens Rea Forensic Accounting" (1990) Meredith Memorial Lectures 405.

EPILOGUE

The interpretation of tax law is evolutionary rather than revolutionary. It was once viewed as a penal statute that should be strictly and literally interpreted without extrinsic aids or policy analysis. Now it is increasingly viewed as a policy statute. *Copthorne Holdings Ltd v Canada (Copthorne)*,[1] the latest decision of the Supreme Court of Canada, illustrates how far we have evolved from strict and literal interpretation to purposive analysis of fiscal legislation.

The *Copthorne* decision is a shot across the bow of tax professionals—lawyers, accountants and CRA officials—who spend long days with their noses buried in the detail of the *Income Tax Act*. There is a danger of not seeing the forest for the trees: *Copthorne*'s message is clear: step back from the technical and convoluted detail of transactions to determine whether an arrangement or scheme abusively undermines the object, spirit and purpose of the tax laws.

Copthorne involved a series of reorganizations of companies controlled by Li Ka-Shing and his son, Victor Li (the Li Family). The transactions are summarized at the end of this Epilogue.

The Li Family also controlled a group of non-resident companies (Li Group), which invested $96.7 million in VHHC Investments Ltd (Canco I), which then purchased the shares of VHHC Holdings Ltd (Canco II) for $67.4 million. Thus, Canco I, with stated and paid-up

---

1   2011 SCC 63 [*Copthorne*].

capital (PUC) of $96.7 million, became the parent company of Canco II, which had stated and PUC of $67.4 million.

Canco II used its capital to invest in the shares of another Canadian company that declined substantially in value and created an unrealized capital loss. Thus, the shares of Canco II fell in value to reflect the decline in the market value of its investment. Of course, Canco II's PUC remained $67 million—the amount equal to Canco I's initial investment.

At this juncture, if Canco I and Canco II amalgamated, the intercompany PUC of $67 million in Canco II would disappear, since it reflected the amount of the investment that a parent had in the subsidiary. Instead, however, in order to simplify the structure of the group and preserve Canco II's PUC, there followed a complex series of amalgamations and reorganizations. The principal feature of the reorganizations was to transfer Canco II's shares to a non-resident parent corporation, which then amalgamated to form yet another new corporation. Further amalgamations and reorganizations occurred. The net effect of all of the reorganizations was that Canco I and Canco II became affiliated corporations rather than the parent and subsidiary companies that they had been initially.

A subsequent horizontal amalgamation of Canco I and Canco II aggregated the PUC of the combined companies ($164 million). Ultimately, a non-resident company set up for the particular purpose redeemed the shares of the amalgamated company for $142 million. Since the redemption price was lower than the PUC of the amalgamated shares, the taxpayers claimed that there was no deemed dividend subject to Canadian withholding tax.

The Minister of National Revenue, however, took a more jaundiced view of the series of transactions. The Minister assessed the withholding tax, alleging that that the PUC of the shares of the amalgamated company should be reduced by $67 million (the amount of Canco I's initial investment in Canco II), which would have been the result had the two companies vertically amalgamated. Thus, the Minister deemed a dividend of $58 million and claimed the withholding tax thereon. The Minister alleged that the series of transactions constituted abusive "surplus stripping" contrary to the general anti-avoidance rule (GAAR) in section 245 of the *Income Tax Act*.

A. SUMMARY OF LAW

The *Income Tax Act* provides for a tax on income, not on capital. Thus, the Act permits shareholders to withdraw their capital from a corporation without any tax being payable.

In corporate law, stated capital is the amount of money that a shareholder commits to the corporation and, in most cases, it represents the shareholder's maximum liability to creditors. Thus, it is the financial measure of the limited liability of shareholders and represents to creditors the amount of funds or assets that the shareholders have invested in the corporation.

In tax law, PUC is analogous to stated capital in corporate law. However, instead of measuring limited liability, it measures the amount of capital that a corporation can return to its shareholders on a tax-free basis.

The *Income Tax Act* deems payments to shareholders in excess of their PUC in the corporation to be dividends. The taxation of dividends depends upon whether the recipient of the dividend is a resident, a non-resident or a corporation. Subject to treaty provisions, dividends to non-residents attract withholding tax, which the paying corporation must remit to the Receiver General of Canada on behalf of the non-resident.

The central issue in *Copthorne* was whether the various corporate reorganizations and amalgamations were a series of transactions that abusively circumvented the PUC and deemed dividend rules to avoid the withholding tax.

An amalgamation is a merger of two or more corporations to form a new corporate entity. Generally speaking, all of the property of the amalgamating corporations becomes the property of the newly amalgamated entity. Similarly, all the liabilities of the amalgamating corporations merge and all of the shareholders of the amalgamating corporations receive shares in the capital stock of the new corporate entity.

In a vertical amalgamation of a parent and its subsidiary corporation, the PUC of the subsidiary corporation is cancelled because it represents the investment of the parent in the subsidiary. In *Copthorne* the total investment was $97 million, of which $67 million was downstreamed into Canco II, the subsidiary.

However, where affiliated corporations (that is, sister and brother corporations) owned by a common parent are amalgamated, their PUC is aggregated and becomes the PUC of the new corporate amalgamated entity. Thus, a horizontal amalgamation creates a much larger PUC that can be withdrawn as a tax-free payment on account of capital.

The Copthorne reorganizations and amalgamations were designed to facilitate the horizontal amalgamation in order to pay a larger tax-free amount when the shares of the amalgamated entity were redeemed. In effect, the taxpayer double-counted the PUC in its affiliated corporations. Having invested only $97 million in Canco I, which reinvested $67 million of the same capital in Canco II, the transactions were designed to facilitate the taxpayer extracting $164 million tax-free on the ultimate redemption of shares by a non-resident shareholder.

The general scheme of section 87 of the Act is to preserve the continuity of PUC on amalgamations and not to permit bump-ups in the PUC that exceed the PUC of the predecessor corporations. Subsection 87(3) provides that where the PUC of the new corporation exceeds the aggregate of the PUC of the predecessor corporations, the PUC of the new corporation must be reduced. Thus, the subsection ensures that the PUC of a new corporation is limited to the aggregate of the PUC of the predecessor corporations. The rule prevents the artificial inflation of PUC on amalgamation. In addition, paragraph 87(9)(b) contains a similar rule that decreases PUC where, on a merger, it is increased by an amount that exceeds the total PUC in respect of the shares of the predecessor corporations that are exchanged for the parent's shares.

None of the individual transactions in the series of reorganizations and amalgamations technically offended the provisions of the Act. The aggregate of the transactions, however, resulted in abusive tax avoidance because their effect was to circumvent the underlying policy of the PUC provisions that seek to prevent artificial increases in PUC, which would facilitate a subsequent tax-free return to the shareholders of the amalgamated corporation. That is exactly what happened in *Copthorne*. Of the total PUC of $164 million, $97 million belonged to Canco I originally and $67 million belonged to its subsidiary, Canco II. The $67 million eventually ended up in a new corporation, Copthorne II, which amounted to double counting.

B. SCHEME OF GAAR

The general scheme of GAAR addresses three questions:

1) Does the transaction (or series of transactions) create a tax benefit?
2) Is the transaction (or series of transactions) that creates the tax benefit an avoidance transaction?
3) Does the avoidance transaction abuse the *Income Tax Act*?

C. TAX BENEFIT?

A tax benefit is defined in subsection 245(1) as "a reduction, avoidance or deferral of tax or other amount payable" under the Act. The Tax Court found that the tax benefit had arisen from the preservation of PUC at the time of the first series of transactions and when it was subsequently distributed to a non-resident shareholder.[2]

The Minister may assume the taxpayer derived a tax benefit. The burden is on the taxpayer to refute the Minister's assumption of the existence of a tax benefit.[3]

The Minister can establish a tax benefit by comparing what the taxpayer did with a reasonable alternative arrangement or transaction that would not produce the same tax benefit. That is, "but for" the tax benefit, what else could the taxpayer have reasonably done in order to achieve its commercial objective?

The "but for" test will almost inevitably result in finding a tax benefit. It would be most unusual in a commercial transaction for a taxpayer to select a route without the tax benefit when the taxpayer could accomplish her objectives in a tax-efficient manner. There would have to be a powerful non-tax commercial benefit that would suggest that the taxpayer did not engage in tax planning.

The Tax Court found that the vertical amalgamation would have been the simpler course of action. However, the potential cancellation of Canco II's PUC on such a reorganization led the taxpayer down its alternative path of restructuring, which ultimately led to the tax benefit in the tax-free redemption of shares. Copthorne did not discharge its burden of proof to show that there was no tax benefit.

D. AVOIDANCE TRANSACTION?

Subsection 245(3) of the Act states that a transaction is an avoidance transaction if it results in a tax benefit, and if it is not undertaken primarily for a *bona fide* non-tax purpose. An avoidance transaction can result from either a single transaction or a series of transactions that electively produce the requisite tax benefit.

If there is a series of transactions, subsection 245(3) applies unless each transaction within the series can "reasonably be considered to have been undertaken or arranged primarily for *bona fide* purposes

---

2   2007 TCC 481.
3   See *Canada Trustco Mortgage Co v Canada*, 2005 SCC 54 at para 63.

other than to obtain" the tax benefit. Thus, a single transaction that is not undertaken primarily for a *bona fide* non-tax purpose contaminates the entire series and results in the series being characterized as an "avoidance transaction."

E. SERIES OF TRANSACTIONS

The concept of a "series of transactions" is integral to GAAR. The concept has two dimensions: common law and statutory.

In common law, a sequence of transactions constitutes a composite whole when the individual components are linked or glued together through firm arrangements or understandings that each component will be completed. In other words, it is well understood that the entire sequence will be completed in a preordained manner.

Preordination does not depend upon strict contractual rights, but on a practical certainty that transactions will be completed as planned.[4] Thus, the first transaction in the sequence should be linked to the last, and then the linked group may be considered a single composite whole. For example, in a sale from A to B and from B to C, at the time that A sells to B, C is identified as the ultimate purchaser and all of the main terms of the sale are agreed to in principle.

The second test, unique to the Canadian GAAR structure, is subsection 248(10), which purports to expand the concept of series to include any related transactions or events completed "in contemplation" of the series. In the above example, the sale from A to B would contemplate the sale to the ultimate purchaser, C.

The Technical Notes to the amending bill that introduced subsection 248(10) state that the subsection, which was introduced two years prior to the enactment of GAAR, was merely to "clarify" the meaning of series of transactions. Senior officials of the government stated that the subsection did no more than accept the concept of series as developed in common law decisions such as *Furniss (Inspector of Taxes) v Dawson.*[5] For example, Michael Hiltz, Director of Re-organizations in the Speciality Rulings Directorate of the CRA, stated:

> [T]he series itself will include a preliminary and a subsequent transaction only if at the time the preliminary transaction is carried out,

---

4   See *Furniss (Inspector of Taxes) v Dawson,* [1984] AC 474 (HL).
5   *Ibid.*

all important elements of subsequent transactions are settled, and the subsequent transaction is eventually carried out.[6]

The legislative intention was to look at subsequent contemplated transactions.

Similarly, David Dodge, then Senior Assistant Deputy Minister of the Department of Finance, wrote in an article in the Canadian Tax Journal:

> [T]he step transaction doctrine, however, when completed by the business purpose test as suggested in . . . *Furniss v Dawson*, represents a coherent and orthodox approach. For that reason, this doctrine has been included in proposed section 245 in the form suggested by these cases.[7]

Thus, there is strong extrinsic evidence that suggests that the legislative intention underlying the phrase "in contemplation of" was to include in a series all the important elements of *subsequent* transactions in the sequence.

In *Canada Trustco Mortgage Co v Canada (Canada Trustco)*,[8] however, the Supreme Court adopted a more expansive approach to the concept of series. Not only does a series include prospective transactions, but it also includes retrospective contemplation of prior transactions.

"Contemplation" is defined as "the action of contemplating or mentally reviewing; the action of thinking about a thing continuously; attentive consideration, study."[9] In *Copthorne*, the Court acknowledges that the more common use of the term "contemplation" is likely prospective.[10]

Although the text and context of subsection 248(10) leave open the question of whether the contemplation should be prospective or retrospective, the Technical Notes and the references to *Furniss (Inspector of Taxes) v Dawson* by senior government officials at the time that the legislation was tabled, and shortly thereafter, strongly suggest that a subsection merely clarifies the common law and does not expand it.

Faced with the choice of reading subsection 248(10) narrowly to include only prospective contemplation, or expansively, to include both prospective and retrospective contemplation, the Supreme Court opted for the expansive interpretation. In doing so, the Court acknowledges

6   Michael Hiltz, "Section 245 of the *Income Tax Act*" (1988) 40 Can Tax Found 7:1 at 7:7.
7   David A Dodge, "A New and More Coherent Approach to Tax Avoidance" (1988) 36 Can Tax J 1 at 15.
8   Above note 3.
9   *Oxford English Dictionary*, 2d ed.
10   Above note 1 at para 50, citing Hiltz, above note 6 at 7:6.

that its decision in *Canada Trustco* was relatively recent and that reversing a recent decision was a step not to be lightly undertaken:

> Before a Court will entertain reversing a recently decided decision, there must be substantial reasons to believe the precedent was wrongly decided. In this case, Copthorne has not met the "high threshold for reversing a precedent" . . . and it is appropriate to reaffirm the *Trustco* interpretation of s. 248(10). [11]

The critical issue in *Copthorne* was whether the share redemption that gave rise to the tax-free return of capital up to the value of the redeemed corporation's PUC was contemplated as part of the same series as the prior sale and amalgamation.

The test to determine whether a transaction is an "avoidance transaction" is objective and fact-based. Copthorne argued that it undertook the transactions for the purpose of simplifying the Li Group companies and utilizing the losses within the amalgamated companies to shelter other gains within other amalgamated companies. However, the additional steps did not explain why the company did not undertake a vertical amalgamation (which would have eliminated Canco II's PUC) and would have permitted the same results.

The taxpayer carries the burden to prove the *bona fide* non-tax purposes of its transactions. The Tax Court found as a fact that the redemption transaction was, with retrospective contemplation, part of the series. The Supreme Court does not easily upset findings of fact.

F. WAS THE AVOIDANCE TRANSACTION ABUSIVE?

The term "abusive" does not imply moral opprobrium concerning the taxpayer's efforts to minimize its taxes. The Supreme Court of Canada has repeatedly endorsed the *Westminster* principle that taxpayers are entitled to select courses of action or enter into transactions that minimize their tax liability. GAAR is a statutory mechanism that superimposes a purpose test in determining the validity of transactions. Thus, GAAR statutorily blunts the doctrine of literal interpretation by focusing on the object, spirit or purpose of tax provisions.

The core of GAAR analysis depends upon determining the object, spirit, purpose or legislative rationale of the technical provisions that the taxpayer uses to obtain a tax benefit.

---

11   *Copthorne, ibid* at para 57.

Purposive analysis does not depend on whether the words of the statute are clear or ambiguous. Even where the words of the Act are clear, a court is entitled to determine the rationale or purpose of the words to determine whether transactions abuse the statute Thus, GAAR analysis requires balancing between two competing interests: the interest of the taxpayer in minimizing his taxes through legitimate means and the legislative interest in ensuring the integrity of the income tax system.

An arrangement is abusive where the transaction (or series of transactions) culminates in an outcome that defeats the purpose of the statutory provisions used to implement it. The burden is squarely on the Minister to demonstrate that the transaction (or series of transactions) is abusive. The benefit of any doubt goes to the taxpayer.

It is trite to say that GAAR creates uncertainty. Of course it does. The Minister only invokes GAAR when he cannot use the specific technical words of tax provisions to assess the taxpayer. If he could use a specific provision, he would assess under the authority of the provision. It is only when the Minister cannot rely on specific provisions that he may rely on GAAR if the transactions undermine the rationale or purpose of the statute. Thus, GAAR was enacted for the very purpose of attacking transactions that escaped the literal meaning of words in provisions, but had the overall effect of frustrating and undermining the purpose of the Act read as a whole. It is inevitable that a broad anti-avoidance provision creates greater uncertainty than a strict literal reading of words or formulae. In *Copthorne*, GAAR trumped the *Westminster* principle.

To be sure, tax law moves like a glacier—imperceptibly, but distinctly obvious in time-lapse photography. The analytical reasoning in *Copthorne* is a signpost to the future.

G. SUMMARY OF TRANSACTIONS[12]

The companies involved in this case are all controlled by Mr. Li Ka-Shing, and his son, Victor Li (the Li Family). They are:

a) Copthorne Holdings Ltd (Copthorne). The case involves three companies named Copthorne Holdings Ltd. While each has the same name, they are not the same, nor are they the same as the appellant at the Supreme Court. The first Copthorne was incorporated under

---

12   The contents of this summary are taken from Appendix A of *Copthorne*, *ibid* at para 129.

the laws of Ontario in 1981, with one share owned by Big City. The second and third companies are amalgamated successor companies that continued business using the name Copthorne Holdings Ltd. I refer to the three companies as Copthorne I, II and III. The appellant in this case is actually the product of a third amalgamation that also continued under the same name.

b) VHHC Investments Ltd (VHHC Investments), an Ontario company incorporated in 1987, owned directly and indirectly by Victor Li, son of Li Ka-Shing.

c) VHHC Holdings Ltd (VHHC Holdings), an Ontario corporation incorporated in 1987, initially owned entirely by VHHC Investments.

d) Big City Project Corporation BV (Big City), a Netherlands company indirectly controlled by Li Ka-Shing.

e) Copthorne Overseas Investment Ltd (COIL), a Barbados company incorporated and owned by Copthorne I.

f) Asfield BV (Asfield), a Netherlands company indirectly owned by a trust whose primary beneficiary was Victor Li.

g) LF Holdings Ltd (LF Holdings), a Barbados company controlled by Li Ka-Shing.

h) VHSUB Holdings Inc (VHSUB), a Canadian company owned by VHHC Holdings.

i) Husky Oil Ltd (Husky), a Canadian company owned in part by the Li Family companies that carried on the business of oil and gas production, refining and distribution.

j) Copthorne International Investment Ltd (CIIL), a British Virgin Islands Company incorporated in 1994.

k) LF Investments (Barbados) Ltd (LF Investments), a Barbados company incorporated in 1994 by LFHoldings.

1) Background

Copthorne I was first incorporated as an Ontario corporation in 1981. It purchased the Toronto Harbour Castle Hotel in 1981 and sold it in 1989 for a substantial capital gain. Its only share was owned by another company within the Li Family group, Big City.

After selling the hotel, Copthorne I incorporated a new company, COIL. COIL carried on a bond-trading business in Singapore.

2) The Creation of the VHHC Companies

In 1987, VHHC Investments was incorporated in Ontario. Victor Li owned the Class A voting common shares, which had a PUC of $100.

He also held 18.75 percent of the Class B non-voting common shares. The rest of the Class B shares were owned by Asfield, which was indirectly owned by Victor Li.

In 1987, 1988 and 1991, Victor Li, Asfield, and LF Holdings further invested in shares of VHHC Investments. As a result of these investments the common and preference shares of VHHC Investments had a total PUC of $96,736,845.

During this time, VHHC Investments in turn used $67,401,279 of the invested funds to purchase common shares of VHHC Holdings. As a result, the shares of VHHC Holdings had a PUC of $67,401,279.

3) The VHHC Companies' Losses From Husky Investments

VHHC Holdings, in turn, invested in Husky directly and through a subsidiary VHSUB. By the end of 1991 the Husky shares had lost substantial value, and as a result VHHC Holdings had suffered a substantial capital loss. VHHC Holdings sold to Copthorne.

In 1992, VHHC Investments sold all of its common shares in VHHC Holdings, which still had a PUC of $67.4 million to Copthorne I for 1 Class A special share of Copthorne I valued at $1,000. This was done in order to shift the capital loss from the Husky investment suffered by VHHC Holdings to Copthorne I to shelter the capital gains from the sale of the hotel. As a result of this sale Copthorne I owned the shares in VHHC Holdings, with the $67.4 million PUC but only a nominal fair market value.

4) The First Series—Amalgamating Copthorne and VHHC Holdings

In 1993, the Li Family decided to amalgamate Copthorne I, VHHC Holdings and two other corporations which it controlled. This was done to simplify the structure of the group of companies and to allow the losses from each of the predecessor corporations' businesses to shelter the profits of others.

However, a direct vertical amalgamation of VHHC Holdings and its parent company, Copthorne I, would result in a cancellation of the $67.4 million PUC in the shares of VHHC Holdings under section 87(3) of the *Income Tax Act*. To avoid this result, the Li Family decided to engage in a number of transactions to protect the PUC.

In July 1993, Copthorne I sold its VHHC Holdings common shares to Big City, Copthorne I's parent company for $1,000. This is referred to as the "1993 Share Sale." This meant that any amalgamation between Copthorne I and VHHC Holdings was "horizontal" not "vertical." This share sale is the transaction that the Minister found was an "avoidance transaction."

On 1 January 1994, Copthorne I, VHHC Holdings, and two other corporations amalgamated to form Copthorne II. The PUC from the common shares of VHHC Holdings was added to $1 of PUC from the single common share of Copthorne I, resulting in a total PUC of approximately $67.4 million distributed evenly between the 20,001,000 common shares of Copthorne II. All of these shares were owned by Big City.

Both the 1993 share sale and the subsequent amalgamation are agreed to be part of a first series of transactions.

5) The Second Series—Amalgamating VHHC Investments With Copthorne II

In 1994, legislative amendments were proposed to the Foreign Accrual Property Income (FAPI) rules of the Act which stood to negatively affect COIL's business. In response to these proposed changes, the Li Family decided to dispose of some of COIL's assets.

A new company, CIIL, was incorporated, to purchase the bond-trading business from COIL. A new Barbados company, LF Investments, was incorporated to purchase all of the shares of Copthorne II from Big City and VHHC Investments from LF Holdings. The two purchased companies were then amalgamated with two other companies to form Copthorne III.

Upon amalgamation, LF Investments received Class D shares of Copthorne III with a PUC that was the sum of the PUC in the common shares of Copthorne II (approximately $67.4 million) and the PUC in the common and preferred shares of VHHC Investments (approximately $96.7 million), for a total PUC of $164,138,025. This PUC was held in 164,138,025 Class D preference shares each having a PUC of $1.

6) The Redemption

Copthorne III then redeemed 142,035,895 of its Class D preference shares held by LF Investments for $142,035,895. As the redemption amount was no more than the total PUC in the shares redeemed by Copthorne III, it was not deemed to be a dividend. Nor did the redemption give rise to a capital gain.

Thus, Copthorne did not withhold or remit any tax on behalf of LF Investments pursuant to section 215(1) of the Act.

The transactions beginning with the incorporation of CIIL and ending with the redemption are agreed to be part of the second series of transactions.

On 1 February 2000, the Minister assessed Copthorne for unwithheld tax under the GAAR. He concluded that Copthorne III was liable for unremitted taxes because the PUC in the shares of Copthorne III should have been calculated to be $96 million, not $164 million. This amounted to $8,748,783.40 in tax which Copthorne III had been obligated to withhold and remit on behalf of LF Investments. Given that Copthorne had not withheld any tax, the Minister assessed this amount against Copthorne III.

PART IX

APPENDICES

THE TIME VALUE
OF MONEY

The fundamental purpose of income tax law is to collect taxes for government expenditures. A taxpayer's obligation for tax arises when he or she earns taxable income. The obligation to pay the tax, however, is determined by a schedule set out in the Act. Thus, the timing of tax payments is key to the efficient collection of revenue.

Time has value. The value is the effect of time on invested money.

We can look at value from two dimensions: future and present. Given a sum of money, we can determine its value at some future date if we know the interest rate at which we will invest the money. Conversely, if we know that we are to receive a sum of money in the future, we can determine its value today if we know the rate at which it is, or can be, invested. Thus, money has "time value."

All assets, tangible and intangible, can be expressed in terms of their future or present value if we can determine the rate at which the asset is invested or discounted. The appropriate rate is usually the market-determined interest or investment rate.

In economic terms, "interest" is the rental cost of borrowing money. The cost of renting money may be fixed in advance, determinable at a future time, or variable according to specified conditions. Thus, interest and time are inextricably related. An interest rate is relevant if, and only if, it is specified in relation to time.

The concept of the time value of money is relevant to all economic transactions. Lawyers deal with assets that have a "time value" in virtually all areas of commercial practice. For example, suppose that a plaintiff's lawyer is offered a choice between a cash settlement of $500,000 or six successive payments of $100,000 payable at the end of each year. Should the lawyer accept the lump-sum settlement or pursue the extended payment plan? Ignoring questions of risk and insolvency, the answer depends upon the prevailing interest rate and income tax considerations associated with the two alternatives. At an interest rate of 10 percent, the six payments of $100,000 have a present value of only $435,300. Hence, the plaintiff would be better off with the lump-sum settlement. If the interest (discount) rate was 4 percent, however, the six payments would have a net present value of $524,000 (see Table A.3).[1]

We arrive at this answer in one of two ways. We can add the present values of each of the payments for six years at 10 percent. The present value of $1 is (see Table A.2):

Year	
1	0.909
2	0.826
3	0.751
4	0.683
5	0.620
6	0.564
	4.353

Hence, the present value of $100,000 payable in six installments would be $435,300.

Alternatively, we arrive at the same answer by looking at Table A.3. Reading down the 10 percent column and across the six year row, we see that the present value of an annuity of $1 payable at the end of each year is $4.35. Hence, the present value of a $100,000 annuity would be $435,000 (rounded). At 4 percent it would be $524,000.

Similarly, a defendant in a lawsuit involving lost profits of a business enterprise may ask the court to reduce the size of any lump-sum award to the plaintiff to take into account the accelerated value of receiving the money today rather than over an extended period of time. For example, if one can establish that the defendant's actions will cause the plaintiff a loss of $100,000 of business profits annually for a period of five years, should the defendant be required to pay the nominal amount of the damages ($500,000) up front or some lesser discounted amount because of the time value of money? At an interest rate of 12 percent, the annual loss of $100,000 spread over five years is worth

---

1   Tables A.1, A.2 and A.3 are at the end of this appendix.

only $360,000 today if paid at the end of each year (see Table A.3). Ignoring the time value of money penalizes the defendant and gives the plaintiff a windfall gain. Thus, time value is essential in structuring damage settlements.

Although we are familiar with the calculation of simple and compound interest, we are less intuitive about the concept of the discounted value of future sums of money. This is because we are taught to think intuitively of investing for the future but not of the present value of future sums. Yet, mathematically speaking, future value and present value are mirror images of each other looked at from different perspectives. The primary purpose of determining future and present values is to measure money in comparable terms across time periods by translating future dollars into economically equivalent current dollars, and *vice versa*.

A. FUTURE VALUE

We determine the future value of money by determining the effect of interest on a principal sum. There are two forms of interest, simple and compound. Interest that is paid only on the amount originally invested, but not on any interest that accrues subsequently, is simple interest.

Simple interest is a function of the principal sum (P) multiplied by rate (R) multiplied by time (n):

$$\text{Interest} = PR(n)$$

For example, if one deposits $10,000 in a guaranteed investment certificate (GIC) for a period of one year at 8 percent, the GIC will be worth $10,800 at the end of the year. The interest earned is $800, or 8 percent of the principal amount for one year. Thus, if simple interest is paid over (n) periods, the total interest payments and the sum originally invested will grow to:

$$F = P\,(1 + R)(n)$$

Where:

F = the future value of money;
P = the present sum of money;
R = net interest rate over a period of time; and
n = the number of periods of time.

Hence, in four years the total sum will equal $13,200.

In contrast, compound interest refers to the process whereby interest is earned not only on the amount originally invested but also on subsequently accrued interest. Compound interest starts out with exactly the same formula as simple interest but extends it to account for the reinvested interest. In other words, the interest on the second and subsequent time periods is calculated not only on the initial principal amount but also on any interest accumulated in preceding time periods.

For example, if one invests $10,000 in a GIC at 8 percent compounded annually for two years, the GIC is worth $11,664 at the end of the second year. At the end of the first year the principal and the interest are $10,800. But the interest for the second year is calculated as 8 percent of $10,800, which is $864.

We arrive at the same result by looking at Table A.1, where we see that the future value of $1 invested at 8 percent for two years is $1.17. In contrast, simple interest for both years would have produced only $11,600. The incremental $64 is due entirely to the fact that the interest in the second year is calculated not only on the initial principal amount but also on the reinvested interest. The $64 is the premium for the compounding of interest. It is the interest on earlier interest.

To summarize, a future amount is determined by the formula:

$$F = P(1 + R)(n)$$

Where:

F = the future value of money;
P = the present sum of money;
R = net interest rate over a period of time; and
n = the number of periods of time.

The formula demonstrates that the longer the time horizon for investment and the more frequent the compounding intervals, the greater the future value of a present sum of money. For example, the future value of $1 invested at 8 percent at the end of years 1 through to 5 is as follows:[2]

Year	
1	$1.080
2	$1.166
3	$1.260
4	$1.360
5	$1.469

If, instead, we compound $10,000 over a period of 8 quarters at 2 percent per quarter (which nominally appears to be the same thing as 8 percent per year), we get a future value of $11,717, or $53 more than

2   Note that Table A.1 is rounded to two decimal places.

in the previous example of compounding only once per year. On a $100 million transaction the difference between annual and quarterly compounding is $530,000. The lesson is simple: a lender will benefit from compounding interest as frequently as possible and the borrower will pay more for frequent compounding. Thus, in an open and competitive market, the borrower and the lender must negotiate both the interest rate and compounding intervals.

There is no such negotiation, however, in tax law. The CRA compounds interest on a *daily* basis on outstanding amounts of taxes payable.[3] In the above example, if the $10,000 was the outstanding amount of a tax assessment, daily compounding of the amount at an equivalent of 8 percent per year would increase the tax payable at the end of two years to $11,735.

Compounding allows us to determine the economic equivalence of money across different time periods. For example, if the market rate of interest is 8 percent, we should be indifferent between paying $1,000 today and $1,469 five years from now because we could invest the $1,000 at 8 percent today and it would grow to $1,469 in five years on a pre-tax basis. The two sums, $1,000 today and $1,469 in five years, are equivalent returns in economic terms if the prevailing rate of interest is 8 percent (see Table A.1.)

B. PRESENT VALUE

We approach the time value of money in two ways: the future value of a present sum of money or the present value of a future sum. Although this may seem obtuse, both values are in fact merely different ways of looking at the same thing. The future value is the sum to which an amount, or a series of periodic and equal amounts, will grow at the end of a certain amount of time if compounded at a particular interest rate. The present value is the discounted value at a particular rate of interest of a sum of money to be received in the future. We can restate the compound interest formula as follows:

$$P = F \div ((1 + R)^n)$$

where:

F = the future value of money;
P = the present sum of money;

---

3   *Income Tax Act*, RSC 1985, c 1 (5th Supp), subs 248(11).

R = net interest rate over a period of time; and

n = the number of periods of time.

The more distant the time when an amount has to be paid on account of tax, the lower its present value. Hence, it pays to delay or defer the payment of taxes as long as possible so as to minimize the present value of the obligation today.

For example, the present value of $1 invested at 8 percent at the end of years 1 through to 5 is as follows (see Table A.2):

Year	
1	$0.926
2	$0.857
3	$0.794
4	$0.735
5	$0.681

When we say that the interest rate is 8 percent per year, we mean that we should be able to exchange in the market 92 cents today in return for $1 a year from now and 86 cents in return for $1 two years from now, and so on. Hence, if we defer the obligation to pay $1,000 in taxes today for five years, the present value of the liability to pay is only $681. Although the face amount of the legal obligation to pay remains the same, namely, $1,000 in five years, its economic value varies depending upon when it is paid. The economic value is only $681 if paid today, $735 if paid a year from now, $794 if paid two years from now, and so on.

Stated another way, if we invested $681 in a deposit that compounded tax free at a rate of 8 percent, we would accumulate $1,000 at the end of five years with which to pay the tax liability. By deferring the tax payable for five years we in effect reduce the tax liability by $319.

To continue with the same example: let us assume that we can defer the tax payable for a period of 50 years. The present value of $1,000 payable in 50 years at a discount rate of 8 percent is $21. In other words, if we invest $21 today and compound it for 50 years on a net 8 percent basis, we will have $1,000 at the end of the investment period. The discounted amount shrinks as a function of two factors: time (n) and the discount rate (R). The longer the period of deferral and the higher the interest rate, the lower the discounted present value. Hence, $1,000 payable in 50 years and discounted at 20 percent has a present value today of (effectively) nil.

In determining present and future values, it is important to specify the assumptions underlying the mathematical calculations. Since time value calculations are premised on an interest rate, an error in estimating the rate can significantly distort results. There is no easy way to minimize this risk other than to rely upon responsible predictions. For example, if one earns 10 percent (instead of 12 percent) over 10 years, $10,000 invested in an RRSP would grow to only $25,900 instead of $31,100. The 2 percent difference in interest rates reduces the investment return by $5,200, a reduction of 16.5 percent over 10 years. The longer the investment horizon, the greater the risk that inaccurate assumptions will creep into the reinvestment formula. Hence, long-term retirement plans should be based on conservative estimates of future reinvestment rates.

It is also important in time value calculations to take into account the income tax effect of payments. As noted above, reinvestment rates can vary substantially depending upon whether the funds are invested in a tax shelter or in a currently taxable investment. With marginal tax rates of 50 percent, ignoring taxes can be even more significant than the miscalculation of anticipated inflation.

Table A.1   Compound Amount of $1: Amount to Which $1 Now Will Grow by End of Specified Year at Compounded Interest

Year	3%	4%	5%	6%	7%	8%	10%	12%	15%	20%
1	1.03	1.04	1.05	1.06	1.07	1.08	1.10	1.12	1.15	1.20
2	1.06	1.08	1.10	1.12	1.14	1.17	1.21	1.25	1.32	1.44
3	1.09	1.12	1.16	1.19	1.23	1.26	1.33	1.40	1.52	1.73
4	1.13	1.17	1.22	1.26	1.31	1.36	1.46	1.57	1.74	2.07
5	1.16	1.22	1.28	1.34	1.40	1.47	1.61	1.76	2.01	2.49
6	1.19	1.27	1.34	1.41	1.50	1.59	1.77	1.97	2.31	2.99
7	1.23	1.32	1.41	1.50	1.61	1.71	1.94	2.21	2.66	3.58
8	1.27	1.37	1.48	1.59	1.72	1.85	2.14	2.48	3.05	4.30
9	1.30	1.42	1.55	1.68	1.84	2.00	2.35	2.77	3.52	5.16
10	1.34	1.48	1.63	1.79	1.97	2.16	2.59	3.11	4.05	6.19
11	1.38	1.54	1.71	1.89	2.10	2.33	2.85	3.48	4.66	7.43
12	1.43	1.60	1.80	2.01	2.25	2.52	3.13	3.90	5.30	8.92
13	1.47	1.67	1.89	2.13	2.41	2.72	3.45	4.36	6.10	10.7
14	1.51	1.73	1.98	2.26	2.58	2.94	3.79	4.89	7.00	12.8
15	1.56	1.80	2.08	2.39	2.76	3.17	4.17	5.47	8.13	15.4
16	1.60	1.87	2.18	2.54	2.95	3.43	4.59	6.13	9.40	18.5
17	1.65	1.95	2.29	2.69	3.16	3.70	5.05	6.87	10.6	22.2
18	1.70	2.03	2.41	2.85	3.38	4.00	5.55	7.70	12.5	26.6
19	1.75	2.11	2.53	3.02	3.62	4.32	6.11	8.61	14.0	31.9
20	1.81	2.19	2.65	3.20	3.87	4.66	6.72	9.65	16.1	38.3
25	2.09	2.67	3.39	4.29	5.43	6.85	10.8	17.0	32.9	95.4
30	2.43	3.24	4.32	5.74	7.61	10.0	17.4	30.0	66.2	237

Year	3%	4%	5%	6%	7%	8%	10%	12%	15%	20%
40	3.26	4.80	7.04	10.3	15.0	21.7	45.3	93.1	267.0	1470
50	4.38	7.11	11.5	18.4	29.5	46.9	117	289	1080	9100

To read Table A.1, determine the compounding rate for the applicable number of compounding periods. For example, each dollar invested at 8 percent for five years yields $1.47 if compounding occurs annually at the end of each year. Compounding semi-annually at 4 percent for 10 time periods yields $1.48.

Table A.2 Present Value of $1: What a Dollar at End of Specified Future Year is Worth Today

Year	3%	4%	5%	6%	7%	8%	10%	12%	15%	20%
1	.971	.962	.952	.943	.935	.926	.909	.893	.870	.833
2	.943	.925	.907	.890	.873	.857	.826	.797	.756	.694
3	.915	.890	.864	.839	.816	.794	.751	.711	.658	.578
4	.889	.855	.823	.792	.763	.735	.683	.636	.572	.482
5	.863	.823	.784	.747	.713	.681	.620	.567	.497	.402
6	.838	.790	.746	.705	.666	.630	.564	.507	.432	.335
7	.813	.760	.711	.665	.623	.583	.513	.452	.376	.279
8	.789	.731	.677	.627	.582	.540	.466	.404	.326	.233
9	.766	.703	.645	.591	.544	.500	.424	.360	.284	.194
10	.744	.676	.614	.558	.508	.463	.385	.322	.247	.162
11	.722	.650	.585	.526	.475	.429	.350	.287	.215	.134
12	.701	.625	.557	.497	.444	.397	.318	.257	.187	.112
13	.681	.601	.530	.468	.415	.368	.289	.229	.162	.0935
14	.661	.577	.505	.442	.388	.340	.263	.204	.141	.0779
15	.642	.555	.481	.417	.362	.315	.239	.183	.122	.0649
16	.623	.534	.458	.393	.339	.292	.217	.163	.107	.0541
17	.605	.513	.436	.371	.317	.270	.197	.146	.093	.0451
18	.587	.494	.416	.350	.296	.250	.179	.130	.0808	.0376
19	.570	.475	.396	.330	.277	.232	.163	.116	.0703	.0313
20	.554	.456	.377	.311	.258	.215	.148	.104	.0611	.0261
25	.478	.375	.295	.232	.184	.146	.0923	.0588	.0304	.0105
30	.412	.308	.231	.174	.131	.0994	.0573	.0334	.0151	.00421
40	.307	.208	.142	.0972	.067	.0460	.0221	.0107	.00373	.000680
50	.228	.141	.087	.0543	.034	.0213	.00852	.00346	.000922	.000109

To read Table A.2, determine the discount rate for the applicable number of discounting periods. For example, each dollar receivable in five years is worth only 68 cents today if the discount rate is 8 percent. If the discount rate is 4 percent semi-annually, the value of each dollar falls to 67 cents.

Table A.3 Present Value of Annuity of $1, Received at End of Each Year

Year	3%	4%	5%	6%	7%	8%	10%	12%	15%	20%
1	0.971	0.960	0.952	0.943	0.935	0.926	0.909	0.890	0.870	0.833
2	1.91	1.89	1.86	1.83	1.81	1.78	1.73	1.69	1.63	1.53
3	2.53	2.78	2.72	2.67	2.62	2.58	2.45	2.40	2.28	2.11
4	3.72	3.63	3.55	3.46	3.39	3.31	3.16	3.04	2.86	2.59
5	4.58	4.45	4.33	4.21	4.10	3.99	3.79	3.60	3.35	2.99
6	5.42	5.24	5.08	4.91	4.77	4.62	4.35	4.11	3.78	3.33
7	6.23	6.00	5.79	5.58	5.39	5.21	4.89	4.56	4.16	3.60
8	7.02	6.73	6.46	6.20	5.97	5.75	5.33	4.97	4.49	3.84
9	7.79	7.44	7.11	6.80	6.52	6.25	5.75	5.33	4.78	4.03
10	8.53	8.11	7.72	7.36	7.02	6.71	6.14	5.65	5.02	4.19
11	9.25	8.76	8.31	7.88	7.50	7.14	6.49	5.94	5.23	4.33
12	9.95	9.39	8.86	8.38	7.94	7.54	6.81	6.19	5.41	4.44
13	10.6	9.99	9.39	8.85	8.36	7.90	7.10	6.42	5.65	4.53
14	11.3	10.6	9.90	9.29	8.75	8.24	7.36	6.63	5.76	4.61
15	11.9	11.1	10.4	9.71	9.11	8.56	7.60	6.81	5.87	4.68
16	12.6	11.6	10.8	10.1	9.45	8.85	7.82	6.97	5.96	4.73
17	13.2	12.2	11.3	10.4	9.76	9.12	8.02	7.12	6.03	4.77
18	13.8	12.7	11.7	10.8	10.1	9.37	8.20	7.25	6.10	4.81
19	14.3	13.1	12.1	11.1	10.3	9.60	8.36	7.37	6.17	4.84
20	14.9	13.6	12.5	11.4	10.6	9.82	8.51	7.47	6.23	4.87
25	17.4	15.6	14.1	12.8	11.7	10.7	9.08	7.84	6.46	4.95
30	19.6	17.3	15.4	13.5	12.4	11.3	9.43	8.06	6.57	4.98
40	23.1	19.8	17.2	15.0	13.3	11.9	9.78	8.24	6.64	5.00
50	25.7	21.5	18.3	15.8	13.8	12.2	9.91	8.30	6.66	5.00

This table is a shorthand extension of Table A.2. It shows the cumulative present value of an annual series of equal payments received at the end of each year. For example, the present value of three annual payments of $1 invested at 8 percent is equal to $2.58 today. We can arrive at the same result from Table A.2 by adding together 0.926, 0.857 and 0.794.

TAX RATES

Table B.1 2011 Federal Personal Tax Credits

Indexed Personal Income Tax Parameters	$
Federal Personal Tax Credit Amounts (Non-Refundable Credits)	
Spouse or common-law partner amount [118(1)B(a) and 118(3.2)]	10,527
Amount for an eligible dependant [118(1)B(b) and 118(3.2)]	10,527
Amount for children under age 18 (maximum per child) [118(1)B(b.1)]	2,131
Basic personal amount [118(1)B(c) and 118(3.1)]	10,527
Caregiver amount [118(1)B(c.1)(iii)]	4,282
Caregiver amount net income threshold [118(1)B(c.1)(iii)D.1]	14,624
Infirm dependant amount [118(1)B(d)(ii)]	4,282
Income threshold at which infirm dependant amount begins to phase out [118(1)B(d)(ii)E]	6,076
Age amount [118(2)]	6,537
Income threshold at which age credit begins to phase out [118(2)B]	32,961
Canada employment amount [118(10)B(a)]	1,065
Maximum adoption expense amount per adoption [118.01(2)B(a)]	11,128
Medical expense tax credit (maximum of 3% of net income) [118.2(1) C, F]	2,052
Disability amount [118.3(1)B]	7,341
Supplement for children with disabilities [118.3(1)C(a)(i)]	4,282
Allowable child care and attendant care expenses threshold [118.3(1) C(a)(ii)(B)]	2,508

Indexed Personal Income Tax Parameters	$
Goods and Services Tax Credit	
Adult maximum [122.5(3)A(a), (b), (c)]	253
Child maximum [122.5(3)A(d), (e)]	133
Single supplement [122.5(3)A(f)]	133
Phase-in threshold for the single supplement [122.5(3)A(f)]	8,209
Family net income at which credit begins to phase out [122.5(3)B]	32,961
Refundable medical expense supplement	
Maximum supplement [122.51(2)A(a)]	1,089
Minimum earnings threshold [122.5(1) "eligible individual"]	3,179
Family net income threshold [122.51(2)B(b)]	24,108
Canada Child Tax Benefit	
Base benefit [122.61(1)A(a)]	1,367
Additional benefit for third child [122.61(1)A(b)]	95
Family net income at which base benefit begins to phase out [122.61(1)B(b)]	41,544
National Child Benefit [NCB] Supplement	
First child [122.61(1)C(a)]	2,118
Second child [122.61(1)C(b)(ii)]	1,873
Third child [122.61(1)C(b)(iii)]	1,782
Family net income at which NCB supplement begins to phase out [122.61(1)G]	24,183
Family net income at which NCB supplement phase-out is complete [122.61(1)G]	41,544
Child Disability Benefit	
Maximum benefit [122.61(1)M]	2,504
Family net income at which benefit begins to phase out [122.61(1)M]	41,544
Old Age Security	
Repayment threshold [180.2(2)A(b)]	67,668

Table B.2 Personal Tax Bracket Thresholds

2011 Federal Income Tax Rates	
Taxable Income	Tax
$41,544 or less	15%
$41,544.01 to $83,088.00	$6,232 + 22% on next $41,464
$83,088.01 to $128,800.00	$15,371 + 26% on next $41,544
$128,800.01 or more	$27,256 + 29% on remainder
Registered Retirement Savings Plan Contribution Limits	
2011	$22,450
2012	$22,970

2011 Federal Income Tax Rates	
Tax-Free Savings Account Contribution Limits	
2011	$5,000
Registered Education Savings Plans Limits for 2011	
Lifetime RESP Contribution Limit	$50,000
Lifetime Canada Education Savings Grant (CESG) Limit	$7,200
Amount of CESG	20% of contributions
Maximum Annual CESG (Application after 2006)	
Where maximum CESG *not* received in prior years:	
Low-income ($41,544 and less)	$1,100
Middle-income ($41,545 to $83,088)	$1,050
High-income ($83,089 and more)	$1,000
Where maximum CESG received in prior years:	
Low-income ($41,544 and less)	$600
Middle-income ($41,545 to $83,088)	$550
High-income ($83,089 and more)	$500
2011 CPP Contribution Rates, Maximums and Exemptions	
Maximum annual pensionable earnings	$48,300
Basic exemption	$3,500
Maximum contributory earnings	$44,800
Employee contribution rate	4.95%
Maximum annual employee contribution	$2,218
Maximum annual self-employed contribution	$4,435
2011 Federal EI Premium Rates and Maximums	
Maximum annual insurable earnings (EI)	$44,200
Rate (Federal)	1.78%
Maximum annual employee premium (Federal)	$787
Maximum annual employer premium (Federal)	$1,101

Table B.3 2011 Provincial Personal Tax Rates

Province	Rate
Alberta	10.00%: $0
British Columbia	5.06% : $0
	7.70%: $36,146
	10.50%: $72,293
	12.29%: $83,001
	14.70%: $100,787
Manitoba	10.80%: $0
	12.75%: $31,000
	17.40%: $67,000

New Brunswick	9.10%: $0
	12.10%: 37,150
	12.40%: $74,300
	12.70%: $120,796
Newfoundland and Labrador	7.70%: $0
	12.50%: $31,904
	13.30%: $63,807
Northwest Territories	5.90%: $0
	8.60%: $37,626
	12.20%: $75,253
	14.05%: $122,345
Nova Scotia	8.79%: $0
	14.95%: $29,590
	16.67%: $59,180
	17.50%: $93,000
	21.00%: $150,000
Nunavut	4.00%: $0
	7.00%; $39,612
	9.00%: $79,224
	11.50%: $128,800
Ontario	5.05%: $0
	9.15%: $37,774
	11.16%: $75,550
Prince Edward Island	9.80%: $0
	13.80%: $31,984
	16.70%: $63,969
Quebec	16.00%: $0
	20.00%: $39,060
	24.00%: $78,120
Saskatchewan	11.00%: $0
	13.00%: $40,919
	15.00%: $116,911
Yukon	7.04%: $0
	9.68%: $41,544
	11.44%: $83,088
	12.76%: $128,800

Table B.4 General Corporate Tax Rates

Jurisdiction	General Rate	M&P Rate
Federal		
2011	16.50%	16.50%
1 January 2012 and thereafter	15.00%	15.00%
Alberta	10.00%	10.00%

Jurisdiction	General Rate	M&P Rate
British Columbia 1 January 2011 and thereafter	10.00%	10.00%
Manitoba 1 July 2009 and thereafter	12.00%	12.00%
New Brunswick		
To 30 June 2011	11.00%	11.00%
1 July 2011–30 June 2012	10.00%	10.00%
1 July 2012 and thereafter	8.00%	8.00%
Newfoundland and Labrador	14.00%	5.00%
Northwest Territories	11.50%	11.50%
Nova Scotia	16.00%	16.00%
Nunavut	12.00%	12.00%
Ontario		
To 30 June 2011	12.00%	10.00%
1 July 2011–30 June 2012	11.50%	10.00%
1 July 2012–30 June 2013	11.00%	10.00%
1 July 2013 and thereafter	10.00%	10.00%
Prince Edward Island	16.00%	16.00%
Quebec	11.90%	11.90%
Saskatchewan	12.00%	10.00%
Yukon	15.00%	2.50%

Table B.5 Small Business Tax Rates and Thresholds

Jurisdiction	Small Business Rate for CCPC	Small Business Thresholds
Federal	11.00%	$500,000
Alberta 1 April 2009 and thereafter	3.00%	$500,000
British Columbia 1 January 2010 and thereafter	2.50%	$500,000
Manitoba 1 December 2010 and thereafter	NIL	$400,000
New Brunswick	5.00%	$500,000
Newfoundland and Labrador 1 April 2010 and thereafter	4.00%	$500,000
Northwest Territories	4.00%	$500,000
Nova Scotia 1 January 2011 and thereafter	4.50%	$400,000
Nunavut	4.00%	$500,000
Ontario 1 July 2010 and thereafter	4.5%	$500,000

Jurisdiction	Small Business Rate for CCPC	Small Business Thresholds
Prince Edward Island 1 April 2010 and thereafter	1.00%	$500,000
Quebec 20 March 2009 and thereafter	8.00%	$500,000
Saskatchewan	4.50%	$500,000
Yukon	4.00%	$500,000

MEASUREMENT OF INCOME

A. GENERAL COMMENT

Every tax system needs a method of measuring the base upon which it imposes taxes. Sales taxes, for example, must identify taxable sales of goods and services. Usage taxes, such as highway tolls, must identify the consumer's use of the particular facility. Thus, the key to a good income tax system is the accurate measurement of the taxable base. In the *Income Tax Act* the taxable base is "income."

We saw in Chapter 4 that "income" is a measure of gain over time. Thus, measuring income requires that we identify the amount of the gain and relate it to the appropriate period when we should recognize the gain for tax purposes. As we will see in this chapter, both of these aspects of measurement can be uncertain processes influenced by law, economics and accounting. The measurement of income is more art than science.

Accounting is the art of measuring and presenting financial information. As such, accounting is the language of financial transactions. Users of financial information need to understand this language, regardless of whether they act for business or represent interests that are adverse to business. Lawyers, for example, must deal with accounting problems in the same way they address other issues, with judgment and analysis. This means that lawyers need to understand accounting to draft financial clauses in contracts, to structure negotiated settlements, for advocacy in litigation, for tax purposes and to negotiate damage awards.

As with all languages, accounting has certain fundamental rules of structure and composition. We refer to these rules as the principles of accounting. Contrary to popular conceptions and, perhaps, most fortunately, accountants did not devise the fundamental structural rules of recording financial data. A Renaissance monk named Pacioli devised the basic process of recording financial data. This process allows us to record information in a methodical manner for analysis and decision making.

It is important to note, however, that the principles of accounting are neither rigid nor uniform. Variations in accounting principles make comparisons of financial information difficult. For present purposes, however, we confine our attention to the basic principles of Canadian accounting.

B. ACCOUNTING PRINCIPLES

A taxpayer's income for a taxation year from a business or property is his or her *profit* therefrom for the year.[1] The term "profit" means *net* profit, that is, the amount of revenue remaining after the deduction of expenses incurred for the purpose of earning the revenue.[2] Thus, we need a system of principled accounting for measuring profit.

We speak of generally accepted accounting principles (GAAP) as the principles that underlie the preparation of financial statements for commercial use. We say "generally accepted" because various professional accounting bodies, regulatory agencies, securities commissions and financial institutions generally accept the principles as appropriate for financial statements. In Canada, the *Canadian Institute of Chartered Accountants (CICA) Handbook* is an authoritative source of GAAP. The *Canada Business Corporations Act* and regulatory statutes recognize it as the benchmark of accounting principles. GAAP, however, encompasses not only the specific recommendations and procedures set out in the *Handbook*, but also broad principles and conventions. Thus, if the *Handbook* does not cover a matter, we use other accounting principles that practitioners accept and that are consistent with the *Handbook*. These accounting principles develop over time and through usage.

When the *Handbook* does not cover a matter, accountants refer to other sources of information. For example, the CICA's Emerging Issues

1   *Income Tax Act*, RSC 1985, c 1 (5th Supp) [*ITA*], subs 9(1); subs 9(2) defines "loss."
2   *Montreal Light, Heat & Power Consolidated v MNR*; *Montreal Coke & Manufacturing Co v MNR*, [1940–41] CTC 217 (Ex Ct), aff'd [1942] CTC 1 (SCC), aff'd [1944] CTC 94 (PC).

Committee (EIC) Abstracts, International Accounting Standards, standards promulgated by the Financial Accounting Standards Board (FASB) in the US and accounting literature are useful sources. Unfortunately, these sources do not always agree on what constitutes GAAP. The *Handbook* addresses such potential differences by saying, "the relative importance of these various sources is a matter of professional judgment in the circumstances." In practice, the order of importance of these sources is as follows:

- *CICA Handbook* and EIC Abstracts;
- CICA accounting guidelines;
- Established Canadian practices;
- Recommendations of the FASB in the US;
- International accounting standards; and
- Literature.

Since GAAP represent authoritative guidelines for the preparation and presentation of financial statements for commercial purposes, we need to clearly understand their fundamental premises. These assumptions are the bedrock upon which we interpret financial information.

Net income essentially comprises two components, namely, revenue and expenses during a period of time. We calculate net profit or net income according to the formula:

$$NI = R - E$$

where:

NI = Net Income
R = Revenues
E = Expenses

All measurement of income for commercial purposes begins with this basic formula. The essence of the income statement is matching revenues and expenses over a period of time, usually one year.

The first step in the calculation of net profit is to look to accounting and commercial principles. In *Daley v MNR*, for example:

> . . . the first enquiry whether a particular disbursement or expense is deductible should not be whether it is excluded from deduction by [paragraph 18(1)(a) or (b)] but rather whether its deduction is permissible by the ordinary principles of commercial trading or accepted business and accounting practice. . . .[3]

---

3   *Daley v MNR* (1950), 50 DTC 877 at 880 (Ex Ct) (fee for call to Bar not deductible expense as preceding commencement of the practice of law). See also

See also *Dominion Taxicab Assn v MNR*:

> The expression "profit" is not defined in the Act. It has not a technical meaning and whether or not the sum in question constitutes profit must be determined on ordinary commercial principles unless the provisions of the *Income Tax Act* require a departure from such principles.[4]

C. ACCOUNTING CONCEPTS

Three basic concepts underlie the preparation and interpretation of financial statements: (1) historical cost accounting, (2) stable dollar value, and the (3) going concern assumption. As we will see in subsequent chapters, these concepts also determine tax results.

1) Historical Cost Accounting

We prepare financial statements using historical and original costs to record transactions. Thus, except for the date when we acquire an asset, its cost does not represent the price for which we can replace (replacement cost) or sell it (fair market value). For this reason, historical cost statements, which trade-off relevance for reliability, are of limited value and we use them with caution.

Canada v Metropolitan Properties Co, [1985] 1 CTC 169 (FCTD) (in absence of specific statutory provisions, generally accepted accounting principles applied); *Imperial Oil Ltd v MNR*, [1947] CTC 353 (Ex Ct) (damages paid on negligence settlement incurred as consequence of operations by which business income earned; damages deemed deductible expenses); *Royal Trust Co v MNR* (1957), 57 DTC 1055 (Ex Ct) (club fees allowed executives to meet new clients; expenses need not be directly related to income); *MNR v Frankel Corp Ltd*, [1958] CTC 314 (Ex Ct) (sale of capital assets of one of four of taxpayer's businesses not taxable as inventory sales but, oddly, taxable as deemed receipt because of diversion tactics); *CGE Co v MNR* (1961), [1962] SCR 3 (debts decreased due to change in foreign exchange rate; profit apportioned amongst tax years rather than upon actual payment of note); *MNR v Irwin*, [1964] SCR 662 (concept of profit for tax purposes clarified); *Quemont Mining Corp v MNR*, [1966] CTC 570 (Ex Ct) (disagreement in formula used to calculate mining taxes paid to province); *MNR v Atlantic Engine Rebuilders Ltd*, [1967] SCR 477 (valuation of inventory consistent and coincidentally correct though original basis of evaluation flawed); *Sherritt Gordon Mines Ltd v MNR*, [1968] CTC 262 (Ex Ct) (generally accepted business and commercial principles used in respect of capitalization of interest expenses during construction period).

4   *Dominion Taxicab Assn v MNR* (1954), 54 DTC 1020 at 1021 (SCC).

Although accountants generally report assets at either historical or depreciated cost, they adjust some assets, such as temporary investments, for upward and downward swings in market values. In other cases, such as inventories, we write down assets when their historical cost exceeds their realizable or fair market values. The theory underlying such adjustments is that we expect to realize (sell) inventories in the current term and, therefore, their market value is more relevant than historical cost.

2) Stable Dollar Value

GAAP treats the dollar as a stable unit of measure. Therefore, if a company owns land that it purchased in 1970 for $25,000 and in 2002 it purchased an identical adjacent tract for $500,000, the lands will appear as $525,000 on the balance sheet. This completely overlooks the fact that during the 32-year period the purchasing power of the dollar has substantially declined. Similarly, if the company sold the first plot of land in 2000 for $500,000, we would record a gain of $475,000 on the income statement, even if the $500,000 has no more purchasing power than the $25,000 in 1970. In other words, historical balance sheet values can be meaningless and we need to evaluate them with care. The rationale for continuing to use a constant dollar as a unit of measure is that historical costs are objective. In contrast, financial statements adjusted for changes in purchasing power require subjective judgments in their preparation. This compromises their reliability. Thus, the balance sheet trades off relevance for reliability.

3) The Going Concern Assumption

The going concern assumption means that the entity expects to continue in operation into the indefinite future and, therefore, will realize its assets and discharge its liabilities in the normal course of business. The entity will continue as a "going concern" into the indefinite future. This assumption supports the historical cost basis of accounting. The business can reasonably expect to recoup the cost of its assets during the course of their useful life. If the assumption is not valid, some other model of accounting, for example, the liquidation basis, may be more appropriate. Thus, the basis of valuing assets (historical cost or liquidation value) on the balance sheet must be consistent with expectations for the entity.

D. ACCOUNTING PRINCIPLES AND TAX LAW

Having determined the appropriate treatment of a receipt or expenditure according to commercial and accounting practice, the next step is to determine whether the Act or case law prescribes a different treatment for tax purposes. The minister cannot insist on a taxpayer using a specific method of paying income taxes if the method the taxpayer uses is permissible under well-accepted business principles and is not prohibited by the Act or by some specific rule of law.[5] Although accounting principles are a guide to interpreting tax law, they cannot be used where the Act prescribes otherwise.[6]

Where the Act specifically prohibits the deduction of an expenditure, the statute obviously prevails over commercial and accounting principles and the expenditure is not deductible in computing profit. For example, under generally accepted accounting principles, a taxpayer may deduct depreciation as an expense in calculating income. Depreciation is the allocation of the historical cost of an asset over its useful life. However, since the Act specifically prohibits the deduction of depreciation, any depreciation calculated for financial statement purposes is not deductible as an expense for tax purposes.[7] Thus, for tax purposes, we add back depreciation to financial net income. As we will see later, the Act allows a taxpayer an alternative deduction to allocate asset costs over their useful life. We refer to this deduction as capital cost allowance.

Similarly, case law may also prohibit the use of a particular method of calculating income that is otherwise acceptable in commercial practice. For example, although the last-in, first-out (LIFO) method of valuing inventory is generally acceptable for financial statement purposes, we cannot use LIFO to calculate income for tax purposes.[8]

The Act can, however, also specifically override a general prohibition against the deduction of a type of an expenditure.[9] For example, interest payable on indebtedness would be a non-deductible payment

---

5   *Canderel Ltd v Canada*, [1998] 1 SCR 147 [*Canderel*].
6   *Canada v Consumers' Gas Co*, [1987] 1 CTC 79 (FCA).
7   *ITA*, above note 1, para 18(1)(b).
8   *MNR v Anaconda American Brass Ltd* (1955), 55 DTC 1220 (PC) [*Anaconda*].
9   See, for example, the general prohibitions in *ITA*, above note 1, paras 18(1)(a) (expenditure must be incurred for the purpose of earning income), 18(1)(b) (expenditure cannot be on account of capital), 18(1)(h) (expenditure cannot be on account of personal or living expenses).

on account of capital[10] were it not for paragraph 20(1)(c), which specifically allows for its deduction in computing income from a business or property. This simply reflects the rule of statutory construction that a specific rule prevails over a general rule.

E. MEASUREMENT AND TIMING

Measurement and timing of income are actually two different concepts. There is, however, an inextricable relationship between the concepts. For example, suppose a business started up in 1900 and closed down in 2010. There might be a number of difficulties involved in measuring the aggregate income of the enterprise over the 110 years. If all we need to know is the net income figure for the 110 years, there is no issue of timing. Serious problems of timing arise, however, if we need to measure income for 2010 only. Then, we need to match 2010 revenues and expenses. Thus, we need to know when we earn revenues, when we recognize the revenues in our financial statements and the principles of matching of revenues and expenses.

We can illustrate these problems by examining the accounting concepts of "realization," "recognition," "accrual," "matching" and "conservatism."

1) Realization

As noted earlier, the measurement of income requires one to calculate gain and relate it to the appropriate time period. Generally, we measure gain at the point of its realization.

A simple definition of "realization" would refer to the point of sale, the time at which X parts with property and receives a real gain in the form of cash. The following examples illustrate the inadequacy of this simple definition. If X sells Black Acre and takes back a mortgage, X realizes a gain that should be recognized for tax purposes. Similarly, we treat an exchange of Black Acre for White Acre, a property of equal value, or for stock in Black Acre Developments Ltd, as a realization. Even if X gives Black Acre away, she will realize a gain. In all these

---

10   *Canada Safeway Ltd v MNR*, [1957] SCR 717 (use of borrowed money important in characterization of interest expense as business or property; acquisition of shares of subsidiary complicated issue); *Interprovincial Pipeline Co v MNR*, [1967] CTC 180 (Ex Ct), aff'd [1968] SCR 498 (tax loophole in treaty cured; incidental interest earned deducted from interest expense to determine loss); *Sherritt Gordon Mines Ltd v MNR*, above note 3.

634 INCOME TAX LAW

cases the rationale is the same: X has parted with her investment in Black Acre, and for tax purposes, we treat X as though she sold the property for cash.

There is a fundamental question, however, as to *when* we "realize" a gain or loss. Suppose, for example that X buys Black Acre for $50,000. By the end of the year the property is worth $60,000. Does X experience a $10,000 gain? Certainly she has a potential gain, a "paper gain," an accrued gain in the Haig-Simons sense. Traditional accounting practice, however, ignores the gain as unrealized.

In the following year, X's property might decline in value to $45,000 or might rise to $70,000. Suppose, in either case, that X then sells the property. According to traditional practice, X is treated as "realizing" a $5,000 loss or a $20,000 gain in the year that the property is sold. In the first case, the $5,000 loss represents a $10,000 paper gain in Year 1 combined with a paper loss of $15,000 in Year 2. In the second case, X had a paper gain of $10,000 in each of the years 1 and 2.

2) Recognition

The second aspect of measurement is to identify the appropriate period in which we wish to recognize the gain for tax purposes. "Recognition" is the taking into account of an amount in computing income under the Act. Some accounting systems would recognize all the "paper" gains and losses in a year even though they are "unrealized." For the most part, however, the Act does not recognize "unrealized" amounts for tax purposes.

There are good reasons for not recognizing paper gains. Accountants, true to the axiom of their conservatism in estimating income, normally disregard such gains because they may prove illusory if values decline in a subsequent period. From the perspective of a taxpayer, the recognition of unrealized gains could prove a hardship. If X were required to recognize a $10,000 paper gain on Black Acre, and to pay tax on it, X would be required to find the money to pay the tax at the end of Year 1. Attempts in the past to tax unrealized gains on certain corporate shares met with considerable taxpayer resistance and only limited success.[11]

On the other hand, the failure to recognize paper gains, and recognition of the entire gain at the point of realization, gives rise to problems of irregularity and "lumping" of income. Delayed realization also allows taxpayers to defer and, therefore, save tax.

---

11   Canada, Department of Finance, *Proposals for Tax Reform* (Ottawa: Finance Canada, 1969) at ss 1.30 and 3.36.

There are some cases in which the Act recognizes unrealized gains. For example, the Act deems a taxpayer who ceases to be a Canadian resident to have disposed of any capital property and realized any accrued gain or loss for tax purposes. In other situations, the Act does not recognize a gain even though it has been realized through an actual disposition. For example, the Act does not recognize realized gains when a person transfers appreciated capital property to his spouse. These exceptions reflect other policy considerations in the tax system that override the accurate measurement of income.

Accountants are not as reluctant to recognize unrealized losses as they are to recognize unrealized gains. Consistent with accounting conservatism in estimating income, and depending upon the nature of the asset concerned, it is sometimes considered good accounting practice to recognize a "paper" loss. Understandably, the revenue authorities usually do not agree that this conservatism should be applied to calculations of income for tax purposes. To forestall the possibility of complete accounting doom and gloom in such matters, the Act does not recognize most paper losses for tax purposes.

We have explored, in a very simple way, the concept of realization of gain. There remains a number of slightly more sophisticated problems concerning the time when gains should be recognized.

Suppose that X starts a business of manufacturing and selling widgets. The business cycle can be broken down into the following steps:

1) Acquisition of inventory of raw metal;
2) Fabrication of metal into an inventory of widgets;
3) Sales activity that results in orders for widgets;
4) Delivery of widgets to customers;
5) Invoicing of customers; and
6) Payment of invoices.

An argument could be made for choosing any one of the last five steps as the point at which X's gain should be recognized for the purposes of calculating income. Our earlier discussion would probably suggest that the gain should not be recognized at any point before step 4. Standard accounting would lead to a choice of step 5 as the point at which X should recognize a gain. In any event, as a matter of usual business practice, steps 4 and 5 are merged. Commonly, the invoice accompanies the delivery of widgets. As we shall see below, if X's business adopts a cash basis of accounting, the gain will not be recognized until step 6, when the business actually receives payment.

One of the most important areas of income measurement is revenue recognition. Revenues derive from the sale of products, fees for services, and the use of intellectual property. Thus, the timing of revenues is the first decision in the measurement process. For accounting purposes, we generally recognize revenues at the point when the earning process is substantially complete. The earning process is substantially complete when we pass title to the product to the purchaser, or when we complete the service. At this point, we have sufficient information to measure revenues objectively. The important point to observe here is that revenue does not necessarily relate in the earnings cycle to when we receive cash for the product or service. For example, if a company sells merchandise on credit (payable in thirty days), we recognize the full sales value when we ship the goods to the customer. The fact that the cash may not come in for thirty days or later does not matter. Indeed, in some cases, the customer might even pay in advance for the purchase of the goods. Nevertheless, we recognize revenues only when we ship the goods and title passes from the company to its customer. Until then, we consider the advance to be a debt owing to the customer. At the point of sale, we transform the debt into revenues.

To be sure, this principle of recognizing revenues at the time of sale and shipment does not make a great deal of difference in most cases, except at the end of the accounting cycle. For example, it matters little to a company with a 31 December year-end whether it takes its revenue for July sales into account in July, August or September when it collects its cash from sales. Since all of the revenue falls in the same accounting period, it matters little for measurement purposes so long as the revenue falls in the current year. The principle, however, is critical at the year-end. It makes a great deal of difference whether revenues from sales for merchandise shipped out in mid-December are taken into the current year's income or in the income of the year following. In this case, the timing of revenues affects the company's bottom-line profit for commercial purposes. Of course, it also affects the company's net income for tax purposes and, therefore, the amount of tax payable in the current year. Thus, we need to match revenues and related expenses in the same period.

3) Accrual

The principles of accrual accounting are central to the matching of revenues and expenses. Accrual accounting requires that we recognize revenues in the period to which they relate, rather than when we collect the cash. Similarly, we recognize expenses in the period when we incur the expense, rather than when we pay for it. For example, assume we purchase merchandise on 20 December of the current year and pay for it on 10 January of the following year. Accrual accounting requires us to recognize the purchase in the current year, even though we did not pay for it until the following year.

As we will see, recognizing expenses in the appropriate period depends upon the nature of the expense. We recognize time-related expenses such as salaries and wages, utilities, interest, etc., at the end of the accounting period to which they relate. This is so even though we have not paid the expenses. Again, this may not make a great deal of difference to expenses we incur in the middle of an accounting period, but it can be important in terms of year-end accounting. Here also, accounting principles do not rely upon the outgoing of cash to determine when we take the expenditure into account in the financial books. The essential concept is matching the expense with revenues in the period in which we derive the benefit of the expense to earn the revenues.

4) Matching

So far we have been discussing the appropriate time to recognize gains and losses. In an accounting sense, gains and losses are measured by reflecting expenditures and receipts. "Gains" or "losses" in themselves are net concepts, as is the "income" of a business, since it reflects all expenditures and all receipts.

Accrual and matching are related. The matching principle requires us to deduct expenses (E) in the same period as they contribute to the earning of revenues (R). Hence, if we incur expenses in one time period but the expenses will benefit several periods, we allocate the expense in some reasonable manner between the various periods. This principle lies at the core of the income equation. In other words, the "R" and "E" in the formula must match each other. The "E" must track the "R" so that both match for accounting purposes. For example, assume that a company orders and receives merchandise on 15 December 2012. We allocate the cost of the merchandise to 2012 or beyond depending upon when we sell the goods and pass title. Hence, if we sell the merchandise and recognize revenues in 2012, we also recognize the expenses (cost of goods sold) of the sale in the same year. If, however, the merchandise remains on hand as inventory, we recognize the cost as an asset in the current year. We then recognize the expense when we sell the merchandise in the following year. Thus, expenses are merely consumed assets.

Matching is essentially an allocation process between time periods. We recognize expenses that benefit the current time period in that period. Expenses that will benefit future time periods are "held" in asset accounts. We recognize them in subsequent time periods when we match them against revenues.

Mismatching of revenues and expenses distorts the net income figure and can seriously mislead users of financial statements. Of course, for tax purposes, mismatching leads to tax deferral if we delay recognizing revenues or accelerate recognizing expenses. From a tax perspective, the most extreme scenario is one where the taxpayer delays recognizing revenues and concurrently accelerates the time when he or she charges off the expenses. This might occur, for example, if the taxpayer receives a lump sum for two years' rental that he or she does not recognize until the second year, but recognizes the rental expenses in the first year. Such mismatching would be wrong both for accounting and tax purposes.

The following example illustrates the resolution of the problem of matching.

Assume that City Dairy Ltd delivers milk door to door and for this purpose requires 100 trucks costing $6,000 each. The trucks will have a useful life of approximately 5 years and will be disposed of for $1,000 each at the end of that time. Thus, over the course of 5 years, each truck represents a $5,000 expense of City Dairy's business. If, however, City Dairy bought and expensed 100 trucks in its first business year, it would dramatically distort its income for the year by recognizing the entire cost of $600,000 as an expenditure for that year. This particular problem is resolved by applying the notion of "depreciation" in order to spread the cost that arises from exhaustion of such assets over an appropriate number of years.

Although "matching" is a well-accepted business principle, it is simply an interpretive aid that assists, but is not determinative, in arriving at an accurate picture of the taxpayer's income.[12] We do not need to match if an expenditure does not directly relate to future revenues, or if it relates to future revenues but also refers to benefits realized in the year of expenditure.

---

12   *Canderel*, above note 5 (tenant inducement payment paid to secure ten-year lease from key tenant deductible entirely in year paid rather than over the period of the lease since sufficient benefit (preserved reputation, ensured future income stream, satisfied interim financing requirements) realized in first year to match expense); *Ikea Ltd v Canada*, [1998] 1 SCR 196 (tenant inducement payment received for signing a ten-year lease taxable as income entirely in year received); *Toronto College Park Ltd v Canada*, [1998] 1 SCR 183 (tenant inducement payment paid to secure lease deductible entirely in year made since amortization over period of lease would not present a more accurate picture of income).

5) Conservatism

Conservatism is attitude. Conservatism refers to the accounting profession's approach to measuring profits. Measuring income means allocating costs and values to time periods and then matching revenues and expenses in the periods. Since we do not always know how much to allocate with absolute certainty, measuring profits requires professional judgment. Conservatism requires a cautious approach in allocating values and recognizing revenues and losses. In effect, conservatism means that an enterprise should not recognize revenues before earning them, but should recognize all anticipated losses even before they actually occur. Some call this a pessimistic approach, others say it is merely being prudent. Regardless of the label, conservatism implies caution and prudence. Recognize no gains in advance of realization but recognize all losses at the earliest signal of trouble.

Conservatism and matching can conflict. For example, should we write off research and development costs over time to match revenues through increased sales? The matching principle requires that we recognize research and development as capital costs that we allocate over time as the new products generate revenues. The concept of conservatism, however, dictates prudence. Should we recognize the research expenditures as early as possible without waiting for future revenues that might never materialize? Thus, measuring profit according to accounting principles is fraught with judgment calls that can materially affect an enterprise's bottom line. Indeed, it is entirely possible for two accountants to look at the same set of numbers and arrive at completely different conclusions on net income. Those responsible for the development of tax policy are fully aware of the variances that occur from discretionary judgments. Thus, we see many provisions in the Act that provide for a particular and specific method of measuring profit, regardless of accounting principles. In almost all cases, the Act prescribes a method of measuring profit that is more onerous than that allowed under accounting principles. This is understandable. Given a choice, why would the tax collector prescribe a method of accounting that produces a better result for the taxpayer?

F. ACCOUNTING STATEMENTS

Financial statements provide information about an economic entity's financial performance, economic resources and legal obligations to investors, creditors, management, tax authorities and other regulators.

Thus, we can use financial statements to assess management's performance, predict the entity's ability to generate future cash flows to meet obligations, assess the return to shareholders, and measure tax liabilities.

Accountants prepare four different financial statements:

- The balance sheet;
- The income statement;
- The statement of retained earnings; and
- The statement of changes in financial position.

The explanatory notes to financial statements are also an integral part of the statements.

The two most common accounting statements for tax purposes are the balance sheet and the income statement (sometimes called a statement of profit and loss).

A balance sheet reflects, *as at a particular date*, the condition of the business as it may be judged by a statement of what the business owns (assets) and a statement of its obligations (liabilities).

The liabilities side of the balance sheet is divided into two parts: (1) a statement of indebtedness to outsiders, and (2) a statement of the owner's equity. All business financing must come from two sources — capital and debt. The owner may make an initial contribution of capital to the business and the business may borrow money from a bank or purchase goods on credit. The traditional balance sheet equation:

$$A = L + E$$

(Assets = Liabilities + owner's Equity)

is true because owner's equity is a constantly shifting amount that represents the difference between assets and liabilities. Whatever the owner of the business may in fact have contributed, that owner's equity at any time is simply this difference:

$$E = A - L$$

A business is a distinct entity for accounting purposes. This is so regardless of its legal status. City Dairy Ltd, for example, is both an accounting entity and a legal entity separate from its incorporators. Assuming that X Widgets is a sole proprietorship carried on by X, it is not a distinct entity in law. It is, however, in terms of accounting treatment.

An income statement is a summary of the receipts and expenditures of a business for a stated period of time.

The two statements, the balance sheet and the income statement, are closely inter-related and must be read together in order to present a complete and meaningful picture of the profitability and solvency of a business.

As an illustration, assume that A and B opened a retail business on 1 January Year 1 with each person contributing $2,500, and a bank loan of $10,000. The opening balance sheet as at 1 January Year 1, would appear as follows:

Balance Sheet			
As at 1 January Year 1			
Assets		Liabilities and Equity	
Cash	$15,000	Bank loan	$10,000
		Owner's equity:	
		Capital A	2,500
		Capital B	2,500
	$15,000		$15,000

The first point to observe is that the balance sheet balances: the left side of the statement that lists all the property owned by the business is exactly equal to the right side of the statement that lists its sources of financing. In other words, the left side of the statement informs the reader as to *what* the business owns (assets), and the right side discloses *how* the assets were financed (liabilities and equity). Hence, the above balance sheet informs any reader without further explanation of the statement that the business entity (the retail business) owned $15,000 of property (assets) as at 1 January Year 1, and that it held it in the form of cash. Further, it informs the reader that the firm was financed from two sources, one external (bank loan $10,000) and the other internal (owner's equity $5,000).

The following transactions illustrate the operation of the fundamental accounting equation $A = L + E$:

On 2 January Year 1, the business leased office space at an annual rent of $6,000 and pays two months' rent on that date.

Balance Sheet			
As at 2 January Year 1			
Assets		Liabilities and Equity	
Cash	$14,000	Bank loan	$10,000
Pre-paid rent	1,000	Owner's equity:	
		Capital A	2,500
		Capital B	2,500
	$15,000		$15,000

On 4 January Year 1, the business acquired office furniture at a cost of $3,000, paying $1,500 in cash with a promise to pay the balance in 90 days.

Balance Sheet
As at 4 January Year 1

Assets		Liabilities and Equity	
Cash	$12,500	Accounts payable	$1,500
Pre-paid rent	1,000	Bank loan	10,000
Office furniture	3,000	Owner's equity:	
		Capital A	2,500
		Capital B	2,500
	$16,500		$16,500

On 15 January Year 1, the business hired two employees at a monthly salary of $1,000 each, and paid their salaries for half a month on 31 January Year 1.

Balance Sheet
As at 31 January Year 1

Assets		Liabilities and Equity	
Cash	$11,500	Accounts payable	$1,500
Pre-paid rent	500	Bank loan	10,000
Office furniture	3,000	Owner's equity:	
		Capital A	1,750
		Capital B	1,750
	$15,000		$15,000

During the month of February Year 1, the business provided services and collected $6,000 in cash, again paying its staff $2,000 in salary.

Balance Sheet
As at 28 February Year 1

Assets		Liabilities and Equity	
Cash	$15,500	Accounts payable	$1,500
Office furniture	3,000	Bank loan	10,000
		Owner's equity:	
		Capital A	3,500
		Capital B	3,500
	$18,500		$18,500

Each of the transactions described has been recorded using the fundamental equation: $A = L + E$. The reader sees that the business owns property (assets) that cost $18,500, now held in two forms, cash and office furniture, and that the firm is financed, as at 28 February Year

1, by outsiders to the extent of $11,500, with insiders (owner's equity) providing the balance of $7,000. The balance sheet does not, however, disclose any information as to how and why the owners' interest in the business increased from $5,000 to $7,000 during the two months of operations. Based on the balance sheet alone it would be difficult, if not impossible, for any user to assess the profitability of the business.

Should the owners, A and B, be required to pay income tax on the increase in their equity of $2,000, or on some other amount? We find the answer only in the income statement. The purpose of the income statement is to disclose how a business has performed between two successive points in time. In this sense, it is a connecting link between successive balance sheets. Whereas a balance sheet informs a reader *where* a business stands as at a given time, an income statement reveals *how* the business moved from the opening balance sheet to the closing balance sheet.

Continuing with the previous illustration, the income statement reveals the following information:

Income Statement		
For the *Two Months* ended 28 February Year 1		
Revenue		$6,000
Expenses		
Wages	$3,000	
Rent	1,000	
Net Income:		(4,000)
		$2,000
Allocation of Net Income		
To A at 50% of $2,000 = $1,000		
To B at 50% of $2,000 = $1,000		

This statement now informs the reader how the owner's equity increased by $2,000. Specifically, the business generated revenues of $6,000 and expended $4,000 in the process of generating those revenues, leaving an excess of revenues over expenses (net income) of $2,000. Thus, the purpose of the income statement is to match revenues earned with expenses incurred to generate the revenue. The statement can usually explain the change in the owners' equity between successive points in time. Accounting principles and conventions deal with the methodology behind the task of matching revenues and expenses.

The net income figure derived from the matching process provides a starting point in calculating a taxpayer's income tax liability. One observes this starting point in subsection 9(1) of the *Income Tax Act*: "a taxpayer's income for a taxation year from a business or property is the taxpayer's profit from that business or property for that year." The terms "income" and "profit" are often used interchangeably, and it is now well established that in the absence of specific statutory provisions or judicial doctrine, "profit" is to be computed in accordance with commercial principles.

G. ACCOUNTING METHODS

To this point, the term "income" has been used to denote the excess of revenues earned over expenses incurred to generate those revenues. Hence, in one sense income is an increase in net wealth; conversely, a loss is a decrease in net wealth. This definition is terse and obvious but mathematically demonstrable. The essence of the concept is thereby reduced to "gain during an interval of time." Thus, "gain" is the *sine qua non* of income. While this definition satisfies the purpose of conceptual explanation, it is necessary to adapt it for use in the preparation of financial statements.

1) Time Intervals

As a preliminary matter, it is essential to select the appropriate "interval of time" between successive financial statements. For no other reason than that of administrative convenience, it has been conventionally established that financial statements should be prepared on an annual basis. Thus, annual financial statements for external reporting and tax purposes are now, with limited exceptions, the general statutory rule. It is this statutory requirement of annual reporting that gives rise to several income measurement problems.

2) Cash vs. Accrual Accounting

The first of these measurement problems is to determine whether financial statements should be prepared on a "cash basis" or on an "accrual basis." The principal distinction between the cash and accrual methods of accounting arises in connection with the treatment of accounts receivable and payable. Accounts receivable from customers and employers are not included in income under the cash method until the taxpayer is actually paid. In contrast, accrual method taxpayers must report their income when services are completed and billed, regardless of when the customer actually pays the account. Thus, the distinction between the two is essentially one of timing.

In cash basis accounting, business transactions are recorded at the time, and in the accounting period, when cash is received or disbursed.

Assuming an accounting period of 1 January to 31 December and the sale of merchandise on 15 December Year 1 for $3,000 with payment received on 15 January Year 2, a cash basis business would record and report the $3,000 revenue earned in Year 2. Further assume that the cost of the merchandise to the business was $1,000, paid in cash at time of purchase on 1 December Year 1. A cash basis business would record and report the cost of merchandise sold in Year 1. The effect of the purchase and sale of merchandise would be reflected in the Income Statements of the business as follows:

(Cash Basis)	Year 1	Year 2	Combined
Sales Revenue	$0	$3,000	$3,000
Cost of Merchandise Sold	(1,000)	0	(1,000)
Net Income (Loss)	$(1,000)	$3,000	$2,000

It is worthy of emphasis that, regardless of the accounting method, the combined net income of the business in the circumstances described would always amount to $2,000. The disadvantage of the cash basis method lies, however, in the mismatching in a particular accounting (fiscal) period of revenues earned and expenses incurred to earn those revenues. Thus, Year 1 shows a net loss of $1,000 due to the combined effect of early expense recognition and delayed revenue recognition. A year later the statement shows net income of $3,000 by ignoring the earlier expense write-off. Each of years 1 and 2 viewed in isolation would present a distorted result of the underlying business transaction: an economic increase of $2,000 in net wealth.

We saw earlier that net income can only be determined with absolute accuracy when the reporting period for financial statements covers the entire life of a business. The selection of a shorter period of time than the life of the business changes the task from income determination to estimation of net income. The sacrifice in mathematical accuracy, however, is well justified by the enhanced administrative and business convenience that results from timely financial statements.

The fact that cash basis accounting, in most situations, distorts the financial statements of an entity and more readily conceals the true impact of business transactions has, with very limited exceptions, led to its rejection as an appropriate method of financial reporting. A notable exception is found in the reporting of employment income, which individuals must report on a cash basis. This requirement results from a balancing of the enhanced administrative convenience to the employee, employer, and the Agency, and the minimal distortion that occurs in measuring employment income on a cash basis.

In contrast with the cash basis of accounting, accrual accounting recognizes revenue when it is realized, and expenses are reported in the same time period as the revenues for which they were incurred. The accrual basis is premised on the rationale that reporting revenues earned and expenses incurred in the same accounting period provides a better "matching," and that such "matching" more accurately depicts the underlying business transaction. Using the same figures as in the previous example, an income statement prepared on an accrual basis would disclose the following:

(Accrual Basis)	Year 1	Year 2	Combined
Sales Revenue	$3,000	$0	$3,000
Cost of Merchandise Sold	(1,000)	0	(1,000)
Net Income (Loss)	$2,000	$0	$2,000

Although the combined net incomes of the two years is the same in both the cash basis and accrual basis methods of reporting, the latter method more accurately reflects the increase in net wealth in each period. (The outstanding accounts receivable of $3,000 as at 31 December Year 1 represented a debt that increased net wealth.)

Regardless of when cash is actually received, accrual accounting requires the reporting of revenue in the fiscal period in which it is realized. The rationale that debt, as much as cash, represents an increase in wealth is one that is particularly appropriate to any modern economy. At the same time, the accrual method requires that expenses incurred to earn revenue be matched with corresponding revenues earned in the same fiscal period. The important task remains to determine the criteria for selection of a given time when revenue may be considered to be realized, and thus recognized as earned, in a particular fiscal period.

The accrual method generally prevents tax deferral. For example, if a person pays five years' worth of lease payments in advance, the lump sum is capitalized and written off over a five-year period. Similarly, the lessor will treat the pre-paid rents as an asset and recognize only 1/5 of the lump sum in each of the five succeeding years. Unfortunately, tax and commercial accounting do not always arrive at the same solution. Tax accounting puts the lessor on the cash method and compels her to recognize the full five-year lump sum payment in the year that she receives it. The lessee, however, is not entitled to deduct the lump sum in the year that she pays it, but must spread it out over five years. This asymmetric policy works to the advantage of the government and against the taxpayer.

3) Tests for Revenue Recognition

Two tests determine the selection of the appropriate time period for revenue recognition. First, the major economic activity concerned with the earning process must have been substantially completed. Second, there should be some objective measurement available. Thus, revenue should only be recognized when major uncertainties in respect of its measurement have been substantially resolved.

When one examines these criteria it is easy to see the rationale for selection of point of sale as the most usual time of revenue recognition. In most merchandising and service businesses, the point of sale represents completion of the major portion of economic activity. In these situations the point of sale is assumed to be the primary economic event and it provides an objective measurement yardstick; namely, sale price.

At the same time a sale generates a flow of assets that converts inventory into accounts receivable. Concurrently with the objective measurement of revenue, related expenses are determinable with reasonable certainty, and any remaining uncertainty is reduced, for pragmatic purposes, to an acceptable level. Finally, the point of sale is clear and determinable. For all these reasons, time of sale is considered to be the point of revenue recognition in most business transactions.

4) Accounting Adjustments

Let us assume that X Widgets is preparing its accounting statements for its fiscal year ending 31 October Year 1. Some special accounting entries are required to implement the system of accruing expenses incurred and revenue earned, in order to comply with the matching principle. In the preceding section we saw that entries are made when an invoice is received or rendered, even though no cash changes hands. At the year-end, some special entries are required to reflect expense or income that has accrued but as to which no transaction is currently taking place. These entries are designed to adjust the "timing" and recognition of expenses and revenue. A further group of entries may also be made to adjust the "measurement" of revenues or expenses.

a) The "Timing" Adjustments
Some transactions that give rise to normal accounting entries represent expense or revenue for a period that straddles the year-end. Assume the following about X Widgets:

1) On 1 July Year 1 it paid a $900 premium for insurance for one year to 30 June Year 2;

2) Its employees are paid monthly on the 15th of the month and the monthly salary expense is $8,000;
3) It holds a Canada Savings Bond that pays $1,200 interest each 30 November;
4) It rents an unused part of the land adjacent to its building to a company that parks its trucks there. The annual rent is $1,200, paid each 31 January and 31 July in advance.

To avoid a misstatement of the expenses and revenues for the year ending 31 October Year 1, four adjustments are necessary:

1) A reduction in insurance expense to reflect the fact that 2/3 of the insurance benefit paid for in July still remains;
2) An increase in salary expense to reflect the ½ month's labour already enjoyed by the business, but which will not be paid for until 15 November;
3) An increase in investment income to reflect the 11/12 of the bond interest accrued to 31 October; and
4) A decrease in rental income to reflect the receipt of three months' rent not yet earned.

The following four adjusting entries will be made:

1) Insurance expense will be reduced by $600 and a balance sheet asset, "prepaid expense," will be set up;
2) Salary expense will be increased by $4,000 and a balance sheet liability, "salary expense payable," will be set up;
3) Investment income will be increased by $1,100 and a balance sheet asset, "accrued bond interest," will be set up; and
4) Rental income will be reduced by $300 and a balance sheet liability, "rent received in advance," will be set up.

b) The "Measurement" Adjustments

It is consistent with accounting conservatism to recognize, at the year-end, that the value of some of the business assets may be overstated and therefore, that business profitability may be exaggerated.

One of the most obvious adjustments to correct for this danger is an allowance for doubtful debts. If X Widgets shows $20,000 in accounts receivable at the year-end, it may well be realistic to predict that some of the debts will never be collected. On that assumption, the balance sheet asset, "Accounts Receivable," would be reduced by an amount (referred to as an allowance for doubtful accounts) that would also reduce the current year's income.

A business may face many contingencies and hazards which a careful accountant and a prudent business manager would like to provide for by making similar "allowances." All of them will have the effect of reducing the statement of current profitability. It may be obvious that the revenue authorities are not prepared to be as gloomy in their forecasting of business hazards, and that the Act will not permit, for the purpose of reporting income for taxation, all of the allowances that the accountant and the business manager might wish.

One adjustment that must be mentioned is the allowance for depreciation. In our earlier hypothetical situation, City Dairy will experience, over five years, a cost of $500,000 in respect of its fleet of trucks. To allocate this cost appropriately in order to match expense and revenue, it may reflect a depreciation expense of $100,000 at the end of each year. This is essentially a "timing" adjustment designed to spread a large cost over the appropriate accounting periods. There is, however, an element of measurement involved: both the assumed useful life of the trucks and their assumed salvage value are based on estimates.

H. OTHER ACCOUNTING METHODS

Some businesses involve such unusual features that the standard accrual basis of accounting fails to achieve an appropriate matching of expenses and revenues. For example, some businesses involve a high volume of sales on terms that call for instalment payments over an extended period of time. Such a business may have significant costs associated with the selling activity but, notionally, a large "profit margin" as judged by the difference between selling price and cost of sales. The incidence of uncollectible accounts in such a business, however, is usually higher than for most other businesses. At best, the accounts are not "receivable" on a current basis, but are going to be received over a much longer period than is usual for businesses generally. This kind of business might adopt the instalment method of accounting which does not recognize the accounts receivable in revenue. In effect, the business uses a hybrid accounting system, which recognizes all expenses except the cost of goods sold on an accrual basis, but recognizes revenue on a cash basis by ignoring its accounts receivable.

Other businesses carry on long-term projects that may involve several years' work to complete. Payment for work completed may be by way of advances or there may be significant delay in receiving payment; and there may be a holdback to satisfy liens or to give the payer a guaranteed opportunity to judge whether the work is satisfactory. Again, because of the difficulty of appropriately matching expenses and revenues, such a business may use a "completed contract" method of accounting.

I.   BASIC INCOME TAX ACCOUNTING

1)   Accounting Period

The division of a business lifetime into arbitrary segments gives rise to problems of accurate income calculation. A taxpayer's lifetime is similarly segmented into annual periods and this segmentation also gives rise to some special problems.

The Act prescribes for individuals a tax year coincident with the calendar year. Corporations are allowed to choose their own fiscal periods for tax purposes.[13]

Businesses carried on in partnership or as a sole proprietorship, although distinct accounting entities, do not have a separate legal personality and are not taxpayers as such. The income from such businesses must be reported by the partners or the proprietor in their personal capacity. The business may, however, use a fiscal period that is different from the calendar year. For example, X Widgets will calculate its income for its fiscal year ending 31 October 2004; that income will be included in X's income for the 2004 taxation year.[14] This means that any income earned in 2004 by X Widgets after 1 November 2004, need not be reported until X files a 2005 tax return in the spring of 2006.

2)   Accounting Methods

a)   General Comment
While employees must report their income according to the cash basis of accounting, businesses are generally required to use the accrual method. The accrual method is considered particularly appropriate for a trading business.[15] There are, however, other methods of accounting that may be more appropriate for some businesses, particularly businesses with peculiar or unique cash flow patterns.

b)   Instalment Sales
As noted above, for tax accounting, a variation of the accrual method may be adopted by certain sales businesses. The instalment method of

---

13   *ITA*, above note 1, subss 249(1) and 249.1.
14   *Ibid*, s 11.
15   *Ken Steeves Sales Ltd v MNR*, [1955] CTC 47 (Ex Ct).

accounting, for example, is considered appropriate for a taxpayer whose business involves instalment sales requiring a small down-payment with the balance due over an extended period.[16]

c) Completed Contract

In contrast, the completed contract method of accounting has been rejected for tax purposes although it might be an appropriate accounting method. Under this method, the taxpayer defers recognition of all expenses and all revenues in respect of long-term contracts until the contract is complete.[17]

d) Cash

Income from office or employment is usually reported on a cash basis. This is confirmed by the use of the words "received" and "enjoyed" in sections 5 and 6 of the Act.

The decision to allow certain taxpayers to use the cash method of accounting is based primarily on a concern for administrative convenience. It would be quite difficult, if not impossible, for millions of employees to prepare their annual income tax returns on an accrual basis of accounting. The accrual basis requires at least some rudimentary knowledge of accounting principles (realization, timing, etc.) that is beyond the inclination of most non-accountants.

It is also important to remember that accrual basis statements require more careful auditing by the tax authorities. Since employee income tax returns represent approximately 80 percent of all tax returns filed, mandatory accrual basis returns from all taxpayers would place an intolerable burden on the CRA's resources. The incremental auditing and accounting fees incurred by both taxpayers and the CRA as a result of accrual accounting cannot be justified by the marginal improvement in the accuracy of annual net income calculations.

Having said that, however, it is important to note that the requirement of cash accounting for employees does allow for some modest amount of tax planning. Employees can, within limits, reduce their immediate tax liabilities by accelerating payment of their expenses and delaying receipt of their income.

It is important to note, however, that in determining income for tax purposes under the cash method, an individual must include not only the cash that he receives in the year, but also any other payments that the individual constructively receives in the year. Thus, the cash

---

16 *MNR v Publishers Guild of Canada Ltd* (1957), 57 DTC 1017 (Ex Ct).
17 *Wilson & Wilson Ltd v MNR*, [1960] CTC 1 (Ex Ct).

method of accounting includes in income both actual and constructive receipts. The essence of the constructive receipts doctrine is that an individual cannot postpone recognizing income simply by failing to exercise his power to collect it. For example, although an individual can delay actual payment beyond the year-end, he cannot avoid including an amount in income merely by waiting until the next year to pick up his paycheque.

The distinction between the two situations is subtle but significant. In the first case, the taxpayer does not have the power to cash, or otherwise control, the cheque because he does not receive it until after the year-end. In the second case, the taxpayer constructively possesses the cheque, but chooses not to exercise his power of possession in order to delay including the amount in income.

These distinctions are particularly important in closely-held corporations. Where an owner-manager of a corporation performs services for the corporation, she is entitled to payment for services. Although the owner exercises discretion as to the timing of the payment, the salary is not considered to be paid until the owner has the corporation's cheque in her possession. Thus, merely because the owner controls the timing of the cheque does not mean that payment to her is accelerated to a point in time before the corporation actually issues the cheque.

To be sure, this allows owner-managers of corporations considerable flexibility in arranging their annual compensation through salary and bonuses. Depending upon the prevailing rates of tax for a particular year, an owner can elect to accelerate or defer salary payments in order to maximize his or her after-tax returns. This form of tax avoidance is a small price to pay for what would otherwise become an impossibly complex accounting system for employees. Similarly, the owner-manager may choose to forego some or all of his or her salary in a year. The amount forgone, however, is not imputed to the individual merely because he or she was entitled to the amount. We do not impute taxable salaries to controlling shareholders.

e) Accrual

In contrast with the requirement of cash basis accounting for employment income, business and property income is usually required to be reported on an accrual basis. The Act does not specifically stipulate a particular method for calculating business or property income. Section 9 says only that a taxpayer's income from a business or property is her profit therefrom. The term "profit," however, has been judicially interpreted to mean profit calculated in accordance with commercial practice, and commercial practice favours accrual accounting for most businesses. Hence, the accrual method is mandated indirectly through the requirement to adhere to generally accepted accounting principles.

f) Modified Accrual

There are certain specific departures from the usual rule that business and property income is calculated in accordance with the rules of accrual accounting. First, an important exception is made in the case of farmers and fishers; these two categories of taxpayers are specifically authorized to use the cash basis method of accounting.[18] The theoretical justification for this particular variation is that, in most circumstances, the distortion of net income when using the cash basis method is minimal and, hence, justifiable in that it is easier for these taxpayers to maintain cash basis books of account.

More pragmatically, one recognizes that it would be politically inconvenient to withdraw a tax concession that has been made available to farmers for so long. If anything, the pull is in the opposite direction. Until 1980 only farmers could use the cash basis of accounting; in that year the cash basis of accounting was extended to fishers, a practice that had been administratively tolerated by the CRA for many years.

A second exception from the accrual basis of accounting is found in the "modified accrual method" applicable to professionals. Professionals, like their business counterparts, are required to calculate income on an accrual basis. Professionals can, however, elect to exclude their work-in-progress in calculating net income for tax purposes.[19]

g) Holdbacks

We have already stated that, in applying the accrual basis of accounting, the time of sale of goods and services is usually the most convenient time to recognize revenue. The time of sale is not, however, the only time for revenue recognition. Certain businesses may deviate from the norm and recognize revenue at some other time. For example, contractors (persons engaged in the construction of buildings, roads, dams, bridges and similar structures) can, by administrative grace, defer recognition of their income until such time as "holdback payments" become legally receivable.[20] This rule varies from the usual accrual accounting test, which does not use legal entitlement as the determining criterion for recognizing revenue. Contractors may, however, also accelerate the recognition of profit by bringing into income amounts that may not be legally receivable by virtue of a mechanics' lien or similar statute.

---

18   *ITA*, above note 1, s 28.
19   *Ibid*, para 34(a).
20   See Interpretation Bulletin IT-92R2, "Income of Contractors " (1 January 1995).

h) Net Worth

To this point, we have discussed the more conventional methods of income determination—cash basis, accrual accounting and modified accrual. There remains one other technique for calculating income, which can be particularly painful to a taxpayer and particularly useful to the CRA. This technique is the "net worth" method of calculating income.

A net worth assessment is usually issued by the CRA when a taxpayer does not file a return or, in some cases, when the Agency does not accept the taxpayer's figures.[21] The theoretical principle underlying the calculation of income using the net worth basis is simple: income is equal to the difference between a taxpayer's wealth at the beginning and at the end of a year, plus any amount consumed by the taxpayer during the year. We saw in Chapter 5 that this principle derives from the Haig-Simons definition of income.

Algebraically, the principle is stated as follows:

$$Income = (WE - WB) + C$$

where:

WE = Wealth at end of year,

WB = Wealth at beginning of year, and

C = Consumption

Note, however, that, unlike the Haig-Simons formulation of income, the formula does not take into account any accrued but unrealized gains in the value of property.

Assume that a taxpayer started out a year owning $100,000 in property, such as a house, car, clothing, furniture, cash, etc. At the end of the year it is estimated that the taxpayer owns $105,000 in property. It is also estimated that the taxpayer spent $45,000 during the year on food, clothing, mortgage payments, vacations, children's education, etc. If the taxpayer has not engaged in any borrowing or repayment of loans, her net income for the year is $50,000; that is, ($105,000–$100,000) + $45,000. If in fact, the taxpayer borrowed $8,000 during the year, her wealth at the end of the year is only $97,000 and her income for the year would be only $42,000.

Notice the resemblance between the net worth basis of determining income and the Haig-Simons concept of income.[22] When a taxpayer does not, or cannot, use conventional accounting records to calculate her income and the CRA does not have any other way of assessing the

---

21   *ITA*, above note 1, subs 152(7).

22   See Chapter 4.

delinquent taxpayer's income, the system must rely on fundamental concepts: income is the money value of the net accretion of economic power between two points of time.

3) Generally Accepted Accounting Principles

The Act determines income from business or property by reference to subsection 9(1):

> Subject to this Part, a taxpayer's income for a taxation year from a business or property is the taxpayer's profit from that business or property for that year.

At one time there was a tentative proposal to incorporate into the Act a general statement to the effect that business profits should be calculated according to GAAP. The proposal was never implemented because of the difficulty in establishing just what GAAP means in all cases. The absence of a statutory provision requiring the computation of profits according to GAAP did not, however, inhibit the development of a similar doctrine in case law. Indeed, if anything, we have arrived at virtually the same result through judicial decisions.

a) Section 9

Although there may be disagreement among accountants concerning the best practice in respect of certain matters, it is now well established that section 9 imports into the Act, at least as a starting point, the standard accounting methods used in the business world. Thorson P dealt with this matter in *Imperial Oil v MNR*,[23] in *Daley v MNR*[24] and in *Royal Trust Co v MNR*.[25] In this last case, dealing with the deductibility of a claimed expenditure, he said:

> . . . it may be stated categorically that . . . the first matter to be determined . . . is whether it was made or incurred by the taxpayer in accordance with the ordinary principles of commercial trading or well accepted principles of business practice.[26]

The important point, however, is that the determination of "net profit" is a question of law and not a matter of generally accepted ac-

---

23   *Imperial Oil v MNR*, above note 3.
24   *Daley v MNR*, above note 3.
25   *Royal Trust Co v MNR*, above note 3; see also *Canada v Metropolitan Properties Co*, above note 3 (GAAP normal rule for measuring income).
26   *Royal Trust Co v MNR*, *ibid* at 1060.

counting principles.[27] Although a court may look at the treatment of particular items by reference to GAAP, they are at best only representative of the principles used for preparing financial statements. GAAP may influence the calculation of income only on a case-by-case basis.[28] To be sure, GAAP may well be influential in determining what is deductible, but they are not the operative legal criteria. Thus, subsection 9(1) represents a starting point and normal accounting practices for tax purposes may be overborne by specific statutory provisions, judicial precedent, or commercial practice.[29]

b) Tax Profits

What is the relationship between accounting profit and profit as determined for income tax purposes? For tax purposes, the starting point requires an examination of generally accepted commercial practice. Is a particular expenditure deductible in computing income according to the rules of general commercial and accounting practice? Or is a particular receipt included in computing income according to commercial rules? Once these preliminary questions are answered, other factors may come into play in determining the appropriate tax treatment.

Take depreciation as an example.[30] The general commercial and accounting rule is that, in calculating net income, a reasonable amount of depreciation can be deducted from revenues. Indeed, commercial practice recognizes many different methods of calculating depreciation (for example, straight-line, declining balance, sum of the years, etc.). Provided that the method is acceptable and the amount is reasonable, depreciation expense is a deductible expense in determining net income for financial statement purposes.

The Act, however, *specifically* prohibits a deduction for depreciation[31] and, therefore, such an expense cannot be taken into account in calculating net income for tax purposes. In lieu of depreciation, the Act allows a deduction for capital cost allowance (CCA) in an amount

---

27 *Symes v Canada*, [1993] 4 SCR 695; *Neonex International Ltd v Canada*, [1978] CTC 485 (FCA).
28 *Canderel*, above note 5.
29 See, generally: *Associated Investors of Canada Ltd v MNR*, [1967] CTC 138 (Ex Ct) [*Associated Investors*]; *Neonex International Ltd v Canada*, above note 27; *Canada v Metropolitan Properties Co Ltd*, above note 23; *MHL Holdings Ltd v MNR*, [1988] 2 CTC 42 (FCTD); *Coppley Noyes & Randall Ltd v MNR*, [1991] 1 CTC 541 (FCTD); and *West Kootenay Power & Light Co v MNR* (1991), 92 DTC 6023 (FCA) [*West Kootenay*].
30 Numerous other examples may be found in Subdivision b of Division B, Part I of the *ITA*, above note 1.
31 *Ibid*, para 18(1)(b).

which may or may not be related to accounting depreciation. Thus, tax profits and accounting income may be substantially different.

c) Statutory Deviations

The Act deviates from accounting principles in many areas. Three important statutory deviations from standard accounting practice are discussed below.

i) Reserves and Allowances

Accountants sometimes prefer to anticipate certain contingencies by setting up an allowance that has the effect of reducing income in the current period. The Act seriously inhibits this conservative and quite normal accounting practice by denying, as a deduction, "an amount transferred or credited to a reserve, contingent account or sinking fund except as expressly permitted by this Part."[32] Instead, the Act sets out a specific and rigid regime in respect of accounting for reserves. Thus, there can be a significant difference between accounting reserves and tax reserves.

ii) Depreciation

At one time, depreciation expense was recognized as a legitimate deduction for tax purposes, subject to showing a sound accounting basis for the deduction. As we have noted, it is indisputable that many capital assets depreciate with use, but the amount of loss in value and the rate at which it occurs are frequently quite speculative. To control the speculations, and to minimize disputes, the Act details a CCA system, which imposes limits on the amount of depreciation deductible in calculating income for tax purposes.

Although, in general, CCA rates are designed to be reasonably realistic, the system is Procrustean. There is no attempt to guarantee that the rates for tax purposes conform to depreciation recognized for accounting purposes. The rates are the same for all taxpayers although their depreciation experience may differ greatly. Further, the CCA system is also used to achieve other socio-economic objectives. It may, for example, be used to stimulate economic activity in depressed regions of the country. Thus, income for tax purposes can differ quite significantly from income reported to shareholders or creditors, and there is nothing unusual or improper in this.

---

32   *Ibid*, para 18(1)(e).

iii) Inventory

A major component of the expenses of some businesses, and thus a major factor in determining income, is the cost of goods sold. To calculate the cost of goods sold, a business must establish its inventory of goods on hand at the year-end, and determine its value. There are a number of accounting approaches to inventory valuation. One method that is commonly used by accountants for financial statement purposes, the last-in, first-out (LIFO), has been judicially rejected for tax purposes as being inappropriate.[33] Here once again, the use of one method for accounting and another for tax purposes can cause a significant difference in the final net income figure.

4) Realization and Recognition of Income

There are many problems relating to realization and the appropriate time to recognize income for tax purposes. Some of these problems are simply difficulties inherent in the nature of the transaction, but others arise from attempts by taxpayers to apply the realization concept to their best advantage.

Stock options are an example of the inherent difficulty in correctly applying the concepts of realization and revenue recognition in tax law. Suppose that ABC Ltd gives employee E an option to buy 1,000 shares of its stock at a price of $10/share, exercisable at any time within three years. The option is given in Year 1 at a time when the stock is trading publicly at $12 per share. E exercises the option in Year 2 when the stock is trading at $15 per share. In Year 3, E sells the stock for $16 per share.

Assuming that the transaction gives rise to income in E's hands, two questions arise: (1) how much income? and (2) in what year? It is arguable that E should be treated as having received $2,000 in Year 1; the company conferred on E, in that year, a benefit in the form of an opportunity to buy for $10,000 what a stranger would pay $12,000 to acquire. It is also arguable, however, that E's benefit is purely potential; if the stock drops below $10 and stays down for three years the option will be worthless.

It could be said that the benefit was received in Year 2 when E actually bought the stock at $5,000 below its market value. Our discussion of the conventional approach to paper gains might suggest, however, as a third alternative, that E should not recognize any income until he or she sells the shares or otherwise parts with them. If the shares rise or fall in value before E parts with them, the actual benefit

---

33   *Anaconda*, above note 8.

to E will be greater or less, accordingly. Using this reasoning, we would tax E in Year 3 on income of $6,000.

The Act provides an arbitrary, but reasonable, solution to the two problems of timing and quantification. Subsection 7(1) generally recognizes E's income in the year in which he or she exercises the option or disposes of it. The amount of income is either the difference between the option price and the current value of the shares or the amount received on disposition of the option.[34] Thus, in our hypothetical situation, E would recognize $5,000 of income in Year 2. This solution really involves identifying the option as the source of E's gain. It is consistent with our basic discussion of realization to say that E's gain is only a paper gain so long as E holds the option, but becomes a real gain when he or she parts with the option by exercising it or disposing of it to someone else.

5) Conformity of Accounting Methods

A taxpayer's income for a taxation year from a business or property is the profit therefrom for the year.[35]

a) Use of Generally Accepted Accounting Principles

The term "profit" means net profit. In the absence of any specific proscription, profit is determined according to commercial and generally accepted accounting principles. Hence, absent an express or implicit statutory or judicial proscription against the use of a particular accounting method, a taxpayer may determine income for tax purposes according to any appropriate accounting method. Thorson P explained the rule in *MNR v Publishers Guild of Canada Ltd*:

> If the law does not prohibit the use of a particular system of accounting then the opinion of accountancy experts that it is an accepted system and is appropriate to the taxpayer's business and most nearly accurately reflects his income position should prevail with the Court if the reasons for the opinion commend themselves to it.[36]

---

34   Actually, *ITA*, above note 1, subs 7(1) is somewhat more complex to provide against artificial dealings through non-arm's length transactions. Further, subs 7(1.1) provides for different treatment in the case of Canadian-controlled private corporations and subs 7(8) addresses shares of publicly listed companies.

35   *Ibid*, subs 9(1).

36   *MNR v Publishers Guild of Canada Ltd*, above note 16 at 1018; see also *Canada v Nomad Sand and Gravel Ltd* (1990), 91 DTC 5032 at 5034–35 (FCA); *Associated Investors*, above note 29; *Maritime Telegraph & Telephone Co v MNR* (1991), 91 DTC 5038 at 5039 (FCTD), aff'd [1992] 1 CTC 264 (FCA) [*Maritime Telegraph*].

Similarly, in *Silverman v MNR*:

> . . . the statute does not define what is to be taken as the profit from
> a business, nor does it describe how or by what method such profit
> is to be computed, though it does contain provisions to which, for
> income tax purposes, any method is subject . . . the method must be
> one which accurately reflects the result of the year's operation, and
> where two different methods, either of which may be acceptable for
> business purposes, differ in their results, for income tax purposes
> the appropriate method is that which most accurately shows the prof-
> it from the year's operations.[37]

Ultimately, however, the measure of profit is a question of law.

b) Conformity of Methods

A taxpayer can use one generally accepted accounting method for financial statement purposes and another for income tax purposes. In
the absence of any statutory requirement that a taxpayer use the same
method of accounting to calculate income both for tax and financial
statement purposes, a taxpayer can select the most appropriate method
of accounting for tax purposes.

The purpose for which income is calculated determines the appropriate method of accounting. An accounting method which is suitable
for a particular purpose is not necessarily the appropriate measure of
income for tax purposes.[38]

What is appropriate for tax purposes? The general rule is to apply
that principle or method which provides the proper picture of net income. In MacGuigan J's words:

---

37   *Silverman v MNR* (1960), 60 DTC 1212 at 1214 (Ex Ct); see also *Bank of Nova
     Scotia v Canada* (1979), 80 DTC 6009 at 6013 (FCTD):

> . . . generally recognized accounting and commercial principles and prac-
> tices are to be applied to all matters of commercial and taxation accounting
> unless there is something in the taxing statute which precludes them from
> coming into play. The legislator when dealing with financial and commercial
> matters in any enactment, including of course a taxing statute, is to be pre-
> sumed at law to be aware of the general financial and commercial principles
> which are relevant to the subject-matter covered by the legislation. The Act
> pertains to business and financial matters and is addressed to the general
> public. It follows that where no particular mention is made as to any varia-
> tion from common ordinary practice or where the attainment of the objects
> of the legislation does not necessarily require such variation, then common
> practice and generally recognized accounting and commercial principles and
> terminology must be deemed to apply.

38   *Friedberg v Canada*, [1993] 4 SCR 285.

... it would be undesirable to establish an absolute requirement that there must always be conformity between financial statements and tax returns and I am satisfied that the cases do not do so. *The approved principle* is that whichever method presents the "truer picture" of a taxpayer's revenue, which more fairly and accurately portrays income, and which "matches" revenue and expenditure, if one method does, is the one that must be followed.[39]

c) A "Truer Picture" of Income?

It is not always easy to apply the rule that a taxpayer may adopt whichever accounting method presents the "truer picture" of revenues and expenses. There are cases where a particular accounting principle presents a "truer picture" for income statement purposes at the expense of some accuracy or relevance in the balance sheet. In other cases, the adoption of a particular accounting method more accurately summarizes a taxpayer's closing balances while sacrificing accuracy on the income statement. *West Kootenay Power & Light Co v MNR*[40] rightly emphasized a proper matching of revenues and expenses and accuracy of the net income figure for tax purposes. Ultimately, however, the computation of profit for tax purposes is a question of law.[41]

A classic example of the conflict between income statement and balance sheet values is seen in accounting for inventory values. Under the last-in, first-out (LIFO) method of inventory accounting, the cost of goods most recently purchased or acquired is the cost that is assigned to the cost of goods sold. Hence, the inventory on hand at the end of an accounting period is valued at the cost that was attributed to the inventory at the beginning of the period (first-in, still here). Any increases in quantity during a period are valued at the cost prevailing during the time the accumulations are deemed to have occurred. Any decreases in quantities are considered to have first reduced the most recent accumulations.[42]

Under the first-in, first-out (FIFO) method, the process is reversed: the cost of goods first acquired is assigned to the first goods sold. The closing inventory comprises the cost of the most recent purchases (last-in, still here).

---

39 *West Kootenay*, above note 29 at 6028 [emphasis added]. See also *Maritime Telegraph*, above note 36 (FCA) ("earned method" of reporting income for accounting and tax purposes produced "truer picture" of taxpayer's income).

40 *West Kootenay*, ibid.

41 *Canderel*, above note 5; *Ikea Ltd v Canada*, above note 12; *Toronto College Park Ltd v Canada*, above note 12.

42 See Canadian Institute of Chartered Accountants, *CICA Handbook*, loose-leaf (Toronto: Canadian Institute of Chartered Accountants, 2010–) at §3030.07.

The use of the FIFO method of accounting for the flow of inventory costs tends to overstate net income during inflationary periods and more accurately reflect the current value of closing inventory on the balance sheet. In contrast, the LIFO method more realistically measures "real" net income, while sacrificing some accuracy in year-end balance sheet values.

Most accountants and business people argue that the use of LIFO for inventory accounting during inflationary periods results in a more meaningful and "truer picture" of business income during inflationary periods. The Privy Council in *MNR v Anaconda American Brass Ltd* (*Anaconda*),[43] however, rejected the use of the LIFO method of inventory valuation for tax purposes. Their Lordships were concerned that the method would permit the creation of hidden reserves:

> . . . the evidence of expert witnesses, that the L.I.F.O. method is generally acceptable, and in this case the most appropriate, method of accountancy, is not conclusive of the question that the Court has to decide. That may be found as a fact by the Exchequer Court and affirmed by the Supreme Court. The question remains whether it conforms to the prescription of the *Income Tax Act*. As already indicated, in their Lordships' opinion it does not.[44]

The accounting principle for selecting the proper method of inventory valuation is clear: the most suitable method for determining cost is that which results in charging against operations those costs that most fairly match the sales revenue for the period. The *CICA Handbook* states the principle as follows:

> The method selected for determining cost should be one which results in the fairest matching of costs against revenues regardless of whether or not the method corresponds to the physical flow of goods.[45]

Anaconda was an unfortunate decision based upon a misunderstanding of accounting methods. The decision rests on two notions: (1) the physical flow of inventory determines values; and (2) the potential for creation of "hidden" reserves. Both premises are fundamentally flawed. The determination of cost does not depend upon the physical flow of goods but on the fairest matching of revenues and expenses. The "fairest" matching of costs against revenues is, presumably, also the method

---

43   *Anaconda*, above note 8.
44   *Ibid* at 1225.
45   See *CICA Handbook*, above note 42 at §3030 and the virtually identical language of the American Institute of Chartered Public Accountants, Accounting Research Bulletin No 43, ch 4.

which presents the "truer picture" of income for tax purposes. Thus, the question is: which method of accounting produces the best and fairest picture of annual profits? Equally, the hidden reserve argument ignores the primary purpose served by the method, namely, the determination of a fair measure of an enterprise's annual income.

6) Non-Arm's Length Transactions

The Act contains stringent anti-avoidance rules to govern transfers of property between persons who do not deal with each other at arm's length. The purpose of these rules is to discourage taxpayers who have close social, family or economic relationships with each other from artificially avoiding tax through the manipulation of transaction values.

Related persons are deemed not to deal with each other at arm's length.[46]

It is a question of fact whether unrelated persons deal with each other at arm's length. Parties are not considered to be dealing with each other at arm's length if one person dictates the terms of the bargain on both sides of a transaction.[47]

The anti-avoidance rules are as follows:[48]

- Where, in a non-arm's length transaction, a purchaser acquires anything for a price in excess of its fair market value, she is deemed to have acquired the property at its fair market value. Consequently, notwithstanding that the purchaser actually paid a price higher than fair market value, the purchaser is deemed to acquire the property at a cost equal to fair market value.

> Example
> A taxpayer buys land from his mother at a cost of $70,000 when, in fact, the land has a fair market value of $50,000 (this may happen if the mother deliberately wants to trigger a higher capital gain to offset unused capital losses). The Act deems the son to have acquired the land at a cost of $50,000. The mother calculates her gain on the basis of her actual proceeds of $70,000.

---

46   *ITA*, above note 1, s 251.
47   *Swiss Bank Corp v MNR*, [1971] CTC 427 (Ex Ct), aff'd (1972), [1974] SCR 1144 (parties acted in concert, exerting considerable influence together; money transactions merely moved funds from one pocket to another); *Millward v MNR*, [1986] 2 CTC 423 (FCTD) (members of law firm who dealt with each other at less than commercial rates of interest not at arm's length); *Noranda Mines Ltd v MNR*, [1987] 2 CTC 2089 (TCC) (existence of arm's-length relationship excluded where one party has *de facto* control over both parties).
48   *ITA*, above note 1, s 69.

- Where, in a non-arm's length transaction, a vendor has disposed of anything at less than its fair market value, the vendor is deemed to have received proceeds equal to fair market value. Thus, notwithstanding that she actually received a lower price, the vendor is taxed on the basis of her deemed proceeds.

> **Example**
>
> A taxpayer sells land that has a fair market value of $50,000 to his daughter for $40,000. Paragraph 69(1)(b) deems the father to have received $50,000. His daughter, however, acquires the property for her actual cost of $40,000, leaving her with the potential of a larger gain when she sells the property.

The overall effect of these rules is that taxpayers can be liable to double taxation in non-arm's length transactions. Section 69 can have a punitive effect. It is structured to discourage non-arm's length parties from dealing with each other at prices other than fair market value.

> **Example**
>
> *Assume*: An individual owns a property to which the following applies:
>
> | | |
> |---|---|
> | Cost | $1,000 |
> | FMV | $5,000 |
>
> She sells the property to her son for $4,000.
>
> *Then:*
>
> Tax consequences to mother:
>
> | | |
> |---|---|
> | Deemed proceeds of sale | $5,000 |
> | Cost | (1,000) |
> | Gain | $4,000 |
>
> If the son sells the property at its fair market value of $5,000, he also realizes a gain of $1,000:
>
> | | |
> |---|---|
> | Actual proceeds of sale | $5,000 |
> | Actual cost of property | (4,000) |
> | Gain | $1,000 |
>
> Total gain:
>
> | | |
> |---|---|
> | Realized by mother | $4,000 |
> | Realized by son | 1,000 |
> | | $5,000 |
>
> Thus, an asset with an accrued gain of $4,000 triggers an actual gain of $5,000. The $1,000 that is exposed to double taxation represents the shortfall between the fair market value of the property ($5,000) and the price at which it is sold ($4,000).

7) Timing of Income

We saw earlier that employment income is generally taxed on a cash basis. In contrast, with a few important exceptions, business and property income are normally calculated on an accrual basis. Thus, generally speaking, income from business and property are recognized for tax purposes when services are performed or goods are sold, rather than when payment for the goods or services is actually received. In other words, although a taxpayer may have to wait for some time to receive payment for goods sold or services rendered, he will be taxed on income in the year in which it is earned.

The accrual method of accounting is the appropriate method of determining profit in most circumstances. It warrants emphasis, however, that this is *not* the only acceptable method for tax purposes. Since subsection 9(1) is silent on the method of accounting that one can use to calculate "profit," a taxpayer is free to use generally accepted accounting principles appropriate to his circumstances if the method is not prohibited by the Act or by judicial precedent.[49]

a) Payments in Advance

The accrual method is modified by the Act for certain payments. For example, payments received in advance of rendering a service or sale of goods are included in income even though the payments represent unearned amounts that would usually be excluded from income for accounting purposes. Under accounting principles, unearned revenue is considered a liability. For tax purposes, unearned revenue is included in income in the year the payment is received, rather than when the revenue is earned. A taxpayer may, however, claim a reserve for goods and services to be delivered in the future.[50]

b) Receivables

A taxpayer is to include in income all amounts receivable by the taxpayer in respect of property sold or services rendered in the course of business carried out during the year.[51]

"Receivable" means that the taxpayer has a clearly established legal right to enforce payment at the particular time under consideration:

---

49 *Oxford Shopping Centres Ltd v Canada*, [1980] CTC 7 (FCTD), aff'd [1981] CTC 128 (FCA).

50 *ITA*, above note 1, paras 12(1)(a) and 20(1)(m).

51 *Ibid*, para 12(1)(b).

In the absence of a statutory definition to the contrary, I think it is not enough that the so-called recipient have a precarious right to receive the amount in question, but he must have a clearly legal, though not necessarily immediate, right to receive it.[52]

For example, in the construction industry, it is usual practice, when work is performed under a contract extending over a lengthy period of time, for interim payments to be made to the contractor. These payments, which are based on progress reports, are usually subject to a percentage holdback to ensure satisfactory completion of the project. In these circumstances, holdbacks need not be brought into income as "receivables" until such time as the architect or engineer has issued a final certificate approving the completion of the project.[53]

An amount is deemed to be receivable on the earlier of the day the account is actually rendered and the day on which it would have been rendered had there been "no undue delay" in rendering the account.

c) Professionals

i) Modified Accrual

The rules in respect of the computation of income of certain professionals (accountants, dentists, lawyers, medical doctors, veterinarians and chiropractors) vary somewhat from the normal accrual basis of accounting. These professional businesses may report income on a so-called modified accrual basis by electing to exclude work in progress in the computation of income.[54] On the sale of the professional business, any work in progress previously excluded is brought into the income of the vendor.[55]

ii) Work in Progress

Generally, if a professional elects to exclude work in progress in the computation of income, her income is computed on the basis of fees billed, subject to any adjustment for undue delay in billing. The election is binding on the taxpayer for subsequent years unless it is revoked with the consent of the minister.[56]

---

52 MNR v John Colford Contracting Co (1960), 60 DTC 1131 at 1135 (Ex Ct), aff'd without written reasons [1962] SCR viii.
53 Ibid.
54 ITA, above note 1, para 34(a).
55 Ibid, para 10(5)(a) and s 23.
56 Ibid, para 34(b); see Interpretation Bulletin IT-457R, "Election by Professionals to Exclude Work-In-Progress from Income" (15 July 1988).

iii) Advance Payments

Amounts received in advance of performance of services are included in income unless the funds are deposited in a segregated trust account.[57] For example, a lawyer who obtains a retainer that must be returned to the client in the event of non-performance of services may exclude the retainer from income if the funds are deposited in a trust account.[58] The taxpayer may, however, claim a deduction in respect of services that will have to be rendered after the end of the year.[59]

d) Farmers and Fishers

Income from a farming or fishing business may be calculated on a cash basis. Thus, the income of a taxpayer from a farming or fishing business is computed by aggregating amounts received in the year and deducting therefrom amounts paid in the year. Accounts receivable are included in income only when they are collected by the taxpayer.[60]

J. RESERVES AND ALLOWANCES

1) Prohibition against Reserves

The term "reserve" is now in disfavour among accountants because it has been applied so widely as to lose any specific meaning. Nevertheless, the term continues to be employed in commercial jargon. The Act specifically sets its face against "reserves."[61]

The general prohibition in paragraph 18(1)(e) of a deduction for any reserve, "contingent account" or "sinking fund," except as specifically permitted by the Act, not only causes accounting for tax purposes to deviate significantly from accounting for other purposes, but it also produces inconsistencies within the system of income tax accounting.

Whether we refer to "reserve," "allowance," "contingency fund" or some other expression, accountants recognize that a simplistic presentation of accrual basis financial statements fails to estimate profitability accurately. The failure results from overlooking future risks or obligations that affect present profitability. An obvious example is depreciation of capital assets. It would be foolish, and poor accounting, to fail to

---

57 *ITA, ibid*, para 12(1)(a).
58 Interpretation Bulletin IT-129R, "Lawyers' Trust Accounts and Disbursements" (7 November 1986).
59 *ITA*, above note 1, para 20(1)(m).
60 *Ibid*, s 28.
61 *Ibid*, para 18(1)(e).

recognize an asset's ultimate obsolescence or exhaustion over a period of time. As already noted, the *Income Tax Act* concedes the wisdom of depreciating capital assets and provides for this by way of the CCA or tax depreciation system.

A clear line must, however, be drawn between depreciation and a decline in the market value of an asset. Although an accountant might think it is prudent for financial statement purposes to recognize a paper loss on investments, the tax system does not allow such an accounting practice for the purpose of determining net income. In *MNR v Consolidated Glass Ltd*,[62] for example, the taxpayer attempted to deduct as a capital loss an amount that reflected the decline in value of the shares of its subsidiary company. A majority of the Supreme Court of Canada held that the taxpayer could not claim a loss in respect of assets of a fluctuating value until such time as the assets were sold or became worthless so that the loss was irrevocable.

2) Doubtful and Bad Debts

Accounts receivable is a major balance sheet asset for many businesses. Receivables are normally recorded on the books at face value; that is, at the value stated on the invoice. As with depreciation, it would be foolish to ignore the obvious risk that all of the accounts of a business are not collected. Every business that sells on credit suffers some credit risk. Although this is the sort of contingent risk that the Act is careful to prevent taxpayers from exploiting, it specifically authorizes a deduction for a reserve for doubtful debts[63] and bad debts.[64]

A taxpayer's doubtful debt reserve may be based on an analysis of the likelihood of collection of individual accounts. Alternatively, it may be stated as a percentage of total accounts receivable. The CRA, however, does not consider percentage-based reserves to be reasonable.[65] In either case, the deduction must be reasonable. The mere fact that a debt has remained unpaid for a considerable time is not determinative that it is bad.[66]

---

62   *MNR v Consolidated Glass Ltd*, [1957] SCR 167.
63   *ITA*, above note 1, para 20(1)(l).
64   *Ibid*, para 20(1)(p).
65   See Interpretation Bulletin IT-442R, "Bad Debts and Reserves for Doubtful Debts" (6 September 1991) at para 24.
66   See *No 81 v MNR* (1953), 8 Tax ABC 82 (factors to consider are time element, history of account, finances of client, taxpayer's past experiences with bad debts, business conditions in locality and in country, and relative sales volume); *No 409 v MNR* (1957), 16 Tax ABC 409 (delay in payment not sufficient to jus-

The deduction for bad debts is in respect of debts "that are established by the taxpayer to have become bad debts in the year."[67]

3) Pre-Paid Income

We can make an adjusting entry to reduce current income by setting up a balance sheet liability to reflect the fact that some income received was unearned. For example, X Widgets sets up a liability, "rent received in advance," for the purpose of moving $300, received in its fiscal period ending 31 October, into the following accounting period. If the prepayment were a deposit and subject to refund on demand, it could be said that X Widgets had not "realized" the amount and should not recognize it in income at that time.

Assuming, however, that X Widgets can retain the $300 even if the payer discontinues use of the rented property, it is nevertheless incorrect, from an accrual accounting point of view, to recognize the $300 in the period ending 31 October.

There are two ways of expressing the accountant's concern that current income is being overstated. One is to say that revenue is overstated because the $300, though received, has not yet been earned. The other is to say that income is overstated as a result of failure to recognize a business liability in the next accounting period; that is, the obligation to make the rented property available for three months. Although these two ways of expressing the matching concept boil down to the same thing in accounting terms, they are not at all alike for income tax purposes.

a) Inclusion in Income

Paragraph 12(1)(a) reads as follows:

> There shall be included in computing the income of a taxpayer for a taxation year as income from a business or property such of the following amounts as are applicable:
>
> (a) any amount received by the taxpayer in the year in the course of a business
>
> (i) that is on account of services not rendered or goods not delivered before the end of the year or that, for any other rea-

tify reserve after two months, in circumstances); *Atlas Steels Ltd v MNR* (1961), 27 Tax ABC 331 (reserve of 3 percent of accounts receivable allowed in circumstances despite unfavourable comparison with company's history of collections). See also CRA Rulings doc 9238377.

67   *ITA*, above note 1, para 20(1)(p).

son, may be regarded as not having been earned in the year
or a previous year, or
(ii) under an arrangement or understanding that it is repayable
in whole or in part on the return or resale to the taxpayer of
articles in or by means of which goods were delivered to a
customer. . . .

Obviously, this requires X Widgets to bring the $300 into income,
whether or not it has been earned. The question which then arises is
whether X Widgets can make an entry to reflect the overstatement of
income. The reference in paragraph 12(1)(a) to amounts "regarded as
not having been earned" confirms that the adjustment cannot be made
directly to the statement of revenues. In any event, normal accrual accounting practice would recognize the receipt and make the adjustment by setting up the liability (unearned income) to reflect the future
obligation to provide the rental property.

b) Deduction from Income

This brings us back to paragraph 18(1)(e), which prohibits all reserves
except those expressly permitted. Fortunately for X Widgets, subparagraph 20(1)(m)(iii) expressly allows "a reasonable amount as a reserve
in respect of . . . periods for which rent or other amounts for the possession or use of land or chattels have been paid in advance."

X Widgets is a simple example of future obligations that affect
current income and can easily be accommodated because the future
obligation can be precisely quantified and its occurrence can be precisely predicted. Thus, there are no problems of measurement or timing. Other examples may be found in the publishing business, which
receives prepaid subscriptions for which the publisher must provide
magazines for a determined future period, and the entertainment business, which sells tickets for future performances with each ticket referable to a specified seat on a specified date.

c) Uncertainty

In other circumstances, however, businesses may legitimately claim
future obligations, but the amount of the obligation may be uncertain
both in respect of quantum and timing. Contrast the sale of season
tickets to hockey games with the sale by a movie theatre chain of gift
books of tickets for cinema performances. In the first case, the hockey
club knows the date of each performance for which ticket revenue has
been received. Whether or not the seats are occupied, the revenue is
earned, and the club's obligation is satisfied on a game-by-game basis
as each game is played. In the second case, the theatre company knows

neither when the gift tickets will be used, nor how many will go forever unused.

There may be an intermediate situation, in which a business cannot accurately predict the amount of its future obligation, but it can at least predict the timing within reasonable limits. An example would be the dinner-of-the-month arrangement under which a group of restaurants participate in a promotional scheme of selling books of tickets for free dinners at participating restaurants. Each book contains twelve tickets; each ticket is usable at a specified restaurant during a specified month. As each ticket entitles the user to a free meal equal in value to another purchased at the same time by the user's dinner partner, Restaurant A cannot be certain of its maximum obligation. Perhaps it can make a reliable estimate based on past experience. In any event, each month, the obligation for that month is determined, and at the end of twelve months the entire obligation has been quantified and satisfied.

A common business situation, rather like the one just described, is that of the insurance agent or broker who receives commissions in respect of insurance contracts extending into a future period. The broker knows that clients will have to be serviced over the period remaining under each contract, but the extent of the potential obligation in each case is highly speculative. Subsection 32(1) resolves the difficulty arbitrarily by allowing the agent or broker to set up a *pro rata* reserve in respect of unearned commissions.

d) Reserve for Future Goods and Services

Paragraph 20(1)(m) authorizes a reserve for a "reasonable amount" for goods or services "that it is reasonably anticipated will have to be delivered [or rendered] after the end of the year."[68] The same provision allows a reasonable reserve for anticipated refunds of deposits made on containers or other "articles in or by means of which goods were delivered to a customer."[69] The uncertainty involved in determining the amount of these future obligations is apparent from the requirement of the provision that the reserve be a "reasonable amount" and that the obligation be "reasonably anticipated."

A special problem of future obligations arises from a certain promotional technique used by some retailing businesses. A customer making a purchase at a Canadian Tire Store, for example, receives some "funny money," a form of scrip that can be applied to future purchases at Canadian Tire. Other businesses have used trading stamps that, after a suf-

---

68 *Ibid*, subparas 20(1)(m)(i) & (ii).
69 *Ibid*, subparas 20(1)(m)(iv) and 12(1)(a)(ii).

ficient quantity were accumulated, could be redeemed for merchandise. For a time, some of the major oil companies issued a card in which a hole was punched on the occasion of a purchase from one of the company stations. When the prescribed number of holes had been punched, the card could be redeemed for a set of dishes or cutlery. In all of these cases, the business is being carried on in such a way that current profitability will be overstated unless the future obligation to redeem the scrip, the trading stamps, or the cards is recognized. The problems inherent in any attempt to determine the amount and the timing of future obligations generated by such promotional schemes are, however, very difficult. The proportion of the trading stamps thrown away or lost is probably high, just as it is very likely that the "funny money" will be carried around in the wallets of Canadian Tire customers for years.

In *Dominion Stores Ltd v MNR*,[70] the minister argued that the taxpayer was not entitled to a deduction under paragraph 20(1)(m), which is conditional upon showing that the reserve is in respect of amounts that have been included in the taxpayer's income pursuant to paragraph 12(1)(a). The minister argued that the "green stamps" given to customers were free, as they were advertised to be, and that the entire payment by the customer was referable to the food and other items being purchased at the time. Accordingly, Dominion Stores had no income in respect of the green stamps and was not entitled to any reserve to recognize the future obligation to redeem them. Justice Cattanach held that the price paid at the checkout desk was a combined price for both the goods being purchased and the green stamps that accompanied them. The taxpayer was, therefore, entitled to take a reserve. It is interesting to note that only this narrow legal issue was submitted to the court. The parties had, by agreement, fixed the appropriate amount of the reserve if the taxpayer was permitted to take it. Obviously, the determination of a "reasonable reserve" would require careful analysis of past experience with green stamp redemptions, and some speculative estimate as to the proportion that would never be redeemed.

K. ACCOUNTING FOR INVENTORY

1) Cost of Goods Sold

The largest single item of expense in a trading or manufacturing business is likely to be the cost of the goods sold. In most businesses that

---

70   *Dominion Stores Ltd v MNR*, [1966] CTC 97 (Ex Ct).

handle a large volume of items that cannot be individually identified, it is neither possible nor desirable to keep a running total of the cost of the goods being sold on a daily basis. The only feasible way to determine the cost of all the goods sold in an accounting period is to add the value of the inventory on hand at the beginning of the period to the cost of inventory purchased during the period and then subtract the value of the inventory on hand at the end of the period. The formula becomes:

Cost of Goods Sold = Opening Inventory + Acquisitions − Closing Inventory

If prices are stable, this formula may give rise to little difficulty. An important problem of valuing opening and closing inventory arises, however, if prices are rising or falling. For example, assume 10,000 units of inventory on hand at the opening of the period, and a current price of $1 per unit;[71] assume 10,000 units on hand at the end of the period and a current price of $4 per unit. Assume also that 100,000 units are traded during the period, the price having risen steadily as the business bought units each month. In many businesses, it will be impossible to say whether the 10,000 units in closing inventory are the same ones as those in the opening inventory, or whether some or none remain from the opening of the period.

If both opening and closing inventory are valued at $10,000, the cost of goods sold will be shown as $30,000 more, and profits will be $30,000 less, than if closing inventory is valued at $40,000.

2) Alternative Methods

The Act permits two general methods of valuing inventory:[72]

1) Valuation at the lower of cost or fair market value for each item of inventory; or
2) Valuation of the entire inventory at fair market value.

A taxpayer's inventory at the beginning of the year must be valued at the same amount at which it was valued at the end of the immediately preceding year.[73]

---

71   Note that we are here assuming a price of $1 to the taxpayer and are ignoring the "value" to the taxpayer in the sense of its current resale price. This would obviously add further complexities to the problem of appropriate valuation of inventory.
72   *ITA*, above note 1, subs 10(1); *Income Tax Regulations*, CRC, c 945, s 1801. Artists and writers may elect a nil value for their inventory under *ITA*, subs 10(6).
73   *ITA, ibid*, subs 10(2).

3) Change of Method

A taxpayer must use the same method of valuation from year to year in the absence of permission from the minister.[74]
Interpretation Bulletin IT-473R provides:

> A change in the method of valuing inventory will generally be approved by the Minister if it can be shown that, considering the circumstances, the new method:
> 1. is a more appropriate way of computing the taxpayer's income;
> 2. will be used for financial statement purposes by the taxpayer; and
> 3. will be used consistently in subsequent years.[75]

L. CONCLUSION

The arbitrary division of a business lifetime into annual segments produces numerous accounting problems. These problems are greatly exacerbated because of the annual accounting for income tax purposes. Under a progressive rate structure, an individual whose income fluctuates widely over a number of years will pay more tax than another taxpayer with the same aggregate income over the period but with little annual fluctuation.

Further, a serious problem occurs when income falls below zero in some years. Without a system of negative income tax and refunds, there is no automatic solution for a taxpayer with a net loss tax year. Some relief is available in section 111 for the carryover of losses from one tax year to another. Loss carryovers and related issues are discussed in Chapters 13 and 14 on the computation of tax.

The measurement of income or profit, which is the foundation of the taxable base on which we impose taxes, is an imperfect art that involves many estimates, assumptions and judgment calls. To be sure, ultimately, net taxable income is a single number on which we impose taxes. The number itself, however, is at best an educated estimate of properly matched revenues and expenses, accounting principles, judicial doctrines and political and tax policy considerations. To understand the measurement of income one must understand law, economics and accounting principles.

---

74   *Ibid*, subs 10(2.1).
75   Interpretation Bulletin IT-473R, "Inventory Valuation" (21 December 1998) at para 8.

FURTHER READINGS

Measurement of Income

ARNOLD, BRIAN J. "Timing and Income Taxation: The Principles of Income Management for Tax Purposes" (1983) 35 Can Tax Found 133.

DROBNY, SHELDON. "Inventory and Accounting Methods: Controversy and Paradoxes" (October 1990) 68 Taxes 764.

HARRIS, EDWIN C. "Measuring Business Income" (1967) 19 Can Tax Found 78.

KAPLOW, LOUIS, & ALVIN C WARREN. "An Income Tax By Any Other Name: A Reply to Professor Strnad"(1985–86) 38 Stan L Rev 399.

ROBERTSON, DA. "Timing Is Everything" (1988) 121:3 CA Magazine 32.

STRNAD, JEFF. "Tax Timing and the Haig-Simons Ideal: A Rejoinder to Professor Popkin [discussion of "Tax Ideals in the Real World: A Comment on Professor Strnad's Approach to Tax Fairness"] (1986) 62 Ind LJ 73.

STRNAD, JEFF. "The Bankruptcy of Conventional Tax Timing Wisdom Is Deeper than Semantics: A Rejoinder to Professors Kaplow and Warren: The Comment" (1987) 39 Stan L Rev 389.

WHITE, ROBERT. "Profits and Prophets: An Accountant's Afterword" (1987) 8 Brit Tax Rev 292.

Basic Income Tax Accounting

COOPER, GRAEME S. "Some Observations of Tax Accounting" (1986) 15 Austl Tax Rev 221.

KNIGHT, RAY, & LEE KNIGHT. "Recent Developments Concerning the Completed Contract Method of Accounting" (1988) 41 Tax Exec 73.

ROBERTS, JR, & WILLIAM LEISS. "Technological and Accounting Innovation: Can They Mesh?" (1986) 36 Can Tax Found 25:1.

STRNAD, JEFF. "Tax Timing and the Haig-Simons Ideal: A Rejoinder to Professor Popkin [discussion of "Tax Ideals in the Real World: A Comment on Professor Strand's Approach to Tax Fairness"] (1986) 62 Ind LJ 73.

Generally Accepted Accounting Principles

DROBNY, SHELDON. "Inventory and Accounting Methods: Controversy and Paradoxes" (October 1990) 68 Taxes 764.

MCDONNELL, THOMAS E. "Falling Between the GAAP's?" (1991) 39 Can Tax J 1313.

MURRAY, KJ, & NICOLE MONDOU. "The Relevance of GAAP in *Cyprus Anvil Mining Corporation* v *The Queen*" (1990) 3 Can Curr Tax P-5.

PADWE, GERALD W. "The Death of G.A.A.P. Reporting: A Tale from the Folks Who Brought You U.S. Tax Reform" (1987) Corp Mgmt Tax Conf 11:1.

STRAIN, WILLIAM J. "Now You See It, Now You Don't: The Elusive Relevance of G.A.A.P. in Tax Accounting" (1985) 37 Can Tax Found 38.

Realization and Recognition of Income

CALLARD, ROSALIND M. "When to Recognize Revenue" (1986) 119 CA Magazine 67.

FREEDMAN, JUDITH. "Profit and Prophets: Law and Accountancy Practice on the Timing of Receipts—Recognition under the Earnings Basis (Schedule D, Cases 1 and 11)" (1987) Brit Tax Rev 61 and 104.

Realization of Income: Timing

ARNOLD, BRIAN J. "Timing and Income Taxation: The Principles of Income Management for Tax Purposes" (1983) 35 Can Tax Found 133.

GROWER, KENNETH W. "Tax Reform and Farmers" (1988) 40 Can Tax Found 24:1.

MCNAIR, DK. "The Taxation of Farmers and Farming" in The Law Society of Upper Canada, *Special Lectures 1986: Income Tax for the General Practitioner* (Don Mills, ON: De Boo, 1986) 77.

———. *Taxation of Farmers and Fishermen*, 2d ed (Toronto: Richard De Boo, 1986).

O'BRIEN, MARTIN L. "Taxation of Profits Derived from Criminal or Illegal Activities" (1988) 2 Can Curr Tax J-85.

ROBERTSON, DA. "Timing is Everything" (1988) 121:3 CA Magazine 32.

TILEY, JOHN. "More on Receivability and Receipt" (1986) Brit Tax Rev 152.

TURNER, PAUL E. "The Reform Down on the Farm'" (July 1990) 24 CGA Magazine 25.

————. "Restricted Farm Losses" (December 1990) 24 CGA Magazine 47.

Reserves and Allowances

CADESKY, MICHAEL. "Corporate Losses" (1990) 42 Can Tax Found 19:1.

FRANKOVIC, JOSEPH V. "Taxing Times: Foreclosures, Default Sales, Debt Forgiveness, Doubtful and Bad Debts" (1991) 39 Can Tax J 889.

KRISHNA, VERN. "Meaning of Allowance" (1986) 1 Can Curr Tax J-144.

LAND, STEPHEN B. "Contingent Payments Are the Time Value of Money" (1987) 40 Tax Lawyer 237.

LOKKEN, LAWRENCE. "The Time Value of Money Rules" (1986) 42 Tax L Rev 1.

Accounting for Inventory

ARNOLD, BRIAN J. "Recent Developments in the Tax Treatment of Inventory" (1979) 31 Can Tax Found 865.

————. "Conversions of Property to and from Inventory: Tax Consequences" (1976) 24 Can Tax J 231.

CADESKY, MICHAEL. "Corporate Losses" (1990) Can Tax Found 19:1.

INNES, WILLIAM I. "The Tax Treatment of Accrued Gains on Inventory at Death" (1992) 12 E & T 122.

LOONEY, STEVE R. "Using L.I.F.O. to Value Costs under the Completed Contract Method: A Tale of Two Accounting Methods" (1986) 39 Tax Lawyer 235.

McDONNELL, THOMAS E. "An Inventory Adventure" (1993) 41 Can Tax J 965.

McQUILLAN, PETER E. "Real Estate Inventory Valuation" (1992) 44 Can Tax Found 5:35.

FREE INTERNET RESOURCES

- AustLII: www.austlii.edu.au/databases.html (Australian and New Zealand caselaw and legislation)
- BAILII: www.bailii.org (British and Irish caselaw and legislation)
- Canada Revenue Agency: www.cra-arc.gc.ca/menu-e.html
- CanLII: www.canlii.org/en/index.php (Canadian caselaw and legislation)
- Supreme Court of India: www.liiofindia.org/in/cases/cen/INSC (decisions from 1950 to the present)
- US Code: www.law.cornell.edu/uscode
- US Supreme Court: www.law.cornell.edu/supct (Supreme Court decisions since 1990)
- US: www.worldlii.org/int/other/GLIN/us (abstracts of US caselaw and legislation)
- WorldLII: www.worldlii.org/databases.html (caselaw and legislation of selected other countries)

GLOSSARY

*Department of Finance definition

Note: Many definitions of accounting terms can be found online at www.ventureline.com/glossary.asp.

*Alternative minimum tax (AMT): A tax levied under the personal income tax to ensure that high-income Canadians claiming preferential tax deductions pay a reasonable amount of tax in any given year.

Arm's length: Arm's length generally refers to the proximity of the relationship between taxpayers. Persons who are related to each other are considered to be non-arm's length with each other. An arm's-length price is a price charged in similar transactions between unrelated parties.

Associated enterprises: The concept of associated enterprises applies typically in tax treaties and encapsulates the arm's-length principle. An enterprise of one contracting state may engage in commercial dealings with an enterprise of the other contracting state that is under common control, management or ownership. If the two enterprises deal under conditions that would not have been imposed on an independent enterprise, a contracting state may include as taxable profits of the enterprise amounts that would have been derived by the enterprise in an arm's-length relationship.

*Average tax rate: The ratio of taxes paid to the tax base. Accordingly, the average income tax rate is the ratio of income tax paid to income.

For example, someone who pays $10,000 in income tax on a taxable income of $50,000 would have an average tax rate of 20 percent.

Branch: A branch of an enterprise is a business carried on through a fixed place of business, which is also referred to as a permanent establishment. A branch is not separately incorporated.

Branch profits tax: The branch profits tax is a tax that may be imposed by the source state on that portion of the business profits of a foreign corporation that is attributable to a permanent establishment therein. The rate of the branch profits tax is determined by the *Income Tax Act* (Part XIV), but is often reduced in Canada's bilateral tax treaties.

*****Capital cost allowance (CCA)**: A tax deduction for business-related capital property that provides for the depreciation of these assets. Businesses can deduct up to a fixed percentage of the depreciated cost each year. CCA may differ from depreciation used for financial statement purposes. For example, in certain cases, the CCA rates at which assets can be written off against income may be faster than the rates used in companies' financial accounts.

*****Capital gain**: An increase in the money value of a capital asset, such as a share, bond, parcel of land, antique or other asset, which results in a profit if the asset is sold. For example, if a share is bought at $26 and sold at $30, there is a capital gain of $4. The taxable capital gain is three-quarters of this amount, or $3.

*****Capital gains tax**: A tax levied on the profits from the sale of capital assets or the deemed sale of capital assets. Capital gains are taxed at one half (2011) of the full income tax rate in Canada. There is a $750,000 exemption for capital gains on small business shares and qualified farm property. A taxpayer's principal residence is not subject to capital gains taxation.

Competent authority: The competent authorities of a country are the persons responsible for its tax administration. Canada Revenue Agency is the competent authority for the purposes of Canadian tax treaties. The competent authorities are responsible for resolving disputes and questions of treaty interpretation.

*****Consolidated Revenue Fund**: The general pool of all income of the federal government, such as tax, tariff and licence fee income, and profits from Crown corporations. All money received by the federal government must be credited to this fund and be properly accounted for.

*Consumption taxes: Taxes on consumption — purchases of goods and services — levied by both the federal and provincial governments. Federal consumption taxes consist mainly of GST and excise taxes on motor fuel, tobacco products and alcoholic beverages. Provincial consumption taxes consist mainly of retail sales taxes, and provincial taxes on motive fuel and tobacco products.

Controlled foreign affiliate: A controlled foreign affiliate is a foreign affiliate controlled by a domestic taxpayer. Control generally refers to a direct or indirect ownership interest of at least 50 percent of the shares.

*Corporate tax: Tax on corporate income in Canada. In addition, Canadian corporations pay a variety of taxes and other levies to the various levels of government in Canada. These include capital and insurance premium taxes; payroll levies (e.g., health taxes, Employment Insurance, Canada Pension Plan, Quebec Pension Plan, Workers' Compensation); property taxes; and indirect taxes, such as sales and excise taxes, levied on business inputs.

Credit method: The credit method provides relief from double taxation by allowing taxpayers a credit for foreign taxes paid by a Canadian resident.

Cross-border transactions: Cross-border transactions are those in which goods and/or services cross over national boundaries. Cross border transactions usually have international tax consequences.

*Deferred taxes: A business accounting concept. Income for tax purposes must always be calculated and taxes paid in accordance with the rules set out in the Income Tax Act. However, businesses' methods of calculating their income for financial statement purposes often differ from those used for tax purposes, and thus companies' income for financial statement purposes will often differ from (and appear greater than) the income on which businesses actually have to pay taxes. In order to reconcile these two amounts in their books, businesses use the accounting concept of deferred taxes.

Dependent agent: The term "dependent agent" is a treaty concept which refers to a person who acts on behalf of another person and who exercises contractual authority on behalf of that other person. The concept of dependent agent is important in determining whether a nonresident person has a permanent establishment in a country.

Dividends: "Dividends" refer to income from shares or other corporate rights (other than debt claims) that participate in profits. In general terms, dividend income must be attributable to the ownership of shares or other units of equity ownership carrying a right to participate in profits.

Economic double taxation: Economic double taxation refers to the taxation of two different taxpayers with respect to the same income (or capital). Economic double taxation occurs, for example, when income earned by a corporation is taxed both to the corporation and to its shareholders when distributed as a dividend.

*Employer-provided health and dental benefits**: The cost of benefits paid by employers on behalf of employees under employer-sponsored health and dental care plans. Such benefits are not included in the employee's employment income.

*Excise tax**: A tax imposed on a particular commodity or service. The tax can be imposed at any trade level and can either be a specific tax or an *ad valorem* tax.

Exemption method: The exemption method provides relief from double taxation by exempting income that is subject to tax in the state of source from tax in the state of residence. The exemption method refers to the amount of income that is subject to tax. Hence, a taxpayer can be affected by the difference in tax rates between the state of source and the state of residence.

Exemption with progression: Under the exemption-with-progression method, the state of residence provides an exemption from its tax for income earned in the state of source, but the residence state retains for itself the right to take the exempt income into account for the purposes of determining the marginal rate at which the taxpayer's non-exempt income is subject to tax. The exemption with progression method prevents a taxpayer from taking advantage of a lower tax bracket in the state of residence by earning income abroad.

*Family income**: For income tax purposes, the combined incomes of both spouses. Family income does not include income of children living at home.

*Family trusts**: Family trust arrangements allow property to be held by a trust for the benefit of beneficiaries under the trust. Trusts are used for many purposes, including succession planning for businesses and dealing with the needs of beneficiaries in special circumstances, such as age and disability.

*Flat tax: A tax levied at the same rate on all income for all individual taxpayers, usually on a broadly defined income base with only a limited number of deductions.

*Flow-through share: A flow-through share is available to mining and petroleum companies to facilitate financing their exploration and development activities. Investors receive an equity interest in the company and income tax deductions associated with new expenditures incurred by the company on exploration and development. Flow-through shares are available to all mining and petroleum companies, but are of greater benefit to non-taxpaying junior exploration companies. These companies are unable to use income tax deductions for exploration and development against their corporate income and are willing to forgo the deduction to new investors.

*Foreign affiliate: A non-resident corporation in which a taxpayer resident in Canada has a significant interest (an equity percentage of not less than 10 percent). A controlled foreign affiliate is generally a foreign affiliate in which the taxpayer has or participates in a controlling interest.

*Foreign trusts: A foreign trust is an entity organized outside Canada which is set up to hold and administer funds or property on behalf of beneficiaries. For example a Canadian taxpayer may transfer funds or property to a foreign trust for the benefit of his children living abroad. However, such arrangements can also be set up for the purpose of reducing income from property for Canadian tax purposes. The *Income Tax Act* contains provisions designed to prevent the avoidance of tax in such cases..

*Goods and Services Tax (GST): The GST is a 5 percent value-added tax applied to the vast majority of goods and services sold in Canada for domestic consumption. The GST does not apply to basic groceries, most medical services and devices, prescription drugs, residential rents, and exports.

*GST rebates: Taxable (including zero-rated) sales by all sectors are eligible for full rebate of tax paid on associated inputs through the input tax credit mechanism. However, certain sectors are also eligible for rebates of a portion of the GST paid on inputs into exempt sales. These rebates go to qualifying public-sector bodies such as municipalities, universities, schools and hospitals (MUSH), as well as to qualifying public service organizations such as charities and non-profit organizations. GST rebates to these institutions minimize the impact of the GST on the cost of providing exempt public services. Other GST rebates include a rebate to foreign tourists for GST paid on hotel accommodation in Canada and goods taken out of the country, as well as a rebate of a portion of the GST paid on the purchase of a new home (excluding rental properties).

*Income: The money and other benefits net of certain expenses flowing to individuals, firms and other groups in the economy. For purposes of the income tax, income is specifically defined to exclude certain types of benefits, such as a capital gain on sale of a principal residence.

*Income testing: A reduction in the level of a benefit based on the recipient's income level.

*Input tax credits: The input tax credit mechanism under the GST effectively provides a refund to registered businesses of all GST paid on inputs involved in the production and sale of taxable goods and services. In this manner, the input tax credit minimizes the amount of indirect tax embedded in the price of Canadian-produced goods and services, making them more competitive internationally and in the domestic market.

Investment income: The income received from investment in securities and property. It includes rent from property, dividends from shares in corporations, and interest from bonds, guaranteed-investment certificates, bank accounts, certificates of deposit, treasury bills and other financial securities.

*Investment tax credit: A tax credit available for investments in scientific research and experimental development and in certain regions.

Juridical double taxation: Juridical double taxation refers to circumstances where a taxpayer is subject to tax on the same income (or capital) in more than one jurisdiction. For example, a resident of Canada who is also considered to be a resident of the United States would be potentially subject to concurrent full taxation in both countries. Bilateral tax treaties generally tend to eliminate (or at least reduce) the possibility of juridical double taxation.

Limitations of benefits: Treaty benefits are generally available only to residents of a contracting state, which, in the case of corporations, includes corporations incorporated in the contracting state. Hence, corporations can engage in "treaty-shopping" by incorporating in a convenient state merely for the purpose of deriving treaty benefits. A limitation on benefits article in a treaty generally limits the ability of third-country residents to shop for a favourable treaty.

*Loss carryovers: Business or investment losses that are incurred in one year that may be used as a deduction from taxable income in another year.

*Manufacturing and Processing (M&P) Tax Credit: A federal tax reduction is provided on Canadian manufacturing and processing income not subject to the small business deduction. This credit has the effect of lowering the tax rate on M&P income from the general federal rate.

*Marginal tax rate: The ratio of the increase in tax to the increase in the tax base (i.e., the tax rate on each additional dollar of income). For example, in the case of an individual facing a marginal income tax rate of 29 percent, each additional dollar of income would be subject to an income tax of 29 cents.

*Net income: Total income minus allowable deductions such as pension contributions, union dues and child care expenses.

Non-resident: A non-resident is a person who does not have a sufficiently close connection with a country to be subject to full tax liability on her worldwide income in the country. Non-residents are usually taxable only on their source income from the country.

OECD commentary: The commentary to the OECD Model Treaty is the official explanation of the Model Treaty by the OECD.

Permanent establishment: A permanent establishment is a fixed place of business through which an enterprise carries on its business in whole or in part. The concept of permanent establishment applies when a state determines that, under its domestic law, the business profits of a resident of another state may be taxable. Tax treaties generally provide that the business profits of an enterprise of one contracting state derived from activities or sources in the other contracting state are not taxable by the source state unless they are attributable to a permanent establishment therein.

*Personal tax: Tax on personal income in Canada, including both personal income taxes and the employee portion of social security contributions (in Canada these are primarily unemployment insurance premiums and Canada/Quebec Pension Plan contributions).

Place of incorporation test: A rule that considers a corporation to be resident in the country in which it is incorporated.

Portfolio investments: Debt or equity investments in a corporation that do not provide the investor with substantial ownership or influence in the management of the corporation. Typically, equity ownership of less than 10 percent of a corporation is considered to be a portfolio investment.

*Receiver General for Canada: The chief financial officer of the federal government, who receives all revenues from the government and deposits them in the Consolidated Revenue Fund.

*Refundable tax credit: Where a tax credit is refundable, a portion of the credit which is not needed to reduce a taxpayer's tax liability (because it is already zero) may be paid to the taxpayer. An example is the refundable investment tax credit.

Resident: A resident is a person who has a sufficiently close connection or nexus with a country to be liable for tax on her worldwide income (full tax liability) in the country.

Royalties: The term "royalties" generally refers to amounts paid for the use of personal property (usually, but not always, intangible property), such as industrial, commercial, scientific or artistic property. Payments for technical assistance are sometimes considered royalties if the technical assistance is related or ancillary to other royalty generating rights.

*Small business deduction (SBD): Corporations that are Canadian controlled private corporations (CCPCs) are eligible for a small business tax rate reduction known as the small business deduction.

*Surtax: An additional tax levied as a percentage of an income tax amount. Both individuals and corporations pay surtaxes in addition to their base amount of federal tax.

*Tax base: The amount on which a tax rate is applied. In the case of personal or corporate income tax, for example, the tax base is taxable income; if some kinds of income are excluded from the definition of taxable income (such as a portion of capital gains, or certain types of benefits), they are said to be excluded from the tax base. In the case of sales taxes, the tax base is the value of items that are subject to tax; basic groceries, for example, are not part of the tax base of the GST. When economists speak of the tax base being broadened, they mean that a wider range of goods, services and income has been made subject to a tax.

*Tax collection agreement: An agreement that enables different governments to have access to a tax field through a single administration and collection agency. For example, the federal government collects personal income taxes on behalf of all provinces (except Quebec) under a tax collection agreement.

*Tax credit: An amount deducted directly from income tax otherwise payable. Examples include the disability credit and the married credit for individuals, and the scientific research and experimental development investment tax credit for corporations.

*Tax deduction: An amount deducted in computing income for tax purposes. Examples include the child care expense deduction and the capital cost allowance.

*Tax deferral: A deferral of income taxes from the current year to a later taxation year through the use of provisions such as deductions for RRSP contributions.

*Tax-exempt goods and services: Some types of goods and services are exempt under the GST. This means that tax is not applied to these sales. However, vendors of exempt products are not entitled to claim input tax credits to recover the GST they paid on their inputs to these products. Examples of tax-exempt goods and services include long-term residential rents, most health and dental care services, day care services, most sales by charities, most domestic financial services, municipal transit and legal aid services.

*Tax expenditure: Forgone tax revenues, due to special exemptions, deductions, credits and deferrals that reduce the amount of tax that would otherwise be payable. Examples of tax expenditures include deductions for pension and RRSP contributions, credits for charitable donations, and incentives for firms to invest in research and development. As these examples indicate, tax expenditures are often designed to encourage certain kinds of activities. They may also serve other objectives, such as providing assistance to lower income or elderly Canadians (e.g., the pension and age credits, the GST credit and the child tax benefit).

*Tax shelter: Tax sparing refers to the allowance of a credit to a domestic tax payer for the amount of foreign taxes that were not paid to a foreign country by virtue of special tax incentive provision in that country or because of a tax holiday in the foreign country.

Tax sparing: Tax sparing refers to the allowance of a credit to a domestic taxpayer for the amount of foreign taxes that were not paid to a foreign country by virtue of special tax incentive provision in that country or because of a tax holiday in the foreign country.

*Taxable income: Net income minus certain other allowable deductions such as the northern residents' deduction.

Thin capitalization: Thin capitalization refers to the ratio of debt to equity. Where a corporation is heavily capitalized by debt claims, it is considered to be thinly capitalized. In certain circumstances, a corporation that is thinly capitalized by non-residents may not be entitled to a full deduction of its interest expense.

*Total income: For income tax purposes, the sum of all income that is potentially subject to tax.

*Trusts: An arrangement under which money or other property is held by one person, often a trust company, for the benefit of another person or persons. These assets are administered according to the terms of the trust agreement. Each province has a trustee act, which regulates the kinds of investments that can be made by the trustees of a trust fund.

*Twenty-one-year deemed disposition rule: A rule requiring that trust assets be treated for tax purposes as if they were disposed of every twenty-one years. This measure accompanied the introduction of capital gains taxation in 1972 to prevent trusts from being used to avoid the taxation of capital gains on death.

Unitary taxation: A system of taxation under which the worldwide profits and losses of multinational enterprises are allocated among its component parts in different countries in accordance with a formula based on multiple factors, such as sales, assets and payroll in each country.

*Wealth tax: Tax imposed either annually (annual net wealth tax) or at death (gift and inheritance or estate tax) on the net value of assets. Property taxes levied by provincial or municipal governments are a form of wealth taxation in Canada. With the general exception of a taxpayer's principal residence, capital gains tax is assessed on the increase in value of assets upon the death of a taxpayer.

Withholding tax: A withholding tax is a tax levied by the country in which income arises (the source country) at a flat rate on the gross amount of the income paid by a resident of the country to a non-resident. The tax is usually collected by the resident taxpayer and remitted to the government on behalf of the non-resident person.

TABLE OF CASES

INDEX

Canadian-controlled private corporations (CCPCs), 18, 115, 169, 412, 414–15, 462
  associated corporations, 440–43
  investment income, taxation structure of, 460
  qualified small business corporations (QSBCs), 291–92
  reassessments, income tax return, 532
  small business corporations, 293–94
  small business deduction and, 387–88, 440
  stock option plans and, 146–47
  tax integration and, 436, 452
Capital assets, expenditures to maintain, 196–201
  legal expenses, 197–99
  repair vs renewal, 199–200
  repairs, maintenance and alterations, 199
  replacements, 200–1
Capital cost allowance (CCA), 44, 149, 151, 212n, 216, 236, 237n, 238–49, 250, 254, 270, 410, 430, 431, 632, 656, 657, 668
  capital cost of property, 242–43
    general, 242–43
  depreciable property, 241–42
  disposition of assets, adjustments on, 245–48
    recapture, 246–48
      capital cost, limited to, 246–47
      deferral, 247–48
      negative balance, 246
    terminal losses, 245
  first year half-rate rule, 248
  general, 238
  structure, 239–41
    classification, 239
    general, 239–40
    permissive, 239
  undepreciated capital cost (UCC), 240, 243–44
  works of art, 248–49
Capital dividend account (CDA), 462–63, 464
Capital expenditures
  current expense vs, 190–202
    general, 190–91

mixed law and fact, 191–202
  capital assets, preservation of, 196–201. *See also* Capital assets, expenditures to maintain
  direct vs indirect consequences, 194–96
  enduring benefit, 193–94
  factual ambiguity, 202
  goodwill, 195–96
  obligations, discharge of, 201
  eligible, 250–51
    eligible capital amount, 250–51
    eligible capital property, 251
    expenditures and receipts, characterization of, 251
Capital gains, 177, 257–95, 421
  adjusted cost base (ACB), 275–80
    cost base, adjustments to, 278–79
    land, acquisition of, 278
    stock dividend and options, 279
    deemed adjusted cost base, 276–78
      Canadian resident, becoming, 277
      change of use, 276
      conversions, 277
      dividends in kind, 277
      identical properties, 276
      lottery prize, 277
      non-arm's length transactions, 277
      options, 277
      stock dividends, 278
    defined, 275
    negative adjusted cost base, 279
    part dispositions, 279–80
  anti-avoidance provisions, 296
  bond discounts and, 177
  business income vs, 159–68
    capital property or investment, meaning of, 160
  capital property, disposition of, 261–62, 266–75
    capital property, types of, 262
    deemed dispositions, 269–74, 294
      bad debts, 273
      change in property use: commercial to personal, 270

general, 359
non-capital losses, 360
restrictions on losses, 360
statutory exceptions, 360
charitable donations by, deductibility
of, 345–52
blended payments, 347
charities, 348–52
political activities, 351–52
tax exempt status, 351
eligible organizations, 347–48
gift, defined, 345–47
computation of tax, 385–88
general tax rate, 385
permanent establishment, 387
provincial tax credit, 386–87
small business deduction, 387–88
tax adjustments, 386
dividends and. *See* Dividends, income from
income tax returns, filing of by, 517
instalment payments, 541–43
balance payable, 542
estimated payments, 541–42
exemption, 542
failure to remit, 542
short fiscal periods, 543
investment income, 452–65. *See also*
Corporate investment income
objects and powers, 166–67
reassessments, income tax return, 532
residence of, 64–71
common law rules, 66–68
dual residence, 67–68
general propositions, 66–67
international tax treaties, 68–71
permanent establishment, 68–69
treaty shopping, 69–71
provincial residence, 73
statutory rules, 65
small business, 112, 115, 116, 159n, 265
business investment losses, 358
capital losses of, 293–94
debt financing, 425
shares of, capital gains from, 291–92
exemption of, 361, 362, 364

subject corporations, 457
transfers/loans to, income attribution
and, 115–16
types of, 413–16
Canadian corporations, 413
Canadian-controlled private corporations (CCPCs), 414–15
exempt corporations, 415–16
other corporations, 415
private corporations, 414
public corporations, 414
special status corporations, 415
taxable Canadian corporations, 413
Counselling benefits, taxation of employee, 148
Criminal charges, deductibility of legal fees for, 188–90
Crown property, taxation and, 11
Cumulative eligible capital account, 249, 251n, 252, 254

Damages, 327–41
breach of contract, 330–41
breach of warranty of authority, 336
claim, nature of, 336
damage principles, 336
employment damages, 333–35
arbitration awards, 335
employment insurance benefits, 335
signing bonuses, 335
wrongful dismissal, 333–34
surrogatum principle, 330–33, 335
capital receipts, 332
global payments, 332
judgments, non-performance, 332–33
tort damages, 337–41
business or investments, 337
capital property, 338
depreciable property, 338
eligible capital property, 338
fatal accidents, 339–40
general, 337
investment income, 340–41
personal injuries, 338–39, 340
cause of action, 328–29